S0-AJW-336

THEORIZING A NEW AGENDA FOR ARCHITECTURE

THEORIZING A NEW AGENDA FOR ARCHITECTURE

AN ANTHOLOGY OF ARCHITECTURAL THEORY 1965–1995

KATE NESBITT, EDITOR

PRINCETON ARCHITECTURAL PRESS
NEW YORK

Published by
Princeton Architectural Press
37 East 7th Street
New York, New York 10003

For a free catalog of books, call 1.800.722.6657.
Visit our web site at www.papress.com.

© 1996 Kate Nesbitt
All rights reserved
Printed and bound in the United States by Thomson-Shore
11 10   10

No part of this book may be used or reproduced in any
manner without written permission from the publisher
except in the context of reviews.

Book design and production by Allison Saltzman

Cover: Atrium of Banco de Credito, Lima, Peru. Arquitectonica
Photo: Timothy Hursley, 1988

Library of Congress Cataloging-in-Publication Data
Theorizing a new agenda for architecture : an anthology of
architectural theory 1965–1995 / Kate Nesbitt, editor.
606 p. : ill. ; 25 cm.
Includes bibliographical references and index.
ISBN 1-56898-053-1 (cloth : alk. paper).
ISBN 1-56898-054-x (paper : alk. paper).
1. Architecture, Modern—20th century.
I. Nesbitt, Kate, 1957–
NA680.T45   1996
720'.1—dc20   95-45968
CIP

CONTENTS

THEORIZING A NEW AGENDA FOR ARCHITECTURE

ACKNOWLEDGEMENTS

This anthology would not have been possible without the help of many people, and it is a pleasure to thank those who supported and assisted me in bringing the project to fruition. I would like to express my deepest gratitude to the contributing authors and illustrators who generously allowed their work to be published here, and to Arquitectonica for the use of the cover image. Thanks to the publishers for their accommodation in reprinting, especially Mary Uscilka and Sarah Miller at MIT Press, Maggie Toy of Academy Editions, Kristin M. Jones at ArtForum International, and Kim Tyner at the Museum of Modern Art. At Princeton Architectural Press, I owe special thanks to Kevin Lippert and Allison Saltzman for their belief in the value of such an anthology and for their encouragement. Among the dedicated staff of the University of Virginia Libraries, Jack Robertson, Lynda White, and Christie D. Stephenson of the Fiske-Kimball Fine Arts Library, and David Seaman of Alderman Library have been particularly forthcoming with their expertise.

I am very grateful to Ken Schwartz, former chair, and Peter Waldman, current chair of the Department of Architecture at the University of Virginia for their confidence in me, for providing graduate assistants, and for release time at two crucial points in the process. I owe thanks to the American Institute of Architects, who provided an AIA/AAF Scholarship for Advanced Study or Research to help support the final year of research and writing, and to the University of Virginia Office of the Vice Provost for Research for a grant to assist with manuscript preparation.

Over the last four years, I have benefitted from discussions about theory with my colleagues at the School of Architecture. I am especially grateful to Robert Dripps, Edward Ford, Judith Kinnard, Dean William McDonough, Elizabeth K. Meyer, Peter Waldman, Camille Wells, C. William Westfall, and Richard Wilson for sharing their insights with me. From other departments within the University of Virginia, Ralph Cohen, Dean Dass, Rita Felski, and Alan Megill were kind enough to provide inter-

I would like to express my sincere appreciation to Kenneth Frampton, Joan Ockman, and Mary McLeod at Columbia University, and to K. Michael Hays at Harvard University, for their comments on the selections and themes. Many of the book's contributors offered important comments and historical perspectives on their work; in this regard my special thanks go to Diana Agrest, Philip Bess, Geoffrey Broadbent, Peter Eisenman, Mario Gandelsonas, Michael Graves, Liane Lefaivre, Juhani Pallasmaa, Demetri Porphyrios, Colin Rowe, Thomas L. Schumacher, Bernard Tschumi, and Alexander Tzonis. Alan Plattus and David Rodowick, who introduced me to contemporary architectural theory and literary theory respectively while I was a graduate student at Yale University, have contributed significantly to the development of my ideas. Similarly, Anthony Vidler's theory lectures at the Institute for Architecture and Urban Studies remain a source of inspiration. Colleagues and friends have read parts of the manuscript; for their helpful suggestions I am very grateful to Joseph Atkins, Lily Chi, Ellen Dunham-Jones, Allison Ewing, Marc Hacker, Barbara Judy, Andrea Kahn, Hope Mauzerall, Kevin Murphy, Kent Puckett, and William Sherman.

Students in my theory classes have shared my enthusiasm for the subject and many have contributed their time to assist with all aspects of the project. In particular, I offer my heartfelt thanks to Whitney Morrill, Adonica Inzer, Chrysanthe Broikos, Lotte Sørensen, Jessie Chapman, Brian Jonas, and Azadeh Rashidi for their assistance with the production of the manuscript. Very special thanks to Janet Cutright, secretary for the Department of Architecture, who proofread the manuscript with great skill and dedication.

Some thanks are more difficult to express. I take great pleasure in dedicating this work to my father, George Nesbitt, whose love of learning has been a model, and to Frank, for his patience and unwavering support.

PREFACE

The publication of Robert Venturi's *Complexity and Contradiction in Architecture* in 1966 radically changed attitudes towards modern architecture. This single book, bearing the imprint of the Museum of Modern Art, opened a Pandora's box of exploration of architectural history in America and abroad, in search of formal principles to guide and enrich contemporary architectural design. Ironically, the same institution that had promoted European modern architecture in the United States under the banner of the International Style became the leader in rejecting it. By the mid 1960s, architecture had been reduced to formulaic repetitions of the canonical works of the Modern Movement, to technological utopias, and to expressionist fantasies. Many other architects contributed to the critique of modernism, some of whom built upon or rejected Venturi's position. It was a contentious period in theory characterized by prodigious publication of books and articles on the professional crisis.

During this time of reexamination of architecture (and of cultural modernity), the influence of extradisciplinary paradigms increased, notably literary paradigms such as semiotics and structuralism. Communication theories and phenomenology presented additional ways to approach the crisis of meaning within architecture. In response to the loss of socially-motivated engagement with the world, Italian Marxism and the Frankfurt School offered political critiques of architecture. No single theory dominated the discourse as academic architects borrowed new thought paradigms from other disciplines. This pluralist, revisionist period can be generally characterized as *postmodern*, an ambiguous, umbrella term which will be discussed in the introduction and by inference, in the essays.

This anthology collects fifty-one of the most important essays on architectural theory since 1965. Several primary-source readers treat architecture up to 1963, but at the outset of this project in 1993, there was no anthology that covered the intervening years. By gathering emblematic essays from two books and from twenty-four journals originating in seven different countries, this collection unites and makes available material that is scattered through libraries. The anthology is specifically designed for an audience of practicing architects, students, and teachers of architecture. In addition, those not familiar with architectural theory will find the book to be an introduction to the important themes and theories of the last three decades. The issues raised are fundamental to understanding the course of architecture in the recent past, and should be of interest to all scholars involved in the analysis and critique of cultural production. In the hands of a diverse group of readers, I hope that this reflective anthology of architectural theory will make a significant contribution to research on architecture since the collapse of the Modern Movement.

In the introduction, I spell out my view of architectural theory as a catalyst for change within the discipline, in both its academic and professional aspects. Theory accomplishes this by acting as a parallel and critical discourse to practice. I have selected the essays for their ability to illuminate theoretical issues and have grouped them in fourteen chapters. The chapters' thematic and paradigmatic (as opposed to chronological) organization is intended to clarify substantive relationships among the different manifestos and polemics; introductions to each piece support these linkages. Because of the complexity and multiplicity of theoretical viewpoints, a coherent presentation of the arguments is urgently needed. Coherence is served by this structure, although admittedly, a number of essays could easily fall in more than one chapter. Rather than seeing this as a fault of the structure, I feel it reveals the intertextual nature of postmodern architectural theory.

The first eight chapters deal with issues of meaning, history, and society. Chapters nine through twelve address these same issues from a common (sometimes subtle) ground in phenomenology, emphasizing nature, place, and tectonics. Finally, the anthology attempts to indicate emerging issues evident in postmodern writings on architecture. Thus, speculations on the body and its experience of architecture comprise chapters thirteen and fourteen. The final sections of the book include notes on contributors, illustration sources, a bibliography organized by chapter headings, and an index.

My commitment to this project stems from study of architectural theory, literary theory, and film theory at Yale University, the Institute for Architecture and Urban Studies (New York), and Copenhagen University. Since coming to the University of Virginia School of Architecture, I have taught the introductory theory class and advanced theory seminars (Theories of Modernism 1800–1945 and Contemporary Architectural Theory: 1965 to the Present). Through these academic experiences, I realized the need for an anthology of contemporary theory, although it is undoubtedly early to be assessing the literature of this period. (I am encouraged that colleagues in art, literature, and cultural criticism have already attempted to forecast what may prove to be significant in the long run. Popular collections exist in these fields: for example, the excellent *Art in Theory: 1900 to 1990*, edited by Harrison and Wood and published in 1993.)

A desire for intensity and brevity, characteristic of the anthology format, restricted the size of this book. My selections are thus not exhaustive and omissions of structure and content are inevitable. Given my background and interests (linguistic theory, psychoanalysis), there is a bias towards works which are interdisciplinary in scope. In addition, an effort was made to include theorists whose production has been substantial and influential. It is not the purpose of this theory anthology to present criticism of specific buildings, so most of the essays selected are not image-dependent. I offer this volume in hope that it will be an impetus to continued reading, discussion, and evaluation of this exciting period. Perhaps it will also provide a basis for understanding the emerging issues at the end of the millennium.

Kate Nesbitt
Charlottesville, Virginia
1995

INTRODUCTION

KATE NESBITT

INTRODUCTION

PART I: THE NECESSITY OF THEORY

Within the discipline of architecture, theory is a discourse that describes the practice and production of architecture and identifies challenges to it. Theory overlaps with but differs from architectural history, which is descriptive of past work, and from criticism, a narrow activity of judgment and interpretation of specific existing works relative to the critic's or architect's stated standards. Theory differs from these activities in that it *poses alternative solutions* based on observations of the current state of the discipline, or offers new thought paradigms for approaching the issues. Its speculative, anticipatory, and catalytic nature distinguishes theoretical activity from history and criticism. Theory operates on different levels of abstraction, evaluating the architectural profession, its intentions, and its cultural relevance at large. Theory deals with architecture's aspirations as much as its accomplishments.

Throughout history, one can identify recurring architectural themes that demand resolution, both conceptually and physically. Physical questions are resolved tectonically, while conceptual or intellectual questions are problematized in the manner of philosophy. Perennial theoretical questions include the origins and limits of architecture, the relationship of architecture to history, and issues of cultural expression and meaning. New theories arise to account for unexamined or unexplained aspects of the discipline.

A survey of architectural theory from the last thirty years finds a multiplicity of issues vying for attention. The lack of dominance of a single issue or a single viewpoint is characteristic of the pluralist period imprecisely referred to as *postmodern*. Evident in all the coexistent and contradictory tendencies is the desire to expand upon the limitations of *modern* theory, including formalism and ideas of functionalism ("form follows function"), the necessity of the "radical break" with history, and the "honest" expression of material and structure. In general, postmodern architectural theory addresses a *crisis of meaning* in the discipline. Since the mid 1960s, architectural theory has become truly interdisciplinary; it depends upon a vast array of critical paradigms. This project of revision of modernism, presented as *Theorizing a New Agenda for Architecture*, is undertaken from political, ethical, linguistic, aesthetic, and phenomenological positions.

While only the first chapter is so titled, postmodernism is in fact the subject and point of reference of the entire book. I hope to make clear that postmodernism is not a singular style, but more a sensibility of inclusion in a period of pluralism. Reflecting this, the selected theoretical essays present a multiplicity of points of view, rather than a nonexistent, unified vision. In some cases, perspectives not represented by essays in my anthology have been mentioned in this introduction to broaden the context of the discussion

I have attempted to construct a coherent discourse from fragmentary texts through the use of a thematic and paradigmatic structure for the book. The fourteen chapters and fifty-one essay introductions provide a framework with which to approach this heterogeneous material and understand the complexities of postmodernism. A chronological structure, while useful in terms of the publication history of the essays, was rejected in favor of clarifying the connections between the themes and positions of different writers, countries, and decades. The themes and theoretical paradigms chosen as chapter headings are recurrent subjects of writings in the postmodern period; they are interrelated and many of the essays could fall under more than one. Together, these themes and paradigms are intended to sketch in the intellectual climate in architecture since 1965 and facilitate comparison of historical positions on the same issues.

I will return in Part II of the introduction to the significant postmodern themes and paradigms that organize the chapters. The discussion of the various types of theory and the general purpose of treatises in the remainder of Part I is intended to situate the authors' recent contributions in relation to the historical body of theory.

PART IA. TYPES OF THEORY

Theory can be characterized by several attitudes towards the presentation of its subject matter: for the most part it is *prescriptive, proscriptive, affirmative,* or *critical.* All of these differ from a "neutral," descriptive position. For instance, a conventional historian might show how others have approached the issues of the moment, without explicitly advocating a position. Such a descriptive history might offer explanations of phenomena that rely on correlation of factual occurrences, like the introduction of new technologies, with resulting changes in design. Nikolaus Pevsner's *Pioneers of Modern Design* is a good example of a conventional, descriptive approach.

Prescriptive theory offers new or revived solutions for specific problems; it functions by establishing new norms for practice. It thus promotes positive standards and sometimes even a design method. This type can be critical (even radical), or affirmative of the status quo (conservative). The tone in either instance is often polemical. Michael Graves's argument in "A Case for Figurative Architecture" (ch. 1) and William McDonough's "Hannover Principles" (ch. 8) are clear prescriptions. The former suggests a return to humanist ideals, and the latter is an ecological manifesto.

Very similar to prescriptive theory is proscriptive theory, which differs in that the standards state what is to be avoided in design. Good architecture or urbanism in proscriptive terms is defined by the *absence* of negative attributes. Functional zoning is an example of proscriptive theory, as is the town planning code for Seaside, Florida by Andres

Duany and Elizabeth Plater-Zyberk, Architects. This code, an instance of conservative instrumental theory, legislates consistent quality by restricting material and style choices, setbacks, and massing.

Broader than descriptive and prescriptive writing, critical theory evaluates the built world and its relationships to the society it serves. This kind of polemical writing often has an expressed political or ethical orientation and intends to stimulate change. Among many possible orientations, critical theory can be ideologically based in Marxism or feminism. A good example of critical theory is architect and theorist Kenneth Frampton's Critical Regionalism, which proposes resistance to the homogenization of the visual environment through the particularities of mediated, local building traditions. Critical theory is speculative, questioning, and sometimes utopian.

PART IB. THE PURPOSE OF THE THEORETICAL TREATISE: DEFINING THE SCOPE OF THE DISCIPLINE

Theoretical treatises are fundamentally concerned with the origins of a practice or of an art. For example, a treatise on *building* might situate the origins of construction practice in the need for shelter. A treatise on *architecture* might place the origins of this disciplinary practice in the imitation of nature, (*mimesis*) and in man's innate desire to improve upon it. In the *Ten Books of Architecture*, Vitruvius hypothesizes that man, being "of an imitative and teachable nature...gradually advanced from the construction of buildings to the other arts and sciences."[1] Architecture is thus asserted as the origin and antecedent of the fine arts. Furthermore, in addition to positing a legitimizing origin, treatises sometimes delineate a clear relationship of difference between architecture and mathematics and the other sciences, in order to assert architecture's disciplinary autonomy.

In addition to the issue of origins, the basic subject matter of architectural treatises can be categorized using the following five points:

1. The requisite qualities of an architect in terms of personality, education, and experience. Alberti offers this mid-fifteenth-century definition of

> what he is that I allow to be an Architect....Him I call an Architect, who, by sure and wonderful Art and Method, is able, both with Thought and Invention, to devise, and, with Execution, to compleat all those Works, which,...can, with the greatest Beauty, be adapted to the Uses of Mankind.[2]

2. The requisite qualities of architecture. For instance, Vitruvius's well known "triad" of firmness, commodity, and delight has served as a set of criteria applied to architecture by treatises since the rediscovery of his work in the Renaissance. The Vitruvian triad has proven difficult to supersede or displace.

3. A theory of design or construction method encompassing technique, constituent parts, types, materials, and procedures. The Abbot Laugier's "Essay on Architecture" (1753) is one such treatise that emphasizes the proper composition of parts.

4. Examples of the canon of architecture, the selection and presentation of which reveal the author's attitude to history. Robert Venturi's use of examplars of Mannerist and Baroque

architecture in his 1966 book was anathema at the time, but compelling in light of his arguments for *Complexity and Contradiction in Architecture*.

5. An attitude about the relationship between theory and practice. Two distinct views on this fundamental subject are represented by architects Bernard Tschumi and Vittorio Gregotti. For Tschumi, "Architecture is not an illustrative art; it does not illustrate theories."[3] His writings suggest that theory's role is one of interpretation and provocation. Gregotti, on the other hand, insists on "theoretical research as a direct foundation of action"[4] in architectural design.

Whether theory must be applicable, "useful knowledge," and whether it must result in predictable outcomes in design is widely debated. If theory must lead to predictable outcomes, then the only acceptable theory is prescriptive or proscriptive. (Not coincidentally, many who pursue predictable outcomes in design espouse neotraditional views of the city and of architecture.) Both aspects of this proposition are challenged by postmodern theorists such as Alberto Perez-Gomez:

> the [modern] belief that theory had to be validated in terms of its applicability...has entailed the reduction of true theory to the status of applied science... This "theory" is oblivious of myth and true knowledge and is exclusively concerned with an efficient domination of the material world.[5]

In an essay on the work of architect and educator John Hejduk, Perez-Gomez argues for the critical power of the unbuilt project, for "paper architecture." Daniel Libeskind and Zaha Hadid are other contemporary architects whose drawings have brought attention to their makers (in their cases, because of the implied new spatial qualities). Earlier examples of significant architectural projects include Étienne-Louis Boullée's monumental "architecture of shadows" and Piranesi's Carceri series, both of which demonstrate the power of the drawn vision. But in general, the role of the theoretical project in the discipline and whether it is part of architecture proper is contested.

In addition to defining the origins and scope of the discipline, theory addresses the following themes, all of which will be covered by essays in this collection: meaning, theories of history, nature, the site, the city, aesthetic issues, and technology. A brief general survey of themes and pertinent questions about each will be followed by a longer discussion of the postmodern period and its particular themes in Part II.

Inherent in the issue of origins is the question of the meaning of architecture and the definition of its essence and limits. For example, function, the programmatic use of shelter, has often been claimed as that which is unique to architecture, and therefore as equivalent to its meaning. But others have argued that accommodating function (in a literal sense) is instead the essence of *building*, as distinguished from *architecture*, which has a larger range of intentions, including symbolic function. This distinction is fundamental to various theoretical constructions of disciplinary boundaries and to the constitution of architecture as art, science, craft, and intellectual activity.

The creation of meaning in architecture has often been studied through the "linguistic analogy." Comparisons to the operation of language raise the following questions: What structures allow for understanding a form of expression? Does meaning not depend on a process of repetition of the familiar, and if so, how can meaning be sustained through innovation and invention? Can there be meaning in form, or only in content? What is appropriate content for architecture?

Because of the durability of buildings, the architectural theorist is always confronted with a historical condition: the simultaneous experience of works dating from vastly different time periods. This necessitates a consideration of one's present relationship with the tradition of the discipline of architecture. What use can one make of past experiences with design and building? Is imitation the best route to beautiful and communicative architecture? Or have standards of beauty and comprehension of form changed, such that *mimesis* leads only to mute form? What is the importance of style? How do technological changes affect the use of prior models of construction?

Theory also addresses the relationship between architecture and nature, as developed through construction of the site. Historically, attitudes have fluctuated from sympathy, harmony, and integration with nature, to hostility and exploitation. Philosophical and scientific paradigms have largely shaped the architect's view of the territory of activity, of the way in which nature (the wilderness) becomes landscape (a cultural artifact) through the designer's efforts. What should the landscape, broadly defined to include urban, suburban, and rural situations, represent of the human place in nature?

The site of a work of architecture in the urban context must also be considered. How is building different in the city? What is the role of the architect in designing for and contributing to the city, understood as a physical, political, economic, and social entity? In the public realm, one encounters the idea of architecture's representational role, which is to find symbolic expression for the institutions that define society. Frampton writes: "the evolution of legitimate power has always been predicated upon the existence of the polis and upon comparable units of institutional and physical form."[6] What should these forms be? Within the process of symbolization are ideas of the relationship of the individual to the collective, often suggested through scale devices and the use of a multiplicity of similar elements in a building.

Through the projection of the human body (symbolic of the perfection of nature) into its form, architecture achieves a proportional harmony that speaks to the issue of scale and the individual. In Renaissance theory as well as in Le Corbusier's Modulor, the body offers a system of interrelated, comparative measurements that seeks to ensure a meaningful experience of architecture. Are these proportional systems, developed in the abstract, really perceptible?

Aesthetics offers criteria for beauty, including proportion, order, unity, and appropriateness. Thus Alberti states in his *Ten Books of Architecture* that architecture should emulate nature, such that no part can be removed or added without compromising the quality of the whole. This is an example of the aesthetic doctrines that characterize architectural theory and address questions such as: How is beauty to be defined in the present moment? How do ornament and decoration figure into beauty? Ornament was maligned by modern purists like Adolf Loos, who considered it decadent and "a crime." Can ornament, structure, and material play significant roles in the construction of meaning?

As discussed in relation to the inclusion of method in treatises, development of technique and technological advances are historically important themes in theory. Modern Movement architects placed high hopes on possibilities for the transformation of society through mass production of affordable objects and housing. Modern theory expressed an unqualified faith in the scientific and industrial revolutions' contributions to human well-being. From our postmodern perspective we ask: Was this faith in technique and technology justified by history?

The preceding survey of the general purpose and content of the theoretical treatise lays the groundwork for the complexity of theory in the postmodern period. It is offered to contextualize the essays in this anthology, which represent the most recent contributions to the discourse of architecture. The discussion shifts now to postmodernism.

PART II: WHAT IS POSTMODERNISM?

Many books and long essays have attempted to answer the question, What is postmodernism? Clearly, it is a term that has different meanings in different contexts. It is thus beyond the scope of my essay to offer a critique or extension of these definitions. Instead, this second part of the introduction approaches postmodernism in architecture from three standpoints: as a historical period with a specific relationship to modernism; as an assortment of significant paradigms (theoretical frameworks) for the consideration of cultural issues and objects; and as a group of themes. The following sections of the introduction overlap each other's boundaries, but nonetheless help to outline postmodernism as a period and as a mode of inquiry with certain recurring themes. The essays are collected in chapters organized by these same paradigms and themes.

PART IIA. POSTMODERNISM AS A HISTORICAL PERIOD

THE HISTORICAL CONTEXT
What is the context within which the crisis of modernism occurred? Cultural theorist Frederic Jameson offers:

> The 1960s are in many ways the key transitional period, a period in which the new international order (neocolonialism, the Green Revolution, computerization, and electronic information) is at one and the same time set in place and is swept and shaken by its own internal contradictions and by external resistance.[7]

This new order is variously known as late capitalism, multinational capitalism, postindustrialization, or the consumer society.[8]

It is easier to define the beginning of the postmodern period than its end, which we have probably not yet reached. Student activism for civil rights, freedom, and the protection of the environment was accompanied by the rise of the anti-war, rock music, and drug culture. Space exploration began gloriously in the 1960s and crashed in the 1980s. Hopes for safe nuclear power were shattered by disastrous accidents at Three Mile Island (1979) and Chernobyl (1986). Radical individualism clashed with repressive religious fundamentalism.

While local military conflicts (motivated by disputes over oil, ethnicity, and religion) have occurred in the aftermath of World War II, in general, peace has reigned in the West for fifty years. The world's population has exploded, and communism has collapsed as a significant force in Eastern Europe, dramatically illustrated in the demolition of the Berlin Wall in 1989.

CHALLENGES TO THE MODERN MOVEMENT IN ARCHITECTURE

In the mid 1960s, challenges to Modern Movement ideology and to a debased and trivialized modern architecture accelerated and proliferated to become known as the postmodern critique. As Frampton notes, "there is little doubt that by the mid-sixties, we were increasingly bereft of a realistic theoretical basis on which to work."[9]

In "Place-form and Cultural Identity," Frampton writes of his growing awareness that modernism needed to be redirected:

> we already saw our task as a qualified restoration of the creative vigor of a movement which had become formally and programmatically compromised in the intervening years....
>
> We had been, in any event, the last generation of students to entertain the projection of utopian urban schemes in both a programmatic and a formal sense.[10]

The demolition of the Pruitt-Igoe housing complex in St. Louis, Missouri in 1972 is widely hailed as marking the failure of modern architecture's vision for housing society. An anti-utopian "derivative which both inspires and deserves destruction," Minoru Yamasaki's "bureaucratic rendition" of the dreams of Le Corbusier, Hilbersheimer, et al[11] was despised by its low-income inhabitants, who undertook to destroy it through vandalism and neglect. The dramatic, intentional bombing of this work of modern architecture (which had been widely celebrated upon opening) was a clear wake-up call to the profession.

The faith of Frampton's generation in continuing the modern project had also been shaken by the appropriation of modern architecture's aesthetic as a progressive sign for corporate headquarters. Stripped of its social program, modern architecture was reduced in the 1950s to a style for reiteration in the commercial sector. This issue was perhaps of less concern to American architects. As Colin Rowe stated with respect to the "New York Five," European modern architecture was imported to America without its ideological component.[12] Furthermore, it was apparent by the 1960s that Europeans had had only limited success implementing their social agenda. A certain disillusionment with social reform had taken hold in the profession. Among the events transpiring in response to this professional crisis are exhibitions, publications, and the rise of theory institutions. Reference to significant instances of each in architecture will define the period of study, 1965 to 1995.

THEORY INSTITUTIONS: NEW YORK, VENICE, LONDON

The institutionalization of architectural theory is evident in the founding of two independent think tanks in New York (1967–85) and Venice (1968–), both of which undertook prodigious publication. Similar in its mission to London's Architectural Association (AA, founded 1847), the cosmopolitan Institute for Architecture and Urban Studies (IAUS) in Manhattan offered a program of lectures, conferences, symposia, panels, and exhibitions. Like the AA and the Venice Institute, the IAUS was established by a board of architects (led by

Peter Eisenman) in opposition to the existing architectural educational system, which in England and Italy is state-run.[13] The IAUS published a newsletter, *Skyline*; two journals, *Oppositions* and *October*; and a series of books under the *Oppositions* imprint.[14] The short-lived book series included the influential English translation of *The Architecture of the City* by Aldo Rossi (1982; Italian, 1966). The Institute's heavy emphasis on discourse and dissemination of theory was characteristic of the postmodern period. (A Chicago Institute for Architecture and Urbanism, the CIAU, revived the IAUS model from 1987 to 1994, when funding dried up.) One of the IAUS's major contributions was to introduce European theorists and architects, many of whom were influenced by linguistic paradigms, to an American audience.[15] While there was no official connection between the IAUS and the Venice Institute, it would be fair to say that the two had many issues in common.

Among the most influential theorists in this period are the Italian architects, gathered around architecture schools in three cities: Rome, Milan, and Venice.[16] In particular, the postwar Istituto Universitario di Architettura di Venezia (Architectural Institute at the University of Venice, IAUV), under the directorship of Giuseppe Samonà from 1945 to 1970, became an important teaching and research venue.[17] In 1968, Manfredo Tafuri (d.1994) founded the Institute of Architectural History at the IAUV, attracting the participation of others interested in critical theory and Marxism. Tafuri's writings, reconsidering the German historiographic method and the relationship between Marxism and architecture, continue to be widely read.

While Milan is the city more often associated with natives Rossi and Gregotti, they are among the neorationalist architects known collectively as the "School of Venice." Both have demonstrated in their careers the importance of simultaneous involvement in different aspects of the architectural profession, including teaching at the IAUV, for instance. Shortly after earning his degree, Rossi also became active editing publications and researching the city at the Venice Institute. Gregotti, editor of *Casabella* since 1982, speaks for many of his contemporaries when he says:

> for an architect to edit a magazine, like teaching, or participating in public debates, is a way of cultivating theoretical reflection, not as a separate activity, but as an indispensable part of design craft. Indeed, theory and history have been and still are, two important constituents of design, at least for my generation.[18]

Through all of these activities, the "School of Venice" has been influential.

PUBLICATIONS: MAGAZINES, ACADEMIC JOURNALS, POLEMICS
Another response to the professional crisis in modern architecture was the blossoming of theoretical literature as new independent magazines and academic journals were established. Unfettered by alliances to professional organizations like the American Institute of Architects or Royal Institute of British Architects, these reviews often took a critical stance in relation to the official journals.

In addition to the output of the Venice Institute, Italy produced three other architectural magazines, all of which are still in print: *Lotus*, *Casabella*, and *Domus*. While the latter two began in 1928, *Lotus* was established in 1963; its sophisticated editorial board has published internationally influential theory in Italian and English. Gregotti again offers some perspective on architecture at the beginning of the postmodern era:

> It is not therefore by chance that the 1960s revealed a new theoretical production marked by a partiality, sufficient to bring to focus new disciplinary questions and aspects, both in Italy and abroad.[19]

For ten years (1985–95), Danish architects under the patronage of Henning Larsen's Copenhagen firm published *Skala: Nordic Magazine of Architecture and Art. Skala's* thirty issues featured most of the major international postmodern figures. Articles and interviews in Danish and English were complemented by an oversized layout using strong graphic design and generous illustrations. Exhibits at the Skala Gallery and lectures by visiting architects made the program a small-scale version of the IAUS for Scandinavia.

Since its founding in 1971, the Japanese *Architecture and Urbanism* (A+U) has published seminal works, both design and text, made accessible to the West by English translations, superb photographs, and graphic design. An international group of advisers and correspondents shapes *A+U's* editorial direction.

Periodicals and thematic "Profiles" from the well-established *Architectural Design* (AD) in London continue to offer timely and provocative presentations of current debates. Many of the same architects serve on the editorial boards of *Lotus, A+U,* and *AD.* With a few exceptions, women have not been well represented in editorial positions or as writers. Exclusion from the masthead may partly explain the dearth of published work by women architects. This can be expected to change now that architecture student bodies are half female and women are moving into faculty positions.

In addition to these commercial publications, university-based architectural journals proliferated in the postmodern period; some were modeled on *Perspecta: The Yale Architectural Journal,* dating from 1952. University of Pennsylvania's *VIA* and the *Architectural Association Quarterly* (AAQ) began publishing in 1968, the year of the manifesto by the student Strike Committee at the École des Beaux Arts.[20] *AAQ* ceased publication in 1982, but reemerged as *AA Files. Modulus* (University of Virginia) and *Precis* (Columbia University) appeared in 1979; the latter ceased publication in 1987. The themes of these topical reviews help chart the period's concerns. For example, the *Harvard Architecture Review* made its debut in 1980 with *Beyond the Modern Movement.* The *Princeton Journal of Architecture* first appeared in 1983, considering *Ritual,* and the *Pratt Journal of Architecture* volume 1, *Architecture and Abstraction* (1985), countered the rise of postmodern historicist representation with modernist abstraction. Some journals have a topical focus, such as *Center* (University of Texas at Austin), which since 1985 has focused on issues broadly related to the study of American architecture.

The earnestness with which subjects (history, the city, monumentality, the landscape, tectonics, ethics, etc.) are tackled by student editors and faculty advisors indicates the depth of the perception of crisis. Postmodern architects turned to the written word to sort out complex issues, as often as they turned to the theoretical project. Extensive academic publishing in this period is indicative of the recent impact and accessibility of desktop publishing in noncommercial markets. But it also reflects the lack of work at the drawing board to occupy architects, especially during the slowdown in building activity precipitated by the 1973 oil embargo and "energy crisis," and the subsequent recessions in the construction industry in the early- and late-1980s and 1990s. During slow periods in the profession, writing theory and designing theoretical projects often sustain architects' interest.

A sampling of emblematic books and articles will now be looked at in greater detail. The reader is also referred to the discussion of the theoretical paradigms and themes in the next sections, and to the individual essay introductions for more background information.

The challenges that arose in the 1950s to the orthodoxy of the Modern Movement came to a head in the mid 1960s with the publication of several substantial treatises in addition to the previously mentioned *The Architecture of the City* and *Complexity and Contradiction in Architecture* (1966). They include Christian Norberg-Schulz's *Intentions in Architecture* (1965), Christopher Alexander's *Notes on the Synthesis of Form* (1964), and Gregotti's *Territory of Architecture* (1966). The latter has not been translated to English in its entirety, but is often referred to by non-Italian writers. (ch. 7) For a discussion of Norberg Schulz and Rossi, see the discussion of place and urban theory in the next section. (ch. 9, 6, 7)

Robert Venturi's *Complexity and Contradiction* (published by the Museum of Modern Art and eventually translated into sixteen languages) prescribes the importance of looking at and using architectural history in contemporary design. (ch. 1) In essence a manifesto for historicist eclecticism, it promotes the anti-modern component (listed first here) of pairs of binary oppositions such as hybrid/pure, distorted/straightforward, and ambiguous/articulated. Venturi is concerned with communication of meaning on numerous levels and avails himself of the associations formed by familiarity with the history of architecture. In a similar fashion, *Learning from Las Vegas* (1972) locates value in the familiar, lowbrow culture of the highway "strip." (ch. 6) His inclusive theory in *Complexity and Contradiction* of "both/and" recognizes explicit and implicit functions, literal and symbolic, and allows for multiple interpretations. In asserting his preference for the "difficult unity of inclusion" (and its resulting tension), Venturi is influenced by several thought paradigms: semiology; Gestalt psychology; and William Empson's literary theory in *Seven Types of Ambiguity*.[21] The last pages of Venturi's text hint at the direction his research will take, as he discovers in the "almost all right" of the American Main Street that "it is perhaps from the everyday landscape, vulgar and disdained, that we can draw the complex and contradictory order that is valid and vital for our architecture as an urbanistic whole."[22] For an architect to celebrate the "ugly and ordinary" in the environment is certainly revolutionary, but will the change be for the better? Is this celebration in fact the populist position he claims to represent?

Philip Johnson (one of Venturi's mentors) recollects the significance of *Complexity and Contradiction* for architectural postmodernism:

> It all came from Bob Venturi's book. We all felt—Venturi, [Robert A.M.] Stern and [Michael] Graves and I—that we should be more connected with the city, and with people. And more contextual: that we should relate to the older buildings.[23]

Within eleven years of its publication, the impact of Venturi's theory was widespread. Robert Stern, who first published an excerpt of *Complexity and Contradiction* as editor of *Perspecta* in 1965, wrote an early (1977) interpretation of the *postmodern historicist* trend. (To differentiate the work Stern describes from postmodernism at large, I refer to it as postmodern historicism.) "New Directions in Modern American Architecture: Postscript at the Edge of Modernism" identifies three areas of focus: the city, the facade, and the idea of cultural memory. (ch. 1) Stern also states corollary principles: the building is a fragment of a larger whole (contextualism); architecture is an act of historical and cultural response; and buildings develop meaning over time.[24] While Stern's "Postscript" may have intended to signal the end of modernism and usher in the postmodern era, it is not a self-proclaimed manifesto like *Complexity and Contradiction*. The essay presents postmodernism as a critique, which Stern identifies as an attempt to resolve the modern split between "rationalism" (encompassing function and technology) and "realism" (history and culture). Interestingly, function and technology are the very things Peter Eisenman identifies with Modern Movement architecture's "realistic" representation in "The End of Classical." (ch. 4) Stern claims that postmodern architectural shapes are "real," not abstract, and are "cognizant of their own purpose and materiality, of their history, of the physical context in which they are built, and of the social, cultural, and political milieu that called them into being."[25] Stern's position, vis-à-vis the social role of building, is stated thus: "buildings are designed to mean something...they are not hermetically sealed objects."[26] In contradiction to this claim of communication and accessibility, postmodern historicist architecture has been strongly criticized as elitist fashion by advocates of social responsibility in architecture.[27]

Also in 1977, Charles Jencks published *The Language of Post-Modern Architecture*, codifying the emerging movement as a style with predictable features. Jencks popularized the term "postmodernism" (which dates from the late 1940s) in architecture, from which it spread to the other arts. In their theoretical work, Jameson and philosopher Jürgen Habermas use Jencks's brand of architectural postmodernism (my postmodern historicism) to point to larger cultural and societal issues.

In 1969, a group of architects calling themselves CASE (the Conference of Architects for the Study of the Environment) held a meeting at the Museum of Modern Art in New York (MoMA). An indirect result of the meeting was the 1972 publication of *Five Architects*, showcasing the abstract, Modern Movement-inspired work of Peter Eisenman, Michael Graves, Charles Gwathmey, John Hejduk, and Richard Meier, who became known as "the New York Five." Introduced by Arthur Drexler (then MoMA curator and Director of Architecture and Design), Rowe, and Frampton, and with a postscript by Johnson, the work of the five gained instant credibility with patrons of architecture. Representing a countertendency of abstraction in relation to Venturi's, Stern's, and Jencks's call for signification of meaning, *Five Architects* was widely influential on architects. Drexler sets the book's tone in his preface, describing the work presented as "only architecture, not the salvation of man and the redemption of the earth:"

> We are all concerned...with social reform....That architecture is the least likely instrument with which to accomplish the revolution has not yet been noticed by the younger Europeans, and in America is a fact.[28]

The common ground was formalist: an interest in the early architecture of Le Corbusier and in the untested possibilities of applying cubist painters' ideas to architecture. The architects' paths have since diverged, but all five remain important figures in academia and the world of practice.

In 1976, Rowe published a collection of his writings since the late 1940s, entitled *The Mathematics of the Ideal Villa and Other Essays*. Many of the pieces had a substantial underground circulation before publication and the book has become a classic, including the influential "Transparency: Literal and Phenomenal," written with Robert Slutzky.[29] *Collage City* (1978), co-authored with Fred Koetter, is discussed in relation to the city, later in this introduction. A version published as an article in 1975 is reprinted in chapter six.

EXHIBITIONS

A series of influential exhibitions have supported the dissemination of postmodern architectural theory. This coincidence of means was also characteristic of the high modern period of the 1920s and 1930s in Europe, with its radical new magazines and frequent exhibitions of housing prototypes. In New York, the Museum of Modern Art (prodded by Johnson) launched the first modern architecture trend in the United States with its International Style exhibition in 1932. This seminal show has counterparts in the postmodern period, when MoMA was the site of three prominent exhibits that charted the changing course of architecture. The Beaux Arts Exhibition in 1975 and its tome-like cat along (which still appeared on some Yale students' desks well into the 1980s) influenced postmodern architectural graphics with its presentation of exquisite watercolor washes of neoclassical projects from the French Academy. The plans also offered models of the use of classical procession, axes, hierarchy, *poché*, and proportion. Four years later, the "Transformations" exhibition presented work from 1969 forward, including a pluralist range similar to that in Jencks's *The Language of Post-Modern Architecture*.[30]

A third MoMA exhibition in the postmodern period, which Johnson curated with Mark Wigley, was "Deconstructivist Architecture" in 1988.[31] The curators attempted the same kind of reorientation of the profession, the same codification of a "movement" as in the previous influential shows. While attracting some attention, the exhibition did not launch another major trend. The disparate appearance of the work and of the intentions of the architects made the gathering seem forced. Mary McLeod suggests in "Architecture and Politics in the Reagan Era: From Postmodernism to Deconstructivism" that some of the architects rejected the "Deconstructivist" label, but nonetheless wished to be included.[32] It seems that "deconstructivism" served as a stylistic label to exhibit some provocative work that may not have had much in common intellectually. The ambiguous term, "deconstructivism," (used only in architecture, to my knowledge) is meant to reflect two sources of influence for the type of postmodern work exhibited: the philosophical deconstruction of Jacques Derrida (see discussion of linguistic theory) and Russian Constructivism. Rem Koolhaas and Zaha Hadid, who used to work together, are perhaps the most committed to formal explorations based on Constructivism. Of the group exhibited, Peter Eisenman and Bernard Tschumi are closest to a deconstructionist position, with their emphasis on critique and dismantling disciplinary boundaries. But Frank Gehry, Steven Holl, and Coop Himmelblau are not really similar to the others mentioned above; they have in common a process of working from intuition and the sensuous properties of materials. Gehry and Holl represent a strong countertendency to postmodern historicism: an almost metaphysical approach to things concrete. In their work and others' of this period, there is an undercurrent of phenomenological thought not always consciously articulated, but quite present as a subtext.

In 1980, the Leo Castelli Gallery in New York solicited designs for private houses from major international architects, recognizing the increasing popularity of architecture with the general public. The eight visionary projects comprising "Houses For Sale" were presented as works of art, and sold rapidly.[33] The Max Protech Gallery in New York featured architecture shows on a regular basis throughout the 1980s.

The architecture section of the Venice Biennale in 1980 was organized by Paolo Portoghesi around the theme, "The Presence of the Past." In his book *Postmodern: The Architecture of the Postindustrial Society*, Portoghesi describes the phenomenon represented in the Biennale:

> The language of Postmodernism...has brought into the domain of the contemporary city an imaginary and humanistic component, and put into circulation fragments and methods of the great historical tradition of the Western world....A new force and a new degree of freedom have entered the world of the architect, where for decades a creative stagnation and an extraordinary indolence had rendered the heredity of the Modern Movement inoperative.[34]

The exhibition was very controversial, being seen by some as nostalgic and "scenographic," and by others like its curator, as breathing new life into architecture. Jürgen Habermas was so affected by visiting the show that he wrote a lecture of protest against this "avant-garde of reversed fronts."[35] Published as "Modernity—An Incomplete Project," his passionate essay has been a rallying point for architects concerned with salvaging the valuable aspects of the program of modern architecture.

PART IIB. POSTMODERNISM'S DEFINING THEORETICAL PARADIGMS

In addition to the growth of architectural theory publications, think tanks, and exhibitions, postmodernism in general is marked by the proliferation of theoretical paradigms, or ideological frameworks, which structure the thematic debates. Imported from other disciplines, the primary paradigms that shape architectural theory are phenomenology, aesthetics, linguistic theory (semiotics, structuralism, poststructuralism, and deconstruction), Marxism, and feminism.

PARADIGM 1: PHENOMENOLOGY

One aspect of this interdisciplinarity is the reliance of architectural theory on the philosophical method of inquiry known as phenomenology. That this philosophical thread underlies postmodern attitudes towards site, place, landscape, and making (in particular, tectonics) is sometimes overlooked and unquestioned. Recent theory has moved towards philosophical speculation by problematizing the body's interaction with its environment. Visual, tactile, olfactory, and aural sensations are the visceral part of the reception of architecture, a medium distinguished by its three-dimensional presence. In the postmodern period, the bodily and unconscious connection to architecture has again become an object of study for some theorists through phenomenology. Husserlian phenomenology, consisting of a "systematic investigation of consciousness and its objects,"[36] is the basis for later philosophers' work.

Prompted by the availability of translations of works by Martin Heidegger and Gaston Bachelard from the 1950s,[37] phenomenological consideration of architecture has begun to displace formalism and lay the groundwork for the emerging aesthetic of the contemporary sublime. Architectural theory typically lags behind cultural theory and the case of the absorption of phenomenology is no exception. Phenomenology's critique of scientific logic, which through positivist ("optimism about the benefits that the extension of scientific method could bring to humanity"[38]) thought had been elevated above and devalued Being, appealed to postmodernists rethinking technology's contributions to modernity in a less enthusiastic light.

Heidegger (1889–1976) studied philosophy under Edmund Husserl. His questionable political alliances during WWII led to a harsh reception of his work by colleagues. Nonetheless, Heidegger's influence is evident on the deconstructionist work of Derrida and on postmodern theorists working on the body.

Heidegger's writing is motivated by concern about modern man's inability to reflect on Being (or existence); this is crucial, he argues, because such reflection defines the human condition. One of the most influential phenomenological works for architecture is "Building Dwelling Thinking," in which Heidegger articulates the relationship between building and *dwelling*, Being, constructing, cultivating, and sparing.[39] Tracing the etymology of the German word *bauen* ("building"), Heidegger rediscovers ancient connotations and broad meanings that express the potential wealth of existence. Dwelling is defined as "a staying with things." When *things* (elements that gather the "fourfold" of earth, sky, mortals, and divinities) are first named, he says, they are recognized. Throughout the essay he maintains that language shapes thought, and thinking and poetry are required for dwelling.

Christian Norberg-Schulz interprets Heidegger's concept of dwelling as being at peace in a protected place. He thus argues for the potential of architecture to support dwelling: "The primary purpose of architecture is hence to make a world visible. It does this as a thing, and the world it brings into presence consists in what it gathers."[40] The Norwegian critic has promulgated the connection between architecture and dwelling in a series of publications dating back to *Existence, Space and Architecture* in 1971. An earlier interest in the experience of things "concrete" is expressed in *Intentions in Architecture* (1965), and hints at his future direction. Norberg-Schulz is widely cited today and is considered the principal proponent of a phenomenology of architecture, that is, a concern with the "concretization of existential space" through the making of *places*. The tectonic aspect of architecture plays a role, especially the concrete detail, which Norberg-Schulz says "explains the environment and makes its character manifest."[41]

Phenomenology in architecture requires deliberate attention to how things are made. As Mies supposedly said, "God is in the details." This influential school of thought not only recognizes and celebrates the basic elements of architecture (wall, floor, ceiling, etc. as horizon or boundary), but it has led to a renewed interest in sensuous qualities of materials, light, and color, and in the symbolic, tactile significance of the joint.

Perez-Gomez proposes extending Heidegger's concept of dwelling to allow for "existential orientation," cultural identification, and a connection with history.[42] By providing an existential "foothold" in "authentic" architecture, man can deal with mortality through the transcendence of "dwelling."[43]

Influenced by phenomenologist Hans-Georg Gadamer, Perez-Gomez claims that the apprehension of architecture as meaningful requires a "metaphysical dimension." This dimension "reveals the presence of Being, the presence of the invisible within the world of the everyday." The invisible must be signified with a symbolic architecture. The emphasis on dwelling is similar to Norberg-Schulz's, but Perez-Gomez is more prescriptive in his requirement for representation: "a symbolic architecture is one that represents, one that can be recognized as part of our collective dreams, as a place of full inhabitation."[44] One can acknowledge potency in the concept of dwelling, while questioning Perez-Gomez's assertion of the necessity for representational, symbolic means to achieve it. Because on the contrary, abstraction is offered by some theorists as more open to interpretations, and therefore as more universally meaningful.

A Finnish phenomenologist, Juhani Pallasmaa, addresses the psychic apprehension of architecture. (ch. 9) He talks about "opening up a view into a second reality of perception, dreams, forgotten memories and imagination."[45] In his work, this is accomplished through an abstract "architecture of silence."[46] While Pallasmaa's investigation of the unconscious parallels the Freudian uncanny, his architecture of silence resonates with the contemporary sublime.

PARADIGM 2: AESTHETIC OF THE SUBLIME

Like phenomenology, aesthetics is a philosophical paradigm that deals with the production and reception of a work of art. This section presents articulations of a single important aesthetic category in the postmodern period. Because of its function as the characteristic expression of modernity,[47] the sublime constitutes the principal emerging aesthetic category in the postmodern period. The sudden rebirth of interest in the sublime is partly explicable in terms of the recent emphasis on the knowledge of architecture through phenomenology. The phenomenological paradigm foregrounds a fundamental issue in aesthetics: the effect a work of architecture has on the viewer. In the instance of the sublime, the experience is visceral.

The emerging definitions of the sublime (such as the uncanny and the grotesque) give shape to the modern aesthetic discourse and coincide with postmodern thought. Contemporary theorists investigating the sublime are reinterpreting a tradition that dates to the first century A.D. and is elaborated during the Enlightenment. Writing at the dawn of modernity, Edmund Burke and Immanuel Kant are significant eighteenth-century sources.[48] A reconsideration of the sublime can be used to re-situate the architectural discourse and to move beyond formalism.

In twentieth-century architecture, any mention of the sublime or the beautiful seems to have been deliberately repressed by theorists and designers anxious to distance themselves from the recent past. To achieve the "radical break" with the history of the discipline that modernism sought, the terms of aesthetic theory had to be changed. A modernist polemic calling for an aesthetic *tabula rasa*[49] (of abstraction) and for the application of scientific principles to design, supplanted the preceding rhetoric. Positivist emphasis on rationality and function marginalized beauty and the sublime as subjective architectural issues. The postmodern recuperation of the sublime (and therefore of its reciprocal, the beautiful) as outlined herein will allow a significant expansion of theory.

Following psychoanalytic and deconstructionist models, several theoreticians argue that the route to a revitalized architecture requires uncovering its repressed aspects. Within the concealed material are often found vulnerable assumptions about the foundations of the discipline. For Anthony Vidler and Peter Eisenman, the uncanny and grotesque, aspects of the sublime, have been repressed. (ch. 14) In Vidler's terms, the "uncanny in this context would be...the return of the body into an architecture that had repressed its conscious presence."[50] Clearly related is Eisenman's grotesque: "the condition of the always present or the already within, that the beautiful in architecture attempts to repress."[51] Their ideas start to define the contemporary sublime in architecture.

The uncanny, as described by Sigmund Freud, is the rediscovery of something familiar that has been previously repressed; it is the uneasy feeling of the presence of an absence. The mix of the known and familiar with the strange, surfaces in the German word for the uncanny, *unheimliche*, which, translated literally, is "unhomely." In Vidler's recent study of *The Architectural Uncanny*, he notes that a common theme is the idea of the human body in fragments.[52] His uncanny is thus the terrifying side of the sublime, with the fear being privation of the integrated body. Vidler sees a "deliberate attempt to address the status of the body in postmodern theory," which is necessitated by the fact that, "The body in disintegration is in a very real sense the image of the notion of humanist progress in disarray."[53] Fragmentation is an important theme in postmodern historicist and deconstructivist architecture, the sources of which may lie in the rejection of anthropomorphic embodiment.[54]

By focusing his phenomenological study on the uncanny, Vidler hopes to discover the "power to interpret the relations between the psyche and the dwelling, the body and the house, the individual and the metropolis."[55] He notes that many architects have selected the uncanny as a powerful "metaphor for a fundamentally unlivable modern condition": homelessness.[56] The uncanny's role in an aesthetic agenda for architecture is to identify and critique significant contemporary issues such as imitation, repetition, the symbolic, and the sublime via the link forged with phenomenology.[57]

Vidler recognizes the use of defamiliarizing "reversals of aesthetic norms, [and] substitutions of the grotesque for the sublime," as avant-garde formal strategies addressing alienation.[58] Perhaps this explains Eisenman's exploration of the grotesque as "the manifestation of the uncertain in the physical."[59] He claims the grotesque offers a challenge to the continuous domination of the beautiful, its repressor since the Renaissance. Eisenman considers the Modern Movement a part of an uninterrupted 500-year-long period he refers to as "the classical." (ch. 4)

In Eisenman's work and in other recent theory, beauty is reemerging in the context of opposition to the sublime (grotesque). He proposes "a containing within," in lieu of reversing the current hierarchy, such that one term (the grotesque) still represses the other (the beautiful).[60] His alternative to the exclusion of oppositional categories recognizes that present within the beautiful is the grotesque: "the idea of the ugly, the deformed, and the supposedly unnatural."[61] The utility of this expanded aesthetic category lies in advancing

Eisenman's usual agenda: he sees the possibility of displacing architecture and its dependence on humanist ideals like beauty, through this complexity.

Perhaps Diana Agrest's model for the relationship of architectural practice and theory can be used to reconfigure the relationship between these two aesthetic categories: if the beautiful is the "normative" discourse of aesthetics, the sublime could be seen as an "analytical and exploratory discourse,"[62] in opposition to beauty. The sublime has been described as a "self-transforming discourse" that influenced the construction of the modern subject.[63] The process-oriented character of the sublime may explain part of its appeal for postmodernists.

The significance of the sublime in the twentieth century is finally being recognized in critical writing, which has dwelt primarily on art and literature. Whether presented as a modern phenomenon capable of social critique, or as an aspect of psychological encounter, the profile of the contemporary sublime is emerging. It encompasses Jean-François Lyotard's and Eisenman's advocacy of disciplinary deconstruction and the indeterminacy of abstraction. Under the rubric of the architectural uncanny, it includes Vidler's phenomenological articulation. These theoretical positions offer ways to remove the mask of avant-garde repression that has limited our ability to see architecture in terms of a continuous dialogue between the sublime and the beautiful. The emphasis Vidler and Eisenman place on the spatial experience of the human *subject* challenges a formalist and nonexperiential reception of architecture.

PARADIGM 3: LINGUISTIC THEORY

A shift in concerns in postmodern cultural criticism has also been effected by the restructuring of thought in linguistic paradigms. Semiotics, structuralism, and in particular post-structuralism (including deconstruction) have reshaped many disciplines, including literature, philosophy, anthropology and sociology, and critical activity at large. A significant introduction of Continental theory to an American audience took place in 1966 at Johns Hopkins University. Among the paper presenters at the International Colloquium on Critical Languages and the Sciences of Man, were Jacques Derrida, Roland Barthes, and Jacques Lacan.[64]

These paradigms, a major influence on thought in the 1960s, paralleled a revival of interest in meaning and symbolism in architecture. Architects studied how meaning is carried in language and applied that knowledge, via the "linguistic analogy," to architecture. They questioned to what extent architecture is conventional, like language, and whether people outside architecture understand how its conventions construct meaning. Among others, Diana Agrest and her partner Mario Gandelsonas in "Semiotics and Architecture," and Geoffrey Broadbent in "A Plain Man's Guide to the Theory of Signs in Architecture," began to ask if a "social contract" exists for architecture. (ch. 2) In a challenge to modern functionalism as the determinant of form, it was argued from a linguistic standpoint that architectural objects have no inherent meaning, but can develop it through cultural convention.[65]

SEMIOTICS

Linguistic theory is an important paradigm for analyzing a general postmodern concern: the creation and reception of meaning. Semiotics and structuralism in particular deal with how language communicates, conceiving of it as a closed system.

Semiotics (Charles Sanders Peirce's chosen term), or semiology (Ferdinand de Saussure's term) approaches language scientifically, as a sign system with a dimension of structure (syntactic) and one of meaning (semantic). Structural relationships bind the signs and their components (signifier/signified) together; syntactic relations are between signs. Semantic relationships have to do with meanings, that is, relations between signs and the objects they denote. Peirce's and de Saussure's initial research in the late-nineteenth and early-twentieth centuries established some principles.

The Swiss linguist de Saussure's lectures on semiology, originally presented in 1906–11, were translated from French to English in 1959, generating a revival of interest in his work. His particular contribution was to study language *synchronically* (in its current use), and to examine the parts of language and the relationships between parts.[66] De Saussure was the inventor of the notions *signifier* and *signified*, whose structural relationship constitutes the linguistic *sign*. As important as the two components of the sign is the idea that: "Language is a system of interdependent terms in which the value of each term results solely from the simultaneous presence of the others."[67]

Applications of semiotic theory to other disciplines proliferated in the 1960s, with especially active practitioners in North and South America, France, and Italy. Umberto Eco, novelist, critic, and semiotician, has written on architecture as a semiotic system of signification. In "Function and Sign: Semiotics of Architecture," Eco claims that architectural signs (morphemes) communicate possible functions through a system of conventions or codes.[68] Literal use or programmatic function is architecture's primary meaning. Signs thus *denote* primary functions, and *connote* secondary functions. His essay "A Componential Analysis of the Architectural Sign/Column/" demonstrates that a single architectural object (in this case, the column) can be a bearer of meaning and therefore a pertinent semantic unit.[69]

In "On Reading Architecture," (1972) an important semiotic investigation published in a mainstream professional magazine (*Progressive Architecture*), Mario Gandelsonas compares the syntactically loaded work of Eisenman with the semantically loaded work of Graves. In general, the theory and practice of Agrest and Gandelsonas is influenced by linguistics; they find in semiotics a way of reading architecture as a field of knowledge production. Gandelsonas's book *The Urban Text* is an example of this analysis.

STRUCTURALISM

Structuralism is a study method that generally claims: "the true nature of things may be said to lie not in things themselves, but in the relationships which we construct and then perceive, *between* them."[70] The world is constituted by language, which is a structure of meaningful relationships between arbitrary signs. Thus, structuralists assert that in linguistic systems, there are only differences, without positive terms.[71]

Structuralism focuses on codes, conventions, and processes responsible for a work's intelligibility, that is, how it produces socially available meaning. As a method, it is not concerned with thematic content, but with "the conditions of signification."[72] While structuralism has its roots in linguistics and anthropology, it is a cross-disciplinary

> investigation of a text's relation to particular structures and processes be they linguistic, psychoanalytic, metaphysical, logical, sociological or rhetorical. Languages and structures, rather than authorial self or consciousness, become the major source of explanation.[73]

The appeal of structuralism for rationalizing architecture is clear from the following explanation of method if one substitutes architectural work for literary work:

> structuralists take linguistics as a model and attempt to develop "grammars"—systematic inventories of elements and their possibilities of combination—that would account for the form and meaning of literary works.[74]

POSTSTRUCTURALISM

Cultural critic Hal Foster marks the transition from modern to postmodern through two ideas borrowed directly from literary and cultural critic Roland Barthes (d. 1980). The latter's ideas of the *work* and the *text* mirror the change of focus in artistic or literary production from the modern creation of a whole or unity, to the postmodern creation of "a multidimensional space,"[75] or "a methodological field."[76] While some[77] would argue that it is difficult to separate structuralism and poststructuralism, Foster also uses the work and text to do so. In his essay, "(Post) Modern Polemics," he associates the structuralist work with the stability of the components of the sign, while the poststructuralist text "reflects the contemporary dissolution of the sign and the released play of signifiers."[78] Barthes's later writings suggest that the signifier has the potential for free play and endless deferrals of meaning, which result from an infinite chain of metaphors.

Poststructuralism thus initiates the "critique of the sign," asking: Is the sign really composed of just two parts (signifier and signified), or does it not also depend on the presence of all the other signifiers it does not engage, from which it differs? Marxist literary theorist Terry Eagleton points out that while structuralism divides the sign from the *referent* (the object referred to), poststructuralism goes a step further and divides the signifier from the signified.[79] The result of this line of thought is that "meaning is not immediately *present* in a sign."[80]

Another way of marking the shift from structuralism to poststructuralism, occurring around 1970, is the move from viewing language objectively, (as an object independent of a human subject), to viewing it as the *discourse* of a subject, or individual. "Discourse," Eagleton explains, "means language grasped as utterance" or "as practice," and is poststructuralism's acknowledgement of the linked roles of speaker and audience, of the important role of dialogue in linguistic communication.[81]

Before structuralism, the act of interpretation sought to discover the meaning which coincided with the intention of the author or speaker; this meaning was considered definitive. Structuralism does not attempt to assign a true meaning to the work (beyond its structure) or to evaluate the work in relation to the canon. In poststructuralism, it is asserted that meaning is indeterminate, elusive, bottomless.

In the absence of relevance of the traditional critical project, Barthes offers, in "From Work to Text," the following ideas for what poststructuralist criticism ought to be. First, critics' search for sources, for influences on which to base their interpretations of an object, causes their work to suffer from the "myth of filiation."[82] In seeking to place modern works of art or architecture in a historical context, critics defy the modernist notion that everything must be original, arising from a *tabula rasa*. A better critical undertaking, Barthes says, is one in which "the critic *executes* the work," in both senses of the word. This double entendre refers to performing the critic's usual interpretive function, and it suggests his oedipal feelings with regard to the literature of the past. Barthes wants the critic, or reader in general, to take an active role as a producer of meaning.

The poststructuralist paradigm raises two main questions pertinent to postmodern architecture, according to Foster in "(Post) Modern Polemics": the status of the subject and its language, and the status of history and its representation. Both are constructs shaped by society's representations of them. In fact, the object of the poststructuralist critique is to demonstrate that all of reality is *constituted* (produced and sustained) by its representations, rather than *reflected* in them. History, for example, is a narrative with implications of subjectivity, of the fictional. Poststructuralism thus supports a proliferation of histories, told from other points of view than that of the power elite. These histories replace the "received" version of a "history of victors."[83]

Poststructuralist thinking similarly problematizes the subject as author, challenging his/her status and power in discussions like Barthes's "The Death of the Author" (1968) and philosopher Michel Foucault's "What is an Author?" (1969).[84] Both suggest that the uniqueness and creativity of the author are just convenient cultural fictions, compared with the selective, reductive role authors actually play in presenting a limited number of issues. In their poststructuralist view, now widely accepted, this "individual" is in fact located within a system of conventions that "speak him/her."

The "romantic artist" as productive "genius" is attacked as an ideological construct like the author, because society's representation conflicts with the artist's function. Like the author, the artist is an exaggerated celebration of individualism. Foucault (d.1984) preferred to look at the author instead as a "function...characteristic of the mode of existence, circulation, and functioning of certain discourses within a society."[85] This perspective allows him to ask more important questions than are raised by traditional criticism, such as: "What are the modes of existence of this discourse? Where has it been used, how can it circulate, and who can appropriate it for himself?"[86]

Many influential practitioners and architectural educators assume poststructuralist stances. Postmodern architectural theory has thus undertaken a reexamination of modern architecture's disciplinary origins (including the tabula rasa notion), and its relationship to history (which could be characterized by Harold Bloom's phrase *The Anxiety of Influence*, 1973), the emphasis on innovation in modernism, and the notion of the individualist, "hero" architect.

The postmodern reorientation of critical priorities, refocusing the object of disciplinary study, occurs with the application of poststructuralist principles to other disciplines. For example, Foucault's consideration of the impact of various discourses leads to a sociological interest in the role of institutions in society. The psychoanalytic criticism of Jacques Lacan and Julia Kristeva is filtered through a poststructuralist lens; in Kristeva's case, it is also layered with feminist thought.

DECONSTRUCTION

One of the most significant poststructuralist manifestations is deconstruction. A philosophical and linguistic practice, deconstruction looks at the foundations of thought in "logocentrism,"[87] and at the foundations of disciplines like architecture. Jacques Derrida, the French philosopher whose work is most often associated with deconstruction, explores the use of rhetorical operations (such as metaphor) to produce the supposed ground or foundation of argument, noting that each concept has been constructed. (ch. 3) For instance, he speculates on what constitutes the "architecture of architecture": If architecture, tectonics, and urban design serve as the fundamental metaphors for other systems of thought, like philosophy, what supports architecture?[88]

Derrida describes his work:

> Deconstruction analyzes and questions conceptual pairs which are currently accepted as self-evident and natural, as if they hadn't been institutionalized at some precise moment....Because of being taken for granted they restrict thinking.[89]

Deconstruction works from the margins to expose and dismantle the oppositions and vulnerable assumptions that structure a text.[90] It then moves on to attempt a more general displacement of the system, by ascertaining what the history of the discipline may have concealed or excluded, using repression to constitute its identity. This strategy is crucial in feminist critiques. (See the discussion on feminism in this introduction.)

The purpose of deconstruction is to displace philosophical categories and attempts at mastery, such as the privileging of one term over the other in binary oppositions, such as presence/absence.[91] The hierarchical binaries are seen not as isolated or peripheral problems, but as systemic and repressive. Derrida sees architecture as aiming at control of the communication and transportation sectors of society, as well as the economy. Deconstruction is part of the postmodern critique; its goal is to end modern architecture's plan of domination.[92]

Tschumi's stated goal for architecture is very close to Derrida's:

> [to achieve the construction of] conditions that will dislocate the most traditional and regressive aspects of our society and simultaneously reorganize these elements in the most liberating way.[93]

In testing the limits of the discipline, discovering its margins, confronting it with other disciplines, and subjecting its premises to radical criticism, Tschumi is the architectural counterpart of Barthes and Derrida.[94] He is interested in the architectural text, as something potentially unlimited, not subsumed within disciplines and traditional genres, but crossing these disciplinary boundaries.

Eisenman has also made proposals (in theory and design) for architecture as text (ch. 4) and his numerous published exchanges with Derrida have been instrumental in introducing architects to deconstruction.

An evolution takes place in the postmodern period, from a structuralist interest in how meaning is created by relationships between signs and components of signs, to the conclusion that determining a definitive meaning is impossible in poststructuralist and deconstructionist thought. Many interesting questions are raised by linguistic theory, and these questions affect the making of architecture, architectural theory, and its critical reception. Is the pursuit of meaning fruitless or nostalgic? If the interpretation of artifacts is not a worthwhile critical practice, what is the purpose of criticism? Ferreting out ideologies? Creative writing? Constructing a parallel narrative which does not claim any particular authority in relation to an artifact?

The architectural concerns of place and meaning are thus threatened by poststructuralist notions like the arbitrariness of the communicative sign. If signs are unreliably interpreted, easily construed in several ways simultaneously, how can architecture express a shared sense of community? And if language is unreliable, can there be agreement on the meaning of architectural "language"? Furthermore, the loss of grand historical narratives, posited by poststructuralists, points to the unattainability of a consensus that might be meaningfully represented in architecture.

PARADIGM 4: MARXISM

The Marxist paradigm is an influential one applied to the study of architecture in the postmodern period, especially for examining the city and its institutions. The postmodern urban critique is supported by the general reconsideration of political questions by Marxist intellectuals and theorists.

Marxist approaches to architectural history and theory (notably among the Italian writers of the "School of Venice"), raise issues of the relationship of class struggle and architecture. Historian Manfredo Tafuri explains his intentions in the conclusion to *Architecture and Utopia* (1973):

> A coherent Marxist criticism of the ideology of architecture and urbanism could not but demystify the contingent and historical realities...hidden behind the unifying terms of art, architecture, and city. (ch. 7)

He defines "the crisis of modern architecture...[as] rather a crisis of the ideological function of architecture." That is, Modern Movement architecture failed to achieve the desired overhaul of the social order because only a *class critique* of architecture is possible. A class architecture cannot cause a general revolution because it depends on and follows this general revolution. Tafuri claims that modern architecture cannot even provide an image of architecture for a liberated society without revisions to its elements: language, method, and structure.

While Tafuri seems to rule out change through architecture, Jameson is more optimistic about the potential of Marxist "enclave theory" for grass-roots resistance to the status quo.[95] This model proposes that marginalized groups, working gradually from the fringes of society, can forge a position as a critical enclave and can initiate change. An example is the student revolutions of May 1968, "the events" in which European (particularly French) students and workers together attempted to overthrow the capitalist system and install Marxism. The students, like women and blacks, embraced the necessity of constituent group radicalism. (Eagleton hypothesizes that the revolutionaries' inability to change the entrenched government may have played a part in the turn to a poststructuralist attack on language.[96] Enclave theory has spawned a number of architectural manifestations, including the above-mentioned Critical Regionalism, which I discuss later. (ch. 11)

These questions of the structure of political power are reinforced by French intellectuals like poststructuralist Michel Foucault, ("Of Other Spaces and Heterotopias") and the influential Frankfurt School, whose members take a modified Marxist position. Foucault's influence has been tremendously widespread, because of his broad analytical studies of the structure of disciplines and professions under the methods of *archaeology* and *geneology* of knowledge. His interdisciplinary approach fuses philosophy, history, psychology, and politics into what he calls a "taxonomy of discourses." Foucault's books *Madness and Civilization*, *The Order of Things*, and *Discipline and Punish* make clear that institutions (and the architectural forms that house them) serve a control function in society. The architectural utopia is even briefly considered in his essay "Of Other Spaces: Utopias and Heterotopias" (1967). In addition to studying the role of institutions, Foucault identifies the role of professional jargon in creating an autonomous, legitimizing, and exclusionary discourse. The postmodern critique of power structures in the late 1960s and 1970s was inspired and facilitated by this analysis.

The Critical Theory of the Frankfurt School is the work of a group within the Institute of Social Research at the University of Frankfurt. It is associated primarily with Max Horkheimer (d.1973), Theodore Adorno (d.1969), both directors of the Institute, and with Herbert Marcuse (d.1979), who remained in the United States after the exiled Institute was reestablished in Germany in the 1950s. Like Foucault, their interdisciplinary approach fuses philosophy, history, and psychology in an effort to accurately describe the phenomena of culture in the context of society and the political economy. Their study of issues such as the rise of authoritarianism and bureaucracy, the changing nature of social relationships, and the relationship of contemporary culture to everyday life, was intended to contribute to the struggle against domination.[97] They were and have continued to be influential with students and progressive thinkers. Walter Benjamin (d.1940), although a peripheral member of the Institute, is now one of the best known. His writings on culture, similar in scope to those of Barthes, have been frequently cited in architectural theory since the late 1970s.

PARADIGM 5: FEMINISM

Activism in the 1960s called attention to the disenfranchisement within ostensibly democratic societies of groups defined by gender, race, or sexual orientation. More recently, it has been highlighted by younger scholars, often gay or female. Critical approaches calling for equity, inclusion, and an end to prejudice, known as "the critique of the Other," are broadening the discussion of architecture and other arts from just formal grounds (which dominate late modernist theory and criticism) to cultural, historical, and ethical grounds. An important instance of this critique of the Other is feminism.

Feminism arose as a political agenda to resist male domination in the postmodern period. This political movement made great strides in achieving social equity, from employment and educational opportunities to legal and financial independence. In the United States, the right to control one's own destiny, which these issues signify, finds its emblem in the ongoing abortion battle.

The exclusionary operations of disciplines and other institutions were successfully challenged in the 1970s by women who had been largely prohibited from full participation in the workforce, politics, and academia. Rejecting sex-based discrimination requires presenting *gender* as unnatural, arbitrary, and irrelevant. To reveal gender as a construction of social control that privileges some members of society at the expense of others, feminists use critical paradigms including post-structuralism, Marxism, and psychoanalysis. Gender has been used historically to isolate or mark "the other." Theorist Chris Weedon points out the origin and implications of gender:

> Psychoanalysis offers a universal theory of the psychic construction of gender identity on the basis of repression [of part of a child's bisexuality]....It offers a framework from within which femininity and masculinity can be understood and a theory of consciousness, language, and meaning. [98]

Architectural theorist Ann Bergren says, "Gender is...a machine for thinking the meaning of sexual difference." [99] She notes that some languages, like English, function without the need for differentiation in gender terms. These kinds of observations have led Bergren to conclude that gender is "subjective in both senses of the term, and thereby rhetorical and political." As a result, feminists are examining the logocentric notion of difference, which originates in gender, and its unacknowledged impact on the built world.

Fundamental to reconsidering cultural constructions like gender is Foucault's "formulation of the subject as pure exteriority, the product of the inscription of the relations of power." [100] In other words, the individual is manipulated into behavioral conformity by explicit political structures and implicit social codes. These structures and codes are precisely the target of feminist attacks.

The feminist critique of architecture aims to engage theory and practice firmly in the sociopolitical reality. Influenced by Freudian and Derridean analysis, Agrest believes the "system" of architecture (the Renaissance theory accounting for classicism that makes up the received "Western tradition") is defined both by what it includes and what it excludes, or represses. In her essay, "Architecture from Without: Body, Logic, Sex," she finds herself and the female body in general to be excluded from this "phallocentric" system. (ch. 13) The pyschoanalytic term "repression" (denial of sex drive leading to neurosis) takes on a spatial meaning here as she describes "an interior of repression," defined by woman and her body, and the system that their repression maintains. She turns the liability of exclusion into an advantage:

> This outside is a place where one can take distance from the closed system of architecture and thus be in...a position to examine [architecture's] mechanisms of closure, its ideological mechanisms of filtration, to blur the boundaries that separate architecture from other practices. [101]

But Agrest also understands the risk that a woman takes in assuming an outside position, in not conforming to the social order: being labeled through history as an ecstatic, a witch, a hysteric, etc. She suggests that a productive extradisciplinary position from which to view architecture and urbanism may be found in film, as it shares with architecture the elements of time and space. The critical point of view Agrest establishes in theory attempts to resituate the female body in postmodern architecture. It is also a significant reminder that the tradition of anthropomorphism was neglected in modern architecture. For more on this concept, see my discussion of the theme of the body.

PART IIC. POSTMODERN ARCHITECTURAL THEMES

Some general themes around which one can cluster issues of postmodern cultural theory are history (the problem of disciplinary tradition), meaning, social responsibility (ethical engagement versus autonomous practice), and the body. In the case of postmodern architectural theory, a strong position is also formulated with respect to the city as cultural artifact, and to *place*, in the phenomenological sense. While most of these themes also characterize architectural theory of the preceding period, one can argue that place and the body were not recognized by the Modern Movement because of its focus on accommodating the collective over the individual, expressed in a language of universality, both technological and abstract. The celebration of the machine as formal model, for instance, excluded the body. Art plays a greater role in postmodern architectural theory than technology, as the pendulum swings again between the poles of architecture as art and architecture as engineering. Vidler says:

> The question of the art of architecture, closed by the functional ethic, may well be opened, with all its disturbing implications, by this attempt in the domain of ideas ....until recently architects [were] more concerned to develop machines for living in than art to wrestle with. The positivistic utopia of modern architecture was in this way based on the repression of death, decay, and the "pleasure principle."[102]

In this period, it often seems that the formal ideas being grappled with first become clear in art, (which is free of the complications of inhabitability, collaboration, and finance), and then trickle down to architecture. For instance, Foster has described how postmodern art creates a destructured object and field, a decentered human subject (both artist and viewer), and causes an erosion of history.[103] These ideas are emphasized in recent theory on the body in architecture.

There is tremendous crossover of issues between postmodern art and art criticism and architectural theory, in part because the same theoretical paradigms (notably poststructuralism) are influential in both disciplines. Common issues include the constellation of ideas surrounding the construction of the artist, such as the definition of his/her role as a producer in society and the reception of the work of art. These issues of making can be summed up as dealing with authorship, authority, and authenticity. Contemporary art curator Howard Fox notes that

> in the 70s art world the authority of certain ideas we associate with modernism had begun to erode: originality, artistic genius, virtuoso workmanship, the notion of the sacrosanctness of the art object.[104]

Many of the ideas now being questioned (holdovers from nineteenth-century romantic conceptions of the artist) are those originally challenged by the work of the surrealists as early as the 1910s. In particular, Marcel Duchamp's "readymades" raise radical, disquieting questions for colleagues about the alchemical, validating artist's signature; the role of the hand in manufacture; ideas of the original and authentic; and the privileged status of places of exhibition. Duchamp's appropriation and presentation of the mass-produced object as *objet d'art* anticipates Benjamin's 1936 essay, "The Work of Art in the Age of Mechanical Reproduction," which acknowledges the changing conditions of making and experiencing art in the industrial era.

Ignasi de Solà-Morales Rubió, the Catalan architectural theorist, cites surrealism as the most committed critical stance against the Modern Movement, thus explaining its fascination for postmodern artists and architects.[105] Another generation of artists and theorists (Robert Morris, Gordon Matta-Clark, Alain Robbe-Grillet, etc.) began to explore this legacy in the mid 1960s. In architecture, Rossi is in the forefront in considering and using surrealism, followed by others who emerged in the 1970s and 1980s, including Tschumi, Koolhaas, and Elizabeth Diller and Ricardo Scofidio.[106]

One of the postmodern strategies for challenging the notion of originality is appropriation: borrowing—even literally reproducing—another person's work with the intent to recontextualize it, or re-present it in a new context. For feminist artists, appropriating a famous male artist's work is a way of calling attention to the marginalization of women in the history of art. It is a controversial way to question the value society places on originality. In Sherrie Levine's work, appropriating and re-presenting the prints of Walker Evans calls attention to the mechanical and serial aspect of photography, and hence its odd relationship to traditional manufacture in the other arts.

THEME 1: HISTORY AND HISTORICISM
That these questions have been raised indicates that modernism has lost its firm, univalent grasp on the art and architecture scene, leaving open the possibility of a multiplicity of theoretical perspectives and forms of expression. It also highlights the self-conscious, analytical, and image-oriented nature of the postmodern period, in which artists and architects concerned themselves with "a history of influence." Postmodern positions call for the reconsideration, if not embrace of disciplinary history, which had been rejected by modern theory. Appropriation is an aggressive way of dealing with the past. Another way is the attitude of self-consciousness of the present as a distinct historical moment, which leads to "periodization," the segregation of works and events into separate chronological or stylistic categories.

Periodization is typical of a *historicist* view of history, defined as seeking to express the *zeitgeist*, or spirit of the age, understood to be unique to the present time and requiring the development of a unique style. (ch. 4) It is clear that the modern idea of style depends upon this theory of history. A historicist culture thus pursues an ever-changing, "emergent ideal" on the model of organic growth or evolution in nature.[107] This nineteenth-century theory of history underlies the relativism of cultural modernity, especially avant-garde ideas about the necessity of a "radical break" with the past.

In "Three Kinds of Historicism," Alan Colquhoun notes: "in the architectural avant-garde this meant the continual creation of new forms under the impulse of social and technological development and the symbolic representation of society through these forms." (ch. 4)

A postmodern critic, Colquhoun discovers two paradoxical aspects of historicism. The primary paradox is that seeking an expression of the zeitgeist condemns one to a pattern of continual change. Habermas deepens the paradox with his suspicion that the "value placed [by modernism] on the transitory, the elusive, and the ephemeral...discloses a longing for an undefiled, immaculate and stable present."[108] Secondly, Colquhoun points out, instead of the fixed ideals and "natural law" of the classical world view, modernism substituted a "flight to the future," an inevitable (positivist) progression of relatively valid expressions of various times. The paradox, for Colquhoun, is that something can be both inevitable and relative. Other questions about historicism include how one can identify the zeitgeist from within history; for Eisenman in "The End of the Classical," (ch. 4) this logical problem suggests the need to find a new purpose for architecture.

Note that historicism has two other definitions that are also relevant in a discussion of postmodern architecture. Colquhoun offers the following: 1) an attitude of concern for the traditions of the past, and 2) the artistic practice of using historical forms. Postmodern historicist architects utilize elements of classical or other past styles in an artistic practice of collage, pastiche, or authentic reconstruction, clearly demonstrating that they feel these forms are superior to contemporary ones because of the associations and meaning they carry.

One of the significant events in recent architectural history is the reappraisal of work not conforming to or contained within the mainstream schools of the Modern Movement. The notion that modern architecture is not singular, but is composed of many distinct tendencies, characterizes the work of the Italian theorists Manfredo Tafuri and Francesco Dal Co. These Marxist architectural historians choose a "dialectical" approach emphasizing the disparate nature of modern works, presented as a plurality of histories. Previously marginalized (as aberrant) buildings and architects are now elevated for comparison with Le Corbusier and Mies van der Rohe as significant exceptions to the hegemony of International Style functionalism (aggressively promoted as the style by the MoMA and historians like Gideion). The postmodern revision also looks for continuities with earlier works, and expresses skepticism about the avant-garde notion of the "radical break": Was it a worthwhile and achievable goal and has it occurred in the twentieth century?

POSTMODERN ATTITUDES IN RELATION TO MODERNITY

Probably the most confusing aspect of postmodern theory is the multiplicity of terms used to describe the various positions taken with regard to the modern condition. The following attempts to simplify the range of possibilities, and to avoid the use of terms that conflict or have different associations outside of this discipline. The two main postmodern attitudes can be classified as either anti-modern or pro-modern. Within this basic schema, one finds critical and affirmative theories, resistant and reactionary, progressive and conservative.

ANTI-MODERN THEORIES

Anti-modern theories seek a "radical break" with modernity, offering alternatives, either future-oriented (critical new visions), or backward-looking (reactionary revivals of tradition). While the former can be seen as "neoavant-garde" in striving for a new expression of a self-consciously defined postmodern time, the latter includes *arrière-garde* (rear-guard) proposals to bypass modernity and return to premodern, preindustrial conditions.

The dominant rear-guard postmodern position calls for the return of history. It reflects skepticism of the extent to which modern artists and architects could actually operate from the tabula rasa they claim as their origin, as well as skepticism about the value of the origin itself. Frequently called "neoconservative" postmodernism, the return to and validation of classicism as transhistorical (not subject to historical change) is one example of the anti-modern position. This reactionary tendency paralleled conservative political developments in the 1980s, with party platforms centered on traditionalism and "family values." In architecture, classical aesthetic values like imitation were championed in this rejection of modernism.

PRO-MODERN THEORIES

The opposite postmodern approach is the progressive position, desiring to extend or complete the modern cultural tradition. The progressivist carries over many ideas from modernism in an effort to transform it. Theorists of this persuasion, such as Foster, feel that the "adversary culture" of the twentieth-century avant-garde has been renounced by reactionary political opponents in order to maintain social control.[109] This conservative strategy of attack relies on equating modernism at large with the aesthetic doctrine of formalism. The reductive presentation of modernism *as formalism*, as occupying a position of "official autonomy," overlooks its potential for social critique. Furthermore, Foster agrees with Clement Greenberg that modernism is "a self-critical program... pledged to maintain the high quality of past art in current production" and to ensure the continuation of the aesthetic as a value.[110]

Habermas, whose work extends that of the Frankfurt School, is among the strongest advocates of this branch of postmodernism. He argues against conservatives' blaming societal ills on cultural modernism, saying (as does Frampton) that it is, in fact, economic and societal *modernization* that causes alienation:

> The neoconservative does not uncover the economic and social causes for the altered attitudes towards work, consumption, achievement and leisure. Consequently, he attributes all of the following—hedonism, the lack of social identification, the lack of obedience, narcissism, the withdrawal from status and achievement competition—to the domain of culture.[111]

To support Habermas's distinction between the effects of modernization and modernism, one can cite the disappointing lack of effectiveness of modern architecture in solving social problems. How can cultural modernism be responsible for social malaise when it cannot affect change? Sounding a Marxist note, Habermas advises resistance to the "autonomous economic system" through the development of checks and balances.

Habermas argues that the Enlightenment project and its liberal values must not be shelved, but renewed with efforts to integrate the three autonomous spheres of reason—art, science, and morality—with each other and with life. The proposed reconciliation of life and art, unsuccessfully attempted by the surrealists, is intended to result in social and personal emancipation.[112]

Also a progressive postmodernist, Jean-François Lyotard explicitly cites Habermas's theoretical work, along with Adorno's *Aesthetic Theory* and Karl Popper's *The Poverty of Historicism* and *The Open Society*, as attempts to continue the project of modernity in specific spheres of art and politics. In their published exchanges, Lyotard disagrees with Habermas's desire for consensus and doubts art's ability "to bridge the gap between cognitive, ethical and political discourses...[and to open] the way to a unity of experience."[113] Lyotard has identified the role of *grand narratives*, or *metanarratives*, which are used to legitimize power structures, ideas such as the hermeneutics of meaning, emancipation of the worker (Marxism's narrative), and the creation of wealth (capitalism), justice, and truth.[114] His efforts to recuperate a critical modernism have discredited the metanarratives by the revelation that they operate to consolidate power. Lyotard claims that technology has taken over all the positions of power. For him and other intellectuals concerned with the ideal of freedom, only *petits recits* ("small stories") and a multiplicity of meanings remain operative in the postmodern period. The collapse of metanarratives thus marks the end of the modern era and of consensus. Lyotard's postmodern task is to wage war on totality (and totalizing intellectual schemes), and to avoid nostalgia for wholeness.

THEME 2: MEANING

Architecture derives its meaning from the circumstances of its creation; and this implies that what is external to architecture—what can broadly be called its set of functions—is of vital importance.[115]

FORM/CONTENT: TYPE, FUNCTION, TECTONICS

Central to the postmodern discussion of meaning is the definition of the essence of architecture, about which there is little consensus. One frequently encounters three elements posited as that which cannot be removed from architecture: type, function, and tectonics. These concerns can be fairly well correlated to the Vitruvian triad of delight (beauty or ideal form), commodity (utility or accommodation), and firmness (durability).

Type is often linked to the other two terms; to function through types based on use, and to tectonics through types based on structural systems. (ch. 5) Typology can also be seen as a catalog of general solutions to problems of architectural arrangement, idealized to the most diagrammatic level. Considered this way, perhaps type constitutes what Derrida has called "the architecture of architecture," or the equivalent of deep structure in language.

The communication of meaning is also part of type because of the redundancy of form, whether the repetition of root forms or invariant elements (archetypes). Consciously or unconsciously perceived, type creates continuity with history, which gives intelligibility to buildings and cities within a culture.

For some postmodernists, the choice between imitation and invention as the origin of form is evaded by accepting the existence of an *a priori* inventory of types available for transformation into models. Since types are too generic (and styleless) to imitate, invention plays a large role in the design process. Type is thus "the interior structure of a form or...a principle which contains the possibility of infinite formal variation and further structural modification of the 'type' itself."[116] Type offers a rational, valueless origin (as opposed to the judgmental choice of a specific historic building as precedent) from which to articulate a design method of transformation.

The writing of Enlightenment theorist Quatremère de Quincy underlies postmodern thinking about typology, such as that of the Italian Neorationalists:

> The foundations of neorationalism lie in its conception of the architectural project, the limits of which are already established by architectural tradition and whose field of action is logically framed by the constant return of types, plans, and basic elements: all synchronically understood as permanent and immutable, rooted in tradition and history.[117]

The architect's role is to transform the ideal or essence that is type, into a physical model. Solà-Morales Rubió calls this process "design figuration," and notes that Rossi's use of type is mediated by his poetic subjectivity and his inspiration from surrealism. Others fuse the typological ideal with the pragmatics of constructional technique, which is sometimes based on regional vernacular building. Giulio Carlo Argan, whose theory allows for the development of new types, suggests a powerful fusion of type with tectonics to create an "inevitable" point of origin for design. (ch. 5)

In the Modern Movement, communication of function is the major expressive issue. Function is seen as rational and scientific, not gratuitous or simply aesthetic. The priority placed on function as content would suggest that it is considered to be the essence of modern architecture. The assumption that architecture's form is derived from or "transparent to" function implies that there can be a direct correspondence between specific forms and specific functions. This correspondence requires codes to create meaning, since meaning is not inherent in the forms, but is culturally constructed. All of these issues and positions are revisited in the postmodern period in essays including Gandelsonas's "Neo-Functionalism," Eisenman's "Postfunctionalism," (ch. 1) Eco's "Function and Sign: Semiotics of Architecture," and Tschumi's "Architecture and Limits" series. (ch. 3)

Eisenman argues that function has been a continuous aspect of architectural theory since the Renaissance, and that this fundamental connection with humanism prevents architecture from moving into modernism. Functionalism, he states, "is really no more than a late phase of humanism." He urges the reader "to recognize that the form/function opposition is not necessarily inherent to any architectural theory and…to recognize the crucial difference between modernism and humanism."

Postmodernism places a higher value on form than on function, deliberately and polemically inverting the modernist dictum: form follows function. The formalist position asserts that form itself is the essence or content of architecture. This emphasis on form as meaning parallels some linguistic developments in structuralism and poststructuralism. In particular, challenges to the notion that language mirrors reality find theoretical counterparts in self-referential architecture. Modern painting had ceased to present recognizable images from life, so why should architecture be bound to present something external to itself? This reasoning underlies the autonomous position which even views function as external to architecture.

Similar debates rage over the centrality of tectonics to architecture. (ch. 12) Some theorists assert that only built work can be considered architecture, while others maintain that physical presence alone is no guarantee. But if a project is to be built, one must confront the issue of tectonics, which highlights again the distinction between building and architecture. Both practices share the need to employ structural systems and resolve material joints, so what elevates architecture above building? Architect Demetri Porphyrios claims that "imitative mediation" in handling raw materials distinguishes architecture; its absence explains why modernism produced only building. Thus, the goal of architecture should be: "To construct a tectonic discourse which, while addressing the pragmatics of shelter, could at the same time represent its very tectonics as myth."[118] For Porphyrios, this assertion leads to the conclusion that classicism is the necessary route to great architecture, based on its ability to mythicize vernacular construction.

Others argue more generally that tectonics is a rich source of meaning. The latter position is sometimes tied to a phenomenological interest in the "thingness" of architecture, in architecture's ability to *gather* (condense meaning in the environment). Part of "a return to things," construction as a process of becoming is a postmodern theme. For example, Faye Jones's Pinecote Pavilion features a partially clad roof that reveals its layered process of construction.

The tectonic emphasis is an important part of the postmodern critique of a sterile, debased modernism and of superficial postmodern historicism. Some architects construct a narrative through material and detail. The narrative is sometimes whimsical (using eclectic borrowing, pastiche, and appliqué), and sometimes pragmatic (taking the required detail as an opportunity for tectonic expressiveness). Gregotti's call for resituating detailing as an architectural problem is seconded by Marco Frascari and Frampton; all three published articles on the subject between 1983 and 1984. Their calls in "The Tell-the-Tale Detail," "Rappel à l'ordre, the Case for the Tectonic," and "The Exercise of Detailing" (ch. 12) have been heeded by the profession. In his search for essence, Frampton suggests "we may return instead to the structural unit as the irreducible essence of architectural form." For him, the structural unit refers to the connection between tectonic components—the joint—which is the "nexus around which building comes into being" and is "articulated as a presence" in phenomenological terms.

REPRESENTATION AND POSTMODERN HISTORICISM

The form versus content debate summarized above is part of postmodernism's consideration of meaning. Representation and figuration are also central to this theme. Postmodern artists reintroduced the human figure and other recognizable forms into their work, ending the long reign of abstraction begun in cubism, constructivism, and suprematism. In postmodern architecture, the use of historic styles or identifiable fragments from specific styles has the same intent: to create form with associations, even to the extent of constructing a narrative. But Gregotti notes in his editorial on detailing that the appearance of the stylistic quotation coincides with a crisis of architectural language. He maintains that the (perverse, radical) historicist quotation is not, however, an adequate substitute for the tectonic detail, which articulates building technique as an expressive component in architectural language.

Graves's work since 1976–77 illustrates his interest in "figurative architecture," by which he means architecture with an associational relationship to nature and the classical tradition. (ch. 1) His suggestive use of historical fragments in the Portland Municipal Building linked his name with a recognizable formal vocabulary or image, which made him a favorite of advertising firms. As McLeod point out, in the status-conscious 1980s, architects were sought-after to design and endorse products from tea kettles to shoes.[119]

The 80s were glamorous years for architects, and the "signature building" was affordable for an affluent society. But the price exacted for mass-market appeal and an imitable style is the commercialization of one's image and the phenomenon of the architectural "knock-off." Developers and builders of strip shopping centers have superficially imitated the Graves style and palette, while entirely missing the point of "figurative architecture." Any critical component of the original is lacking in the commercial version.

This work and its assimilation by the marketplace indicate that there may be some validity to the idea that architecture can act as a semiotic sign system. This pertains primarily to work concerned with the stylistic dimension of architecture, whether it be classical or vernacular in inspiration. A good example is Stern's portfolio of neotraditional houses for affluent, conservative clients. The designs capitalize on associations of nineteenth-century architectural styles with wealth, status, and aristocratic lifestyles. In Stern's view, following Rossi, a form's meaning is understood to accrue over time through the function of cultural memory. But this is not to suggest other similarities in their approaches to their work

A characteristic postmodern historicist compositional strategy is pastiche, the eclectic quotation of fragmented historical elements. Foster has discussed this phenomenon as appropriation of the past for present purposes. Presented as a critique of uncommunicative minimalism, he doubts whether a decontextualized history of emblematic fragments is any more accessible than abstraction. Pastiche tends to be accompanied by an attitude of parody towards the historical fragments, which belies a genuine respect for the past. Phillip Johnson's AT&T Building (1978) illustrates the kind of tongue-in-cheek games postmodern historicist architects play, in this case, exploding the scale of a Chippendale highboy to become a Manhattan skyscraper. What should we take to be the meaning of a building envelope resembling a piece of furniture?

Stern has pointed out the "ornamentalist" tendency of postmodern historicist architecture, which relies on the decorated wall plane to convey meaning. (ch. 1) This observation implies that the postmodern *facade* as concealing mask replaces the modernist *elevation* revealing the interior. (The change in terminology for the wall surface is indicative of postmodern historicist interest in the Beaux Arts tradition.) Recently, decorative energy has also been focused on materials and detail as expressive episodes in a building.

Predictably, some critiques of postmodern historicism focus on the prominent issue of representation. Removing stylistic fragments from their historical context results in what Frampton and others have called scenographic effects from de-historicizing architecture. In addition to "make-believe classical," Porphyrios identifies two other distinct postmodern architectural manifestations: "make-believe high tech" and the "transgression" of deconstruction. His article "The Relevance of Classical Architecture" criticizes all postmodern "culture" as founded on an unstable ground comprised of the primacy of context and the "rhetoric of style," an eclectic attitude of looking at styles as communicative devices. (ch. 1) The resulting postmodern historicist architecture is scenographic kitsch, epitomized by Robert Venturi and Denise Scott Brown's "decorated shed."

Porphyrios also feels that parody and pastiche are inappropriate to architectural investigation. His alternative is the authentic classical revival, with meaning derived from the logic of construction and its mythification. He finds further justification for classicism on the basis of ecology, urbanism, and culture.

Some theorists, including Diane Ghirardo, argue that postmodern historicist architecture tends to selectively misread history and to ignore larger ecological, political, and social responsibilities. She criticizes this abdication in pursuit of formalism. As an example, Ghirardo points out that in America in the 1970s, unemployed architects did not turn to designing social utopias, but retreated instead to fetishistic "paper architecture." (ch. 8)

In opposition to the often superficial appropriation of images from architectural history by postmodern historicists, other architects asserted the positive values of abstraction in their writing and projects. For instance, the inaugural volume of the *Pratt Journal* presented various discussions of the continuing validity of abstraction. Similarly, Lyotard's contemporary sublime challenges the notion that abstraction is without content, offering as an illustration modern artists' attempts to "present the unpresentable" from the realm of ideas.

THEME 3: PLACE

> During the last decades it has become increasingly clear that this pragmatic approach [functionalism] leads to a schematic and characterless environment with insufficient possibilities for human dwelling. The problem of meaning in architecture has therefore come to the fore.[120]

MAN, ARCHITECTURE, AND NATURE

The relationship between man and nature is a long-standing philosophical problem that has been highlighted by phenomenologists like Norberg-Schulz. In Western thought, nature as "the other" in relation to culture has been a stabilizing theme for centuries. For instance, the human struggle against a threatening nature characterizes Enlightenment ideas of the sublime.

Since the Industrial Revolution, advanced technology has reduced the urgency of this survival struggle. In fact, it has been suggested by deconstructionists that the ancient nature/culture opposition has been displaced, rendered irrelevant, along with all other binaries. If this is true, has the binary structure been eliminated? Some have argued that having conquered nature, the challenge to culture now comes from the opposite end of the spectrum: from man's knowledge and its instrumentalized form, technology. Along with technological advancement, for example, mankind has created a global environmental crisis.

Architecture literally and symbolically overcomes the forces of nature to provide shelter. In the pre-industrial past, the production of meaning in architecture relied upon structured references to and associations with nature. Modern architecture embraced the machine analogy instead of the organic analogy. Although machines are often designed on the basis of natural systems, their use as a formal model prevented architecture from referring directly to nature. This is problematic because despite technological advances, symbolizing man's position within the natural world remains one of architecture's roles.

PLACE AND GENIUS LOCI

Albert Einstein defines place as "a small portion of the earth's surface identifiable by a name...a sort of order of material objects and nothing else."[121] Architectural historian Peter Collins accepts this definition and develops its implications:

> Now this is precisely the kind of space involved in architectural design, and one might contend that a "place" (plaza, piazza) is the largest space that an architect is able to deal with as a unified work of art.[122]

Theories of *place*, arising from phenomenology and physical geography,[123] emphasize the specificity of spatial experience and in some cases, the idea of the *genius loci*, or unique spirit of the place. Place offers a way to resist the relativism in modern theories of history through the engagement of the body and its verification of the particular qualities of a site.

Heidegger's position that the relationship to nature is crucial to rich human experience is shared by many contemporary architects and theorists including Gregotti, Raimund Abraham, Tadao Ando, and Norberg-Schulz. The latter claims the architect's responsibility is to discover the genius loci, and design in a way (place-making) that accounts for this singular presence. (ch. 9) In other words, Norberg-Schulz calls for man's intervention to intensify the natural attributes of the situation. Certain significant elements of architecture have been celebrated by phenomenologists as "embodiments of difference": "Boundary and threshold are constituent elements of place. They form part of a figure which discloses the spatiality in question."

Gregotti elevates place-making to the primal architectural act, the origin; laying a stone on the ground is the beginning of "modifications" that turn place into architecture. (ch. 7) He sees architecture as constituted by structural relationships (in particular, differences) in the environment, which, similar to structure in language, allow understanding. This notion of difference explains his emphasis on the measurement of intervals, rather than the presence of isolated objects. The architect's task is to reveal nature by situating and utilizing the landscape. The current interest in constructing the site[124] reflects the desire to make a place, as promoted by Norberg-Schulz and Gregotti.

CONFRONTATION AND DWELLING

Abraham's inscribing the site clearly demonstrates an attitude of aggressive intervention in the landscape. Describing his process in "Negation and Reconciliation," Abraham says:

> It is the conquest of the site, the transformation of its topographical nature, that manifests the ontological roots of architecture. The process of design is only a secondary and subsequent act, whose purpose is to reconcile the consequences of the initial intervention, collision, and negation. (ch. 10)

Abraham's design and theoretical work reveal a commitment to the principle of engagement between architecture and landscape. There are perhaps less violent ways to conceptualize and realize this interaction, such that the design process is more than a remediation of the "conquest." Other postmodern architects, for example Ando, assert a larger and more positive role for design than Abraham does.

Heidegger's "Building Dwelling Thinking" suggests a responsible relationship with regard to nature in his notion of *sparing*, or nurturing the earth. Sparing frees something to its own essence. It may mean clearing a place for inhabitation, or respecting a place as it is found. Ando feels "the necessity of discovering the architecture which the site itself is seeking" because "The presence of architecture—regardless of its self-contained character—inevitably creates a new landscape." (ch. 10)

There is another way in which contemporary architects and landscape architects establish a responsible relationship with nature: their work provides a frame for its spiritual apprehension, considered fundamental to a meaningful existence. In a recent polemic entitled "Toward New Horizons in Architecture," Ando underscores the primary role of his architecture in allowing for the presence of nature in modern urban life. He proposes that "architecture becomes a place where people and nature confront each other under a sustained sense of tension...that will awaken the spiritual sensibilities latent in contemporary humanity." Heidegger's notion of dwelling comes to mind again in this context.

PLACE AND REGIONALISM

Based in part on phenomenology, Frampton's Critical Regionalism seeks the possibility of dwelling in an architecture of greater experiential meaning. (ch. 11) He espouses recognition of regional, vernacular building and its sensitivity to light, wind, and temperature conditions, all of which dictate an architectural response befitting the particular place. Critical Regionalism promotes the notion that climatically specific designs will be successful aesthetically and ecologically, and will offer resistance to the homogenizing forces of modern capitalism. Following Heidegger, Frampton resists universalizing forces by marking a bounded precinct on the earth and under the sky. An architectonic approach emphasizing the site's topography often characterizes his exemplars.

Another common aspect of Critical Regionalist work is a critical attitude towards the use of mass-produced building products. Without arguing for a return to primitive means of construction, Frampton recalls Semper's poetic understanding of the differences inherent in the frame (aerial) and the bearing wall (earthen, "telluric") building systems. (ch. 12) The richness that can result from the contrast between the two systems and the articulation of their juncture, is fundamental to tectonic communication. Instead of scenographic images, a meaningful narrative can be conveyed by the elements of construction and their thoughtful assembly.

Not all theorists are in agreement about the value of place. For example, although his writings suggest a phenomenological position, Perez-Gomez criticizes the genius loci as an "empty postmodern simulation, incapable of revelatory depth" in the context of our cities of shopping malls and traffic networks.[125] He suggests instead an emphasis on reinventing the site as open and liberative.

The possibility that phenomenological place is nostalgic and outmoded is also raised by theorists of postindustrial culture. Jean Baudrillard, Christine Boyer, and Ellen Dunham-Jones, among others, have addressed the issues of the transformation and dematerialization of the physical world by new electronic media. Gatherings such as "Between Digital

Seduction and Salvation" (Pratt, 1992) and "Buildings and Reality: A Symposium on Architecture in the Age of Information" (University of Texas, 1986) have offered opportunities to reflect on the meaning of these changes. As Peter Eisenman says in "Visions' Unfolding: Architecture in the Age of Electronic Media": "The electronic paradigm directs a powerful challenge to architecture because it defines reality in terms of media and simulation, it values appearance over existence." (ch. 13) Our attitude toward place is bound to be affected by the substitution of a virtual paradigm of experience for the body's spatial and tactile experience.

These critiques indicate one of the emerging issues in architectural theory: changing definitions of reality. Will making or marking a physical place, expressive of an ordered private or public realm, be irrelevant, redundant, or rhetorical in the future? What will be the effect of the electronic dematerialization of communication on architecture, whose production symbolizes solidity, permanence, and cultural community? What will be the effect on landscape architecture, which is ephemeral, temporal, and dynamic? Are place and meaning endangered by the electronic "global village"? In a recent opinion piece, architect Ezra Ehrenkrantz predicted drastic social and economic consequences for American cities based on the dispersal of population as receivers on the information superhighway.[126] His concerns are complemented by a range of urban theories that arose when postmodern architects rediscovered the city as a ground for architectural activity on numerous levels; socioeconomic, political, historical, formal, poetic, and artistic.

THEME 4: URBAN THEORY

By the 1960s, urban renewal and drastic modern interventions had rent the urban fabric beyond recognition. Architects, having focused mainly on creating freestanding "object" buildings (such as the Guggenheim Museum and the Seagram Building in New York) for forty years, began to realize that there was no ground against which to read these objects. Instead, their buildings floated in an endless, undifferentiated modern "open space." The development of building sites into landscape or garden had been neglected in the twentieth century, slowing the steady evolution of the 400-year-long tradition of landscape architecture. Furthermore, a general consensus can be established for Rowe and Koetter's claim that "the city of modern architecture...has not yet been built. In spite of all the good will and good intentions of its protagonists, it has remained either a project or an abortion."[127]

This crisis situation is noted by planners, and by architects who often blame planners for poor implementation of good ideas. For example, functional zoning (first implemented in New York City in 1916) comes under fire by postmodernists for its negative approach to planning. In separating disparate land uses from each other via legislation, zoning aims at protecting property values and occupants from harmful conflicts of use. But zoning also increases distances between homes and grocery stores and other necessities of life, thereby increasing society's dependence on the automobile. Furthermore, design standards for roads privilege movement of the car, often at the expense of pedestrian circulation and a sense of neighborhood.

In the United States, the pursuit of ownership of the single-family house, along with the automobile, has contributed to megalopolitan sprawl, as retail areas crop up to serve new, widespread residential markets. Eventually, office spaces are built further out into the suburbs to reduce commuting time from congested locales in which mass transit is absent. The problems of sprawl—faceless development, loss of nature, disorientation—and the likelihood that suburbs and cities will eventually expand until they touch each other, were predicted by novelist Italo Calvino in his depiction of "continuous" cities:

> You advance for hours and it is not clear to you whether you are already in the city's midst or still outside it...outside Penthesilea does an outside exist? Or, no matter how far you go from the city, will you only pass from one limbo to another, never managing to leave it?[128]

He could be describing the eastern seaboard of the United States and its "Bos-Wash megalopolis."

Journalists also joined the postmodern critique of the city; bracketing this period are books reacting against modern urbanism. Jane Jacobs's *The Death and Life of Great American Cities* (1961) urges a reconsideration of the practices of urban renewal. She argues that institutionalized planning has not proven itself capable of predicting the outcomes of its initiatives. From her perspective, it is evident that planning results in the degeneration of the environment, perhaps attributable to the profession's lack of observation of the "real" city. Some twenty years later, James Howard Kunstler, author of *The Geography of Nowhere* (1993), rails against the American pattern of land use that has continued unabated since WWII: suburban sprawl and the commercial development along the highway. His lectures urge an embrace of neotraditional urbanism as an antidote to contemporary urban ills, many of which he blames on the automobile. He stresses that the solution to alienation, crime, and environmental degradation is small-scaled, pedestrian-friendly communities modeled on the American Main Street town.

The critique of the modern city begun in the 1960s includes utopian designs, large-scale "reconstructions," prescriptive theories and urban design codes, and defenses of unrealized modern urban objectives. Of these many proposals, this anthology presents three postmodern urban positions, selected for their influence or relevance in America: contextualism, represented by Rowe, Koetter, and Thomas Schumacher; "populism," or the American Main Street, represented by Venturi, Scott Brown, and Steven Izenour (with the firm VSBA); and a global, "contemporary city" model, represented by Koolhaas. (ch. 6) In addition to bringing forth ideas from these three positions, this introduction outlines aspects of European neorationalism, American urban design codes, and the application of semiology to the city.

Both contextualism and populism can be seen as developments from within academia, in that they are cultivated by teams of faculty and students analyzing the city and making proposals for new design strategies. Whether an appreciation of the piazzas of Rome, or the commercial highway strip of Las Vegas, Cornell and Yale design students contributed to the formulation of influential theories, later published by their professors. In fact, Rowe's student Schumacher published an article on the "collage" method of urban design before his mentor.

Similarly, Koolhaas's provocative and animated interpretation of Manhattan in *Delirious New York* (1978, 1994) was aided by the work of his students at the IAUS. Less a critique than a celebration of New York's "Culture of Congestion," it has a common attitude with VSBA's treatment of Las Vegas. The book is "an argument for a second coming of Manhattanism, this time as an explicit doctrine that can transcend the island of its origins to claim its place among contemporary urbanisms."[129] Like *Learning from Las Vegas*, this book's intention is to counteract the overwhelmingly negative views of New York within the architectural profession. Koolhaas's analysis of the city's defining formal feature is indicative of his approach:

> The Grid is, above all, a conceptual speculation....in its indifference to topography, to what exists, it claims the superiority of mental construction over reality. Through the plotting of its streets and blocks it announces that the subjugation, if not obliteration, of nature is its true ambition.[130]

The allure of a city which has "remove[d] its territory as far from the natural as humanly possible" becomes evident in the evocative, dreamlike narrative sequences and projects that Koolhaas presents. In the 1980s, he extended his optimism to urban studies of the "edge cities" of Atlanta, Seoul, and the periphery of Paris.

CONTEXTUALISM

Rowe and Koetter's seminal article, "Collage City," (1975) offers the influential analytical and designs strategies still promulgated in some schools of architecture today. It begins with Rome:

> offered here as some sort of model which might be envisaged as alternative to the disastrous urbanism of social engineering and total design....the physique and politics of Rome provide perhaps the most graphic example of collisive fields and interstitial debris. (ch. 6)

Special emphasis on figure-ground and Nolli plans, and on Hadrian's Villa earns them emblematic stature in the postmodern period. The villa's similarities to the formal organization of seventeenth-century Rome lead to "that inextricable fusion of imposition and accommodation,...which is simultaneously a dialectic of ideal types plus...empirical context." This conjunction of opposites, expanded in their book to include order/disorder, simple/complex, private/public, innovation/tradition, is similar in form and intention (which could be summarized as "accommodation and coexistence") to Venturi's inclusive argument in *Complexity and Contradiction*. Rowe, Koetter, and Venturi are all influenced by the positive view of ambivalence in Gestalt theory, which permits a multiplicity of readings. (Rowe also emphasized ambivalence in the aforementioned "Transparency: Literal and Phenomenal" article.)

Imperial Rome evidences the essence of what Rowe and Koetter call the "bricolage mentality," an unscientific, unsystematic tinkering that resists any dangerous totalizing impulse in urban planning. Among other phenomena, they criticize the attempt to apply positivist logic to something as imprecise as architecture and urban design. Alexander's *Notes on the Synthesis of Form* is cited by the authors for its admirable, if unattainable effort at erasing values and personal prejudice from the design process to ensure universality. The anti-totalitarian position that dominates their discourse is supported by sociologist Karl Popper's pro-democracy writings. Rowe and Koetter propose a more genuinely populist position than VSBA's *Learning from Las Vegas*.

Rowe and Koetter distinguish bricolage (a term borrowed from Claude Lévi-Strauss) from collage, in which "objects and episodes are obtrusively imported and, while they retain the overtones of their source and origin, they gain also a wholly new impact from their changed context." One can see the persuasive appeal of collage as a postmodern urban technique when it is defined as "a way of giving integrity to a jumble of pluralist references," which "can allow Utopia to be dealt with as image, to be dealt with in fragments." The graphic techniques of reading developed by Rowe and the Cornell School offer a vocabulary (built on solid/void relations) and syntax of continued validity for describing and understanding the city.

The term "contextualism" is not used by Rowe and Koetter, but was applied to their theory by Schumacher in his 1971 essay, "Contextualism: Urban Ideals and Deformations." Since then, contextualism has come to mean little more than "fitting in with existing conditions," according to Richard Ingersoll, who describes it as a "Teflon ideology."[131] Schumacher reflected recently on the distortions the term has suffered:

> After the so-called Postmodern revolution the term "contextualism" began to attach itself to stylistic manifestations—as do most co-opted ideas in architecture. It referred to red brick buildings being built in red brick neighborhoods and gingerbread matching gingerbread.[132]

THEORIES OF READING AND MEANING

In the postmodern period, semiology has also had an impact on the perception of the city, through such works as Barthes's "Semiology and Urbanism," (1967) which suggests a process of reading the city as a text. It applies a linguistic model of meaning derived from structured relationships between objects in the city. Thus he says:

> a city is a fabric...of strong elements and neutral [nonmarked] elements,...(we know that the opposition between the sign and the absence of sign, between full degree and zero degree, is one of the major processes in the elaboration of meaning).[133]

Linguistics is embraced by postmodern architects as a way of codifying architectural meaning into a system. But in this essay, evidencing a move towards poststructuralist thinking, Barthes notes the "erosion of the notion of the lexicon," which had promised a one-to-one correspondence between signifiers and signifieds, on which ideas of symbolism rest. Despite this erosion, the city will continue to signify. This analogy summarizes his view of the urban condition:

> Every city is constructed, made by us, somewhat in the image of the ship Argo, every piece of which was replaced over time but which always remained the Argo, that is, a set of quite legible and identifiable meanings.[134]

The application of these structuralist and poststructuralist ideas to urban design has been investigated by Agrest and Gandelsonas. Barthes's interdisciplinary model of critique is also evident in their writings, especially in several of Agrest's essays on urbanism.

Interestingly, both Agrest and Tschumi propose the study of filmic representation and the use of film techniques as ways of approaching the experience of architecture in the city. Agrest says:

at the beginning of this century—the [artistic] referent for architecture has been painting. This referent is not productive enough when we approach architecture from the urban field. A more powerful referent is film, a complex system that develops in time and through space.[135]

Tschumi has chosen to emphasize a different aspect of Barthes's discussion of the city: the overlooked "erotic dimension" of the city identified (by Barthes) as the attraction the center city holds for the periphery. Barthes's "Semiology and Urbanism" and Le plaisir du texte (1973) are clear influences on Tschumi's "The Pleasure of Architecture." (ch. 13)

IMAGE OF THE CITY
It is interesting to compare these ideas of reading the city with those of urban planner Kevin Lynch, whose influential Image of the City (1960) described how people orient themselves in the environment. An early critique of the post-WWII city, Lynch insisted on the necessity of a memorable visual order in man's surroundings. Imageability or legibility of form thus became important attributes sought by urban designers and architects concerned with the issue of communication of meaning. Meaning is located in the distinctiveness of path, edge, node, district, and landmark, according to Lynch. Barthes cites Lynch as having "gotten closest to the problems of an urban semantics," but notes that his "conception of the city remains more 'gestaltic' than structural." Lynch's ideas are used by Norberg-Schulz and other phenomenologists to support positions asserting the significance of place.

EUROPEAN URBANISM: NEORATIONALISM AND TYPOLOGY
Rossi also credits Lynch with shaping his idea that spatial orientation in the city derives from experiencing significant episodes, such as monumental precincts. The structuralist idea that the city is legible through the repetition of elemental (irreducible, archetypal) components, given meaning through collective memory, defines Rossi's poetic reading of the city. Rossi also investigates the function of type in the European city as the repository of collective memory. He compares the operation of these permanent urban elements to the function of the fixed linguistic structures of Ferdinand de Saussure. In The Architecture of the City (1966), Rossi spells out his intention to write a manifesto on typology and urban design as a reaction against the modernist city. He treats the city as an artifact, an evolving man-made object, and the representation of cultural values.

Rossi's reminder of what the city symbolizes was extremely important in refocusing attention on the idea of making architecture in an urban context: "The contrast between particular and universal, between individual and collective, emerges from the city and from its construction, its architecture."[136]

Rossi also reintroduced the notion of typology as an analytic tool and as the rational basis for a design process of transformation. In emphasizing that "type is the very idea of architecture, that which is closest to its essence,"[137] Rossi reveals his belief in the underlying idea of fixed laws, of a priori types, which had been dismantled in the modern period. Permanent urban aspects like housing and monuments are contrasted with "catalytic" primary elements that "retard or accelerate the process of urbanization."[138] His writing, teaching, and influential built works like the Teatro del Mondo, Segrate Town Center, and Modena Cemetery established Rossi as the leader of the Italian neorationalist movement, La Tendenza. In his introduction to The Architecture of the City, Eisenman contests a reception of the ideas as contextual:

> In light of the recent development of a so-called contextual urbanism which has come to dominate urban thought some fifteen years after the original publication of this book, Rossi's text can be seen as an anticipatory argument against the "empty formalism" of context reductively seen as a plan relationship of figure and ground.[139]

Architect Leon Krier takes a different view of the range of available types than Rossi, while agreeing in principle on their importance in constituting the urban realm. His source of types is Enlightenment neoclassicism and the preindustrial, eighteenth-century city. Through a taxonomy of urban building types (including spaces, buildings, and construction methods) and using a deliberately limited and rationalized range of building materials, he hopes to reintroduce rigor to architecture and urbanism. The re-creation of the public realm requires significant places and monuments, both of which need the support of a taut surround of "fabric" buildings.

While Rossi is concerned primarily with making an intervention in the context of the city, Krier has taken on the large-scale reconstruction of the European city as a critical project. In fact, he has argued forcefully that the unbuilt project is the most responsible way to engage architectural thinking given the current socio-economic conditions: "architectural reflection can at this precise moment only be undertaken through the practical exercise in the form of a critique or in the form of a critical project."[140] The possibility for utopian, visionary work remains open in his opinion, and is required by the degradation of contemporary urbanism. In particular, he is concerned with the reconstitution of well defined, exterior public spaces—the street, square, etc.—as "part of an integral vision of society, ...part of a political struggle."[141] The public place symbolizes the ethical responsibilities of the citizen.

Krier also takes on the modernist myth that industrializing the building process would liberate the worker. Ironically, he says:

> Industrialization has neither created quicker building techniques nor a better building technology. Far from having improved the physical conditions of the worker, it has reduced manual labour to a stultifying and enslaving experience. It has degraded a millennial and dignified craft to a socially alienating exercise.[142]

This supports Krier's decision not to build, which he later reversed when given the chance to build his own house in Seaside, Florida. He suggests using industrially produced materials with an exaggerated tectonic sensibility intended to recall the mythification of construction embodied in classical details.

LEARNING FROM LINGUISTICS

While *Complexity and Contradiction* uses European precedents, *Learning from Las Vegas* accepts as a given the American highway strip development and expounds a more ostensibly populist point of view. In *Learning from Las Vegas*, Venturi, Scott Brown, and Izenour (VSBA) are also influenced by communication theory and in particular, semiotics. Their discussion of the "duck" and the "decorated shed" is in essence an argument about reincorporating symbolic function with literal function as a necessary part of architecture. The issue then becomes how to accomplish symbolization: through expression in three-dimensional form with the "sign as building" (the modern functionalist "duck"), or through a two-dimensional sign fronting the building (the postmodern "shed")? It should also be noted that symbolic aspects of modern architecture were not acknowledged at the time, since functionalist theory holds that architecture simply works through a scientific analysis of program to determine and house the needs of the client.[143] That many modern masterpieces are "ducks" is a dramatic charge from these postmodern theorists.

Given the significance of the automobile in VSBA's study of Las Vegas, many decisions are made from the vantage point of the vehicle moving along the highway. Thus, the authors determine that billboards of tremendous scale operate efficiently to convey messages, commercial as well as civic ("I am a monument"), to 55-mile-an-hour traffic. They also privilege one part of the Vitruvian triad, commodity, which includes the idea of convenience, and which further supports their choice of the sign on the shed. They insist that the sign applied to a "dumb box" of a building is the most economical, and therefore the most honest and appropriate way to communicate.

This argument—founded on existing conditions including the market economy, construction practice, and urbanism (or rather the lack thereof)—is not neutral. It affirms the status quo of development in late-twentieth-century America, and hence is conservative. Furthermore, VSBA's idea of architectural theory or design "philosophy" emerges as quite utilitarian and prescriptive: it is only useful if "it helps you relate forms to requirements."[144] As an example of the function of the book as *apologia*, the duck versus shed discussion condenses their point of view of accommodation. They assess the American reaction to the built environment and find a lack of demand for quality over kitsch. They assume this indicates satisfaction with the existing conditions and that their approach should reflect this. In comparison with the arrogant Modern Movement "hero" architect, VSBA's approach is quite modest. While clearly they attempt to correct for the overly negative view of the world and its objects characteristic of the Modern Movement, their uncritical approach also misses the mark. Setting up a comparison between two equally ludicrous extremes is a rhetorical strategy that VSBA has used to great effect in many instances. In the case of the strip, perhaps VSBA's real goal is to find a position between total rejection and total acceptance.

EDGE CITIES: THE CONTEMPORARY PATTERN OF DEVELOPMENT

Koolhaas's recent theoretical writings also generously accept the given conditions of limitless sprawl and placelessness. He seeks to discover the virtues within the situation at the edge of the city, which others have overlooked in favor of the better-defined center. He distinguishes his research in "Towards the Contemporary City" from other current, postmodern investigations as "a paramodern alternative." Koolhaas also advocated a different strategy in planning the IBA (International Building Exhibition) housing project in Berlin. Other architects saw IBA as an opportunity for the massive reconstruction of the city, along the neotraditional lines proposed by Krier, while Koolhaas suggested allowing the war-torn city to continue to present its history and "to make of the city a sort of territorial archipelago—a system of architectural islands surrounded by forests and lakes in which the infrastructures could play without causing damage." (ch. 6) Like postmodern historicist theorists, Koolhaas defends the nineteenth-century idea of "remodeling without destroying the preexisting city." The differences come in the choice of what and how to build. His basic strategy is to intensify and clarify the existing conditions through a contrast between open space and dense development.

Koolhaas would approve of the approach to American edge cities taken by Stephen Holl.[145] Holl has designed a *proun*-inspired aerial complex for Phoenix, which he calls "spatial retaining bars," and triangles of intense architectural development interspersed with triangles of greenery for the city of Cleveland. These projects, which resist sprawl through the deliberate construction of boundaries, are consistent with Holl's phenomenological interest in the specificity of place, articulated in his book *Anchoring* (1989). The significance of boundaries as noted by Heidegger becomes fundamental to a reconsideration of modern space. (See Harries, ch. 8) The value placed on anonymous, uninterrupted Cartesian space, an expression of freedom, must be weighed against the human need for the familiar and the security of limits. Holl's large-scale works and more intimate interiors (Fukuoka housing's flexible arrangement: "hinged space") play off this dialectic. Projects like his "Spiroid Sectors" for Dallas function as a critique on many levels: of master planning, of the current dependence on the automobile and the resultant environmental problems, of the hegemony of the American suburban dream, and of existing construction materials and methods.

NEW AMERICAN URBANISM: DESIGN CODES

One of the recent theoretical manifestations mistakenly described as contextualism is that of the "neotraditionalists," who convene regularly as the Congress for the New Urbanism.[146] These postmodern urban theorists argue that architects must resist the dominance of the contemporary edge city. The prescriptive code-writing for new towns that characterizes the work of Andres Duany and Elizabeth Plater-Zyberk, Architects (DPZ), the acknowledged leaders in this movement, aims for stylistic coherence (often to a Victorian ideal) as well as consistency in setbacks, roof and fence lines, and building types. Their partially built community of Seaside has both garnered praise and generated tremendous debate, on occasion forcing the architects into a defensive position vis-à-vis its ecological, social, and stylistic implications.[147] While DPZ maintains that their work is not about style, most of their support comes from postmodern historicist architects. And of course, from developers in many states who rush to commission DPZ and their CNU colleagues to design new towns in suburban locations. These developments appeal to the paradoxical, nostalgic American desire for a simulacrum of tradition (and its associated values), while living in a brand new home built with the latest petrochemical simulations of materials.

THEME 5: POLITICAL AND ETHICAL AGENDAS

The postmodern urban critique has been mirrored by the consideration of larger political and ethical questions by architectural theorists. At the heart of the debate is what kind of role architecture as a discipline is to play in society. Four possible roles come to mind right away: 1) architecture can be indifferent to social concerns and their expression and representation; or 2) architecture can be an affirmative actor supporting the status quo and accepting existing conditions; or 3) architecture can gently guide society in a new direction; or 4) architecture can radically criticize and remake society. The choice of model depends on the answer to the following basic question: Is architecture primarily an art or a service profession? The various opinions represented here by a series of articles written since 1975 are part of the growing political and ethical debate in architectural theory.

The issue of architecture's societal role is often framed in terms of the possibility and morality of an autonomous position. A pervasive theme in the writings of this period, autonomy is seen variously as being neutral, critical, or reactionary. Autonomy in architecture is usually associated with the creation of form by an internal, self-referential discourse. This usage of autonomy is roughly synonymous with formalism, defined as an overriding concern with issues of form, to the exclusion of sociocultural, historical, or even material and constructional issues. Such an autonomous position can be taken by the maker of a work, or by a viewer or interpreter. The resulting architectural object is often abstract, nonrepresentational. To identify an autonomous position, postmodern architectural theory struggles to define which elements are internal or unique to the discourse: Are form, function, materiality, or type essential? Can architecture about architecture communicate to a community at large? Can it be critical?

Tschumi suggests that architecture can never be completely self-referential. In "Architecture and Transgression, " he says, "architecture...thrives on its ambiguous location between cultural autonomy and commitment, between contemplation and habit."[148] While the art object is contemplated for itself in the artificial surrounds of the gallery, architecture becomes a backdrop for life. Tschumi certainly refers to Walter Benjamin's comments about the reception of architecture in "a state of distraction," which is the habitual mode in the modern city.

Tschumi may also be referring to another Frankfurt School member, Adorno, and his theory on *committed* art, art that is progressive and overtly political. A neo-Marxist, Adorno writes in the essay "Commitment" (1962) that political resistance in art can be achieved only through autonomy. Through removal from the fray, outside the normal conditions of representation, one can establish a site of resistance. The autonomous work of art is governed by its own inherent structure, not by its reception. This way, the critical function can be sustained longer. Adorno rejects committed art because it will be too easily assimilated or "co-opted" by conservatives. Politically committed art builds on familiar territory, and thus has an "entente" with the world. It can be used by all manner of parties at both ends of the political spectrum, which again diminishes its critical potential. He writes: "The notion of a 'message' in art, even when politically radical, already contains an accommodation to the world..."[149] Adorno believes a position of silence, distinct from the aestheticist "art for art's sake," will prove a more fruitful vehicle of resistance.

Architecture by its nature is socially embedded, experienced by habit, not deliberation. Thus the applicability of Adorno's ideas to the realm of architecture is difficult, since architecture has this problematic entente with the world. Can one move outside the conventions of representation in architecture to create an architecture of resistance? Ando for one, argues that abstraction and austerity of means in architecture *will* awaken the viewer to a more conscious experience of architecture and to his/her own spirituality. This is the foundation of his critical, autonomous position.

Other theorists, including the editors of *VIA* 10, *Ethics and Architecture*, take a position against autonomy in architecture, asserting: "Because architecture aims to be understood and used by its society, it cannot be autonomous and still maintain its relevance. Architecture, in this sense, can never be value-free."[150] In other words, architecture must communicate and within the content of the communication are embedded values, of which the architect must be cognizant. To this end, the editors advocate a return to the study of ethics, which "questions what is appropriate, and more importantly, how we determine what is appropriate."[151] They offer the following definition of ethics:

> Ethics is the study of moral problems and judgments which form the bases for conduct in society. A consistent set of moral judgments enables us to determine a purpose, and thus to act intentionally....Ethical knowledge, the understanding of these values, is gained by practice and action in culture.[152]

In line with their emphasis on ethical knowledge is architect Philip Bess's article, in which he claims there is a "genuine and intrinsic relationship between architecture and ethics" in that buildings and cities embody an ethic, either communitarian or individualist. (ch. 8) He focuses on the necessity of shared values for the successful functioning of community. Bess argues that narcissistic personal development has outweighed socialization (at least in democratic societies), resulting in a culture of Nietzschean radical individualism. He blames the absence of a sense of community in contemporary life on the powerful influence of individualism. While individualism is surely part of the modern zeitgeist, one could argue more broadly for its basis in the values of scientific positivism, in capitalism, and in the American "frontier mentality." Noting that the traditional city symbolized legitimate authority and civic virtue, Bess suggests that communities today need to revive the idea of the "common good," and represent it in architecture. (Belief in the common good is essential to the success of the environmental movement, which asks for voluntary behavior changes, possibly involving hardship or inconvenience, to promote global betterment.)

A pressing political question for the ethical positions just outlined is the attainability of a societal consensus which can be represented by architecture. In light of the diversity of society, this goal appears increasingly elusive and naive to many theorists, and totalitarian and threatening to others.

PROFESSIONAL ETHICS

The AIA Code of Ethics and Professional Conduct (1993) is interesting with regard to the issue of consensus. It lays out a set of *nonbinding* recommendations for conduct for its members, all of whom have agreed to abide by the code. The document's scope includes such broad goals as: consider the social and environmental impact of architectural activities (for example, avoid discrimination); respect and conserve the natural and cultural heritage; strive to improve the environment and quality of life; uphold human rights; and be involved in civic affairs. The fact that all these important points are nonbinding indicates that they are also the most difficult to define, to enforce, and on which to develop consensus in the architectural community.

Another branch of ethics in postmodern architectural theory calls for engagement in the political realm. This takes many forms, including calls for the resuscitation of a social welfare role for architecture, like that of the high modern period. Emblematic of this past idealism are the *seidlung*, housing estates designed by the leading architects of the 1920s and erected in Germany and Holland. Reviving this model of political and ethical engagement is one way of rescuing architecture, according to Ghirardo.

Ghirardo's recent writings, such as "Architecture of Deceit," raise provocative questions about whether architecture's primary role is art or service. Ghirardo clearly says it is the latter and adopts a critical position demanding political and social responsibility. Architects, she insists, should investigate the power structures in society that shelter their affluent clients, instead of retreating to a position reliant on the "purity" of the art of architecture.

Noting that the built world is not autonomous of the market economy, she sets out to "discern the relationship between political intentions, social realities, and building." (ch. 8) In other words, she suggests that members of the profession need to question the politics of building: who builds what, where, for whom, and for what price. To not question authority, for Ghirardo, is to be complicit with the status quo. And in the face of homelessness, racism, and sexism, she argues, such complicity is unethical.

This kind of analysis of the physical manifestations of power structures has always interested urban planners and Marxist critics. In the postmodern period, it also surfaces in the writing and projects of socially responsible architects. Ghirardo's model of political and ethical engagement offers a compelling alternative to "traditional art historical" approaches that highlight formal concerns to the exclusion of all others, risking degeneration to a discussion of style.

Ghirardo is also suspicious of other critics' unconscious deployment of ideology, and of reactionary efforts to denigrate the utopianism of the twentieth-century architectural avant-garde. While recognizing that the avant-garde's dreams and plans for social change were flawed and naive, she nonetheless applauds the optimistic and energetic engagement of modern architects in social, political, and economic issues. It is precisely this engagement she finds lacking in postmodern architecture of all stylistic types. Her conclusion is that "only when architects, critics, and historians accept the responsibility for building— in all of its ramifications—will we approach an architecture of substance."

ENVIRONMENTAL ETHICS

An emerging political agenda is represented by the "green architecture" movement, which proposes the need for an environmental ethics of building. Such recent theory aims to develop a less antagonistic relationship with nature by resisting sprawl through high-density development, and through the use of renewable, non-polluting, and recycled materials. The "sustainability" movement is supported by the phenomenological idea that a relationship with nature is essential to full human self-realization on this planet.

William McDonough, architect and environmentalist, argues that the ethical implications of architectural work include acknowledging the rights of future generations and of other species to a healthy environment. He takes the AIA ethical guidelines very seriously and feels that the profession's status will improve if it takes a broader view of the services it provides. Like many of the other ethical positions, environmentalism embodies a critique of both modern architecture and the material conditions of modernity.

For McDonough, the continuation of current habits of architectural practice, in light of the known toxicity of building materials and processes, is negligent. His radical position calls for new definitions of prosperity, productivity, and quality of life. It begins with coming to peace with man's place in the natural world. The understanding that nature is not immutable requires an attitude of integration with and a commitment to renewing and restoring the earth and its living systems.

THEME 6: THE BODY

The body and nature, two organic systems, both existed in an antagonistic relationship to modernism. Among modernists, Le Corbusier was almost alone in pursuing a human-based proportional system, the Modulor. The relationship between the body and architecture was for the most part neglected by functionalist architects except in the pragmatic accommodation of human form in shelter. Another postmodern route to a revitalized architecture thus converges on the human body as the site of architecture. The current interest in the body appears in several forms: phenomenological, poststructuralist, and feminist.

BODY, SUBJECT, AND OBJECT

The body is the physical substance of the human being, often portrayed as opposite to the mind or soul. Some philosophers define the "person" or "self" as an entity constituted by the body and soul.[153] The psychic component, considered as subject, receives attention in modern psychology, psychiatry, and in epistemology. Epistemologically, the subject is an individual "knower," an ego, or an act of awareness. In the other fields, the subject is an "individual subjected to observation."[154] This meaning, with its political overtones, is common to the work of poststructuralists including Foucault, who offers this definition: "There are two meanings of the word "subject": subject to someone else by control and dependence; and tied to his own identity by a conscience or self-knowledge."[155]

THE BODY IN CLASSICAL ARCHITECTURE: PROJECTION AND ANTHROPOMORPHISM

In classical architecture, the human body serves as part of a myth of origin through its use as a figural and proportional model for projection into plan organization, facade, and detail. Vidler points out that the body's image can be "mathematically inscribed" via proportions and scale, or "pictorially emulated."[156] The body metonymically represents nature in general, and nature's elegant way of organizing complex functions.

THE END OF HUMANIST PROJECTION

Among the challenges to the classical, anthropocentric world view and to its construction of the human subject is the existentialist position that verification of man's existence is found in and depends on the material world. Jean-Paul Sartre claims in *Being and Nothingness* (1959) that the body derives knowledge of itself from objects in the world. Eisenman explains that what characterizes the shift from humanism to modernism is:

> a displacement of man away from the center of his world. He is no longer viewed as an
> *originating agent*. Objects are seen as ideas independent of man. In this context, man is
> a discursive function among complex and already-formed systems of language. (ch. 1)

Since the demise of the classical tradition, Vidler observes a steady retreat of the body from the building. The process, which results in "the loss of the body as an authoritative foundation for architecture," is marked by three increasingly abstract scenarios of bodily projection: the building is a body; the building represents or "embodies" states of body or mind; the environment has bodily or organic attributes.[157] This distancing tendency during modernism is also due to an obvious turning away from figuration and towards an agenda of abstraction, which was certainly influenced by the industrialization of building.

THE POSTMODERN RENOVATION OF THE BODY

There are several different postmodern reactions to the modern treatment of the body. First, Graves's historicist work comments on the loss of meaning resulting from the end of the humanist ideal of anthropocentrism. Man cannot feel centered in the continuous space of modernism, he argues, even in an exemplary work like the Barcelona Pavilion, which suffers from the lack of clearly differentiated elements like floor, ceiling, wall, and window. In "A Case for Figurative Architecture," he writes:

> The Modern Movement based itself largely on technical expression—internal language—
> and the metaphor of the machine dominated its building form. In its rejection of the human
> or anthropomorphic representation of previous architecture, the Modern Movement under-
> mined the poetic form in favor of nonfigural, abstract geometrics. (ch. 1)

The role of architecture's poetic language is to provide orientation in the environment. In its absence, "the cumulative effect of non-figural architecture is the dismemberment of our former cultural language of architecture." Graves's architecture aims to reintroduce anthropomorphism through the use of significant classical devices, which establish and symbolize man's relationship to nature and the cosmos.

Perez-Gomez makes a phenomenological proposal for the "renovation of the body" as "our undivided possession, which allows access to reality" (defined as the body-world continuum) and gives the world its appearance through projection. Perez-Gomez notes that great works of modern architecture necessarily refer to a different body image than did classical architecture, which was based on "an objectified unitary body." A postmodern form of reference as practiced by Hejduk points instead to "the qualities of the *flesh*." Perez-Gomez explains his idea:

> Our renovated body image can only be grasped analogically, indirectly, through the very instruments and objects that mediate between the body and the world, capturing the footprint of the embodied consciousness.[158]

He concludes that "An authentic interest in architectural meaning in our times must be accompanied by a conscious or unconscious renovation of the body."

As discussed, Vidler's contribution to the question of the body is a study of the uncanny, which "opens up the unsettling problems of identity around the self, the other, the body and its absence."[159] He notes that the experience of the uncanny, like Perez-Gomez's "bodying forth," is the projection of the mental state of the individual that "elides the boundaries of the real and the unreal to provoke a disturbing ambiguity."[160] As a critical tool, Vidler uses the uncanny to focus on anthropomorphic embodiment, gender, and the Other. The end of anthropomorphic embodiment in architecture has led to an uncanny sense of the presence of an absence and to "the building in pain."[161]

Tschumi also comments on the absence of the body. In "Architecture and Limits III," he critiques "The usual exclusion of the body and its experience from all [contemporary] discourse on the logic of form" as characteristic of reductive (formalist) interpretations of architecture. (ch. 3) The avoidance, even repression, of the body is an aspect of puritanism that he has observed in modern architecture, too. In place of reduction, Tschumi offers Dionysian "excess" and the transgression of rational limits to reveal the useless (positively so), excessive eroticism of space. Aspects of his essay "The Pleasure of Architecture" have phenomenological overtones: he describes the body's orientation in the spatially different conditions of plane and cavern, street and living room, and admits that "taken to its extreme, the pleasure of space leans toward the poetics of the unconscious." (ch. 13)

POSTSTRUCTURALIST NOTIONS OF THE BODY AS SITE

Other theorists, having rejected anthropocentrism, are seeking to establish a poststructuralist understanding of the relationship between the body and the physical environment. Opposed to the concept of the projection of *interiority* (the mental state of the subject), are poststructuralist challenges to the centrality of man in the cosmos that this interiority assumes. The humanist ideal of man creating order in the world by projecting his bodily image is inverted by Foucault's notion of *exteriority*: that the external world of institutions and conventions determines the man. The projection of interiority thus collapses.

Agrest's claim that the body of woman is repressed by the "system" of architecture was noted in the earlier discussion of the essay "Architecture from Without: Body, Logic, and Sex." It is worth examining the mechanism of symbolic appropriation by which the repression of the female body is accomplished. Agrest explains:

> In a rather complex set of metaphorical operations throughout these [Renaissance] texts, the gender of the body and its sexual functions are exchanged in a move of transsexuality whereby man's ever-present procreative fantasy is enacted. (ch. 13)

Thus, the navel, as the center of the (male or female) body, "becomes a metonymic object or a *shifter* in relation to gender." Agrest borrows the idea of the shifter, a "signifier which opens to other systems,"[162] from linguist Roman Jakobson. The recuperation of the female body as central to architecture requires opening up the system, for instance, by allowing the shifter to transform the body into geometry, and nature (associated with the feminine) into architecture. Feminists play an important role in reintroducing the body into theory.

A posthumanist view of the body/world relationship underlies the projects of architects Diller and Scofidio. In the article "Body Troubles," Robert MacAnulty cites their recent theoretical investigations of the spatial structures and social customs that order our bodies, such as habits of domesticity. He writes: "Here again we are confronted with a model of space wherein the body's significance is not as a figural source of mimetic projection, but as site for the inscriptions of power."[163] Based on this critical work, MacAnulty suggests reformulating the body in "spatial, inscriptive, and sexual terms" instead of the "figural, projective, and animistic" terms of phenomenologists.

Eisenman raises a similar challenge to the body's projection which he identifies as taking place through our primary faculty, vision. (ch. 13) His analysis indicates that vision has *determined* architectural drawing, especially perspective, and that drawing conventions then limit ideas of space. Perez-Gomez concurs with Eisenman that "the main assumption [which needs to be rethought] is that architectural drawings are necessarily projections."[164] Recalling a familiar theme, Eisenman claims that architecture will never move beyond the Renaissance world view, unless it challenges representation.[165] He seeks a new kind of non-projective drawing capable of confronting the anthropocentric bias of the Western culture. Furthermore, Eisenman advocates that architecture problematize vision in order to critique its dominance and to come to a new understanding of space.

CONCLUSION: THE NECESSITY OF POSTMODERN THEORY

Despite its confusing aspects, there are many reasons to study postmodern theory. The writings of 1965 to 1995 embrace a wealth of architectural themes, which are framed by fascinating theoretical paradigms. They help to illuminate the heterogeneous production of architecture during the last thirty years, and to explain its relationship to modern architecture.

Postmodern theory is critical, optimistic, and intellectual, it challenges and celebrates the capacity of the mind, and it offers models of critical and ethical thinking. In this regard, theory can pedagogically demonstrate comparative analysis of writers' positions and the logic of their arguments. The ethical component also establishes a model for responsible behavior as an architect, emphasizing the link between the designer's activity and society.

The postmodern essays in this anthology are related to the larger tradition of architectural theory by virtue of a continuity of themes, such as architecture's meaning and its relationship to nature, the city, technology, and historical precedent. The *weighting* of these concerns, and the positions taken about the relationship between architecture and these themes, are what differ from previous theoretical endeavors. This difference is due to the influence of powerful, extradisciplinary theoretical paradigms on the discipline of architecture. For example, the idea that theory can be a catalyst for social change is inspired by Marxism and the neo-Marxist Frankfurt School critique.

The anthology attempts to present a balanced view of the prevalent postmodern ideologies; no single school of thought has been, or could be, chosen to represent this pluralist period. Instead, the authors of the essays are introduced and allowed to debate among themselves. This seems to be the most honest way to depict the situation. Some writers appear frequently in these pages, in part because of their ubiquitous involvement in the architectural profession: here, acting as editor, there as faculty member, dean, or curator. And in any case, writing. The genre of choice is the essay, which is a "sample, example, rehearsal; an attempt; a composition of moderate length on any particular subject, or branch of a subject, originally implying want of finish."[166]

The result of all the fluidity in the profession during these years is a discourse at once provocative, anticipatory, speculative, and open-ended. The results of this theory are unpredictable and varied. The critical orientation of much of the New Agenda is shaped by the social climate of the time, which encompassed political activism for expanded rights for women, blacks, gays, and even endangered species. Resistance to all totalizing structures, institutions, and modes of thought was the battle cry in the 1960s and 1970s. While the scale of the causes advocated seemed scaled back in the 1980s, the critical impulse persisted. The postmodern critique of modern architecture has been carried on by those powerfully entrenched in institutions, and by voices of the marginalized "Other."

Three themes of critical theory appear to be emergent in the mid 1990s: feminism and the problem of the body in architecture, the aesthetic of the contemporary sublime, and environmental ethics. From positions outside the mainstream of discourse and within, operating with the fragmentary essay as their tool, postmodern theorists approach the recurrent and emergent themes of architecture.

1   Marcus Vitruvius Pollio, *The Ten Books of Architecture* (New York: Dover, 1960), 39–40.
2   Leon Battista Alberti, *The Ten Books of Architecture* (London: Tiranti, 1965), ix.
3   Bernard Tschumi, "Six Concepts," in *Architecture and Disjunction* (Cambridge: MIT Press, 1995), 259.
4   Vittorio Gregotti, "The Necessity of Theory," *Casabella* no. 494 (September 1983): 13.
5   Alberto Perez-Gomez, "The Renovation of the Body: John Hejduk and the Cultural Relevance of Theoretical Project," *AA Files* 13, no. 8 (Autumn 1986): 29.
6   Kenneth Frampton, "Towards a Critical Regionalism: Six Points for an Architecture of Resistance," in Hal Foster, ed., *The Anti-Aesthetic: Essays on Postmodern Culture* (Port Townsend, WA.: Bay Press, 1983), 25.
7   Frederic Jameson, "Postmodernism and Consumer Society," in *The Anti-Aesthetic*, op. cit., 113.
8   Ibid.

9   Kenneth Frampton, "Place-form and Cultural Identity," in John Thackara, ed., *Design after Modernism: Beyond the Object* (New York: Thames and Hudson, 1988), 51–52.
10 Ibid.
11 Colin Rowe and Fred Koetter, "Collage City," *AR* no. 942, vol. 158 (August 1975): 72.
12 Colin Rowe, "Introduction," in *Five Architects* (New York: 1972), 15.
13 On the mission of the AA, see their brochure, which states "The Architectural Association was founded in 1847 in opposition to a system of education controlled by the Crown. It was created to democratize the practice of architecture, to cultivate individual imaginations by means of a self-directed independent education." The mission of the IAUS is described in an article in *Casabella* no. 359–360 (1971): 100–102. David Stewart describes the Italian scenario: "the dispute between the government and the schools of architecture culminated in 1970–71 in the removal of Rossi and others from their teaching posts at the Polytechnic in Milan." Venice existed outside the interference of government. "The Expression of Ideological Function in the Architecture of Aldo Rossi." *A+U* no. 65 (May 1976): 110.
14 The journal *Oppositions* was published from vol. 1 in September 1973 to vol. 26 in 1984. See Joan Ockman, "Resurrecting the Avant-Garde: The History and Program of Oppositions," in Beatriz Colomina, ed., *ArchitectureProduction* (New York: Princeton Architectural Press, 1988), 181–199.
15 The conspicuous overlap of IAUS fellows and Princeton faculty can probably be explained by the fact that Peter Eisenman, Director of the Institute, taught at Princeton as well.
16 See Ignasi de Solà-Morales Rubió, "Neo-Rationalism and Figuration," *Architectural Design* 45, no. 5–6 (1984): 15–20.
17 Joan Ockman, *Architecture Culture 1943–1968* (New York: Rizzoli, 1993), 449.
18 Gregotti, "The Necessity of Theory," op. cit.: 13.
19 Ibid.
20 Ockman, *Architecture Culture*, op. cit., 457–458.
21 Venturi cites Empson in *Complexity and Contradiction in Architecture* (New York: Museum of Modern Art, 1966), 22.
22 Ibid., 104.
23 Jo Ann Lewis, "It's Postmodern and if You Don't Get It, You Don't Get It," *Washington Post* (27 March 1994): G7.
24 Robert A.M. Stern, "New Directions in Modern American Architecture: Postscript at the Edge of Modernism," *Architectural Association Quarterly* 9, no. 2–3, (1977): 67–68.
25 Ibid.
26 Ibid.: 69.
27 Diane Ghirardo, "Past or Post Modern in Architectural Fashion," *Journal of Architectural Education* 39, no. 4 (Summer 1986): 2–6.
28 "Preface," in *Five Architects*, op. cit., 1.
29 "Transparency: Literal and Phenomenal," (1955–56) first published in *Perspecta* (1963).
30 At MoMA, 1979. Cited by Frampton in "Place-form," op. cit., 53.
31 See catalog of same name.
32 Mary McLeod, "Architecture and Politics in the Reagan Era: From Postmodernism to Deconstructivism," *Assemblage* 8 (1989): 44.
33 The "Houses for Sale" show ran from 18 October to 22 November 1980. Some images are reproduced in Paolo Portoghesi, *Postmodern: The Architecture of the Postindustrial Society* (New York: Rizzoli, 1983), 110–111.
34 Ibid., 6.
35 Jürgen Habermas, "Modernity—An Incomplete Project," in *The Anti-Aesthetic*, op. cit., 3.
36 Antony Flew, *A Dictionary of Philosophy* (New York: St. Martin's Press, 1984), 157.
37 Gaston Bachelard, *The Poetics of Space*, Maria Jolas, trans. (Boston: Beacon Press, 1969) and Martin Heidegger, "Building Dwelling Thinking," from *Poetry, Language, Thought*, Albert Hofstadter, trans. (New York: Harper & Row, 1971), 145–229.
38 Flew, *A Dictionary*, op. cit., 283
39 Its significance for architects is evident in its publication in English and Italian in *Lotus* vol. 9 (February 1975): 208–210.
40 Christian Norberg-Schulz, "Heidegger's Thinking on Architecture," *Perspecta* 20 (1983): 67.
41 Christian Norberg-Schulz, "The Phenomenon of Place," *Architectural Association Quarterly* 8, no. 4 (1976): 6.
42 Alberto Perez-Gomez, "Architectural Representation in the Age of Simulacra," *Skala* 20 (1990): 42.
43 Perez-Gomez, "The Renovation of the Body," op. cit.: 27–28.
44 Perez-Gomez, "Architectural Representation," op. cit.: 42.
45 Juhani Pallasmaa, "The Social Commission and the Autonomous Architect," *Harvard Architecture Review* 6 (1987): 119.

46 The architect in a lecture at the University of Virginia, 1993.
47 Jean-François Lyotard, "The Sublime and the Avant-garde," *ArtForum* 20, no. 8 (April 1982): 38. See also "Presenting the Unpresentable: The Sublime," *ArtForum* 22, no. 8 (April 1984) and "Appendix" in *The Postmodern Condition: A Report on Knowledge*, Geoffrey Bennington and Brian Massumi, transl. (Minneapolis: University of Minnesota Press, 1984).
48 Edmund Burke, *An Inquiry into our Ideas of the Sublime and the Beautiful* (New York: Oxford University Press, 1987) and Immanuel Kant, *Observations on the Feeling of the Beautiful and the Sublime*, John T. Goldthwait, trans. (Berkeley: University of California Press, 1981).
49 Modernist idea that, to be "of its time," everything in artistic practice has to be original, beyond history, i.e., to start from a "clean slate," or *tabula rasa*.
50 Anthony Vidler, *The Architectural Uncanny* (Cambridge: MIT Press, 1992), 79.
51 Peter Eisenman, "En Terror Firma: In Trails of Grotextes," in *Form; Being; Absence: Architecture and Philosophy, Pratt Journal of Architecture* 2 (New York: Rizzoli, 1988): 114.
52 Anthony Vidler, "Theorizing the Unhomely," *Newsline* 3, no. 3 (1990): 3. Lacanian developmental psychology has revealed that children do not immediately understand themselves as integrated beings. But once having perceived themselves as bodily unities, (via the mirror stage), the idea of the fragmented or "morselated" body is banished to the unconscious. This hidden knowledge, when reencountered, explains the impact of horror films and dismemberment fantasies.
53 Vidler, *The Architectural Uncanny*, op. cit., 79.
54 Ibid., xi.
55 Vidler, "Theorizing," op. cit.: 3. The writing here echoes the chapter on "The House" in Bachelard's classic *Poetics of Space*.
56 Vidler, *The Architectural Uncanny*, op. cit., x.
57 Ibid., 12.
58 Ibid., 13.
59 Eisenman, "En Terror Firma," op. cit.: 114.
60 Ibid.: 115.
61 Ibid.: 114.
62 Diana I. Agrest, *Architecture from Without: Theoretical Framings for a Critical Practice* (Cambridge: MIT Press, 1993), 1.
63 Peter de Bolla, *The Discourse of the Sublime: Readings in History, Aesthetics, and the Subject* (New York: Oxford University Press, 1989), 12.
64 Josüe Harari, *Textual Strategies: Perspectives in Post-Structuralist Criticism* (Ithaca: Cornell University Press, 1979), 444.
65 Diana Agrest and Mario Gandelsonas, "Semiotics and Architecture," *Oppositions* 1 (Summer 1976): 97.
66 Terence Hawkes, *Structuralism and Semiotics* (Berkeley: University of California Press, 1977), 20.
67 Ferdinand de Saussure, *Course in General Linguistics* (New York: McGraw-Hill, 1966), 114.
68 Umberto Eco, "Function and Sign: Semiotics of Architecture," in Broadbent, Bunt, Jencks, eds., *Signs, Symbols and Architecture* (New York: John Wiley, 1980), 11–70. Originally published in 1973.
69 Umberto Eco, "A Componential Analysis of the Architectural Sign/Column/," in *Signs, Symbols and Architecture*, op. cit., 232.
70 Hawkes, *Structuralism and Semiotics*, op. cit., 17.
71 Jonathan Culler, *On Deconstruction: Theory and Criticism after Structuralism* (Ithaca: Cornell University Press, 1982), 28.
72 Ibid., 20.
73 Ibid., 21.
74 Ibid., 22.
75 Hal Foster, "(Post) Modern Polemics," *Perspecta* 21 (1984): 150.
76 Roland Barthes, "From Work to Text," in *Image Music Text*, Stephen Heath, trans. (New York: Hill and Wang, 1977), 157.
77 Culler, *On Deconstruction*, op. cit., 25.
78 Foster, "(Post) Modern Polemics," op. cit.
79 Terry Eagleton, *Literary Theory: An Introduction* (Minneapolis: University of Minnesota Press, 1983), 128.
80 Ibid.
81 Ibid., 114–115.
82 Barthes, "Work," op. cit., 160.
83 Foster, "(Post) Modern Polemics," op. cit.: 146.
84 Roland Barthes, "The Death of the Author," in *Image Music Text*, op. cit., 142–148, and Michel Foucault, "What is an Author?" in Harari, *Textual Strategies*, op. cit., 141–160.
85 Foucault, "What is an Author?" op. cit., 148.
86 Ibid., 160.
87 The tendency in metaphysical philosophy to seek a foundation, or an origin. Logocentric thought sets up binary oppositions, like presence/absence, which privilege one term over the other.

Culler says: "Logocentrism thus assumes the priority of the first term [associated with identity and presence], and conceives of the second in relation to it, as a complication, a negation, a manifestation, or a disruption of the first." Culler, *On Deconstruction*, op. cit., 92–93.

88   Jacques Derrida, "Point de folie—Maintenant l'architecture," *AA Files* no. 12 (Summer1986): 65.

89   Jacques Derrida, interviewed by Eva Meyer, "Architecture Where Desire Can Live," *Domus* no. 671 (April 1986): 18.

90   Eagleton, *Literary Theory*, op. cit., 133.

91   Culler, *On Deconstruction*, op. cit., 85.

92   Ibid., 24.

93   Tschumi, "Six Concepts," op. cit., 260.

94   Anthony Vidler, "The Pleasure of the Architect," *A+U* no. 288 (September 1988): 17.

95   Frederic Jameson, *Architecture Criticism Ideology* (Princeton. Princeton Architectural Press, 1985), 70.

96   Eagleton, *Literary Theory*, op. cit., 142.

97   David Held, *Introduction to Critical Theory* (Berkeley: University of California Press, 1980), 33–39.

98   Chris Weedon, *Feminist Practice and Poststructuralist Theory* (Cambridge: Blackwell Publishers, 1987), 43, 46.

99   Ann Bergren, "Architecture Gender Philosophy," in *Strategies in Architectural Thinking* (Cambridge: MIT Press, 1992), 12.

100 Robert McAnulty, "Body Trouble," in *Strategies in Architectural Thinking*, op. cit., 191.

101 Agrest, *Architecture from Without*, op. cit., 3.

102 Anthony Vidler, introduction to Bernard Tschumi's "Architecture and Transgression," *Oppositions 7* (Winter 1976): 55

103 Foster, "(Post) Modern Polemics," op. cit.: 151.

104 Lewis, "It's Postmodern..." op. cit.: G6.

105 Solà-Morales Rubió, "Neo-Rationalism," op. cit.: 19.

106 See *AD Profile* 11: *Surrealism and Architecture. Architectural Design* 48, no. 2–3, (1978), with articles by Tschumi, Frampton, and Koolhaas. See also my article on Duchamp's influence on contemporary architects, "Construction/Demolition, Object/Process" in *Proceedings of the 1991 ACSA Southeast Regional Conference* (Charlotte: University of North Carolina, 1992), 42–47.

107 See Alan Colquhoun, "Three Kinds of Historicism." (ch. 4)

108 Habermas, "Modernity," op. cit., 5.

109 Foster, "Preface," in *The Anti-Aesthetic*, op. cit., ix–xvi.

110 Foster, "(Post) Modern Polemics," op. cit.: 151.

111 Habermas, "Modernity," op cit., 7

112 Ibid., 11.

113 Lyotard, *The Postmodern Condition*, op. cit., 72.

114 Ibid., xxiii.

115 Alan Colquhoun, "Postmodernism and Structuralism," in *Modernity and the Classical Tradition* (Cambridge: MIT Press, 1989), 254.

116 Giulio Carlo Argan, "On the Typology of Architecture," *Architectural Design* no. 33 (December 1963): 565.

117 Solà-Morales Rubió, "Neo-Rationalism," op. cit.: 18.

118 Demetri Porphyrios, "Classicism is Not a Style," *Architectural Design* no. 5–6 (1982): 56.

119 McLeod, "Architecture in the Reagan Era," op. cit.: 43.

120 Norberg-Schulz, "Heidegger's Thinking on Architecture," op. cit.: 68.

121 Peter Collins, *Changing Ideals in Modern Architecture 1750–1950* (London: Faber and Faber, 1965), 289.

122 Ibid.

123 D.W. Meinig, ed., *The Interpretation of Ordinary Landscapes: Geographical Essays* (New York: Oxford University Press, 1979).

124 Carol Burns, "On Site: Architectural Preoccupations," in Andrea Kahn, ed., *Drawing/Building/Text: Essays in Architectural Theory* (New York: Princeton Architectural Press, 1991), 146–168.

125 Perez-Gomez, "Architectural Representation," op. cit.: 43.

126 Ezra Ehrenkrantz, "Superhighway's Urban Dangers," *Architecture* 84, no. 5 (May 1995): 51, 53, 55.

127 Colin Rowe and Fred Koetter, *Collage City* (Cambridge: MIT Press, 1978).

128 Italo Calvino, *Invisible Cities* (New York: Harcourt Brace Jovanovich, Inc., 1974), 156–158.

129 Rem Koolhaas, *Delirious New York: A Retroactive Manifesto for Manhattan* (New York: Monacelli Press, 1994), 10.

130 Ibid., 20.

131 Richard Ingersoll, *Design Book Review* 17 (Winter 1989): 3.

132 Thomas L. Schumacher, unpublished statement, May 1995.

133 Roland Barthes, "Semiology and Urbanism," in *Structures Implicit and Explicit, VIA* 2 (1973): 155.

134 Ibid.: 157.

135 Agrest, *Architecture from Without*, op. cit., 4.
136 Aldo Rossi, *The Architecture of the City* (Cambridge: MIT Press, 1982), 21.
137 Ibid., 41.
138 Peter Eisenman, "Introduction," in *The Architecture of the City*, op. cit., 6.
139 Ibid.
140 Leon Krier, "The Reconstruction of the City," in *Rational Architecture: The Reconstruction of the European City* (Brussels: Archives of Modern Architecture Editions, 1978), 38.
141 Ibid., 39.
142 Ibid., 41.
143 Alan Colquhoun, "Sign and Substance: Reflections on Complexity, Las Vegas, and Oberlin," in *Essays in Architectural Criticism: Modern Architecture and Historical Change* (Cambridge: Oppositions Books and MIT Press, 1985), 139–151.
144 Denise Scott Brown, "On Ducks and Decoration," in *Architecture Culture*, op. cit., 447.
145 Kate Nesbitt, "Cities of Desire/Boundaries of Cities," *Arquitectura* no. 288 (August 1991): 116–121.
146 First meeting, 8 October 1993, cited in Peter Katz, *The New Urbanism* (New York: McGraw-Hill, Inc., 1994), 241.
147 "Seaside and the Real World: A Debate on American Urbanism," *Architecture New York* no. 1 (July/August 1993).
148 Bernard Tschumi, "Architecture and Transgression," *Oppositions 7* (Winter 1976): 61.
149 Theodor Adorno, "Commitment," in Andrew Arato and Eike Gebhardt, eds., *The Essential Frankfurt School Reader* (New Tork: Urizen Books, 1978), 317.
150 "Postscript," *Ethics and Architecture, VIA* 10, John Capelli, Paul Naprstek, Bruce Prescott, eds. (1990): 164.
151 Ibid.
152 Ibid.
153 Runes, *A Dictionary*, op. cit., 54.
154 Ibid., 320.
155 Michel Foucault, "The Subject and Power," Brian Wallis, ed., *Art After Modernism* (New York: New Museum of Contemporary Art, 1984), 420.
156 Vidler, *The Architectural Uncanny*, op. cit., 69.
157 Ibid., 70.
158 Perez-Gomez, "Renovation," op. cit.: 29.
159 Vidler, "Theorizing the Unhomely," op. cit.: 3.
160 Ibid.: 3.
161 Quote is a Vidler lecture title cited in MacAnulty, "Body Troubles," op. cit., 196.
162 Diana Agrest, "Design versus Non-Design," in *Architecture from Without*, op. cit., 55.
163 McAnulty, "Body Troubles," in *Strategies in Architectural Thinking*, op. cit., 196.
164 Perez-Gomez, "Architectural Representation," op. cit.: 40.
165 Eisenman, "Visions' Unfolding." (ch. 13)
166 *The Compact Edition of the Oxford English Dictionary* (New York: Oxford University Press, 1984), 896.

1. POSTMODERNISM
ARCHITECTURAL RESPONSES TO THE CRISIS WITHIN MODERNISM

Complexity and Contradiction in Architecture:
Selections from a Forthcoming Book
Robert Venturi

The material included here, "Complexity versus
Picturesqueness," is an excerpt from the first publication of a manifesto that drastically changed the
face of twentieth-century architecture. When
Complexity and Contradiction in Architecture
appeared as a Museum of Modern Art book in
1966, it launched the first important American
architectural trend since the International Style,
also introduced by MoMA in 1932. The influential manifesto, published in sixteen languages,
established Robert Venturi as a major postmodern
theorist. He is credited with initiating the
American critique of the hegemony of corporate
modernism and with the recovery of historical
precedent. Among those who make such claims
for Venturi's book are Yale architectural historian
Vincent Scully, who urgently felt the need for a
critique of modernism,[1] and Scully's protégé,
Robert A.M. Stern, who published this excerpt as
student editor of *Perspecta: The Yale Architectural
Journal.*

The problem with modern architecture and
urbanism, Venturi claims, is that it is too reductive.
By carefully limiting the problems it would solve,
modern architecture produced solutions that were
pure, but boring. As a result, modern architecture
is not on a level with modern science, poetry, or
art, all of which recognize complexity and contradiction. (Peter Eisenman makes similarly unfavor-
able comparisons between modern architecture
and modern works in other disciplines in "Post-
Functionalism.") Venturi's critique of reductionism
offers instead an inclusive theory, expressed in his
terms of "both/and," "double-functioning elements," "more is not less," and "the difficult unity
of inclusion." Inclusiveness, he argues, produces
positive artistic tension and leads to a rich
condition of multiple interpretations.

Venturi's position in *Complexity and
Contradiction* is influenced by semiotics, Gestalt
(perceptual) psychology, and by literary theory
proposing the poetic value of ambiguity. He also
finds support for his emphasis on complexity in

evolutionary theory and psychology. Concerned with communication on numerous levels, Venturi finds the locus of architectural meaning in associations formed by familiarity with the history of the discipline. He admits that the book is an *apologia* for his design work and expresses his preferences in European architectural history, especially for mannerism and the baroque. Part of his theoretical contribution is the renewed consciousness, if not the embrace, of history, which underlies all postmodern architecture and distinguishes it from modern architecture. But the uses made of this recuperated tradition by lesser postmodern historicist architects have not all been successful. Thus, the appearance of Venturi's theory, encouraging an eclectic, image-oriented appropriation of history, can be likened to opening a Pandora's box of styles.

Among the targets of Venturi's criticism in *Complexity and Contradiction in Architecture* is the modernist steel-frame building with curtain wall cladding, which separates structure and enclosure. In suggesting the reintegration of these two functions, Venturi prepares the way for recent work that embraces the load-bearing wall as phenomenologically and tectonically rich and significant. (ch. 9, 12)

Towards the end of the book, Venturi begins to discuss American urbanism in the form of the Main Street town. His attitude towards the commercial highway "strip" and its symbolism is developed in *Learning from Las Vegas* (co-authored with Denise Scott Brown and Steven Izenour, 1972), which urges an acceptance of and accommodation to given conditions. (ch. 6)

1   Robert Venturi, *Complexity and Contradiction in Architecture* (New York: Museum of Modern Art, 1966).

ROBERT VENTURI

COMPLEXITY AND CONTRADICTION IN ARCHITECTURE
SELECTIONS FROM A FORTHCOMING BOOK

COMPLEXITY VERSUS PICTURESQUENESS

Complexity must be constant in architecture. It must correspond in form and function. Complexity of program alone breeds a formalism of false simplicity; complexity of expression alone tends toward formalism of multiplicity—an over-simplification rather than a simplicity on the one hand—a mere picturesqueness rather than complexity on the other. We no longer argue over the primacy of form or function; we cannot ignore their interdependence, however.

Orthodox modern architects have tended to recognize complexity either insufficiently or inconsistently. In their attempt to break with tradition and start all over again, they idealized the primitive and elementary at the expense of diversity and sophistication. As participants in a revolutionary movement, they acclaimed the newness of modern function over its complexity. In their role as reformers, they puritanically worked for the separation and exclusion of elements over the inclusion of diverse elements and their juxtapositions. Complexity of program has often accompanied a simplicity of form like early Le Corbusier's "great primary forms...which are distinct...and without ambiguity." Modern architecture, with few exceptions, eschewed ambiguity. More recent rationalizations for simplicity in architecture—subtler than the earlier arguments of modern architecture—are the various expansions of Mies's magnificent paradox, "less is more." Paul Rudolph has recently stated the implications of Mies's point of view: "All problems can never be solved, indeed it is a characteristic of the twentieth century that architects are highly selective in determining which problems they want to solve. Mies, for instance, makes wonderful buildings only because he ignores many aspects of a building. If he solved more problems, his buildings would be far less potent."[1]

From *Perspecta: The Yale Architectural Journal* 9/10 (1965): 19–20. Courtesy of the author and publisher.

The doctrine "less is more" bemoans complexity and justifies exclusion for expressive purposes. It does, indeed, permit the artist to be "highly selective in determining which problems [he wants] to solve." But the architect, if he must be "completely committed to his particular way of seeing the universe"[2]—that is, selective in *how* he approaches problems—he must not select *which* problems to approach. He can exclude important problems only at the risk of separating his architecture from the experience of life and the needs of society. And if some of his problems in an inclusive kind of architecture prove insoluble, he can express this; there is room in architecture for the fragment, for contradiction and improvisation and their attendant tensions.

Mies's exquisite pavilions have indeed had valuable implications for architecture, but is not their selectiveness of content and language their limitation as well as their strength? I question analogies to pavilions, especially Japanese pavilions in our recent house architecture. Such forced simplicity is oversimplification. [Philip] Johnson's Wiley House, for instance, separates and articulates the "private functions" of living below and the open social function above, but the building borders on the diagrammatic. It becomes a dry duality—an abstract theory of either or—before it is a house. Where simplicity cannot work, simpleness results. Blatant simplification means bland architecture. Less is a bore.

The recognition of complexity and contradiction in architecture does not negate what [Louis] Kahn has called "the desire for simplicity." But aesthetic simplicity, which is a satisfaction to the mind if valid and profound, derives from inner complexity. The Doric temple's simplicity to the eye is achieved through the famous subtleties and precision of its distorted geometry. [Jaquelin] Robertson has pointed out the contradictions and tensions implied in the unique position of the corner triglyphs at the end of the architrave and off center of the columns, and the consequent enlarged end metope.[3] The Doric temple could achieve apparent simplicity through real complexity.

Kenneth Burke has referred to oversimplification as a valid process in analysis: "We over-simplify a given event when we characterize it from the standpoint of a given interest."[†] But this is not the process of art. Literary critics have emphasized the complexity of the language of art, which is as inherently unsimple as its content. Others have characterized the interpretation of a work of art as the conscious play between the perception of what it seems and the conception of what it is. Its very meaning is in the discrepancies and contradictions of a complex juxtaposition.

I referred to some justifications for simplicity in early modern architecture—its exaggerated clarity as a technique of propaganda—its exclusive, almost puritanical, narrowness as an instrument of reform. But another reason is that things were simpler then. Solutions were more obvious if not easier to attain; the resolute Wright grew up with the motto "truth against the world." Such a slogan no longer seems adequate and our position is more likely, that described by August Hecksher:

The movement from a view of life as essentially simple and orderly to a view of life as complex and ironic is what every individual passes through in becoming mature. But certain epochs encourage this development; in them the paradoxical or dramatic outlook colors the whole intellectual scene....Amid simplicity and order rationalism is born, but rationalism proves inadequate in any period of upheaval. Then equilibrium must be created out of opposites. Such inner peace as men gain must represent a tension among contradictions and uncertainties....A feeling for paradox allows seemingly dissimilar things to exist side by side, their very incongruity suggesting a kind of truth.[4]

And Edmund W. Sinnott has referred to complexity in organic evolution: "Evolution has been primarily a process of increase in size and complexity. Natural selection, I think, has not put a premium on form *as such* but rather on the increased differentiation and division of labor that make an organism more efficient and likely to survive. This process has *necessarily* resulted in an increased elaboration of form, the laws of matter and energy being what they are."[5]

An architecture of complexity and contradiction, I reaffirm, does not mean picturesqueness or willful expressionism. If I am against purity, I am also against picturesqueness. False complexity currently counters false simplicity, and parallels other current architecture, which one of its authors calls serene. This reaction represents a new formalism usually as unconnected with experience and program as the former cult of simplicity. On the level of detail even, it cannot parallel a facility and exuberance of technique like the valid showing-off of late Gothic tracery or northern Mannerist strap work.

Our best architecture sometimes has rejected a simplicity through reduction in order to promote a complexity within a whole; the work of [Alvar] Aalto, Le Corbusier (who sometimes disregards his polemical writings), and, sometimes, [Frank Lloyd] Wright are examples. But characteristics of complexity and contradiction in their work are often ignored or misunderstood. Critics of Aalto, for instance, have liked him mostly for some of his other characteristics, such as sensitivity to natural materials and fine detailing. I do not consider Aalto's church at Vvokenniska picturesque, nor even an example of a justifiable quasi-expressionism like Giovanni Michellucci's Church of the Autostrada. Aalto's complexity is part of the program and the structure of the whole rather than an expressive device justified only by the desire for expression. Complexity must be the result of the program at least rather than the will of the author. The complex building creates a vivid whole despite its variety.

1   Paul Rudolph, "Rudolph," *Perspecta* 7 (1961): 51.
2   Ibid.: 51.
3   D.S. Robertson, *Greek and Roman Architecture* (Cambridge: 1959).
4   August Heckscher, *The Public Happiness* (New York: 1962), 102.
5   Edmund W. Sinnott, *The Problem of Organic Form* (New Haven, 1963), 195.

†   [Kenneth Burke, *Permanence and Change* (Los Altos: Hermes Publications, 1954).—Ed.]

INTRODUCTION

Post-Functionalism
Peter Eisenman

In this editorial from the Institute for Architecture and Urban Studies journal *Oppositions*, Director Peter Eisenman takes issue with the term "postmodernism," on the grounds that modern architecture never happened, making postmodern architecture an impossibility. Eisenman bases his unusual claim on the idea that the *relationship* between function and form has been a defining characteristic of architecture since the Renaissance. Humanist architecture sought a balance between programmatic accommodation and the "articulation of ideal themes in form," also known as type. (ch. 5) Industrialization, however, introduced new functions of such challenging complexity that typological solutions were inadequate to the design task, and function began to dominate in the "form follows function" model. By this century, the theory of functionalism had evolved to mean that the programmatic use of a building could and should determine the form and massing of the building. Twentieth-century functionalism, Eisenman says, emphasizing the determination of form by function, is thus an extension of humanist beliefs, and is therefore not truly modern. He then notes that in lieu of a period called postmodernism, we are in the midst of a 500-year continuity, or "classical episteme." The idea of a continuous period since the Renaissance, which challenges the defining of historical periods on the basis of stylistic appearance, is expanded in his essay, "The End of the Classical." (ch. 4)

Although cultural modernism has recognized the end of humanism and anthropocentrism, these changes have yet to be registered in architecture. Other artistic disciplines for which Eisenman has great respect have managed to express notions such as the decentered subject, essential to the posthumanist world view. In order to create an architectural manifestation of "the modernist sensibility," Eisenman says one must break with function as a foundational principle, or origin. His alternative to postmodernism, "post-functionalism," advocates a dialectic between humanist typology and fragmentation of typical forms into signs.

A partially post-functionalist position is established in Robert Venturi and Denise Scott Brown's preference for the "decorated shed" over the "duck." Like Eisenman, they reject modern functionalism's literal and exaggerated expression of program in the form and massing of the building; the duck is their caricature of this uneconomical approach. Their modest alternative, the decorated shed, rejects function as the determinant of form by housing all functions in the same "dumb" box. The only significant difference between buildings, Venturi and Scott Brown suggest, should be the sign on the surface of the box. Despite their proposal to cease literally constructing the function of the building in three-dimensional form, their signage and supergraphics still intend to present the shed's function. In other words, these architects continue to accept function as worthy of representation, as a *meaning* of architecture.

Novelist and semiotician Umberto Eco, who asserts that function *is* the primary meaning signified by architectural elements (behaving like signs), would probably disagree with Eisenman's proscription of function as origin.[1] To take away the signified aspect of architecture, that to which the sign refers, would eliminate communication.

Eisenman acknowledges that other postmodernists reject "the modern sensibility" as problematic, while maintaining the connection to function. He claims that these opponents of his position fail to recognize the differences between humanism and modernism. But in fact, some are quite cognizant of the differences, and prefer humanism. For example, while Eisenman advocates a break with humanism, Michael Graves's "figurative architecture" intends a reconciliation. Similarly, Demetri Porphyrios suggests a return to authentic, tectonic classicism that represents humanist values.

1   Umberto Eco, "Function and Sign: Semiotics in Architecture," *Via* 2: *Structures Implicit and Explicit* (1973).

PETER EISENMAN
POST-FUNCTIONALISM

The critical establishment within architecture has told us that we have entered the era of "post-modernism." The tone with which this news is delivered is invariably one of relief, similar to that which accompanies the advice that one is no longer an adolescent. Two indices of this supposed change are the quite different manifestations of the "Architettura Razionale" exhibition at the Milan Triennale of 1973 and the "École des Beaux Arts" exhibition at The Museum of Modern Art in 1975. The former, going on the assumption that modern architecture was an outmoded functionalism, declared that architecture can be generated only through a return to itself as an autonomous or pure discipline. The latter, seeing modern architecture as an obsessional formalism, made itself into an implicit statement that the future lies paradoxically in the past, within the peculiar response to function that characterized the nineteenth century's eclectic command of historical styles.

What is interesting is not the mutually exclusive character of these two diagnoses and hence of their solutions, but rather the fact that *both* of these views enclose the very project of architecture within the *same* definition: one by which the terms continue to be function (or program) and form (or type). In so doing, an attitude toward architecture is maintained that differs in no significant way from the 500-year-old tradition of humanism.

The various theories of architecture which properly can be called "humanist" are characterized by a dialectical opposition: an oscillation between a concern for internal accommodation—the program and the way it is materialized—and a concern for articulation of ideal themes in form—for example, as manifested in the configurational significance of the plan. These concerns were understood as two poles of a single, continuous experience. Within pre-industrial, humanist practice, a balance between them could

From *Oppositions* 6 (Fall 1976): unpaginated. Courtesy of the author.

be maintained because both type and function were invested with idealist views of man's relationship to his object world. In a comparison first suggested by Colin Rowe, of a French Parisian *hôtel* and an English country house, both buildings from the early nineteenth century, one sees this opposition manifested in the interplay between a concern for expression of an ideal type and a concern for programmatic statement, although the concerns in each case are differently weighted. The French *hôtel* displays rooms of an elaborate sequence and a spatial variety born of internal necessity, masked by a rigorous, well-proportioned external façade. The English country house has a formal internal arrangement of rooms which gives way to a picturesque external massing of elements. The former bows to program on the interior and type on the façade; the latter reverses these considerations.

With the rise of industrialization, this balance seems to have been fundamentally disrupted. In that it had of necessity to come to terms with problems of a more complex functional nature, particularly with respect to the accommodation of a mass client, architecture became increasingly a social or programmatic art. And as the functions became more complex, the ability to manifest the pure type-form eroded. One has only to compare William Kent's competition entry for the Houses of Parliament, where the form of a Palladian Villa does not sustain the intricate program, with Charles Barry's solution where the type form defers to program and where one sees an early example of what was to become known as the *promenade architecturale*. Thus, in the nineteenth century, and continuing on into the twentieth, as the program grew in complexity, the type-form became diminished as a realizable concern, and the balance thought to be fundamental to all theory was weakened. (Perhaps only Le Corbusier in recent history has successfully combined an ideal grid with the architectural promenade as an embodiment of the original interaction.)

This shift in balance has produced a situation whereby, for the past fifty years, architects have understood design as the product of some oversimplified form-follows-function formula. This situation even persisted during the years immediately following World War II, when one might have expected it would be radically altered. And as late as the end of the 1960s, it was still thought that the polemics and theories of the early Modern Movement could sustain architecture. The major thesis of this attitude was articulated in what could be called the English Revisionist Functionalism of Reyner Banham, Cedric Price, and Archigram. This neo-functionalist attitude, with its idealization of technology, was invested with the same ethical positivism and aesthetic neutrality of the prewar polemic. However, the continued substitution of moral criteria for those of a more formal nature produced a situation which now can be seen to have created a functionalist predicament, precisely because the primary theoretical justification given to formal arrangements was a *moral* imperative that is no longer operative within contemporary experience. This sense of displaced positivism characterizes certain current perceptions of the failure of humanism within a broader cultural context.

There is also another, more complex, aspect to this predicament. Not only can functionalism indeed be recognized as a species of positivism, but like positivism, it now can be seen to issue from within the terms of an idealist view of reality. For functionalism, no matter what its pretense, continued the idealist ambition of creating architecture as a kind of ethically constituted form-giving. But because it clothed this idealist ambition in the radically stripped forms of technological production, it has seemed to represent a break with the pre-industrial past. But, in fact, functionalism is really no more than a late phase of humanism, rather than an alternate to it. And in this sense, it cannot continue to be taken as a direct manifestation of that which has been called "the modernist sensibility."

Both the Triennale and the Beaux Arts exhibitions suggest, however, that the problem is thought to be somewhere else—not so much with functionalism *per se*, as with the nature of this so-called modernist sensibility. Hence, the implied revival of neo-classicism and Beaux Arts academicism as replacements for a continuing, if poorly understood, modernism. It is true that sometime in the nineteenth century, there was indeed a crucial shift within Western consciousness: one which can be characterized as a shift from humanism to modernism. But, for the most part, architecture, in its dogged adherence to the principles of function, did not participate in or understand the fundamental aspects of that change. It is the potential difference in the nature of modernist and humanist theory that seems to have gone unnoticed by those people who today speak of eclecticism, post-modernism, or neo-functionalism. And they have failed to notice it precisely because they conceive of modernism as merely a stylistic manifestation of functionalism, and functionalism itself as a basic theoretical proposition in architecture. In fact, the idea of modernism has driven a wedge into these attitudes. It has revealed that the dialectic form and function is culturally based.

In brief, the modernist sensibility has to do with a changed mental attitude toward the artifacts of the physical world. This change has not only been manifested aesthetically, but also socially, philosophically, and technologically—in sum, it has been manifested in a new cultural attitude. This shift away from the dominant attitudes of humanism that were pervasive in Western societies for some four hundred years took place at various times in the nineteenth century in such disparate disciplines as mathematics, music, painting, literature, film, and photography. It is displayed in the non-objective abstract painting of [Kazimir] Malevich and [Piet] Mondrian; in the non-native, atemporal writing of [James] Joyce and [Guillaume] Apollinaire; the atonal and polytonal compositions of [Arnold] Schönberg and [Anton] Webern; in the non-narrative films of [Hans] Richter and [Viking] Eggeling.

Abstraction, atonality, and atemporality, however, are merely stylistic manifestations of modernism, not its essential nature. Although this is not the place to elaborate a theory of modernism, or indeed to represent those aspects of such a theory which have already found their way into the literature of the other humanist disciplines, it can simply be said that the symptoms to which one has just pointed suggest a displacement of man away from the center of his world. He is no longer viewed as an *originating agent*. Objects are seen as ideas independent of man. In this context, man is a discursive function among complex and already-formed systems of language, which he witnesses but does not constitute. As [Claude] Lévi-Strauss has said, "Language, an unreflecting totalization, is human reason which has its reason and of which man knows nothing." It is this condition of displacement which gives rise to design in which authorship can no longer either account for a linear development which has a "beginning" and an "end"— hence the rise of the atemporal—or account for the invention of form—hence the abstract as a mediation between pre-existent sign systems.

Modernism, as a sensibility based on the fundamental displacement of man, represents what Michel Foucault would specify as a new *épistème*. Deriving from a non-humanistic attitude toward the relationship of an individual to his physical environment, it breaks with the historical past, both with the ways of viewing man as subject and, as we have said, with the ethical positivism of form and function. Thus, it cannot be related to functionalism. It is probably for this reason that modernism has not up to now been elaborated in architecture.

But there is clearly a present need for a theoretical investigation of the basic implications of modernism (as opposed to modern style) in architecture. In his editorial "Neo-Functionalism," in *Oppositions* 5, Mario Gandelsonas acknowledges such a need. However, he says merely that the "complex contradictions" inherent in functionalism—such as neo-realism and neo-rationalism—make a form of neo-functionalism necessary to any new theoretical *dialectic*. This proposition continues to refuse to recognize that the form/function opposition is not necessarily inherent to any architectural theory and so fails to recognize the crucial difference between modernism and humanism. In contrast, what is being called post-functionalism begins as an attitude which recognizes modernism as a new and distinct sensibility. It can best be understood in architecture in terms of a theoretical base that is concerned with what might be called a modernist dialectic, as opposed to the old humanist (i.e., functionalist) opposition of form and function.

This new theoretical base changes the humanist balance of form/function to a dialectical relationship within the evolution of form itself. The dialectic can best be described as the potential co-existence within any form of two non-corroborating and non-sequential tendencies. One tendency is to presume architectural form to be a recognizable transformation from some pre-existent geometric or platonic solid. In this case, form is usually understood through a series of registrations designed to recall a more simple geometric condition. This tendency is certainly a relic of humanist theory. However, to this is added a second tendency that sees architectural form in an atemporal, decompositional mode, as something simplified from some pre-existent set of non-specific spatial entities. Here, form is understood as a series of fragments—signs without meaning dependent upon, and without reference to, a more basic condition. The former tendency, when taken by itself, is a reductivist attitude and assumes some primary unity as both an ethical and an aesthetic basis for all creation. The latter, by itself, assumes a basic condition of fragmentation and multiplicity from which the resultant form is a state of simplification. Both tendencies, however, when taken together, constitute the essence of this new, modern dialectic. They begin to define the inherent nature of the object in and of itself and its capacity to be represented. They begin to suggest that the theoretical assumptions of functionalism are in fact cultural rather than universal.

Post-functionalism, thus, is a term of absence. In its negation of functionalism it suggests certain positive theoretical alternatives—existing fragments of thought which, when examined, might serve as a framework for the development of a larger theoretical structure—but it does not, in and of itself, propose to supply a label for such a new consciousness in architecture which I believe is potentially upon us.

INTRODUCTION

A Case for Figurative Architecture
Michael Graves

One of the famous "Five Architects," Michael Graves's conversion to postmodern historicism was gradual and influential. Even in his "White" (modern) projects, he evidences an interest in figuration, in the representational potential of architecture. Under the sway of Le Corbusier and analytic cubism (in particular, of the painter Juan Gris) in the years prior to 1976–77, his suggestive use of color, and later of loaded, historical fragments should perhaps come as no surprise. These interests surface in his paintings and set designs, as well as in his architecture.

As suggested in Mario Gandelsonas's article "On Reading Architecture," Graves is drawn to classical art and architecture in part because of the way they structure humanity's relationship to nature "through the assimilation of the underlying laws of nature."[1] The enduring theme of architecture and landscape appears in the form of idealized classical gardens projected for suburban New Jersey, clearly inspired by Graves's stay at the American Academy in Rome. For the "Grey" (postmodern) Graves, the spatial hierarchy established by anthropomorphic and cosmological references (especially to earth and sky) in classicism is far superior to the alienating continuous space of modernism. In a recent statement reflecting on his essay he says, "figurative architecture,...for me is a way of describing a humanistic architecture that expresses the myths and rituals of our society."[2]

Graves's harsh critique of modernism is also based on the inarticulateness of abstraction. Modernism lacks *character*, which he claims is:

> what finally gives us our sense of identity within a place, a building, or a room....Character and characteristics of buildings are part story-telling, part memory, part nostalgia, part symbol.[3]

Important to his theory of representation is the notion that language and (by an admittedly difficult extension,) art share two forms of communication: standard and poetic. He employs the "linguistic analogy" to stress the applicability of this idea to architecture. (ch. 2) The standard form of language is that which is serviceable and *conventional*, while the poetic operates at the *limits* of convention. (See Bernard Tschumi, ch. 3)

Graves equates the standard versus poetic forms respectively with *building* versus *architecture*, a distinction many postmodernists make based on the intention of the architect. Building, for Graves, encompasses instrumental aspects inherent to its practice, while architecture strives to symbolically represent culture and its myths. It is significant that Graves identifies this symbolic function as responding to cultural issues, in contrast to others' (Peter Eisenman's) desire for an autonomous architecture, or one based in philosophy or literary criticism. Graves and Eisenman are considered representatives of polar positions in "On Reading Architecture." The article compares the autonomous, abstract, "syntactic" approach of Eisenman to Graves's figural, "semantic" architecture.

Graves elaborates on his method:

> I attempt to design with a wide palette, rephrasing the traditional language of architecture with its recognizable forms and simultaneously drawing on the lessons of modern composition, all in response to the program, the site, and the client's aspirations. My architecture takes a fresh look at both classicism and modernism, as they both contain allusions that are part of our contemporary culture.[4]

These allusions rely on the function of the associative plane of expression. Graves's work, because of its strong quality as image, is subject to appropriation and manipulation by builders and others who package shelter as a commodity. (See Kenneth Frampton, ch. 12) The critical capacity of postmodern historicist architecture with regard to building in general, sought in Michael's Graves's case through the poetic form of language, is quickly exhausted.

1 Mario Gandelsonas, "On Reading Architecture," in Geoffrey Broadbent, Richard Bunt, and Charles Jencks, eds., *Signs, Symbols and Architecture* (Chichester, UK: John Wiley & Sons Ltd., 1980), 255.
2 Michael Graves, "Current Thoughts on Design," unpublished statement, May 1995.
3 Ibid.
4 Ibid.

MICHAEL GRAVES

A CASE FOR FIGURATIVE ARCHITECTURE

A standard form and a poetic form exist in any language or in any art. Although analogies drawn between one cultural form and another prove somewhat difficult, they nevertheless allow associations that would otherwise be impossible. Literature is the cultural form which most obviously takes advantage of standard and poetic usages, and so may stand as a model for architectural dialogue. In literature, the standard, accessible, simple ranges of daily use are expressed in conversational or prose forms, while the poetic attitudes of language are used to test, deny, and at times, to further support standard language. It seems that standard language and poetic language have a reciprocal responsibility to stand as separate and equal strands of the greater literary form and to reinforce each other by their similarity and diversity. Through this relationship of tension, each form is held in check and plays on the other for its strength.

When applying this distinction of language to architecture, it could be said that the standard form of building is its common or internal language. The term internal language does not imply in this case that it is non-accessible, but rather that it is intrinsic to building in its most basic form—determined by pragmatic, constructional, and technical requirements. In contrast, the poetic form of architecture is responsive to issues external to the building, and incorporates the three-dimensional expression of the myths and rituals of society. Poetic forms in architecture are sensitive to the figurative, associative, and anthropomorphic attitudes of a culture. If one's goal is to build with only utility in mind, then it is enough to be conscious of technical criteria alone. However, once aware of and responsive to the possible cultural influences on building, it is important that society's patterns of ritual be registered in the architecture.

From Karen Vogel Wheeler, Peter Arnell, and Ted Bickford, eds., *Michael Graves: Buildings and Projects 1966–1981* (New York: Rizzoli, 1982), 11–13. Courtesy of the author and publisher.

Could these two attitudes, one technical and utilitarian and the other cultural and symbolic, be thought of as architecture's standard and poetic languages?

Without doubt, the inevitable overlap of these two systems of thought can cause this argument to become somewhat equivocal. However, the salient tendencies of each attitude may be distinguished and reasonably discussed. This is said with some critical knowledge of the recent past. It could be maintained that dominant aspects of modern architecture were formulated without this debate about standard and poetic language, or internal and external manifestations of architectural culture. The Modern Movement based itself largely on technical expression—internal language—and the metaphor of the machine dominated its building form. In its rejection of the human or anthropomorphic representation of previous architecture, the Modern Movement undermined the poetic form in favor of nonfigural, abstract geometries. These abstract geometries might in part have been derived from the simple internal forms of machines themselves. Coincident with machine metaphors in buildings, architecture in the first half of this century also embraced aesthetic abstraction in general. This has contributed to our interest in purposeful ambiguity, the possibility of double readings within compositions.

While any architectural language, to be built, will always exist within the technical realm, it is important to keep the technical expression parallel to an equal and complementary expression of ritual and symbol. It could be argued that the Modern Movement did this, that as well as its internal language, it expressed the symbol of the machine and therefore practiced cultural symbolism. But in this case, the machine is retroactive, for the machine itself is a utility. So this symbol is not an external allusion but rather a second, internalized reading. A significant architecture must incorporate both internal and external expressions. The external language, which engages inventions of culture at large, is rooted in a figurative, associational, and anthropomorphic attitude.

We assume that in any construct, architectural or otherwise, technique, the art of making something, will always play a role. However, it should also be said that the components of architecture have not only derived from pragmatic necessity, but also evolved from symbolic sources. Architectural elements are recognized for their symbolic aspect and used metaphorically by other disciplines. A novelist, for example, will stand his character next to a window and use the window as a frame through which we read or understand the character's attitude and position.

In architecture, however, where they are attendant to physical structure, basic elements are more frequently taken for granted. In this context, the elements can become so familiar that they are not missed when they are eliminated or when they are used in a slang version. For instance, if we imagine ourselves standing adjacent to a window, we expect the window sill to be somehow coincident with the waist of our body. We also expect, or might reasonably ask, that its frame help us make sense not only of the landscape beyond but also of our own position relative to the geometry of the window and to the building as a whole. In modern architecture, however, these expectations are seldom met and instead the window is often continuous with the wall as horizontal banding or, more alarmingly, it becomes the entire surface. The naming of the "window wall" is a prime example of the conflation or confusion of architectural elements.

Architectural elements require this distinction, one from another, in much the same way as language requires syntax; without variations among architectural elements, we will lose the anthropomorphic or figurative meaning. The elements of any enclosure include wall, floor, ceiling, column, door, and window. It might be wondered why these elements, given their geometric similarity in some cases (for example, floor and ceiling) must be understood differently. It is essential in any symbolic construct to identify the thematic differences between various parts of the whole. If the floor as ground is regarded as distinct from the soffit as sky, then the material, textural, chromatic, and decorative inferences are dramatically different. Yet in a formal sense, these are both horizontal planes.

We as architects must be aware of the difficulties and the strengths of thematic and figural aspects of the work. If the external aspects of the composition, that part of our language which extends beyond internal technical requirements, can be thought of as the resonance of man and nature, we quickly sense an historical pattern of external language. All architecture before the Modern Movement sought to elaborate the themes of man and landscape. Understanding the building involves both association with natural phenomena (for example, the ground is like the floor), and anthropomorphic allusions (for example, a column is like a man). These two attitudes within the symbolic nature of building were probably originally in part ways of justifying the elements of architecture in a prescientific society. However, even today, the same metaphors are required for access to our own myths and rituals within the building narrative.

Although there are, of course, instances where the technical assemblage of buildings employs metaphors and forms from nature, there is also possibility for a larger, external natural text within the building narrative. The suggestion that the soffit is in some sense celestial, is certainly our cultural invention, and it becomes increasingly interesting as other elements of the building also reinforce such a narrative. This type of cultural association allows us "into" the full text or language of the architecture. This is in contrast to modern examples which commonly sacrifice the idea or theme in favor of a more abstract language. In these instances, the composition, while perhaps formally satisfying, is based only on internal references. A de Stijl composition is as satisfying turned upside down as it is right side up, and this is in part where its interest lies. We may admire it for its compositional unity, but as architecture, because of its lack of interest in nature and gravity, it dwells outside the reference systems of architectural themes. A de Stijl building has two internal systems, one technical and the other abstract.

In making a case for figurative architecture, we assume that the thematic character of the work is grounded in nature and is simultaneously read in a totemic or anthropomorphic manner. An example of this double reading might be had by analyzing the character of a wall. As the window helps us to understand our size and presence within the room, so the wall, though more abstract as a geometric plane, has over time accommodated both pragmatic and symbolic divisions. Once the wainscot or chair rail is understood as being similar in height to the window sill, associations between the base of the wall (which that division provides) and our own bodies are easily made. As we stand upright and are, in a sense, rooted in the ground, so the wall through its wainscot division, is rooted relative to the floor. Another horizontal division takes place at the picture molding, where the soffit is dropped from its horizontal position to a linear division at the upper reaches of the wall. Although this tripartite division of the wall into base, body, and head does not literally imitate man, it nevertheless stabilizes the wall relative to the room, an effect we take for granted in our bodily presence there.

The mimetic character that a wall offers the room, as the basic substance of its enclosure, is obviously distinct from the plan of the room. While we see and understand the wall in a face to face manner, we stand perpendicular to the plan. The wall contributes primarily to the character of the room because of its figurative possibilities. The plan, however, because it is seen perspectively, is less capable of expressing character and more involved with our spatial understanding of the room. While space can be appreciated on its own terms as amorphous, it is ultimately desirable to create a reciprocity between wall and plan, where the wall surfaces or enclosures are drawn taut around a spatial idea. The reciprocity of plan and wall is finally more interesting than the distinctions between them. We can say that both wall and plan have a center and edges.

The plan alone, however, has no top, middle, and base, as does the wall. At this point, we must rely on the reciprocal action or volumetric continuity provided by both. Understanding that it is the volumetric idea that will be ultimately considered, we can analyze, with some isolation, how the plan itself contributes to a figurative architectural language.

For the purposes of this argument, a linear plan, three times as long as it is wide, might be compared to a square or centroidal plan. The square plan provides an obvious center, and at the same time, emphasizes its edges or periphery. If the square plan is further divided, like tic-tac-toe, into nine squares, the result is an even greater definition of corners, edges, and a single center. If we continue to elaborate such a geometric proposition with freestanding artifacts such as furniture, the locations of tables and chairs will be not only pragmatic, but also symbolic of societal interactions. One can envision many compositions and configurations of the same pieces of furniture, which would offer us different meanings within the room.

Predictably, the three-square composition will subdivide quite differently from the centroidal plan. While the rectangular composition will distinguish the middle third of the room as its center, and the outer third as its flanks, we are less conscious here of occupiable corners. The corners of the square composition contribute to our understanding of the center and are read as positive. In contrast, the corners of the rectangular plan are remote from its center and are seemingly residual. Our culture understands the geometric center as special and as the place of primary human occupation. We would not typically divide the rectangular room into two halves, but rather, more appropriately, would tend to place ourselves in the center, thereby precluding any reading of the room as a diptych. In analyzing room configurations, we sense a cultural bias to certain basic geometries. We habitually see ourselves, if not at the center of our "universe" at least at the center of the spaces we occupy. This assumption colors our understanding of the differences between center and edge.

If we compare the understanding of the exterior of the building to that of its interior volume, another dimension of figurative architecture arises. A freestanding building such as Palladio's Villa Rotunda, is comprehensible in its objecthood. Furthermore, its interior volume can be read similarly—not as a figural object but as a figural void. A comparison between such an "object building" and a building of the Modern Movement, such as Mies van der Rohe's Barcelona Pavilion, allows us to see how the abstract character of space in Mies's building dissolves any reference to or understanding of figural void or space. We cannot charge Mies with failing to offer us figurative architecture, for this is clearly not his intention. However, we can say that, without the sense of enclosure that the Palladio example offers us, we have a much thinner palette than if we allow the possibility of both the ephemeral space of modern architecture and the enclosure of traditional architecture. It could be contended that amorphic or continuous space, as understood in the Barcelona Pavilion, is oblivious to bodily or totemic reference, and we therefore always find ourselves unable to feel centered in such space. This lack of figural reference ultimately contributes to a feeling of alienation in buildings based on such singular propositions.

In this discussion of wall and plan, an argument is made for the figural necessity of each particular element and, by extension, of architecture as a whole. While certain monuments of the Modern Movement have introduced new spatial configurations, the cumulative effect of nonfigurative architecture is the dismemberment of our former cultural language of architecture. This is not so much an historical problem as it is one of a cultural continuum. It may be glib to suggest that the Modern Movement be seen not so much as an historical break but as an appendage to the basic and continuing figurative mode of expression. However, it is nevertheless crucial that we re-establish the thematic associations invented by our culture in order to fully allow the culture of architecture to represent the mythic and ritual aspirations of society.

The Relevance of Classical Architecture
Demetri Porphyrios

A manifesto for the revival of authentic classicism,
architect Demetri Porphyrios's essay begins by taking the
Modern Movement to task for failures at the scale of the
building and the city. His critique, developing arguments
from his *Classicism is Not a Style* (1982), goes beyond
aesthetics to attack the ideological basis of modern
architecture. Both the article and the book were published by the British journal *Architectural Design*, the
source of a significant amount of postmodern theory.

Porphyrios points out that the results of realizing the
modernist urban program advanced by Le Corbusier
and CIAM were the "mathematical abstraction" of the
city and the extinction of symbolic meaning, also recognized by Robert Venturi and Denise Scott Brown. (ch. 6)
The separation of functions under zoning, and the ubiquitous "tower in the park," led to distortions in the scale
and experience of the modern city. Object buildings created sprawl and deprived the city of meaningful hierarchies. Porphyrios proposes to address modernism's failures with what Kevin Lynch would call the "imageability"
of the traditional city. Reestablishing the dense rhythm of
street, square, and block of the European town, he
claims, will end urban disorientation. This aspect of
Porphyrios's polemic positions him in the postmodern
urban critique along with Leon and Rob Krier.

Just as significant to Porphyrios's argument is the
critical stance he takes towards both modern and postmodern buildings. He sees the former as mute, unable
to transcend their materiality to aspire to architecture,
while the latter are scenographic, eclectic kitsch, resulting from the postmodern "rhetoric of style." All the obvious manifestations of postmodernism (whether High-
Tech, Classical, or Deconstructionist) are cynical and
destructive of the culture of architecture, he asserts.
Porphyrios would thus disapprove of the built work of
all of his colleagues in this chapter, although not of
Michael Graves's humanist intentions stated in his theory of "figurative architecture."

Porphyrios's alternative is a broadened ethical
role for architects and the mythification of construction
as a renewed foundation for the discipline. (ch. 8, 12)
Through reliance on the tectonic, rather than stylistic,
justification of classicism, Porphyrios effectively distinguishes his design work from other postmodernists.

DEMETRI PORPHYRIOS

THE RELEVANCE OF CLASSICAL ARCHITECTURE

In the last twenty-five years architects have articulated a devastating critique of the ideological assumptions of Modern architecture. The critique concerns both the aesthetics of architecture and the organization of the city. For the Modernists, the ideal of reductive purity was ideologically charged and in this sense Modernist buildings were seen not only as things of beauty but also as anticipations of the radiant universal city of the future; in other words, of a city that would stand as a symbol of liberated and non-hierarchic society. In that sense, Modernism has been the only avant-garde movement of our century. This avant-garde commitment to such a goal of an emancipatory social liberation required, among other things, a refusal to look back to the various architectural traditions, all of which were supposed to have connotations of authoritarian domination. The old stylistic differences, whether regional, historical, or attributable to class distinctions, were soon to dissolve. Style meant ornament, it meant decoration and since it symbolized status seeking, conspicuous consumption and display it was bound to be socially and morally objectionable, intellectually indefensible and aesthetically corrupt.

As regards urban design, we know that the Modernist approach was a radically rationalist *tabula rasa*, a clean slate: zoning, the city in the park, the free-standing building, the disappearance of the street, and the square, the destruction of the urban block. In short, it meant the destruction of the urban fabric of the city. All that was systematically hailed by the Modernists as an ingenious advance in urban social engineering. Take, for example, Hilbersheimer who claimed that "every exception and every nuance must be cancelled out; abstract, mathematical order must reign so that it may constrain chaos to become form." Hilbersheimer was neither the first nor the last Modernist planner. In the mid-nineteenth century, Jules Borie had spoken of similar crystalline palaces for the

From *Architectural Design* 59, no. 9–10 (1989): 53–56. Courtesy of the author and publisher.

brave new world and, I suppose, as late as 1969 designers like Superstudio still believed that their "landscrapers" could be socially regenerative.

In my book on Alvar Aalto I have stressed this double objectivism of Modern architecture: the objectivism that aimed on the one hand at the mathematical abstraction of the city and on the other at the extinction of symbolic meaning. I discussed how Alvar Aalto emerged as a significant figure in the 50s and 60s exactly because he adopted strategies which appeared to undermine this double objectivism. In that sense, Aalto was the first modern eclectic and by extension the first Post-Modernist. In fact, Aalto had a catalytic effect in the debates which took place in the mid-60s between the Whites and Greys. Out of these debates two major concerns emerged: the importance of the rhetoric of style and the primacy of context. The whole Post-Modernist culture was indeed founded on these two concerns. Architectural thinking slowly moved away from Modernist planning towards contextual strategies and eventually towards a re-kindled interest in traditional urbanism.

The re-orientation which took place in the 60s and which later developed into Post-Modernism was and still remains based on an eclectic attitude. Much like nineteenth-century eclecticism, the aim of modern eclecticism has been to look at historical styles merely as communicative devices, as labels and clothing. Style itself was seen as having no natural relationship to the tectonics of building. Since this eclectic mood had nothing to do with the values of revivalism, it soon became clear that there could be no common criteria of aesthetic evaluation. Hence a pluralism that sprung out of "an age of conciliatory culture, widespread, visiting the beliefs of all countries and all ages, accepting everything without fixing any part, since truth is everywhere in bits and nowhere in its entirety."

Many, including myself, have discussed the architecture of the last twenty-five years as historicism, contextualism, relativism, or the aesthetics of accommodation. I don't want to take issue here with any of these interpretations. In a sense, all these accounts are accurate evaluations of our contemporary mood. If we are to understand, however, the phenomenon of Post-Modern architecture we must look at the distinctive use of its stylistic devices and conventions.

Modernism as an avant-garde made us familiar with the idea of showing rather than concealing the conventions and devices which are used in constructing a work of art. I refer here to what the Russian Formalists called the foregrounding of the device; an idea found in the alienation effect, for example, of [Bertolt] Brecht. This idea of estrangement and foregrounding the device so characteristic of Modernism is maintained by Post-Modernism. Post-Modernism works show themselves for the contrivance they are, but in doing so they also state that everything else in life is a contrivance and that simply there is no escape from this. Hence the self-referential circularity of the Post-Modern quotation and the extreme fascination with parody and meta-linguistic commentary. Let me look now at the three major meta-linguistic idioms of Post-Modernism today: Post-Modern High-Tech, Post-Modern Classical, and Post-Modern Deconstructionist.

The engineer's language of the nineteenth century had a direct relationship to the contingencies of construction and shelter. The social vision of the Polytechnicians gave it a futuristic aura which was to be exploited ever after by the so-called High-Tech architects. But as we know, Ferdinand Dutert's Palais des Machines was indeed a High-Tech building in the sense that it pushed the engineering skill of its time to its limits for a socially purposeful brief. On the contrary, contemporary so-called High-Tech buildings are only make-believe simulations of High-Tech imagery. It is in this sense that we can say that High-Tech acts today as a meta-language. The device, namely technologism, is shown here for the contrivance it is. In a culture where the frontiers of technology have moved away from building towards space and genetics, the idea of a High-Tech building can only be either wishful thinking or a make-believe.

The second idiom of Post-Modernism today is that of the Post-Modern Classical. [Theophilus] Hansen's nineteenth-century Academy in Athens was a reworking of the Classical language where the principles of commodity, firmness, and delight were all respected. On the contrary, Post-Modern Classicists use the device of parody. They favour playful distortion, citation, deliberate anachronism, diminution, oxymoron, etc. Ultimately, this is yet another make-believe cardboard architecture.

Finally, Deconstruction today is marketed as a recent avant-garde. But it is neither recent nor an avant-garde. It is but another version of the Post-Modern movement. The language adopted is that of the Constructivist avant-garde. But whereas the aesthetics of the Constructivists, say [Iakov] Chernikhov, were ultimately grounded in the social vision of an emancipated urban proletariat and in the hoped-for technology of the new industrial state, Post-Modern Deconstructionists today exploit the graphics of the avant-garde so that they may benefit by association and promote themselves as a new critical wave. They loudly reject such ideas as order, intelligibility, and tradition. Architecture is supposed to become an experience of failure and crisis. And if crisis is not there, well then it must be created. In this respect, Post-Modern Deconstructivists lack a socially-grounded critical platform. If anything, Deconstruction today is a version of aestheticism. And let me add: those who claim amnesia have systematically resorted to historicism.

These three versions of the Post-Modern—Post-Modern High-Tech, Post-Modern Classical and Post-Modern Deconstruction—differ widely in their stylistic preferences, symbolic content and social constituencies but they share a similar scenographic view of architecture. This view of architecture as scenography can be summarized in [Robert] Venturi's principle of the "decorated shed": construction (firmness), shelter (commodity), and symbolism (delight) are distinct and unrelated concerns. They do not influence each other. Construction, shelter, and symbolism are each governed by their own rules and they share no common aim. This scenographic attitude in the production of a building coupled with the fascination with parody I mentioned earlier are the two fundamental characteristics of the Post-Modern. Confronted with Post-Modern architecture one has a feeling somehow that all values have been researched and rejected. We are of this or that opinion just for the fun of it.

I have great respect for the inventive ingenuity of the Post-Modernists but I have repeatedly in the past criticized the Post-Modernists as regards exactly these two points: the principle of the "decorated shed" and the aesthetics of parody. The self-paralysing parodies they thrive on, when unwrapped from their intellectualist idiom, are but dispirited commonplaces. If my view has been that of a Classicist, it has been so not because of a transcendental belief in the immutable nature of the orders but because I have come to realise that *Classicism is not a style.*

Let me clarify what I mean here. The critique launched by contemporary Classicists starts, quite significantly, not with the aesthetics of architecture but with the strategies of urban design. In other words, the critique addresses the destruction of the traditional urban fabric, the progressive abstraction of the city through zoning and the excremental experience of the Las Vegas Strip. The twentieth-century city, argue the Classicists, works well from the sewers up to the sky-scrapers as long as one considers the wastage in human and natural resources as a concommittant to the sustaining of the overall edifice.

Instead, the Classicists propose the wisdom of the traditional city: English, European, American, or otherwise. The issue here is not one of stylistics but of ecological balance: to control the sprawl of our cities, to reconsider the scale and measure of the urban block, to emphasise the typological significance of design, to establish hierarchies between public and private realms, and to re-think the constitution of the open spaces of the city.

As regards the aesthetics of architecture, the Classicists adopt the theory of imitation. Art, it is argued, imitates the real world by turning selected significant aspects of it into mythical representations. Consider the following comparison. A documentary record of the atrocities of civil war can be contrasted with [Francisco] Goya's or [Peter Paul] Rubens's "Atrocities of War" that depict Saturn devouring his children. The documentary record can only provoke disgust. Goya's imitative representation of the real world, however, does afford us aesthetic pleasure. This is so exactly because it establishes a distance from reality which allows us to contemplate our universal human predicament.

Similarly, a Classicist would argue, architecture is the imitative celebration of construction and shelter qualified by the myths and ideas of a given culture. Such myths might have to do with life, nature or the mode of production of a given society. Ultimately, architecture speaks of these myths and ideas but always through the language of construction and shelter, celebrating construction and shelter by means of tectonic order.

Surely, many Modernists have spoken about "honest construction." But I want to stress here that Classical imitation has nothing in common with the structural functionalism of Modern architecture. Modernism does *not* imitate construction and shelter; it simply uses raw building material without any imitative mediation. In that sense, Modernism has produced buildings but, as yet, no architecture. The result has been a century of mute realism in the name of industrial production. On the contrary what makes Classical architecture possible is the dialogic relationship it establishes between the craft of building and the art of architecture. Our imagination traverses this dialogic space between, say, a pergola and a colonnade, and establishes hierarchies, levels of propriety, and communicable systems of evaluation.

Classical architecture needs also another dialogic relationship: this time the relationship between one building and another. This point is very important. Today the market ethic of the original and authentic is based on the pretense that every work of art is an invention singular enough to be patented. As a consequence of this frame of mind, demonstrating the debt of, say, Giulio Romano to Bramante is today called scholarship but it would have been denounced as plagiarism were Giulio Romano still alive. I think it is unfortunate that it is not only the inexperienced Modern architect who looks for a residual originality as a hallmark of talent. Most of us today tend to think of an architect's real achievement as having nothing to do with the achievement present in what he borrows. Since we have been educated as Modernists we tend to think that our contribution comprises solely in that which is different. We therefore tend to concentrate on peripheral issues of stylistics.

What I am suggesting here is that the real contribution of an architect lies in what he/she chooses to borrow. Let us think for a moment of the greatness, say, of [Leon Battista] Alberti. His greatness lies in the fact that he gave a new life to the humanist theme itself which he passed on to the fifteenth century from the sources of antiquity. The world of Alberti was very different from that of antiquity; the technology was different, the politics were different, the *haute couture* had changed, but the great humanist theme of commodity-firmness-delight was still alive and will stay alive.

Let me finish by saying that architecture has nothing to do with "novelty-mania" and intellectual sophistries. Architecture has nothing to do with transgression, boredom, or parody. It has nothing to do with parasitic life, excremental culture of the cynical fascination with the bad luck of others. Architecture has to do with decisions that concern the good, the decent, the proper. Decisions about what Aristotle called the *EY ZEIN*, the good and proper life. Surely, what constitutes proper life varies from one historical period to another. But it is our responsibility to define it anew all the time. If we choose to embrace the tradition of the Classical we will find no recipes but we will encounter again and again a kind of genius for practical life, a kind of genius that is actually less of a gift than a constant task of adjustment to present contingencies. It is in this sense that we can speak of the Classical as that which endures; but this defiance of time is always experienced as a sort of historical present.

Versions of this paper were read at the Classicism Symposium at the Tate Gallery, London, 1988, and at Neocon 21, Chicago, 1989.

INTRODUCTION

New Directions in Modern American Architecture:
Postscript at the Edge of Modernism
Robert A.M. Stern

Published in the British journal *Architectural
Association Quarterly* in 1977, architect Robert
Stern's piece is an early interpretation of the
American postmodern architectural trend. In this
article, he identifies Robert Venturi and Charles
Moore as originators of postmodern historicism,
which shifted the emphasis in theory from
autonomous, modern formalism to a search for
meaning. Stern finds three main areas of concern
to these postmodern architects, all of which relate
to the production of meaning: the facade, the
city, and the idea of cultural memory. He calls the
three practices or principles which address these
concerns Ornamentalism, Contextualism, and
Allusionism.

 Crediting the idea of Allusionism to Venturi,
Scott Brown and Associates (VSBA) in *Learning
from Las Vegas*, Stern notes that forms accrue
meaning over time, making architecture comprehensible. Stern clearly states that buildings should
convey meaning, or signify, within society; "they
are not hermetically sealed objects." (In this
regard, Stern's position opposes Peter Eisenman's
in chapter four.) Postmodern historicist architecture
intends to signify in large part through recourse to
historic precedent or type.

 In the intervening years since VSBA's book
appeared, Stern asserts, two additional principles
have emerged. One is Contextualism, the idea
that the building is a fragment of a larger urban
whole, which is associated in Stern's mind with
Romaldo Giurgola. To Europeans, the renewed
interest in "The City" would be credited to Aldo
Rossi's impassioned *Architecture of the City*,
which however, did not appear in English until
1982. (ch. 6, 7)

 Stern's third principle, Ornamentalism, is
not as clear as it could be. In essence, Stern
observes a revival of interest in the facade as
carrier of architectural meaning. Citing the
example of Michael Graves, he stresses the
importance of figuration and the compositional
use of historical fragments rich in associations.

One could also mention VSBA's semiotic consideration of the wall as *sign* in their discussion of the "duck" and the "decorated shed," as part of Ornamentalism.

As opposed to later readings of postmodern historicism emphasizing its fantasy, Stern claims a "realism" for the forms of the movement which he says recognize "the social, cultural, and political milieu that called them into being." Stern is clearly under the influence of Venturi and historian Vincent Scully in arguing for communicative buildings. All three of Stern's principles suggest an important role for history in the production of meaning in postmodern architecture. His statement that "appropriate references to historical architecture can enrich new work and thereby make it more familiar, accessible, and possibly even more meaningful," is similar to asserting that architecture functions as a sign system. (ch. 2)

ROBERT A.M. STERN
NEW DIRECTIONS IN MODERN AMERICAN ARCHITECTURE
POSTSCRIPT AT THE EDGE OF THE MILLENIUM

I began my book *New Directions in American Architecture* in 1969 by posing a debate between the group of architects whom I described as "exclusivist" and a new "inclusivist" group, a debate that continues to be the central focus of my concern in writing this postscript.[1] In 1969 I saw the inclusivists—since 1974 often referred to as the "grey" architects—as third-generation modernists. At the present time, however, I see their position rather differently: they are the first post-modern generation of architects, establishing a position that marks a significant break with the three generations of the Modern Movement and its so-called International Style, that is with the first generation of Le Corbusier and Mies; the second generation of [Philip] Johnson, [Kevin] Roche, and [Paul] Rudolph; and the third represented by Richard Meier, Charles Gwathmey, and Peter Eisenman.

Although the idea of "modernism" has long been intertwined with a belief that art is shipwrecked in a commercial society, the second generation of the Modern Movement continues to ride the crest of the enormous prosperity that engulfed American architecture in the wake of World War II.[2]

While the heroic ambitions of some and the technological bravura of others among this group no longer embodies for many Americans the same mystique of power and progress they once did, a market for this work still exists, particularly in those so-called "developing" countries whose vision of America remains rooted to the values that most of us rejected the night Lyndon Johnson told the nation that we could have guns and butter, war in Vietnam, peace and progress at home.[3]

The third generation of the Modern Movement—the so-called "white" architects —has emerged as much in the reaction to the permissive inclusivism of the "grey"

From *Architectural Association Quarterly* 9, no. 2 and 3 (1977): 66–71. Courtesy of the author and publisher.

architects as to the dilution of the fundamental values and forms of modernism that has characterized the largely commercial work of the second generation. This third generation seeks to revitalize the Modern Movement by a process of purification based on a return to the philosophical idealism that motivated European Modernism in the 1920s and 1930s and to the most abstract aspects of its form-making: the mechanomorphological cubism of Le Corbusier, and the rigorous, highly cerebral constructs of such architects as Hannes Meyer and Giuseppe Terragni.[4]

To some degree, the debate between "white" exclusivism and "grey" inclusivism can be seen as a battle of styles not unlike the one that took place in America during the last great economic depression, when International Style modernism struggled for acceptance against the prevailing progressive traditionalist modes.[5] But the battle of the 1970s is not without irony: the brave-new-world modernism of fifty years ago is now seen by the insurgent post-modernists as orthodox, stifling, and not a little irrelevant while the third-generation modernists seek to return to the forms and values of the pioneer Modernism of the 1920s, even though their built work often comes closer to the provincial, pragmatic, and derivative American International Style of the 1930s, than to the purer and more rigorously abstract European prototypes.[6]

Richard Meier, perhaps the best known, and certainly the most established of the "white" architects, has built his reputation on the design of several elegant private houses. Though they never achieve the luminous resolution of perceived and implied ideas about space and shape that characterizes Le Corbusier's work of the 1920s, these meticulously conceived objects infuse a sense of drama into the traditional Modernist dialectic between open (public) and closed (private) spaces, and between load-bearing and non-load-bearing elements.

Meier's high-density apartment complex in the Bronx is his most culturally engaged work to date. Here he incorporates lessons about ordinary composition and contextual responsibility observed in the work of [Robert] Venturi, as well as strategies for the integration of tower and slab and to some extent for site organisation that characterise the Coronado condominium project of Charles Moore. In the handling of the outdoor spaces between the buildings and beneath the raised slabs, however, the scheme remains plagued by the "socially problematic" modernist concept of the "open city" and its freed ground plane.[7]

Charles Gwathmey, together with his partner Robert Siegel, has also established his reputation with work at the domestic scale. Gwathmey's first notable success, the house built for his parents at Amagansett, combining influences from Le Corbusier and from the American Shingle Style, exhibits a superb sense of craftsmanship and a fresh attitude toward the use of traditional wood frame construction. The additions which have been made over the past ten years, first the studio and then a second house built on an adjacent lot, elaborate with remarkable success the propositions advanced in the original house, as they suggest the limited urbanistic capabilities of the method.[8] In later house groupings, where the sites and the buildings are much bigger, the confusion of intersecting shapes and geometries renders inapplicable the splendid sculptural activity of the Amagansett group without producing a readily comprehensible order of their own. Subsequent attempts at clarification and simplification at the residential scale, such as the Cogan House, in which references to Le Corbusier's villa at Garches and his High

Court at Chandigarh are combined, seem dry and alienated from issues of programme, site, and context.

In the work at a more public scale, Gwathmey has also posed serious questions. In the renovation of Whig Hall, his removal of an exterior wall to reveal the neo-cubism of the interior remodeling is characteristically modernist and suggests an ambivalence about the value of the new one. While it is too soon to measure the success of the recently completed housing at Perinton under the impact of actual use, the separation between "public" and "private," "habitable" and "non-habitable" rooms (when the latter include kitchens and baths) seems (cf Gerald Allen) diagrammatic, while the continuous white stucco buildings appear incongruous in their typical suburban context.[9]

Peter Eisenman has articulated a most important critique of the pseudo-functionalism of first- and second-generation modernism, and on the basis of his anti-functionalist stance he claims with some justification to be the first true Modernist. Eisenman's "post-functionalism" offers a valuable critique of the direction which the Modern Movement took as its early abstractions were compromised by the realities and practicalities implicit in the commercialism of the post-World War II period. But in its rigorous iconoclasm and its refusal to regard both user and technique as significant in the process of design, Post-Functionalism trivialises the meaning of architecture as a humanistic discipline.[10]

Post-Functionalism insists on the autonomous nature of architecture. It claims to be an architecture independent of history and culture, content to speak only its own language and eschewing any communication of ideas other than its own—a point of view that inevitably offers few lessons for a public architecture. It is therefore not surprising that in his work on housing, Eisenman has been unable to escape the historical culture of architecture and has made explicit reference to the forms of orthodox modernism of the 1920s and 1930s.

Third-generation modernism seeks to revivify modernism by drawing back from its present-day commercialism and by returning to the forms, if not always to the philosophy of its founders in the 1920s, though Richard Meier and Charles Gwathmey have produced admirable work for commercial clients. Post Modernism on the other hand, seeks to resolve the modernist split between "rationalism" (that is, function and technology) and "realism" (that is, history and culture).[11] It sides with philosophical pragmatism and aesthetic pluralism, recognising both the general and the particular, the inherent and the explicit, the Form and its Design or Shape.[12] For Post-Modernism, architectural shapes are distinctly real rather than abstract; they are cognizant of their own utilitarian purpose and materiality, of their history, of the physical context in which they are to be built, and of the social, cultural, and political milieu that called them into being.[13]

Robert Venturi and Charles Moore laid the foundation of Post-Modernism in their emphasis on "meaning" and their recognition of the disfunction between a reductive architecture and a complex culture. Romaldo Giurgola has added to this the philosophy of the building as a fragment of a larger whole; Michael Graves has noted the power of the fragment as an element of composition.

Now, twenty years after its initial formulation in the work of Moore and Venturi, Post-Modernism begins to take on the aspects of a style. Three principles, or at least attitudes, characterise Post-Modernism at this time:

CONTEXTUALISM
The individual building as a fragment of a larger whole
Renouncing what Colin Rowe has called the "object fixation" of modernist architecture, Post-Modernism prefers incomplete or compromised geometries, as manifested in Venturi and Rauch's Guild House and Yale Mathematics Building; in Mitchell/Giurgola's Boston City Hall and AIA projects and their University Museum, which draws upon the language of Wilson Eyre and his colleagues fifty years later to produce work that seems at once old and new; in Charles Moore's Citizen Federal Savings and Loan Association; and in Allan Greenberg's additions to the Hartford Court House.

Particularly important in this context is the explicit recognition of the growth of buildings over time, as can be seen in Venturi and Rauch's Football Hall of Fame and North Canton City Hall projects and in their Humanities and Social Science Buildings at the State University at Purchase, New York.

ALLUSIONISM
Architecture as an act of historical and cultural response[14]
Allusionism is not to be confused with the simplistic eclecticism that has too often in the past substituted pat, predigested typological imagery for more incisive analysis. The principle is rather that there are lessons to be learned from history as well as from technological innovation and behavioural science, that the history of buildings is the history of meaning in architecture. Moreover, for the Post-Modernist these lessons from history go beyond modes of spatial organization or structural expression to the heart of architecture itself: the relationship between form and shape and the meanings that particular shapes have assumed over the course of time. This Post-Modernist examination of historical precedent grows out of the conviction that appropriate references to historical architecture can enrich new work and thereby make it more familiar, accessible, and possibly even more meaningful to the people who use buildings. It is, in short, a cue system that helps architects and users communicate better about their intentions.

This inclusion of explicit references to the past has been handled in a number of ways by the Post-Modernists. One of these is the inclusion of particular fragments from earlier buildings. This can be seen in Moore's use of wooden Tuscan columns to support his house at Orinda; and Mexican patio tiles reconstituted in plastic at the Burns House; in Venturi and Rauch's incorporation of Gothic tracery in the Yale Mathematics Building, and Palladian windows in the Trubek House; and in our own fabrication of mouldings in the Lang House, and pilasters for a New York town house.

A second manifestation of Post-Modernist historical allusionism can be seen in the infusion of the design of entire buildings with the mood of a previous moment in history. So it is that Charles Moore's Piazza d'Italia, commissioned by a group of Italian-Americans as an embellishment to the forecourt of an undistinguished office tower, as much evokes the genuine monuments of Italy—not to mention the extravaganza to Victor Emmanuel in Rome—as it does the images of that country we have received on celluloid from Hollywood. Venturi and Rauch's houses for the Brant family are in distinctly different moods or styles: one, in Bermuda, evokes the vaguely Spanish Bermuda cottages that were built by the English (though its vigour also recalls the neo-Spanish of Santa Barbara's George Washington Smith); the other, a ski house in Colorado, looks like what a good Viennese Secessionist architect might have done with the commission in about 1910.

ORNAMENTALISM
The wall as the medium of architectural meaning
Though ornament is often the handmaiden of allusionism, the decoration of the vertical plane need not be justified in historical or cultural terms; the decorated wall responds to an innate human need for elaboration and for the articulation of the building's elements in relation to human scale. This aspect of ornamentalism can be seen in Michael Graves's work, e.g. his Claghorne House addition of 1974.

While it is true that Modernism rejected applied ornamentation, it never abandoned ornament itself. Mies ornamented the Barcelona Pavilion through the juxtaposition of richly veined, book-matched marbles, woods, polished chrome fittings, and tinted glass. In Mies's later work, such as the Seagram Building, virtually his entire design energies were expended in the decorative elaboration of structure on the facade. Le Corbusier, having learned a bitter lesson at Pessac, where his only decorative gesture had been the relatively impermanent and sparing use of paint, in later works such as the Monastery at La Tourette, manipulated the individual spaces of the building to achieve highly particularised forms and experimented with crudely-finished and rough-textured concrete, so defying the user's ability to affect change.[15]

Typical within the second-generation Modernist search for richness is the over-elaboration of structure exemplified by Philip Johnson's Kline Science Tower or Louis Kahn's placement of mechanical functions at the exterior of Richards Medical Laboratories, a laboratory being one of the few building types where such a strategy could be justified semantically. In his Art and Architecture Building at Yale, Paul Rudolph, taking lessons from Kahn and Le Corbusier among others, pushed and pulled all the elements of the building, combining corrugated concrete walls, boldly articulated mechanical, stair and toilet towers and a plan with forty-three different levels on seven floors to produce a building that is, in a certain sense, a total work of integral decoration.

Venturi first used applied ornament to give a large and appropriately public scale to a modestly sized institutional building in Ambler, Pennsylvania. The introduction of super-graphics by Moore and his associates at Sea Ranch has become a standard decorating response to the inarticulate modernist interior. In his own house in New Haven, Moore used layered plywood panels to make ornament at a variety of scales and provided places for the inclusion of those personal possessions so often banished in the service of Modernist minimalism.

James Polshek has demonstrated that available functional paradigms—in this case, Davis, Brody's Riverbend—can be successfully adapted to new situations largely through the use of applied ornament. Venturi and Rauch's Brant House at Greenwich, Connecticut, is a veritable handbook of Post-Modernist attitudes toward ornament: the brick pattern emphasises frontality, giving the house an "estate" image; the clapboarding de-emphasises the rear and connects it with New England cottages; the green colour fuses the house with the landscape without sacrificing its integrity as a man-made object. In Whitman Village, Moore uses a variety of decorative devices to heighten the articulation of the individual dwelling units, to relate the scale of the buildings to that of the inhabitants and to mediate between the architecture of a low-income housing project and the architecture of its affluent sub-urban context. The contrast of attitudes to such issues as public and private open space, individuality and communality, image and context, as they are to be seen at Perinton and at Whitman Village should make emphatic the differences between late Modernist and Post-Modernist positions.

Post-Modernism recognises that buildings are designed to mean something, that they are not hermetically sealed objects. Post-Modernism accepts diversity; it prefers hybrids to pure forms; it encourages multiple and simultaneous readings in its efforts to heighten expressive content. Borrowing from forms and strategies of both orthodox modernism and the architecture that preceded it, Post-Modernism declares the past-ness of both; as such it makes a clear distinction between the architecture of the Modern period, which emerged in the middle of the eighteenth century in western Europe, and that puritanical phase of the Modern period which we call the Modern Movement. The layering of space characteristic of much Post-Modernist architecture finds its complement in the overlay of cultural and art historical references in the elevations. For the Post-Modernist, "more is more."

The emergence of the "inclusivist" Post-Modernist position should be seen against the political framework of the period since 1960. Post-Modernism's confidence in the philosophical validity of pluralism was nurtured in the optimism of the Kennedy years. In the increasingly restrictive climate of the late Johnson period, and especially in the time of Nixon, that faith in pluralism took on an almost tragic dimension, one that can be read in the poignant, ironically undercut monument at Valley Forge that Allan Greenberg has designed for the Sons of the American Revolution. Just as the nation's Centennial triggered the emergence of a great synthesising attitude toward form, as seen in the works of [Frank] Furness, [Henry Hobson] Richardson, [Louis] Sullivan, and [Frank Lloyd] Wright an attitude representing the first great American contribution to the evolution of modern architecture, so its Bicentennial celebration, an event that miraculously transcended ballyhoo and star-spangled paper plates, may also foster the establishment of a new position, a new way of gathering up the diverse threads of the architecture and the culture of our polyglot nation, and trigger the release of shapes, spaces, and styles distinctly and appropriately our own.[16]

1   My use of these terms derived from Charles Moore who had in turn picked them up from Robert Venturi, *Complexity and Contradiction in Architecture*, 22–23.
2   See Vincent Scully, "Introduction," in Robert Venturi, *Complexity and Contradiction in Architecture*, 15–16; Henry-Russell Hitchcock, "Introduction" in Yukio Futagawa, *Kevin Roche/John Dinkeloo Associates 1962–75* (Tokyo: ADA Edita, 1975); Paul Goldberger, "High Design at a Profit," *New York Times Magazine* (14 November 1976): 78–79; William Marlin, "Penzoil Place," *Architecture Record* CLX, no. 7 (November 1976): 101–110. The "silver" architecture of such West Coast architects as Cesar Pelli and Anthony Lumsden seems at this writing not much more than an extension of second-generation modernism. The work of Eugene Kupper, another member of that loose affiliation, seems very closely related in intention to the architecture of the "whites," while Thomas R. Vreeland's work not unexpectedly connects up with that of the "greys." See "Images from a Silver Screen," *Progressive Architecture* LVII, no. 10 (October 1976): 70–77, and Thomas R. Vreeland Jr., "The New Tradition," *LA Architect* (October/November 1976).

3   On the architecture of "developing" countries see John Morris Dixon, "1001 Paradoxes," *Progressive Architecture* LVII, no. 10 (October 1976): 6; Sharon Lee Ryder, "A Place in Progress," *Progressive Architecture* LVII, op. cit.: 49–55; Suzanne Stephens, "The Adventures of Harry Barber in OPEC Land," *Progressive Architecture* LVII, op. cit.: 56–65.

4   Arthur Drexler, "Preface," in Peter Eisenman et al, *Five Architects* (New York: Wittenborn, 1972), 1; See also Colin Rowe, "Introduction," ibid., 3–7; Kenneth Frampton, "Criticism," ibid., 9–17; Robert A.M. Stern, Jaquelin Robertson, Charles Moore, Allan Greenberg, and Romaldo Giurgola, "Five on Five," *Architectural Forum* CXXXVIII (May 1973): 46–57; David Morton, "Richard Meier," *Global Architecture* no. 22 (1973): 2–7; Peter Eisenman, "From Object to Relationship II: Giuseppe Terragni—Casa Giuliani Frigerio; Casa del Fascio," *Perspecta* 13/14 (1971): 36–65; Richard Meier, "Les Heures Claires," *Global Architecture* no. 13: 2–7.

5   See Peter Eisenman and Robert A.M. Stern, "White and Grey," *Architecture and Urbanism* no. 52 (April 1975): 3–4, 25–180; Robert A.M. Stern, George Howe, *Towards a Modern American Architecture* (New Haven: Yale University Press, 1975), ch. 6.

6   I first made this point in my *40 Under 40, Young Talent in Architecture* (New York: American Federation of Arts, 1966); see also Manfredo Tafuri, "European Graffiti: Five x Five = Twenty Five," *Oppositions* 5 (Summer 1976): 35–73; Robert Venturi, Denise Scott Brown, and Steven Izenour, *Learning from Las Vegas* (Cambridge: MIT Press, 1972), 47; Vincent Scully, *The Shingle Style Today or the Historian's Revenge* (New York: Braziller, 1974), 38–40; Arthur Drexler, "Preface," to *The Architecture of the École des Beaux-Arts* (New York: Museum of Modern Art, 1975).

7   Kenneth Frampton, "Introduction," in *Richard Meier, Architect* (New York: Oxford University Press, 1976), 7–16; see also Stuart Cohen, "Physical Context/Cultural Context: Including It All," *Oppositions* 2 (January 1974): 1–40.

8   Jaquelin Robertson, "Machines in the Garden," *Architectural Forum* CXXXVIII, no. 4 (May 1973): 49–53.

9   Gerald Allen, "Discrimination in Housing Design," in Charles Moore and Gerald Allen, *Dimensions* (New York: McGraw Hill, Architectural Record Books, 1976), 131–142; on Whig Hall, see Manfredo Tafuri, "American Graffiti..."

10   Peter Eisenman, "Post-Functionalism," *Oppositions* 6 (Autumn 1976); see also Douglas Davis, "Real Dream Houses," *Newsweek* LXXXVIII (4 October 1976): 66–69; "House III," *Progressive Architecture* LV, no. 5 (May 1974): 92–98; John Morris Dixon, "Editorial," *Progressive Architecture* LIII, no. 3 (March 1972): 67; Mario Gandelsonas, "On Reading Architecture," *Progressive Architecture* LIII, op. cit.: 68–86; Scully, *Shingle Style Today*, op. cit., 39; Charles Jencks, "Fetishism and Architecture," *Architectural Design* (August 1976): 492–495.

11   See my "Grey Architecture: Quelques variations post-modernistes autour de l'orthodoxie," *L'Architecture d'Aujourd'hui* no. 186 (August/September 1976): 83; Charles Jencks, "The Rise of Post-Modern Architecture," *Architectural Association Quarterly* vol. 7 (October/December 1975): 3–14.

12   The phrase "Form and Design" is Kahn's; "Shape" has been suggested in place of "Design" in Kahn's sense, by Charles Moore: Moore and Allen, *Dimensions*, op. cit., 11–15.

13   Vincent Scully linked the concepts of inclusivism and realism in relation to a "school of design" in his "Foreword" to John W. Cook and Heinrich Klotz, eds., *Conversations with Architects* (New York: Praeger, 1973), 7–8; See also Mario Gandelsonas, "New-Functionalism," *Oppositions* 5 (Summer 1976); and Denise Scott Brown, "On Architectural Formalism and Social Concern: A Discourse for Social Planners and Radical Chic Architects," *Oppositions* 5, op. cit.: 99–112.

14   The first use of the concept of "allusionism" in Post-Modernist design I know of is in Robert Venturi et al., *Learning from Las Vegas*, op. cit., 58; See also John Morris Dixon, "Revival of Historical Allusion," *Progressive Architecture* LVI no. 4 (April 1975): 59; plus additional articles in the same issue by Charles Moore, Jim Murphy, Sharon Lee Ryder, and myself.

15   For a discussion of Le Corbusier's Pessac project, see Philippe Boudon, *Lived-In Architecture* (Cambridge: MIT Press, 1972).

16   See Scully, *Shingle Style Today*, op. cit., 8–11, 42; Also Scully's "Forword" in Cook and Klotz, eds., *Conversations with Architects*, op. cit., 7–8; Scully, *Modern Architecture* rev. ed. (New York: Braziller, 1974), 50.

BIBLIOGRAPHY

Appleyard, Donald et al. *The View from the Road.* Cambridge: MIT Press, 1963.

Blake, Peter. *God's Own Junkyard: The Planned Deterioration of America's Landscape.* New York: Holt, Rinehard and Winston, 1964.

Brolin, Brent C. *The Failure of Modern Architecture.* New York: Van Nostrand Reinhold, 1976.

Cohen, Stuart E. *Chicago Architects.* Chicago: Swallow Press, 1976.

Collins, Peter. *Architectural Judgement.* Montreal: McGill University Press, 1971.

Cook, John W. and Heinrich Klotz, eds. *Conversations with Architects.* New York: Praeger, 1973.

Drew, Philip. *Third Generation: The Changing Meaning of Architecture.* New York: Praeger, 1972.

Eisenman, Peter et al. *Five Architects.* New York: Wittenborn, 1972.

Giurgola, Romaldo and Maimini Meheta. *Louis I Kahn.* Zurich: Artemis, 1975.

Gutman, Robert, ed. *People and Buildings.* New York: Basic, 1972.

Hall, Edward T. *The Hidden Dimension.* New York: Doubleday, 1966.

———. *The Silent Language.* New York: Doubleday, 1959.

Halprin, Lawrence. *Cities.* New York: Reinhold, 1963.

———. *Freeways.* New York: Rienhold, 1966.

———. "New York, New York: A Study of the quality, character, and meaning of open space in urban design," prepared for the City of New York, March 1968.

Huxtable, Ada Louise. *Kicked a Building Lately?* New York: New York Times, Quadrangle, 1976.

———. *Will They Ever Finish Bruckner Boulevard?* New York: Macmillan Co., 1970.

Jacobs, Jane. *The Death and Life of Great American Cities.* New York: Random House, 1961.

Jacobus, John. *Philip Johnson.* New York: George Braziller, 1962.

———. *Twentieth-Century Architecture: The Middle Years 1940–1965.* New York: Praeger, 1966.

Jencks, Charles. *Architecture 2000.* New York: Praeger, 1971.

———. *Modern Movements in Architecture.* Garden City: Anchor, 1973.

Jencks, Charles and George Baird, eds. *Meaning in Architecture.* New York: Braziller, 1970.

Johnson Philip. *Architecture 1949–1965.* New York: Holt, Reinhard and Winston, 1966.

Le Corbusier. *The Radiant City.* Pamela Knight, Eleanor Levieux, and Derek Coltman, trans. New York: Orion Press, 1967; French edition 1933.

Lynch, Kevin. *The Image of the City.* Cambridge: MIT Press, 1960.

Mayor's Task Force. *The Threatened City, A Report on the Design of the City of New York.* New York, 1967.

Meier, Richard. *Richard Meier, Architect.* New York: Oxford University Press, 1976.

Meyerson, Marten et al. *The Face of the Metropolis: The Building Developments that are Reshaping Our Cities and Suburbs.* New York: Random House, 1963.

Moore, Charles, Gerald Allen, and Donlyn Lyndon. *The Place of Houses.* New York: Holt, Rinehard and Winston, 1974.

Nairn, Ian. *The American Landscape: A Critical View.* New York: Random House, 1974.

Norberg-Schulz, Christian. *Intentions in Architecture.* Cambridge: MIT Press, 1961.

Rowe, Colin. *The Mathematics of the Ideal Villa and Other Essays.* Cambridge: MIT Press, 1976.

Ruscha, Edward. *Some Los Angeles Apartments.* Los Angeles: Wittenborn, 1965.

———. *The Sunset Strip.* Los Angeles: Wittenborn, 1966.

———. *Twenty-Six Gasoline Stations.* Los Angeles: Wittenborn, 1962.

Schwab, Gerhard. *The Architecture of Paul Rudolph.* New York: Praeger, 1970.

Scully, Vincent. *American Architecture and Urbanism.* New York: Praeger, 1969.

———. *Louis I. Kahn.* New York: Braziller, 1962.

———. *Modern Architecture.* New York: Braziller, rev. ed, 1974.

——. *The Shingle Style Today or the Historian's Revenge*. New York: Braziller, 1974.

Temko, Allen. *Eero Saarinen*. New York: Braziller, 1962.

Venturi, Robert. *Complexity and Contradiction in Architecture*. New York: Museum of Modern Art, 1966.

——, Denise Scott Brown, and Steven Izenour. *Learning from Las Vegas*. Cambridge: MIT Press, 1972.

—— and Rauch. *Signs and Symbols in the American City*. Washington, DC: Renwick Gallery; New York: Aperture, 1976.

Von-Eckardt, Wolf. *A Place to Live: The Crisis of the Cities*. New York: Seymour Lawrence/ Delacorte Press, 1967.

Wolf, Peter. *The Future of the City. New Directions in Urban Planning*. New York: Watson Guptill, 1974.

Wolfe, Tom. *Kandy-Kolored Tangerine-Flake Streamline Baby*. New York: Farrar, Straus and Giroux, 1965. (See Chapter 1 on Las Vegas).

2. SEMIOTICS AND STRUCTURALISM
THE QUESTION OF SIGNIFICATION

INTRODUCTION

Semiotics and Architecture: Ideological
Consumption or Theoretical Work
Diana Agrest and Mario Gandelsonas

The postmodern period saw a revival of interest
in meaning in architecture and a self-consciousness about the terms in which the discipline was
described. These two issues coincided in the
"linguistic analogy," the idea that architecture
could be seen as a visual language. It was recognized in the 1960s that this common assumption needed further scrutiny with regard to the
following question: to what extent is architecture
conventional, like language, and are its conventions so widely understood that there exists a
"social contract" vis-à-vis architecture? Both this
article and the following, by Geoffrey Broadbent,
emphasize the problems and potential of applying the linguistic analogy to architecture.

Diana Agrest and Mario Gandelsonas's
essay condenses a longer article published in
Semiotica entitled "Critical Remarks on Semiology
and Architecture." Appearing in 1973 in the first
volume of *Oppositions*, the journal of the Institute
for Architecture and Urban Studies, the version of
the essay reprinted here set a high standard for
critical discourse. It evidences the influence of
Marxism and of linguist Ferdinand de Saussure's
work in Agrest and Gandelsonas's formulation of
a theoretical position. Educated in architecture at
the University of Buenos Aires, the two studied
structural linguistics in Paris in the late 1960s—
a time of great student activism. Roland Barthes's
influence is also evident in their theoretical work
(ch. 13); one example is the idea of "reading"
the city, which Gandelsonas investigates in
The Urban Text.

Agrest and Gandelsonas are careful to distinguish between the current interest in communication theory and semiotics; the distinction lies
in the object of study of each field. Semiotics
(roughly synonymous with semiology) is the
science of the different systems of linguistic *signs*.
It is concerned with the nature of signs and the
rules governing their behavior within a system.
Semiotics is thus involved with *signification*, or the
production of meaning, which is accomplished

via the relation between the two components of the sign: the signifier (such as a word) and the signified (the object denoted). In contrast, communication theory deals with the use and effects of signs, with their function and reception by people involved in the transmission of a *message*. Agrest and Gandelsonas note that confusion regarding this distinction has led to some questionable applications of semiotic theory by architects and critics.

The authors see semiotics as a way to deepen the understanding of the production of meaning in architecture. They suggest that semiotics be conceived as part of a larger project, and not simply as an unmediated importation of concepts from an outside discipline. Thus, semiotics might be useful as a weapon against ideology, or "adaptive [architectural] theory," which allows the perpetuation of the economic and political status quo. Agrest and Gandelsonas hope that *critical* theory, devoted to the production of knowledge on architecture and to the critique of ideology, will replace this adaptive norm. (The critique of ideology reappears in Manfredo Tafuri's essay in chapter seven.)

DIANA AGREST AND MARIO GANDELSONAS
SEMIOTICS AND ARCHITECTURE
IDEOLOGICAL CONSUMPTION OR THEORETICAL WORK

Theories of architecture and design have largely been oriented towards the perpetuation of the fundamental structure of Western society, while seeking at the same time to maintain design as a valid operation within this established order. The authors challenge this adaptive role of architectural theory through their analysis of the absorption of semiotics as a "theoretical blockade," and argue that theory can only be considered a production of knowledge when its ideological basis is totally transformed.

In the last twenty years the production of "theories" of architecture and design has dramatically accelerated in a way that emphasizes the particular role of architectural theory as it has been continuously developed over five centuries. The function of these "theories," now as always, has been to adapt architecture to the needs of Western social formations,[1] serving as the connection between the overall structure of a society and its architecture.[2] In this way architecture has been modified to respond to *changing* social demands; architecture thereby *becoming* assimilated to society through "theoretical" operations. The corresponding changes introduced by "theory" into architectural practice serve to perpetuate the basic structure of the society and at the same time maintain architecture itself as an institution within Western social formations.[3]

In a previous article[4] we established the process of production of knowledge as a theoretical project which is aimed neither at adapting architecture to the "needs" of the social formations nor to maintaining the architectural institution as we know it. At this juncture one is concerned with *theory* in a strict sense, as opposed to the adaptive "theory," which we call *ideology*.

Ideology can be seen as a certain set of representations and beliefs—religious, moral, political, aesthetic—which refer to nature, to society, and to the life and activities of men

From *Oppositions* 1 (September 1973): 93–100. Courtesy of the authors.

in relation to nature and society. Ideology has the social function of maintaining the overall structure of society by inducing men to accept in their consciousness the place and role assigned to them by this structure. At the same time it works as an *obstacle* to real knowledge by preventing both the constitution of theory and its development.

Its function is not to produce knowledge but to actively set itself against such production. Ideology in a way alludes to reality, but it only offers an illusion of this reality.[5] The summation of Western architectural "knowledge" in its entire range, from commonplace intuition to sophisticated "theories" and histories of architecture, is to be recognized as ideology rather than as theory. This ideology has explicitly claimed to serve the *practical* needs of society, by ordering and controlling the built environment. Nevertheless, we hold that the underlying function of this ideology is in fact the pragmatic one of both serving and preserving the overall structure of society in Western social formations. It serves to perpetuate the capitalist mode of production, and architectural practice as part of it. Thus, even if ideology affords knowledge of the world, it is a *certain* knowledge, which is limited and distorted by this overriding function.

We propose that there is a need for a theory, which should be clearly distinguished from the adaptive "theory" or, what we call here architectural ideology. In these terms architectural theory is the process of production of knowledge which is built upon a *dialectical* relationship with architectural ideology, that is, it grows out of this ideology and at the same time is in radical opposition to it. It is this dialectical relationship which distinguishes and separates theory from ideology.

In opposition to ideology, we propose a *theory* of architecture, which is necessarily placed outside ideology. This theory describes and explains the relationships between society and the built environments of different cultures and modes of production.[6] The theoretical work uses as its raw material no real or concrete things but beliefs, notions and concepts regarding these things. These notions are transformed by means of certain conceptual tools, the consequent product being knowledge of things.[7] Architectural ideology, considered as part of a bourgeois society and culture, provides part of the raw material on which the conceptual tools must be brought to work.

The relationships between theory and ideology might be viewed as a continuous struggle where ideology defends a type of knowledge whose major effect is the preservation of existing social systems and their institutions, rather than the explanation of reality. There have been many examples in history of this relationship. Ptolemy's theory of the universe, which corroborated Biblical texts, was supported by the Church for centuries against any other models which could explain more accurately the same reality. In opposition, Copernicus's theory was the result of a conceptual mutation within such an ideology. He literally destroyed Ptolemy's notion of geocentrism, and he separated his theory from this ideology by "projecting the earth into the skies."[8] In return, the condemnation of Copernicus by the Church through its attempt to suppress a new concept of the world where man was no longer the center of the world, and where the Cosmos was no longer ordered around him, shows another aspect of this struggle. The theoretical ideology, which originally opposed the Copernican conception, finally *absorbed* it to reaccommodate the theoretical structure. In this process of dialectical relationship between theory and ideology two different stages must be distinguished: the first is that of *productive transformation*, when the ideology is initially transformed to provide a theoretical basis; the second is that of *methodological reproduction*, when the theory is developed as an entity separated from ideology. In this sense, Copernicus's studies correspond to the first stage, where the theoretical work consists essentially in the subversion of a given ideology.

In architecture, we have yet to see a Copernicus to introduce the first stage of theoretical explanation. Indeed we have only recently begun to perceive the need to analyze the relationships between theory and ideology.

Several architectural ideologies have had a more or less systematized appearance, which has been emphasized through the ambiguous title of "theory." In recent years this ambiguity has been accentuated by several pseudo-theoretical developments that use models from different fields, such as mathematics, logic, behaviorism, or philosophy. When these models are applied, they introduce a superficial order while leaving the basic ideological structure unchanged. This introduction of models from other fields is to be regarded as ideological consumption, and may be witnessed as temporary fashion at the level of technique.[9] *But the consumption of theories, which can be considered in themselves tools for the development of theory on architecture, acts as a special form of ideological obstacle, which we call theoretical blockade.*

Many theories pretending to be theory in a strict sense are in fact the precise opposite. They function as an *obstacle* to theoretical production. But the many "semiotic theories of architecture" which have been produced in recent years, serve only to consume a theory of semiotics—that in our opinion might provide a range of tools for the production of knowledge *on* architecture. They constitute the essence of a theoretical blockade.

This transposition of linguistic and semiotic concepts to the field of architecture only maintains architectural ideology. Such a procedure cannot be confused with a theoretical process which must be based on the critique and subversion of the ideological notions. In our opinion, semiotics can help in this critical task, as an important tool for the *production of knowledge*, only if we understand the semiotic concepts in relation to a general semiotic theory and not as isolated formulas. This implies that semiotic concepts related to a semiotic theory must be distinguished from similar concepts related to other theoretical fields. For example, while the concept of "code" belongs both to semiotics and communication theory, it performs a different role in each theory. Most present uses of semiotics fail to develop explicitly the distinction between notions belonging to different theoretical fields—semiotics, communication theory, and traditional semantics— which they use in a random and arbitrary fashion.

One aspect of theoretical blockade seems to us to arise in a situation when those responsible for developing "theory" neither distinguish nor relate with sufficient precision distinctly different discourses whose epistemological base and orientation is patently divergent. This can be seen in the existing confusion in the use of the notions of communication and signification. To understand more clearly the nature of this confusion one can look at George Baird's "La Dimension Amoureuse in Architecture."[10] Baird writes, for example, "In the most modern sense of the distinction, the langue of a social phenomenon is considered to be its 'code,' and the parole its 'message.' In some respects, this distinction is the most interesting because it introduces into semiology a number of precise mathematical techniques of analysis, commonly grouped under the name 'information theory.'"[11] The confusion here is that langue and parole are related to the notion of signification, and code and message to the notion of communication. Langue-parole and code-message can only be cross-linked in very few and exceptional cases. The confusion between these two notions produces a situation where there is no clear defin-ition and distinction made between communications theory and semiotics considered as a theory of signification. This problem can be seen in another statement by Baird where these two theoretical fields are again considered to be interchangeable: "Taking its cue from [Claude] Lévi-Strauss's structural anthropology, modern *semiology* looks on all social phenomena as communication systems; not only the obvious ones...but also... architecture."[12]

If semiotics is to become an important tool for the development of architectural theory, it would seem important to clarify the distinction between the notion of *com-munication* and the notion of signification, and their particular relevance for architecture.

Semiotics, the theory of the different systems of signs, is considered to be only a first stage towards a future general theory of ideologies.[13] In this present stage semiotics not only can provide models, but it can also suggest theoretical strategies in our battle against a specific ideology, architectural ideology.

In the definition of semiotics as given by [Ferdinand de] Saussure,[14] the notion of *communication* does not appear for the precise reason that it is a different and distinct phenomenon from *signification*. The study of the phenomenon of communication, which analyzes how signs are sent and received, differs from and cannot be confused with a study which analyzes "what the signs consist of" or "what laws determine them."[15]

The notion of communication in fact is related to a characteristic that is common to all systems of signs; namely that they provide a means for communicating between individuals. In contrast, the notion of signification depends on the particular internal structure within a given cultural system, such as that appointed to architecture, cinema or literature. The particular structure of such cultural phenomena stems from their *exis-tence* as social institutions and not from their *use* by individuals. In architecture, for example, the particular signification of Japanese buildings is related to the internal struc-ture of an architectural system of signs which is determined by the social and cultural context, and not by their functional use, which is similar to the use of buildings in other cultures, i.e., shelter, gathering, etc. In other words, the notion of communication is related to the function and use of a system whereas the notion of signification indicates internal relation within a system. Communication is concerned with the *use* and *effects* of signs, while signification is concerned with the *nature* of signs and the *rules* governing them.[16] This difference implies, first, that even if we understand the factors which are part of the process of communication, we may still not know anything about the nature of signification itself; secondly, that since signification depends on the specific nature of the different systems of signs, it has to be redefined for each different semiotic system according to the way its internal structure works and according to what makes each internal structure different. This, then, is precisely the subject matter of semiotics —to consider the different semiotic systems as devices which produce signification, and to determine how this signification is produced.

Saussure's procedure for defining semiotics, linguistics, and linguistic signification demands examination both as a device for the discussion of ideological notions and to establish the heuristic value of semiotic concepts and procedures as a tool for the production of a theory *on* architecture. In Saussure, language itself is subsumed by the notion of semiotics. The definition of linguistics requires a simultaneous definition of semiotics. Saussure defines semiotics (*semiologie*) as the science of the different systems of signs and the study of "langue" (the system of language) as the study of only one of the various semiotic systems. He then defines the concept of "sign" (the units of the system) as a double entity composed of a "signifier" (the acoustic image) and "signified" (the concept). Following this, signification is defined as a relation, internal to the sign, linking signifier and signified. He then demonstrates the arbitrary character of signification in the sign and shows how it is determined by another relation—the relationship between signs external to the signs themselves, which Saussure calls *value*.

With this definition Saussure opposes the concept of signification in traditional semantics. In traditional semantics, as shown, for example, in the semiological triangle of [Charles Kay] Ogden and [Ivor Armstrong] Richards, it is the particular conjunction of a form and a meaning which gives rise to the word; that is, meaning itself is considered as inherent to the word.[17] For Saussure, on the other hand, words only take meaning according to their place within language considered as a semiotic system; that is, the word has no inherent meaning in itself. Saussure is opposed to the thesis of inherent meaning, where the meanings of the components of language mirror their content, or in other words, where language is seen as a representation of a thought that exists before or independent of any linguistic realization.[18] Saussure postulates language as being a device—and not a mirror—for communication. This device is seen as a system of signs, which in turn is structured upon an internal, arbitrary relationship. As [Roland] Barthes remarks: "Starting from the fact that in human language the choice of sounds is not imposed on us by the meaning itself (the *ox* does not determine the sound *ox*, since in any case the sound is different in other languages), Saussure had spoken of an *arbitrary* relation between signifier and signified."[19] Instead of considering this relation—as determined by *thought*—Saussure considers it as the result of a social contract. "The association of sound and representation is the outcome of a collective training."[20]

The consideration of architecture as a system of signs has theoretical validity if it is used as a negative conceptual tool; that is, only when notions such as *arbitrariness* or *value* are used for a critique of architecture as an ideology. Saussure defines arbitrariness as a tool to oppose and criticize the ideological conception of language as representation. This thesis of arbitrariness allows Saussure to do away with the representative thesis about the nature of language. Because he understands language as a system which is not determined by its content, he establishes the conditions for the definition of an autonomous, theoretical object of linguistics: the langue. The importance of arbitrariness in language rests not only with the notion itself, but with the introduction of sociocultural hypotheses in linguistics that replace the naturalistic hypothesis. The concept of arbitrariness has not yet been introduced in semiotic theories of architecture, just as the distinction between traditional semantics and semiotics has never been made in architecture.

Traditional semantics makes explicit an implicit conception of meaning which has served as a basis for architectural ideology from classical treatises to the functionalist approach. In the sense of traditional semantics, *objects* in the environment have been understood to have *inherent meaning*. Traditional semantic concepts therefore only reinforce and maintain architectural ideology in its function as an obstacle to the production of knowledge. The conception of inherent meaning is incompatible with the semiotic conception of meaning as determined by system. Because of this, important semiotic concepts such as arbitrariness and value are lost. It is also difficult to establish the notion of arbitrariness in architecture because it contradicts ideological notions, such as function or expression, which are understood to be naturally communicated by architectural objects, as if their meanings were inherent to objects. To postulate the linkage between object and meaning as arbitrary, implies a denial of the supposed natural linkage between the function and the form of an object, which in turn exposes its socio-cultural nature. That is, to attribute a certain function to an architectural fact implies an underlying *convention*. In other words, an architectural object is understood as such, not because it has a certain inherent meaning which is "natural" to it, but because meaning has been attributed to it as the result of cultural convention.

This analysis of the arbitrary linkage between architectural object and function or other meanings invalidates the notion of function as the unique determinant of the form of the object. It also invalidates the idea of meaning as inherent to the object. Consequently, it is necessary to modify the traditional notion of meaning. The consideration of meaning introduced in a theory of architecture through the notion of *arbitrariness* must oppose ideological notions such as function or inherent meaning. The fact that these two notions serve as an obstacle for the introduction of arbitrariness explains, first, why there has been no suggestion for its application to the field of architecture and, second, why a notion such as *motivation* has been introduced instead. For example, Charles Jencks, in "Semiology and Architecture," says, "this is perhaps the most fundamental idea of semiology and meaning in architecture: the idea that any form in the environment or sign in language is motivated, or capable of being motivated."[21] Such a notion perpetuates the understanding of the built environment as a result of functional demands, or as communicating a meaning which is determined by what has "motivated it." This merely reinforces ideological views which emphasize the natural or causal character of architectural form while denying its conventional and socio-cultural nature. The notion of arbitrariness which shows that the form-function pair cannot be explained in itself, indicates the necessity to explain it in terms of its relationships with other pairs within a system of conventions. In general, we can say that if any sign would be an imitation of what it represents, then one could explain it in itself, without the necessity of its having a relation with other signs in a system. But as this is not the case, we must investigate the nature of this relation.[22]

As we said above, the relationship between signs, which links them within a system, is defined by Saussure as *value*. It is possible to say that with the notion of value Saussure breaks from traditional semantics into the field of modern linguistics. Here meaning is no longer an intrinsic property of an isolated sign; rather, it is defined by the differences or the relation of values that are established between signs within a formal system of relations: the *langue*.

For the definition of value Saussure compares language and economics: "*For a sign* (or an economic 'value') to exist...it must be possible, on the one hand, *to exchange dissimilar* things (work and wage) and on the other, to *compare* similar things with each other. That is, one can *exchange* five dollars for bread, soap or a cinema ticket, but one can also compare this five dollars with ten or fifty dollars, etc.; in the same way, a *'word' can be 'exchanged' for an idea* (that is, for something dissimilar); *but it can also be compared with other words* (that is, something similar): in English the word mutton derives its value only from its co-existence with *sheep*; the meaning is truly fixed only at the end of this double determination: signification and value."[23] Value, therefore, comes "from the reciprocal situation of the pieces of the language." It is even more important than signification. "What quantity of idea or phonic matter a sign contains is of less importance than what there is around it..."[24]

Is it possible to construct a system in the domain of objects using this semiotic procedure? We think it is. However, we think the definition of that system requires a series of methodological precautions.

First it is necessary to define the specific characteristics of the "architecture" with which we are going to deal. In other words, which "architecture" are we going to deal with in terms of its situation? Is it Western architecture or Indian architecture? Or are we going to define architecture by a time sequence, such as Renaissance or Modern? A comparative analysis of the concept of value within Western architecture, with the concept of value within other systems of the same culture (the natural language, for example) might be helpful in determining some specific characteristics of architecture. What should be avoided in this analysis is the mechanical application of the model of language to architecture—an operation which has occurred in several semiotic studies. The mechanical application of this model, which was specifically developed for language, to other semiotic systems, such as architecture, only acknowledges the recognition of what is similar to language on the ideological level but does not define the *differences* in inner structure between language and the other semiotic systems. Even if it is possible to see the langue as a complex system of underlying rules, and therefore to compare it with the explicit and implicit systems of rules in architecture, architectural rules are determined by a certain sect belonging to a determined social class, while the langue is the property of everyone in general and no one in particular. These architectural systems of rules do not show any of the properties of those of the langue—they are not finite, they are not organized in a simple way, nor do they determine the manifestation of the system. Moreover, architectural rules are in a constant state of flux and change radically.

The mechanical application of the model langue/speech to Western architecture reinforces architectural ideology by denying the differences between architecture and language and by ignoring the place of natural language in architecture.[25] Moreover, and perhaps more important, it denies that "something" which defines a major difference between architecture and language—that is, the creative aspect of architecture. In language the individual can *use* but not *modify* the system of language (langue). In contrast to language, the architect can and does modify the system, which is fabricated on a system of conventions. The result of applying in a mechanical way the concept of langue to architecture is that the fabricated, conventional character of the system is hidden, appearing instead as if it were natural, as in language. The model langue/speech does not explain but overlooks creativity in architecture. Creativity in architecture is a complex play of conservation and variation of shapes and ideological notions within certain determined limits.[26] In our opinion an analysis of creativity could more properly be based on the notion of value. It must begin by using as raw material the ideological systems of rules which assign and maintain certain value relationships between shapes and meanings, for their design, use or interpretation. The description of the structure of these rules is a first necessary step of semiotic analysis, where the concepts and the adequate tools capable of overcoming specific ideological obstacles must be produced. This preliminary work of description, which is our immediate concern, must be distinguished, however from the *explanation* of the underlying system of rules which produce the ideological structure, a task which is our ultimate objective.[27]

The discussion of ideological notions by means of semiotic conceptual tools comprises another problem which also must be faced. Ideology works as an obstacle to the production of theory, not only by virtue of the fact that it perpetuates ideological notions, such as function or inherent meaning, but also by virtue of the fact that it perpetuates traditional boundaries defining the various fields—ideological regions—such as literature, urban design, and architecture, where those notions function.[28] Ideological notions always imply an ideological region to which they belong, and conversely, any ideological region is built upon an apparently more or less systematized set of ideological notions.

What we call theoretical blockade is related not only to the misuse of semiotic concepts but also to a more general problem— a confusion between an ideological region and an object of study. The application of semiotic concepts to architecture, as we have indicated, supposes a semiotic theory and method being applied to architecture. In our view it makes little sense to build a semiotics of architecture, which presupposes a theory divided according to the existing divisions of painting, literature, cinema, urban design, architecture, etc. An ideological approach which identifies a semiotics of architecture implies the acceptance of the existing division of the above practices and denies the fact that such divisions have an institutional and conventional character. Consequently, the theoretical system or object of study is confused with real, concrete, and singular objects. This difference between theoretical and real object can be seen in social sciences such as linguistics or historic materialism. For example, the theoretical object of structural linguistics is not speech but the concept of *langue*, which is developed through the study of real objects—i.e different languages. The theoretical object of historic materialism is not a given social formation such as France or England but the concept of *history*, which is developed through the study of different modes of production in real social formations. In a similar way the theoretical object of a semiotics of the built environment must be the development of an abstract conceptual structure which explains the production of signification in the configuration of the built environment, which in turn will produce knowledge of concrete objects such as Western architecture. The production of this conceptual structure requires conceptual tools which in the present initial stage do not exist and which must be elaborated according to *demands* of the theoretical work. This elaboration will be made on the basis of semiotic abstract concepts and semiotic theoretical strategies employed as heuristic devices. In our conception of theory, its ultimate *raison d'être* is the knowledge of concrete objects, in this case of the built environment in a certain time and place. But this knowledge is only a result of a process of transformation of notions belonging to an architectural ideology. A theory as production of knowledge, as we have indicated, is only to be developed through a constant struggle with ideology. The production of knowledge can only be done by disassembling not only ideological notions but also through methodically erasing the boundaries separating different practices within a culture and through looking towards other cultures and situated at other points in time. Theoretical work cannot be realized from inside architectural ideology, but from a theoretical "outside" separated from and against that ideology. This must be the first step in the construction of a materialist dialectic theory of architecture as part of a more general theory of ideology.

1   Social formation (*formation sociale*) is a Marxist concept denoting "society." "Social formation is the concrete complex whole comprising economic practice, political practice, and ideological practice at a certain place and stage of development." Louis Althusser, *For Marx* (New York: First Vintage Books, 1970), 251.

2   There are other functions of architecture and design theories to which we do not refer in this article, i.e., the theory that has the function of establishing a certain ordering of design operations within architectural practice.

3   Transformations in society introduce reforms that allow the existing system to survive. However, these are never real changes—since the structural relationships are not being touched—but are merely transformations of that system. For example, the development of the capitalist mode of production through various different stages—mercantilism, industrial capitalism, imperialism, etc.—has been based on a series of transformations achieved in different domains which did not in any way modify the fundamental class structure.

4   Diana Agrest and Mario Gandelsonas, "arquitectura/Arquitectura," *Materia, Cuadernos de Trabajo* (Buenos Aires: 1972).

5   To be more precise we should say ideologies (plural) even if in this article we refer to a particular ideology, bourgeois ideology.

6   This is only a partial definition related to the specific subject of this article: the relationship between theory and architectural ideology. This partial character stems from the fact that the important theoretical problem of the relation existing between architectural practice and the "unconscious" (Freud) has not been considered in this article.

7   We try to follow here the chapter "Methodology" in Karl Marx, *Introduction to Political Economics* recently elaborated upon by Althusser in *For Marx*. We consider these works a fundamental basis for any dialectic materialist approach to theory as opposed to any form of idealistic conception of theory. See Althusser's qualification of idealistic theory under the categories of "empiricism" and "formalism." We use the term theory, however, in such a way as to contrast it with what must now be considered only the Western conception of theory and to emphasize its present provisory character as only a stage in the development of a more general theory of ideologies.

8   Alexander Koyre, *La Révolution Astronomique* (Paris: Hermann, 1961), 16.

9   Diana Agrest, "Epistemological Remarks on Urban Planning Models," lecture, IAUS, New York, 1972.

10 Charles Jencks and George Baird, *Meaning in Architecture* (New York: Braziller, 1970).

11 Ibid., 82.

12 Ibid., 87.

13 Julia Kristeva, "Le Lieu Semiotique," in J. Kristeva, J. Rey-Devove, and J. K. Umiker, eds., *Essays in Semiotics* (The Hague and Paris: Mouton, 1971). See also Eliseo Veron, "Condiciones de produccion modelos generativos y manifestacion ideologica," in *El Proceso Ideologico* (Buenos Aires: Ed. Tiempo Contemporaneo, 1971).

14 Ferdinand de Saussure, *Course in General Linguistics* (New York: McGraw-Hill, 1966).

15 Ibid., 16.

16 Paolo Valesio, "Toward a Study of the Nature of Signs," *Semiotica* III, 2 (1971): 160.

17 John Lyons, *Introduction to Theoretical Linguistics* (Cambridge, UK: Cambridge University Press, 1968), 404.

18 Oswald Ducrot and Tzvetan Todorov, *Dictionarie Encyclopédique des Sciences du Langage* (Paris: Seuil, 1972), 15–16.

19 Roland Barthes, *Elements of Semiology* (New York: Hill and Wang, 1968), 50.

20 Ibid.

21 Jencks and Baird, *Meaning in Architecture*, op. cit.., 11.

22 This comparison does not refer to the similarities of form-function pairs and signs but to the similarities of the relationships between form-function pairs and the value relationships between signs. To take the concept of value for theoretical development in architecture can be justified not only on the basis of recent analyses which demonstrate its validity (Jacques Derrida, *De la Grammatologie* [Paris: Ed. du Minuit, 1967]) but also from Roman Jakobson's writings on metaphor and metonymy in R. Jakobson, *Essais de linguistique générale* (Paris: Ed. du Minuit, 1963). A similar position is taken by Christian Metz in various works on "the semiotics of movies."

23 Barthes, *Elements*, op. cit., 55.

24 Ibid.

25 Mario Gandelsonas, "Beyond Function," in preparation.

26 Mario Gandelsonas, "Linguistics in Architecture," *Casabella* 374 (February 1973).

27 Diana Agrest and Mario Gandelsonas, "Critical Remarks on Semiology and Architecture," to be published in *Semiotica* VI (1973).

28 Julia Kristeva, "Le Texte Clos," *Languages* 12 (Paris: Didier-Larousse, 1968). See also Jean Louis Scheffer's review of L. Marin, "Elements pour une Semiologie Picturale," *Semiotica* IV, 5 (1971).

INTRODUCTION

A Plain Man's Guide to the Theory of Signs
in Architecture
Geoffrey Broadbent

Geoffrey Broadbent's article from 1977 is a part
of the postmodern critique published by the British
journal *Architectural Design*. Broadbent, an architect and educator, presents the argument that
buildings carry meaning and that architects
should understand the processes by which such
meaning is ascribed. Creating meaning intentionally, he claims, prevents accidental readings. He
argues, for instance, that modern functionalism
failed in its attempt at a "machine-like and meaning-free" architecture because of architecture's
"inescapable semantic dimension."

The study of semiotics (the system of *signs*) is
one way to approach the question of meaning.
Charles Sanders Peirce identifies two dimensions
of the system: *semantic and syntactic*, corresponding to Ferdinand de Saussure's *associative* and
syntagmatic, which are roughly equivalent to
meaning and structure. Broadbent finds the
semantic aspect of the system more crucial for
architecture, and offers as examples of semanti-
cally-oriented work the postmodern historicism of
Robert Venturi, Michael Graves, Robert Stern, and
Charles Moore.

Like Diana Agrest and Mario Gandelsonas,
Broadbent recognizes the importance of the
"social contract" in language; it is a set of conventions that allows the linguistic *sign* to function,
and produces consensus about meaning.
Nevertheless, Broadbent writes that the social
contract is absent from architecture and that this
absence is what differentiates architecture from
language. Paradoxically, he maintains that buildings can "undoubtedly" be read as *signs* in the
way de Saussure intended.

Broadbent provides an overview of the fields
of linguistic and communication theory, as well as
behavioral and environmental psychology. In
addition to the semiotic approaches of Peirce and
de Saussure, he presents numerous, dissimilar theoretical paradigms including those of Noam
Chomsky, Louis Hjelmslev, and Charles Kay
Ogden and Ivor Armstrong Richards. He endorses

the latters' addition of the *referent* to the signifier/signified pair. Broadbent rightly points out the appeal for architects of Chomsky's structuralist theory concerning the formation of expression using the generative and transformational rules of grammar. The potential of these syntactic ideas as a basis for a rational design method is clear, and their impact can be seen in Italian neorationalism (ch. 7) and in the syntactic work of Peter Eisenman. The syntactic influence lingers on in architecture school pedagogy today.

Despite his interest in the linguistic analogy, Broadbent notes that architecture should not just be read visually. Unlike Agrest and Gandelsonas's essay, he stresses that architecture affects all of the senses. The importance of the body in architecture is further investigated in chapters thirteen and fourteen.

GEOFFREY BROADBENT

A PLAIN MAN'S GUIDE TO THE THEORY
OF SIGNS IN ARCHITECTURE

Geoffrey Broadbent offers a considered discussion of architectural semiotic, in which he demystifies this jargon-ridden and complex discourse and presents a succinct argument for architects once again intentionally designing meaning into their buildings.

It is ten years now since George Baird wrote the first article in English on the Theory of Signs as applied to architecture.[1] He met with a fair amount of hostility from people like Reyner Banham,[2] who felt that in suggesting that buildings "carry" meaning, Baird was simply advocating a new, elitist monumentality. Like the rest of us, Baird's critics had been brought up to believe in a "functional" architecture, designed with machine-like precision around a particular brief, and realised three-dimensionally according to the latest available technology: in steel frame, concrete frame, or—Banham's preference at the time—some kind of inflatable. Both articles were later reprinted in the first book in English on the subject—*Meaning in Architecture*—edited by Baird and Charles Jencks.[3] That too met with a fair amount of hostility when it was published in 1969.

But times have changed. It is perfectly possible now for people like the Venturis,[4,5] Charles Moore,[6] Brent Brolin,[7] Charles Jencks,[8] and many others to suggest that architecture designed with deliberate meaning is taking over from functionalism and to be taken seriously in saying so. There are at least three new books coming out on the subject—by [Juan] Bonta,[9] by Broadbent, Jencks and Bonta,[10] and by Broadbent and [Thomas] Llorens[11] so obviously it is something of a growth industry. Of course, there had been conscious attempts to give meaning to buildings in the past. The clearest probably were the

From *Architectural Design* 47, no. 7–8 (July/August 1978): 474–482. Courtesy of the author and publisher. First presented as a lecture at an Art Net forum in London to launch Charles Jencks's *The Language of Post-Modern Architecture*, May 1977.
Starred notes contain captions for illustrations not reprinted herein.

great eighteenth-century picturesque landscape gardens such as Stourhead in Wiltshire, which, with its splendid arrangement of temples, grottoes, and bridges, peering through the trees around a lake, actually "tells" a story, or rather two separate stories simultaneously. The individual buildings symbolise certain incidents in the life of Henry Hoare—who made the garden—together with certain events in Homer's *Iliad*. Hoare was drawing parallels between the vicissitudes of his own life and those of Aeneas.[12]

But the functionalist ethic has been with us for so long that most people still have a sneaking feeling that it was morally "right." Architects such as Le Corbusier,[13] [Walter] Gropius,[14] and Mies,[15] not to mention historians such as [Sigfried] Giedion,[16] [Nikolaus] Pevsner,[17] and [J. M.] Richards,[18] had told us most forcibly that architecture shouldn't be a matter of mere superficial styling, applied cosmetically to the outside of buildings. Actually the word "functional" became attached specifically to steel and concrete frame buildings, simple and rectangular in form and clad in white stucco, grey concrete, or glass. The curious thing is that when one analyses them according to any sensible concept of "function" (the best one I know is still Bill Hillier's:[19] that buildings enclose space in ways which may facilitate or inhibit a particular range of activities, filter out the external environment, consume resources and act as cultural symbols, whether one likes it or not. See my article in Dennis Sharp's new book on *The Rationalists*[20]) they prove to be some of the worst buildings in history in terms of fitness for purpose, solar overheating, heat loss, noise penetration, costs in use, and so on. It so happens that hardly any of the pioneering "functionalist" buildings of the 20s actually remain in their original state. Those which do remain have mostly been altered to fit them for continued habitation, and whilst Le Corbusier's Maison la Roche and his Villa Savoye at Poissy have been restored to approximately their original states, it is so they could be used as museums!

Yet whatever they lack in terms of practical functioning, these buildings certainly are magnificent symbols of the 1920s. In other words, they *are* the very thing they were not supposed to be, which is hardly surprising because, like it or not, *all* buildings symbolise, or at least "carry" meaning. Even Pevsner admits this now—on the last page of his *A History of Building Types*[21] he writes: "every building creates associations in the mind of the beholder, whether the architect wanted it or not." He calls this "evocation" whilst insisting still that the International Modern "conveys clarity, precision, technological daring and a total denial of superfluity." There is no getting away from it; just as Chartres Cathedral carries meanings, so does the meanest garden shed. That is why the functionalists' dream of a machine-like and meaning-free architecture never was anything more than a dream.

If all buildings inevitably carry meaning, then we should do well to see how they do it. At the very least, that will help us to understand all buildings better. And if our buildings are going to symbolise anyway—despite our best (or worst) intentions—then an understanding of how they do so *may* help us design them to do it better. The most promising way of looking at these things seems to be the Theory of Signs which has been developing from the work of Ferdinand de Saussure, a Swiss philosopher whose lectures at the University of Geneva in 1906–1911 were later collated by his students and published as the *Course in General Linguistics*,[22] and Charles Sanders Peirce, an American surveyor whose voluminous collected papers (1860–1908)[23] amount already to eight massive volumes.

Peirce and Saussure both wanted to set up a general theory of signification: how one thing, anything—a word, a picture, a diagram, rain clouds, smoke, or a building—"stands for," "reminds us of" another, a theory which they called respectively, *Semiotic* (Peirce), and *Semiology* (Saussure). (Most people these days seem to prefer Peirce's term.) Unfortunately, the profusion and conflict of terminology within this field has probably proved the greatest stumbling block, certainly in the Anglo-Saxon world, to the acceptance of the whole field itself as being worthy of study. Many people indeed have made the point that the word "semiotic" reminds them of—is itself a *sign* for—"idiotic."

And so they have been put off, which is a pity now that the basic quarrying has been done, from Peirce as well as from Saussure. And the range of terms one uses need not be all that formidable. Mario Pei's *Glossary of Linguistic Terminology*[24] contains some 1800 entries, most of which are concerned specifically with the mechanisms of language—they are largely irrelevant to semiotic as a whole. Indeed, Peirce's most important terms are missing, largely because until recently—due to lack of translations—they had made little impact in Continental linguistic circles. But even if the whole of Pei were relevant—which it is not—that would still form a favourable contrast, say, with building. *The Penguin Dictionary of Building*[25] contains 5400 plus entries, most of which (around ninety percent) will be familiar to *anyone* who has spent some time in architectural practice. I had never heard of words such as *caul* and *commarone*, *dunter* and *dyker*, *fillister*, *jedding*, *kerk*, and *peen*. Nor did I know about *combinations*, *nicker*, not to mention *Lesbian rule* (OK); but I certainly would not, because of these unfamiliar words (and there were about thirty more) dismiss the whole field of building as being irrelevant because I could not be bothered to learn its significant terms. What a philistine profession ours has become if it dismisses fields like semiotic because at first sight its terminology seems difficult. But whereas one could not survive on a building site without, say, at least half of the *Penguin Dictionary*'s vocabulary (not to mention a little of the more robust vernacular) one can work in semiotic with some nine basic terms (*pragmatic, syntactic, semantic, signifier, signified,* and *referent; icon, index,* and *symbol*). One can become positively fluent with another twenty or so, whilst one could venture into the most sophisticated realms of rhetoric with perhaps a dozen more.

BASIC DIVISIONS OF THE FIELD

The first set of terms comes not from Peirce or Saussure, but from one of the former's disciples, Charles Morris who, like his master, was the most flagrant coiner of jargon. But this basic division of semiotic[26] into the three levels, *pragmatic, semantic,* and *syntactic,* is most useful for our purposes. He says:

Pragmatic "deals with the origins, uses (by those who actually make them) and the effects of signs (on those who interpret them) within the (total range of) behaviour in which they occur."

Semantic "deals with the signification of signs in all modes of signifying" that is, with the ways in which they actually "carry" meanings.

Syntactic "deals with the combination of signs (such as the ways in which words are put together to form sentences) without regard to their specific significations (meanings) or their relations to the behaviour in which they occur" thus ignoring the effects those meanings have on those who interpret them.

Morris envisages these three levels as "nesting" within each other. Thus the basic study of signs will be a *pragmatic* matter, the study of meaning (*semantics*) will be part of this, and the study of *syntax* (the actual "structure" of sign-systems) will in turn be part of semantics. So let us look at each of these in turn with particular reference to architecture.

PRAGMATICS

Architectural pragmatics obviously consist of looking at all the ways in which architecture, as a sign system, actually affects those who use buildings. At this pragmatic level, architecture probably is the most interesting and complex sign-system of all. Words act on one sense at a time—either we listen to them being spoken *or* we read them off the printed page. Music obviously affects the sense of hearing more than any of the others; but architecture, inevitably, affects a wide range of senses simultaneously: seeing, hearing, smell, heat, and cold (through the skin), not to mention such esoteric senses as equilibrium and those of position and movement in our muscles and joints (kinaesthetic). I tried in *Design in Architecture*[27] to present all this in diagrammatic form. Some architectural semioticians tend to "read" architecture as an entirely visual matter, ignoring all the other ways in which architecture "carries" meaning for us, and thus, in my view, they trivialise it. Even [John] Ruskin admitted in *The Seven Lamps of Architecture*[28] that he "always found it impossible to work in the cold interiors of our cathedrals" and went on to ascribe certain deficiencies of his own (aesthetic) judgment to that "state of weakened health" to which the chill of Salisbury had reduced him.

So, if architecture "means" something to each of the senses, how do the messages get through? One of the most useful devices for explaining this was developed by Claude Shannon[29] for analysing the ways in which messages are transmitted along telephone lines. He called it the information channel, for which G. K. Koenig considered the implications in an essay,[30] and I also developed for *Design in Architecture.*[*] Anything which conveys information physically—a telephone line, a book, a drawing, or a building—is an information channel. Any building is constantly sending out "messages"—visual, acoustic, thermal and so on—which can be received by one of the senses and "decoded" according to the observer's personal experience. It's a perceptual matter, which is why we all attach different levels of importance to the levels at which the different senses are stimulated in people—those half suffocated or half frozen in a typical "Miesian" building can still find it *visually* beautiful, whilst others may find its appearance too redolent of filing cabinets, matchboxes, or whatever to offer them any visual delight.

If that is what happens generally, how can we actually analyse architecture pragmatically—that is, in terms of the *effects* it will have on people? Physiologists, psychologists, and physicists obviously can work through all the senses and plot the effects which things have on them. They have indeed done this, suggesting certain norms for human comfort in terms of lighting, temperature, noise, and other levels. They have shown that

---

[*] The concept of information channel was developed by telephone engineers for the analysis of efficiency in telephone systems, but the principles apply to any medium—radio, television, film, books, drawings. Buildings convey meanings to their users through many such channels, acting simultaneously on one's personal experience tastes, predilections, etc. (John Wiley and Sons)

most of us will be satisfied at certain levels, comfortable at others, and delighted even at others again. Already we could use this knowledge to generate a new kind of architecture, based on known requirements for environmental control, by designing buildings specifically as environmental filters. The psychologists also have moved towards a more conventional analysis of what things "mean" to people—moving in fact, towards semantics. This work has taken a number of forms:

1) Attempts to measure directly what people say about cities, individual buildings, or rooms—that is, their verbal responses.

2) Attempts to measure the attitudes underlying what people actually say. A great deal of work in these areas has been published in various journals and conference proceedings, and there is a vast literature in the subject by now, of which the most accessible summaries probably are those by [Harold] Proshansky, [William] Ittelson and [G. R.] Rivlin,[31] [Fergus I.M.] Craik,[32] [Irwin] Altman,[33] [David V.] Canter,[34,35] and [Terence] Lee.[36]

Such work covers the whole range of people's physiological, psychological and social reactions to buildings; some of it naturally is concerned with what buildings *mean* to people—or, at least, with what they say they mean. A range of techniques has been used in this research, such as Osgood's Semantic Differential, which enables one to plot with some accuracy the meanings which people attach to certain concepts in a three-dimensional "semantic space." [R. G.] Hershberger[37] tried to establish a basic set of scales for such work for use in environmental research, whilst [Carl Axel] Acking[38] and [Basil] Honikman[39] devised such scales and put them to different uses. Acking projected photographic slides of interiors to his subjects and asked them to mark each room against his concept scales. He then analysed these scales and measured feelings of comfort and security, estimations of social status, physical appearance, degree of originality, and so on. Honikman also asked his subjects to look at pictures of rooms and to rate them against scales: bad/good, dirty/clean, dark/light, and so on.

One problem with Semantic Differential, as many experimenters see it, is that the scales in use are set up by the experimenter. This raises the obvious problems of any social survey: that the scales themselves may *suggest* things to people which otherwise they might never have thought of. At the same time, they may ask people to think of things (including buildings) in ways which they find quite impossible. It was to answer such objections that George Kelley developed his Repertory Grid technique[40]—originally for the investigation of what people thought about other people. He asked each subject to write onto cards the names of certain very familiar people: father, mother, sister, brother, favourite teacher, most hated teacher, etc. Then he worked systematically through the cards, grouping them into threes and asking his subject to name any quality shared by two of the people which the third one did not share. They thought of "constructs" such as friendly, helpful, intelligent, and so on. Having thus listed the "constructs" by which his subject thought about people, Kelley then asked further questions by which the subject ranked the constructs in order of importance for him—is it more important to be "friendly" than "intelligent," and so on. Honikman[41] and others have adapted this technique to establish the constructs against which people "construe" the built environment or, in this case, photographs of rooms.

But there is a fundamental problem in applying the results of such research. Suppose we could establish—for a particular population—that a particular room type, house form, or whatever actually *was* overwhelmingly more popular than another, should we then build only that type? Of course not, if we did that it would become so boring that people no longer preferred it. Yet Semantic Differential and repertory grid techniques may be useful for quite different purposes, in establishing the degree to which architect and client, student and teacher, or even architect and psychologist, agree or disagree on fundamental issues concerning architecture. Chris Abel[42,43] has done a certain amount of work in this area already with architectural students and teachers, attempting to relate students' architectural constructs to the designs they actually produce and the tutor's constructs to the ways in which they criticise those designs.

SYNTAX

Syntax, of course, is concerned with the *structure* of sign-systems, such as the ways in which words are grouped together to form sentences. Saussure actually draws an architectural analogy to show how the syntactic (he uses the adjective "syntagmatic") and the semantic (he calls it "associative") dimensions interrelate:

> From the associative and syntagmatic point of view a linguistic unit is like a fixed part of a building, eg: a column. On the one hand the column has a certain relation to the architrave that it supports; the arrangement of the two units in space suggests the syntagmatic relation. On the other hand, if the column is Doric, it suggests a mental comparison of this style with others (Ionic, Corinthian, etc): although none of these elements is present in space; the relation is associative.

Most of us sat through tedious lessons at school, parsing irrelevant sentences into their various parts—nouns, adjectives, verbs—and some linguists such as [Jerzy] Pelc[44] have developed such studies of syntax into the most tortuous kinds of exercise in symbolic logic. But the whole subject received a tremendous boost in the 1950s, after Noam Chomsky had first published his *Syntactic Structures*.[45] Chomsky suggested that each of us possesses an innate capacity for generating sentences. We possess certain understandings of the world, which he calls "deep structures," which underlie every sentence it is possible to utter.[46] They are raised to form the "surface structure" by which we express our ideas by means of certain *generative rules*. They give us a basic sentence form, such as:

The boy sees the girl

But before we actually utter it we can also apply certain transformational rules such as: transformation into the passive:

(The girl was seen by the boy)
transformation into the negative:
(The boy did not see the girl)
interrogative: (Did the boy see the girl?)
affirmative: (The boy did see the girl!)
predictive: (The boy will see the girl)

and so on.

Like other syntacticians before him, Chomsky analyses his sentences into forms such as noun (N), verb (V), Noun Phrase (NP)– –Noun Phrase: The + Noun; Verb Phrase (VP): Verb + NP, and so on. His basic sentence therefore can be analysed as follows:

Deep Structure

```
        NP                    VP
      /    \                /    \
    T        N            V        NP        Generative rules
                                  /    \
                                T        N
```

The boy sees the girl   Surface structure

He never quite describes what he means by "deep structure," which is unfortunate because one really needs to know just how deep these structures might be. Others have made their own versions, and a simple, but perfectly adequate one was presented by the English linguist C. T. Onions as long ago as 1904.[47] He suggested that *all* our relationships with the world outside ourselves *could* be expressed in one of the following forms:

He waits (he is merely there, in the environment)
He is a Frenchman (he has certain describable characteristics)
He eats ortolans (he has a direct, physical effect on other things in the environment)
He gives me some (he engages in a transaction with me)
He pleases me (his actions have an emotional effect on me).

But if he fails in this particular respect, Chomsky cannot be accused of neglecting to describe the workings of his generative and transformation rules. He describes them in the form of algorithms—that is fixed sets of rules of a kind familiar to computer scientists, such that, provided they are "fed" with the correct data, they will generate automatically a "correct" solution.

Some architects, naturally, have tried to work in this way. Peter Eisenman, for instance, has drawn directly on Chomsky to describe the way in which he has personally developed a complex of rules for the generation (and transformation) of architectural forms.[48] In a typical case (House II) Eisenman started with a cube of space. He then subdivided it with a 3 x 3 grid to give a total of nine "compartments" on each floor. This notional grid could then be realised physically by rows of columns, a system of parallel walls, or both. Eisenman therefore decided on a further, diagonal division of his cube with a wall "system" running towards it from one side and a column "system" from the other. He then looked at the "negative" spaces left between his walls and gradually developed an extraordinarily complex system of interlocking spaces each of which *then* could be dedicated to a certain living activity. Eisenman's primary concern, in other words, was with the abstract perfection of his system. Once the form had been determined, then the

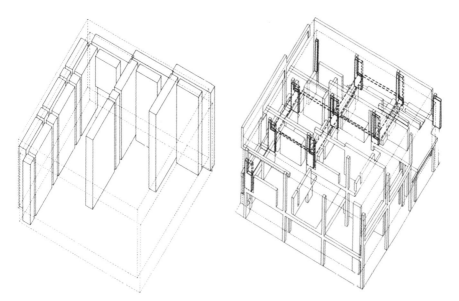

Eisenman developed his House II design according to a set of syntactic rules. He divided the basic "cube" of space by a 3 x 3 grid which could be "built" with columns or parallel walls. He decided to use both systems, meeting against a diagonal division of his cube. He then looked at the "negative" spaces thus formed and allocated them to various functions of living. But the result looks like a Le Corbusier villa.

functions might (hopefully) follow. He has continued this ruthless pursuit of abstraction to such an extent that in House VI, for instance, the "system" demanded an oblong slot along the centre of the master bedroom. The (single) beds, of course, have to be arranged on either side, suggesting that those who use them are expected to lead such disciplined lives that they never will risk life (and limb) by trying, impulsively, to cross the gap.

Curiously enough, Eisenman is by no means the first architect to deal in such complex syntax. No less an architect than Sir Edwin Lutyens was working towards the end of his life on an *Armature of Planes*[49] which his son Robert describes as follows,

> a building is made up of solids and voids...which...are geometrically related...to state this relationship it is first of all necessary to visualise space...as divided along three planes, mutually at right angles, into a number of cubical...cells. One series of planes is horizontal...the two other series...are vertical, at right angles to one another.
> This visualisation of a space divided in all directions becomes an "armature of planes," or foundation of three-dimensional relationships. It should be thought of not as a grid or frame of three intersecting sets of lines...but as almost invisible "lines of cleavage," the whole being like a glass cube made up of smaller glass cubes.

And a Venezuelan architect, Domingo Alvarez, demonstrated this quite independently: what it would be like to be in Lutyen's "glass cube." Alvarez found it difficult to describe to his students just what he meant by "space" so he made small mirror-lined boxes to demonstrate this. Once these had proved successful, he built a series of three-metre internally mirrored, walk-in cubes. In one case, the "lines of cleavage" are made by etching narrow strips of translucent glass over the surface of three of the mirrors—one horizontal (the ceiling) and two vertical—at right angles to one another. These strips are then illuminated from behind with coloured light: red, green, and blue. The experience of being inside Alvarez's cube certainly brings one nearer to inhabiting a pure spatial syntax than any other kind of built reality ever could.

Yet even this by no means exhausts the fascination which spatial syntax seems to exercise for some people. [Lionel] March and [Philip] Steadman for instance, demonstrate a whole range of possibilities for *describing* architecture in such syntactic terms, in their *Geometry of Environment*,[50] and most of those concerned with computer-aided design find themselves, sooner or later, dealing in grids, lattices, and with systems of coordinates for locating points in space. Some, such as [William] Hillier and [Arthur] Leaman,[51*] believe that the whole of architecture can be explained in terms of the rules by which individual spaces can be clustered together, whilst others, such as Steadman and [William J.] Mitchell and [Robin S.] Liggett[52] have examined—with equivalent conviction—the rules by which whole spaces can be divided up.[**] Such work with its severe mathematical basis does throw light on what kinds of planning are *possible*.

But whilst syntactic rules obviously are important for the analysis of underlying "structures" in architecture, it seems to me that those who pursue syntax for its own sake, at the expense of the semantic dimensions, finally are doomed to the same kind of failure as the "functionalists" themselves. Eisenman, not to mention the Italian Rationalists such as Aldo Rossi,[53] have made it their declared aim to *make* an architecture of pure syntax with no semantic content whatever. Yet with the notable exception of Alvarez—whose mirrored boxes "remind us" only of themselves—everyone else who has tried to build a "syntactic" architecture has stumbled against the reality of three-dimensional expression. Thus Lutyens clad his "armature of planes" with a pared-down Classicism; Eisenman clad his "surface structures" with unmistakable evocations of white-walled 1920s International Style. Chomsky himself seems to have hung back from defining his deep structures *because* they had semantic implications. But finally we cannot ignore these implications, which is why so many semioticians have concentrated their attentions on the semantic dimension.

---

[*] Hillier and Leaman believe that all possible architectural forms can be developed by the clustering of forms according to a set of syntactic rules which determine how spaces can be placed together. (After Hillier and Leaman)

[**] Steadman, Mitchell and Liggett demonstrate that architectural forms can also be developed by subdividing spaces according to a set of syntactic rules.

SEMANTICS

It happens however, that one of Saussure's most basic concepts was anticipated by none other than Vitruvius himself, who wrote:

> ...in all matters, but particularly in architecture, there are those two points: the thing signified and that which gives it significance. That which is signified is the subject of which we may be speaking; and that which gives it significance is a demonstration of scientific principles.[54]

Saussure's concept of a sign is exactly like this. He thinks of it as a two-part entity, consisting of a *signifier* and a *signified,* formally united by social contract.[*] The signifier in this case consists of some material representation—the speech sounds, marks on paper, and so on—from which, maybe, a word is formed; whilst the signified consists of the concept to which that word refers. Initially, the relationship between word and concept was quite arbitrary. There was no particular reason why the English should call a certain animal "bull" the French call it "boeuf" whilst the German call it "ochs." A particular animal which happened to be grazing on the Franco-German border might well be called by both names, simultaneously. But *because* the relationship between signifier and signified initially was arbitrary it must be respected by everyone. No one can change it unilaterally; a social contract now exists between all English speaking people that we shall use the word "bull" whenever we want to refer to that particular animal. If one of us used some other word, or coined a new word for the purpose, no one could understand him; he would have broken the social contract. Let us note in passing that with a few exceptions, no such social contract exists to the meaning of architecture, this is a fundamental difference between architecture and language.

Others since Saussure have developed his concept of sign in various ways. [Charles Kay] Ogden and [Ivor Armstrong] Richards[55] for instance felt his two-part entity to be by no means adequate. They took his signifier (they called it *symbol*) and his signified (which they called thought or *reference*) and added a third element, the *referent,* which is the actual object, person or event to which one is referring; hence their semiological triangle:

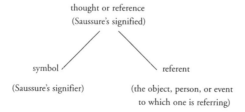

thought or reference
(Saussure's signified)

symbol   referent

(Saussure's signifier)   (the object, person, or event
                          to which one is referring)

[*] Magritte demonstrates Saussure's fundamental point that the relationship between a signifier and a signified is quite arbitrary. There was no reason, initially, why the words he used should not have been attached to the objects he painted. But they were not. Magritte broke the social contract and what he says, literally, is nonsense. He communicates nothing to us therefore, except for the fact that he is playing semantic games. (René Magritte, "The Key of Dreams," 1936.)

This has gained a certain currency in linguistic circles, but [Louis] Hjelmslev[56] felt that it also was inadequate. He postulated the sign as four-part structure which takes the following form (I have plotted equivalents in the Saussurean and the Ogden/Richards schemes):

Hjelmslev:		Saussure:	Ogden & Richards:
	form	signified	referent
Plane of content:	substance		thought
Plane of expression:	substance		reference
	form	signifier	symbol

There *may* be advantages in splitting the concept which links signifier and referent in this way, because it allows for a process of encoding between one's immediate thought about the object and the way one chooses to refer to it by means of words or other signifiers.

Buildings undoubtedly can be read as signs in the way that Saussure intended. The possibilities for a semiology of architecture were first explored by Italian theorists such as [Carlo Ludovico] Ragghianti,[57] although the floodgates opened up after [Roberto] Pane's book of 1948.[58] Their successors, however, have spent a considerable amount of time disagreeing with each other as to the levels at which concepts from the analysis of language should be drawn into the analysis of architecture. [Renato] De Fusco and [Maria Luisa] Scalvini, for instance,[59] equated the exterior of a building (Palladio's Rotunda at Vicenza) with Saussure's *signifier* and the interior with his *signified*, a simple scheme which they develop with some subtlety. [Umberto] Eco, however,[60] took quite a different view. The *signifier* for him might be a staircase signifying the act of walking up—which thus becomes the signified. Both of those interpretations add something of value to architectural debate, and I have suggested a third,[61] following Ogden and Richards: that any building, at any time, can be signifier, signified or *referent*—or all three simultaneously—in their three-part scheme. The Parthenon exists obviously, as a referent, an object, still standing on the Acropolis in Athens, but it also exists as a *signified*—by photographs, diagrams, and words—in any book which describes such buildings. And for many people still it is also a *signifier* of all that was best in ancient Greek democracy. We ought to make sure in discussing it whether the Parthenon as a *signified* actually *is* that arrangement of stones—the partial reconstruction which exists currently on the Acropolis; or the building in its former, more ruined state—familiar from photographs of the 1930s; or the Parthenon as built by Ictinus and Callicrates in its pristine form, circa 450 BC, with garishly coloured sculpture, gilding, and the rest. Or is it—for many people—a "symbol" of perfection in architecture which never actually existed?[*] Not that architecture

---

[*] The Barcelona Pavilion no longer exists as a referent. It was demolished at the end of the Exhibition in 1929, but it is still an extremely potent signifier of another kind of perfection, which is signified as the Parthenon also is in countless words, and reproductions of photographs. [The Barcelona Pavilion has since been reconstructed.—Ed.]

need be "there" physically, even to symbolise perfection. As Bonta points out[62] the Barcelona Pavilion no longer exists as a physical thing, a complex of steel, glass, marble. But it certainly exists as signifier of another kind of architectural perfection, and as a signified in the twenty or so photographs which survive from 1929.

It should be pointed out that certain theorists, including Eco,[63] are by no means happy with this extension of Saussure's sign to include the referent. They point out, rightly, that there is no necessary relationship between a signifier, a signified, and a referent. A particular sign vehicle (signifier) may signify a fictitious object (such as a unicorn), or merely a set of abstract thoughts (signifiers) for which no object exists. Eco's problem can be solved quite simply by taking his referent as a "thing"—provided one uses, say the Oxford Dictionary definition of "thing": What is *or may be* an object of perception, knowledge, or *thought*—(my italics).

Of course there is more to it than that, but even the most extreme of metaphysical philosophers these days now seem to admit that a real, physical world actually exists. Whatever else sign systems may or may not do, they aren't of much interest if they don't refer to it.

In terms of the way the brain works, it hardly matters whether the "thing" is a "real" object in the physical world or something we dreamed about. We shall subject it to processes of thinking in just the same way. However, our ideas of it somehow arose in the brain, so let us agree with Ogden and Richards that the referent *is* a thing, (but) whilst realising that a "thing" can be real or imaginary.

As for Eco's insistence that the referent should be a whole class of things, rather than one particular example, this merely confuses two perfectly ordinary terms in linguistics: connotation and denotation. Eco does this quite wilfully. He says "The difference between denotation and connotation is not (as many authors maintain) the difference between 'univocal' and 'vague'...signification....What constitutes connotation as such is the connotative code which establishes it..." Those "many authors" whom Eco dismisses probably would accept Pei's much simpler definitions:

Denotation The meaning which a form has for all who use it (the intrinsic meaning of water).

Connotation The special shades of meaning (based on emotional or other factors) that a form has for its individual user (the evil connotation of profits for labour leaders as against its favourable connotations for management...).

So whilst one need not necessarily dismiss Eco's *Theory* as does his *Times Literary Supplement* reviewer (1977), as "a more or less gratuitous expression of an Italian *esprit de système*—it is much too interesting and stimulating for that—one cannot accept his dismissal of such patently useful concepts, nor his attempt to complexify what can be fairly straightforward.

Peirce's semiotic is much more complex than Saussure's semiology. At one time, Peirce identified 59,049 (3^{10}) different classes of sign, which he later reduced considerably in number. There are scattered references to them in various of his collected papers, but they are difficult to extract. The papers themselves are often confused, ambiguous, and self-contradictory; in addition to these, Peirce presents us with two other difficulties. Firstly he was an inveterate "trichotomiser," grouping everything taxonomically into sets of threes; and secondly, he constantly flouted Saussure's social contract, coining a new word or term for every concept which occurred to him. He wrote, for instance, of first-ness, secondness, and thirdness; of abstractives, concretives, and collectives; of Phemes, Semes, and Delemes; of Potisigns, Actisigns, and Famisigns; of qualisigns, sinsigns, and legisigns. Of all his trichotomies, however, that which classifies signs into Icons, Indices, and Symbols has proved to be the most fruitful. He defines them as follows:

> 'An *icon* is a sign which refers to the Object that it denotes by virtue of certain charac-ters of its own and which it possesses just the same, whether any such object actually exists or not.'
> A *symbol* is 'a sign which refers to the object that it denotes by virtue of law, usually any associations of general ideas, which operates to cause that symbol to be interpreted as referring to that object,' and
> An *index* is a sign, or representation 'which refers to its object not so much because of any similarity of, or analogy with it, nor because it is associated with general characters which that object happens to possess, but because it is in dynamical (including spatial) connection, both with the individual object on the one hand and with the senses or memory of the person for whom it acts as a sign.'

Peirce's *icon* is an object which exists in its own right but which has certain elements in common with some other object, and can therefore be used to represent that object. Maps, photographs, and algebraic signs are icons in this sense, so are architects' draw-ings. Unfortunately though, Peirce's definitions of icons are so ambiguous that a gener-ation of semioticians is still concerned with trying to unravel which he actually meant by an iconic sign: Eco,[64] Volli,[65] [Tomás] Maldonado,[66] Broadbent,[67] and others have con-tributed to this particular debate.

So in considering the architectural implications we ought to start with Peirce's rather more straightforward index, a sign which indicates some particular object or cir-cumstance in terms of a physical relationship. A pointing finger indicates which way to go, the pole star indicates north, a weather vane indicates which direction the wind is blowing from.

As for buildings as indices, one can think of many art galleries, museums, exhibi-tion pavilions and even houses—such as Le Corbusier's Maison la Roche of 1923—which are planned about a set route. Such buildings *indicate* to us which way we should go in moving around them, so certainly they are indices. The "functional" building also was intended to be an index, indicating by its form the functions which it houses. This may be possible in the case, say, of an oil refinery, a gas cracking plant, or a nuclear power sta-tion; but most so-called "functional" buildings are merely symbols of modernity. Peirce's symbol is even more straightforward: it is a sign which "carried" some general meaning; thus a badge symbolises the fact that someone belongs to an organisation, a railway tick-et symbolises the fact that they have paid to travel. Ordinary words, in Peirce's terms, are symbols in this sense. A church obviously symbolises Christianity. Peirce's *symbol* has the specific quality that whatever relationship exists between the symbol itself and the enti-ty which it symbolises has to be *learned*, both by the user of symbols and those to whom its meaning is important. In this sense it closely resembles Saussure's *sign*, a signifier and a signified with a learned relationship between them.

Buildings certainly can be symbols in Peirce's senses.[*] The Gothic cathedral obviously is a *symbol* of the Christian faith; most of us in the Western cultures have learned the essential relationship between a building of that form and the religion which it symbolises. We even share a social contract as to *conventional* church form.

As for building as *icon*: any drawing, model, or photograph of a building is an icon in Peirce's sense, but the building itself also may be an icon—if it "reminds" us of something else. I have described elsewhere[68] certain buildings which were designed by visual analogy with forms from nature—as in the case of Le Corbusier's crab-shell roof at Ronchamp; or the hands in prayer analogy which suggested the roof-form of [Frank Lloyd] Wright's Chapel at Madison Wisconsin; or the analogy with modern painting, as in the case of de Stijl architecture, and so on. Such buildings obviously can be iconic signs of the forms from which they were derived. One of the clearest is the duck-shaped poultry stand on Long Island to which Peter Blake and Robert Venturi have drawn our attention.

Charles Jencks[69] suggests that icons of this kind (he insists on calling them metaphors) are too simple, banal, and direct; that their use can lead to an architecture— he calls it "univalent"—which is just as boring as anything by Mies. I agree with him, whilst objecting to his use of metaphor to describe straight, simple, visual analogies. I have previously tried to distinguish between these subtle terms[70] so let me use one of Jencks's examples to point this distinction further. Jencks chooses the Casa Battló of Antoni Gaudí as an example of architecture which carries a rich variety of meanings on a number of levels. The first two floors have a curious colonnade formed by visual analogy with human bones. The main facade, with its undulating forms in brown, green, and blue ceramics, obviously is an icon for the sea, whilst Jencks points out the boldly tiled roof actually "looks like" a dragon. It is dominated by a pinnacle bearing a Christian cross. Bones, sea, and dragon are all icons at the level of simple visual analogy, but as Jencks also points out the whole thing is an expression of Catalan nationalism in which the dragon of Castille has been slain by St. George—the patron Saint of Barcelona. The bones of course represent those of the martyrs who have died in the cause. Now obviously this represents a "higher" level of meaning—shading towards say illusionism— which certainly is not revealed by a direct reading of the simple, visual analogies. *This* is metaphor, and we should do well to reserve the word for such deep and subtle meanings, rather than applying it, indiscriminately, to simple, visual analogy.

But there is also another kind of architectural icon—the kind of likeness between buildings which depends on some underlying structure, rather than on simple, observable, visual likeness. Probably the clearest example of this is that suggested by March and Steadman, who took three Frank Lloyd Wright plans—the Life House, the Ralph Jester House, and the Vigo Sundt House—and showed that despite the obvious differences in the appearances of their plans (the first is based on rectangular geometry, the second on

[*] The trouble with symbolism is that because it is culture-based and has to be learned, its meanings also can change. When Karl Friedrich Schinkel chose a neo-classical form with Greek Ionic columns for his Altes Museum in Berlin (1822), it symbolised ideas of enlightenment and liberal democracy. But when Paul Troost chose a similar form for Hitler's Museum of German Art in Munich (1936), it symbolised something quite different.

circular, and the third on triangular), there was nevertheless a pattern of relationships between living rooms and terrace, terraces and pools, bedrooms and bathrooms, etc, which underlay them all. In this sense each was an icon for the other.

So what does all this tell us? Well, first of all the pragmatics of meaning can have and have had, effects on how buildings were designed. Any attempt to design buildings consciously for the effects they now have on their users in this sense was a pragmatic affair. Certainly that was true of eighteenth-century picturesque; it is also true of more recent architecture in which sensory effects on people have been taken into account. Secondly, and obviously, there is, and has been, a considerable traffic in architectural syntactics. Any attempt to generate architecture according to some geometric system obviously is syntactic in this sense. And thirdly, all buildings "carry" meaning in the semantic sense. Now that we accept this as inevitable, we might as well make sure that they do it properly. A number of architects—such as the Venturis, Charles Moore, Bob Stern, the Taller de Arquitectura—have been trying to do just that.

It is hardly surprising, given the way in which architectural meaning has been suppressed so severely over the past fifty years or so, that some of their attempts, to say the least, are rather halting. They still do not seem sure just how buildings "carry" meaning. That is why the various concepts from Saussure, from Peirce, and from others promise to be so helpful in suggesting with greater precision just how the meaning can be carried.

1   G. Baird, "La Dimension Amoureuse," *Arena, Architectural Association Journal* (June 1967); reprinted in C. Jencks and G. Baird, *Meaning in Architecture* (London: Barrie and Rockliffe, 1969).
2   R. Banham, "The Architecture of Wampanoag," in C. Jencks and G. Baird, *Meaning in Architecture*, op. cit.
3   C. Jencks and G. Baird, *Meaning in Architecture*, op. cit.
4   R. Venturi, *Complexity and Contradiction in Architecture* (New York: Museum of Modern Art, 1966).
5   R. Venturi, D. Scott Brown, and S. Izenour, *Learning From Las Vegas* (Cambridge: MIT Press, 1972).
6   C. Moore, *The Place of Houses* (New York: Holt, Reinhart and Winston, 1974).
7   B. Brolin, *The Failure of Modern Architecture* (London: Studio Vista, 1976).
8   C. Jencks, *The Language of Post Modern Architecture* (London: Academy, 1977).
9   J.P. Bonta, *Expressive Systems in Architecture* (London: Lund Humphries, forthcoming).
10 G. Broadbent, C. Jencks, and D. Bunt, *Signs, Symbols and Architecture* (London: J. Wiley and Sons, forthcoming).
11 G. Broadbent and T. Llorens, *Meaning in the Built Environment* (London: J. Wiley and Sons, London, forthcoming).
12 K. Woodbridge, *The Stourhead Landscape* (London: The National Trust, 1971).
13 Le Corbusier, *Vers une Architecture* (Paris: Editions Cres, 1923); *Towards a New Architecture*, Etchells, trans. (London: Architectural Press, 1927).
14 W. Gropius, *Scope of Total Architecture* (London: Allen & Unwin, 1956).
15 L. Mies van der Rohe, "Industrielles Bauen," *G.* no. 3 (June 1924); *Form* no. 3, N. Bullock, trans. (December 1966).
16 S. Giedion, *Space, Time and Architecture* (London: Oxford University Press, 1967).
17 N. Pevsner, *Pioneers of the Modern Movement* (London: Faber, 1936). Reprinted as *Pioneers of Modern Design* (Harmondsworth: Penguin, 1960, 1964).
18 J.M. Richards, *Modern Architecture* (Harmondsworth: Penguin).

19   W.R.G. Hillier, J.E. Musgrove, and P. O'Sullivan, "Knowledge and Design," *EDRA* 3, W.J. Mitchell, ed. (1972).

20   D. Sharp, *The Rationalists* (London: Architectural Press, 1977).

21   N. Pevsner, *A History of Building Types* (London: Thames and Hudson, 1976).

22   F. de Saussure, *Course in General Linguistics* (1906–11), W. Baskin, trans. (New York: Philosophical Library; London: Peter Owen, 1959).

23   C. Hartshorne and P. Weiss, eds., *The Collected Papers of Charles Sanders Peirce* 8 vols. (Cambridge: Harvard University Press, 1974).

24   M. Pei, *Glossary of Linguistic Terminology* (New York: Anchor, 1966).

25   J.S. Scott, ed., *Penguin Dictionary, A Dictionary of Building* (Harmondsworth: Penguin, 1964).

26   C. Morris, "Foundations of the Theory of Signs," *International Encyclopedia of Unified Science* vol. 2 (Chicago: Chicago University Press, 1938).

27   G. Broadbent, *Design in Architecture* (London: J. Wiley and Sons, 1974).

28   J. Ruskin, *The Seven Lamps of Architecture* (London, 1849).

29   C.E. Shannon and W. Weaver, *The Mathematical Theory of Communication* (Urbana: University of Illinois Press, 1949).

30   G.K. Koenig, *Architetture e Communicazione* (Florence: Editrice Fiorentina 1964).

31   H. Prohansky, W. Ittelson, and G.R. Rivlin, *Environmental Psychology: Man and his Physical Setting* (New York: Holt, Reinhart and Winston).

32   I.C.A. Craik, "Environmental Psychology," *Annual Review of Psychology* 24 (1973).

33   I. Altman, *The Environment and Social Behaviour* (Belmont, CA; Wandsworth, 1975).

34   D. Canter, *Psychology for Architects* (London: Applied Science, 1974).

35   D. Canter, *The Psychology of Place* (New York: St. Martins Press, 1977).

36   T. Lee, *Psychology and the Environment* (London: Methuen, 1976).

37   R.G. Hershberger, "A Study of Meaning in Architecture," Sanoff and Cohn, eds., *Proceedings of the first Environmental Design Research Association (EDRA) conference, 1972.*

38   C.A. Acking, "Perception of the Human Environment," B. Honikman, ed., *Proceedings of the Architectural Psychology Conference at Kingston Polytechnic, RIBA, London, 1969.*

39   B. Honikman, "An Investigation of the Relationship Between Construing an Environment and its Physical Town," *EDRA* 3, W.J. Mitchell, ed. (1972).

40   G.A. Kelley, "A Theory of Personality," extract from *The Psychology of Personal Constructs* (New York: W. W. Norton, 1963).

41   B. Honikman, "Personal Construct Theory and Environmental Evaluation," in Preiser, *Environmental Design, proceedings of the third Environmental Design Research Association (EDRA) conference, Virginia, 1973.*

42   C. Abel, "The Learning of Architectural Concepts," paper to *EDRA 6 Conference, University of Kansas, 1975.*

43   C. Abel, "Instructional Simulation of Client Construct Systems," paper to British Architectural Psychology Conference, Sheffield, 1975.

44   J. Pelc, "Semiotics and Logic," contribution to First Congress of the International Association for Semiotic Studies, Milan, 1974.

45   N. Chomsky, *Syntactic Structures* (The Hague: Mouton, 1957).

46   N. Chomsky, *Aspects of the Theory of Syntax* (Cambridge: MIT Press, 1965).

47   C.T. Onions, *An Advanced English Syntax* (London, 1904).

48   P. Eisenman, "Notes on Conceptual Architecture II: Dual Deep Structure," lecture notes, 1972. See also M. Gandelsonas, "On Reading Architecture," *Progressive Architecture* (March 1972), and M. Tafuri, "American Graffiti Five x Five = 25," *Oppositions* 6 (Summer 1976).

49   R. Lutyens, *Sir Edwin Lutyens: An Appreciation in Perspective* (London: 1942).

50   L. March and P. Steadman, *The Geometry of Environment* (London: RIBA).

51   W. Hillier and A. Leaman, *Space Syntax* (London: University College School of Environmental Studies, 1976).

52   P. Steadman, W. Mitchell, and R. Liggett, "Synthesis and Optimisation of Small Rectangular Floor Plans," *Environment and Planning* (January 1976).

53   A. Rossi, *l'Architettura della Citta* (Padua: Marsilio, 1966).

54   Vitruvius, *The Ten Books on Architecture*, M.H. Morgan, trans., 1914 (New York: Dover Publications, 1960).

55   C.K. Ogden and I.A. Richards, *The Meaning of Meaning* (London: Routledge and Kegan Paul, 1966).

56   L. Hjelmslev, *Prolegomenon to a Theory of Language* (Baltimore: Indiana University Publications in Anthropology and Linguistics, 1953).

57   Ragghianti, "Saggio di analisi linguistics del Arquitettura Moderna," *Casabella* no. 116 (1937).

58   R. Pane, "Architettura e letteratura," *Architettura e arti figurative* (Venice, 1948).

59   R. De Fusco and K.L. Scalvini, *Se Segni e Simboli del Tempietto de Bramante* (1970).

60   U. Eco, *La Struttura Assente. Introduzione all ricera Semiologica* (Milano: Bompiani, 1968).

61   G. Broadbent, *Meaning in Architecture*, op. cit.

62   J.P. Bonta, *Mies van der Rohe, Barcelona 1929. An Anatomy of Architectural Interpretation* (Barcelona: Gili, 1975).

63   U. Eco, *A Theory of Semiotics* (Bloomington: Indiana University Press, 1976).

64   U. Eco, "Introduction to a Semiotics of Iconic Signs," *Versus* 2 (January 1972).

65   U. Volli, "Some Possible Developments of the Concept of Iconism," *Versus* 3 (February 1972): 14–30.

66   T. Maldonado, "On Iconism," contribution to the First Congress of the International Association for Semiotic Studies, Milan, 1974.

67   G. Broadbent, "Building as an Iconic Sign System," paper to the first Congress of the International Association for Semiotic Studies, Milan.

68   G. Broadbent, *Design in Architecture*, op. cit.

69   C. Jencks, *The Language of Post Modern Architecture*, op. cit.

70   G. Broadbent, *Design in Architecture*, op. cit.

3. POSTSTRUCTURALISM AND DECONSTRUCTION
THE ISSUES OF ORIGINALITY AND AUTHORSHIP

INTRODUCTION

Architecture Where Desire Can Live
Jacques Derrida interviewed by Eva Meyer

In this interview from the Italian architecture magazine *Domus*, philosopher and literary critic Jacques Derrida raises some important questions, beginning with the relationship between theory and practice. He asks, What is architectural thinking? Does architecture constitute an embodiment of thinking and can it be other than a representation of thought? This frames the issue of whether architecture is an art (mimetic or otherwise), or merely a technique for instrumentalizing architectural thinking. He indicates that unlike the other fine arts, architecture is not concerned with the representation of something already existing.

Despite (or perhaps because of) his position outside the discipline, Derrida and deconstruction have influenced architectural theory and design since the 1980s, when his exchanges with Peter Eisenman and Bernard Tschumi were published. The subsequent interest in the philosopher's work is typical of the postmodern questioning of meaning and the search for theoretical paradigms from outside the discipline with which to approach architecture.

Derrida has called attention to the intersection of philosophy and architecture, in that philosophical thought relies on architectonic and urban models. It is precisely the *language* of architectural metaphors (such as "the foundation of philosophy," or even "the architecture of architecture") which Derrida sets out to deconstruct or dismantle, along with the fundamental *oppositions* ("binaries") on which language and meaning are based. The deconstructive practice analyzes these received pairs of terms to reveal that they are not natural, but have in fact been culturally created, or "institutionalized," at a specific historical moment. Their promotion and acceptance as natural are seen as ideological, that is, deceptive, and restrictive of thinking. Derrida sees architecture as aiming at control of the sectors of communication, transportation, and the economy. His postmodern critique of architecture proposes the end of this "plan of domination."

Derrida and Tschumi are both interested in *place*, in the "taking place" of an event, and in the temporal dimension of experience in space. (ch. 9, 13) Two archetypes are discussed in Derrida's piece, and their usual roles are somewhat conflated: the Tower of Babel is conventionally used as a metaphor for the incomprehensibility of language, while the labyrinth represents an unintelligible spatial condition. Derrida allows the labyrinth to appropriate and superimpose this metaphoric association of the tower, despite the striking formal differences between the two. (Derrida may refer here to Tschumi's "Questions of Space,"[1] in which an important opposition is set up between the labyrinth as model of experiential, sensory space versus the pyramid, representing the theoretical, linguistic aspect of architecture.) For Derrida, the tower and labyrinth archetypes lead to a confrontation with the sublime because of the impossibility of apprehending them. (ch. 14) He leaves open the possibility that "there may be an undiscovered way of thinking belonging to the architectural moment, to desire, to creation." Such thought "could only be conveyed by...the sublime."

1   Bernard Tschumi, "Questions of Space," *Studio International* 190, no. 977 (September/October 1975): 136–142.

JACQUES DERRIDA INTERVIEWED BY EVA MEYER

ARCHITECTURE WHERE DESIRE CAN LIVE

Jacques Derrida (JD): Let us consider architectural thinking. By that I don't mean to conceive architecture as a technique separate from thought and therefore possibly suitable to represent it in space, to constitute almost an embodiment of thinking, but rather to raise the question of architecture as a possibility of thought, which cannot be reduced to the status of a representation of thought.

Since you refer to the separation of theory and practice, one might start by asking oneself how this working separation came about. It seems to me that from the moment one separates Theorem and Pratem, one considers architecture as a simple technique and detaches it from thought, whereas there may be an undiscovered way of thinking belonging to the architectural moment, to desire, to creation.

Eva Meyer (EM): If one is going to envisage architecture as a metaphor and thereby constantly point to the necessity of the embodiment of thinking, how can it be reintroduced into thinking in a non-metaphorical way? Possibly not necessarily leading to an embodiment, but which remain along the way, in a labyrinth for example?

JD: We will talk about the labyrinth later. First of all, I would like to outline how the philosophical tradition has used the architectural model as a metaphor for a kind of thinking which in itself cannot be architectural. In [René] Descartes for instance you find the metaphor of the founding of a town, and this foundation is in fact what is supposed to support the building, the architectonic construction, the town at the base. There is consequently a kind of urbanistic metaphor in philosophy. The "Meditations," the "Discourse on Method" are full of these architectonic representations which, in

From *Domus* no. 671 (April 1986): 17–24. Courtesy of the author and publisher.

addition, always have political relevance. When Aristotle wants to give an example of theory and practice, he quotes the "architekton": he knows the origin of things, he is a theorist who can also teach and has at his command the labourers who are incapable of independent thought. And with that a political hierarchy is established: architectonics is defined as an art of systems, as an art therefore suitable for the rational organisation of complete branches of knowledge. It is evident that architectural reference is useful in rhetoric in a language which in itself has retained no architecturality whatsoever. I consequently ask myself how, before the separation between theory and practice, between thinking and architecture, a way of thinking linked to the architectural event could have existed. If each language proposes a spatialisation, an arrangement in space which doesn't dominate it but which approaches it by approximation, then it is to be compared with a kind of pioneering, with the clearing of a path. A path which does not have to be discovered but to be created. And this creation of a path is not at all alien to architecture. Each architectural place, each habitation has one precondition: that the building should be located on a path, at a crossroads at which arrival and departure are both possible. There is no building without streets leading towards it or away from it; nor is there one without paths inside, without corridors, staircases, passages, doors. And if language cannot control these paths towards and within a building, then that only signifies that language is enmeshed in these structures, that it is "on the way." "On the move towards language" ([Martin] Heidegger), on the way to reaching itself. The way is not a method, that must be clear. The method is a technique, a procedure in order to gain control of the way, in order to make it viable.

EM: And what is the way, then?

JD: I refer once more to Heidegger who says that "odos," the way, is not "méthodos," that there is a way which cannot be reduced to the definition of method. The definition of the way as a method is interpreted by Heidegger as an epoch in the history of philosophy starting with Descartes, [Gottfried] Leibniz, and [G. W. F.] Hegel and concealing its nature of being a way, making it slip into oblivion, whereas in fact it indicates infinity of thinking: thinking is always a way. If thinking doesn't rise above the way, if the language of thinking or the thinking system of the language is not understood as metalanguage on the way, that means that language is a way and so has always had a certain connection with habitability, and with architecture. This constant "being on the move," the habitability of the way offering no way out entangles you in a labyrinth without any escape. More precisely, it is a trap, a calculated device, such as [James] Joyce's labyrinth of Dedalus.

The question of architecture is in fact that of the place, of the taking place in space. The establishing of a place which didn't exist until then and is in keeping with what will take place there one day, that is a place. As [Stéphane] Mallarmé puts it, ce qui a lieu, c'est le lieu. It is not at all natural. The setting up of a habitable place is an event, and obviously the setting up is always something technical. It invents something which didn't exist beforehand and yet at the same time there is the inhabitant, man or God, who requires the place prior to its invention or causing it. Therefore one doesn't quite know where to pin down the origin of the place. Maybe there is a labyrinth which is neither natural nor artificial and which we inhabit, within the history of graeco-occidental philosophy where the opposition between nature and technology originated. From this opposition arises the distinction between the two labyrinths. Let us return to the place, to spatiality and to writing. For some time, something like a de-constructive procedure has been establishing itself, an attempt to free oneself from the oppositions imposed by the history of philosophy, such as "physis/techne/God/man, philosophy/architecture." De-construction therefore analyses and questions conceptual pairs which are currently accepted as self-evident and natural, as if they hadn't been institutionalised at some precise point, as if they had no history. Because of being taken for granted they restrict thinking.

Now the concept of de-construction itself resembles an architectural metaphor. It is often said to have a negative attitude. Something has been constructed, a philosophical system, a tradition, a culture, and along comes a de-constructor and destroys it stone by stone, analyses the structure and dissolves it. Often enough this is the case. One looks at a system—Platonic/Hegelian—and examines how it was built, which keystone, which angle of vision supports the building; one shifts them and thereby frees oneself from the authority of the system. It seems to me, however, that this is not the essence of de-construction. It is not simply the technique of an architect who knows how to de-construct what has been constructed, but a probing which touches upon the technique itself, upon the authority of the architectural metaphor and thereby constitutes its own architectural rhetoric. De-construction is not simply—as its name seems to indicate— the technique of a reversed construction when it is able to conceive for itself the idea of construction. One could say that there is nothing more architectural than de-construction, but also nothing less architectural. Architectural thinking can only be de-constructive in the following sense: as an attempt to visualize that which establishes the authority of the architectural concatenation in philosophy. From this point we can go back to what connects de-construction with writing: its spatiality, thinking in terms of a path, of the opening up of a way which—without knowing where it will lead to—inscribes its traces. Looking at it like that, one can say that the opening up of a path is a writing which cannot be attributed to either man, or God, or animal since it designates in its widest sense the place from which this classification—man/God/animal—can take shape. This writing is truly like a labyrinth since it has neither beginning nor end. One is always on the move. The opposition between time and space, between the time of speech and the space of the temple or the house has no longer any sense. One lives in writing. Writing is a way of living.

EM: At this point I would like to bring into play the forms of writing of the architect himself. Since the introduction of the orthogonal projection, ground plan and sectional drawings have become the primary means of notation in architecture. They also provide the principles according to which architecture is defined. Looking at floor plans by Palladio, Bramante, Scamozzi, one can read the transition from a theocentric to an anthropocentric world view, in that the shape of the cross opens up increasingly in platonic squares and rectangles, to be finally totally resolved in them. Modernism on the other hand distinguishes itself by a criticism of this humanistic position. Le Corbusier's Maison Domino is an example of this: a new type of construction made of cubic elements, with a flat roof and large windows, rationally articulated without any constructional ornaments. In short, an architecture which no longer represents man but which—as Peter Eisenman puts it—becomes a self-referential sign. A self-explanatory architecture gives information on what is inherent in itself. It reflects a fundamentally new relationship between man and object, house, and inhabitants. One possibility of representing such an architecture is axonometry: a guide to the reading of a building which doesn't presuppose its habitability. It seems to me that this self-reflection of architecture within architecture shows a development which can be connected with your work on deconstruction because of its starting point which is deeply critical of methodology and therefore also of a philosophic nature. If the house in which one feels "at home" becomes open to imitation and intrudes upon reality then a changed concept of building has been introduced, not as an application but as a condition of thinking. Would it be conceivable that the theocentric and the anthropocentric world view together with its "being a place" could be transformed into a new and more diversified network of references?

JD: What emerges here can be grasped as the opening of architecture, as the beginning of a non-representative architecture. In this context it might be interesting to recall the fact that, at the outset, architecture was not an art of representation, whereas painting, drawing and sculpture, can always imitate something which is supposed to already exist. I would like to remind you once more of Heidegger, and above all of the "Origin of the work of art" in which he refers to the "Riß" (rip-break-up drawings). It is a "Riß" which should be thought of in its original sense independently of modifications such as "Grundriß" (ground plan), "Aufriß" (vertical section), "Skizze" (draft). In architecture there is an imitation of the "Riß," of the engraving, the action of ripping. This has to be associated with writing.

From here originates the attempt of modern and postmodern architecture to create a different kind of living which no longer fits the old circumstances, where the plan is not oriented towards domination, controlling communication, the economy, and transport etc. A completely new rapport between surface—the drawing—and space—architecture—is emerging. This relationship has long been important. In order to talk about the impossibility of absolute objectivation, let us move from the labyrinth to the building of the Tower of Babel. There too the sky is to be conquered in an act of name-giving, which yet remains inseparably linked with the natural language. A tribe, the Semites, whose name means "name," a tribe therefore called "name" want to erect a tower supposed to reach the sky, according to the Scriptures, with the aim of making a name for itself. This conquest of the sky, this taking up of a position in the sky means giving oneself a name and from this power, from the power of the name, from the height of the meta-language, to dominate the other tribes, the other languages, to colonise them. But God descends and spoils this enterprise by uttering one word: Babel and this word is a name which resembles a noun meaning confusion. With this word he condemns mankind to the diversity of languages. Therefore they have to renounce their plan of domination by means of a language which would be universal.

The fact that this intervention in architecture, with a construction and that also means: de-construction—represents the failure or the limitation imposed on a universal language in order to foil the plan for political and linguistic domination of the world says something about the impossibility of mastering the diversity of languages, about the impossibility of there being a universal translation. This also means that the construction of architecture will always remain labyrinthine. The issue is not to give up one point of view for the sake of another, which would be the only one and absolute, but to see a diversity of possible points of view.

If the tower had been completed there would be no architecture. Only the incompletion of the tower makes it possible for architecture as well as the multitude of languages to have a history. This history always has to be understood in relation to a divine being who is finite. Perhaps it is characteristic of postmodernism to take this failure into account. If modernism distinguishes itself by the striving for absolute domination, then postmodernism might be the realisation or the experience of its end, the end of the plan of domination. The postmodernism could develop a new relationship with the divine which would no longer be manifest in the traditional shapes of the Greek, Christian, or other deities, but would still set the conditions for architectural thinking. Perhaps there is no architectural thinking. But should there be such thinking, then it could only be conveyed by the dimension of the High, the Supreme, the Sublime. Viewed as such, architecture is not a matter of space but an experience of the Supreme which is not higher but in a sense more ancient than space and therefore is a spatialisation of time.

EM: Could this "spatialisation" be thought of as a postmodern conception of a process involving the subject in its machination to such an extent that it cannot recognise itself in it? How can we understand this as a technique if it does not imply any reacquisition, any dominion?

JD: All the questions we have raised so far point to the question of doctrine and that can only be placed in a political context. How is it possible, for instance, to develop a new inventive faculty that would allow the architect to use the possibilities of the new technology without aspiring to uniformity, without developing models for the whole world? An inventive faculty of the architectural difference which would bring out a new type of diversity with different limitations, other heterogeneities than the existing ones and which would not be reduced to the technique of planning?

At the "Collège International de Philosophie," a seminar is held where philosophers and architects work together because it became evident that the planning of the "Collège" also has to be an architectural venture. The "Collège" cannot take place if one cannot find a place, an architectural form for it which bears resemblance to what might be thought in it. The "Collège" has to be habitable in a totally different way from university. Until now, there has been no building for the "Collège." You take a room here, a hall there. As architecture, the "Collège" does not exist yet and perhaps never will. There is a formless desire for another form. The desire for a new location, new arcades, new corridors, new ways of living and of thinking.

That is a promise. And when I said that the "Collège" does not exist as architecture yet, it might also mean that the community it requires does not exist yet and therefore the place is not being constituted. A community must accept the commitment and work so that architectural thinking takes place. A new relationship between the individual and the community, between the original and the reproduction is emerging. Think of China and Japan for example, where they build temples out of wood and renew them regularly and entirely without them losing their originality, which obviously is not contained in the sensitive body but in something else. That too is Babel: the diversity of relationships with the architectural event from one culture to another. To know that a promise is being given even if it is not kept in its visible form. Places where desire can recognise itself, where it can live.

INTRODUCTION

Architecture and Limits I
Bernard Tschumi

In 1980 and 1981, *ArtForum*, the New York art magazine, published a series of three features on architecture, coordinated and introduced by Bernard Tschumi.[1] Most of the articles in the "Architecture and Limits" series are written by authors represented here, including Peter Eisenman, Rem Koolhaas, Anthony Vidler, Raimund Abraham, and Kenneth Frampton.

Tschumi's brief introductions summarize the current issues in theory at that time. He touches upon the following: What is the unique characteristic or essence of architecture as a discipline? Is it the use (function) or the process of building? How are architecture's boundaries established? Does one have to choose between *genius loci* and *zeitgeist*, as promoted by phenomenologists and historicists, (ch. 4, 9) or between social concerns and autonomy? (ch. 8)

A recurring theme in all three introductory essays, which gives them relevance to theory and design today, is the critique of formalism. In "Architecture and Limits I," Tschumi advocates resisting "The narrowing of architecture as a form of knowledge into architecture as mere knowledge of form." In general, he finds contemporary theory and criticism to be reductive and limited by "ideologies" such as formalism, functionalism, and rationalism.

The series title is significant in its use of the concept of *limits*. As Tschumi explains in the first essay, "limits are the strategic areas of architecture," the base from which one can launch a critique of existing conditions. This idea is fundamental to poststructuralist and deconstructionist thought, both of which posit that the contents of the margins (of texts or disciplines) are more important than their location indicates. The implication of this idea is that through careful efforts, one can disclose the repressed contents of a work and gain access to a new interpretation. Tschumi advocates use of this critical approach to challenge "reductionist" attitudes, which operate to eliminate differences and attack works at the limits. Linear (cause-and-effect-based) histories of architecture exemplify reductionist thinking. Tschumi maintains that without limits, architecture could not exist: "Cancelling limits…is cancelling architecture altogether." Nonetheless, these necessary limits seem to invite transgression, which he has described as a valid critical practice.

One of Tschumi's more controversial statements, which he investigates more fully in "The Pleasure of Architecture," (ch. 13) is that usefulness may not, strictly speaking, be necessary to architecture. He admits, however, that utility (utilitas) is a component of building. He further distinguishes building and architecture on the basis of their relationship to drawing: while architecture depends on the existence of drawings and texts, building does not. Finally, architecture goes beyond building to become knowledge. Many of his postmodern contemporaries also articulate the difference between building and architecture.

"Architecture and Limits II" revisits aspects of the disciplinary tradition to determine whether parts of the tradition are restricting architecture's development, and "Architecture and Limits III" focuses on new definitions of the architectural program.

1   The journal was then interdisciplinary and theoretical in outlook, publishing, for example, postmodern theorist Jean-François Lyotard's significant articles on the sublime and modern art, listed in my bibliography.

BERNARD TSCHUMI

ARCHITECTURE AND LIMITS I

In the work of remarkable writers, artists, or composers one sometimes finds disconcerting elements located at the edge of their production, at its limit. These elements, disturbing and out of character, are misfits within the artist's activity. Yet often such works reveal hidden codes and excesses hinting at other definitions, other interpretations.

The same can be said for whole fields of endeavor: there are productions at the limit of literature, at the limit of music, at the limit of theater. Such extreme positions inform us about the state of art, its paradoxes, and its contradictions. These works, however, remain exceptions, for they seem dispensable—a luxury in the field of knowledge.

In architecture, such productions of the limit are not only historically frequent, but indispensable: architecture simply does not exist without them. For example, architecture does not exist without drawing, in the same way that architecture does not exist without texts. *Buildings* have been erected without drawings, but architecture itself goes beyond the mere process of building. The complex cultural, social, and philosophical demands developed slowly over centuries have made architecture a form of knowledge in and of itself. Just as all forms of knowledge use different modes of discourse, so there are key architectural statements that, though not necessarily built, nevertheless inform us about the state of architecture—its concerns and its polemics—more precisely than the actual buildings of their time. [Giovanni Battista] Piranesi's engravings of prisons, [Étienne-Louis] Boullée's washes of monuments, have drastically influenced architectural thought and its related practice. The same could be said about particular architectural texts and theoretical positions. This does not exclude the built realm, for small constructions of an experimental nature have occasionally played a similar role.

From *ArtForum* 19, no. 4 (December 1980): 36. Courtesy of the author and publisher.

Alternately celebrated and ignored, these works of the limit often provide isolated episodes amidst the mainstream of commercial production, for commerce cannot be ignored in a craft whose very scale involves cautious clients and carefully invested capital. Like the hidden clue in a detective story, these works are essential. In fact, the concept of limits is directly related to the very definition of architecture. What is meant by "to define?"—"To determine the boundary or limits of," as well as "to set forth the essential nature of."[1]

Yet the current popularity of architectural polemics and the dissemination of its drawings in other domains have often masked these limits, restricting attention to the most obvious of architecture's aspects, curtailing it to a *Fountainhead* view of decorative heroics. By doing so, it reduces architectural concerns to a *dictionnaire des idées reçues*, dismissing less accessible works of an essential nature or, worse, distorting them through association with the mere necessities of a publicity market.

The present phenomenon is hardly new. The twentieth century contains numerous reductive policies aimed at mass media dissemination, to the extent that we now have two different versions of twentieth-century architecture. One, a maximalist version, aims at overall social, cultural, political, programmatic concerns, while the other, minimalist, concentrates on sectors called style, technique, and so forth. But is it a question of choosing one over the other? Should one exclude the most rebellious and audacious projects, those of [Konstantin] Melnikov or [Hans] Poelzig for example, in the interest of preserving the stylistic coherence of the Modern Movement? Such exclusions, after all are common architectural tactics. The Modern Movement had already started its attack on the Beaux-Arts in the 1920s by a tactically belittling interpretation of nineteenth-century architecture. In the same way, the advocates of the International Style reduced the Modern Movement's radical concerns to homogenized iconographic mannerisms. Today, the most vocal representatives of architectural postmodernism use the same approach, but in reverse. By focusing their attack on the International Style, they make entertaining polemics and pungent journalism, but offer little new to a cultural context that has long included the same historical allusions, ambiguous signs, and sensuousness they discover today.

Architectural thought is not a simple matter of opposing *Zeitgeist* to *Genius Loci*, conceptual concerns to allegorical ones, historical allusions to purist research. Unfortunately, architectural criticism remains an underdeveloped field. Despite its current popularity in the media, it generally belongs to the traditional genre, with "personality" profiles and "practicality" appraisals. Serious thematic critique is absent, except in the most specialized publications. Worse, critics, there, are partial to current reductive interpretations and often pretend that plurality of styles makes for complexity of thought. Thus it is not surprising that a solid critique of the current frivolity of architecture and architectural reporting hardly exists. "The bounds beyond which something ceases to be possible or allowable"[2] have been tightened to such an extent that we now witness a set of reductions highly damaging to the scope of the discipline. The narrowing of architecture as a form of knowledge into architecture as mere knowledge of form is matched only by the scaling down of generous research strategies into operational power broker tactics.

The current confusion comes clear if one distinguishes, amidst current Venice or Paris Biennales, mass-market publications and other public celebrations of architectural polemics, a worldwide battle between this narrow view of architectural history and research into the nature and definition of the discipline. The conflict is no mere dialectic, but a real conflict corresponding, on a theoretical level, to practical battles that occur in everyday life within new commercial markets of architectural trivia, older corporate establishments and ambitious university intelligentsia.

Modernism already contained such tactical battles and often hid them behind reductionist ideologies (formalism, functionalism, rationalism). The coherence these ideologies implied has revealed itself full of contradictions. Yet this is no reason to strip architecture again of its social, spatial, conceptual concerns and restrict its limits to a territory of "wit and irony," "conscious schizophrenia," "dual coding," and "twice-broken split-pediments."

Such reduction occurs in other, less obvious ways. The art world's fascination with architectural matters, evident in the obsessive number of "architectural reference" and "architectural sculpture" exhibitions, is well matched by the recent vogue among architects for advertising in reputable galleries. These works are useful only insofar as they inform us about the changing nature of the art. To envy architecture's "usefulness" or, reciprocally, to envy artists' freedom shows in both cases naiveté and misunderstanding of the work. Building may be about usefulness, architecture not necessarily so. To call architectural those sculptures that superficially borrow from a vocabulary of gables and stairs is as naive as to call paintings some architects' tepid watercolors or the P.R. renderings of commercial firms.

Such reciprocal envy is based on the narrowest limits of outmoded interpretations, as if each discipline were inexorably drawn toward the other's most conservative texts. Yet the avant-garde of both fields sometimes enjoys a common sensibility, even if their terms of reference inevitably differ. It should be noted that architectural drawings, at their best, are a mode of working, of thinking about architecture. By their very nature, they usually refer to something *outside* themselves (as opposed to those art drawings that refer only to themselves, to their own materiality and devices).

But back to history. The pseudo-continuity of architectural history, with its neatly determined action-reaction episodes, is based on a poor understanding of history in general and architectural history in particular. After all, this history is not linear and certain key productions are far from enslaved to artificial continuities. While mainstream historians have dismissed numerous works by qualifying them as "conceptual architecture," "cardboard architecture," "narrative," or "poetic" spaces, the time has come to systematically question their reductive strategies. Questioning them is not purely a matter of celebrating what they reject. On the contrary, it means understanding what borderline activities hide and cover. This history, critique and analysis remains to be done. Not as a fringe phenomenon (poets, visionaries or, worse, intellectuals) but as central to the nature of architecture.

REPRESENTATION

I have called "reductionist" those attitudes that negate differences and limits. Cancelling limits (through pluralism, for example) is cancelling architecture altogether, for these limits are the strategic areas of architecture. We have seen that architectural drawings generally refer to something outside themselves, as opposed to drawings that refer only to themselves. A similar distinction occurs at another level *within* architecture, when the question becomes whether built architecture refers to some expressive meaning or symbolic content exterior to architecture, or whether it speaks only of itself, of its nature and its intrinsic condition. The question is, of course, one of representation. As the first of a series in *ArtForum*, two key works are introduced here: a set of drawings by John Hejduk and an argument by Anthony Vidler. John Hejduk works on the elements of the language of architecture as well as on its means of representation. By pushing them to their respective limits, he suggests here archetypal correlations between materials, function and representation. Anthony Vidler's analyses open a methodological field where the history of ideas, the history of language, the history of science all intersect and mingle with the history of architecture. Together with a few others, but each independently, they have significantly and continually contributed to "things having some quality or attribute of the highest possible degree,"[3] constantly redefining the limits influencing the development of architectural thought, in order not "to bring it to an end."[4]

1   *Oxford English Dictionary*, "to define."
2   Ibid., "limit."
3   Ibid., "limit,"
4   Ibid., "to define."

INTRODUCTION

Architecture and Limits II
Bernard Tschumi

This essay is the second in a three-part series
that appeared in *ArtForum* between December
1980 and September 1981. In "Architecture and
Limits II," Bernard Tschumi attempts to define the
limits of the discipline by asking if scale, proportion, symmetry, composition, form/function, ideal
types/programmatic organization, or the Vitruvian
triad are architecture's limiting themes. Tschumi
says it is likely that these elements are either
essential to architecture, or liabilities to be
displaced. Point by point, he considers the status
of each of Vitruvius's three principles of accommodation (*commoditas*), "structural stability"
(*firmitas*), and beauty (*venustas*). He concludes
that beauty has disappeared, structure no longer
limits architecture, and that attitudes about accommodating the body in space have shifted. The
body in space sustains his interest for the remainder of the essay.

   In pointed comments, Tschumi criticizes
modern ideas about "honesty of materials," and
postmodern nostalgia for poché and the mass
wall. These tectonic or even "builderly" concerns,
he suggests in "Architecture and Limits I," are not
central to architecture. He proposes that an alternative way to look at "the materiality of architecture...is in its solids and voids, its spatial
sequences, its articulations, its collisions." This
poetic possibility emphasizes the *choreographic*
aspect of the body's experience of architecture,
which Tschumi sometimes describes as "cinematic" in order to stress movement and its temporal
dimension. Significant to his proposal for architecture "as event" is the idea that bodies *construct*
space through movement. For example, pageants
and spectacles involving large numbers of people
clearly generate a changed spatial condition in
an urban street.

   Tschumi speaks of *space* enthusiastically,
and variously as mental, physical, and social
space. His conceptions of space and place
(see Derrida, this chapter) bear little relation to
that of phenomenologists like Christian Norberg-
Schulz, who promotes *place* to counteract the

deficiencies of modernist space. Tschumi would claim that the problem is not with the space, but with its programming in terms of function rather than event.

Tschumi's literacy in linguistic theory, post-structuralism, and psychoanalysis emerge in this part of his ongoing attempt to define an interdisciplinary architecture. But the connection he suggests between beauty and structural linguistics is not clear. Nor is the relationship he intends between the pairs thought and space, theoretical and practical. The latter pair he discusses at length in "Questions of Space,"[1] in terms of the way architecture brings together the opposites conception and experience, material and immaterial. His growing body of built work aims to fuse theoretical notions and spatial experience. To that end, he embraces "Events, drawings, texts [that] expand the boundaries of socially justifiable constructions."

1   Bernard Tschumi, "Questions of Space," *Studio International* 190, no. 977 (September/October 1975): 136–142.

BERNARD TSCHUMI
ARCHITECTURE AND LIMITS II

The limits of architecture are variable: each decade has its own ideal themes, its own confused fashions. Yet each of these periodical shifts and digressions raises the same question: are there recurrent themes, constants that are specifically architectural and yet always under scrutiny—an architecture of limits?

As opposed to other disciplines, architecture rarely presents a coherent set of concepts—a definition—that displays both the continuity of its concerns and the more sensitive boundaries of its activity. However, a few aphorisms and dictums that have been transmitted through centuries of architectural literature do exist. Such notions as "scale," "proportion," "symmetry," and "composition" have specific architectural connotations. The relation between the abstraction of thought and the substance of space— the Platonic distinction between "theoretical" and "practical"—is constantly recalled; to perceive the architectural space of a building is to perceive something-that-has-been-conceived. The opposition between form and function, between ideal types and pro-grammatic organization, is similarly recurrent, even if both terms are viewed, increasingly, as independent.

One of the more enduring equations is the Vitruvian trilogy *venustas, firmitas, utilitas*—"attractive appearance," "structural stability," "appropriate spatial accom-modation." It is obsessively repeated throughout centuries of architectural precepts, though not necessarily in that order. Are these possible architectural constants, the inherent limits without which architecture does not exist? Or is their permanence a bad mental habit, an intellectual laziness observed throughout history? Does persistence grant validity? If not, does architecture fail to realize the displacement of limits it has held for so long?

From *ArtForum* 19, no. 7 (March 1981): 45. Courtesy of the author and publisher.

The twentieth century has disrupted the Vitruvian trilogy, for architecture could not remain insensitive to industrialization and the radical questioning of institutions (whether family, state, or church) at the turn of the century. The first term—attractive appearance (beauty)—slowly disappeared from the vocabulary, while structural linguistics took hold of the architect's formal discourse. Yet early architectural semiotics merely borrowed codes from literary texts, applied them to urban or architectural spaces, and inevitably remained descriptive. Inversely, attempts to construct new codes meant reducing a building to a "message" and its use to a "reading." Much of the current vogue for quotations of past architectural symbols proceeds from such simplistic interpretations.

In recent years, however, serious research has applied linguistic theory to architecture, adding an arsenal of selection and combination, substitution and contextuality, metaphor and metonymy, similarity and contiguity, following the terms of [Roman] Jakobson, [Noam] Chomsky, and [Émile] Benveniste. Although exclusively formalist manipulation often exhausts itself if new criteria are not injected to allow for innovation, its very excesses can often shed new light on the elusive boundaries of the "prison-house" of architectural language.[†] At the limit, this research introduces preoccupations with the notion of "subject" and with the role of "subjectivity" in language, differentiating language as a system of signs from language as an act accomplished by an individual.

The concern for the next term—structural stability—seems to have disappeared during the 1960s without anyone realizing or discussing it. The consensus was that anything could be built, provided you could pay for it. And concern with structure vanished from conference rosters and dwindled in architectural courses and magazines. Who, after all, wants to stress that the Doric pilasters of current historicism are made of painted plywood or that appliqué moldings are there to give metaphorical substance to hollow walls?

The progressive reduction of building mass over a period of centuries meant that architects could arbitrarily compose, decompose and recompose volumes according to formal rather than structural laws. Modernism's concern for surface effect further deprived volumes of material substance. Today, matter hardly enters the substance of walls that have been reduced to sheetrock or glass partitions that barely differentiate inside from outside. The phenomenon is not likely to be reversed, and those who advocate a return to "honesty of materials" or massive poché walls are often motivated by ideological rather than practical reasons. It should be stressed, however, that any concern over material substance has implications beyond mere structural stability. The materiality of architecture, after all, is in its solids and voids, its spatial sequences, its articulations, its collisions. (One remark in passing: some will say concern for energy conservation replaced the concern for construction. Maybe. Research in passive and active energy conservation, solar power, and water recycling, certainly enjoys a distinct popularity, yet does not greatly affect the general vocabulary of houses or cities.)

The sole judge of the last term of the trilogy, "appropriate spatial accommodation" is, of course, the body, your body, my body—the starting point and point of arrival of architecture. The Cartesian body-as-object has been opposed to the phenomenological body-as-subject and the materiality and logic of the body has been opposed to the materiality and logic of spaces. From the space of the body to the body-in-space—the passage is intricate. And that shift, that gap in the obscurity of the unconscious, somewhere between body and Ego, between Ego and Other....Architecture still has not begun to analyze the Viennese discoveries at the turn of the century, even if architecture might one day inform psychoanalysis more than psychoanalysis has informed architecture.

The pervasive smells of rubber, concrete, flesh; the taste of dust; the discomforting rubbing of an elbow on an abrasive surface; the pleasure of fur-lined walls and the pain of a corner hit upon in the dark; the echo of a hall—space is not simply the three-dimensional projection of a mental representation, but it is something that is heard, and is acted upon. And it is the eye that frames—the window, the door, the vanishing ritual of passage....Spaces of movement—corridors, staircases, ramps, passages, thresholds; here begins the articulation between the space of the senses and the space of society, the dances and gestures that combine the representation of space and the space of representation. Bodies not only move in, but generate spaces produced by and through their movements. Movements—of dance, sport, war—are the intrusion of events into architectural spaces. At the limit, these events become scenarios or programs, void of moral or functional implications, independent but inseparable from the spaces that enclose them. So a new formulation of the old trilogy appears. It overlaps the three original terms in certain ways, while enlarging them in other ways. Distinctions can be made between mental, physical, and social space, or, alternatively, between language, matter, and body. Admittedly, these distinctions are schematic. Although they correspond to real and convenient categories of analysis ("conceived," "perceived," "experienced"), they lead to different approaches and to different modes of architectural notation.

A change is evident in architecture's status, in its relationship to its language, its composing materials, and its individuals or societies. The question is how these three terms are articulated, and how they relate to each other within the field of contemporary practice. It is also evident that since architecture's mode of production has reached an advanced stage of development, it no longer needs to adhere strictly to linguistic, material, or functional norms but can distort them at will. And, finally, it is evident from the role of isolated incidents—often pushed aside in the past—that architecture's nature is not always found within building. Events, drawings, texts expand the boundaries of socially justifiable constructions.

The recent changes are deep and little understood. Architects-at-large find them difficult to accept, intuitively aware as they are that their craft is being drastically altered. Current architectural historicism is both a part of and a consequence of this phenomenon—both a sign of fear and a sign of escape. To what extent do such explosions, such changes in the conditions of the production of architecture *displace the limits of* architectural activities in order to correspond to their mutations?

THREE LIMITS

In Europe and in America, certain works are symptomatic of these recent changes. Variously decried for their lack of practicality, their iconoclasm or for being out of touch with architectural practice, they are both a positive consequence of, and a contributing factor in, these transformations. They are not a matter of "style" or "generation." They do not encourage imitators and blind followers by proposing "how to design a house," or "how to reconstruct the city," with simple rules and well-drawn instructions. On the contrary, they each attempt to push back the limits architecture bears upon itself.

Raimund Abraham's seminal series of architectural drawings explores clashes between boundaries, oppositions between inside and outside, void and solid, artifice and nature. The ironical "collisions" shown here play on both the power of mass and the sensuality of contrasts. Peter Eisenman's research on the nature of architecture and its language is fundamental; it both fills a gap and reaches for extremes. The excerpts from the transformational diagrams of *Houses* presented here are only a part of a large body of theoretical studies and writings. Kenneth Frampton's role as a critical historian emphasizes the social and cultural circumstances of architecture. His fragmentary polemic on the body covers a nearly "forbidden" ground in the field of architectural thought.

†   [Frederic Jameson, *Prison House of Language* (Princeton: Princeton University Press, 1972)—Ed.]

INTRODUCTION

Architecture and Limits III
Bernard Tschumi

In this, the final of three *ArtForum* essays, Bernard Tschumi returns to the issue of form and content, which in architecture is often framed as form versus function. The author states that neither modernism nor postmodern historicism (to which his hostility is evident in labeling it "a false polemic") has addressed the problem of function or "programmatic concerns." Both modernism and postmodernism are solely concerned with formal or stylistic manipulation, based on the conception of the architectural work as object: "Form still follows form; only the meaning and frame of reference differ."

After examining the discipline's response to the need for new building types in the nineteenth century, Tschumi describes a recourse to "mediating factors like ideal types." Among other things, this leads him to conclude that:

> there was no necessary causal relationship between function and a subsequent form, or between a given building type and a given use.

A most interesting comparison can be made to Peter Eisenman's editorial "Post-Functionalism," (ch. 1) to which Tschumi apparently refers in the opening paragraph. While Eisenman agrees with Tschumi's conclusion about the lack of connection between form and function (and has gone out of his way to test this in his work), in "Post-Functionalism," he asserts that increased programmatic complexity in the nineteenth century *ruled out* the use of types. Thus, for Eisenman, function dominated form, a situation which must be addressed by a truly modern architecture.

As Tschumi sees it, around 1980 function is rejected by "neomodernists" (including Eisenman) as a lingering part of the humanist tradition, and by postmodern historicists (who might be called "neohumanists") as being part of the modern tradition.

He says:

> Programmatic concerns have been dismissed as both remnants of humanism and as morbid attempts to resurrect now-obsolete functionalist doctrines.

This double rejection is motivated by the desire on both parts to elevate formalism and exclude social concerns from postmodern architecture's agenda. Eisenman, however, will argue that his motivation is to bring architecture back to its primary, internal concerns. (ch. 4.)

In opposition to these two formalist positions, Tschumi's critique seeks to replace notions of the nineteenth-century functional program with the idea of program accompanying a performance or an event. Tschumi suggests that one should conceive of architecture not as object (or *work*, in structuralist terms), but as an "interaction of space and events." He finds that the application of semiotics to architecture has exacerbated the habit of objectification of the singular work, while ignoring its complex "intertexuality."[1] Tschumi argues for architecture as a human activity, or as an open-ended *text*, in poststructuralist terms. Citing the example of pageants and spectacles, the author hopes to see the human body as central to questions of space. The experience of the moving body in space distinguishes architecture from art. The author more explicitly engages the body in "The Pleasure of Architecture." (ch. 13)

Tschumi's position as a poststructuralist is influenced by Michel Foucault (in adopting the idea of the "epistemological break," a break between discontinuous periods of knowledge) and by Jacques Derrida's deconstruction. The appeal of poststructuralism and deconstruction for him is that:

> they challenged the idea of a single unified set of images, the idea of certainty, and of course, the idea of an identifiable language.[2]

An identifiable language is not necessary, since he has stated that architecture does not illustrate thoughts. Tschumi asserts that architecture as illustration is but one of the many reductive interpretations which architecture must abandon to supercede the modern.

---

1   This idea is borrowed from Roland Barthes and Julia Kristeva: "intertexuality" is a web or network of relations between the components of a *sign*, or between an individual work and the works which precede or surround it, on which it relies for meaning.

2   Bernard Tschumi, "Six Concepts," in *Architecture and Disjunction* (Cambridge: MIT Press, 1994), 87.

BERNARD TSCHUMI

ARCHITECTURE AND LIMITS III

Program: a descriptive notice, issued beforehand, of any formal series of proceedings, as a festive celebration, a course of study etc. (...), a list of the items or "numbers" of a concert etc., in the order of performance; hence the items themselves collectively, the performance as a whole....[1]

An architectural program is a list of required utilities; it indicates their relations, but suggests neither their combination nor their proportion.[2]

To address the notion of the program today is to enter a forbidden field, a field architectural ideologies have consciously banished for decades. Programmatic concerns have been dismissed both as remnants of humanism and as morbid attempts to resurrect now-obsolete functionalist doctrines. These attacks are revealing in that they imply an embedded belief in one particular aspect of modernism—the preeminence of formal manipulation to the exclusion of social or utilitarian considerations, a preeminence that even current post-modernist architecture has refused to challenge.

But let us briefly recall some historical facts that govern the notion of the program. Although the eighteenth century's development of scientific techniques based on spatial and structural analysis had already led architectural theorists to consider use and construction as separate disciplines, and hence to stress pure formal manipulation, the program long remained an important part of the architectural process. Implicitly or explicitly related to the needs of the period or the state, the program's apparently objective requirements by and large reflected particular cultures and values. This was true of the Beaux Arts' "Stables for a Sovereign Prince" of 1739 and the "Public Festival for the

From *ArtForum* 20, no. 1 (September 1981): 40. Courtesy of the author and publisher.

Marriage of a Prince" of 1769. Growing industrialization and urbanization soon generated their own programs. Department stores, railway stations, and arcades were nineteenth-century programs born of commerce and industry. Usually complex, they did not readily result in precise forms, and mediating factors like ideal building types were often required, risking a complete disjunction between "form" and "content."

The Modern Movement's early attacks on the empty formulas of academicism condemned these disjunctions, along with the decadent content of most Beaux Arts programs, which were regarded as pretexts for repetitive compositional recipes. The concept of the program itself was not attacked, rather, the way it reflected an obsolete society. Instead, closer links between new social contents, technologies, and pure geometries announced a new functionalist ethic. At the first level, this ethic emphasized problem-solving rather than problem-formulating; good architecture was to grow from the objective problem peculiar to building, site, and client, in an organic or mechanical manner. On a second and more heroic level, the revolutionary urges of the futurist and constructivist avant-gardes joined those of early nineteenth-century utopian social thinkers to create new programs. "Social condensers," communal kitchens, workers' clubs, theaters, factories, or even *unités d'habitation* accompanied a new vision of social and family structure. In a frequently naive manner, architecture was meant to both reflect and mold the society to come.

Yet by the early 1930s in the United States and Europe, a changing social context favored new forms and technologies at the expense of programmatic concerns. By the 1950s modern architecture had been emptied of its early ideological basis, partially due to the virtual failure of its utopian aims. Architecture also found a new base in the theories of modernism developed in literature, art, and music. "Form follows form" replaced "form follows function," and soon attacks on functionalism were voiced by neo-modernists for ideological reasons, and by post-modernists for esthetic ones.

In any case, enough programs managed to function in buildings conceived for entirely different purposes to prove the simple point that there was no necessary causal relationship between function and subsequent form, or between a given building type and a given use. Among confirmed modernists, the more conventional the program, the better; conventional programs, with their easy solutions, left room for experimentation in style and language, much as Karl Heinz Stockhausen used national anthems as the material for syntactical transformations.

The academization of constructivism, the influence of literary formalism, and the example of modernist painting and sculpture all contributed to architecture's reduction to simple linguistic components. When applied to architecture, Clement Greenberg's dictum that content be "dissolved so completely into form that the works of art or literature cannot be reduced in whole or in part to anything but itself...subject matter or content becomes something to be avoided like a plague" further removed considerations of use. Ultimately, in the 1970s, mainstream modernist criticism, by focusing on the intrinsic qualities of autonomous objects, formed an alliance with semiotic theory to make architecture an easy object of poetics.

But wasn't architecture different from painting or literature? Could use or program be part of form rather than a subject or content? Didn't Russian Formalism differ from Greenbergian modernism in that, rather than banishing considerations of content, it simply no longer opposed form to content, but began to conceive of it as the *totality* of the work's various components? Content could be equally formal.

Much of the theory of architectural modernism (which, notably, emerged in the 1950s rather than in the 1920s) was similar to all modernism in its search for the specificity of architecture, for that which is characteristic of architecture alone. But how was such specificity defined? Did it include, or exclude use? It is significant that architectural postmodernism's challenge to the linguistic choices of modernism has never assaulted its value system. To discuss "the crisis of architecture" in wholly stylistic terms was a false polemic, a clever feint aimed at masking the absence of concerns about use.

While it is not irrelevant to distinguish between an autonomous, self-referential architecture that transcends history and culture and an architecture that echoes historical or cultural precedents and regional contexts, it should be noted that both address the same definition of architecture as formal or stylistic manipulation. Form still follows form; only the meaning and the frame of reference differ. Beyond their diverging esthetic means, both conceive of architecture as an object of contemplation, easily accessible to critical attention, as opposed to the interaction of space and events, which is usually unremarked upon. Thus walls and gestures, columns and figures are rarely seen as part of a single signifying system. Theories of reading, when applied to architecture, are largely fruitless in that they reduce it to an art of communication or to a visual art (the so-called single-coding of modernism, or the double-coding of postmodernism), dismissing the "intertextuality" that makes architecture a highly complex human activity. The multiplicity of heterogeneous discourses, the constant interaction between movement, sensual experience, and conceptual acrobatics refute the parallel with the visual arts.

If we are to observe, today, an epistemological break with what is generally called modernism, then it must also question its own formal contingency. By no means does this imply a return to notions of function versus form, to cause-and-effect relationships between program and type, to utopian visions, or to the varied positivist or mechanistic ideologies of the past. On the contrary, it means going beyond reductive interpretations of architecture. The usual exclusion of the body and its experience from all discourse on the logic of form is a case in point.

The *mise-en-scènes* of Peter Behrens, who organized ceremonies amidst the spaces of Josef Maria Olbrich's *Mathildenhoehe*; Hans Poelzig's sets for *The Golem*; László Moholy-Nagy's stage designs, which combined cinema, music, sets, and actions, freezing simultaneities; El Lissitsky's displays of electromechanical acrobatics; Oskar Schlemmer's gestural dances; and Konstantin Melnikov's "Montage of Attractions," which turned into real architectural constructions—all exploded the restrictive orthodoxy of architectural modernism. There were, of course, precedents—Renaissance pageants, Jacques-Louis David's revolutionary fêtes, and, later and more sinister, [Albert] Speer's Cathedral of Ice and the Nuremberg Rally.

More recently, departures from formal discourses and renewed concerns for architectural events have taken an imaginary programmatic mode.[3] Alternatively, typological studies have begun to discuss the critical "affect" of ideal building types that were historically born of function but were later displaced into new programs alien to their original purpose. In this last installment of a series of three, *Architecture and Limits* presents three architects[†] whose concerns for events, ceremonies, and programs suggest a possible distance vis-à-vis both modernist orthodoxy and historicist revival.

1   *Oxford English Dictionary.*

2   Julien Guadet, *Éléments et théorie de l'architecture* (Paris: 1909).

3   Such projects began to emerge during the past decade, and range from Superstudio's
     Ideal Cities to John Hejduk's Thirteen Towers of Canareggio.

†   [Tschumi, Rem Koolhaas, and Alan Plattus.—Ed.]

INTRODUCTION

Introduction: Notes Towards a Theory of
Architectural Disjunction
Bernard Tschumi

This brief essay integrates the deconstructionist
themes of displacement and dislocation with
Bernard Tschumi's design work. It served as an
introduction to Tschumi's method, synthesizing theory and design, and to the four projects which
were published with it in *Architecture and
Urbanism*. His continued interest in discovering
and working at the limits of architecture leads to
a strategy of disjunction: the deployment of trans-
formative operations such as compression, insertion, transference, superposition, distortion, and
de-centering. Disjunction leads to a rejection of
synthesis or totality and correlates with the emphasis on process in Peter Eisenman's writings. By
resisting the condition of stasis, Tschumi deliberately achieves critical, destabilizing relations of
conflict. Disjunctions are retained, for example,
between man/object, object/events, and
events/space.
    Another way in which Tschumi attempts to
expand the discipline of architecture is through
the transgression of its boundaries. (See
"Architecture and Limits I, II, III," this chapter.)
He imports the editing techniques of "dissolve"
and "montage" from film to challenge conventional graphic representations. By virtue of its temporal duration, film offers possibilities for narrative
and can present extraordinary relationships
between events and space. His Parc de la Villette
and its "cinematic promenade" have been highly
influential, both as a prize-winning international
competition entry and as a built part of the
Mitterand government's *"Grands Projets."*

BERNARD TSCHUMI

INTRODUCTION: NOTES TOWARDS A THEORY OF ARCHITECTURAL DISJUNCTION

ORDER

Any theoretical work, when "displaced" into the built realm, still retains its role within a general system or open system of thought. As in the theoretical projects *The Manhattan Transcripts*, 1981, and the current *Parc de la Villette*,[†] what is questioned is the notion of unity. As they are conceived, both works have no beginnings and no ends. They are operations, composed of repetitions, distortions, superimpositions, and so forth. Although they have their own internal logic—they are not aimlessly pluralistic—their operations cannot be described purely in terms of internal or sequential transformations. The idea of order is constantly questioned, challenged, pushed to the edge.

STRATEGIES OF DISJUNCTION

Although the notion of disjunction is not to be seen as an architectural concept, it has effects that are impressed upon the site, the building, even the program, according to the dislocative logic governing the work. If one were to define disjunction, moving beyond its dictionary meaning, one would insist on the idea of limit, of interruption. Both the *Transcripts* and *La Villette* employ different elements of a strategy of disjunction. This strategy takes the form of a systematic exploration of one or more themes: for example, frames and sequences in the case of the *Transcripts*, superimposition and repetition in that of *La Villette*. Such explorations can never be conducted in the abstract, *ex nihilo*; one works within the discipline of architecture, although with an awareness of other fields: literature, philosophy, or even film theory.

From *Architecture and Urbanism* no. 216 (September 1988): 13–15. Courtesy of the author and publisher.

LIMITS

The notion of the limit is evident in the practice of [James] Joyce, and [Georges] Bataille and [Antonin] Artaud, all of whom worked at the edge of philosophy and nonphilosophy, of literature and nonliterature. The attention paid today to Jacques Derrida's deconstructive approach also represents an interest in the work at the limit: concepts in the most rigorous and internalized manner, but also their analysis from without, so as to question what these concepts and their history hide, as repression or dissimulation. Such examples suggest that there is a need to consider the question of limits in architecture. They act as reminders (to me) that my own pleasure has never surfaced in looking at buildings, at the great works of history or the present of architecture, but, rather in dismantling them. To paraphrase Orson Welles: "I don't like architecture, I like making architecture."

NOTATION

The work on notation undertaken in *The Manhattan Transcripts* was an attempt to deconstruct the components of architecture. The different modes of notation employed were aimed at grasping domains that, though normally excluded from most architectural theory, are indispensable to work at the margins, or limits of architecture. Although no mode of notation, whether mathematical or logical, can transcribe the full complexity of the architectural phenomenon, the progress of architectural notation is linked to the renewal of both architecture and its accompanying concepts of culture. Once the traditional components have been dismantled, reassembly is an extended process; above all, what is ultimately a transgression of classical and modern canons should not be permitted to regress towards formal empiricism. Hence the disjunctive strategy used both in the *Transcripts* and at *La Villette*, in which facts never quite connect, and relations of conflict are carefully maintained, rejecting synthesis or totality. The project is never achieved, nor are the boundaries ever definite.

DISJUNCTION AND THE AVANT-GARDE

As Derrida points out, architectural and philosophical concepts do not disappear overnight. The once fashionable "epistemological break" notwithstanding, ruptures always occur within an old fabric that is constantly dismantled and dislocated in such a way that its ruptures lead to new concepts or structure. In architecture such disjunction implies that at no moment can any part become a synthesis or self-sufficient totality; each part leads to another, and every construction is off-balance, constituted by the traces of another construction. It could also be constituted by the traces of an event, a program. It can lead to new concepts, as one objective here is to understand a new concept of the city, of architecture.

If we were to qualify an architecture or an architectural method as "disjunctive," its common denominators would be the following:

Rejection of the notion of "synthesis" in favor of the idea of dissociation, of disjunctive analysis;

Rejection of the traditional opposition between use and architectural form in favor of a superposition or juxtaposition of two terms that can be independently and similarly subjected to identical methods of architectural analysis;

Emphasis placed, as a method, on dissociation, superposition, and combination, which trigger dynamic forces that expand into the whole architectural system, exploding its limits while suggesting a new definition.

The concept of disjunction is incompatible with a static, autonomous, structural view of architecture. But it is not anti-autonomy or anti-structure: it simply implies constant, mechanical operations that systematically produce dissociation (Derrida would call it *différance*) in space and time, where an architectural element only functions by colliding with a programmatic element, with the movement of bodies or whatever. In this manner, disjunction becomes a systematic and theoretical tool for the making of architecture.

†   [Now under construction.—Ed.]

INTRODUCTION

Architecture and the Problem of
the Rhetorical Figure
Peter Eisenman

This essay, from the Japanese magazine
Architecture and Urbanism, was originally presented as a lecture at Yale University on February 20,
1987. Peter Eisenman introduces his material with
a quote from Sigmund Freud, thereby announcing
his psychoanalytic orientation. The quote reflects on
the diachronic nature of the city of Rome, comparing it to the inscribed psyche of an individual.
Freud's analogy would certainly seem fertile to
Roland Barthes (in "Semiology and Urbanism") and
Aldo Rossi (in *The Architecture of the City*), for
whom the city is a repository for collective memory.
Eisenman returns to this idea towards the end of
the piece in proffering *trace*: a "condition of
absence [that] acknowledges the dynamic reality
of the living city." Trace (a concept borrowed from
Jacques Derrida's deconstruction) becomes part of
the perpetual, arbitrary process with which
Eisenman proposes to resist traditional goal- and
object-oriented design strategies. Process is more
specifically addressed in his earlier and more substantial essay, "The End of the Classical." (ch. 4)

Eisenman prepares his argument for the
"rhetorical figure" by reviewing the ground of
semiotic and structuralist assumptions with regard
to architecture. The rhetorical figure is a hybrid
form synthesizing presence and absence; it contains its own absence. It differs from what
Eisenman calls a "representational figure," which
refers to an absent thing. As an example,
Eisenman interprets Robert Venturi and Denise
Scott Brown's "duck" and "decorated shed"
notions, suggesting that the duck is representational, and the shed rhetorical. As a second example, he cites Michael Graves's work in pursuit of
a "figurative" architecture. Eisenman ascribes
"authority" to Graves's figures: "they are texts of
authority" which "work to narrow the suggestive
(or rhetorical) nature of the sign." He points out
that this narrowing of the linguistic *sign* separates
architectural postmodernism (which is classical or
traditional, as in Graves's case) from literary (poststructuralist) or philosophical postmodernism.

Eisenman sees limited inventive potential in Graves's use of traditional figures, and seeks instead to discover different, postmodern rhetorical figures. Proposing the notion of site as *palimpsest*, rhetorical figures may be used to reveal a repressed text (or self-conscious "fiction") of site-specific meanings. The site is thus analogous to a manuscript with visible traces of previous texts. Eisenman's design work builds on the site as layered, by using superposition. This process (also common in Bernard Tschumi's work) is the key to Eisenman's challenge to the notions of beginning and end, origin and destination.

PETER EISENMAN

ARCHITECTURE AND THE PROBLEM
OF THE RHETORICAL FIGURE

> Now let us, by a flight of imagination, suppose that Rome is not a human inhabitation, but a physical entity with a similarly long and copious past—an entity, that is to say, in which nothing that has once come into existence will have passed away and all the earlier phases of development continue to exist alongside the latest one.
> Sigmund Freud, "Civilization and its Discontents"

Sigmund Freud, in an unintended cultural repression, assumes later in the same text that "if we want to represent historical sequence in spatial terms we can only do it by juxtaposition in space....The same space," he says, "cannot have two different contents." But this is only true if we assume that architecture is place, time, and scale specific. What if this is not the case? What if this assumption merely represents five hundred years of a cultural repression known as Classical Architecture? What if it is possible to reinvent a Rome, a Rome free of these repressions, a Rome which is no longer place, time, and scale specific? But first, what is the nature of these repressions?

They assume the metaphysics of architecture (that is, shelter, aesthetics, structure, and meaning), and the vocabulary (elements such as columns, capitals, etc.) to have the status of natural law. The assumed factual nature of this assumption stems from the fact that it is the nature of architecture, unlike any other discipline, to establish center, to manifest presence, to be the agent of reality—bricks and mortar, shelter and function, house and home. Architecture, because it *is* bricks and mortar, holds out the promise of reality, authenticity, and genuine truth in a surreal world where truth is a managed item developed by committees, produced by writers, and sold by media spokesmen. Our only source of value today is a memory of value, a nostalgia; we live in a relativist world, yet

From *Architecture and Urbanism* no. 202 (July 1987): 16–22. Courtesy of the author and publisher.

desire absolute substance, something that is incontrovertibly real. Through its being, architecture has become, in the unconscious of society, the promise of this something real. But it is also true that architecture, more than any other discipline, must confront and dislocate this deeply-rooted perception in order to be. This is because, contrary to popular opinion, the status quo of dwelling does not define architecture. What defines architecture is the continuous dislocation of dwelling, in other words, to dislocate what it in fact locates.

To dislocate dwelling, architecture must continually reinvent itself. Architecture accomplishes this out of itself, out of the stuff that holds it together. Palladio did not know what a country villa was. He invented it out of architecture. One could almost say that architecture is the continuing invention of dwelling. It is the need to dislodge dwelling that has maintained architecture throughout history. It is the power of architecture's nature to center that renders its task to decenter and thus recenter so difficult.

Architecture creates institutions. It is a constructive activity. Architecture, by its very creation, is institutionalizing. So for architecture to be, it must resist what it must in fact do. In order to be, it must always resist being. It must dislocate without destroying its own being, that is, it must maintain its own metaphysic. This is the paradox of architecture. Thus in order to reinvent a site whether it be a city or a house, the idea of site must be freed from its traditional places, histories, and systems of meanings. This involves the dislocation of the traditional interpretation of its elements so that its figures can be read rhetorically as opposed to aesthetically or metaphorically. What does it mean to read rhetorically? What is a rhetorical figure?

Traditionally in language there is a relationship between a sign and what it stands for. For example, a cat, c-a-t, has a fixed relationship to an animal which walks around on four legs and meows. It is not a question of how the letters look. If you change the letters around from c-a-t to a-c-t, they are the same letters, but now it does not mean a four-legged animal. It means something else. So there is a fixed relationship within the structure of the letters and a fixed relationship between that particular fixed structure to an object. Now it has been suggested that it is possible to cut the fixed and supposedly immutable relationship between sign and signified. That is, the relationship which always has been, which is thought to be as much a natural law as architectural elements are to architecture. Cutting this relationship would produce what might be called free floating signs without necessary meanings or the necessary relationship to their object—cut from cultural, historical, accumulated meaning. Now the difference between literature and architecture is enormous. Linguistic signs are traditionally transparent. That means that with "cat" we do not look at the letters c-a-t and examine the relationship between the c and the a; we go right away to the four-legged animal. What literature tries to do is to dam up this transparency of signs. So that what the art of writing—poetry—attempts to do is make less transparent the relationship between the sign and the signified. Language can do this because it has a very elaborate syntax, that is, it can dam up the transparency and make the words opaque, giving them substance in themselves. Now (paradoxically) that substance is like a cutting. When you start to make words opaque, you start cutting the relationship between the sign and the signified. You cut or obscure or deny the easy flow from the word to its meaning. Jacques Derrida has suggested that traditionally, language suppresses the aesthetic in favor of the rhetorical.

Now in architecture, it is almost the reverse. The presence in the object is dominated by the aesthetic; the absence, or the rhetorical quality is repressed. Thus we do not have either an agreed-upon sign system or an elaborated grammar. In fact, architecture is perhaps the least representative of all the arts. In architecture, when you build a wall, not only is it really opaque, but its relationship to a signified is very difficult to articulate. A wall is a wall, it is not a word, it *is*, it is never *about*. It is the thing that the word "wall" refers to, it is the opposite condition of a word: words are transparent whereas walls are opaque. In this opacity, walls also have traditional meanings as elements of a thought-to-be immutable vocabulary of architecture. When Michael Graves says that what Peter Eisenman is doing is not architecture, he means that it is outside what he assumes to be the natural vocabulary of architecture. Outside of the traditional associative feelings about the content of a wall. If we want to make a wall more of a sign—that is, more rhetorical—we have to reduce its traditional opacity, that is its traditional elemental, structural, and aesthetic content. This requires the introduction of an absence in the is of architecture, an absence in its presence. Absence has been traditionally repressed by presence. This requires a strategy.

Let us go back to our words "cat" and "act" and suggest another relationship. If we add a third term, the verb "is," we have the forms "cat is" and "act is." Now, if we superpose them and produce a third form "cactis," it is a sign which does not mean anything in itself. While it is similar to "cactus," it does not in itself represent or suggest the plant or the desert. This process first fragments and recombines the fragments like a new word. There is both loss and gain in each transaction. The new form contains the loss of the prior forms as well as the loss of its own meaning. Therefore there is an absence. This is what I am calling provisionally a rhetorical figure. This is in order to distinguish the metaphorical figure which is both rhetorical but also representational, from what I define as a rhetorical figure. This is in reality a catachresis which is thus not representational as will be explained later. Now how does this operate in architecture? The representational figure stands for something outside. So there is also an absence. But this absence is about, it is outside, it is not contained within the *is*. The rhetorical figure, like the cactis, stands for its own absence—it does not refer outside—its own absence *is*. Architecture has always assumed that like language and like art, it has signs, i.e., that figuration is representational. But this idea of rhetorical figuration in architecture is not representational. A representational figure represents a thing in its absence. A rhetorical figure contains its absence, that is, it contains its openendedness.

The classical history of architecture is not without rhetorical figures, but this implicit rhetoric was always univocal, spoken in the classical language of architecture, understanding that rhetoric in itself is not culturally free. The attempt here is to loosen the culture of architecture from the monotony of classical architectural rhetoric, that is, to use the freedoms that architecture potentially makes available. In his use of the "duck" and the "decorated shed," Robert Venturi actually made this attempt to distinguish between representational rhetorical, although he did not explicitly define it as such. A duck is a representational figure; the decorated shed a rhetorical figure. Venturi actually initiated post-modern historicizing in architecture by condemning representational ducks. This is because the rhetorical decorated shed uses (or represents) the traditional vocabulary of architecture.

In Graves, there is a rhetorical and a representational aspect of his figures. Graves's rhetorical figures differ from mine in that he assumes that the vocabulary of architecture is the vocabulary of architecture. His work is similar to the traditional literary aspects of rhetoric (that is, it is rhetorical in a traditional representational mode). Traditional architecture has by its very nature been writing one text of authority—that is, its reality was seen as history or aesthetic in an attempt to reduce anxiety. Graves's figures are texts of authority. What Graves does not acknowledge is that columns or capitals did not always exist in the conventional vocabulary of architecture. They were invented out of the rhetorical potential of architecture.

Now today, Graves's work presents a very interesting case because while it is artfully presented to look like invention, in the assumption of the givenness of the column and the capital, that is in the givenness of the vocabulary of architecture, he in fact works to end the possibility of invention. This is because the representational figure, like its predecessor, the abstract figure, works to narrow the suggestive (or rhetorical) nature of the sign.

What one is arguing thus far:

1) That postmodernist impulse in architecture quite rightly restored figuration.

2) In doing so, it copied the idea of figuration as a linguistic invocation; that figuration was aesthetically, rather than rhetorically, based.

3) That when its figural sign was rhetorically based, as in the case of Graves, it was done within and accepting the traditional and elemental vocabulary of architecture (i.e. columns, beams, walls, doors). It assumes this to be natural.

4) Thus what we know as postmodern architecture is not postmodernist in any conventional linguistic or literary (or even philosophical) sense. It is merely another kind of classical or traditional figuration. Thus one must now search for a postmodernist rhetorical figure in architecture which is not emarginated or repressed.

The idea of the rhetorical figure which is being proposed here is rhetorical in two senses. First, because it writes texts other than the approved texts of architecture. Second, because it writes texts other than texts of presence. That is, other than texts of elemental scale, original value, and aesthetic or metaphorical meaning.

In my proposal for rhetorical figures, architecture is no longer seen as merely aesthetic or functional elements, but rather as an *other* grammatical counter, proposing an alternate reading of the idea of site and object. In this sense, a rhetorical figure will be seen to be inherently contextual in that the site is treated as a deeply scored palimpsest. But traditional contextualism is representational and analytic, treating place as a physical presence known as a culturally determined idea containing powerful symbolic and evocative meanings. The analogic or rhetorical, rather than analytic, character of this process dislocates site implications from their culturally predetermined meanings by superposing two old contents to create a new content. In the resulting rhetorically, as opposed to aesthetically, structurally, or historically determined figuration, there is the revelation in the site of a repressed text. This text suggests that there are other meanings which are site-specific by virtue of their pre-existence, however latent, within the context.

For example, traditionally an axis represented a linear progression in time, a continuous and indifferent movement between two (or more) points which in themselves contain meaning and relate to each other in a hierarchical way. Through the process of superposition, elements of such an axial progression are dislocated continuously, appearing at once at a different scale and in a different place. By superposing the endpoints of any three different length segments, and thus making them the same length, we reveal their analogous relationships as endpoints of different segments of an axis. When these segments become the same length, they obviously become different scales. This in turn dislocates the traditional notion of scale as given by the human body or the human eye. Each of these segments now lose their real dimension, location, place, and time; ultimately, the whole notion of the axis as a form bound to linear time, hierarchy, and continuity is subverted. More importantly, because elements along each of these axes are relocated, they begin to also superpose on other elements to reveal unexpected correspondences which in their former reality would have remained unintelligible. What is revealed from the initial superpositions cannot be predicted. These are the so-called "repressed texts" that are found by reading these new rhetorical figures. Superpositions result in a dislocation of origin and destination, of time and space. By incorporating in any site the assemblage from disparate but analogous elements of other sites, the two figures occupy origin and destination contemporaneously. At the same time, movement along an axis toward a destination results in a return to origin. The misreading suggested by these figures hints at other misreadings of place. In this way, the idea of place is both reinforced and denied. While new places are created the traditional notion of place is undercut because each place is actually many places at once. The result is a text which displaces the traditional notion of time and space. It denies traditional and privileged ideas of context and aesthetic presence. It recognizes that absence is an essential condition of a rhetorical figure, but not absence as the opposite site of presence, rather absence in presence (the only constant truth now about the idea of a thing is that it is not the thing itself, and therefore, contains the presence of the absence of the thing). Any site contains not only presences, but the memory of previous presences and the immanences of a possible presence. The physical difference between a moving thing (dynamism) and a still one (stasis) is that the moving one contains the trace of where it has been and where it is going. The introduction of this trace, or condition of absence acknowledges the dynamic reality of the living city.

This process assembles this repressed text as a fiction. These rhetorical figures are fictional because while the elements of the site seem to be in their original position, that is, they seem to be located according to their previous condition of formal structure (axes and events at the beginning, middle, and end of such axes), they in fact are not. Origin and destination are perceived contemporaneously while movement toward the destination results in a return to origin. The perception at one point of all the elements of the progression, rearranged in scale and distance dislocates the relationship between time and space. In the same way, one might proceed along the axis encountering the same elements several times. Time and space, form and figure are thus collapsed as interdependent entities, space becomes independent of time (actual and historical), and space (more precisely, place and locus) becomes independent of form. This allows the conception of these elements, time, space, place, form, figure, in a system, which contains the possibility of its own contradiction. The meaning of space of time is freed from a symbolized representation: the definition of time as linear or circular, and of space as dynamic or static, now has no meaning in the traditional sense. The system of meaning (cultural structure) of a form is denied without denying the form: but now the forms in themselves have no transcendental or *a priori* meaning. They are cut off from their former givenness. The meaning is in the relationship; the architecture is between the signs. These seeming conditions of presence make these analogies coexistent with their precedents and yet suspends them in a condition of absence. It dislocates the conceptual essence of their previous typical structures (hierarchy, time, space, place, etc.). The elements are now devoid of their "original" meaning, they are not embedded in culture, history, place, scale, or time. They are both the "new" and the "old," now timeless, place-less, and spaceless in terms of scale, distance, and direction. This means that their form and figure do not relate directly to an inevitable structure of time and place.

This repressed text is a fiction which recognizes its own fictive condition. In its way, it begins to acknowledge the fictional quality of reality and the real quality of fiction. Culture, history, and ultimately architecture are not fixed and merely additive, but are a continual process of reiteration and simultaneous dislocation which at every moment modifies the previous instant of meaning and structure.

INTRODUCTION

Derrida and Beyond
Robert Mugerauer

A philosopher and urban planning professor, Robert Mugerauer presents an introduction to and explication of the ideas of Jacques Derrida, and looks at several architects whose work is affected by deconstruction. This essay in *Center*, the journal of the University of Texas School of Architecture, was originally a lecture for "Buildings and Reality: A Symposium on Architecture in the Age of Information" held in Austin in 1986. Of the conference participants, Karsten Harries, Peter Eisenman, and Anthony Vidler are represented in various chapters of this anthology.

Mugerauer's essay supports a phenomenological line of resistance (focused on *place*) to deconstruction's positing of the lack of objective reality. (ch. 9–12) Harries, another philosopher, also represented the phenomenological position at the symposium. Influenced by Martin Heidegger, both Mugerauer and Harries maintain that the authenticity of *dwelling* is powerful enough to overcome the reasoning of Derrida. The symposium thus functioned as a platform for showcasing these two prominent adversarial positions in contemporary theory.

Mugerauer situates Derrida's deconstruction as a continuation of Nietzsche's nihilist project: dispensing with the pursuit of an ultimate reality, or objective truth, to be revealed. In fact, deconstruction presents the radical idea that there is no permanent reality to be known, and thus, all truth can be revealed as error. This has challenging implications for the task of interpretation. According to Derrida, interpretation is not a search for truth, but an activity of *displacement* ("a violent situating of difference"), aiming to unseat cultural dominants. In particular, this involves scrutinizing the *oppositions* (such as male/female, nature/culture, science/art) which are perpetuated by and sustain culture, "by periodically elevating one binary term and suppressing the other."

Although his own position still relies on the notion of presence (besieged by deconstruction as the basis of metaphysical thought), Mugerauer understands deconstruction's critical possibilities. The deconstructive process exposes cultural "fictions" to prevent empowerment based on prejudice, such as ethnocentrism or sexism. In the realm of architecture, this displacement might take the form of inverting the domination of culture over architecture, implicit in the widely received Idea that the built world must *represent* culture. Proposals by the architects included in this chapter and by Derrida suggest a desire to move beyond presenting or representing anything. Their alternative is to privilege process over object (terms common to Eisenman and Bernard Tschumi), allowing buildings to be interpreted and used as critical *events*. But with his emphasis on place and authenticity, and presumably stability, Mugerauer finds these process-oriented proposals Inadequate

ROBERT MUGERAUER
DERRIDA AND BEYOND

What do buildings and reality have to do with one another as we enter the last phase of the modern era? We might suppose that buildings themselves, unlike, say, stories, are quintessentially real, that they have a meaning we can discover, or that they embody something you can count on. But over the last 100 years, a line of Postmodern theorists and critics have contended that such "naive" beliefs misconstrue the situation. Indeed, French philosopher Jacques Derrida now appears to be completing the project that Frederick Nietzsche began: the nihilistic and subjectivistic devaluation and annulment of what traditionally has been taken as the truth about reality.

According to the now dominant view, our culturally built world is a desire that imposes itself as a false comfort and oppression. *Our posturing takes the form of pretending that there is some permanent transcendental-metaphysical "reality" to be known, whereas there is not.* Consequently, since access to any objective, privileged meaning is illusory, philosophical or scientific truth is unmasked as a kind of error.

Art alone suffices to retain and enhance the power we desire to unfold for ourselves, while simultaneously freeing us from the tyranny of deceptions of "objectivity." Therefore, architecture, as an embodiment of will and meaning, can function both to avoid the error of posturing values and to prescribe for itself the environment that increases our power and satisfaction. For instance, the architectural gestures of Peter Eisenman, Coop Himmelblau, Emilio Ambasz, and I. M. Pei are Postmodern and radical precisely because they *deconstruct* "naive" assumptions about buildings and reality.

The question, then, of the relation of buildings and reality becomes the question of whether Postmodern architectural processes and buildings can escape the realm of

From *Buildings and Reality: Architecture in the Age of Information, Center* 4 (1988): 66–75. Courtesy of the author and publisher.

reality-as-convention by becoming unreality and, in some sense, free. Or, insofar as they successfully embody new conventions of discourse, will they inevitably arc back to pose as new realities?

THE SITUATION

Perhaps more than any other contemporary thinker, Jacques Derrida points a way to architectural deconstruction as a situational strategy.[1] According to Derrida, Western culture is built on the assumption that there are intelligible first grounds or causes. In its most powerful form, the first principle has been called *presence*: the enduring of what is present to us. We proceed from a series of seemingly primal dimensions that have logical and metaphysical priority: *presence* vs. absence; *being* vs. beings; *identity* vs. difference; *truth* vs. fiction; *life* vs. death. Our culture unfolds as the development of these privileged dimensions.

Playing out the critique of the Western metaphysical tradition to an extreme, Derrida contends that the very foundational dimensions or concepts noted above are themselves nothing more than strategies that enable us to assume and act as if the world were intelligible. By means of metaphysics, the West has concealed from us its own unintelligibility, its own fictive character.

Derrida argues that there is no transcendental reality or meaning and thus these privileged dimensions only feign sovereignty. Though such reality and meaning—and our knowledge of them—would appear to govern our science and philosophy, our arts and technology, they are unable to provide any foundation at all. Derrida points to the rupture effected in the discourse of our time which discloses a destructive displacement. Our Western enterprise has no viable center, even while one is absolutely necessary. Our need and wish for objective reality has led to such fictional namings as "substance" and "God."

What metaphysics conceals is that it rests on a supposition; the desired objective center is achieved only insofar as a more primal situation is concealed. A more fundamental, but complex, *difference* ("*différance*") is suppressed and concealed by the dominating metaphysics. Derrida holds that difference itself—the binary tensed difference or pairing of presence/absence, Being/beings, identity/difference—is what makes possible the seeming priority of only one member of each pair, of only one dimension (for example, presence, Being or identity). This *différance* is primal but is no ground in itself; it necessarily has no origin or end but is just continuing difference.

"Différance," as Derrida uses it, has two senses. It means differ and defer. To *differ* means to be spatially separate (nothing, not even the present or consciousness, is self-present or identical; there is no original identity). To *defer* means to temporally separate (nothing ever is wholly present; even the present is always delayed). Since what we take to be objective reality is fundamentally spatial and temporal—think of what we mean by the built environment, for example—Derrida is claiming that there is no moment when anything is given as itself, in full self-present identity; there is always a gap, an absence in the heart of reality. Indeed, it is this *difference* which is primal.

Metaphysics erases the primal difference in order to suppress absence, beings, death, and so on; that is, in order to provide us with a false comfort, both in the most rigorous activities of high culture and in the everydayness within which we are submerged.

Derrida contends that we need to face up to the dangers of living a sham; we need to confront the unintelligibility and non-decidable nature of the world. The false comfort of the illusion of what appears to be established and unchangeable should give way to scrupulous honesty about the situation. In short we need to be liberated. Derrida calls the freeing technique *deconstruction*, which aims to show the fictive nature of these constructs which attempt to transcend and regulate. *To be liberated, we would need to deconstruct the relationships of the built environment and culture, since the built environment and culture are built things; that is, our culturally built world is a sham of social, historical embodiments of the metaphysics of presence.*

BUILT THINGS

But if there is no objective reality, what about things and buildings, for example? Are there no things in themselves, no primary facts that are given to be understood? Strategically, Derrida is not so much interested in the arguments as to whether objects exist independently as he is in exploring how nothing exists as *simply and wholly* present to be understood.

We might suppose that a house or city were an objective reality that "governs" the signifying words we use to refer to them or even the whole structure of interpretive texts. But that is too simple; it is an example, according to Derrida, of the metaphysical sham—supposing that a referred-to house has a metaphysical priority. Given the principle of difference (that is, that absence always comes with presence), we can see that what we conveniently call a thing is itself a sign or referent where there is no final identity or authoritatively determining presence. What we call a house has its sense or meaning in a whole web of references. Actually, the entire world (including all things and buildings) is, for Derrida, *a text.*

> ...the world is a texture of traces which exist autonomously as "things" only as they refer to or relate to each other. They are therefore "signs" in that, like signs, their "being" always lies elsewhere (because a sign is always the sign of something else; it cannot refer to something other....No entity...has a unique being...apart from the web of relations and forces in which it is situated. The thing itself always escapes.[2]

We suppose we understand the meaning of a picture of pyramids by visiting the pyramids themselves. But when we do so, the pyramids are not fully present to us; we know their original meaning is lost to us, only partially guessed at. We try to recover that original meaning by referring to other artifacts or documents that tell of the originary, grounding act of the pharaoh or even the gods. But without those documents the pyramids would be monuments whose original meaning is lost. Thus cut off from the present, the past would be absent—held onto only by webs of language. Any built structure is this way: in itself it is partially absent since it is kept present and meaningful only by the web of meaning or discourse we weave around it and onto which we try to hold.

LANGUAGE

The question of the character of building and things leads, then, for Derrida, to language. To interpret things requires an interpretation of language, not only because we interpret things by using language but because things and world are themselves webs of signs.

What is language? Tradition holds that language, or some language, has access to an ultimately grounding reality. This would occur, for example, in philosophy or the sciences (which make possible engineering and architecture). Indeed, our Western tradition depends on this claim. But Derrida holds that the traditional assertion—that language represents objective reality—is a problematic maneuver that itself creates the illusion that a non-linguistic objective realm is mirrored in language.

Difference in its linguistic mode would show that sign and signified always differ (the present sign is a sign of what is absent—a missing presence) and involve delay (the deferred is a supposed ontological ground of the sign). That is, the fundamental position for Derrida is that sign and signified never coincide, nor are they given together. Signifiers never coincide with any transcendent signified thing or concept: in principle, there are no self-identical things or concepts. This means that the difference and delay never stop. The signifiers go in an endless chain.

Consequently, language is a closed infra-referential system of signs whose meanings are constituted by their place in historical systems of differences. Entire systems are unstable, shifting and drifting into obscurity. For example, according to Derrida, because the basic binary character of the total web of differences is all but obscured, it is in vain that we try to understand nature without culture or theory separate from practice. All we have to understand, interpret and live within is the endless web of differences of historically masked systems of signifiers. We cannot go outside of language to establish an orderly ground or center; there is nothing outside of discourse. Honesty, Derrida insists, requires a *decentering*.

CULTURE

We might suppose, in saying that all meaning is referential and that we are inescapably caught within language, that Derrida claims that all meaning is cultural—a standard kind of relativism. Actually he takes a much more radical approach. His claim is that 1) culture *per se* is a posture, its authority and accomplishments all maneuvers with no basis, and 2) although this is an unavoidable sham, there is no alternative.

Culture sustains itself and proceeds by periodically elevating one binary term and suppressing the other. The historical process of imposing honorific concepts in the name of presence and identity, subsequently to substitute them, *is* our culture.

This also is to say that, for all our grim seriousness in imposing and enforcing dominant terms and consequential practices, culture is merely the play (the going on with no ground) of all differentiated relationships. *Recognition of decentered situations, then, leads to free play.* We extend, self-consciously now, the free play of signification. As we realize how the signified is a fiction, not meaningful except as different from the sign, we can free ourselves from the illusion of objective referents and also see that the sign need not—cannot—take its place. So the signifier is not a meaningful identity in itself either; neither signified nor sign as final signification need to be held on to. *We are liberated into the free play of signs.*

INTERPRETATION

At this point, we can see how Derrida would claim that all we have is interpretation. We are imprisoned in vast historical systems of language and prior interpretation. Since illusory attempts to know objective reality need in all honesty to be rejected, we can be open only to new possible references, that is, to participating self-consciously in the free-play of differences. With no prospect of arriving at any thing like final, definitive, "true" interpretation, our interpretation always remains open and underway and needs to become an affirmation of the play of signification.

Derrida's interpretation, then, is not a theory—theory is pointless. Rather, it is an activity. It is a strategy meant to free us from the tyranny of traditional metaphysical interpretation and to overcome the belief in a temporal origin or original which we can recover.

The tactic is to find ways into earlier and other interpretations, contexts and concealments so as to undo the imposition and concealment, that is, to expose the differences. We can do this by finding flaws in the metaphysical construction, marginal cases, exceptions, undecided, or ambiguous points in the texts (built environments) themselves.

Derrida holds that texts undercut themselves: since the imposition of the master term depends on the supposition of its binary, one would expect to find rifts and traces of what is hidden. These flaws or fissures are exploited.

Derrida's deconstruction proceeds by way of *displacement,* a strategy which is a violent situating of difference. The fundamental move in displacement is to reverse the relationship of binary terms and call into question the preceding system. For example, whereas in the West the binary pair "signified/signifier" has been hidden insofar as priority has been given to the "signified" as the objective and transcendent reality, which is followed by the subsequent and dependent "signifier," we have seen that Derrida up-ends the relationship of the two, explaining the signified as absent (different from the present signifier and always delayed). That is, the signified is itself a signifier. Thus *the traditionally subservient term becomes the dominant one for interpretation of the other, and differance is momentarily emphasized (although not restored).*

Each displacement leads to others in the system. Since all meaning is infra-referential and since fissures in a text indicate the opening of an intervening text, the displacement once begun, spreads systematically. Since, as we have seen, the interpretation of all systems of signifiers is nothing except another system, there is inherent violence to the dominant tradition, which pretends to elucidate things with signs. Derrida would interrupt that pretense.

This is a process of displacing or dislodging any culturally dominant element and, even more radically, of removing the seeming ground for traditional understanding by not recognizing the master term as such, seeing it instead as a special case of what was excluded or outside the dominant system. *The strategy is to subvert the system of sham meaning and operation, to refuse the falsely comforting reconciliations or identities by which the tradition has swallowed difference.* This displacement of the metaphysics of presence is nothing less than a reversal and dislodging of these traditional hierarchies of power.

Note, however, that Derrida is not claiming or attempting to *destroy* the center or dominant terms or to end the metaphysical tradition: the fiction of a center and dominance by some terms is necessary and unavoidable if we are to have or be a culture.

[Derrida] does not attempt to put an end to fiction for he does not think that there is anything other than fictions, contingencies, alterable configuration of the code of respectability—but only to dispel the ring of illusion which we weave around them.[3]

What matters is situating the binaries (for example, consciousness and the material, nature and culture) and especially the dominance of one term in the large linguistic system, thereby allowing it to continue to function but without illusion or the attendant harm of empowerment (ethnocentrism, sexism, totalitarianism). The objection that such a view of interpretation is skeptical, if not cynical, is met with Derrida's claim that it simply is scrupulous, albeit disconcerting, honesty.

To be liberated from the delusion of false comforts, we would need to deconstruct the relation of the built environment and culture since both buildings and cultures are man-made things. Culture and the built environment form a fundamental binary difference (as do nature and culture). Clearly the binary has been worked out so we understand culture as the dominant term: culture, we hold, is what makes the built environment possible, even necessary, in the first place. The built environment is but one of many aspects of culture and is meant to be of service to culture.

To deconstruct the binary, we could explore the inversion of the terms, seeing how culture erases its difference from the built by pretending it is not itself something built; culture does this by positing itself as generative and as an autonomous transcendent object to be studied by the human sciences. But *culture can be seen as a special case of built form and environment. A deconstruction through architecture would involve exploiting the fiction that cultural presence is instantiated in building by showing how the built-up undercuts or discloses fissures in the goals of presence and identity desired by culture.*

Here we need an interpretation of the built environment as a displacement of the cultural desire for presence as a means to deconstructing the relation of built form and culture. Of course, this involves other differences; the larger scope of differences between nature and the built, and between nature and culture.

Certainly Derrida's approach is central to understanding modern and Postmodern architecture. Postmodern architecture in particular was a deconstruction of our traditional understanding of design, of forms and prototypes, and in some ways of the act of building. What we need now, and are approaching is the deconstruction of architecture itself.

EISENMAN

One case of recent architectural deconstruction worth studying is Peter Eisenman's "Museum for California State University at Long Beach" project. Indeed, over the years Eisenman has been the theoretician and designer who most explicitly works with Derrida's ideas, contending that reality is what we reassemble after dissembling the illusion of the beliefs, stories, and norms of the traditional past. The ordinary world of Western common sense and science, for Derrida and for Eisenman, is precisely the realm to be unmasked as unreality, the posturing of prior fiction as supposed reality. The only authentic gesture would be the acknowledgment and announcement of fiction.

As Eisenman explains his process, deconstructive architecture proceeds by a continual set of "dislocations," to produce a place that is no place, no object, and no shelter, and that has no scale, no time. At Long Beach, design is begun by deconstructing super-imposed texts or fictions: traces of water at the site (river, coastline, channel), traces of the fault-line, traces of the first white settlement of 1849, and of the first land division in 1949. Transferring each of the tracings, or mapped fictions, to a computer makes possible the swift rotation and rescaling of all superpositions, until one hits upon the "best" combination. In the final steps, the building is filled in, not as a mass or set of fixed, functional elements, but as a continuation of the game. The old architecture is gone, and in its stead one has a new formal ploy, uncertainty, and enigmatic meaning.

Clearly we are considering the *power* of artists to conjure appearances, and, indeed, Eisenman acknowledges that the issue is one of this kind of control. The object is the transformation of self and environment from the vantage point of the culture of architects, not that of patrons or users. We may never know whether Eisenman's Museum for California State University is livable or not.

But the deconstruction and transformation of ordinary reality is not totally accomplishable. Eisenman's work, as a series of projects, attests to that; each settles for being unsettling or, if built, uncomfortable. By choosing one possibility he lets go of the others, of course. Is a stronger position necessary to adequately demonstrate the illusion that Derrida says is reality? Is it possible to keep the choices always open and difference perpetually presented?

COOP HIMMELBLAU

Coop Himmelblau (Wolfgang Prix and Helmut Swiczinsky) can be understood as advocating a more radical position—leaving in tension what cannot be settled: the modern urban experience.[4] For architects and users alike, the openness and freedom is to be maintained not only in the creative process of design but in the building's inhabitation.

Insistently stripping away the pretense of safe, completed architecture requires a continuous mode of deconstruction expressed formally, and the refusal to assert determinate spaces for proper programmed use. Prix and Swiczinsky strive to burst through illusion and pretense to stay free.

Freedom involves continuing tension, both in the buildings and, prior to that, in the design process, which would need to accept and sustain the tension resulting from unresolved openness and choice. Coop Himmelblau's working procedure maps Derrida's account of the generative power of language. The partners proceed from prolonged discussions that end when, in one communicative act, rough sketches are produced and a model straightforwardly follows. From the Word comes Design. The design itself is an enormously complex superimposition of multiple views and cross-sections, where the multiform ambiguities of the design and sketch are rendered now as structural components, now as complex, alternative flowpaths and spaces for possible users. "Resolution" lies not in reduction, but in discerning valid, still-open choices.

The inner logic of Atelier Bauman, for example, refuses resolution, holding off by enduring the tension—a logic manifested in the taut envelope, facade, and exterior, which gives neither one way or another. The tension of multiple dimensions, of future choices, are held. And because the entire building so vigorously holds onto openness and freedom, accepting their tensions, the overall effect is powerful. The feeling of distortion and "twist" is like the experience of a sheet of winter ice groaning under pressure, ready to shatter and pile upon itself.

In their attempt to locate architecture at the center of the experience of our unresolvable situation, Coop Himmelblau is held back, in part, by an ideology it would need to transcend in order to succeed. With Derrida, in the modern voice, the architects insist that "there is no truth"; yet, simultaneously, they affirm the acceptance of the city as it is and advocate representing a tattered urban reality. The insistence on urban industrial materials—corrugated metal doors and interior wall panels, steel and chrome rails, concrete and asphalt, in The Red Angel discloses at its center, as Derrida held it would, that just when we admit there is no truth or resolution or intrinsic beauty, we inevitably desire them the more, and find them.

Coop Himmelblau, despite its best efforts, cannot sustain itself with the mere destruction of convention without, in the end, reconstituting space according to conventions of its own—as Eisenman also found. A more sophisticated and more adequate deconstruction is called for, one that still would emphasize differences with previous conventions and yet also would assume responsibility for a reassembly that might serve as a new, and perhaps more necessary, cultural fiction. In short, true deconstruction requires both displacement of posturing superiority and its replacement with a new, habitable, if equally fictional, reconstruction, rather than an endless, frozen posture of locked struggle.

AMBASZ

Emilio Ambasz's Lucile Halsell Conservatory in San Antonio[5] challenges a cultural posture—the relation of culture and nature—by a series of logico-spatial inversions rather than evident attack. In addition, he goes on to reinstate the new built complex as an autonomous cultural realm with its own conventions.

The official text describing the project[6] does not disclose its radical nature. Stressing continuity with local places, the new complex is said to be integrated with the surrounding hills and climate and with the community's interest in ceremony and processions (a religious allusion). Then, too, having it all ways, the project announces that it maintains and enhances the diversity already there.

Yet, even a first glance at the building complex makes it clear that the Conservatory is very different from the rest of the existing garden complex. One obvious way in which the new project might be said to "fit" would be as an element in a heterogeneous garden. The juxtaposition of different forms in a collective "garden" is not unusual. The unity, parallel to that of a fair, comes from the idea of "themes," a "variety of garden elements"— formal gardens (rose, herb, old-fashioned, sacred, for the blind), Texas natural settings (Hill Country, East Texas Pineywoods, South Texas Plains), Gazebo Hill Overlook, Outdoor Theater, Xeriscape, and Conservatory Complex. At this mundane level of ensemble, the Conservatory does work: surely it is a formal *tour de force*, a most "different" and curious building. The building complex and its plants surely will be a major attraction.

But Ambasz's project operates at two deeper levels. The Conservatory reverses the dominant concepts and forms of the traditional garden culture and, finally, asserts its own reversal. That is, the building and its discourse constitute a new fictive text that deconstructs its predecessors and establishes itself as the replacement.

In a first decentering, the identity of a botanical garden is undone. It seems that Ambasz has proposed a building complex intelligible as a continuation of the tradition of greenhouses. In the West, we have used technology to cultivate exotic and interesting plants in hostile climates (or during hostile times of the year). Glass and glazing have long been techniques to overcome the natural processes that otherwise would prevent our cultivation and enjoyment of the vegetative realm. With the greenhouse, we assert culture over nature.

Ambasz, however, does not continue this tradition of straightforward domination of culture over nature. He plays with the relationship, establishing the difference between his garden and the traditional forms of greenhouse, rather than identity and continuity.

In Ambasz's Conservatory, the earth itself becomes a container, protecting plants from the sun. Here the traditional relationship is unexpectedly inverted: hot sun, not cold earth, is the threat; earth, not glass, is the container. In Derrida's terms, Ambasz replaces the traditional identities of greenhouse-garden and the presence of sun with the difference of his building project and the reduction or "absence" of sun. Of course, nature does not *re*place culture in Ambasz's Conservatory. But nature (earth) temporarily *dis*places culture (greenhouse), only to be immediately transformed, in turn, into its own opposite: nature becomes a technological element or instrument used to culturally overcome nature—that is, itself. But unlike nature transformed as sand is to glass, *this earth is transformed and nonetheless appears left as earth: a deft double deconstruction accomplishes the final semblance of matters unchanged.*

A second displacement is carried out in regard to the cultural norms, or typology, of the botanical garden. Again, the official text describing the project asserts "continuity" with the surrounding regional forms, referring, for example, to the "garden patio or courtyard characteristics of Texas." But the new addition bears no resemblance to what is already there or anything Texan. No unity is promoted. The vaunted courtyard form strongly contrasts with the already existing gathering place on the site. The open, grassed area articulated by the limestone walls from the old reservoir of the 1890s and a wooden arbor have a simplicity and power of entirely different order. Here, the new complex's contrast and discontinuity with local tradition could not be stronger. Similarly, the evocation of cultural tradition, with its religious overtones, is not borne out in the building. The text tells us the Conservatory is a "secular temple" with a strong sense of procession. What identifications are evoked? The strong Roman Catholic tradition of the area? The earlier indigenous religious traditions with their pyramids? Or the Egyptian pyramids, as quoted in the Palm House?

Not unexpectedly, on closer inspection, the Conservatory has no correlate or final grounding referent. The building-as-text means nothing by way of reference to, or continuation of, objective natural or cultural tradition. What the building and its discourse accomplish first appears to be an opening to some new mode of building; the signified is deferred and the building remains as a pure sign.

Through its double inversion and assertion of difference, Ambasz's Conservatory establishes its own fictive meaning, hence, the eerie effect of the models—the outward look of desert, palm, and temple; the inward realm of oasis and tropical vegetation. These images of the Conservatory's new forms in the landscape recall projects for outer space, such as the terraforming of NASA or Ettore Sottsass's "High-Tech Star" or "Amphitheater brought down to Earth." What postures as contextualism for the Southwest instead accomplishes a new earthscape, not on another planet but at the very site which the building's displacements have cleared for itself. In spinning its own tale, the Conservatory establishes itself as a unique place to be.

Ambasz's Conservatory as architectural fiction, then, goes beyond the work of Peter Eisenman and Coop Himmelblau cited here. It not only dissembles the traditional presences and identities upon which it is built, but, forsaking the attempt to remain a totem of destruction, it completes a needed assertion of new cultural presence and identity.

Architecture proceeds as deconstruction by remaining a strategy in process, not by denying habitable space or interpretable symbolism. The deepest architectural deconstruction, then, can dissemble past architectural and cultural prototypes and end with a subtly different, but disturbing, reconstruction.

I. M. PEI

I. M. Pei's recent project for the Louvre accomplishes one of Postmodernism's most sophisticated projects of deconstruction. Pei's design is for a glazed pyramid, based on the proportions at Giza, to be sited in the middle of the Court of Napoleon at the Louvre. The pyramid, surrounded by three smaller pyramids and seven pools, will provide ground level access to the surrounding buildings. The glazed surface, according to the architect, "would reflect the skies of Paris by day and be lit like a vast lantern at night."[/]

According to traditional methods of interpretation, the project would be evaluated according to categories such as historical context, formal relation to surrounding architecture, or the creativity of the architect. No doubt "creative," these pyramids are apt to be seen either as a display of the true genius of Pei in the vicinity of one of the major collections of Western art or as a show of egotism of one who would compare his work with that of the masters.

Formally, however, it seems clear that the pyramids appear to shatter the unity of their context, resulting in conflict and tension rather than harmony and resolution out of some rich additive complexity. Although the fusion of disparate elements can create polysemous meaning, as in metaphor, the mere juxtaposition here might appear to be more of a bad joke.

Yet if we recall the deeper foundations of French art and architecture, specifically the geometrical basis of great works, whether in [Jacques-Louis] David or [Paul] Cezanne, Pei's pyramid may appear to be more meaningful. For now, let us propose as true that the purity of pyramid, cylinder, sphere, and square could be said to be the common basis for classic French art, of whatever period and style. Moreover, let us claim that such pure forms have linked French art to their origin in antiquity. Pei's project would then evoke that heritage—appropriate for the Louvre, the focus on the great classical tradition. The new project is now grounded in the past (that is, in identity and presence).

Thus, it could be argued that the project is intelligible when interpreted in light of deconstruction. The creative dimension would be a struggle for presence and immortality; the historical and formal dimensions would embody contentions over presence and identity. Pei's pyramid does not function merely as a historical quotation of the classic tradition of pyramidal forms, but as the active assertion of presence and identity at the expense of the modernist "tradition of change."

On the other hand, by commissioning a change in the Louvre in the first place, and one that appears to fracture its historical repose and aesthetic wholeness to boot, the Mitterand Government is attempting to assert that what matters is not the conservation of masterpieces from the past, whose physical condition and meanings deteriorate despite our best techniques of preservation, but, rather, the continuous, present achievement of creativity which is the French artistic and cultural accomplishment. The Louvre, then, would not be all institutional Dorian Gray, but would witness French identity as a creative power actively (still) present.

The pyramid's displacement of meaning also can be seen at a deeper level. Pei's pyramid, in its *relation to light and life*, is altogether opposite the traditional Egyptian pyramid and other earlier uses of the form.

Recall that the pyramids of Egypt gathered and held the divine force of life, which emanated from the sun god, Ra, to his son, the pharaoh, and thus to the kingdom, as did the rays of the sun. Accordingly, for the Egyptians light had cosmic significance. The soul lived, plants grew and people saw, that is, light was efficacious, because it was, above all, sacred power. The pyramids focused and reflected such sacred light from their gold capstones and closed out profane, ordinary light from their permanently darkened interior passages and chambers. Inside the sealed pyramid, the pharaoh's *ka* (the vital force of life as the principle soul) remained in union with the sun god and moved about, continuing his action in his eternal dwelling.

In sharp contrast, Pei's pyramid at the Louvre deals with light as a fully natural phenomenon. (What else would it be for contemporary architecture?) It allows light to enter into the building, it reflects the city's sky, it lets light shine out—it vanquishes the meaning of the Egyptian pyramids and their supposed ground in sacred light.

The Egyptian pyramids symbolically reflected the vital force which the gold capstone physically reflected in reiteration; that is, they showed not the pyramid's profane surroundings but the sacred cosmos. The pyramids in Paris reflect the surrounding human and natural environment, the city's lights and passing weather. No physical light emanated from the Egyptian pyramids; but because the pharaoh lived eternally within, he continued to disperse to the kingdom the vital force which he alone possessed as the gift from the sun god. Pei's pyramidal "lantern" shows our power: even when the sun is gone we generate light, light that we have created, and thus provide for our own culture and way of life.

And, of course, Pei's pyramids simultaneously dislocate earlier French uses of the pyramid. With this building, the Mitterand Government would assert itself as a monument of great men (Mitterand), current French culture, and perhaps Pei, to be admired and emulated, conferring a sort of cultural immortality upon them. But that shows that the eighteenth-century, Neo-classical architectural memorials designed by [Étienne-Louis] Boullée, [Léon] Dufourny, and others fail to sustain their supposed earlier accomplishment: their meaning as access to sublime nature and thus timeless divinity no longer is operative; their testimony to the triumph of almost forgotten individuals over death is not credible. If the Neo-classical vision of architecture really had the meaning it purported, it would be powerful today. Here it is not, except by contrast.

Therefore, what is necessary is the repetition of the *act*. As the French earlier had appropriated the antique and classical to assert their presence and identity, so it must be done again, all over. As King Louis XIV, for example, asserted his and France's presence, identity and life in rebuilding the Louvre's Petite Gallery (continuing the process of reconstructing the Louvre begun by Charles V in the thirteenth century), as Napoleon asserted it in his day with power over past empires, the Egyptian pyramids and the Sphinx themselves, as Boullée, [Jacques] Rousseau, [Jacques-François] Blondel, and [Claude-Nicolas] Ledoux had at the end of the eighteenth century with their monuments of power and memory today, Mitterand and Pei do again in "late modern" style.

Pei's pyramids give no hint of support for such bankrupt ideas as the eternal presence of divinity. In this regard, the Louvre is the perfect site for Pei's pyramids; earlier, the scene of assertion of the Sun-King's power (as Louis XIV identified himself with the sun as symbol of the presence of divine right in the tradition—succession?—of the pharaoh empowered by his sun-god Ra), now it is the site for the claim of current power and identity which is accomplished by building over a thereby incorporated tradition.

Understood as the displacement of the earlier traditional architecture of eternal presence by continuous reaffirmation of temporal presence, Pei's pyramids have their meaning as part of our posture and strategy for today's power. We have a way, then, to interpret Pei's own gloss on his pyramids, as noted by an architectural reporter: "He described it, rather enigmatically, as having an architectural presence while being less than architecture."[8]

The displacement of the earlier meaning of the same forms by deconstructive inversions accomplishes for us what earlier buildings attempted to do in their time. We are shown the futility of expecting final success, much less the experience of any eternal presence. We are shown one, perhaps the only, strategy we have to establish and maintain an identity and presence as part of a living city and tradition of symbols. Where better to celebrate the triumph and limitations of our lives and the power of our art and architecture than in the center of the Court of Napoleon? How better than with displaced pyramids?

THE POSTMODERN CONDITION AND THE FUTURE

It seems that in the Postmodern era the task of thinking and building is to remain free from "naive" illusions. Not only our modes of discourse but the very built environment, whether woven by gestures of the media or architecture, are fictions for which we need to take responsibility. The cultural project is to renew the coming of fresh meaning by elevating process over object, so that buildings become interpreted and used as critical events. The architect's task is to devise strategies whereby we hold off a building's reification and concretization as conventional meaning systems. Even if we know that in the end we will fail to hold, the goal is to keep deconstructing and reconstructing, forever weaving our environment afresh.

The freedom from the illusion of the metaphor and metaphysics of presence, both in theory and philosophy, should be a permanent gain. The question of how to go on remains to be continually asked, however, since it is not clear how the act of deconstruction can persist. How can deconstruction remain continuously an event? As we have seen, destruction is not enough; we must necessarily generate our own discourse and new conventions, which assume the position of being meaningful, in turn needing to be undone. Derrida acknowledges that his work, too, is such a strategic fiction, which has no privilege and should not (could not, since he is self-consistent) become a new presence. If Derrida is right, it would mean that the only available next move is through and beyond "deconstruction."

Is there yet a way in our time to recover a genuine belonging with reality and truth? It would have to result from a deconstruction and overcoming of Derrida.

The strongest line of thinking for the task emerges from the work of Martin Heidegger, which shows how neither Nietzsche nor Derrida is radical enough! Because their inversions or metaphysical ideas still remain tied to the metaphysical system, they remain necessarily within its history, even as they approach its end. The task, according to Heidegger, is to move to the no-longer-metaphysical.

Heidegger agrees that the illusions of the past need to be displaced and stripped away. Yet, *against Derrida and Nietzsche, Heidegger contends that the revelation of the power of our fictive grasp of the world simultaneously conceals within itself—and from itself—the reality and truth of the natural and cultural world. The world itself needs to be brought into "unconcealment."* In such a move beyond deconstruction, reality and truth are not understood as some reassembly after our dissembly of the false, posturing relations of sign and signified. Rather, Heidegger advances the interpretation of truth as the disclosure of the dynamic unfolding of natural, human and sacred dimensions of the cosmos, somewhat like the best science. Further, according to Heidegger, it is possible to establish a genuine belonging with what-is-given-to-us, rather than an ironic or alienated relationship with it.

We can say yes to a self-releasement from the prison of willful power *and* purely fictive discourse; thoughtfully and responsibly we can remain open to the possibility of true dwelling and authentic building. Such openness calls for a new mode of building.

We could no longer build as in the past, nostalgically replicating historical forms; both Heidegger and Derrida would agree. Architecture, as a primal mode of interpreting the world, brings forth order, setting out an individual's place in nature and the community.[9] We have some hints as to what a post-deconstructive architecture would look like. To note one example, Karsten Harries calls for a recovery of architecture's natural symbols. In our life as participants in the world, we have access to the meaning of the body's matrix of motion and orientation, to the sense of boundary and center, of vertical and horizontal, of darkness and light, of inside, outside, and between. Because things do still speak to us, we can achieve an architectural vocabulary of doors, columns, roofs, and so on, which is non-arbitrary. In its power to transform space into place, building could provide a dwelling place where we could belong in a community, in a specific—regional—landscape.

The agreement that the best architecture must sweep away cultural posturing and nostalgia leaves us with the final—still open—questions: Is Derrida or is Heidegger the more insightful about truth and reality? Should building be deconstruction as Eisenman, Coop Himmelblau, Ambasz, and Pei indicate, or the attempt at recovery of place as Harries and others advocate?

1   The most central writings of Jacques Derrida are: "Interview," *Domus* 671 (April 1986): 17–24; *Of Grammatology* (Baltimore: Johns Hopkins University Press, 1976); *Writing and Difference* (Chicago: University of Chicago Press, 1978).
2   Jacques Derrida, *Speech and Phenomena* (Evanston: Northwestern University Press, 1973), 104.

3   John D. Caputo, "From the Deconstruction of Hermeneutics to the Hermeneutics of Deconstruction," in John Bailiff, ed., *Proceedings: Eighteenth Heidegger Conference* (Stevens Point, WI: University of Wisconsin—Stevens Point, 1984), 83. Caputo's "From the Primordiality of Absence to the Absence of Primordiality," in Hugh J. Silverman and Don Ihde, eds., *Hermeneutics and Deconstruction* (Albany: SUNY Press, 1985), also informs a deconstruction of deconstruction.

4   On Coop Himmelblau, see Frank Werner, *Architektur ist Jetzt*; quotations are from the lecture by the same title, delivered in Frankfurt and London, November 1984 and covered in *Architectural Review* 180, no. 1074 (August 1986): 17–24.

5   On Ambasz's Conservatory, see *Progressive Architecture* 66, no. 1 (January 1985): 120–121, and *Domus* 667 (December 1985): 14–17.

6   Ibid.

7   *Architect's International* 179, no. 7 (15 February 1984): 38.

8   Ibid.

9   Karsten Harries, "Thoughts on a Non-Arbitrary Architecture," *Perspecta* 20 (1983): 16; cf. Christian Norberg-Schulz, *Genius Loci* (New York: Rizzoli, 1985).

4. HISTORICISM
THE PROBLEM OF TRADITION

Three Kinds of Historicism
Alan Colquhoun

Architect and theorist Alan Colquhoun's essay
explains the difficult and ambiguous uses of the
term "historicism," which encompasses various
ways of grappling with the problem of tradition.
A theory of history with its roots in late-eighteenth-
century German romanticism, *historicism* is a
modern concept commonly linked with the *zeitgeist*, or "spirit of the age." The primary definition
of historicism is the study of society's institutions
"in the context of their historical development" on
the basis of an organic model of growth and
change.
    This modern view of history contrasts with
the classical view. The latter is based on a distinction between natural law, which is essential,
universal, and enduring, and history, which is
contingent or transitory. Colquhoun points out that
relative values replaced eternal ones because of
the rise of positivism in the age of reason. The
philosophical underpinnings of positivism are thus
important to the formulation of avant-garde theory
in art and architecture, which insists on the "radical break." The break, a historical rupture, is
necessary because of the connection between
freedom and the "new," as posited by the
avant-garde.
    Colquhoun's essay lucidly exposes the para-
doxes of the historicist view, in particular the
belief in inevitable progress towards some true
expression of the time. He describes this belief as
the substitution of an "emergent ideal" for the
fixed ideals of classical world view. The role of
historicist thinking in the concepts of architectural
style and periodization is also noted.
    Colquhoun's other two types of historicism, an
attitude and an artistic practice, help explain postmodern architecture's eclectic pluralism. The attitude is one of sympathy towards the culture and
customs of the past. The artistic practice is sampling forms and imagery freely from the various
historic styles, all styles being conceived as equally valid. Both attitude and practice underlie the
phenomenon of postmodern architecture embracing the use of historical form in the late 1970s.

(To avoid confusion with other contemporaneous work, I refer to this work as *postmodern historicism*.)

Writing in 1983, Colquhoun notes that postmodern historicist architects were assailing modernism's call to express the *zeitgeist*. Some, including Aldo Rossi and Michael Graves, suggested the need to return to the eternal values embodied in classical architecture. Furthermore, postmodern historicists rejected the avant-garde pursuit of social revolution and favored a formalist emphasis. These factors and attempts to resituate their work in relation to a classical view of history led to postmodern historicist architecture's reputation as a reactionary movement. This reading is supported by looking at the conservative patrons who commissioned their work.

Although sympathetic in principle to the recuperation of tradition, Colquhoun criticizes postmodern historicism's questionable theoretical grounding. Appearing in both *Architectural Design* and *Oppositions*, his essay was a call to the fledgling movement for more rigorous thinking. He concludes by identifying evolving postmodern attitudes: history is not teleological (aiming towards predetermined ends), and acceptance of tradition is the necessary condition for the production of architectural meaning. The latter represents his own belief that knowledge of <u>history is fundamental to the understanding the present</u>. Colquhoun's proposal is similar to the position Eisenman advocates in "The End of the Classical" (this chapter) in one respect: both advance architecture as an autonomous discipline that internalizes its tradition.

ALAN COLQUHOUN

THREE KINDS OF HISTORICISM

The title of this essay is simply the starting point for an attempt to clarify the confusion that surrounds the word *historicism* in modern architectural criticism, and through this to throw some light on the present situation in architecture, in which a new consciousness of history has replaced the antihistorical bias of the Modern Movement.

Dictionary definitions (and general usage) suggest that there are three interpretations of *historicism*: 1) the theory that all sociocultural phenomena are historically determined and that all truths are relative; 2) a concern for the institutions and traditions of the past; 3) the use of historical forms. The word *historicism* therefore can be applied to three quite separate objects: the first is a theory of history; the second, an attitude; the third, an artistic practice. There is no guarantee that the three have anything in common. I will investigate them to see how, if at all, they *are* related and then to see what light they throw on the phenomenon sometimes referred to as the *neo-avant-garde*.

The idea that values change and develop with historical time is by now so ingrained in common wisdom that it is difficult to imagine a different point of view. Yet the idea is, historically speaking, of fairly recent origin. It began to take shape in Europe as a whole in the seventeenth century, but was not given a consistent philosophical or historiographic formulation until the rise of the romantic movement in Germany in the late eighteenth century. The word *historicist*, as it applies to our first definition, comes from the German word *historismus*. It used to be translated as *historism*, but, probably under the influence of Benedetto Croce, was changed to *historicism*—from the Italian *storicismo*—in the early years of this century.

From *Oppositions* 26 (Spring 1984): 29–39. First published in *Architectural Design* 53, no. 9/10 (1983). Also in *Modernity and the Classical Tradition* (Cambridge: MIT Press, 1989). Courtesy of the author and MIT Press.

In the German movement, historicism was connected with idealism and neo-platonism. But the "Idea" had connotations different from those associated with the classical thought of the seventeenth and eighteenth centuries. According to classical thought, cultural values derived from natural law. Indeed, the value of history for historians like Hume and Montesquieu was that it provided evidence of the existence of this natural law. It was necessary, when studying history, to strip away the inessential and accidental and to expose the essential and universal. Through the study of history one learned with David Hume that "human nature was always and everywhere the same." It followed from this that what was of value in the cultural products of this human nature—art and architecture, for example—was equally fixed. Architecture, no less than painting, was an imitation of Nature through the intuition of her underlying laws. History, as the story of the contingent, merely had the effect of obscuring these laws. It is true that the rise of empirical science in the seventeenth century led certain theorists to question the immutable laws of architecture enshrined in the writing of Vitruvius (for instance, Claude Perrault went so far as to say that the rules of proportion and the orders owed their authority to custom), but this was not a universally held view. The majority of architects and theorists of the seventeenth and eighteenth centuries still held the view that good architecture obeyed immutable natural laws. Even Langier, writing at a time when the notion of taste had already undermined the classical certainties, claimed that Perrault was prompted by the spirit of contrariness and that the rules of architecture could be deduced from a few self-evident axioms based on our observation of nature. The best architecture was that which was close to nature, and that which was closest to nature could be found in the building of the ancients—though sometimes even they had been mistaken, in which case archaeology had to be supplemented with reason.

The idealism of the neoclassical view of architecture was therefore absolutist and depended on a combination of authority, natural law, and reason. Although in many ways the doctrines of neoclassicism differed from those of the Renaissance, the two held that the values of architecture referred to fixed laws, exemplified in Greco-Roman buildings.

The historicist view disputed the epistemology on which this view of architecture depended and gave an entirely different interpretation of the Ideal. According to historicism, the classical conception of a fixed and immutable ideal was, in fact, a false realism; and it tried to apply to the works of man the same objective standards that it applied to the natural world as a whole. But man belonged to a different category from that of inorganic or organic nature. Man and his institutions could be studied only in relation to the context of their historical development. The individual and the social institutions he constructed were governed by a vital, genetic principle, not by fixed and eternal laws. Human reason was not a faithful reflection of abstract truths; it was the rationalization of social customs and institutions, which had evolved slowly and which varied from place to place and from one time to another. The ideal was therefore an aim that emerged from historical experience and contingency. Although it might have been necessary to postulate an ideal that would be ultimately the same for all cultures, it could not be rationally grasped. We could give it only the names that belonged to the values of a local culture at its particular stage of development. Every culture therefore contained a mixture of truth and falsehood when measured against the ideal; equally, each culture could adhere only to its own notion of the true and the false, through values that were immanent in particular social and institutional forms.

In this view, society and its institutions were analogous to the individual. The individual can be defined only in terms unique to himself. Though he may be motivated by what he and his society see as objective norms of belief and conduct, his own essence cannot be reduced to these norms; it is constituted by the contingent factors of his birth and is subject to a unique development. The value of his life cannot be defined in a way that excludes his individuality. It is the same with societies, cultures, and states: they develop according to organic laws which they have internalized in their structures. In them, truth cannot be separated from destiny.

Based on a new notion of history, this view found its chief expression in the field of historiography. The aim of the historian became to research into the past of a particular society for its own sake, not in order to confirm *a priori* principles and provide exemplars, as had been the case with the English and French historians of the eighteenth century. This new project was undertaken in the German-speaking countries in reaction against the French rationalism that had dominated European thought for two centuries, and it coincided with the rise of German national consciousness. In the work of Leopold von Ranke, the first great historian of this school, the writing of history is characterized by two equally important tendencies: the objective and exhaustive examination of facts, and the attempt to penetrate the essential spirit of the country or period being studied. The dialectic between these two aims (which one might call the positivist and the idealist) had already been stated clearly by Wilhelm von Humboldt in his famous essay "On the Historian's Task" of 1821. According to von Humboldt, the events of history are given purpose and structure by a hidden spirit or idea, just as the idea or form is hidden in the infinitely variable forms of the visible world. It is the historian's task to reveal the idea beneath the empirical surface of historical events, just as it is the artist's task to reveal the ideal beneath the accidental appearance of bodies. At the same time, the idea can become apparent only through the detailed study of these events. Any imposition on history of an *a priori* purpose will inevitably distort *reality*, and it is this reality that is the object of historical study.

An ideal that emerges from particular historical events entails a relativizing of cultures, since aspects of the ideal to be revealed will differ from case to case; and this relativizing of the historical view is obviously connected in some way with eclecticism in the practice of art and architecture. Yet eclecticism did not, in itself, result necessarily in a doctrine of relativism. It was the product of an interest in history which developed in the early eighteenth century—a phenomenon of the history of taste before it became connected with German historical theory. Indeed, *returning* to an architecture based on nature—a notion so foreign to the spirit of historicism—was itself one of the products of this new interest in, and attitude toward, history.

The attitude toward history in the eighteenth century was, in fundamental ways, different from that of the Renaissance. The Renaissance had a strong faith in its contemporary world. In returning to classical modes, it picked up the threads of a world that was more modern than recent medieval culture. In the eighteenth century the return to classicism was always accompanied by elements of poetic reverie, nostalgia, and a sense of irretrievable loss. Within the context of this type of historical consciousness, eclecticism took two forms which at first might seem incompatible. On the one hand, different styles could exist side by side, as when one finds a classical temple next to a Gothic ruin at Stowe. On the other hand, one style could come to stand for a dominant moral idea and be connected with an idea of social reform. This happens, for example, in the second half of the eighteenth century in France, when the desire to reform society initiates a return to austere classical forms, such as one finds in the architecture of [Claude-Nicolas] Ledoux or the paintings of [Jacques-Louis] David. What is common to both forms of eclecticism is a strong feeling for the past, a awareness of the passage of historical time, and the ability of past styles to suggest certain poetic or moral ideas. The same motif can be the expression of private taste and the symbol of public morality. Robert Rosenblum[1] gives the example of the Doric temple front forming the entrance to a cave, which was a folly in the garden of the banker Claude Bernard Saint-James before it became an emblem of Revolution in a pageant at Lyon some years later.

Eclecticism depends on the power of historical styles to become the emblems of ideas associated with the cultures that produced them. No doubt this relationship first made itself felt in the Renaissance, but by the late eighteenth century historical knowledge had vastly extended its range of cultural models. An interest in Gothic architecture and in the architecture of the orient existed alongside the classical tradition, which was itself augmented by the discovery of Greek architecture. The idea of a return to a strict and primitive classicism based on *a priori* principles and natural law was one aspect of a new situation giving rise to the new possibility of choice. Choice implies a standard of taste and a decision as to the correct norm—whether this norm is based on a relative scale or on an absolute standard.

Returning to our definitions, we see that the "concern for the institutions of the past" and the "use of historical forms" belong to a broader category of historical phenomena than the historicist theory that "all sociocultural phenomena are historically determined." It was not until the historicist theory was formulated that the idea of the relativism of culture values became an issue. The theory made it impossible, in principle, to favor one style over another, since each style was organically related to a particular spatiotemporal culture and could not be judged except on its own terms. Yet historicist thought was not able to accept all that its theory implied. The historian Friedrich Meinecke[2] pointed out that there were two ways in which historicism attempted to avoid the implications of relativism: by setting up one period as a paradigm and by what he called the "flight into the future."

Representing a historical period as a paradigm would seem contrary to the principles of historicism and, in doing so, historical thought was clearly reverting to eclectic practice. But there was a difference: eclecticism had never severed completely its connections with the classical tradition. It had merely qualified this tradition with examples from other styles, either using these styles to give variety to classical themes or using them to purify the notion of classicism itself—as in the case of Gothic and Greek architecture. With romanticism and historicism, the break from classicism was complete. The style now set up as paradigmatic was Gothic, since Gothic represented not just a particular set of poetic associations, but a type of "organic" society. Here we see a coincidence between positivism and historicism similar to that which I have noted already in Leopold von Ranke. For instance, in seeking the essence of Gothic architecture, [Eugène Emmanuel]

Viollet-le-Duc reduced it to a set of instrumental principles that could provide a dynamic model for contemporary practice.

The other method by which historicism tried to overcome relativism—the flight into the future—depended upon a different set of ideas. One of the essential notions of historicism was, as I have said, the idea of development. Not only were various cultures the result of geographical and temporal displacement, not only were cultures unique and irreducible to a single set of principles, but they were also subject to a law of growth and change. The notion of genetic development was essential. Without it, the various guises in which the ideal appeared in history would be entirely random and arbitrary, since there was no longer any absolute ideal against which to measure them. It was necessary to replace the notion of a fixed ideal, to which historical phenomena should conform, with the notion of a *potential* ideal, which historical events were *leading up to*. Carried to its extreme, this view led to the idea of history as a teleological process, in which all historical events were determined by final causes. History was now oriented toward an apocalyptic future and no longer toward a normative past. It was the philosophers of historicism, particularly [G. W. F.] Hegel, who stressed in this way the determinism of history, not the historians themselves. Indeed, [Leopold] von Ranke (following von Humboldt) warned against the tendency of philosophy to schematize history by resorting to final causes. To him this was just as unacceptable as the classical notion of natural law because it denied what to the historians was the basis of historical development—the spiritual independence of the historical subject and the operation of free will in history.

Hegelian idealism, with its emphasis on historical teleology, replaced the will of the historical subject with the suprapersonal will of history itself. The ideal was not seen as informing the individual protagonists of history, as von Humboldt and von Ranke taught; it constituted an implacable historical will, of which the historical subject was the unconscious agent.

The Hegelian notion of historical determinism, however much it was misunderstood,[3] had a profound influence on the framework of thought characteristic of the artistic avant-garde in the late nineteenth and early twentieth centuries. Art and architecture could fulfill their historical destinies only by turning their backs on tradition. Only by looking toward the future could they be faithful to the spirit of history and give expression in their works to the spirit of the age. In architecture this meant the continual creation of new forms under the impulse of social and technological development, and the symbolic representation of society through these forms. Historians of the modern movement, such as [Sigfried] Giedion, [Nikolaus] Pevsner, and [Reyner] Banham, have tended to emphasize this developmental aspect of the avant-garde.

But this mode of thought was not the only, and perhaps not the most important, ingredient of the twentieth-century avant-garde. Another influence was what Philippe Junod, in his book *Transparence et opacité*,[4] has called "gnosiological idealism," whose principal theoretician was the nineteenth-century philosopher Konrad Fiedler. Growing out of the general atmosphere of historicist tradition, this theory systematically sought to exclude from artistic creation the last traces of the idea of *imitation*. It rejected the notion that the work of art is a mirror in which one sees something else. Hegel himself was the principal victim of this radical idealism, since he held the view that the work of art was a reflection of an idea external to itself. The notion of the "opacity" of the work of art was developed further by the Russian Formalists of the 1920s, and it became an essential component of avant-garde thinking.

At the opposite extreme, there was in modernism the idea of natural law and a return to the basic principles of artistic form, which was close to the primitive neoclassicism of the Enlightenment. The tension between this and historicism is particularly noticeable in the writings and buildings of Le Corbusier.

It is not these two aspects of modernism that its critics have attacked, but rather the idea of historical determinism. They have correctly pointed out that a blind faith in the future has the effect of handing over control of the architectural environment to market forces and their bureaucratic representatives. A movement that started as the symbolic representation of utopia has ended by becoming a tool of everyday economic practice. Critics have also shown (and equally correctly) that the systematic proscription of history as a source of architectural values cannot be sustained once the initial utopian impetus of modernism has been lost.

What these "postmodernist" critics have been unable to establish is a *theory of history* that will give a firm basis for this newfound historical consciousness. Because their attack has been restricted mostly to two aspects of modernism—historical determinism and historical amnesia—all they have been able to propose is the reversal of these two ideas: 1) history is not absolutely determined; 2) the acceptance of tradition, *in some form*, is the condition of architectural meaning. These two propositions, being reactions to other propositions, remain negative, and lack a systematic and legitimate basis of their own.

The fact that history cannot be considered as determined and teleological in any crude sense leaves open to question the relation between the historicity of all cultural production, on the one hand, and the cumulative and normative nature of cultural values, on the other. We can hardly expect to return to a classical interpretation of history in which a universal natural law is an *a priori* against which one measures all cultural phenomena. One of the chief reasons why this would be inconceivable is that today we have a different relation to history from that of the eighteenth century. In the eighteenth century the dominant classes were well read in the classics and were able to interpret their culture in terms of classical culture, using it to provide examples and models for their conduct. We have seen that the notion of universal norms was a product of a lively and concrete sympathy for the historical past. Today, our knowledge of the past has increased vastly, but it is the province of specialists and is equal and opposite to a widespread ignorance and vagueness about history in our culture. The more our knowledge of the past becomes objective, the less the past can be applied to our own time. The use of the past to supply models for the present depends upon the ideological distortion of the past; and the whole effort of modern historiography is to eliminate these distortions. In this sense, modern historiography is the direct descendant of historicism. As such, it is committed to a relativistic view of the past and resists the use of history to provide direct models.

On the other hand, it is equally difficult to imagine a culture that ignores the historical tradition altogether. The flight into the future, which characterized the phase of historicism that directly affected modernism, deliberately tried to instill a forgetfulness of history. In so doing, it brought to light what may be considered two weaknesses in nineteenth-century historicist thought. First, it did not take account of cultural borrowing. In its concern to stress the uniqueness of each culture, it overlooked the extent to which all cultures, even the most "indigenous," are based on the ideas and principles of other, pre-existent cultures. There has never been such a thing as an absolutely pure culture; to demonstrate this, one has only to mention the attraction that various proto-renaissances exerted on the medieval world and the influence that the classical world never ceased to exert on European culture.

The second weakness of historicism (closely related to the first) is that it tended to suppress the role that the establishment of norms and types has always played in cultural development. It confused two things that are, in fact, unrelated: it confused the way in which cultures might be studied with the way in which cultures operate. While it might be fruitful to study history as if the culture under examination were a unique organism, it does not follow that it was such an organism in fact. How, for instance, could a historicist study a culture that believed in natural law, and in the principle of the imitation of the idea, without somehow contradicting his own method? To do this, historical analysis would have to reconcile two contradictory principles within itself. Paradoxical as this may seem, this is an important principle that must be faced. It suggests that our culture—and our architecture, as one of its manifestations—must make the same reconciliation. The uniqueness of our culture, which is the product of historical development, must be reconciled with the palpable fact that it operates within a historical context and contains within itself its own historical memory.

In what way can cultural memory manifest itself in architecture today? In my opinion it cannot do this by reverting to eclecticism, if by eclecticism we mean something belonging to eighteenth- and nineteenth-century culture. I have tried to show that in the eighteenth and nineteenth centuries eclecticism depended on the power of architectural style to become a sign or emblem for a certain set of ideas. But this depended on a knowledge of, and sympathetic identification with, the styles of the past and an ability to subject those styles to ideological distortions—distortions that were nonetheless predicated on a thorough knowledge of the styles themselves. Architecture is a form of knowledge by experience. But it is precisely this element of inward knowledge and experience that is lacking today. When we try to recover the past in architecture, we cross a chasm—the chasm of the late nineteenth and early twentieth centuries, during which the power of architectural style to convey definite meanings disappeared entirely. Modern eclecticism is no longer ideologically active, as it was in the nineteenth century. When we revive the past now, we tend to express its most general and trivial connotations; it is merely the "pastness" of the past that is evoked. The phenomenon was already recognized eighty years ago by Aloïs Riegl, who drew attention to the two popular attitudes toward artistic works then prevalent: "newness" and "oldness." As an emblem of "pastness," modern historical recovery actually resists too accurate a memory of past styles; it is only in this way that it can become an item of cultural consumption. As modernism itself was recuperated by capitalism, so is "postmodernism" in all its guises. Modernism and "postmodernism" are two sides of the same coin. They are both essentially "modern" phenomena and are equally remote from the attitude toward history of the eighteenth and nineteenth centuries.

Given the fact that what we produce today is bound to be specifically modern, no matter how we incorporate the past into our work, we should look at that other tradition—the tradition of modernism—to see which of its elements inevitably persist in our attitude toward works of art and architecture. I have mentioned two aspects that are independent of the notion of historical determinism and the flight into the future: the opacity of the work of art and the search for primitive sources. Opacity denies that the work of art is merely a reflection or imitation of some model, whether this model is thought of as a platonic form or as consisting of the "real" world. In this sense it resists both realist idealism and naturalism. But it is not inconsistent with the idea of historical memory. By giving priority to the autonomy of artistic disciplines, it allows, even demands, the persistence of tradition as something that is internalized in these disciplines. The artistic tradition is one of the "objective facts" that is transformed by the creative act.

It seems to me, therefore, that it is valid to approach the problem of tradition in architecture as the study of architecture as an autonomous discipline—a discipline which incorporates into itself a set of aesthetic norms that is the result of historical and cultural accumulation and which takes its meaning from this. But these aesthetic values can no longer be seen as constituting a closed system of rules or as representing a fixed and universal natural law. The notions of the opacity of the work of art and the search for basic principles do not presuppose that architecture is a closed system which has no contact with outside life, with the nonaesthetic. The aesthetic comes into being anew through the existence of a particular material situation, even if it is not wholly conditioned by this situation. Today's historians tend toward investigation of material conditions of the artistic production of the past; today's architects should be equally aware of the transformation of the tradition brought about by these conditions.

What I have said implies that historicism, considered as the theory by which all sociocultural phenomena are historically determined, must still form the basis of our attitude toward history. But the sleight of hand by which historicist idealism replaced the fixed ideal with an emergent idea can no longer be accepted. Such a unitary and mystical concept is bound to lead to systems of thought—both political and artistic—that presuppose what, in fact, remains to be proved: that any given historical system is an organic unity leading inevitably to the progress of mankind.

On the contrary, all systems of thought, all ideological constructs, are in need of constant, conscious criticism; and the process of revision can come about only on the assumption that there is a higher and more universal standard against which to measure the existing system. History provides both the ideas that are in need of criticism and the material out of which this criticism is forged. An architecture that is constantly aware of its own history, but constantly critical of the seductions of history, is what we should aim for today.

1   Robert Rosenblum, *Transformations in Late Eighteenth-Century Art* (Princeton: Princeton University Press, 1967), 127.

2   Friedrich Meinecke, "Geschichte und Gegenwart" (History in relation to the present) (1933), in *vom Geschichtlichen Sinn und vom Sinn der Geschichte*, 2nd ed. (1939), 14ff; cited by Karl Hinrichs in Friedrich Meinecke, *Historism. The Rise of a New Historical Outlook*, J.E. Anderson, trans. (London: Routledge and Kegan Paul, 1972), li.

3   In the Introduction to the *Philosophy of World History*, Hegel lays greater stress on the need for an empirical approach than is often supposed.

4   Philippe Junod, *Transparence et opacité* (Lausanne: L'Age d'homme, 1976).

The End of the Classical: The End of the
Beginning, the End of the End
Peter Eisenman

In this significant article from 1984, Peter
Eisenman introduces the idea that architecture
has lost its legitimacy in a time of general crisis of
values, precipitated by the revealing of
Enlightenment "modes of knowing" as simply
"a network of value-laden arguments." Underlying
his thinking is the deconstructionist critique of
rationalizing techniques like measurement, and
of philosophical logic based on assumptions of
causality.

His main argument is concerned with
historical periodization: architecture for the last
500 years, notwithstanding modernism's
purported "radical break," can be seen as
continuous, as "the classical episteme." Here,
he borrows Michel Foucault's term *episteme*, but
inverts his categories of classical and modern.
So in the absence of the epistemological break
posited by the avant-garde, what has in fact tran-
spired? Eisenman answers that architecture has
suffered the illusions of three "fictions" or simulations, due to its continued reliance on origins and
ends, and on strategically oriented processes of
composition.

He develops his critique of the "fictions"—
reason, representation, and history—and offers
alternatives to origins in type, function, or any
other values "external" to architecture. In the early
Oppositions editorial "Post-Functionalism," (ch. 1)
Eisenman claims that function limits the possibilities of architecture. In place of these false origins,
he proposes here the condition of the "not-classical," that is, architecture as an independent discourse, or as a meaning-free, arbitrary, and timeless *text*. Is Eisenman attempting to effect an epistemological break between the classical and "not-
classical" epistemes? In substituting a perpetual
process for object, graft for origin, motivation for
strategy, will he be the first modern architect?

PETER EISENMAN

THE END OF THE CLASSICAL
THE END OF THE BEGINNING, THE END OF THE END

Architecture from the fifteenth century to the present has been under the influence of three "fictions." Not withstanding the apparent succession of architectural styles, each with its own label—classicism, neoclassicism, romanticism, modernism, postmodernism, and so on into the future—these three fictions have persisted in one form or another for five hundred years. They are *representation, reason,* and *history.*[1] Each of the fictions had an underlying purpose: representation was to embody the idea of meaning; reason was to codify the idea of truth; history was to recover the idea of the timeless from the idea of change. Because of the persistence of these categories, it will be necessary to consider this period as manifesting a continuity in architectural thought. This continuous mode of thought can be referred to as *the classical.*[2]

It was not until the late twentieth century that the classical could be appreciated as an abstract system of relations. Such recognition occurred because the architecture of the early part of the twentieth century itself came to be considered part of history. Thus it is now possible to see that, although stylistically different from previous architectures, "modern" architecture exhibits a system of relations similar to the classical.[3] Prior to this time, the "classical" was taken to be either synonymous with "architecture" conceived of as a continuous tradition from antiquity or, by the mid-nineteenth century, an historicized style. Today the period of time dominated by the classical can be seen as an "episteme," to employ Foucault's term—a continuous period of knowledge that includes the early twentieth century.[4] Despite the proclaimed rupture in both ideology and style associated with the Modern Movement, the three fictions have never been questioned and so remain intact. This is to say that architecture since the mid-fifteenth century aspired to be a paradigm of the *classic,* of that which is

From *Perspecta: The Yale Architectural Journal* 21 (1984): 154–172. Courtesy of the author and publisher.

timeless, meaningful, and *true.* In the sense that architecture attempts to recover that which is classic, it can be called "classical."[5]

THE "FICTION" OF REPRESENTATION: THE SIMULATION OF MEANING

The first "fiction" is representation. Before the Renaissance there was a congruence of language and representation. The meaning of language was in a "face value" conveyed within representation; in other words, the way language produced meaning *would be represented* within language. Things were; truth and meaning *were* self-evident. The meaning of a romanesque or gothic cathedral was in itself; it was *de facto.* Renaissance buildings, on the other hand—and all buildings after them that pretended to be "architecture"—received their value by representing an already valued architecture, by being simulacra (representations of representations) of antique buildings; they were *de jure.*[6] The *message* of the past was used to verify the *meaning* of the present. Precisely because of this need to verify, Renaissance architecture was the first simulation, an unwitting fiction of the object.

By the late eighteenth century historical relativity came to supersede the face value of language as representation, and this view of history prompted a search for certainty, for origins both historical and logical, for truth and proof, and for goals. Truth was no longer thought to reside in representation but was believed to exist outside it, in the processes of history. This shift can be seen in the changing status of the orders: until the seventeenth century they were thought to be paradigmatic and timeless; afterwards the possibility of their timelessness depended on a necessary historicity. This shift, as has just been suggested, occurred because language had ceased to intersect with representation—that is, because it was not *meaning* but a *message* that was displayed in the object.

Modern architecture claimed to rectify and liberate itself from the Renaissance fiction of representation by asserting that it was not necessary for architecture to represent another architecture; architecture was solely to embody its own *function.* With the deductive conclusion that form follows function, modern architecture introduced the idea that a building should express—that is, look like—its function, or like an *idea* of function (that it should manifest the rationality of its processes of production and composition).[7] Thus, in its effort to distance itself from the earlier representational tradition, modern architecture attempted to strip itself of the outward trappings of "classical" style. This process of reduction was called *abstraction.* A column without a base and capital was thought to be an abstraction. Thus reduced, form was believed to embody function more "honestly." Such a column looked more like a *real* column, the simplest possible load-carrying element, than one provided with a base and capital bearing arboreal or anthropomorphic motifs.

This reduction to pure functionality was, in fact, not abstraction; it was an attempt to represent reality itself. In this sense functional goals merely replaced the orders of classical composition as the starting point for architectural design. The moderns' attempt to represent "realism" with an undecorated, functional object was a fiction equivalent to the simulacrum of the classical in Renaissance representation. For what made function any more "real" a source of imagery than elements chosen from antiquity? The idea of function, in this case the message of utility as opposed to the message of antiquity, was raised to an originary proposition—a self-evident starting point for design analogous to typology or historical quotation. The moderns' attempt to represent realism is, then, a manifestation of the same fiction wherein meaning and value reside outside the world of an architecture "as is," in which representation is about its own *meaning* rather than being a *message* of another previous meaning.

Functionalism turned out to be yet another stylistic conclusion, this one based on a scientific and technical positivism, a simulation of efficiency. From this perspective the Modern Movement can be seen to be continuous with the architecture that preceded it. Modern architecture therefore failed to embody a new value in itself. For in trying to *reduce* architectural form to its essence, to a pure reality, the moderns assumed they were transforming the field of referential figuration to that of non-referential "objectivity." In reality, however, their "objective" forms never left the classical tradition. They were simply stripped down classical forms, or forms referring to a new set of givens (function, technology). Thus, Le Corbusier's houses that look like modern steamships or biplanes exhibit the same referential attitude toward representation as a Renaissance or "classical" building. The points of reference are different, but the implications for the object are the same.

The commitment to return modernist abstraction to history seems to sum up, for our time, the problem of representation. It was given its "Post-Modern" inversion in Robert Venturi's distinction between the "duck" and the "decorated shed."[8] A duck is a building that looks like its function or that allows its internal order to be displayed on its exterior; a decorated shed is a building that functions as a billboard, where any kind of imagery (except its internal function)—letters, patterns, even architectural elements—conveys a *message* accessible to all. In this sense the stripped-down "abstractions" of modernism are still referential objects: technological rather than typological ducks.

But the Post-Modernists fail to make another distinction which is exemplified in Venturi's comparison of the Doges' Palace in Venice, which he calls a decorated shed, and [Jacopo] Sansovino's library across the Piazza San Marco, which he says is a duck.[9] This obscures the more significant distinction between architecture "as is" and architecture as message. The Doges' Palace is not a decorated shed because it was not representational of another architecture; its significance came directly from the meaning embodied in the figures themselves; it was an architecture "as is." Sansovino's library may seem to be a duck, but only because it falls into the history of library types. The use of the orders on Sansovino's library speaks not to the function or type of the library, but rather to the representation of a previous architecture. The facades of Sansovino's library contain a message, not an inherent meaning; they are sign boards. Venturi's misreading of these buildings seems motivated by a preference for the decorated shed. While the replication of the orders had significance in Sansovino's time (in that they defined the classical), the replication of the same orders today has no significance because the value system represented is no longer valued. A sign begins to replicate or, in Jean Baudrillard's term, "simulate" once the reality it represents is dead.[10] When there is no longer a distinction between representation and reality, when reality is only simulation, then representation loses its *a priori* source of significance, and it, too, becomes a simulation.

THE "FICTION" OF REASON: THE SIMULATION OF TRUTH

The second "fiction" of postmedieval architecture is *reason*. If representation was a simulation of the meaning of the present through the message of antiquity, then reason was a simulation of the meaning of the truth through the message of science. This fiction is strongly manifest in twentieth-century architecture, as it is in that of the four preceding centuries; its apogee was in the Enlightenment. The quest for origin in architecture is the initial manifestation of the aspiration toward a rational source for design. Before the Renaissance the idea of origin was seen as self-evident; its meaning and importance "went without saying"; it belonged to an *a priori* universe of values. In the Renaissance, with the loss of a self-evident universe of values, origins were sought in natural or divine sources or in a cosmological or anthropomorphic geometry. The reproduction of the image of the Vitruvian man is the most renowned example. Not surprisingly, since the origin was thought to contain the seeds of the object's purpose and thus its destination, this belief in the existence of an ideal origin led directly to a belief in the existence of an ideal end. Such a genetic idea of beginning/end depended on a belief in a universal plan in nature and the cosmos which, through the application of classical rules of composition concerning hierarchy, order, and closure, would confer a harmony of the whole upon the parts. The perspective of the end thus directed the strategy for beginning. Therefore, as [Leon Battista] Alberti first defined it in *Della Pittura*, composition was not an open-ended or neutral process of transformation, but rather a strategy for arriving at a predetermined goal; it was the mechanism by which the idea of order, represented in the orders, was translated into a specific form."

Reacting against the cosmological goals of Renaissance composition, Enlightenment architecture aspired to a rational process of design whose ends were a product of pure, secular reason rather than of divine order. The Renaissance vision of harmony (faith in the divine) led naturally to the scheme of order that was to replace it (faith in reason), which was the logical determination of form from *a priori* types.

[J.-N.-L.] Durand embodies this moment of the supreme authority of reason. In his treatises formal orders become type forms, and natural and divine origins are replaced by rational solutions to the problems of accommodation and construction. The goal is asocially "relevant" architecture; it is attained through the rational transformation of type forms. Later, in the late nineteenth and early twentieth centuries, function and technique replaced the catalogue of type forms as origins. But the point is that from Durand on, it was believed that deductive reason—the same process used in science, mathematics, and technology—was capable of producing a truthful (that is, meaningful) architectural object. And with the success of rationalism as a scientific method (one could almost call it a "style" of thought) in the eighteenth and early nineteenth centuries, architecture adopted the self-evident values conferred by rational origins. If an architecture *looked* rational—that is, *represented* rationality—it was believed to *represent* truth. As in logic, at the point where all deductions developed from an initial premise corroborate that premise, there is logical closure and, it was believed, certain truth. Moreover, in this procedure the primacy of the origin remains intact. The rational became the moral and aesthetic basis of modern architecture. And the representational task of architecture in an age of reason was to portray its own modes of knowing.

At this point in the evolution of consciousness something occurred: reason turned its focus onto itself and thus began the process of its own undoing. Questioning its own status and mode of knowing, reason exposed itself to be a fiction.[12] The processes for knowing—measurement, logical proof, causality—turned out to be a network of value-laden arguments, no more than effective modes of persuasion. Values were dependent on another teleology, another end fiction, that of rationality.

Essentially, then, nothing had really changed from the Renaissance idea of origin. Whether the appeal was to a divine or natural order, as in the fifteenth century, or to a rational technique and typological function, as in the post-Enlightenment period, it ultimately amounted to the same thing—to the idea that architecture's value derived from a source outside itself. Function and type were only value-laden origins equivalent to divine or natural ones.

In this second "fiction" the crisis of belief in reason eventually undermined the power of self-evidence. As reason began to turn on itself, to question its own status, its authority to convey truth, its power to prove, began to evaporate. The analysis of analysis revealed that logic could not do what reason had claimed for it—reveal the self-evident truth of its origins. What both the Renaissance and the modern relied on as the basis of truth was found to require, in essence, faith. Analysis was a form of simulation; knowledge was a new religion. Similarly, it can be seen that architecture never embodied reason; it could only state the desire to do so; there is no architectural image of reason. Architecture presented an aesthetic of the experience of (the persuasiveness of and desire for) reason. Analysis, and the illusion of proof, in a continuous process that recalls Nietzsche's characterization of "truth," is a never-ending series of figures, metaphors, and metonymies.

In a cognitive environment in which reason has been revealed to depend on a belief in knowledge, therefore to be irreducibly metaphoric, a classical architecture—that is, an architecture whose processes of transformation are value-laden strategies grounded on self-evident or a priori origins—will always be an architecture of restatement and not of representation, no matter how ingeniously the origins are selected for this transformation, nor how inventive the transformation is.

Architectural restatement, replication, is a nostalgia for the security of knowing, a belief in the continuity of Western thought. Once analysis and reason replaced self-evidence as the means by which truth was revealed, the classic or timeless quality of truth ended and the need for verification began.

THE "FICTION" OF HISTORY: THE SIMULATION OF THE TIMELESS

The third "fiction" of classical Western architecture is that of history. Prior to the mid-fifteenth century, time was conceived nondialetically; from antiquity to the middle ages there was no concept of the "forward movement" of time. Art did not seek its justification in terms of the past or future; it was ineffable and timeless. In ancient Greece the temple and the god were one and the same; architecture was divine and natural. For this reason it appeared "classic" to the "classical" epoch that followed. The classic could not be represented or simulated, it could only be. In its straightforward assertion of itself it was nondialectical and timeless.

In the mid-fifteenth century the idea of a temporal origin emerged, and with it the idea of the past. This interrupted the eternal cycle of time by positing a fixed point of beginning. Hence the loss of the timeless, for the existence of origin required a temporal reality. The attempt of the classical to recover the timeless turned, paradoxically, to a time-bound concept of history as a source of timelessness. Moreover, the consciousness of time's forward movement came to "explain" a process of historical change. By the nineteenth century this process was seen as "dialectical." With dialectical time came the idea of the zeitgeist, with cause and effect rooted in presentness—that is, with an aspired-to timelessness of the present. In addition to its aspiration to timelessness, the "spirit of the age" held that an *a priori* relationship existed between history and all its manifestations at any given moment. It was necessary only to identify the governing spirit to know what style of architecture was properly expressive of, and relevant to, the time. Implicit was the notion that man should always be "in harmony"—or at least in a non-disjunctive relation—with his time.

In its polemical rejection of the history that preceded it, the Modern Movement attempted to appeal to values for this (harmonic) relationship other than those that embodied the eternal or universal. In seeing itself as superseding the values of the preceding architecture, the Modern Movement substituted a universal idea of relevance for a universal idea of history, analysis of program for analysis of history. It presumed itself to be a value-free and collective form of intervention, as opposed to the virtuoso individualism and informed connoisseurship personified by the post-Renaissance architect. Relevance in modern architecture came to lie in embodying a value other than the natural or divine; the zeitgeist was seen to be contingent and of the present, rather than as absolute and eternal. But the difference in value between presentness and the universal—between the contingent value of the zeitgeist and the eternal value of the classical—only resulted in yet another set (in fact, simply the opposite set) of aesthetic preferences. The presumedly neutral spirit of the "epochal will" supported asymmetry over symmetry, dynamism over stability, absence of hierarchy over hierarchy.

The imperatives of the "historical moment" are always evident in the connection between the representation of the function of architecture and its form. Ironically, modern architecture, by invoking the zeitgeist rather than doing away with history, only continued to act as the "midwife to historically significant form." In this sense modern architecture was not a rupture with history, but simply a moment in the same continuum, a new episode in the evolution of the zeitgeist. And architecture's representation of its particular zeitgeist turned out to be less "modern" than originally thought.

One of the questions that may be asked is why the moderns did not see themselves in this continuity. One answer is that the ideology of the zeitgeist bound them to their present history with the promise to release them from their past history; *they were ideologically trapped in the illusion of the eternity of their own time.*

The late twentieth century, with its retrospective knowledge that modernism has become history, has inherited nothing less than the recognition of the end of the ability of a classical or referential architecture to express its own time as timeless. The illusory timelessness of the present brings with it an awareness of the *timeful* nature of past time. It is for this reason that the representation of a zeitgeist always implies a simulation; it is seen in the classical use of the *replication* of a *past time* to invoke the timeless as the *expression* of a *present time*. Thus, in the zeitgeist argument, there will always be this unacknowledged paradox, a simulation of the timeless through a replication of the timeful.

Zeitgeist history, too, is subject to a questioning of its own authority. How can it be possible, from within history, to determine a timeless truth of its "spirit"? Thus history ceases to be an objective source of truth; origins and ends once again lose their universality (that is, their self-evident value) and, like history, become fictions. If it is no longer possible to pose the problem of architecture in terms of a zeitgeist—that is if architecture can no longer assert its relevance through a consonance with its zeitgeist—then it must turn to some other structure. To escape such a dependence on the zeitgeist—that is, the idea that the *purpose* of an architectural style is to embody the spirit of its age—it is necessary to propose an alternative idea of architecture, one whereby it is no longer the purpose of architecture, but its inevitability, to express its own time.

Once the traditional values of classical architecture are understood as not meaningful, true, and timeless, it must be concluded that these classical values were *always* simulations (and are not merely seen to be so in light of a present rupture of history or the present disillusionment with the zeitgeist). It becomes clear that the classical itself was a simulation that architecture sustained for five hundred years. Because the classical did not recognize itself as a simulation, it sought to represent extrinsic values (which it could not do) in the guise of its own reality.

The result, then, of seeing classicism and modernism as part of a single historical continuity is the understanding that there are no longer any self-evident values in representation, reason, or history to confer legitimacy on the object. This loss of self-evident value allows the timeless to be cut free from the meaningful and the truthful. It permits the view that there is no one truth (a timeless truth), or one meaning (a timeless meaning), but merely the timeless. *When the possibility is raised that the timeless can be cut adrift from the timeful (history), so too can the timeless be cut away from universality to produce a timelessness which is not universal.* This separation makes it unimportant whether origins are natural or divine or functional; thus, it is no longer necessary to produce a classic—that is, a timeless—architecture by recourse to the classical values inherent in *representation, reason,* and *history.*

THE NOT-CLASSICAL: ARCHITECTURE AS FICTION

The necessity of the quotation marks around the term "fiction" is now obvious. The three fictions just discussed can be seen not as fictions but rather as simulations. As has been said, fiction becomes simulation when it does not recognize its condition as fiction, when it tries to simulate a condition of reality, truth, or non-fiction. The simulation of representation in architecture has led, first of all, to an excessive concentration of inventive energies in the representational object. When columns are seen as surrogates of trees and windows resemble the portholes of ships, architectural elements become representational figures carrying an inordinate burden of meaning. In other disciplines representation is not the only purpose of figuration. In literature, for example, metaphors and similes have a wider range of application—poetic, ironic, and the like—and are not limited to allegorical or referential functions. Conversely, in architecture only one aspect of the figure is traditionally at work: object representation. The architectural figure always alludes to—aims at the representation of—some *other* object, whether architectural, anthropomorphic, natural, or technological.

Second, the simulation of reason in architecture has been based on a classical value given to the idea of truth. But [Martin] Heidegger has noted that error has a trajectory parallel to truth, that error can be the unfolding of truth.[13] Thus to proceed from "error" or fiction is to counter consciously the tradition of "mis-reading" on which the classical unwittingly depended—not a presumedly logical transformation of something *a priori*, but a deliberate "error" stated as such, one which presupposes only its own internal truth. Error in this case does not assume the same value as truth; it is not simply its dialectical opposite. It is more like a *dissimulation*, a "not-containing" of the value of truth.

Finally, the simulated fiction of Modern Movement history, unwittingly inherited from the classical, was that any present-day architecture must be a reflection of its zeitgeist; that is, architecture can simultaneously be about presentness and universality. But if architecture is inevitably about the invention of fictions, it should also be possible to propose an architecture that embodies an *other* fiction, one that is not sustained by the values of presentness or universality and, more importantly, that does not consider its purpose to reflect these values. This *other* fiction/object, then, clearly should eschew the fictions of the classical (representation, reason, and history), which are attempts to "solve" the problem of architecture rationally; for strategies and solutions are vestiges of a goal oriented view of the world. If this is the case, the question becomes: What can be the model for architecture when the essence of what was effective in the classical model the presumed rational value of structures, representations, methodologies of origins and ends, and deductive processes—has been shown to be a simulation?

It is not possible to answer such a question with an alternative model. But a series of characteristics can be proposed that typify this aporia, this loss in our capacity to conceptualize a new model for architecture. These characteristics, outlined below, arise from that which can *not be*; they form a structure of *absences*.[14] The purpose in proposing them is not to reconstitute what has just been dismissed, a model for a theory of architecture—for all such models are ultimately futile. Rather what is being proposed is an expansion beyond the limitations presented by the classical model to the realization of *architecture as an independent discourse*, free of external values—classical or any other; that is, the intersection of the *meaning-free*, the *arbitrary*, and the *timeless* in the artificial.

The meaning-free, arbitrary, and timeless creation of artificiality in this sense must be distinguished from what Baudrillard has called "simulation":[15] it is not an attempt to erase the classical distinction between reality and representation—thus again making architecture a set of conventions simulating the real; it is, rather, more like a *dis*simulation.[16] Whereas simulation attempts to obliterate the difference between real and imaginary, dissimulation leaves untouched the difference between reality and illusion. The relationship between dissimulation and reality is similar to the signification embodied in the mask: the sign of pretending to be *not* what one is—that is, a sign which seems not to signify anything besides itself (the sign of a sign, or the negation of what is behind it). Such a dissimulation in architecture can be given the provisional title of the *not-classical*. As dissimulation is not the inverse, negative, or opposite of simulation, a "not-classical" architecture is not the inverse, negative, or opposite of classical architecture; it is merely different from or other than. A "not-classical" architecture is no longer a certification of experience or a simulation of history, reason, or reality in the present. Instead, it may more appropriately be described as an *other* manifestation, an architecture as is, now as a fiction. It is a representation of itself, of its own values and internal experience.

The claim that a "not-classical" architecture is necessary, that it is proposed by the new epoch or the rupture in the continuity of history, would be another zeitgeist argument. The "not-classical" merely proposes an end to the dominance of classical values in order to reveal other values. It proposes, not a new value or a new zeitgeist, but merely another condition—one of reading architecture as a text. There is nevertheless no question that this idea of the reading of architecture is initiated by a zeitgeist argument: that today the classical signs are no longer significant and have become no more than replications. A "not-classical" architecture is, therefore, not unresponsive to the realization of the closure inherent in the world; rather, it is unresponsive to representing it.

THE END OF THE BEGINNING

An origin of value implies a state or a condition of origin before value has been given to it. A beginning is such a condition prior to a valued origin. In order to reconstruct the timeless, the state of *as is*, of face value, one must begin: begin by eliminating the time-bound concepts of the classical, which are primarily origin and end. The end of the beginning is also the end of the beginning of value. But it is not possible to go back to the earlier, prehistoric state of grace, the Eden of timelessness before origins and ends were valued. We must begin in the present—without necessarily giving a value to presentness. The attempt to reconstruct the timeless today must be a fiction which recognizes the fictionality of its own task—that is, it should not attempt to simulate a timeless reality.

As has been suggested above, latent in the classical appeal to origins is the more general problem of cause and effect. This formula, part of the fictions of reason and history, reduces architecture to an "added to" or "inessential" object by making it simply an effect of certain causes understood as origins. This problem is inherent in all of classical architecture, including its modernist aspect. The idea of architecture as something "added to" rather than something with its own being—as adjectival rather than nominal or ontological—leads to the perception of architecture as a practical device. As long as architecture is primarily a device designated for use and for shelter—that is, as long as it has origins in programmatic functions—it will always constitute an effect.

But once this "self-evident" characteristic of architecture is dismissed and architecture is seen as having no *a priori* origins—whether functional, divine, or natural—alternative fictions for the origin can be proposed: for example, one that is *arbitrary*, one that has no external value derived from meaning, truth, or timelessness. It is possible to imagine a beginning internally consistent but not conditioned by or contingent on historic origins with supposedly self-evident values.[17] Thus, while classical origins were thought to have their source in a divine or natural order and modern origins were held to derive their value from deductive reason, "not-classical" origins can be strictly arbitrary, simply starting points, without value. They can be artificial and relative, as opposed to natural, divine, or universal.[18] Such artificially determined beginnings can be free of universal values because they are merely arbitrary points in time, when the architectural process commences. One example of an artificial origin is a *graft*, as in the genetic insertion of an alien body into a host to provide a new result.[19] As opposed to a collage or a montage, which lives within a context and alludes to an origin, a graft is an invented site, which does not so much have object characteristics as those of process. A graft is not in itself genetically arbitrary. Its arbitrariness is in its freedom from a value system of non-arbitrariness (that is, the classical). It is arbitrary in its provision of a choice of reading which brings no external value to the process. But further, in its artificial and relative nature a graft is not in itself necessarily an achievable result, but merely a site that contains *motivation* for action—that is the beginning of a process.[20]

Motivation takes something arbitrary—that is, something in its artificial state which is not obedient to an external structure of values—and implies an action and a movement concerning an internal structure which has an inherent order and an internal logic. This raises the question of the motivation or purpose from an arbitrary origin. How can something be arbitrary and non-goal oriented but still be internally motivated? Every state, it can be argued, has a motivation toward its own being—a motion rather than a direction. Just because architecture cannot portray or enact *reason* as a value does not mean that it cannot argue systematically or reasonably. In all processes there must necessarily be some beginning point; but the value in an arbitrary or intentionally fictive architecture is found in the *intrinsic* nature of its action rather than in the direction of its course. Since any process must necessarily have a beginning and a movement, however, the fictional origin must be considered as having at least a methodological value—a value concerned with generating the internal relations of the process itself. But if the beginning is in fact arbitrary, there can be no direction toward closure or end, because the motivation for change of state (that is, the inherent instability of the beginning) can never lead to a state of no change (that is, an end). Thus, in their freedom from the universal values of both historic origin and directional process, motivations can lead to *ends* different from those of the previous value-laden *end*.

THE END OF THE END

Along with the end of the origin, the second basic characteristic of a "not-classical" architecture, therefore, is its freedom from *a priori* goals or ends—the end of the end. The end of the classical also means the end of the myth of the end as a value-laden effect of the progress or direction of history. By logically leading to a potential closure of thought, the fictions of the classical awakened a desire to confront, display, and even transcend the end of history. This desire was manifest in the modern idea of utopia, a time beyond history. It was thought that objects imbued with value because of their relationship to a self-evidently meaningful origin could somehow transcend the present in moving toward a timeless future, a utopia. This idea of progress gave false value to the present; utopia, a form of fantasizing about an "open" and limitless end, forestalled the notion of closure. Thus the modern crisis of closure marked the end of the process of moving toward the end. Such crises (or ruptures) in our perception of the continuity of history arise not so much out of a change in our idea of origins or ends than out of the failure of the present (and its objects) to sustain our expectations of the future. And once the continuity of history is broken in our perception, any representation of the classical, any "classicism," can be seen only as a belief. At this point, where our received values are "in crisis," the end of the end raises the possibility of the invention and realization of a blatantly fictional future (which is therefore non-threatening in its "truth" value) as opposed to a simulated or idealized one.

With the end of the end, what was formerly the process of composition or transformation ceases to be a causal strategy, a process of addition or subtraction from an origin. Instead, the process becomes one of *modification*—the invention of a non-dialectical, non-directional, non-goal oriented process.[21] The "invented" origins from which this process receives its motivation differ from the accepted, mythic origins of the classicists by being *arbitrary*, reinvented for each circumstance, adopted for the moment and not forever. The process of modification can be seen as an open-ended tactic rather than a goal-oriented strategy. A strategy is a process that is determined and value-laden before it begins; it is *directed*. Since the arbitrary origin cannot be known in advance (in a cognitive sense), it does not depend on knowledge derived from the classical tradition and thus cannot engender a strategy.

In this context architectural form is revealed as a "place of invention" rather than as a subservient representation of another architecture or as a strictly practical device. To invent an architecture is to allow architecture to be a cause; in order to be a cause, it must arise from something outside a directed strategy of composition.

The end of the end also concerns the end of object representation as the only metaphoric subject in architecture. In the past the metaphor in architecture was used to convey such forces as tension, compression, extension, and elongation; these were qualities that could be seen, if not literally in the objects themselves, then in the relationship between objects. The idea of the metaphor here has nothing to do with the qualities generated between buildings or between buildings and spaces; rather, it has to do with the idea that the internal process itself can generate a kind of non-representational figuration in the object. This is an appeal, not to the classical aesthetic of the object, but to the potential *poetic* of an architectural text. The problem, then, is to distinguish texts from representations, to convey the idea that what one is seeing, the material object, is a text rather than a series of image references to other objects or values.

This suggests the idea of architecture as "writing" as opposed to architecture as image. What is being "written" is not the object itself—its mass and volume—but the *act* of massing. This idea gives a metaphoric body to the act of architecture. It then signals its reading through an other system of signs, called *traces*.[22] Traces are not to be read literally, since they have no other value than to signal the idea that there is a reading event and that reading should take place; trace signals the idea to read.[23] Thus a trace is a partial or fragmentary sign; it has no objecthood. It signifies an action that is in process. In this sense a trace is not a simulation of reality; it is a dissimulation because it reveals itself as distinct from its former reality. It does not simulate the real, but represents and records the action inherent in a former or future reality, which has a value no more or less real than the trace itself. That is, trace is unconcerned with forming an image which is the representation of a previous architecture or of social customs and usages; rather, it is concerned with the marking—literally the figuration—of its own internal processes. Thus the trace is the record of motivation, the record of an action, not an image of another object-origin.

In this case a "not-classical" architecture begins actively to involve an idea of a reader conscious of his own identity as a reader rather than as a user or observer. It proposes a new reader distanced from any external value system (particularly an architectural-historical system). Such a reader brings no *a priori* competence to the act of reading other than an identity as a reader. That is, such a reader has no preconceived knowledge of what architecture should be (in terms of its proportions, textures, scale, and the like); nor does a "not-classical" architecture aspire to make itself understandable through these preconceptions.[24]

The competence of the reader (of architecture) may be defined as the capacity to distinguish *a sense of knowing from a sense of believing*. At any given time the conditions for "knowledge" are "deeper" than philosophic conditions; in fact, they provide the possibility of distinguishing philosophy from literature, science from magic, and religion from myth. The new competence comes from the capacity to read per se, to know how to read, and more importantly, to know how to read (but not necessarily decode) architecture as a text. Thus the new "object" must have the capacity to reveal itself first of all as a text, as a reading event. The architectural fiction proposed here differs from the classical fiction in its primary condition as a text and in the way it is read: the new reader is no longer presumed to know the nature of truth in the object, either as a representation of a rational origin or as a manifestation of a universal set of rules governing proportion, harmony, and ordering. But further, knowing how to decode is no longer important; simply, language in this context is no longer a code to assign meanings (that *this* means *that*). The activity of reading is first and foremost in the recognition of something as a language (that *it is*). Reading, in this sense, makes available a level of *indication* rather than a level of meaning or expression.

Therefore, to propose the end of the beginning and the end of the end[25] is to propose the end of beginnings and ends of value—to propose an *other* "timeless" space of invention. It is a "timeless" space in the present without a determining relation to an ideal future or to an idealized past. Architecture in the present is seen as a process of inventing an artificial past and a futureless present. It remembers a no-longer future.

This paper is based on the non-verifiable assumptions or values: timeless (originless, endless) architecture; non-representational (objectless) architecture; and artificial (arbitrary, reasonless) architecture.

1   Jean Baudrillard, "The Order of Simulacra," "Simulations," New York City, Semiotext(e) (1983), 83.
2   The term "classical" is often confused with the idea of the "classic" and with the stylistic method of "classicism." That which is classic, according to Joseph Rykwert, invokes the idea of "ancient and exemplary" and suggests "authority and distinction"; it is a model of what is excellent or the first rank. More importantly, it implies its own timelessness, the idea that it is first rank at any time. Classicism, as opposed to the classical, will be defined here as a method of attempting to produce a "classic" result by appealing to a "classical" past. This accords with the definition given by Sir John Summerson, for whom classicism is not so much a set of ideas and values as it is a *style*. He maintains that while much of Gothic architecture was based on the same proportional relationships as the "classical" architecture of the Renaissance, no one could confuse a Gothic cathedral with a Renaissance palazzo; it simply did not have the look of classicism. In contrast, Demetri Porphyrios argues that classicism is not a style, but instead has to do with rationalism: "as much as architecture is a tectonic discourse, it is by definition transparent to rationality...the lessons to be learned today from classicism, therefore, are not to be found in classicism's stylistic wrinkles but in classicism's rationality." Porphyrios here confuses classicism with the classical and the classic,

that is, with a set of values privileging the "truth" (that is, rationality) of tectonics over "expression" and error. The fallacy of this approach is that classicism relies on an idea of historical continuity inherent in the classical; therefore it does not produce the timelessness characteristic of the classic. The classical, by implication, has a more relative status than the classic; it evokes a timeless past, a "golden age" superior to the modern time or the present.

3   Michel Foucault, *The Order of Things* (New York: Random House, 1973). It is precisely Michel Foucault's distinction between the classical and modern that has never been adequately articulated in relationship to architecture. In contrast to Foucault's epistemological differentiation, architecture has remained an uninterrupted mode of representation from the fifteenth century to the present. In fact, it will be seen that what is assumed in architecture to be classical is, in Foucault's terms, modern, and what is assumed in architecture to be modern is in reality Foucault's classical. Foucault's distinction is not what is at issue here, but rather the continuity that has persisted in architecture from the classical to the present day.

4   Foucault, *The Order of Things*, op. cit., xxii. While the term "episteme" as used here is similar to Foucault's use of the term in defining a continuous period of knowledge, it is necessary to point out that the time period here defined as the classical episteme differs from Foucault's definition. Foucault locates two discontinuities in the development of Western culture: the classical and the modern. He identifies the classical, beginning in the mid-seventeenth century, with the primacy of the intersection of language and the representation: the value of language, "its meaning," was seen to be self-evident and to receive its justification within language; the way language provided meaning could be represented within language; the way language provided meaning could be represented within language. On the other hand, Foucault identifies the modern, originating in the early nineteenth century, with the ascendance of historical continuity and self-generated analytic processes over language and representation.

5   "The End of the Classical" is not about the end of the classic. It merely questions a contingent value structure which, when attached to the idea of the classic, yields an erroneous sense of the *classical*. It is not that the desire for a classic is at an end, but that the dominant conditions of the classical (origin, end, and the process of composition) are under reconsideration. Thus it might be more accurate to title this essay "The End of the Classical as Classic."

6   Franco Borsi, *Leon Battista Alberti* (New York: Harper and Rowe, 1977). The facade of the church of Sant' Andrea in Mantua by Alberti is one of the first uses of the transposition of ancient building types to achieve both verification and authority. It marks, as Borsi says, "a decisive turning away from the vernacular 'to the Latin.'" (p. 272) It is acceptable in the "vernacular" to revive the classical temple front because the function of the temple in antiquity and the church in the fifteenth century was similar. However, it is quite another matter to overlay the temple front with the triumphal arch. (See R. Wittkower, *Architectural Principles in the Age of Humanism* [New York: Norton, 1971], and also D. S. Chambers, *Patrons and Artists in the Renaissance* [London: MacMillan & Co., 1970].) It is as if Alberti were saying that with the authority of God in question, man must now resort to the symbols of his own power to verify the church. Thus the use of the triumphal arch becomes a message on the facade of Sant' Andrea rather than an embodiment of its inherent meaning.

7   Jeff Kipnis, from a seminar at the Graduate School of Design, Harvard University, 28 February 1984. "Form cannot follow function until function (including but not limited to use) has first emerged as a possibility of form."

8   Robert Venturi, Denise Scott Brown, and Steven Izenour, *Learning from Las Vegas: The Forgotten Symbolism of Architectural Form*, rev. ed. (Cambridge: MIT Press, 1977), 87.

9   See the film "Beyond Utopia: Changing Attitudes in American Architecture," (New York: Michael Blackwood Productions, 1983).

10   Baudrillard, "The Order of Simulacra," "Simulations," op. cit., 8, 9. In referring to the death of the reality of God, Baudrillard says "...metaphysical despair came from the idea

that the images concealed nothing at all, and that in fact they were not images,...but actually perfect simulacra..."

11   Leon Battista Alberti, *On Painting* (New Haven: Yale University Press, 1966), 68–74.

12   Morris Kline, *Mathematics, The Loss of Certainty* (New York: Oxford University Press, 1980), 5.

13   Martin Heidegger, "On the Essence of Truth," in *Basic Writings* (New York: Harper & Row, 1977). "Errancy is the essential counter-essence to the primordial essence of truth....Errancy and the concealing of what is concealed belong to the primordial essence of truth."

14   Gilles Deleuze, "Plato and the Simulacrum," *October* no. 27 (Winter 1983). Deleuze uses a slightly different terminology to address a very similar set of issues; he discusses the Platonic distinction between model, copy, and "simulacrum" as a means of assigning value and hierarchical position to objects and ideas. He explains the overthrow of Platonism as the suspension of the *a priori* value-laden status of the Platonic *copy* in order to: "raise up simulacra, to assert their rights over icons or copies. The problem no longer concerns the distinction Essence/Appearance or Model/Copy. This whole distinction operates in the world of representation....The simulacrum is not degraded copy, rather it contains a positive power which negates both original and copy, *both model and reproduction.* Of the at least two divergent series interiorized in the simulacrum neither can be assigned as original or as copy. It doesn't even work to invoke the model of the Other, because no model resists the vertigo of the simulacrum." (pp. 52, 53) Simulation is used here in a sense which closely approximates Deleuze's use of copy or icon, while dissimulation is conceptually very close to his description of the pre-Socratic simulacra.

15   Baudrillard, "The Order of Simulacra," "Simulations," op. cit., 2. In the essay "The Precession of Simulacra" Baudrillard discusses the nature of simulation and the implication of present-day simulacra on our perception of the nature of reality and representation: "Something has disappeared; the sovereign difference between them (the real and... simulation models) that was the abstraction's charm."

16   Ibid., 5. Distinguishing between simulation and what he calls dissimulation, Baudrillard says that "to dissimulate is to feign not to have what one has. To simulate is to feign to have what one hasn't....'Someone who feigns an illness can simply go to bed and make believe he is ill. Someone who simulates an illness produces in himself some of the symptoms (Littre)' Thus feigning...is only masked; whereas simulation threatens the difference between 'true' and 'false,' between 'real' and 'imaginary.' Since the simulator produces 'true' symptoms, is he ill or not?" According to Baudrillard, simulation is the generation by models of a reality without origin; it no longer has to be rational, since it is no longer measured against some ideal or negative instance. While this sounds very much like my proposal of the not-classical, the not-classical is fundamentally different in that it is a dissimulation and not a simulation. Baudrillard discusses the danger in the realization of the simulacra—for when it enters the real world it is its nature to take on the "real" attributes of that which it is simulating. Dissimulation here is defined differently: it makes apparent the simulation with all of its implications on the value status of "reality" without distorting the simulacra or allowing it to lose its precarious position, posed between the real and the unreal, the model and the other.

17   What is at issue in an artificial origin is not motivation (as opposed to an essential or originary cause, as in an origin of the classical) but rather the idea of self-evidence. In deductive logic reading backward inevitably produces self-evidence. Hence the analytic process of the classical would always produce a self-evident origin. Yet there are no *a priori* self-evident procedures which could give one origin any value over any other. It can be proposed in a *not-classical* architecture that any initial condition can produce self-evident procedures that have an internal motivation.

18   The idea of arbitrary or artificial in this sense must be distinguished from the classical idea of architecture as artificial nature or from the idea the arbitrariness of the sign in language. Arbitrary in this context means having no natural connection. The insight that origins are a contingency of language is based on an appeal to reading; the origin can be arbitrary because it is contingent on a reading that brings its own strategy with it.

19 Jonathan Culler, *On Deconstruction: Theory and Criticism after Structuralism* (Ithaca: Cornell University Press, 1982). This is basically similar to Jacques Derrida's use of graft in literary deconstruction. He discusses graft as an element which can be discovered in a text through a deconstructive reading: "deconstruction is, among other things, an attempt to identify grafts in the texts it analyses: what are the points of juncture and stress where one scion or line or argument has been spliced with another?...Focusing on these moments, deconstruction elucidates the heterogeneity of the text." (p. 150) The three defining qualities of graft as it is used in this paper are 1) graft begins with the arbitrary and artificial conjunction of 2) two distinct characteristics which are in their initial form unstable. It is this instability which provides the motivation (the attempt to return to stability) and also allows modification to take place. 3) In the incision there must be something which allows for an energy to be set off by the coming together of the two characteristics. Culler's discussion of deconstructive strategy contains all of the elements of graft: it begins juxtaposed in such a way as to create movement, and the deconstruction (graft) is identifiable in terms of that motivation. This paper, which concentrates on transposing these ideas from a pure analytic framework to a program for work, is more concerned with what happens in the process of consciously making grafts than finding those that may have been placed unconsciously in a text. Since a graft by definition is a process of modification, it is unlikely that one could find a static or undeveloped moment of graft in an architectural text; one would be more likely to read only its results. Graft is used here in a way that closely resembles Culler's analysis of Derrida's method for deconstruction of opposition: "To deconstruct an opposition...is not to destroy it....To deconstruct an opposition is to undo and displace it, to situate it differently." (p. 150) "This concentration on the apparently marginal puts the logic of supplementarity to work as an interpretive strategy: what has been relegated to the margins or set aside by previous interpreters may be important precisely for those reasons that led it to be put aside." (p. 140) Derrida emphasizes graft as a non-dialectic condition of opposition; this paper stresses the processual aspects which emerge from the moment of graft. The major differences are of terminology and emphasis.

20 Ibid., 99. "The arbitrary nature of the sign and the system with no positive terms gives us the paradoxical notion of an 'instituted trace,' a structure of infinite referral in which there are only traces—traces prior to any entity of which they might be the trace." This description of "instituted trace" relates closely to the idea of *motivation* as put forth in this paper. Like Derrida's "instituted trace," motivation describes a system which is internally consistent, but arbitrary in that it has no beginning or end and no necessary or valued direction. It remains a system of differences, comprehensible only in terms of the spaces between elements or moments of the process. Thus, motivation here is similar to Derrida's description of *difference* it is the force within the object that causes it to be dynamic at every point of a continuous transformation. Internal motivation determines the nature of modification for the object and is rendered readable through trace.

21 Jeff Kipnis, "Architecture Unbound," unpublished paper, 1984. Modification is one aspect of extension which is defined by Kipnis as a component of decomposition. While extension is any movement from an origin (or an initial condition), modification is a specific form of extension concerned with preserving the evidence of initial conditions (for example, through no addition or subtraction of materiality). On the other hand, synthesis is an example of extension which does not attempt to maintain evidence of initial conditions but rather attempts to create a new whole.

22 The concept of trace in architecture as put forward here is similar to Derrida's idea in that it suggests that there can be neither a representational object nor representable "reality." Architecture becomes text rather than object when it is conceived and presented as a system of differences rather than as an image or an isolated presence. Trace is the visual manifestation of this system of differences, a record of movement (without direction) causing us to read the present object as a system of relationships to other prior and subsequent movements. Trace is to be distinguished from Jacques Derrida's use of the term,

for Derrida directly relates the idea of "difference" to the fact that it is impossible to isolate "presence" as an entity. "The presence of motion is conceivable only insofar as every instant is already marked with the traces of the past and future...the present instant is not something given but a product of the relations between past and future. If motion is to be present, presence must already be marked by difference and deferral." (Culler, *On Deconstruction*, op. cit., 97.) The idea that presence is never a simple absolute runs counter to all of our intuitive convictions. If there can be no inherently meaningful presence which is not itself a system of differences then there can be no value-laden or *a priori* origin.

23 We have always read architecture. Traditionally it did not induce reading but responded to it. The use of arbitrariness here is an idea to stimulate or induce the reading of traces without references to meaning but rather to other conditions of process—that is, to stimulate pure reading without value or prejudice, as opposed to interpretation.

24 Previously, there was assumed to be an *a priori* language of value, a poetry, existing within architecture. Now we are saying that architecture is merely language. We read whether we know what language we are reading or not. We can read French without understanding French. We can know someone is speaking nonsense or noise. Before we are competent to read and understand poetry we can know something to be language. Reading in this context is not concerned with decoding for meaning or for poetic content but rather for indication.

25 C.F. Franco Rella, "Tempo della fine e tempo dell'inizio," (The Age of the End and the Age of the Beginning) *Casabella* 489/499 (January/February 1984): 106–108. The similarity of the title of Franco Rella's article is coincidental, for we use the terms "beginning" and "end" for entirely different purpose. Rella identifies the present as the age of the end, stating that the paradoxical result of progress has been to create a culture that simultaneously desires progress and is burdened with a sense of passing and the chronic sense of irredeemable loss. The result is a culture which "does not love what has been but the end of what has been. It hates the present, the existing, and the changing. It therefore loves nothing." Rella's article poses the question of whether it is possible to build today, to design in a way that is *with* rather than *against* time. He desires the return to a sense of time-boundedness and the possibility of living in one's own age without attempting to return to the past. The mechanism by which he proposes to re-create this possibility is myth. He differentiates myth from fiction, and it is this difference which illuminates the opposition between his proposal and the propositions of this paper. Myth is defined as a traditional story of ostensibly historical events that serves to unfold part of the worldview of a people in the traditional value-laden sense, giving history and thus value to timeless or inexplicable events. Rella dismisses fiction as verisimilitude, merely creating the appearance of truth. Instead of attempting to return to the past, myth attempts to create a new beginning merely situating us at an earlier, and less acute, state of anxiety. But a myth cannot alleviate the paradox of progress. Against both of these, "The End of the Beginning and The End of the End" proposes dissimulation, which is neither the simulation of reality as we know it nor the proposal of an alternate truth, which appeals to the identical verifying structures of belief—that is, origins, transformations, and ends. "The End of the Classical" insists on maintaining a state of anxiety, proposing fiction in a self-reflexive sense, a process without origins or ends which maintains its own fictionality rather than proposing a simulation of truth.

INTRODUCTION

From Contrast to Analogy: Developments in the
Concept of Architectural Intervention
Ignasi de Solà-Morales Rubió

This essay from the Italian magazine *Lotus
International* is by a member of its editorial board,
Ignasi de Solà-Morales Rubió. He continues a discussion of the theories of design method begun in
his *Architectural Design* essay, "Neo-rationalism
and Figuration." The author, who studied architecture and philosophy in his native Barcelona,
addresses in particular the problem of adding to
the urban context, which is of great importance to
neorationalist members of the "School of Venice"
and the American Cornell School. (ch. 6, 7)
"Intervention" is the term commonly used to
describe such strategies of addition in the traditional city. The conscious formation of an attitude
to history, implied by the architect's intervention, is
a second component of the essay, which explains
its inclusion in this chapter on historicism.

Whether the intervention contrasts with or is
analogous to the existing context, Solà-Morales
Rubió notes that "it...produces a genuine interpretation of the historical material with which it has to contend." While contrast between the ancient and the
new was sanctioned by modernists (in CIAM's
Charter of Athens of 1933), the author finds more
complexity in the postmodern relationship to the past:

> The cultural crisis is a crisis of universal models
> ...it is not possible today to formulate an aes-
> thetic system with sufficient validity to make it
> applicable beyond the individual circumstances.

The loss of a universal system is due to changes
in ideas of meaning, whether influenced by psychology (he emphasizes the significance of
gestalt) or philosophy (modern relativism replacing
eternal laws). Gestalt psychology supports the
strategy of contrast because:

> it was even asserted that the phenomenon of
> meaning in any field of the visual arts is pro-
> duced through juxtaposition, interrelation,
> and contrast of fundamentally heterogeneous
> shapes, textures, or materials.

Similarly, photomontage and collage representations derive their impact from the contextual construction of meaning via these suggested formal procedures. It is evident that similar discoveries about the fundamentally important operation of *difference* in language link linguistic structuralism to postmodern architectural theories of meaning.

Solà-Morales Rubió points to a shift in which contrast no longer dominates approaches to intervention, but remains one option among several "rhetorical figures." (See Eisenman, ch. 3) He defines the analogical operation as a comparison allowing difference and repetition to be simultaneously present. Analogy encompasses narrative and relationships of affinity, and dimensional, typological, and figurative correspondence. For instance, Aldo Rossi's analogical architecture relies on the use of type and its transformation. (ch. 7)

Analogy has an open-ended, nonprescriptive quality that dovetails with Solà-Morales Rubió's poststructuralist-influenced position. Like Jacques Derrida and Jean-François Lyotard, he suggests the importance of an aesthetic of the sublime:

> in the present, post-Freudian era, creation appears...to be the clear confrontation between the dreadful and its artistic sensibility.

Peter Eisenman and Anthony Vidler have also offered notions of the dreadful, the dark side of the sublime: the grotesque and the uncanny. (ch. 14)

IGNASI DE SOLÀ-MORALES RUBIÓ
FROM CONTRAST TO ANALOGY
DEVELOPMENTS IN THE CONCEPT OF ARCHITECTURAL
INTERVENTION

The relationship between a new architectural intervention and already existing architecture is a phenomenon that changes in relation to the cultural values attributed both to the meaning of historic architecture and to the intentions of the new intervention.

Hence it is an enormous mistake to think that one can lay down a permanent doctrine or still less a scientific definition of architectural intervention. On the contrary, it is only by understanding in each case the conceptions on the basis of which action has been taken that it is possible to make out the different characteristics which this relationship has assumed over the course of time. The design of a new work of architecture not only comes physically close to the existing one, entering into visual and spatial rapport with it, but it also produces a genuine interpretation of the historical material with which it has to contend, so that this material is the object of a true interpretation which explicitly or implicitly accompanies the new intervention in its overall significance.

When Mies van der Rohe presented his project for skyscrapers on Friederichstrasse to the authorities in Berlin, in 1918, the form of the new buildings in Alexanderplatz in 1921, and the other ones by Ludwig Hilbersheimer of the center of Berlin in 1927 or by Le Corbusier for the central zone of Paris in 1936, just to mention the best-known examples, have in common not only the same technique of representation but also the same sensitivity in the definition of a particular type of relationship between existing architecture and what is projected as new.

The technique of photomontage, or analogous perspective drawings, is particularly suited to emphasizing the *contrast* between old and new architecture. But this contrast which reveals differences in texture, materials and geometry, as well as in the density of

From *Lotus International* no. 46 (1985): 37–45. Courtesy of the author and publisher.

the urban grid, makes no pretence of being a negative judgement, a repudiation of historic architecture. On the contrary, as Le Corbusier commented on his project, "the new modern dimensions and the showing to advantage of historic treasures produce a delightful effect."[1]

It is often claimed that the avant-garde architecture of the Modern Movement completely ignored the architecture of the past, and that this lack of interest was the sign of a purely negative evaluation of it. It is true that the architecture of that time was the product of a formal system which claimed to be self-sufficient, at least in its programmatic expressions, based on the abstract geometry of form and simple three-dimensional shapes. But even this attitude could not help but make its own interpretation of the material presented to it by the city and by history, defining in paradigmatic fashion a type of relationship that is characterized by preponderance of the effect of *contrast* over any other type of formal category.

At the beginning of the century, Aloïs Riegl had analyzed the modern attitude to the problems of the monumental heritage in a series of penetrating and illuminating articles. In one written in 1903, Riegl described a typical category of the new sensitivity with regard to historical monuments.[2]

Alteswert, the quality of antiquity, is different from *Denkmalswert*, monumental value or monumentality, and from *kunsthistorisches Wert*, the historic-artistic value of buildings as it had been expressed in pre-twentieth-century culture. Since the Renaissance, European culture has developed a system of evaluation based not only on the current value that works of art might have, but also on their exemplary value as prior models of the good art of the past. From the nineteenth century onwards an additional value came into play, the historical value of the building or monument as a record of a positive and documented situation. The dichotomy between monumental value and documentary value emerged with the positivistic culture of the nineteenth century. But for Riegl, who started out from the crisis in positivism and in the objectivity of the new culture's language at the end of the century, the beginning of the twentieth century would be characterized by another situation. It was a question, to some extent, not only of a new relationship but also a more radical one between historical and monumental material and the cultural value assigned to it. Antiquity or the value of oldness, giving this term the ambiguity and lack of precision that it itself inspires, is a novelty typical of contemporary sensibility, in an attitude which makes the establishment of any kind of artistic standard relative and which ignores the positive significance of the information contained within a work of art.

Antiquity is a subjective quality that produces a purely psychological satisfaction derived from a view of the old as a manifestation of the passing of historical time.

Riegl, from the perspective of mass psychology, realized that the modern citizen is not interested in erudite information that can be decoded in the detail of an ornament or the arrangement of a colonnade, but in a more sweeping view. What attracts him is the testimony to a certain age offered by the monument. Precisely because the prime value of urban culture was, and still is, the finished perfection of new building, and given that new buildings have value only to the extent that they present a challenge to the passing of time, an image of intangibility to the erosion of history and a permanence in their form, colour, and finishing, this same subjective and mass sensitivity, little inclined towards rational cognition, finds in antiquity the all-embracing value in terms of which it can interpret historical architecture. It is in the necessary alternation between new and ancient architecture that fundamental aesthetic satisfaction is produced.

What typifies the new sensitivity, the new *Kunstwollen* or will to art of the twentieth century is the contrast between *Neuheitswert* or novelty value and *Alteswert*, or oldness as value. That is to say, the contrast between newness and oldness.

But this value attributed to what is ancient has a psychological key which Riegl explains in the same text with great precision. It is a purely perceptual satisfaction, which seeks no precise gain in knowledge, expressing itself as pure feeling of a subjective, vague and comforting character.

Comparison with the late classical attitude and with the religious subjectivism that characterized early Imperial culture served Riegl to define, in greater detail, the type of perceptibiliy to which he was referring. A more than tactile viewpoint and one that is more interested in the condition of life expressed by the monument than in this concrete specification, the search for antiquity represents a certain renunciation of knowledge, but also the affirmation of a collective and synthetic sensitivity which characterizes metropolitan man *en masse*.

Riegl's accurate description serves to explain what type of sensitivity it is that is revealed in the examples cited at the start of this article and in the special way in which the *contrast* between old and new architectural materials is established, as happens in those avant-garde projects that have to contend with the architecture of the past.

In order to back up the theory of *contrast* at the level of perception, as it is formulated by Riegl, it would not be difficult to draw too on the theoretical models utilized by intellectuals of the day when they were piecing together the history of architecture or looking for its psychological foundations in the *Gestalttheorie* that theoreticians and protagonists of the new art used as a basis for their own aesthetic experiences.

In the case of historiography it is clear that beginning with Riegl and at least up until [Sigfried] Giedion, but significantly in the works of [Gustav Adolf] Platz and Kurt Behrendt as well, the history of the architecture of the past is analyzed as a product of the past, bringing out its *novelties* and *differences* with respect to the architecture of the present.[3] Not only did they get over the reluctance about using the past in order to experience the more immediate and contemporary present, but they realized that this explanation served above all to show up the radical opposition, the contrast, between the ancient and the new, between history and current events.

In the treatises on the psychology of form by [Wolfgang] Köeller in 1929 and by [Kurt] Koffka in 1935, one finds a systematic organization of the more general principles of a conception in which the notions of ground-form and of contrast are fundamental to an explanation of perception and of its significance.[4]

In fact in the same years the teachings of [Wassily] Kandinsky, [Joseph] Albers, [László] Moholy-Nagy, and even Paul Klee during the early phase of the Bauhaus made use of just the same psychological categories for the training of draughtsmen and designers. Not only was architecture described—by Moholy-Nagy—as a phenomenon that is perceived three-dimensionally on the basis of a geometry and texture, thereby making a clean sweep of any kind of meaning, but it was even asserted that the phenomenon of meaning in any field of the visual arts is produced through juxtaposition, interrelation, and contrast of fundamentally heterogeneous shapes, textures, or materials.

Just as *collage* and *photomontage* develop techniques of extracting new and specific meanings from the confrontation of autonomous fragments, architecture, by contrasting ancient with new structures, finds the ground and the form in which the past and the present recognize each other.

But if there is a clear relationship between Riegl's diagnosis, the positions of historiography and the psychology of aesthetics, and the work of the architects of the Modern Movement when confronted with historical materials, it is also worth calling attention to the connections with a field that would seem to have little to do with avant-garde debate. That is that of the conservators and professional restorers who were developing a conception of the restoration of monuments in their specialized publications and debates that in its way had something in common with the idea of *contrast* as a fundamental category of the relationship between old and new architecture.

If ever since the end of the nineteenth century the theoretical literature produced by experts in restoration, such as Camillo Boito, defended a criterion of clear-cut differentiation in those interventions of restoration that involved an element of construction, it is this very idea that became one of the fundamental principles laid down in the 1931 Athens charter of restorers. More than once in the ten fundamental points into which this charter is divided, the clear conception of the *contrast* that must be produced between the protected historical buildings and new interventions is defended. Not just by recommending that modern materials should be used on certain occasions, but above all by the repeatedly expressed criterion according to which difference is noted in the different arrangement of added elements, in the use of different materials and in the absence of decorations in new constructions, in their geometrical and technological simplicity. Thus it can be said that the Athens charter accepted in a generalized and standardized fashion the criteria and approaches already elaborated in that period by architects. Architects who, whether they belonged to the world of avant-garde experimentation or the academic one of restoration, were subject to an identical historical sensibility. When the other Athens charter, that of the men of the CIAM in 1933, also insisted on the impossibility of accepting the historical pastiche and appealed to the *Zeitgeist* to justify their demand that new interventions in historical zones be made in the language of present-day architecture, this was not in reality so far from what had been asserted two years earlier by other professionals with whom they appeared to have very few things in common. Indeed, the two bodies were distinguished by the militant and progressive character of one and the historicist and conservative interests of the other.

But at a distance of fifty years, the differences between the two professional categories were not of such an absolute nature as it was in the interest of the protagonists to have people believe at the time.

Beneath the obvious differences there was a common attitude towards historical material and its interpretation. In both cases their guiding principle was formed by the late Romantic taste for rough textures and for the patina left by time on old buildings, without precise ornamental or stylistic distinctions, in overall contrast with the limpid, precise, and abstract geometry of the new works of architecture. In this way, the *contrast* between old and new was transformed not just in the outcome of radically opposing approaches, but also the perceptual procedure through which each kind of architecture established, reciprocally, its dialectical significance in the metropolitan city, was changed.

The predominance of the category of *contrast* as a fundamental principle of aesthetics in problems of intervention already belongs to the past. At least one cannot speak today of its privileged position. The effects of *contrast* remain in work of recent intervention, both as vestiges of the poetics of the Modern Movement in a few of today's architects and, in any case, as one of the many rhetorical figures that are used in the new and more complex relationship that current sensibility has established with the architecture of the past.

Let us take a number of examples that we find expressive of the new situation. Examples which, even though they are not all recent, seem to typify the new sensitivity with regard to this problem.

The project that [Erik Gunnar] Asplund worked on over a long period, from 1913 to 1937, for the extension to the Göteborg town hall, cannot be explained on the basis of a simple notion of *contrast*. On the contrary, what seems to characterize the line taken by the Swedish architect over the course of five successive projects is his interpretation of dominant features in the old building in order that they should find an echo in the part that was to be added on.

As much in the organization of the plan, extending the system of arcades, as in the lay-out of the facade, prolonging the pattern of empty spaces and pillars, in one case and in the other by extending the horizontal tripartite division as a dominant formal structure, in all the successive versions the approach to a satisfactory solution was developed through similarity between what were considered to be outstanding elements in the old structure and the forms that were proposed for the new extension. Difference and repetition were seen simultaneously through a controlled handling of the relations between similarity and diversity that are proper to any *analogical* operation.

When Carlo Scarpa turned Castelvecchio in Verona into a museum of the city he too had to deal with the prestige of the mediaeval building and the need to adapt it to requirements of a modern museum. Not so much through a comprehensive analysis of its composition as by means of a narrative and fragmentary development, Scarpa's intervention introduces historicist figures into the historical authenticity of the existing building. Through a display of cinematographic kind, he accumulates redesigned images of architectural works of the past, both from the Middle Ages and from other periods perhaps with far-off mediaeval origins but conjuring up more recent European experiences, such as those of the turn of the century in Glasgow or Vienna.

Here the *analogical* procedure is not based on the visible synchronism of interdependent orders of form, but on the association made by the observer over the course of time. By this means situations of affinity are produced, and thanks to the connotative capacity of the languages evoked in the intervention, relations or links are established between the historic building—real and/or imaginary—and the elements of design that serve to make the building effectively dependent.

Some of Giorgio Grassi's finest theoretical writing sets out to explain his approach to the restoration of the castle of Abbiategrasso, in 1970.[5] Basing himself on writings by Ambrogio Annoni and on the most cultivated tradition of restoration and the highest level of professionalism, Grassi found that the methodological key to organization of the intervention lay in the very architecture of the existing building. This was a correction of the kind of idealism practised by [Eugène Emmanuel] Viollet-le-Duc, who tried to find the basis for intervention in the *idea* hidden within the building. Grassi transformed this into a realism completely bound up with the spatial, physical, and geographical materiality of the artifact on which he was operating.

Drawing from typological analysis a first approximation to its internal laws, the project turns out as a compromise between the modes proper to the modern tradition based on the independence of new and old structure, and the dimensional, typological, and figurative correspondence between old and new parts in an attempt to create a mutual correlation that would unify the totality of the complex. Again it is a dialectical way of expressing the synchronism of similarity and difference.

Rafael Moneo's 1980 project for expansion of the Banco de España building in Madrid lies almost at the opposite extreme. Like Grassi, Moneo follows in the narrow track marked out by the laws of the building itself, by the logic of its composition and by the existing organization of structure and space. *Leaving almost no room for irony* and without any kind of separation to delimit the characteristics of each aesthetic operation, Moneo's project completes the existing building while effacing itself to the utmost and emphasizing to just what extent the existing building imposed its own exigencies. Here *analogy* becomes tenuous, almost imperceptible, turning into mere tautology.

The four examples analyzed so far have a series of characteristic traits in common. The cultural crisis is a crisis of universal models. The difference between the present situation and that of academic culture or modern orthodoxy lies in the fact that it is not possible today to formulate an aesthetic system with sufficient validity to make it applicable beyond the individual circumstances.

[Friedrich] Nietzsche's critique of metaphysics and [Ludwig] Wittgenstein's critique of language have stripped away all pretence of generality or permanence in the processes of culture. It is the same radically historical situation that post-Foucaultian knowledge acknowledges in itself. While academic culture has been able to create universally applicable procedures of intervention through the notion of style and modern culture has been able to create an interwoven system of fragments by means of psychological subjectivism, it is difficult in the present situation to recognize anything but the factual nature, on the one hand, of the concrete work with which one has to deal and on which one has to operate and, on the other, the infinite system of referents with which the collective imagery of architecture is studded.

The liberal optimism of Colin Rowe may still have faith in the effectiveness of collage when he thinks that a fragmentary dismemberment does not conflict with a certain kind of comprehensive strategy that allows some measure of control over the city and its architecture.[6] But what happens to Colin Rowe with the collage is the same as happened to the terrified Pandora, Epimetheus's wife, when she let all the evils that afflict humanity out of her golden box and was left with nothing in her hands but the container in which she still counted on keeping hope.

But the hope of collage rests solely, as a technique, on a *Gestalt* composition of which today's barbarous artists of *frottage* and *dripping* have given a good account. The current reality is, in a sense, more reductive in that it is more critical. But for the very same reason it is more precise at the moment of acting, with an acute awareness of what the building is telling us and what the history of architecture teaches us.

In recent years knowledge of the intimate structures of buildings has led to the development of techniques and tools that are as sophisticated as they are accurate.

The typo-morphological analysis championed by Aldo Rossi in his writings of the sixties has resulted, on the one hand, in a genuinely encyclopaedic culture of representation, dimensional comparison, and structural awareness of all the problems of form presented by existing buildings. Since the sixties architectural culture has been imbued with an authentic obsession with analysis, making use of cartographic, planimetric, and three-dimensional instruments of extraordinary effectiveness.

But it is no less true that we are today in a position to know just how little this analytical mechanism has to do with creating a sufficient condition for the project. While the analytical protocols of the project have been refined to limits virtually impossible to achieve in other historical eras, this very precision has revealed that creativity of design represents a level of operation completely untrammeled by and independent of the need for analysis.

Instrumental knowledge of the object does not allow us to evade the risk of the project and, in this case, the risk of the representation and new linguistic structures which the intervention will have to introduce.

But in this situation history is not, as it once was, *magistra vitae*. Nor is it a logical instrument for tendentious explanation of the present. On the contrary, running parallel to the drastic historicizing of the present there is a polycentric dispersion of historical awareness.

Since the Sixties we have seen an unmasking of the illusions of an ideological history that tended not only to dispel the anxiety of the present, but also to justify its choices. That history can no longer hang on to a pretence of veracity. There is no guiding thread leading from the past to the present. Manfredo Tafuri, the most decisive thinker with regard to the holistic nature of the cycle of architectural history in the modern era, has constructed a model that is as effective for criticism as it is tautological for representation of the passing of historical time. If on the one hand, the idea of the origin of modernity has been pushed back ad infinitum, no longer stopping in the last century or at the Enlightenment but reaching back to the well-springs of modern culture in the Renaissance, on the other, the problems that are raised in [Filippo] Brunelleschli turn up in Mannerism and in the culture of the Counter-Reformation, as well as in the crisis in enlightened thought or the decline of the avant-garde.

The idea that architecture and architects give birth at one and the same time to their affirmation and their negation, and therefore to the meaning and the contradiction of their logic, represents not only a central hypothesis of his work, but also the dominant paradigm in the majority of recent architectural historiography.

Historical awareness, like the analytic techniques of the project, is caught in the contradiction between the sophisticated development of its areas of knowledge and the most absolute impoverishment of methodology. Microhistory, anthropological history or the history of mentality are, at bottom, private, reductive, and fragmentary responses to the impossibility of defending interpretive models of a wider range.[7]

In his book *Lo bello y lo siniestro*, Eugenio Trias discusses the meaning and scope of contemporary aesthetic production.[8] If the whole of European aesthetics after [Immanuel] Kant is experienced from the barriers which Kant himself placed on the aesthetic object, in the sense that only the dreadful had to be estranged from the field of creation, in the present, post-Freudian era, creation appears, instead, to be the clear confrontation between the dreadful and its artistic expression.

The disorder that contemporary thought finds in reality lies at the origin of the experience of the dreadful. The task of art is that of the veil of Maya, a chaste covering that wraps the horror of Chaos in transparent material and displays it at the same time as covering it.

The linguistic comprehension of artistic phenomena, which originates in formalistic linguistics, has made it possible to understand with greater precision the conditions in which the meaning can shift, be transformed, and undergo metamorphosis through structural relationship. This linguistic structure which, recognized in the tissue of objects, permits their liberation and play, is also the one which in the field of architectural intervention defines the situation of the present day.

The meanings suggested to us by the works that we discussed at the beginning of this article are not explicable without the greatest liberty in the manipulation of the sense, and at the same time, the structures of meaning that the concrete building displays, exist only as a support for this manipulation. To this must be added the accumulation of historical references that replace the ancient systematic and efficient knowledge of history with a multiple stock of imagery.

As an aesthetic operation, the intervention is the imaginative, arbitrary, and free proposal by which one seeks not only to recognize the significant structures of the existing historical material but also to use them as *analogical* marks of the new construction.

Comparison, as difference and similarity, from within the only possible system, that particular system defined by the existing object, is the foundation of every *analogy*. On this *analogy* is constructed every possible and unpredictable meaning.

1   Le Corbusier, *Oeuvre Complète, 1934–1939* (Zurich: 1946).
2   A. Riegl, *Der moderne Denkmalkultus, sein Wesen, seine Entstehung (Enleitung zum Denkmalschutzgesetz)* (Vienna: 1903).
3   Analysis of the early historiography linked to the fortunes of the Modern Movement has been carried out by M.L. Scalvini and M. Gaudi, in *L'immagine storiografica dell'architettura contemporanea. Da Platz a Giedion* (Rome: 1984).
4   W. Köeller, *Gestalt Psychology* (New York: 1929); K. Koffka, *Principles of Gestalt Psychology* (New York: 1935).
5   G. Grassi, "Il progetto di intervento sul castello di Abbiategrasso e la questione del restauro," *Edilizia Popolare* no. 113 (Milan: 1973). Now in the book *La arquitectura como oficio y otros escritos* (Barcelona: 1980).
6   C. Rowe, *Collage City* (Cambridge: 1979).
7   J. Le Goff, *La nouvelle histoire* (Paris: 1979).
8   E. Trias, *Lo bello y lo siniestro* (Barcelona: 1982).

5. TYPOLOGY AND TRANSFORMATION

INTRODUCTION

On the Typology of Architecture
Giulio Carlo Argan

In the postmodern period, theorists reconsidered the notion of type as the essence of architecture, seen in some cases as comparable to linguistic deep structure. After its revival by architectural historian Giulio Carlo Argan in this essay, architects including Aldo Rossi and Rafael Moneo investigated Quatremère de Quincy's definition of type: "the idea of an element which should itself serve as a rule for the model." Moneo interprets it as the inherent structural and formal order that allows architectural objects to be grouped together, distinguished, and repeated.[1]

Typology is valued by Rossi and Leon Krier as a precise analytical tool for architecture and urban form, which also provides a rational basis for design. The interest in type is part of the larger postmodern search for meaning because it establishes continuity with history—increasingly seen as necessary to give architecture legibility within a culture. In discussions of urban morphology, type is credited with the capacity to create a legible urbanism, promoted by postmodernists as the remedy for the "object-in-a-field" modernist city. In the 1970s, urban legibility was sought by recreating the building forms and figural public spaces of the traditional European city.

Giulio Carlo Argan's types, approximating archetypes, are regressed or reduced to a common "root form" from specific works in a particular culture, which have obvious analogous formal and functional properties. His theory also allows for the creation of new types in response to sociocultural and technological changes. Thus, type for Argan is more a principle allowing for variation, than an *a priori* set of fixed entities. As he defines it, type operates on the levels of formal configuration, structure, and decorative elements. Argan concludes that linking typology to tectonics will make it an "inevitable" basis for formal exploration; his proposed structural level of type constitutes such a link.

Argan's consideration of type is relevant to the process of design in general, and to the production of individual works. Thus he engages the modern architect's concerns in confronting the tradition of the discipline, expressed by literary critic Harold Bloom as "the anxiety of influence." While the use of a specific model or precedent requires the exercise of judgement in selection, Argan considers the generic type to be neutral and value-free. He can then work convincingly around the problem of influence and imitation.

Argan's brief article leaves some interesting questions unanswered: What are the (unidentified) "fundamental profound problems" that type addresses? What is type's "constant ideological base"? Why have so few significant modern types evolved?

1   Rafael Moneo, "On Typology," *Oppositions* 13 (Summer 1978), 22–43

GIULIO CARLO ARGAN

ON THE TYPOLOGY OF ARCHITECTURE

This article appeared first in a volume of essays (edited by Karl Oettinger and Mohammed Rassem) offered to Professor Hans Sedlmayr on his sixty-fifth birthday, and published in Munich by C. H. Beck in 1962. It seemed to the translator to approach a subject which is central to speculation about architectural theory both in this country and in America—but to do so from a rather unfamiliar standpoint and so contribute a new element to current discussion.
Joseph Rykwert

Most modern critics who depend ultimately on some form of idealistic philosophy would deny that an architectural typology could in any way be valid. They are right in so far as it would be absurd to maintain that the formal value of a circular temple is increased as it approaches an ideal "type" of circular temple. Such an ideal "type" is only an abstraction; so it is inconceivable that an architectural "type" could be proposed as a standard by which the individual work of art could be valued. On the other hand it cannot be denied that architectural typologies have been formulated and passed down in theoretical treatises and the work of famous architects. It is therefore legitimate to postulate the question of typology as a function both of the historical process of architecture and also of the thinking and working processes of individual architects.

There is an obvious analogy between architectural typology and iconography: typology may not be a determining factor of the creative process, but it is always in evidence much as iconography is in figurative arts, though its presence is not always obvious. How does an architectural "type" appear? Those critics who would admit that "types" have a certain importance are those who explain architectural forms in relation to a symbolism or to a ritual pattern connected with them. This kind of criticism has not

From *Architectural Design* no. 33 (December 1963): 564–565. Translated by Joseph Rykwert. Courtesy of the publisher.

resolved (and cannot resolve) a crucial problem: does symbolic content exist before the creation of the "type" and determine it—or is it just a subsequent deduction? This question of precedence is, however, not decisive where it is considered in the context of an historical process; when symbolic content precedes the "type" and determines it, this content is only transmitted in connection with certain architectural forms; in the same way when the reverse happens, the succession of forms transmits the symbolic content in a more or less conscious manner. There are cases in which symbolic content is sought for consciously as a link to an ancient formal tradition; such a procedure may become an important consideration by virtue of its historical and aesthetic function. Two test cases of a conscious linking of architectural form with ideological content are those of the symbolism of centralized religious building of the Renaissance studied by [Rudolf] Wittkower; and that of a Baroque architectural allegory studied by [Hans] Sedlmayr.

Quatremère de Quincy gives a precise definition of an architectural "type" in his historical dictionary. The word "type," he says, does not present so much an image of something to be copied or imitated exactly as the idea of an element which should itself serve as a rule for the model...

the model understood as part of the practical execution of art is an object which should be imitated for what it is the "type" on the other hand is something in relation to which different people may conceive works of art having no obvious resemblance to each other. All is exact and defined in the model; in the "type" everything is more or less vague. The imitation of "types" therefore has nothing about it which defies the operation of sentiment and intelligence....

The notion of the vagueness or generality of the "type" which cannot therefore directly affect the design of buildings or their formal quality, also explains its generation, the way in which a "type" is formed. It is never formulated *a priori* but always deduced from a series of instances. So the "type" of a circular temple is never identifiable with this or that circular temple (even if one definite building, in this case the Pantheon, may have had and continues to have a particular importance) but is always the result of the confrontation and fusion of all circular temples. The birth of a "type" is therefore dependent on the existence of a series of buildings having between them an obvious formal and functional analogy. In other words, when a "type" is determined in the practice or theory of architecture, it already has an existence as an answer to a complex of ideological, religious, or practical demands which arise in a given historical condition of whatever culture.

In the process of comparing and superimposing individual forms so as to determine the "type," particular characteristics of each individual building are eliminated and only those remain which are common to every unit of the series. The "type" therefore, is formed through a process of reducing a complex of formal variants to a common root form. If the "type" is produced through such a process of regression, the root form which is then found cannot be taken as an analogue to something as neutral as a structural grid. It has to be understood as the interior structure of a form or as a principle which contains the possibility of infinite formal variation and further structural modification of the "type" itself. It is not, in fact, necessary to demonstrate that if the final form of a building is a variant of a "type" deduced from a preceding formal series, the addition of another variant to the series will necessarily determine a more or less considerable change of the whole "type."

Two salient facts show that the formative process of a typology is not just a classifying or statistical process but one carried out for definite formal ends. Firstly: typological series do not arise only in relation to the physical functions of buildings but are tied to their configuration. The fundamental "type" of the circular shrine for instance, is independent of the functions, sometimes complex, which such buildings must fulfill. It was only in the second half of the nineteenth century that an attempt was made to set up a typology based on the order of physical functions (typical plans for hospitals, hotels, schools, banks, etc.) which, however, has not produced any important formal results. Historical "types," such as centrally planned or longitudinal temples, or those resulting from a combination of the two plans, are not intended to satisfy contingent, practical requirements; they are meant to deal with more profound problems which—at least within the limits of any given society—are thought fundamental and constant; it is, therefore, essential to lay claim to all the experience matured in the past in order to be able to conceive forms in such a way that they will continue to be thought valid in the future. However much a "type" may allow of variation, the ideological content of forms has a constant base, though this may—indeed should—assume a particular accent or character at any particular time. Secondly, although an infinite number of classes and sub-classes of "types" may be formulated, formal architectural typologies will always fall into three main categories; the first concerned with a complete configuration of buildings, the second with major structural elements and the third with decorative elements. Examples of the first category are centrally or longitudinally planned buildings; of the second, flat or domed roofs, traviated or arcuated systems; and of the third, orders of columns, ornamental details, etc. Now, it is clear that a classification so constituted follows the succession of the architect's working process (plan, structural system, surface treatment) and that it is intended to provide a typological guide for the architect to follow in the process of conceiving a building. So that the working out of every architectural project has this typological aspect; whether it is that the architect consciously follows the "type" or wants to depart from it; or even in the sense that every building is an attempt to produce another "type."

But if the "type" is a schema or grid and the schema inevitably embodies a moment of rigidity or inertia, the presence of such a schema needs to be explained in the context of an artist's creative process. This leads one back naturally to the general problem of the relation between artistic creation and historical experience, since it is from historical experience that the "type" is always deduced. What requires further explanation, however, is the proposition that at least a part of that historical experience presents itself to an architect who is designing a building in the form of a typological grid. The "type," so Quatremère de Quincy has said, is an "object" but "vague or indistinct"; it is not definite form but a schema or the outline of a form; it also carries a residue of the experience of forms already accomplished in projects or buildings, but all that makes for their specific formal and artistic value is discarded. More precisely in the "type" they are deprived of their character and of their true quality as forms; by sublimation into a "type" they assume the indefinite value of an image or a sign. Through this reduction of preceding works of art to a "type," the artist frees himself from being conditioned by a definite historical form, and neutralizes the past. He assumes that what is past is absolute and therefore no longer capable of developing. Accepting Quatremère de Quincy's definition, one might say that the "type" arises at the moment at which the art of the past no longer appears to a working artist as a conditioning model.

The choice of a model implies a value judgment: a recognition that a certain definite work of art is perfect and has to be imitated. When such a work of art re-assumes the schematic and indistinct nature of a "type," the individual action of the artist is no longer bound to a value judgment; the "type" is accepted but not "imitated" which means that the repetition of the "type" excludes the operation of that kind of creative process which is known as mimesis. In fact, the acceptance of the "type" implies the suspension of historical judgment and is therefore negative; although also "intentioned," directed to the formulation of a new kind of value in as much as it demands of the artist—in its very negativity—a new formal determination.

It is true that the assumption of a "type" as a starting point for the architect's working process does not exhaust his involvement with historical data: it does not stop him from assuming or rejecting definite buildings as models.

Bramante's tempietto of San Pietro in Montorio is a classic instance of such a process; it obviously depends on a "type": the peripteral circular temple described by Vitruvius (Book IV, Chapter 8) which integrates the abstraction of the "type" through historical "models" (for instance, the temple of Sybil at Tivoli), and so appears to claim for itself the status of both model and "type." Indeed it is characteristic of Bramantesque classicism to aspire to a syncretic union of ideal antiquity (which is essentially "typical") and of historical antiquity which has a status of a formal model. An instance of a diametrically opposed attitude is that of neoclassical architects who assume classical architectural typology, not classical architectures, as a model so that the movement produces works which are merely three-dimensional transcriptions of "type." If the concept of typology could in some way be brought back to that of "techtonics" as recently defined by Cesare Brandi (*Eliante o della archa*, 1956), one might say that typology is a notional base on which formal development of the artist must inevitably rest.

It will, therefore, be clear that the position of the artist vis-à-vis history has two aspects, the aspect of typology and that of formal definition. That of typology is not problematic: the artist assumes certain data, taking as a premise of all his work a group of common notions, or a heritage of images with all their more or less explicit content and their ideological overtones. This aspect may be compared to the iconographic and compositional treatment of themes in figurative art. The aspect of formal definition, on the other hand, implies a reference to definite formal values of the past on which the artist explicitly arrives at a judgment. This judgment, however, must itself imply a typology since, whenever a value judgment on given works of art is passed, a judgment must also be passed about the way in which the artist, in creating them, had dealt with the relevant typological scheme.

The question of the value of architectural typology has recently been examined by Sergio Bettini (*Zodiac* no. 5) and by G. K. König (*Lezioni del Corso di Plastica*, Florence: Editrice Universitaria, 1961). In these writings the opinion prevails that an architectural "type" must be treated as a schema of spatial articulation which has been formed in response to a totality of practical and ideological demands. From this one might deduce that the formal invention which overcomes the "type" is a response to immediate demands in reference to which the "type" had lost any real value. A recourse to the "type" would therefore occur when the immediate demand which the artist is called to answer has its roots in the past. A significant instance is provided by the comparison between modern religious and industrial architecture. Industrial architecture which deals with altogether new demands has created new "types" which have, in many cases, great importance for the later development of architecture. Religious architecture which answers demands rooted in the past has resulted in typological repetition (artistically valueless) or in attempts at freeing the artist of all typological precedent (as, for instance, Le Corbusier at Ronchamp). These have led to the proposing of counter-types, mostly ephemeral or unacceptable—there are few instances of modern developments of historical "types."

The conclusion must be that the typological and the inventive aspect of the creative process are continuous and interlaced—the inventive aspect being merely that of dealing with the demands of the actual historical situation by criticizing and overcoming past solutions deposited and synthesized schematically in the "type."

INTRODUCTION

Typology and Design Method
Alan Colquhoun

This essay is a classic of the postmodern period, having appeared in four different publications. From its first printing in the British journal *Arena* in 1967, to its reprinting in *Perspecta*, Yale University's esteemed architectural journal, and in two anthologies, Alan Colquhoun's questioning of modernist design methods has had significant impact. In addition, the piece is one of the earliest postmodern writings on typology in English, asserting that "Recourse to some kind of typological model is...necessary."

Colquhoun, an architect, theorist, and educator, comes to this conclusion after an examination of the Modern Movement's supposedly "objective" or scientific design methodology. He finds in its two components an inherent contradiction. The primary component, "biotechnical determinism," takes a teleological view of the evolution of forms in architecture. But since this approach does not help with "determining the actual configuration," architects must then turn to the second and incompatible component, intuition, an important element in modern expressionist theories. Intuition is used in making choices in the design process, choices which together constitute the designer's intention. The author turns to the Italian theorist Tomás Maldonado's idea

> that the area of pure intuition must be based on a knowledge of past solutions applied to related problems, and that creation is a process of adapting forms derived either from past needs or from past aesthetic ideologies to the needs of the present.

Colquhoun sees the transformation of past solutions (i.e., using typology as design method) as a means of acknowledging the role of precedent in design. This is a radical break with the Modern Movement, which rejected type and theories of imitation in favor of innovation.

In a later piece entitled "Modern Architecture and Historicity," written as the introduction to his collection of essays for *Oppositions*, Colquhoun goes further, to assert that typology, as an instrument of cultural memory, is a *condition* of architectural meaning. It is the context within which new work is understood. In line with the contemporaneous structuralist thought of Roland Barthes and Claude Lévi-Strauss, Colquhoun reads architectural artifacts as coded by layers of cultural signification. Typology is a mechanism to retrieve this signification, used by the neorationalists Aldo Rossi (ch. 7) and Leon Krier.

ALAN COLQUHOUN

TYPOLOGY AND DESIGN METHOD

During the last few years a great deal of attention has been given to the problem of design methodology and to the process of design as a branch of the wider process of problem-solving. Many people believe—not without reason—that the intuitive methods of design traditionally used by architects are incapable of dealing with the complexity of the problems to be solved and that without sharper tools of analysis and classification the designer tends to fall back on previous examples for the solution of new problems— on type-solutions.

One of the designers and educators who has been consistently preoccupied with this matter is Tomás Maldonado. At a seminar at Princeton University in the fall of 1966, Maldonado admitted that in cases where it was not possible to classify every observable activity in an architectural program, it might be necessary to use a typology of architectural forms in order to arrive at a solution. But he added that these forms were like a cancer in the body of the solution and that as our techniques of classification become more systematic, it should be possible to eliminate them altogether.

Now, it is my belief that beneath the apparently practical and hard-headed aspect of these ideas lies an aesthetic doctrine. It will be my purpose to show this to be the case and, further, to try to show that it is untenable without considerable modification.

One of the most frequent arguments used against typological procedures in architecture has been that they are a vestige of an age of craft. It is held that the use of models by craftsmen became less necessary as the development of scientific techniques enabled man to discover the general laws underlying the technical solutions of the preindustrial age.

From *Essays in Architectural Criticism: Modern Architecture and Historical Change* (Cambridge: Oppositions Books and MIT Press, 1981), 43–50. First published in *Arena* 83 (June 1967). Republished in *Perspecta* 12 (1969). Also published in Charles Jencks and George Baird, eds., *Meaning in Architecture* (New York: Braziller, 1969), 267–277. Courtesy of the author and MIT Press.

The vicissitudes of the words "art" and "science" certainly indicate that there is a valid distinction to be drawn between artifacts that are the result of the application of the laws of physical science and those that are the result of mimesis and intuition. Before the rise of modern science, tradition, habit, and imitation were the methods by which all artifacts were made, whether these artifacts were mainly utilitarian or mainly religious. The word "art" was used to describe the skill necessary to produce all such artifacts. With the development of modern science, the word "art" was progressively restricted to the case of artifacts which did not depend on the general laws of physical science but continued to be based on tradition and the idea of the final form of the work as a fixed ideal.

But this distinction ignores the extent to which artifacts have not only a "use" value in the crudest sense but also an "exchange" value. The craftsman had an image of the object in his mind's eye when starting to make it. Whether this object was a cult image (say, a sculpture) or a kitchen utensil, it was an object of cultural exchange, and it formed part of a system of communication within society. Its "message" value was precisely the image of the final form which the craftsman held in his mind's eye as he was making it and to which his artifact corresponded as closely as possible. In spite of the development of the scientific method, we must still attribute such social or iconic values to the products of technology and recognize that they play an essential role in the generation and development of the physical tools of our environment. It is easy to see that the class of artifacts which continues to be made according to the traditional methods (for example, paintings or musical compositions) has a predominantly iconic purpose, but such a purpose is not so often recognized in the creation of the environment as a whole. This fact is concealed from us because the intentions of the design process are "hidden" in the overt details of the performance specifications.

The idolization of "primitive" man and the fundamentalist attitude which this generates have also discouraged the acceptance of such iconic values. There has been a tendency since the eighteenth century to regard the age of primitive man as a golden age in which man lived close to nature. For many years, for instance, the primitive hut or one of its derivatives has been taken as the starting point for architectural evolution and has been the subject of first-year design programs in the schools, and it would not be an exaggeration to say that frequently a direct line of descent is presumed to exist from the noble savage through the utilitarian crafts to modern science and technology. Insofar as it is based on the idea of the noble savage, this idea is quite baseless. The cosmological systems of primitive man were very intellectual and very artificial. To take only kinship systems, the following quotation from the French anthropologist Claude Lévi-Strauss will make the point clear: "Certainly," he says,

> the biological family is present and persists in human society. But what gives to kinship its character as a social fact is not what it must conserve of nature; it is the essential step by which it separates itself from nature. A system of kinship does not consist of objective blood ties; it exists only in the consciousness of men; it is an arbitrary system of representations, not the spontaneous development of a situation of fact.[1]

There seems to be a close parallel between such systems and the way modern man still approaches the world. And what was true of primitive man in all the ramifications of his practical and emotional life—namely, the need to *represent* the phenomenal world in such a way that it becomes a coherent and logical system—persists in our own organizations and more particularly in our attitude toward the man-made objects of our environment. An example of the way this applies to contemporary man is in the creation of what are called socio-spatial schemata. Our senses of place and relationship in, say, an urban environment, or in a building, are not dependent on any objective fact that is measurable; they are phenomenal. The purpose of the aesthetic organization of our environment is to capitalize on this subjective schematization and make it socially available. The resulting organization does not correspond in a one-to-one relationship with the objective facts but is an artificial construct which *represents* these facts in a socially recognizable way. It follows that the representational systems which are developed are, in a real sense, independent of the quantifiable facts of the environment, and this is particularly true if the environment is changing very rapidly.

However, no system of representation, no metalanguage, is totally independent of the facts which constitute the objective world. The Modern Movement in architecture was an attempt to modify the representational systems which had been inherited from the preindustrial past and which no longer seemed meaningful within the context of a rapidly changing technology. One of the main doctrines at the root of this transformation was based essentially on a return to nature, deriving from the Romantic movement but ostensibly changed from a desire to imitate the surface of natural forms, or to operate at a craft level, to a belief in the ability of science to reveal the essence of nature's mode of operation.

Underlying this doctrine was an implied belief in biotechnical determinism. And it is from this theory that the current belief in the supreme importance of scientific methods of analysis and classification derives. The essence of the functional doctrine of the Modern Movement was not that beauty or order or meaning was unnecessary, but that it could no longer be found in the deliberate search for final forms. The path by which the artifact affected the observer aesthetically was seen as short-circuiting the process of formalization. Form was merely the result of a logical process by which the operational needs and the operational techniques were brought together. Ultimately these would fuse in a kind of biological extension of life, and function and technology would become totally transparent. The theory of Buckminster Fuller is an extreme example of this doctrine.

The relation of this notion to Spencerian evolutionary theory is very striking. According to this theory the purpose of prolonging life and the species must be attributed to the process as a whole, but at no particular moment in the process is it possible to see this purpose as a conscious one. The process is therefore unconscious and teleological. In the same way, the biotechnical determinism of the Modern Movement was teleological, because it saw the aesthetic of architectural form as something which was achieved without the conscious interference of the designer but as something which nonetheless was postulated as his ultimate purpose.

It is clear that this doctrine contradicts any theory which would give priority to an intentional iconic form, and it attempts to absorb the process by which man tries to make a representation of the world of phenomena back into a process of unconscious evolution. To what extent has it been successful, and to what extent can it be shown to be possible?

It seems evident, in the first place, that the theory begs the whole question of the iconic significance of forms. Those in the field of design who were—and are—preaching pure technology and so-called objective design method as a necessary and sufficient means of producing environmental devices persistently attribute iconic power to the creations of technology, which they worship to a degree inconceivable in a scientist. I said earlier that it was in the power of all artifacts to become icons, no matter whether or not they were specifically created for this purpose. Perhaps I might mention certain objects of the nineteenth-century world of technology which had power of this kind—steamships and locomotives, to give only two examples. Even though these objects were made ostensibly with utilitarian purposes in mind, they quickly became gestalt entities, which were difficult to disassemble in the mind's eye into their component parts. The same is true of later technical devices such as cars and airplanes. The fact that these objects have been imbued with aesthetic unity and have become carriers of so much meaning indicates that a process of selection and isolation has taken place which is quite redundant from the point of view of their particular functions. We must therefore look upon the aesthetic and iconic qualities of artifacts as being due, not so much to an inherent property, but to a sort of availability or redundancy in them in relation to human feeling.

The literature of modern architecture is full of statements which indicate that after all the known operational needs have been satisfied, there is still a wide area of choice in the final configuration. I should like to cite two designers who have used mathematical methods to arrive at architectural solutions. The first is Yona Friedman, who uses these methods to arrive at a hierarchy of organization in the program. Friedman, in describing methods of computing the relative positions of functions within a three-dimensional city grid, has acknowledged that the designer always faced, after computation, with a choice of alternatives, all of which are equally good from an operational point of view.[2]

The second is Yannis Xenakis, who, in designing the Philips Pavilion while he was in the office of Le Corbusier, used mathematical procedures to determine the form of the enclosing structure. In the book which Philips published to describe this building, Xenakis says that calculation provided the characteristic form of the structure but that after this, logic no longer operated, and the compositional arrangement had to be decided on the basis of intuition.

From these statements it would appear that a purely teleological doctrine of technico-aesthetic forms is not tenable. At whatever stage in the design process it may occur, it seems that the designer is always faced with making voluntary decisions and that the configurations which he arrives at must be the result of an *intention* and not merely the result of a deterministic process. The following statement of Le Corbusier tends to reinforce this point of view. "My intellect," he says,

> does not accept the adoption of the modules of Vignola in the matter of building. I claim that harmony exists between the objects one is dealing with. The chapel at Ronchamp perhaps shows that architecture is not an affair of columns but an affair of plastic events. Plastic events are not regulated by scholastic or academic formulae; they are free and innumerable.

Although this statement is a defense of functionalism against the academic imitation of past forms and the determinism it denies is academic rather than scientific, it nonetheless stresses the release that follows from functional considerations rather than their power of determining the solution.

One of the most uninhibited statements of this kind comes from László Moholy-Nagy. In his description of the design course at the Institute of Design in Chicago, he makes the following defense of the free operation of intuition. "The training," he says,

> is directed toward imagination, fantasy, and inventiveness, a basic conditioning to the ever-changing industrial scene, to the technology-in-flux....The last step in this technique is the emphasis on integration through a conscious search for relationships.... The intuitive working mechanics of the genius gives a clue to this process. The unique ability of the genius can be approximated by everyone if only its essential feature be apprehended: the flashlike act of connecting elements not obviously belonging together ....If the same methodology were used generally in all fields we would have the key to our age—seeing everything in relationship.[3]

We can now begin to build up a picture of the general body of doctrine embedded in the Modern Movement. It consists of a tension between two apparently contradictory ideas—biotechnical determinism on the one hand and free expression on the other. What seems to have happened is that, in the act of giving a new validity to the demands of function as an extension of nature's mode of operation, a vacuum has been left where previously there was a body of traditional practice. The whole field of aesthetics, with its ideological foundations and its belief in ideal beauty, has been swept aside. All that is left in its place is permissive expression, the total freedom of the genius which, if we but knew it, resides in us all. What appears on the surface as a hard, rational discipline of design turns out rather paradoxically to be a mystical belief in the intuitional process.

I would like now to turn back to the statement by Maldonado which I mentioned earlier. He said that so long as our classification techniques were unable to establish all the parameters of a problem, it might be necessary to use a typology of forms to fill the gap. From the examples of the statements made by modern designers, it would seem that it is indeed never possible to state all the parameters of a problem. Truly quantifiable criteria always leave a choice for the designer to make. In modern architectural theory this choice has been generally conceived of as based on intuition working in a cultural vacuum. In mentioning typology, Maldonado is suggesting something quite new and something which has been rejected again and again by modern theorists. He is suggesting that the area of pure intuition must be based on a knowledge of past solutions applied to related problems, and that creation is a process of adapting forms derived either from past needs or from past aesthetic ideologies to the needs of the present. Although he regards this as a provisional solution—"a cancer in the body of the solution"—he nonetheless recognizes that this is the actual procedure which designers follow.

I suggest that this is true and, moreover, that it is true in all fields of design and not only that of architecture. I have referred to the argument that the more rigorously the general physical or mathematical laws are applied to the solution of design problems the less it is necessary to have a mental picture of the final form. But, although we may postulate an ideal state in which these laws correspond exactly to the objective world, in fact this is not the case. Laws are not found in nature. They are constructs of the human mind; they are models which are valid so long as events do not prove them to be wrong. They are models, as it were, at one remove from pictorial models. Not only this. Technology is frequently faced with different problems which are not logically consistent. All the problems of aircraft configuration, for example, could not be solved unless there was give-and-take in the application of physical laws. The position of the power unit is a variable; so is the configuration of the wings and tail plane. The position of one affects the shape of the other. The application of general laws is a necessary ingredient of the form. But it is not a sufficient one for determining the actual configuration. And in a world of pure technology this area of free choice is invariably dealt with by adapting previous solutions.

In the world of architecture this problem becomes even more crucial, because general laws of physics and the empirical facts are even less capable of fixing a final configuration than in the case of an airplane or a bridge. Recourse to some kind of typological model is even more necessary.

It may be argued that, in spite of the fact that there is an area of free choice beyond that of operation, this freedom lies in the details (where, for instance, personal "taste" might legitimately operate). This could probably be shown to be true of such technically complex objects as airplanes, where the topological relationships are largely determined by the application of physical laws. But it does not seem to apply to architecture. On the contrary, because of the comparatively simple environmental pressures that operate on buildings, the topological relationships are hardly at all determined by physical laws. In the case of the Philips Pavilion, for example, it was not only the acoustic requirements which established the basic configuration but also the need for a building which would convey a certain impression of vertigo and fantasy. It is in the details that these laws become stringent and not in the general arrangement. Where the designer decides to be governed by operational factors, he works in terms of a thoroughly nineteenth-century rationalism, for example in the case of the office buildings of Mies van der Rohe and Skidmore, Owings and Merrill, where purely pragmatic planning and cost considerations converge on a received neoclassical aesthetic to create simple cubes, regular frames, and cores. It is interesting that in most of the projects where form determinants are held to be technical or operational in an avant-garde sense, rationalism and cost are discarded for forms of a fantastic or expressionist kind. Frequently, as in the case of Archigram, forms are borrowed from other disciplines, such as space engineering or Pop Art. Valid as these iconographic procedures may be—and before dismissing them one would have to investigate them in relation to the work of Le Corbusier and the Russian Constructivists, who borrowed the forms of ships and engineering structures—they can hardly be compatible with a doctrine of determinism, if we are to regard this as a modus operandi, rather than a remote and utopian ideal.

The exclusion by modern architectural theory of typologies and its belief in the freedom of intuition can at any rate be partially explained by the more general theory of expression which was current at the turn of the century. This theory can be seen most clearly in the work and theories of certain painters—notably Wassily Kandinsky, both in his paintings and in his book *Point and Line to Plane*, which outlines the theory on which his paintings are based. Expressionist theory rejected all historical manifestations of art, just as modern architectural theory rejected all historical forms of architecture. To it these manifestations were an ossification of technical and cultural attitudes whose raison d'être had ceased to exist. The theory was based on the belief that shapes have physiognomic or expressive content which communicates itself to us directly. This view has been subjected to a great deal of criticism, and one of its most convincing refutations occurs in E. H. Gombrich's book *Meditations on a Hobby Horse*. Gombrich demonstrates that an arrangement of forms such as is found in a painting by Kandinsky is, in fact, very low in content, unless we attribute to these forms some system of conventional meanings not inherent in the forms themselves. His thesis is that physiognomic forms are ambiguous, though not wholly without expressive value, and that they can only be interpreted within a particular cultural ambience. One of the ways he illustrates this is by reference to the supposed affective qualities of colors. Gombrich points out in the now famous example of traffic signals that we are dealing with a conventional and not a physiognomic meaning, and he maintains that it would be equally logical to reverse the meaning system so that red indicated action and forward movement, and green inaction, quietness, and caution.[4]

Expressionist theory probably had a very strong influence on the Modern Movement in architecture. Its application to architecture would be even more obvious than to painting because of the absence, in architecture, of any forms which are overtly representational. Architecture has always, with music, been considered an abstract art, so that the theory of physiognomic forms could be applied to it without having to overcome the hurdle of anecdotal representation, as in painting. But if the objections to expressionist theory are valid, then they apply to architecture as much as to painting.

If, as Gombrich suggests, forms by themselves are relatively empty of meaning, it follows that the forms which we intuit will, in the unconscious mind, tend to attract to themselves certain associations of meaning. This could mean not only that we are not free from the forms of the past and from the availability of these forms as typological models but that, if we assume we are free, we have lost control over a very active sector of our imagination and of our power to communicate with others. It would seem that we ought to try to establish a value system which takes account of the forms and solutions of the past if we are to gain control over concepts which will obtrude themselves into the creative process, whether we like it or not.

There is, in fact, a close relationship between the pure functionalist or teleological theory that I have described and expressionism, as defined by Professor Gombrich. By insisting on the use of analytical and inductive methods of design, functionalism leaves a vacuum in the form-making process. This it fills with its own reductionist aesthetic—the aesthetic that claims that "intuition," with no historical dimension, can arrive spontaneously at forms which are the equivalent of fundamental operations. This procedure postulates a kind of onomatopoeic relationship between forms and their content. In the case of a biotechnico-determinist theory, the content is the set of relevant functions—functions which themselves are a reduction of all the socially meaningful operations within a building—and it is assumed that the functional complex is translated into forms whose iconographic significance is nothing more than the rational structure of the functional complex itself. The existent facts of the objective functional situation are the equivalent of the existent facts of the subjective emotional situation, in the case of expressionist theory. But traditionally in the work of art, the existent facts, whether subjective or objective, are less significant than the values we attribute to these facts or to the system of representation which embodies these values. The work of art, in this respect, resembles language. A language which was simply the expression of emotions would be a series of single-word exclamations; in fact, language is a complex system of representation in which the basic emotions are structured into an intellectually coherent system.[5] It would be impossible to conceive of constructing a language a priori. The ability to construct such a language would have to presuppose the language itself. Similarly a plastic system of representation such as architecture has to presuppose the existence of a given system of representation. In neither case can the problem of formal representation be reduced to some preexistent essence outside the formal system itself, of which the form is merely a reflection. In both cases it is necessary to postulate a conventional system embodied in typological problem-solution complexes.

My purpose in stressing this fact is not to advocate a reversion to an architecture which accepts tradition unthinkingly. This would imply that there was a fixed and immutable relation between forms and meaning. The characteristic of our age is change, and it is precisely because this is so that it is necessary to investigate the part which modifications of type-solutions play in relation to problems and solutions which are without precedent in any received tradition.

I have tried to show that a reductionist theory according to which the problem solution process can be reduced to some sort of essence is untenable. One might postulate that the process of change is carried out, not by a process of reduction, but rather by a process of exclusion, and it would seem that the history of the Modern Movement in all the arts lends support to this idea. If we look at the allied fields of painting and music, we can see that in the work of a Kandinsky or a [Arnold] Schoenberg, traditional formal devices were not completely abandoned but were transformed and given a new emphasis by the exclusion of ideologically repulsive iconic elements. In the case of Kandinsky it is the representational element which is excluded; in the case of Schoenberg it is the diatonic system of harmony.

The value of what I have called the process of exclusion is to enable us to see the potentiality of forms as if for the first time and with naiveté. This is the justification for the radical change in the iconic system of representation, and it is a process which we have to adopt if we are to keep and renew our awareness of the meanings which can be carried by forms. The bare bones of our culture—culture with its own characteristic technology—must become visible to us. For this to happen a certain scientific detachment toward our problems is essential and with it the application of the mathematical tools proper to our culture. But these tools are unable to give us a ready-made solution to our problems. They only provide the framework, the context within which we operate.

1   *Structural Anthropology*, Claire Jacobson and Brooke Grundfest Schoepf, trans. (New York: Basic Books, 1963), 50.

2   Friedman discussed this issue at a lecture given at the Architectural Association in 1966.

3   *Visions in Motion* (Chicago: Paul Theobald, 1947), 68.

4   It is interesting that since his book came out it has been reported that the Chinese have, in fact, reversed the meanings of their traffic signals.

5   For the study of language as a system of symbolic representation, see Ernst Cassirer, *The Philosophy of Symbolic Forms*, Ralph Manheim, trans. (New Haven: Yale University Press, 1957). For a discussion of language in relation to literature (metalanguage), see Roland Barthes, *Essais Critiques* (Paris: Éditions du Seuil, 1964).

INTRODUCTION

The Third Typology
Anthony Vidler

Anthony Vidler, a founding editor of *Oppositions*, is an architectural historian who writes frequently on Enlightenment architecture. In this essay, he locates the foundations of typology in the ideal of nature (during the Enlightenment), in the order of industrial production (during modernism), and in the city (during the advent of postmodernism). For Vidler, type is inextricably linked to the origins of architecture.

This editorial (one of four position statements by members of the board)[1] in *Oppositions*, the journal of the Institute for Architecture and Urban Studies, emphasizes the operation of type within the city as an important "emerging" third typology in the 1970s. The new typology, "like the first two, is clearly based on reason and classification as its guiding principles." But beyond these similarities, the typologies differ.

The earlier typologies, based on nature ("the organic analogy"), and industry ("the machine analogy"), can be seen as *external* legitimizations that bring cultural relevance to architecture. This "third typology" of the neorationalists (ch. 7) seeks both its inspiration and its forms *internally*, in the physical patterns of the synchronic city. These self-referential, autonomous types are exclusively formal, and "emptied of specific social content." Typology thus returns architectural theory to the problem of form. But the city as the source of postmodern architectural types ensures that "political implications" and "meanings" are not lost in the transformation of urban forms. Vidler's discussion deals primarily with the work of Aldo Rossi, although he also cites Leon and Rob Krier in passing. He interprets their transformational use of Enlightenment urban form and space types as "explicitly critical" of Modern Movement urbanism. Such aspects of the traditional city as "continuous fabric, the clear distinction between public and private marked by the walls of street and square," celebrated by Rossi in *The Architecture of the City*, make up the third typology. Vidler also implies that this type may operate as a critical alternative to the English "townscape" and American Main Street ("strip-city") movements. As such, he finds it to be a promising and rational, nonarbitrary alternative, free of nostalgia and eclecticism. Vidler's essay is one of the many *Oppositions* writings that introduced Rossi and Italian neorationalism to an American audience.

1   Joan Ockman, in her history of the journal, describes how each editor took the stand and expressed his views on the most significant issue of the moment. These position statements began with Kenneth Frampton, "On Reading Heidegger," in *Oppositions* 4 (October 1974): unpaginated, (ch. 9) and proceeded through Mario Gandelsonas, "Neo-Functionalism," *Oppositions* 5 (Summer 1976): unpaginated, and Peter Eisenman: "Post-Functionalism," *Oppositions* 6 (1976): unpaginated, (ch. 1) to conclude with this by Vidler. See Ockman, "Resurrecting the Avant-Garde: The History and Program of Oppositions," in Beatriz Columina, ed., *Architectureproduction* (New York; Princeton Architectural Press, 1988), 196–197.

ANTHONY VIDLER
THE THIRD TYPOLOGY

From the middle of the eighteenth century, two distinct typologies have informed the production of architecture.

The first, developed out of the rationalist philosophy of the Enlightenment, and initially formulated by the Abbé Laugier, proposed that a natural basis for design was to be found in the model of the primitive hut. The second, growing out of the need to confront the question of mass production at the end of the nineteenth century, and most clearly stated by Le Corbusier, proposed that the model of architectural design should be founded in the production process itself. Both typologies were firm in their belief that rational science, and later technological production, embodied the most progressive "forms" of the age, and that the mission of architecture was to conform to, and perhaps even master these forms as the agent of progress.

With the current questioning of the premises of the Modern Movement, there has been a renewed interest in the forms and fabric of pre-industrial cities, which again raises the issue of typology in architecture. From Aldo Rossi's transformations of the formal structure and typical institutions of the eighteenth-century city, to the sketches of the brothers [Leon and Rob] Krier that recall the primitive types of the Enlightenment *philosophes*, rapidly multiplying examples suggest the emergence of a new, third typology.

We might characterize the fundamental attribute of this third typology as an espousal, not of an abstract nature, nor of a technological utopia, but rather of the traditional city as the locus of its concern. The city, that is, provides the material for classification, and the forms of its artifacts provide the basis for re-composition. This third typology, like the first two, is clearly based on reason and classification as its guiding

From *Oppositions* 7 (Winter 1976): 1–4. Republished in *Rational Architecture: The Reconstruction of the European City* (Brussels: Archives of Modern Architecture Editions, 1978). Courtesy of the author.

principles and thus differs markedly from those latter-day romanticisms of "townscape" and "strip-city" that have been proposed as replacements for Modern Movement urbanism since the fifties.

Nevertheless, a closer scrutiny reveals that the idea of type held by the eighteenth-century rationalists was of a very different order from that of the early modernists and that the third typology now emerging is radically different from both.

The celebrated "primitive hut" of Laugier, paradigm of the first typology, was founded on a belief in the rational order of nature; the origin of each architectural element was natural; the chain that linked the column to the hut to the city was parallel to the chain that linked the natural world; and the primary geometries favored for the combination of type-elements were seen as expressive of the underlying form of nature beneath its surface appearance.

While the early Modern Movement also made an appeal to nature, it did so more as an analogy than as an ontological premise. It referred especially to the newly developing nature of the machine. This second typology of architecture was now equivalent to the typology of mass production objects (subject themselves to a quasi-Darwinian law of the selection of the fittest). The link established between the column, the house-type, and the city was seen as analogous to the pyramid of production from the smallest tool to the most complex machine, and the primary geometrical forms of the new architecture were seen as the most appropriate for machine tooling.

In these two typologies, architecture, made by man, was being compared and legitimized by another "nature" outside itself. In the third typology, as exemplified in the work of the new Rationalists, however, there is no such attempt at validation. The columns, houses, and urban spaces, while linked in an unbreakable chain of continuity, refer only to their own nature as architectural elements, and their geometries are neither scientific nor technical but essentially architectural. It is clear that the nature referred to in these recent designs is no more nor less than the nature of the city itself, emptied of specific social content from any particular time and allowed to speak simply of its own *formal* condition.

This concept of the *city* as the site of a new typology is evidently born of a desire to stress the continuity of form and history against the fragmentation produced by the elemental, institutional, and mechanistic typologies of the recent past. The city is considered as a whole, its past and present revealed in its physical structure. It is in itself and of itself a new typology. This typology is not built up out of separate elements, nor assembled out of objects classified according to use, social ideology, or technical characteristics: it stands complete and ready to be de-composed into fragments. These fragments do not re-invent institutional type-forms nor repeat past typological forms: they are selected and reassembled according to criteria derived from three levels of meaning—the first, inherited from meanings ascribed by the past existence of the forms; the second, derived from choice of the specific fragment and its boundaries, which often cross between previous types; the third, proposed by a re-composition of these fragments in a new context.

Such an "ontology of the city" is indeed radical. It denies all the social utopian and progressively positivist definitions of architecture for the last two hundred years. No longer is architecture a realm that has to relate to a hypothesized "society" in order to be conceived and understood; no longer does "architecture write history" in the sense of particularizing a specific social condition in a specific time or place. The need to speak of function, of social mores—of anything, that is, beyond the nature of architectural form itself—is removed. At this point, as Victor Hugo realized so presciently in the 1830s, communication through the printed word, and lately through the mass media has released architecture from the role of "social book" into its specialized domain.

This does not of course mean that architecture in this sense no longer performs any function, no longer satisfies any need beyond the whim of an "art for art's sake" designer, but simply that the principal conditions for the invention of object and environments do not necessarily have to include a unitary statement of fit between form and use. Here it is that the adoption of the city as the site for the identification of the architectural typology becomes crucial. In the accumulated experience of the city, its public spaces and institutional forms, a typology can be understood that defies a one-to-one reading of function, but which, at the same time, ensures a relation at another level to a continuing tradition of city life. The distinguishing characteristic of the new ontology beyond the specifically formal aspect is that the city, as opposed to the single column, the hut-house, or the useful machine, is and always has been political in its essence. The fragmentation and re-composition of its spatial and institutional forms thereby can never be separated from the political implications.

When a series of typical forms are selected from the past of a city, they do not come, however dismembered, deprived of their original political and social meaning. The original sense of the form, the layers of accrued implication deposited by time and human experience cannot be lightly brushed away; and certainly it is not the intention of the Rationalists to disinfect their types in this way. Rather, the carried meanings of these types may be used to provide a key to their newly invested meanings. The technique, or rather the fundamental compositional method suggested by the Rationalists is the transformation of selected types—partial or whole—into entirely new entities that draw their communicative power and potential critical force from the understanding of this transformation. The City Hall project for Trieste by Aldo Rossi, for example, has been rightly understood to refer, among other evocations in its complex form, to the image of a late eighteenth-century prison. In the period of the first formalization of this type, as [Giovanni Battista] Piranesi demonstrated, it was possible to see in *prison* a powerfully comprehensive image of the dilemma of society itself, poised between a disintegrating religious faith and a materialist reason. Now, Rossi, in ascribing to the city hall (itself a recognizable type in the nineteenth century) the affect of prison, attains a new level of signification, which evidently is a reference to the ambiguous condition of civic government. In the formulation, the two types are not merged: indeed, city hall has been replaced by open arcade standing in contradiction on prison. The dialectic is clear as a fable: the society that understands the reference to prison will still have need of the reminder, while at the very point that the image finally loses all meaning, the society will either have become entirely prison, or, perhaps, its opposite. The metaphoric opposition deployed in this example can be traced in many of Rossi's schemes and in the work of the Rationalists as a whole, not only in institutional form hut also in the spaces of the city.

This new typology is explicitly critical of the Modern Movement; it utilizes the clarity of the eighteenth-century city to rebuke the fragmentation, de-centralization, and formal disintegration introduced into contemporary urban life by the zoning techniques and technological advances of the twenties. While the Modern Movement found its hell in the closed, cramped, and insalubrious quarters of the old industrial cities, and its Eden in the uninterrupted sea of sunlit space filled with greenery—a city become a garden—the new typology as a critique of modern urbanism raises the continuous fabric, the clear distinction between public and private marked by the walls of street and square, to the level of principle. Its nightmare is the isolated building set in an undifferentiated park. The heroes of this new typology are therefore to be found not among the nostalgic, anti city utopians of the nineteenth century nor among the critics of industrial and technical progress of the twentieth, but rather among those who, as the professional servants of urban life, direct their design skills to solving the questions of avenue, arcade, street and square, park and house, institution and equipment in a continuous typology of elements that together coheres with past fabric and present intervention to make one comprehensible experience of the city.

For this typology, there is no clear set of rules for the transformations and their objects, nor any polemically defined set of historical precedents. Nor should there be; the continued vitality of this architectural practice rests in its essential engagement with the precise demands of the present and not in any holistic mythicization of the past. It refuses any "nostalgia" in its evocations of history, except to give its restorations sharper focus; it refuses all unitary descriptions of the social meaning of form, recognizing the specious quality of any single ascription of social order to an architectural order; it finally refuses all eclecticism, resolutely filtering its "quotations" through the lens of a modernist aesthetic. In this sense, it is an entirely modern movement, and one that places its faith in the essentially public nature of all architecture, as against the increasingly private visions of romantic individualists in the last decade. In it, the city and typology are reasserted as the only possible bases for the restoration of a critical role to an architecture otherwise assassinated by the apparently endless cycle of production and consumption.

6. URBAN THEORY AFTER MODERNISM

CONTEXTUALISM, MAIN STREET, AND BEYOND

INTRODUCTION

Collage City
Colin Rowe and Fred Koetter

In the postmodern period, one of the most influential American urban theories is Colin Rowe and Fred Koetter's *Collage City*, written in 1973 and published in 1978. This excerpt appeared in the British monthly, *Architectural Review*, in 1975, and contains these sections: "After the Millenium," "Crisis of the Object: Predicament of Texture," "Collision City and the Politics of 'Bricolage,' " and "Collage City and the Reconquest of Time." The problems of modern urbanism addressed by the architects' proposal were later summarized by Rowe in mock psychoanalytic terms as "object fixation, *zeitgeist* worship, physics envy [pseudo science], and stradaphobia."[1]

The authors' "diagnosis" stems from the research of Cornell students and faculty in Rome, a city widely admired as the model of traditional urbanism. The group's adoption of the tool of the figure/ground plan for urban analysis led to a revival of interest in the 1748 Nolli Plan of Rome. These drawings emphasize the role of public and private space in determining the character of the city. The Cornell group's main discovery was that modern architecture had inverted the ratio of built to "open" space with disastrous results at the street level. By privileging the object building, modernism left desolate fields of nonurban space that divided neighborhoods, isolated people, and stranded buildings. These wastelands, although convenient for the automobile, lacked an inscription of human scale, and the quality of enclosure so characteristic of the premodern European public realm. (ch. 9)

Rowe and Koetter's critique continues with a review of utopian urban schemes circa 1965, ranging from "nostalgic" to "prophetic." These diverse manifestations are important when considered relative to one another, but separately, are dismissed as extreme. In their place, Rowe and Koetter offer the idea of *collage*, as a technique, and as a "state of mind" tinged with irony. The authors promote this fragmentary method as a solution to the problem of the "new," without sacrificing the possibility of a democratic pluralism:

"the city of collage...might be a means of accommodating emancipation and allowing all parts of a pluralist situation their own legitimate expression."[2]

The political aspect of their theory depends on the pro-democratic writings of the twentieth-century Austrian philosopher Karl Popper for its defense of the necessity to avoid coercive, totalizing schemes. This anti-totalitarian reasoning connects the authors with postmodern thinkers like Jürgen Habermas, Jacques Derrida, and Jean-François Lyotard.

Rowe and Koetter's notion that building inevitably involves value judgements and represents "the ethical content of the good society" is reiterated by Philip Bess and Karsten Harries. (ch. 8) While both "Collage City" and Venturi's *Complexity and Contradiction* (ch. 1) make inclusive arguments (for order/disorder, "accommodation and coexistence," both/and, etc.), Rowe and Koetter's pluralist approach needs to be distinguished from Venturi's. The form and intention of the oppositions (summarized as "accommodation and coexistence") is indeed similar. Rowe, Koetter, and Venturi are all influenced by the positive view of ambivalence in Gestalt theory, which permits a multiplicity of readings.

But the differences emerge more clearly in Venturi's later book, *Learning from Las Vegas*, written with Denise Scott Brown and Steven Izenour. (See excerpt, this chapter) The "populist" position they articulate deliberately avoids the political implications of their research by refusing to make value judgements about the Las Vegas strip. Because of their willingness to engage ethical issues, Rowe and Koetter are more genuinely enthusiastic about a pluralistic society and an urbanism allowing for change.

1   Colin Rowe, "The Present Urban Predicament,"
     Cornell Journal of Architecture 1 (1981): 17.
2   Ibid.: 17, 18.

COLIN ROWE AND FRED KOETTER
COLLAGE CITY

AFTER THE MILLENIUM

The city of modern architecture which, now that it seems to have become an almost irre-sistible reality, has begun to invite so much criticism, has, of course, prompted two quite distinct styles of reaction which are neither of recent formulation. Perhaps in its origins this city was a gesture to social and psychological dislocations brought about by the First World War and the Russian Revolution: and one style of reaction has been to assert the inadequacy of the initial gesture. Modern architecture did not go far enough. Perhaps dislocation is a value in itself: perhaps we should have more of it: perhaps, hopefully embracing technology. We should now prepare ourselves for some kind of computerised surf ride, over and through the tides of Hegelian time, to some possibly ultimate haven of emancipation.

Such might seem to be the approximate inference of the Archigram image: but we wish to parallel it with an image of which the inference is completely the reverse. As an exhibition of townscape, the Harlow town square involves a conscious attempt to placate and console. The first image is ostensibly forward looking, the second deliberately nos-talgic: and, if both are highly random, the randomness of the one is intended to imply all the vitality of an unprejudiced imaginary future, while the randomness of the other is intended to suggest all the casual differentiations which might have been brought about by the accidents of time. The implication of the second image is of an English market place (imaginably it could also be Scandinavian) which, though it is absolutely of the moment (the moment being c.1950) is also a product of all the accumulations and vicissitudes of history.

Excerpt from "Collage City" *Architectural Review* 158, no. 942 (August 1975): 66–90. Courtesy of the authors and the publisher.

Superstudio.

Which is not to comment upon the respective quality of these images, nor to propose the question: *which of them is the more necessary:* but which may be allowed to preface a somewhat analogous confrontation. Its two parts are, in the one case, Italian and, in the other, American: Brave New World (the obtrusive themes of emancipation and love played out in a desert—with impressive mountain backdrop) and Brave Old World (a confection which insists that things are now, but absolutely, far more like they used to be than they ever were before). The one is a product of Superstudio, exhibited fairly recently at the Museum of Modern Art, and the other is a model for Disneyworld's Main Street.

And the argument can be quite simple. Superstudio professes to conceive of objects, of buildings, of all artificial physical form, as coercive and tyrannical, as operating to limit a, probably, Marcusean freedom of choice. Objects, buildings, physical forms are, and must be considered, dispensable: and the ideal of life must be seen as unrestricted and nomadic—all that we need are a set of Cartesian co-ordinates (representative of a universal electronic structure) and then, plugged into this grid of freedom (or skipping around within it), an equilibrated and happy existence will, *ipso facto*, ensue.

Now, if this is may be to traduce the poetry of the Superstudio image, it is not seriously to distort its idea. Freedom is freedom from objects—freedom from all the clutter of Venice, Florence, Rome, freedom to range in an endless Arizona of the mind, to range hopefully supported by the occasional cactus—and the idea of such ultimate simplicity can only be seductive. All of Le Corbusier's funny buildings have gone away, all of the technological extravaganzas of Archigram have been declared obsolete; and, instead, here we are just as we are, naked, natural, without excuse and with nobody going to be hurt—except, of course, that, around the corner we may be pretty certain about the superior restaurant and the Lamborghini which is waiting to take us there.

Given the suppositions from which it derives, one may concede the logic of the Italian image: but, as the ultimate upstaging of science fiction, it may still permit the consideration of Disneyworld as a *reductio ad absurdum*, of townscape. For here is not any Arizona of the mind, tragic in spite of all, but rather a Main Street of musical comedy.

Deprivation can, apparently, take a variety of forms; and, whatever abstract freedom might be (*Don't fence me in* or *Please do fence me in just a little bit*), freedom in Florence is, conceivably, not quite the same thing as freedom in Dubuque. But this is simply to intuit that, just as there is a sense of surfeit in Italy, there is a sense of deprivation in Iowa. For, where the absolute Cartesian grid of cities, of rural roads, or fields, has long been a preponderant reality and, where it has been equipped with the minimum of interpolations, then both grid and interpolations assume a different consequence from what might elsewhere obtain. The grid ceases to be a desirable ideal, the interpolations cease to be a disagreeable reality; the grid becomes a slightly fatiguing fact of life, the interpolations a long awaited distraction; and, if this argument is in any way permissible, then, just possibly, we might arrive at two conclusions:

1) That the success of Walt Disney Enterprises rests in its provision of significant and particular interpolations in the all-embracing and egalitarian grid; and

2) That the Utopian world which is proposed by such an outfit as Superstudio can only operate as some sort of green light for the Disney-like entrepreneurs of the future.

In other words, the ultimate grid of freedom—which is like the ultimate grid of Nebraska or Kansas—whether propounded as an idea or as a convenience, will produce a more or less predictable reaction and the deliberate elimination of local detail—whether spatial or psychological—is likely to be counter-balanced by its simulation. Which is to intimate that images like these two are sequentially bound together (like a Free University of Berlin and a Port Grimaud) in a chain of cause and effect.

However, an important issue, *the* important issue, remains the exclusiveness of both these images, the presumption of prophecy by the one, the assumption of nostalgia by the other. Like the two English images previously observed, the one is nearly all anticipation, the other almost all recollection; and, at this stage, it surely becomes relevant to propose the deep absurdity of this particular split which seems to be more a matter of heroic posture than of anything else.

Certainly it is a type of schism all the more gross because, on each side, there is an entirely false psychology assumed—a type of schism which scarcely helps. For, given that the fantasy of the comprehensive city of deliverance has lead to a situation which is abominable, the problem remains what to do. Reductionist Utopian models will certainly founder in the cultural relativism which, for better or worse, immerses us and it would seem only reasonable to approach such models with the greatest circumspection: the inherent debilitations of any institutionalised *status quo* (more of Levittown, more of Wimbledon, even more of Urbino and Chipping Campden) would also seem to indicate that neither simple "give them what they want" nor unmodified townscape are equipped with sufficient conviction to provide more than partial answers; and, such being the case with reference to all of the prominent models, it becomes necessary to envisage a strategy which might, hopefully and without disaster, accommodate the ideal and which, plausibly and without devaluation, might respond to what the real might be supposed to be.

In a recent book, *The Art of Memory*,[1] Francis Yates speaks of Gothic cathedrals as mnemonic devices. The bibles and the encyclopedias of both the illiterate and the literate, these buildings were intended to articulate thought by assisting recollection: and, to the degree that they acted as Scholastic classroom aids, it becomes possible to refer to them as having been *theatres of memory*. And the designation is a useful one, because, if today we are only apt to think of buildings as necessarily prophetic, such an alternative mode of thinking may serve to correct our unduly prejudiced naiveté. The building as *theatre of prophecy*, the building as *theatre of memory*—if we are able to conceive of the building as the one, we must, also inherently be able to conceive of it as the other: and, while recognising that without benefit of academic theory, these are both of them the ways in which we habitually interpret buildings, this memory-prophecy theatre distinction might then be carried over into the urbanistic field.

Having said just so much and no more, it goes almost without saying that exponents of the city as prophecy theatre will likely be thought of as radicals, while exponents of the city as memory theatre will, almost certainly, be described as conservatives; but, if there might be some degree of truth in such assumption, it must also be established that block notions of this kind are not really very useful. The mass of mankind is likely to be, at any one time, both conservative and radical, to be preoccupied with the familiar and diverted by the unexpected: and, if we all of us both live in the past and hope for the future (the present being no more than an episode in time), it would seem reasonable that we should accept this condition. For, if without prophecy there can be no hope, then, without memory there can be no communication.

Obvious, trite and sententious though this may be, it was—happily or unhappily—an aspect of the human mind which the early proponents of modern architecture were able to overlook—happily for them, unhappily for us. But, if without such distinctly perfunctory psychology "the new way of building" could never have come into being, there cannot any longer be an excuse for the failure to recognise the complementary relationship which is fundamental to the processes of anticipation and retrospection. Interdependent activities we cannot perform without exercising them both: and no attempt to suppress either in the interest of the other can ever be protractedly successful. We may receive strength from the novelty of prophetic declamation: but the degree of this potency must be strictly related to the known, the perhaps mundane and the necessarily memory-laden context from which it emerges.

The dichotomy of memory-prophecy, so important for modern architecture, might therefore be regarded as entirely illusory, as useful up to a point but academically absurd if pressed: and, if such may be allowed and, if it seems plausible that the ideal city which we carry in our minds should accommodate our known psychological constitution, it would seem to follow that the ideal city which might now be postulated should, at one and the same time, behave as both theatre of prophecy and theatre of memory.

CRISIS OF THE OBJECT: PREDICAMENT OF TEXTURE

We have so far attempted to specify two versions of the Utopian idea: Utopia as an, implicit, object of contemplation and Utopia as an, explicit, instrument of social change: we have then deliberately muddied this distinction by the introduction of fantasies of architecture as anticipation and architecture as retrospection: but briefly to forget these secondary issues: it would be facetious further to indulge speculation in the area of Utopian concern without first directing some attention to the evaluations of Karl Popper. For present purposes these are two essays of the late 1940s, "Utopia and Violence" and "Towards a Rational Theory of Tradition":[2] and it must be a matter of surprise that neither of these seems, so far, to have been cited for its possible commentary upon the architectural and urbanistic problems of today.[3]

Popper, as might be expected, is hard on Utopia and, correspondingly, soft on tradition: but these essays should also be placed in the context of that massive criticism of simple inductivist visions of science, of all doctrines of historical determinism and of all theorems of the closed society which he has continuously conducted and which increasingly begins to appear as one of the more important twentieth-century constructs. The Viennese liberal, long domiciled in England and using what appears to be a Whiggish theory of the state as the cutting edge of an attack upon Plato, Hegel, and, not so incidentally, the Third Reich, it is in terms of this background that Popper must be understood as the critic of Utopia and the exponent of tradition's usefulness.

For Popper tradition is indispensable—communication rests upon tradition: tradition is related to a felt need for a structured social environment; tradition is the critical vehicle for the betterment of society; the "atmosphere" of any given society is related to tradition: and tradition is somewhat akin to myth—or, to say it in other words, specific traditions are somehow incipient theories which have the value, however imperfectly, of helping to explain society.

But such statements also require to be placed alongside the conception of science from which they derive, the conception of science as not so much the accumulation of facts but as the rigorous criticism of hypotheses. It is hypotheses which discover facts and not *vice versa*; and, seen in this way—so the argument runs—the role of traditions in society is roughly equivalent to that of hypotheses in science. That is: just as the formulation of hypotheses or theories results from the criticism of myth.

"Similarly traditions have the important double function of not only creating a certain order or something like a social structure, but also of giving us something on which we can operate; something that we can criticise and change. (And) just as the invention of myth or theories in the field of natural science has a function—that of helping us to bring order into the events of nature—so has the creation of traditions in the field of society."[4]

And it is presumably for such reasons that a rational approach to tradition becomes contrasted by Popper with the rationalist attempt to transform society by the agency of abstract and Utopian propositions. These are "dangerous and pernicious." Utopia proposes a consensus about objectives: and "It is impossible to determine ends scientifically. There is no scientific way of choosing between two ends..." This being so

> the problem of constructing a Utopian blue print cannot possibly be solved by science
> alone; since we cannot determine the ultimate ends of political actions scientifically

...they will at least partly have the character of religious differences. And there can be no tolerance between these different Utopian religions...the Utopianist must win over or else crush his competitors."[5]

In other words, if Utopia proposes the achievement of abstract goods rather than the eradication of concrete evils, it is apt to be coercive since there can far more easily be a consensus about concrete evils than there can be about abstract goods; and, if Utopia introduces itself as a blueprint for the future, then it is doubly coercive since the future *cannot* be known to us. But, in addition to this, Utopia is particularly dangerous since the invention of Utopias is likely to occur in periods of rapid social change; and urban Utopian blueprints are liable to be rendered obsolete before they can be put into practice, then it is only too probable that the Utopian engineers will proceed to inhibit change—by propaganda, by suppression of dissident opinion, and, if necessary, by physical force.

It is perhaps unfortunate in all this that Popper makes no distinction between Utopia as metaphor and Utopia as prescription; but, this being said, what we are here presented with (though the treatment of tradition is, perhaps, unduly sophisticated and the handling of Utopia certainly a little bitter and abrupt) is, by inference, one of the most completely devastating critiques of the twentieth-century architect and planner.

It is also the critique of a certain contemporary "orthodoxy" which is quite generally diffused. The Popperian position which, in the face of scientism and historicism, insists upon the fallibility of all knowledge *ought* to be reasonably well known; but, if Popper is evidently concerned—in terms of their probable practical results—with certain largely unthinking procedures and attitudes, the intellectual situation which, persistently, he has felt compelled to review is comparatively easy to exhibit.

The announcement by the White House on 13 July 1969 of the creation of the National Goals Research Staff stated the following:

> There are increasing numbers of forecasting efforts in both public and private institutions, which provide a growing body of information upon which to base judgements of probable future developments and of choices available.
>
> There is an urgent need to establish a more direct link between the increasingly sophisticated forecasting now being done and the decision making process. The practical importance of establishing such a link is emphasised by the fact that virtually all the critical national problems of today could have been anticipated well in advance of their reaching critical proportions.
>
> An extraordinary array of tools and techniques has been developed by which it becomes increasingly possible to project future trends—and thus to make the kind of informed choices which are necessary if we are to establish mastery over the process of change. These tools and techniques are gaining widespread use in the social and physical sciences, but they have not been applied systematically to the science of government. The time is at hand when they should be used and when they must be used.[6]

"The science of government," "tools and techniques" which "*must* be used," "sophisticated forecasting," "the kind of informed choices which are necessary if we are to establish mastery over the process of change": this is [Claude-Henri] Saint-Simon and [G. W. F.] Hegel, the myths of potentially rational society and inherently logical history installed in the most unlikely of high places: and in its naively conservative but simultaneously Neo-Futurist tone, as a popular rendition of what is by now folklore, it might almost have been designed as a target for Popper's critical strategies. For, if "mastery over the process of change" may indeed sound heroic, the strict lack of sense of this idea can only be emphasised: and if this is the simple fact that "mastery over the process of change" would necessarily eliminate all but the most minor and extrinsic changes, then this is the real burden of Popper's position. Simply that in so far as the form of the future depends upon future ideas, this form is not to be anticipated: and that, therefore, the many future oriented fusions of Utopianism and historicism (the ongoing course of history to be subject to rational management) can only operate to restrain any progressive evolution, any genuine emancipation. And it may be at this point that one does distinguish the quintessential Popper, the libertarian critic of historical determinism and strictly inductivist views of scientific method who, surely more than anyone else, has probed and discriminated that crucial complex of historico-scientific fantasies which, for better or worse, has been so active a component of twentieth-century motivation.

The 1969 statement of the White House (which has been so ironically falsified by events) we conceive of as far from merely an American absurdity. It is a type of statement which is likely to be issued by almost any government of the present day (we can imagine its French and its English editions): and, apart from its "decisionism," it is a statement only too horribly close in its basic presumptions to the general tone of modern architecture and then to the derivative attitudes of the planner.

The roads into the future are, at last, to be well oiled and accident free: there are no longer to be hidden bumps and erratic chicanes: the final truth has been divulged: free from dogmatic presupposition we now, logically, consult only the "facts": and, consulting the "facts," we are able, finally, to project the all-encompassing and never-to-be-disrupted ultimate solution of *total design*. Something a little like this was, and continued to be, modern architecture's *Leitmotif*: and, if whatever it has to do with society may be distinctly mysterious, one can still be left contemplating the respective affiliations of *total politics* and *total architecture*.

Probably, when the account is finally rendered, they will be discovered to have been much the same: but something of total politics and total architecture are present, of necessity, in all Utopian projections. Utopia has never offered options. To repeat: the citizens of Thomas More's Utopia *could not fail to be happy because they could not chose but be good*: and the idea of dwelling in goodness, without capacity for moral choice, has been prone to attend most fantasies, whether metaphorical or literal, of the ideal society.

The maintained endorsements of Utopia are one thing, its criticism is another: but for the architect, of course, the ethical content of the good society has always been something which building was to make evident. Indeed it has, probably, always been his primary reference: for, whatever other controlling fantasies may have merged to assist him—antiquity, tradition, technology—these have invariably been conceived of as aiding and abetting a, in some way, benign or decorous social order.

Thus, not to retreat backwards all the way to Plato and, instead, to find a much more recent *quattrocento* springboard, [Antonio Averlino] Filarete's Sforzinda contains all

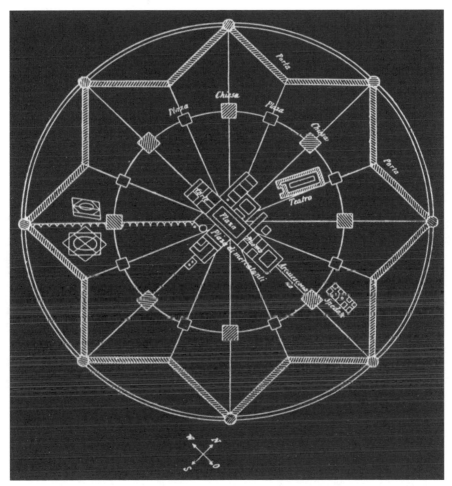

Filarete's plan for the city of Sforzinda (from Codex Maglia Beccianus) is an enduring symbol of humanist order. It assumed that all human situations were susceptible to rules that ensured a hierarchical, well-ordered city.

the premonitions of a situation assumed to be entirely susceptible to rule. There is a hierarchy of religious edifices, the princely *regia,* the aristocratic palace, the mercantile establishment, the private residence: and it is in terms of such a gradation—an absolute ordering of status and function—that the well-conducted city became conceivable.

But it still remained an idea and there was to be no question of its literal and immediate application. For the medieval city represented an intractable nucleus of habit and interest which could, in no way, be directly breached: and, accordingly, the problem of the new became one of subversive interjection within the city—Palazzo Massimo, Campidoglio, etc.—or of polemical demonstrations outside the city—the garden discloses what the city ought to be.

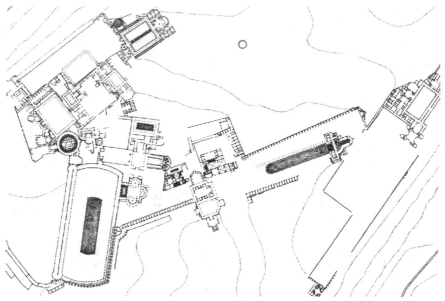

While Versailles is a built version of one idea, the Villa Adriana at Tivoli is an accumulation of several ideas. The Villa Adriana presents the demands of the ideal and recognises at the same time the needs of the *ad hoc*. Here are the beginnings of collage.

The garden as a criticism of the city—a criticism which the city later abundantly acknowledged—has not, as yet, received sufficient attention: but, if outside Florence, for instance, this theme is profusely represented, its most extreme affirmation can only be at Versailles, that seventeenth-century criticism of medieval Paris which [Eugène Georges] Haussmann and Napoleon III later so energetically took to heart.

As a prophetic vision of the city, an enormous rendition of Filarete-style Utopia in which trees have come to serve as buildings, as a very literal exaggeration of Utopian decorum. Versailles must now serve as some kind of gear change to initiate a further phase of argument. We have unambiguous, unabashed Versailles. The moral is declared to the world and the advertisement can scarcely be refused. This is total control and the glaring illumination of it. It is the triumph of generality, the prevalence of the over-whelming idea, the suppression of the exception: and the obvious parallel to mount alongside it, for present purposes, is the Villa Adriana at Tivoli. For, if Versailles may be a sketch for total design in a context of total politics, the Villa Adriana attempts to dis-simulate all reference to any single controlling idea. The one of them is all unity and con-vergence: the other is all disparity and divergence: the one supposes itself to be an organ-ism, entire and complete: the other presents itself as an animated dialectic of parts: com-pared with the single-mindedness of Louis XIV. Hadrian, who proposes the reverse of any "totality," seems only to need an accumulation of the most various fragments.

They are both of them, no doubt, aberrations: they are both of them the prod-ucts of absolute power, but they are both of them the products—almost the clinical illustrations—of absolutely different psychologies; and the Louis XIV-Hadrian confrontation perhaps might best be interpreted by a quotation from Isaiah Berlin. In his famous essay Berlin discriminates two personalities: the hedgehog and the fox. *The fox knows many things but the hedgehog knows one big thing.* This is the text which is chosen for elaboration and made to serve as a pretext for the following:

> ...there exists a great chasm between those, on one side, who relate everything to a single central vision, one system less or more coherent or articulate, in terms of which they understand think and feel—a single, universal, organising principle in terms of which all that they are and say has significance—and, on the other side, those who pursue many ends, often unrelated and even contradictory, connected, if at all, only in some *de facto* way, for some psychological or physiological cause: related by no moral or aesthetic principle: these last lead lives, perform acts, and entertain ideas which are centrifugal rather than centripetal, their thought is scattered or diffused, moving on many levels, seizing upon the essence of a vast variety of experiences and objects for what they are in themselves, without, consciously or unconsciously seeking to fit them into or exclude them from any one unchanging...at times fanatical, unitary inner vision. The first kind of intellectual and artistic personality belongs to the hedgehogs, the second to the foxes...[7]

And the great ones of the earth divide fairly equally: Plato, Dante, [Fyodor] Dostoevsky, [Marcel] Proust are, needless to say, hedgehogs. Aristotle, [William] Shakespeare, [Aleksandr] Pushkin, [James] Joyce are foxes. This is the rough discrimination: but, if it is the representatives of literature and philosophy who are the critical concern, the game may be played in other areas also. [Pablo] Picasso, a fox, [Piet] Mondrian, a hedgehog, the figures begin to leap into place; and, as we turn to architecture, the answers are almost entirely predictable. Palladio is a hedgehog, Giulio Romano, a fox; [Nicholas] Hawksmoor, [John] Soane, Philip Webb are probably hedgehogs. [Christopher] Wren, [John] Nash, Norman Shaw almost certainly foxes; and, closer to the present day, while [Frank Lloyd] Wright is unequivocally a hedgehog, [Edwin] Lutyens is just as obviously a fox.

But, to elaborate the results of, temporarily, thinking in such categories, it is as we approach the area of modern architecture that we begin to recognise the impossibility of arriving at any symmetrical balance. For if [Walter] Gropius, Mies, Hannes Meyer, Buckminster Fuller are clearly eminent hedgehogs, then where are the foxes whom we can enter into the same league? The preference is obviously one way. The *single central vision prevails.* One notices a predominance of hedgehogs: but, if one might sometimes feel that fox-like propensities are surrounded with dubiety and, therefore, not to be disclosed, of course there still remains the job of assigning to Le Corbusier his own particular slot, "*whether he is a monist or a pluralist, whether his vision is of one or of many, whether he is of a single substance or compounded of heterogeneous elements.*"[8]

These are questions which Berlin asks with reference to [Leo] Tolstoy—questions which (he says) may not be wholly relevant: and then, very tentatively, he produces his hypothesis:

> that Tolstoy—as by nature a fox, but believed in being a hedgehog: that his gifts and achievement are one thing, and his beliefs, and consequently his interpretation of his

own achievement, another: and that consequently his ideals have led him, and those whom his genius for persuasion has taken in, into a systematic misinterpretation of what he and others were doing or should be doing.[9]

Like so much other literary criticism shifted into a context of architectural focus, the formula seems to fit: and, if it should not be pushed too far, it can still offer partial explanation. There is Le Corbusier, the architect, with what William Jordy has called "*his witty and collisive intelligence.*"[10] This is the person who sets up elaborately pretended Platonic structures only to riddle them with an equally elaborate pretence of empirical detail, the Le Corbusier of multiple asides, cerebral references, and complicated *scherzi*: and then there is Le Corbusier, the urbanist, the deadpan protagonist of completely different strategies who, at a large and public scale, has the minimum of use for all the dialectical tricks and spatial involutions which, invariably, he considered the appropriate adornment of a more private situation. The public world is simple, the private world is elaborate: and, if the private world affects a concern for contingency the would-be public personality long maintained an almost too heroic disdain for any taint of the specific.

But, if the situation of *complex house-simple city* seems strange (when one might have thought that the reverse was applicable) and, if to explain the discrepancy between Le Corbusier's architecture and his urbanism one might propose that he was, yet again, a fox assuming hedgehog disguise for the purposes of public appearance, this is to build a digression into a digression. We have noticed a relative absence of foxes at the present day; but, though this second digression may later be put to use, the whole fox-hedgehog diversion was initiated for ostensibly other purposes. It was initiated to establish Hadrian and Louis XIV as, more or less, free-acting representatives of these two psychological types who were autocratically equipped to indulge their inherent propensities, and then to ask of their products: which of these two might be felt the more exemplary for today—the accumulation of set pieces in collision or the total coordinated display?

The Villa Adriana is a miniature Rome. It plausibly reproduces all the collisions of set pieces and all of the random empirical happenings which the city so lavishly exhibited. It is a conservative endorsement of Rome where Versailles is a radical criticism of Paris. At Versailles all is design, total and complete, but at Tivoli, as in the Rome of Hadrian, design and non-design qualify and amplify their respective statements. Hadrian is one of Françoise Choay's "culturalists," concerned with the emotive and the usable; but for Louis XIV, the "progressivist" (assisted by [Jean-Baptiste] Colbert), it is the rationalisable present and future which exhibit themselves as the exacting idea. Random idiosyncrasy, local diversity, have little to say to this state of mind: and it is when the rationalisations of a Colbert become handed down by [Anne-Robert-Jacques] Turgot to Saint-Simon and [Auguste] Comte that one begins to see something of Versailles' prophetic enormity.

For certainly, there, at Versailles, was anticipated all the myth of the rationally ordered and "scientific" society, the accident-free society ruled by knowledge and information in which debate has become superfluous; and, if we then proceed to drench this myth with fantasies of historical evolution and further to charge it with the threat of damnation or the cult of crisis, we might begin to approach a state of mind not too remote from that which presided over the origins of modern architecture. But, if it becomes increasingly hard not to smile at the old story that, in order to avert impending doom, the enterprises of mankind must be brought into closer alignment with the inevitable forces of blissful destiny, then, if we are emancipated by our derision, it might become possible (the idea is advanced with all due hesitation) to consult the promotings, first of all of taste and, secondly, commonsense.

Taste is, of course, no longer—and was, perhaps never—a serious or substantial matter and talk of commonsense should equally inspire reservations: but, if both of them are the crudest of concepts, they may still appropriately serve as the crudest of blunt instruments for yet another approach to the Villa Adriana. Thus, given two conditions of equal size and endlessness as those at Versailles and Tivoli, it is almost certain that the uninhibited aesthetic preference of today is for the structural discontinuities and the multiple syncopated excitements which the Villa Adriana presents; and, in the same way, whatever may be the conscientious and contemporary concern for *the single central vision*, for a condition of complete, holistic and novel continuity, it should be apparent that the manifold disjunctions of Hadrian's villa, the sustained inference that it was built by several people (or régimes) at different times, its seeming combination of the schizoid and the reasonable, might recommend it to the attention of political societies where political power frequently—and mercifully—changes hands.

Given the anti-Utopian polemic of Karl Popper, given the—fundamentally—anti-hedgehog innuendo of Isaiah Berlin, the bias of this argument should now be clear: it is better to think of an aggregation of small, and even contradictory set pieces (almost like the products of different régimes) than to entertain fantasies about total and "faultless" solutions which the condition of politics can only abort. Its implication is an installation of the Villa Adriana as some sort of model presenting the demands of the ideal and the needs of the *ad hoc*; and its further implication is that some such installation begins, politically, to be necessary.

But, of course, the Villa Adriana is not simply a physical collision of set pieces. It is not merely a reproduction of Rome. For it also presents an iconography as complex as its plan. Here the reference is supposed to be to Egypt, there we are supposed to be in Syria, and, elsewhere, we might be in Athens: and thus, while *physically* the villa presents itself as a version of the Imperial metropolis, it further operates as an ecumenical illustration of the mix provided by the Empire and, almost, as a series of mementos of Hadrian's travels. Which is to say that, in Villa Adriana, apart from physical collisions (though dependent on them), we are, above all else, in the presence of a highly impacted condition of symbolic reference: and which is further to introduce an argument that must be deferred: the argument that, in Villa Adriana, we are in the presence of something like what, today, it is customary to speak of as *collage*.

COLLISION CITY AND THE POLITICS OF BRICOLAGE

The cult of crisis in the inter-war period: before it is too late society must rid itself of outmoded sentiment, thought, technique: and if, in order to prepare for its impending deliverance, it must be ready to make *tabula rasa*, the architect as key figure in this transformation, must be ready to assume the historical lead. For the built world of human habitation and venture is the very cradle of the new order and, if he is properly to rock it, the architect must be ready to come forward as a front-line combatant in the battle for humanity. Perhaps, while claiming to be scientific, the architect had never previously operated within quite so fantastic a psycho-political milieu: but, if this is to parenthesise, it was for such reasons—Pascalian reasons of the heart—that the city became hypothesised as no more than the result of "scientific" findings and a completely glad "human" collaboration. Such became the activist Utopian total design. Perhaps an impossible vision: and for those who, during the past fifty or sixty years (many of them must be dead) have been awaiting the establishment of this city, it must have become increasingly clear that the promise—such as it is—cannot be kept. Or so one might have thought: but, although the total design message has had a somewhat spotted career and has often elicited scepticism, it has remained, and possibly to this day, as the psychological substratum of urban theory and its practical application. Indeed it has been so little repressible that, in the last few years, a newly inspired and wholly literal version of this message has been enabled to appear as renditions of the "systems" approach and other "methodological" finds.

We have largely introduced Karl Popper to support an anti-Utopian argument with which we do not wholly agree; but in our interpretation of the activist Utopia our indebtedness to Popper's position should surely be evident. It is a position which, particularly when stated at length as in *The Logic of Scientific Discovery* (1934) and *The Poverty of Historicism* (1957),[11] is hard to evade; and one might have thought that the idea of modern architecture as science, as potentially part of a unified comprehensive science, ideally like physics (the best of all possible sciences) could scarcely have protracted itself to survive into a world which also included the Popperian critique of just such fantasies. But this is to misunderstand the hermetic and retarded nature of architectural debate: and, in those areas where Popperian criticism appears to be unknown and where the "science" of early modern architecture is also presumed to be painfully deficient, it goes without saying that the problem-solving methods proposed are laborious and often extended.

One has only to contemplate the scrupulousness of the operation in a text such as *Notes on the Synthesis of Form*[12] to get the picture. Obviously a "clean" process dealing with "clean" information, atomised, cleaned, and then cleaned again, everything is ostensibly wholesome and hygienic; but, resulting from the inhibiting characteristics of commitment, especially physical commitment, the product seems never to be quite so prominent as the process. And something comparable might be said about the related production of stems, webs, grids, and honeycombs which, in the later '60s, became so conspicuous an industry. Both are attempts to avoid any imputation of prejudice: and if, in the first case, empirical facts are presumed to be value-free and finally ascertainable, in the second, the co-ordinates of a grid are awarded an equal impartiality. For, like the lines of longitude and latitude, it seems to be hoped that these will, in some way, eliminate any bias, or even responsibility, in a specification of the infilling detail.

But, if the ideally neutral observer is surely a critical fiction, if among the multiplicity of phenomena with which we are surrounded we observe what we wish to observe, if our judgements are inherently selective because the quantity of factual information is finally indigestible, and if any literal usage of a "neutral" grid labours under approximate problems, the myth of the architect as eighteenth-century natural philosopher, with all his little measuring rods, balances, and retorts, as both messiah and

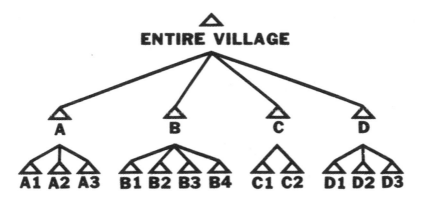

A1 contains requirements 7, 53, 57, 59, 60, 72, 125, 126, 128.
A2 contains requirements 31, 34, 36, 52, 54, 80, 94, 106, 136.
A3 contains requirements 37, 38, 50, 55, 77, 91, 103.
B1 contains requirements 39, 40, 41, 44, 51, 118, 127, 131, 138.
D2 contains requirements 30, 35, 46, 47, 61, 97, 98.

Diagram from Christopher Alexander's *Notes on the Synthesis of Form.*

scientist, Moses and [Isaac] Newton (a myth which became all the more ludicrous after its annexation by the architect's less well-pedigreed cousin, the planner), must now be brought into proximity with *The Savage Mind* and with everything which bricolage represents.

"There still exists among ourselves," says Claude Lévi-Strauss,

an activity which on the technical plane gives us quite a good understanding of what a science we prefer to call "prior" rather than "primitive" could have been on the plane of speculation. This is what is commonly called "bricolage" in French;[13]

and he then proceeds to an extended analysis of the different objectives of *bricolage* and science, of the respective roles of the "bricoleur" and the engineer.

In its old sense the verb "bricoler" applied to ball games and billiards, to hunting, shooting, and riding. It was however always used with reference to some extraneous movement: a ball rebounding, a dog straying, or a horse swerving from its direct course to avoid an obstacle. And in our time the "bricoleur" is still someone who works with his hands and used devious means compared to those of the craftsman.[14]

Now there is no intention to place the entire weight of the argument which follows upon Lévi-Strauss's observations. Rather the intention is to promote an identification which may, up to a point, prove useful: and, so much so, that, if one may be inclined to recognise Le Corbusier as a fox in hedgehog disguise, one may also be willing to envisage a parallel attempt at camouflage: the "bricoleur" disguised as engineer.

> Engineers fabricate the tools of their time....Our engineers are healthy and virile, active, and useful, balanced and happy in their work...our engineers produce architecture for they employ a mathematical calculation which derives from natural law.[15]

Such is an almost entirely representative statement of early modern architecture's most conspicuous prejudice. But then compare Lévi-Strauss:

> The *bricoleur* is adept at performing a large number of diverse tasks: but, unlike the engineer, he does not subordinate each of them to the availability of raw materials and tools conceived and procured for the purpose of the project. His universe of instruments is closed and the rules of his game are always to make do with "whatever is at hand," that is to say with a set of tools and materials which is always finite and is also heterogeneous because what it contains bears no relation to the current project, or indeed to any particular project, but is the contingent result of all the occasions there have been to renew or enrich the stock or to maintain it with the remains of previous constructions or destructions. The set of the *bricoleur's* means cannot therefore be defined in terms of a project (which would pre-suppose besides, that, as in the case of the engineer, there were, at least in theory, as many sets of tools and materials, or "instrumental sets," as there are different kinds of projects). It is to be defined only by its potential use...because the elements are collected or retained on the principle that "they may always come in handy." Such elements are specialised up to a point, sufficiently for the *bricoleur* not to need the equipment and knowledge of all trades and professions, but not enough for each of them to have only one definite and determinate use. They represent a set of actual and possible relations; they are "operators," but they can be used for any operations of the same type.[16]

For our purposes it is unfortunate that Lévi-Strauss does not lend himself to reasonable laconic quotation. For the *bricoleur*, who certainly finds a representative in the "odd job man," is also very much more than this. "*It is common knowledge that the artist is both something of a scientist and of a 'bricoleur'*";[17] but, if artistic creation lies mid-way between science and *bricolage*, this is not to imply that the *bricoleur* is "backward." "*It might be said that the engineer questions the universe while the 'bricoleur' addresses himself to a collection of oddments left over from human endeavours*";[18] but it must also be insisted that there is no question of primacy here. Simply the scientist and the *bricoleur* are to be distinguished

> by the inverse functions which they assign to events and structures as means and ends, the scientist creating events...by means of structures and the "bricoleur" creating structures by means of events.[19]

But we are here, now, very far from the notion of an exponential, increasingly precise "science" (a speedboat which architecture and urbanism are to follow like highly inexpert water skiers); and, instead, we have not only a confrontation of the *bricoleur*'s "savage mind" with the "domesticated" mind of the engineer, but also a useful indication that these two modes of thought are not representatives of a progressive serial (the engineer illustrating a perfection of the *bricoleur*, etc.) but are, in fact, necessarily co-existent and complementary conditions of the mind. In other words, we might be about to arrive at some approximation of Lévi-Strauss's "pensée logique au niveau du sensible."

For, if we can divest ourselves of the deceptions of professional *amour propre* and accepted academic theory, the description of the *bricoleur* is far more a "real-life" specification of what the architect-urbanist is and does than any fantasy deriving from "methodology" and "systemics." Indeed the predicament of architecture which, because it is always in some way or another, concerned with amelioration, with by some standard, however dimly perceived, making things better, with how things ought to be, is always hopelessly involved with value judgements and can never be scientifically resolved—least of all in terms of any simple empirical theory of "facts." And, if this is the case with reference to architecture, then, in relation to urbanism (which is not even concerned in making things stand up) the question of any scientific resolution of its problems can only become more acute. For, if the notion of a "final" solution through a definitive accumulation of all data is, evidently, an epistemological chimera, if certain aspects of information will invariably remain undiscriminated or undisclosed, and if the inventory of "facts" can never be complete because of the rates of change and obsolescence, then, here and now, it surely might be possible to assert that the prospects of scientific city planning should, in reality, be regarded as equivalent to the prospects of scientific politics.

For, if planning can barely be more scientific than the political society of which it forms an agency, in the case of neither politics nor planning can there be sufficient information acquired before action becomes necessary. In neither case can performance await an ideal future formulation of the problem as it may, at last, be resolved; and, if this is because the very possibility of that future where such formulation might be made depends on imperfect action now, then this is only once more to intimate the role of *bricolage* which politics so much resembles and city planning surely should.

But are the alternatives of "progressivist" total design (propelled by hedgehogs?) and "culturalist" *bricolage* (propelled by foxes?) genuinely, at the last analysis, all that we have available? We believe that they are; and we suppose that the political implications of total design are nothing short of devastating. No ongoing condition of compromise and expediency, of wilfulness and arbitrariness, but a supremely irresistible combination of "science" and "destiny," such is the unacknowledged myth of the activist or historicist Utopia: and, in this complete sense, total design was, and is, make believe. For, on a mundane level, total design can only mean total control, and control not by abstractions relating to the absolute value of science or history but by governments of man; and, if the point scarcely requires emphasis, it can, still, not be too strongly asserted that total design (however much it may be loved) assumes for its implementation a level of centralised political and economic control which, given the presumption of political power as it now exists anywhere in the world, can only be considered thoroughly unacceptable.

"The most tyrannical government of all, the government of nobody, the totalitari-anism of technique." Hannah Ahrendt's image of a horror may also now come to mind: and, in this context, what then of "culturalist" *bricolage*? One may anticipate its dangers; but, as a deliberate recognition of the deviousness of history and change, of the certain-ty of future sharp temporal cacsuras, of the full tonality of societal gesture, a conception of the city as intrinsically, and even ideally, a work of *bricolage* begins to deserve serious attention. For, if total design may represent the surrender of logical empiricism to a most unempirical myth and if it may seem to envisage the future (when all will be known) as a sort of dialectic of nondebate, it is because the *bricoleur* (like the fox) can entertain no such prospects of conclusive synthesis, because, rather than with one world—infinitely extended though subjected to the same generalisations—his very activity implies a will-ingness and an ability to deal with a plurality of closed finite systems (*the collection of oddments left over from human endeavour*) that, for the time being at least, his behaviour may offer an important model.

Indeed if we are willing to recognise the methods of science and *bricolage* as con-comitant propensities, if we are willing to recognise that they are, both of them, modes of address to problems, if we are willing (and it may be hard) to concede equality between the "civilised" mind (with its presumptions of logical seriality) and the "savage" mind (with its analogical leaps), then, in re-establishing *bricolage* alongside science, it might even be possible to suppose that the way for a truly useful future dialectic could be prepared.

A truly useful dialectic? The idea is simply the conflict of contending powers, the almost fundamental conflict of interest sharply stipulated, the legitimate suspicion about others' interests, from which the democratic process—such as it is—proceeds: and then the corollary to this idea is no more than banal: if such is the case, that is if democracy is compounded of libertarian enthusiasm and legalistic doubt, if it is inherently a colli-sion of points of view and acceptable as such, then why not allow a theory of contend-ing powers (all of them visible) as likely to establish a more ideally comprehensive city of the mind than any which has, as yet, been invented?

With the Villa Adriana already in mind, the proposition leads us (like Pavlov's dogs) automatically to the condition of seventeenth-century Rome, to that inextricable fusion of imposition and accommodation, that highly successful and resilient traffic jam of intentions, an anthology of closed compositions and *ad hoc* stuff in between which is simultaneously a dialectic of ideal types, plus a dialectic of ideal types with empirical context; and the consideration of seventeenth-century Rome (the complete city with the assertive identity of its sub-divisions: Trastevere, Sant' Eustachio, Borgo, Campo Marzo, Campitelli...) leads to the equivalent interpretation of its predecessor where forum and *thermae* pieces lie around in a condition of inter-dependence, independence, and multi-ple interpretability. And Imperial Rome is, of course, far the more dramatic statement. For, with its more abrupt collisions, more acute disjunctions, its more expansive set pieces, its more radically discriminated matrix and general lack of "sensitive" inhibition, Imperial Rome, far more than the city of the High Baroque, illustrates something of the *bricolage* mentality at its most lavish—an obelisk from here, a column from there, a range of statues from somewhere else, even at the level of detail the mentality is fully exposed: and, in this connection, it is amusing to recollect how the influence of a whole school of

Seventeenth-century Rome exemplifies the dialectic of ideal urban types. It is a complete city where the corporate parts assert their own identity.

historians was, at one time, strenuously dedicated to presenting the ancient Romans as inherently nineteenth-century engineers, precursors of Gustave Eiffel, who had somehow, and unfortunately, lost their way.

So Rome, whether Imperial or Papal, hard or soft, is here offered as some sort of model which might be envisaged as alternative to the disastrous urbanism of social engineering and total design. For, while it is recognised that what we have here are the products of a specific topography and two particular, though not wholly separable cultures, it is also supposed that we are in the presence of a style of argument which is not lacking in universality. That is: while the physique and the politics of Rome provide perhaps the most graphic example of collisive fields and *interstitial debris*, there are calmer versions.

Rome, for instance, is—if you wish to see it so—an imploded version of London: and the Rome-London model may, of course, perfectly well be expanded to provide a comparable interpretation of a Houston or a Los Angeles. But to introduce detail would be, unduly, to protract the argument: and simply to terminate: rather than any Hegelian "indestructible bond of the beautiful and the true," rather than ideas of a permanent and future unity, we would prefer to consider the complementary possibilities of consciousness and sublimated conflict: and, if there is here urgent need for both the fox and the *bricoleur*, it is just possible that, in the face of prevailing scientism and conspicuous *laissez aller*, their activities could provide the true and constant *Survival Through Design*.

COLLAGE CITY AND THE RECONQUEST OF TIME

The tradition of modern architecture, always professing a distaste for art, has characteristically conceived of society and the city in highly conventional artistic terms—unity, continuity, system: but there is an alternative and apparently far more "art" prone method of procedure which, so far as one can see, has never felt any need for such literal alignment with "basic" principles. This alternative and predominant tradition of modernity—one thinks of such names as Picasso, [Igor] Stravinsky, [T.S.] Eliot, Joyce—exists at a considerable remove from the ethos of modern architecture: and, because it makes of obliquity and irony a virtue, it by no means conceives itself to be equipped with a private pipe line to either the truths of science or to the patterns of history.

"I have never made trials nor experiments." "I can hardly understand the importance given the word research." "Art is a lie which makes us realise the truth, at least the truth it is given us to understand." "The artist must know the manner of convincing others of the truthfulness of his lies."[20] With such statements as these of Picasso's one might be reminded of [Samuel Taylor] Coleridge's definition of a successful work of art (it might also be the definition of a successful political achievement) as that which encourages "*a willing suspension of disbelief.*" The Coleridgean mood may be more English, more optimistic, less drenched with Spanish irony: but the drift of thought—the product of an apprehension of reality as far from tractable—is much the same: and, of course, as soon as one begins to think of things in this way, all but the most entrenched pragmatist gradually becomes very far removed from the advertised state of mind and the happy certainties of what is sometimes described as modern architecture's "mainstream." For one now enters a territory from which the architect and the urbanist have, for the most part, excluded themselves. The vital mood is now completely transformed. One is no less in the twentieth century; but the blinding self-righteousness of unitary conviction is at last placed alongside a more tragic cognition of the dazzling and the scarcely to be resolved multiformity of experience.

The two formulations of modernity which elaborate themselves may thus be more or less characterised; and, allowing for two contrasted modes of "seriousness," one may now think of Picasso's *Bicycle Seat* (Bull's Head) of 1944:

> You remember that bull's head I exhibited recently? Out of the handlebars and the bicycle seat I made a bull's head which everybody recognised as a bull's head. Thus a metamorphosis was completed; and now I would like to see another metamorphosis take place in the opposite direction. Suppose my bull's head is thrown on the scrap heap. Perhaps some day fellow will come along and say: "why there's something that would come in very handy for the handlebars of my bicycle..." and so a double metamorphosis would have been achieved."[21]

Remembrance of former function and value (bicycles and minotaurs); shifting context: an attitude which encourages the composite; an exploitation and re-cycling of meaning (has there ever been enough to go around?): desuetude of function with corresponding agglomeration of reference: memory: anticipation: the connectedness of memory and wit: this is a laundry list of reactions to Picasso's proposition: and, since it is a proposition evidently addressed to "people," it is in terms such as these, in terms of pleasures remembered and values desired, of a dialectic between past and future, of an impacting of iconographic content, of a temporal as well as a spatial collision, that, resuming an earlier argument, one might proceed to specify an ideal city of the mind.

With Picasso's image one asks: what is "false" and what is "true," what is "antique" and what is "of today": and it is because of inability to make half-way adequate reply to this pleasing difficulty that one is obliged, finally, to identify the problem of composite presence (already prefigured at the Villa Adriana) in terms of *collage*. Collage and the architect's conscience, collage as technique and collage as state of mind: Lévi-Strauss tells us that "*the intermittent fashion for 'collages,' originating when craftsmanship was dying, could not...be anything but the transposition of 'bricolage' into the realms of contemplation*":[22] and, if the twentieth-century architect has been the reverse of willing to think of himself as a bricoleur, it is in this context that one must also place his frigidity in relation to a major twentieth-century discovery. Collage has seemed to be lacking in sincerity, to represent a corruption of moral principles, an adulteration. One thinks of Picasso's *Still Life with Chair Caning* of 1911–12, his first collage, and begins to understand why.

In analysing this production, Alfred Barr speaks of:

> ...the section of chair caning which is neither real nor painted but is actually a piece of oil-cloth facsimile pasted on to the canvas and then partly painted over. Here in one picture Picasso juggles reality and abstraction in two media and at four different levels or ratios. (And) if we stop to think which is the most "real" we find ourselves moving from aesthetic to metaphysical contemplation. For what seems most real is most false and what seems most remote from everyday reality is perhaps the most real since it is *least an imitation*.[23]

And the oilcloth facsimile of chair caning, an *objet trouvé* snatched from the underworld of "low" culture and catapulted into the superworld of "high" art, might illustrate the architect's dilemma. For collage is simultaneously innocent and devious.

Indeed, among architects, only that great straddler Le Corbusier, sometimes hedgehog, sometimes fox, has displayed any sympathy towards this kind of thing. His buildings, though not his city plans, are loaded with the results of a process which might be considered more or less equivalent to that of collage. Objects and episodes are obtrusively imported and, while they retain the overtones of their source and origin, they gain also a wholly new impact from their changed context. In, for instance, the Ozenfant studio one is confronted with a mass of allusions and references which it would seem are all basically brought together by collage means.

Disparate objects held together by various means, "*physical, optical, psychological*,"

> the oilcloth with its sharp focused facsimile detail and its surface apparently so rough yet actually so smooth,...partly absorbed into both the painted surface and the painted forms by letting both overlap it:[24]

Le Corbusier as collagiste in his solarium for the De Beistégui penthouse.

with very slight modifications (for oilcloth facsimile substitute fake industrial glazing, for painted surface substitute wall, etc.), Alfred Barr's observations could be directly carried over into interpretation of the Ozenfant studio. And further illustrations of Le Corbusier as *collagiste* cannot be hard to find: the too obvious De Beistégui penthouse: the roofs-capes—ships and mountains—of Poissy and Marseilles, random rubble at the Porte Molitor and the Pavillon Suisse; an interior from Bordeaux-Pessac; and particularly, the Nestlé exhibition pavilion of 1928.

But, of course beyond Le Corbusier the evidences of this state of mind are sparse and have been scarcely well received. One thinks of [Berthold] Lubtetkin at Highpoint 2 with his Erectheion caryatids and pretended imitations of the housepainter imitating wood: one thinks of Moretti at the Casa del Girasole with its simulated antique frag-ments in the *piano rustico*; and one thinks of [Franco] Albini at the Palazzo Rosso. Also one may think of Charles Moore. But the list is not extensive and its briefness makes admirable testimony. It is a commentary upon exclusiveness. For collage, often a method of paying attention to the leftovers of the world, of preserving their integrity and equip-ping them with dignity, of compounding matter of factness and cerebrality, a convention and a breach of convention, necessarily operates unexpectedly. A rough method, "a kind of *discordia concors*, a combination of dissimilar images, or discovery of occult resem-blances in things apparently unlike," Samuel Johnson's remarks upon the poetry of John Donne, which could also be remarks upon Stravinsky, Eliot, Joyce, upon much of the programme of Synthetic Cubism, are indicative of the absolute reliance of collage upon a juggling of norms and recollections, upon a backward look which, for those who think of history and the future as exponential progression towards ever more perfect simplici-ty, can only prompt the judgement that collage, for all its psychological virtuosity (Anna Livia, all alluvial), is a wilfully interjected impediment to the strict route of evolution.

And the argument is obviously that between two conceptions of time. On the one hand time becomes the metronome of progress, its serial aspects are given cumulative and dynamic presence; while, on the other, though sequence and chronology are recognised for the facts which they are, time, deprived of some of its linear imperatives, is allowed to re-arrange itself according to experimental schemata. In terms of the one argument the commission of an anachronism is the ultimate of all possible sins. In terms of the other the conception of date is of minor consequence. [Filippo] Marinetti's:

> When lives have to be sacrificed we are not saddened if before our minds shines the magnificent harvest of a superior life which will arise from their deaths....We are on the extreme promontory of the centuries! What is the use of looking behind...we are already living in the absolute, since we have already created eternal omnipresent speed. We sing of great crowds agitated by work; the multi-coloured and polyphonic surf of revolution.[25]

and his later:

> The victory of Vittorio Veneto and the coming to power of Fascism constitute the real-Isation of the minimum Futurist programme...
> Futurism is strictly artistic and ideological....Prophets and forerunners of the great Italy of today, we Futurists are happy to salute in our not yet forty-year-old prime minister a marvellous Futurist temperament

might be a *reductio ad absurdum* of the one argument: and Picasso's

> To me there is no past and no future in art....The several manners which I have used in my art must not be considered as an evolution or as steps towards an unknown ideal of painting....All I have ever made was made for the present and with the hope that it will always remain in the present.[26]

could be allowed to represent an extreme statement of the other. In theological terms, the one argument is eschatological, the other incarnational; but, while they both of them may be necessary, the cooler and more comprehensive nature of the second argument might still excite attention. *The second argument might include the first; but the reverse can never be true*; and, with so much said, one might now approach collage as a serious instrument.

Presented with Marinetti's chronolatry and Picasso's a-temporality: presented with Popper's critique of historicism (which is also Futurism/futurism): presented with the difficulties of both Utopia and tradition, with the problems of both violence and atrophy: presented with alleged libertarian impulse and alleged need for the security of order; presented with the sectarian tightness of the architect's ethical corset and with more reasonable visions of catholicity; presented with contraction and expansion; we ask what other resolution of social problems is possible outside the limitations of collage. Limitations which should be obvious enough; but, still, admitted limitations which prescribe and ensure an open territory.

It is suggested that a collage approach, an approach in which objects (and attitudes) are conscripted or seduced from out of their context is—at the present day—the only way of dealing with the ultimate problems of either or both Utopia and tradition; and the provenance of the architectural objects introduced into the social collage need not be of great consequence. It relates to taste and conviction. The objects can be aristocratic or they can be "folkish," academic, or popular. Whether they originate in Pergamum or Dahomey, in Detroit or Dubrovnik, whether their implications are of the twentieth or the fifteenth century, need be no great matter. Societies and persons assemble themselves according to their own interpretations of absolute reference and traditional value; and, up to a point, collage accommodates both hybrid display and the requirements of self-determination.

But up to a point: for if the city of collage may be more hospitable than the city of modern architecture, if it might be a means of accommodating emancipation and allow-ing all parts of a pluralist situation their own legitimate expression, it cannot any more than any other human institution be completely hospitable. For the ideally open city, like the ideally open society is just as much a figment of the imagination as its opposite. The open and the closed society, either envisaged as practical possibilities, are both of them the caricatures of contrary ideals: and it is to the realm of caricature that one should choose to relegate all extreme fantasies of either emancipation or control. Thus, the bulk of Popper's arguments in favour of the emancipatory interest and the open society must surely be conceded; but, while the need for the reconstruction of an operative critical theory after its long negation by scientism, historicism, psychologism, should be evident, if we are concerned with the production of an open city for an open society, we may still be concerned with an imbalance in Popper's general position comparable to that in his critiques of tradition and Utopia. This can seem to be a too exclusive focus on what, after all, are highly idealised empirical procedures: and a corresponding unwillingness to attempt any construction of positive ideal types.

It was the lavish perspectives of cultural time, the historical depths and profundities of Europe (or wherever else culture was presumed to be located) as against the exotic insignificance of "the rest," which most furnished previous ages of architecture: and it has been the opposite condition which has distinguished that of our own—a willingness to abolish almost all the taboos of physical distance, the barriers of space, and then, alongside this, an equal determination to erect the most impervious of temporal fron-tiers. One thinks of that chronological iron curtain which in the minds of the devout, quarantines modern architecture from all the infections of free-wheeling temporal asso-ciation: but, while one may recognise its former justification (identity, incubation, the hot house), the reasons for artificially maintaining such a temperature of enthusiasm can now only begin to seem very remote. But when one recognises that restriction of free trade, whether in space or time, cannot forever, be profitably sustained, that without free trade the diet becomes restricted and provincialised, the survival of the imagination endangered, and that, ultimately, there must ensue some kind of insurrection of the sens-es, this is only to identify one aspect of the situation—a likely aspect, an aspect as it might be conceived by Popper, and an aspect from which the reasonably sensitive might well shrink. For is an acceptance of free trade to imply absolute dependence upon it: and are the benefits of free trade to be followed by no more than a rampage of the libido?

Up to a point the Popperian social philosophy is sympathetic. It is an affair of attack and *détente*, of attack upon attitudes not making for *détente*. But such an intellectual position which, simultaneously, envisages the existence of heavy industry and Wall Street (as traditions to be criticised) *and* postulates the existence of an ideal theatre of argument (a Rousseau version of the Swiss canton complete with organic *Tagesatzung*?) may also inspire scepticism.

The [Jean-Jacques] Rousseau version of the Swiss canton (which had very little use for Rousseau), the comparable New England town meeting (white paint and witch hunt?), the eighteenth-century House of Commons (not exactly representative), the ideal academic faculty meeting (what to say about that?): undoubtedly these—along with miscellaneous soviets, kibbutzim, and other references to tribal society—belong to the few theatres of logical and equal discourse so far projected or erected. But, if there should obviously be more of them, then, while one speculates about their architecture, one is also compelled to ask whether these are simply *traditional* constructs. Which is first to intrude the ideal dimension of these various theatres; and which is then to ask whether *specific* traditions (awaiting criticism) are in any way conceivable without that great body of anthropological tradition involving magic, ritual, and the centrality of ideal type, and presuming the Utopian mandala as incipient presence.

Since, though it may not be entirely apparent, we talk about a condition of active equilibrium, the ideal Swiss canton of the mind and the New England community of the picture postcard must now clamour for at least a brief attention. The ideal Swiss canton of the mind, trafficked but isolated, and the New England village of the picture postcard, closed but open to all the imports of mercantile venture, are reputed to have always maintained a stubborn and calculated balance of identity and advantage. That is: to survive they could only present two faces. Which, because it is a qualification that must be laid upon the ideas of free trade and the open society, could, at this point, allow occasion to recall Lévi-Strauss's precarious "balance between structure and event, necessity and contingency, the internal and the external..."[27]

Now a collage technique, by intention if not by definition, insists upon the centrality of just such a balancing act. A balancing act? But:

> Wit, you know, is the unexpected copulation of ideas, the discovery of some occult relation between images in appearance remote from each other: and an effusion of wit, therefore, presupposes an accumulation of knowledge; a memory stored with notions, which the imagination may cull out to compose new assemblages. Whatever may be the native vigour of the mind, she can never form many combinations from few ideas, as many changes can never be rung upon a few bells. Accident may indeed sometimes produce a lucky parallel or a striking contrast; but these gifts of chance are not frequent, and he that has nothing of his own, and yet condemns himself to needless expenses, must live upon loans or theft.[28]

Samuel Johnson, again, provides a far better definition of something very like collage than any we are capable of producing. His observations propose a commerce in which all components retain an identity enriched by intercourse, in which their respective roles may be continually transposed, in which the focus of illusion is in constant fluctuation with the axis of reality; and surely some such state of mind should inform all approaches to both Utopia and tradition.

We think again of Hadrian. We think of the "private" and diverse scene at Tivoli. At the same time we think of the Mausoleum (Castel Sant' Angelo) and the Pantheon in their metropolitan locations. And particularly we think of the Pantheon, of its oculus. Which may lead one to contemplate the publicity of necessarily singular intention (keeper of Empire) and the privacy of elaborate personal interests—a situation which is not at all like that of *ville radieuse* versus Garches.

Habitually Utopia, whether Platonic or Marxian, has been conceived of as *axis mundi* or as *axis istoriae*; but, if in this way it has operated like all totemic, traditionalist and uncriticised aggregations of ideas, if its existence has been poetically necessary and politically deplorable, then this is only to assert the idea that a collage technique by accommodating a whole range of *axis mundi* (all of them vest pocket Utopias—Swiss canton, New England village, Dome of the Rock, Place Vendôme, Campidoglio, etc.) might be a means of permitting us the enjoyment of Utopian poetics without our being obliged to suffer the embarrassment of Utopian politics. Which is to say that, because collage is a method deriving its virtue from its irony, because it seems to be a technique for using things and simultaneously disbelieving in them, it is also a strategy which can allow Utopia to be dealt with as image, to be dealt with in *fragments* without our having to accept it *in toto*, which is further to suggest that collage could even be a strategy which, by supporting the Utopian illusion of changelessness and finality, might even fuel a reality of change, motion, action and history.

1   Frances Yates, *The Art of Memory* (London and Chicago: 1966), 79.
2   Karl Popper, *Conjectures and Refutations* (New York: 1962).
3   Stanford Anderson, "Architecture and Tradition That Isn't Trad Dad," *Architectural Association Journal* vol. 80, no. 892 (1965) constitutes a significant exception.
4   Popper, *Conjectures and Refutations*, op. cit., 131.
5   Ibid., 358–360.
6   *Public Papers of the Presidents of the United States, Richard Nixon,* 1969, no. 265. Statement of the Establishment of the National Goals Research Staff.
7   Isaiah Berlin, *The Hedgehog and the Fox* (New York: 1957), 7.
8   Ibid., 10.
9   Ibid., 14.
10   William Jordy, "The Symbolic Essence of Modern European Architecture of the Twenties and its Continuing Influence," *Journal of the Society of Architectural Historians* vol. XXII, no. 3 (1963).
11   Karl Popper, *The Logic of Scientific Discovery* (New York: 1959), originally published as *Logik der Forschung* (Vienna: 1934); *The Poverty of Historicism* (London: 1957).
12   Christopher Alexander, *Notes on the Synthesis of Form* (Cambridge: 1964).
13   Claude Lévi-Strauss, *The Savage Mind* (Chicago: 1969), 16.
14   Ibid., 16.
15   Le Corbusier, *Towards a New Architecture* (London: 1927), 18–19.
16   Lévi-Strauss, *The Savage Mind*, op. cit., 17–18.
17   Ibid., 22.
18   Ibid., 19.
19   Ibid., 22.
20   Alfred Barr, *Picasso: Fifty Years of His Art* (New York: 1946), 271.

21 Ibid., 241.
22 Lévi-Strauss, *The Savage Mind*, op. cit.
23 Barr, *Picasso*, op. cit., 79.
24 Ibid., 79.
25 F.T. Marinetti, from the Futurist Manifesto 1909 and from appendix to A. Bellramelli, *L'uomo Nuovo* (Milan: 1923). Both quotations extracted from James Joll, *Three Intellectuals in Politics* (New York: 1960).
26 Barr, *Picasso*, op. cit., 79–80.
27 Lévi-Strauss, *The Savage Mind*, op. cit., 30.
28 Samuel Johnson, *The Rambler* no. 194 (25 January 1752).

INTRODUCTION

Contextualism: Urban Ideals + Deformations
Thomas L. Schumacher

This manifesto presents the evolving ideas (circa 1970) of Colin Rowe and his graduate students in the Cornell University Urban Design Studio with regard to building in the context of the city. Their reappraisal of modern urbanism called for an end to the destruction of center city areas by new construction, and proposed an alternate strategy of "contextualism," a term coined by the students to describe Rowe's theory. Thomas Schumacher, one of Rowe's students, recently recollected:

> In fact, the term originally used by Steven Hurtt and Stuart Cohen was *Contexturalism*, a conflation of *Context* and *Texture*. We were interested in urban texture, what Italians call the *tessuto urbano* (more literally "Urban Fabric"), and urban form. We were not interested in style....our representative projects sought to reconcile modern urbanism with the traditional city....the inadequacies and problems of modern architecture are *urban*, not *stylistic*....It *is* possible to make good cities using modern architecture, as the Amsterdam School proved back in the 1930s.[1]

This article is one of the first statements of the principles of Rowe's "collage city" approach, which Schumacher lays out prescriptively. One of the most important ideas is that both urban solids (building masses) and voids (the spaces of street and square) can be figural. The use of analytical figure/ground plan diagrams made clear the significance of the form of public spaces in creating the character of the city. European cities are characterized by well defined, figural public spaces including streets and squares, while American cities tend to have open, unbounded planes, like greens, malls, and commons.

A second important component of contextualist theory is the idea of the "differentiated building." Schumacher acknowledges a debt to Robert Venturi's *Complexity and Contradiction* for the development of this notion; he refers no doubt to Venturi's statement that the building should

accommodate difficult conditions without concealing the accommodation. The "differentiated
building" synthesizes ideal and circumstantial,
deforming to the conditions of the site, and
accommodating many pressures without losing
its Gestalt "imageability."

Contextualism offers a middle-ground position between an unrealistically frozen past with
no future development permitted, and urban
renewal with the total loss of the urban fabric.
Schumacher presents the traditional city's compositional strategy of gradual accretion as an alternative model to the massive bulldozing and new
construction of the 1950s and 1960s. The
collage city model has been extremely influential
in American schools of architecture including the
Institute for Architecture and Urban Studies, where
Rowe was a Fellow from 1967 to 1969.

1   Thomas L. Schumacher, unpublished statement,
     May 1995.

THOMAS L. SCHUMACHER

CONTEXTUALISM: URBAN IDEALS AND DEFORMATIONS[1]

The time is ripe for construction, not foolery.
Le Corbusier, 1922

We can work it out.
The Beatles, 1966

If one momentarily puts aside most of our urban problems (overcrowding, transportation, economics, etc.), if one places himself in the unlikely position of abstracting a small aspect of reality, he can examine the shape of the modern city independent of its many functions. The twentieth-century town is physically a combination of two simple concepts: the traditional city of corridor streets, grids, squares, etc., and the city-in-the-park. The traditional city is primarily an experience of spaces defined by continuous walls of building which are arranged in a way that emphasizes the spaces and de-emphasizes the building volumes. It is an experience which can be thought of as resulting from a subtractive process in which spaces have been carved out of solid masses. By contrast, the city-in-the-park (a phenomenon most clearly articulated by Le Corbusier as the "Ville Radieuse"), is compositionally the reverse of the traditional city. Composed of isolated buildings set in a parklike landscape, the city-in-the-park presents an experience which emphasizes the building volumes and not the spaces which the buildings define or imply.

Although the division of urban form into two types is somewhat arbitrary, it approximates reality. Because the twentieth-century town is an unhappy combination of the traditional city and various misconceptions of the Ville Radieuse, contextualism has attempted to resolve this dilemma and made the city as we find it a viable form in a future which promises enormous expansion. Faced with the reality that orgies of construction at economically

From *Casabella* no. 359–360 (1971): 79–86. Courtesy of the author and publisher.

ripe times have made a mess of our urban life, it seems imperative to stop and reflect.

So far, modern theories of urbanism and their applications have tended to devalue the traditional city.[2] Yet we have not broken our ties to it. We respect and enjoy the charm and human scale of the picturesque medieval town, while we destroy—in the name of progress—what little traditional urbanism we possess. The criterion of economic obsolescence overrides all others. If a building doesn't keep paying for itself, it goes. "Big ball" renewal projects have created a chasm between the existing and the new preventing either from offering any reasonable amenity.[3] Modern architecture promised a utopia fashioned after the machine. The promise hasn't been kept. One could, at this point, understandably argue for a revisionist philosophy and a return to traditional city ideas. Yet this alone does not solve so many of our real problems. Land values and the economic necessities of grouping people in high concentrations have greatly limited the flexibility of the capitalist city. Economic pressures and design preferences, for example, have led to the typification of housing as packages which can be assembled only as the city-in-the-park, endlessly repetitive and based on profit rather than need. The results are urban configurations which relate neither to the human being nor to the neighborhood which they interrupt.

Obviously some middle ground is needed. To retreat to a hopelessly artificial past is unrealistic, but to allow a brutalizing system to dominate and destroy traditional urbanism is irresponsible. Contextualism, professing to be a reconciliation of the above ideas, has attempted such a middle ground. But before any specific discussion of these ideas can be made, it is necessary to state a few of the basic assumptions which have formed the groundrules for this approach to solving urban problems. Very briefly, the argument might be stated as follows: because form need not follow function, building programs and uses need not be expressed in the configuration of buildings and towns. This renders out-of-context comparisons feasible. Hence a church plan and a housing block can be rationally compared. The manipulation of forms at large scale relates directly to the organizational patterns of buildings. Such smaller scale works serve as analogue models for larger projects. Thus, urban form is seen as possessing a life of its own, irrespective of use, culture, and economic conditions. Formal continuities transcending periods therefore become an important consideration.[4] Moreover, the communicative nature of architecture as a mimetic art is given new importance. This attitude depends upon the proposition that the modern-movement concept of utility and economy of means as expressed in functionalist theory is inadequate to cope with the complexities of modern experience, and that an "overplus" of communication is a necessary constituent of both buildings and cities.[5] Thus, "...the various forms of architecture...are above all structures or representation; which means in actual terms that architecture, like every other art, is both reality and representation."[6]

The validity of these assumptions cannot be tested. While they do not appear to relate directly to the solution of so many of our urban problems, it can be argued that those problems cannot be solved by architecture (or urban design) as a medium of direct communication but more likely by a social and economic process of which architecture is only a part. One is not arguing against social relevance. One "is" arguing that after a certain point in the planning process other criteria surface which allow us to make judgments about the final form of our cities. And although it is just as easy to leave out this phase (indeed, today it is always left out), it is the application of such criteria (either consciously or unconsciously) which give many cities their particular ambiences.

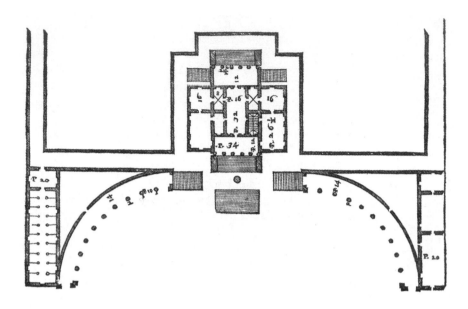

Andrea Palladio, Villa Badoer.

A building is like a soap bubble. This bubble is perfect and harmonious if the breath has been evenly distributed from the inside. The exterior is the result of the interior.
Le Corbusier, *Towards a New Architecture*, 1923

In contrast to frontalism, born out of a static conception of life, the new architecture will reach a great richness by developing an "all-sided plastic" way in space and time.
Theo van Doesburg, "24 Points of the New Architecture," 1924

The above statements typify an attitude toward architectural form which, while it gave modern architecture and urbanism some of its important peculiarities as a style, also created many of the problems we face today in the siting of buildings and the design of cities. The concept that a building should exist in the round, isolated from its neighbors, multi-sided and without preferential faces, is of course not new.[7] What was new for modern architecture was the insistence that this type of configuration be typical for all building types rather than special to particularly important building uses.

The development of Renaissance architecture is generally described as the historical progression from the Loggia degli Innocenti of [Filippo] Brunelleschi to the Tempietto of Bramante. This progression is presented as the continuing refinement of motifs from inscribed forms to real forms—from surface to volume—culminating in a cylindrical temple capped by a dome. Independent of context, round and idealized (almost without function) this little pavilion represented an ideal scarcely attainable in buildings with only slightly more complicated programs and site conditions. Allusions to the perfection

T. van Doesburg, C. van Eesteren, Project for a Private House.

of the Tempietto are common in buildings up to the twentieth century. Certainly Santa Maria della Consolazione in Todi approaches this condition. But in most cases architects have been required to soften the ideal and conform to both use and the situation.[8] The Villa Badoer of Palladio is an example of the alterations made to an "ideal," multi-sided form in order to accommodate the attendant functions housed in the wings. This building still lacks the site restrictions which promote the elaborate formal disguises that urban buildings do often possess.

By comparison, [Theo] van Doesburg's and [Cornelis] van Eesteren's project for a private house, 1922, represents an intent similar to that of the Tempietto, and can be contrasted to the Villa Badoer. Van Doesburg's construction is a multi-sided figural building which is dependent upon separation from its context. But aside from being figural (like the Villa Badoer), it is also "non"-frontal. Lacking any plane of reference as face and thereby lacking flanks, this project approaches the state of idealization of the Tempietto. Like the Tempietto this project is a prototype. Such idealization of buildings has been a

Giorgio Vasari, Uffizi, Florence.

Le Corbusier, Unité d'Habitation, Marseille.

constant imperative of modern architecture either as a purely formal preference like the de Stijl prospects, or as representing a functional unit or a program, as in the Bauhaus projects and buildings. The image of the building as an object in the round is so much a part of the modern architect's vision that he is prone to see all ages of building in these "sculptural" terms. Hence the modern architect is often disappointed in the buildings he visits which do not reflect this pre-conception.

The notion that some ideal forms can exist as fragments, "collaged" into an empirical environment, and that other ideal forms can withstand elaborate deformations in the process of being adjusted to a context have largely eluded the modern architect. This attitude was recognized and deplored by Robert Venturi who called for elements which were "...hybrid rather than 'pure,' distorted rather than 'straightforward,' ambiguous rather than 'articulated'..."[9]

It is precisely the ways in which idealized forms can be adjusted to a context or used as "collage"[10] that contextualism seeks to explain, and it is the systems of geometric organization which can be abstracted from any given context that contextualism seeks to divine as design tools.

To return to the question of the city as solids "in" voids and voids "in" solids, a comparison of the Uffizi in Florence and the Unité d'habitation in Marseilles, provides a useful analogy. The Unité is a rectangular prism, oblong and solid. The Uffizi is a rectangular prism, oblong and void. Both may be seen as "figures" surrounded by a "ground," and each represents a way of looking at the city. An archetypal void seen as a figure in plan is a conceptual ambiguity since figures are generally thought of as solid. Yet when a void has the properties of a figure it is endowed with certain capabilities which "ground" voids lack. While the Piazza Barberini in Rome, a "ground" void, functions well as a distributor of traffic but not as a collector of people, the Piazza Navona, a figural void, collects pedestrians easily.

In an unpublished masters thesis at Cornell University,[11] Wayne Copper has explored the nature of void as figure and solid as ground. "Once it is recognized that figure and ground are conceptually reversible, it follows quite naturally that their roles are interdependent." To consider a famous urban space without the back-up solid which provides its "ground" is to render an incomplete picture. Obviously the Piazza San Marco in Venice owes much of its vitality as a figural space and collector of people to the densely packed areas around it which feed it people and provide the contrast of solid to its void. When seen reversed in an all black and white drawing, the ambivalence of solid and void is obvious, and the tension created by the equality of the visual "weight" poses some interesting questions: does a regular space require irregular back-up solids? Can any norm of size relationships between streets and squares be abstracted from examining such spaces? But mainly, is this all simply irrelevant since building heights vary and the actual surfaces which define space "really" give urbanism its particular ambience? (The old idea that the Sistine Chapel is simply a barn without its painted-on architecture comes to mind here). Yet, as Copper argues, "...it would be absurd to attempt to analyze midtown Manhattan with only one level of plan...although with Rome, it would not." Obviously this abstraction does not provide the whole story, and for New York this is almost meaningless. As a tool of analysis, however, the figure-ground drawing does involve us immediately with the urban structure of a given context.

The abstraction of ideas via the concept of figure-ground and figure-ground reversal (or ambivalence) proceeds to the examination of ideal forms which have become "classic urbanism" as well as to the contexts into which these ideals are placed. The ideal city of the Renaissance, for example, begins as a medieval town containing a collection of idealized buildings and culminates as a geometric abstraction devised to accept all forms of individually idealized structures. Between the two is the reality of the Renaissance city, a medieval town which both deforms and is deformed by the Renaissance buildings it hosts. The "città ideale" of Peruzzi should be contrasted to the siting of the Palazzo Rucellai. The palace is in a narrow street where it is impossible to ever achieve a frontal view of the facade. While this is contrary to Renaissance intentions for the city, it is necessary to accept the condition and allow oneself the luxury of his perceptual ability to "lift" the building out of context.

In a constricted environment, the siting of culturally important buildings for which specific deformations are created is important to note. S. Agnese in Piazza Navona is perhaps the quintessential example. The basic parti is that of a centralized cross surmounted by a dome (not unlike S.M. della Consolazione), a basically figural building. The insistently flat façade of the Piazza implied the need for a building which adhered to the existing geometry, contrary to the ideal parti type. S. Agnese is both. The façade of the Piazza is maintained and at the same time is warped in such a way that its integrity is not broken while the dome is perceptually thrust forward into the prominence it requires as a symbol. The deformations of a particular building parti which maintain a reading of the building as an ideal form is not solely a function of the pressures exerted by a tight context. The differentiation of the faces of completely figural buildings is also of interest. Colin Rowe has stated that the absolute idealization of any useful building is logically impossible because, if no other pressures influence its design, at least entrance and orientation must act as deforming pressures.

The deforming pressures of an entry sequence may be seen in Le Corbusier's Pavillon Suisse which has been widely misconceived and emulated as a nonhierarchical, two-faced slab. It is in fact a two-sided slab, but it has a clearly defined front and back, which are treated as differently as possible within the limits of a flat surface. The entrance façade is prefaced by two curved surfaces, one rough and one smooth, that heighten the flatness of the block itself which is basically solid. The "garden" facade, by contrast, is a transparent flat curtain wall.

If the Pavillon Suisse is an example of a building "distorted" by a relatively loose context, an example of the opposite (an undistorted building within a tight context) is the CBS building of Eero Saarinen. Confined within the tight grid of New York City and placed at the end of a block, the CBS tower takes no account of the fact that its four façades face different conditions. The two streets, the wide avenue, and the adjacent buildings have in no way been recognized. Indeed, the site pressures have been so well camouflaged that the entrances to the building are almost impossible to find. The interaction of the idealized parti with its environment may be further seen in a small scale analogy, a detail in the Palazzo Farnese of Antonio da Sangallo the younger. In the entry sequence, the central aisle of a three-aisled entrance, is the width of the typical bays of the courtyard arcade. The side aisles, however, are narrower, thus leaving a discrepancy where they meet the courtyard. This is accommodated by a fan-like forced perspective band at the inner courtyard facade. Here the two conflicting forms are brought together in a resolution that not only solves an otherwise awkward intersection, but also does not completely disguise the existence of the problem. It is a kind of "75% solution" to a compositional problem that, through its incompleteness, enriches the entire composition.

Although this example is not literally a microcosm of problems of urban form (particularly plan problems), the nature of the solution is analogous and contextualism attempts to create a milieu in which abstractions of this kind and great jumps in scale can be useful tools for breaking sets.

At a larger scale, the siting of the Palazzo Borghese and the adjustments made to it in order to accommodate a complex condition explain the urban implication of Sangallo's moves in the Palazzo Farnese. This sort of adjustment differs from that of S. Agnese in the way the configuration and building are more complicated and in the way more responses are made to site pressures. Here the archetypal renaissance cortile is embedded in an oddly shaped configuration. The geometric inconsistencies are resolved by the addition of new geometries which "collect" and absorb the odd directions.

The above examples, S. Agnese in the Piazza Navona and the Palazzo Borghese, represent configurations in which fragmentary responses are made to appear as part of the parti. A second type of urban configuration, where buildings are put together with elements which relate directly to the context and only haphazardly to the building itself, is seen in the complex of S. Giovanni in Laterano. Growing slowly over many centuries and responding to specific pressures, the Lateran complex (an urban "megastructure" of moderate scale) exhibits the characteristics of a collage. The principle facade relates to the portal of S. Giovanni, the benediction loggia relates to the Via Merulana (the Sixtus V axis from Santa Maria Maggiore), and the Palazzo Laterano relates to the Piazza S. Giovanni. All of the elements are tacked on to the body of the church which does "not" respond to their pressures but remains internally the archetypal basilica almost without deformation.

Similar to S. Giovanni in its local accommodation of context is the Cathedral of Florence. Here the concept of building as both figure and ground is exploited. The major façade serves as ground to the Baptistry which is totally figural and to the Piazza S. Giovanni. The rear of the Cathedral acts as a figure which intrudes into and activates the Piazza del Duomo. It is this sort of differentiated building which can respond to many pressures created by a context without losing its imageability as a Gestalt. This type of building is rare in modern architecture ([Alvar] Aalto's Pensions Institute in Helsinki is a noticeable exception, as are many of Le Corbusier's works). It is different from the typical picturesque modern building which "...separates function into interlocking wings or connected pavilions."[12]

If we relate the urban pressures recognized in the aforementioned examples to the concept of idealization through programmatic requirements (i.e., if we deform Le Corbusier's soap bubble), we can arrive at a logically balanced "contextual" building. The office building type, although most often idealized as a point block, can assume any number of functioning shapes. A beautiful example of this flexibility is [Erik] Gunnar Asplund's 1922 competition for the Royal Chancellery in Stockholm. Produced at the same time that Le Corbusier was creating his "Ville Contemporaine," Asplund's project presented an opposite point of view. In the "Ville Contemporaine," the office building

Florence Cathedral. Wayne Copper, "The Figure-Grounds."

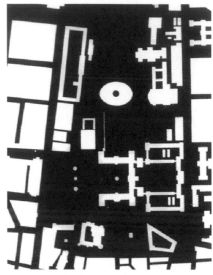

Stuttgart. Wayne Copper, "The Figure-Grounds."

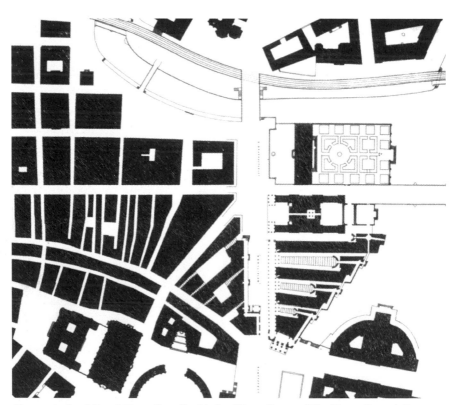

Gunnar Asplund, Royal Chancellery, Stockholm. Wayne Copper, "The Figure-Grounds."

was idealized as a cruciform tower—a collection of concepts about a building type—presented in almost cartoon fashion. To Asplund, the specific symbolic impact of the building type was subordinate to the relationship of the building and site. The resulting parti ties the building inextricably to the context in a manner that tends to disguise the limits of the actual building lot. Here the relative symbolic importance of the complex in the town is accomplished locally, by the placement of the entrance portico of the major axis. This portico functions in a manner similar to the benediction loggia of S. Giovanni in Laterano. The chancellery configuration begins to imply a strategy of "progressive substitution" in which successive elements relate directly to the adjacent elements. Although the building complex responds to its site context, it is by no means a simple catalogue of site pressures. On the contrary, Asplund's scheme is in the best tradition of Venturi's idea of "Both-And." It is both responsive and assertive, both figure and ground, both introverted and extroverted, and both idealized and deformed.

A further jump in scale leads to the study of "zones" and "fields"[13] within particular city plans. When abstracted, these are obvious organizing devices for further development as well as conceptually prototypical schemes for buildings in deformations. The plans for Stuttgart and Munich exhibit the presence of zones generally related to certain periods of development. The figure-ground abstractions show how accident, important buildings, and major spaces tend to section the city into a series of phenomenally transparent fields, the organizations of which are not unlike those of a cubist painting. "Within cubist painting," Copper asserts, "pictorial space has been shattered into an endless collage of overlapping elements rarely complete in themselves," which "find their organization via reference to larger elements often superimposed over them..." In urban groupings, "...a field of objects would be seen as a unit when they are defined by some dissimilar means of organization, or when, via some idiosyncrasy of form, polarize themselves into a cogent grouping."

As in cubist painting, when the organizational geometries do not reside in the objects themselves, the possibilities of combining various buildings within a system of order which attributes to each piece a bit of the organization become almost infinite. To limit the range of possibilities the use of the grid systems has been traditional. The interaction of grids and diagonals and curved systems has been explored in the Urban Design Department at Cornell University under the direction of Colin Rowe. In the plan for the Buffalo waterfront prepared by students under Professor Rowe's guidance, the existing city grids of Buffalo have been exploited, and moves have been made to bring the grids into a condition of spatial overlap in order to facilitate movement and "sense of place."[14] The plan represents a careful use of cubist-like order and specific deformations of idealized buildings. The system works almost as a straight line process. Fields are identified through the abstraction of the town via figure-ground drawings. Those considered useful in terms of activity and location are reinforced and clarified. The areas of collision are brought into sharp focus as needing resolution. In this case the city hall area was taken as the focus of two major grid systems, one of which relates to the waterfront, and the other of which relates to the existing town. These are brought together through the use of overlapping zones and geometrically multi-functioning buildings.

A further development of this approach, but in a more rigid context, was the Cornell team's Harlem plan, part of an exhibit sponsored by the Museum of Modern Art:

"New Cities, Architecture and Urban Renewal."[5] The scheme dealt with the particularities of the Manhattan Grid. Virtually without hierarchy, the grid offers no inherent possibilities for specific important building sites or centers of activity. Nor are any particular intersections given real prominence over others. This has the opposite effect of that in a medieval town. Because all streets are the same, initial orientation changes and becomes disorientation. No sense of "place" occurs because no place is different from any other place. The medieval town is, of course, the reverse. Initially impossible to fathom, it ultimately offers total orientation with familiarity. In the case of Harlem, the uneven terrain and the diagonal of St. Nicholas Avenue provide the only resources for enlivening the grid. Furthermore, the intrusion of vast wastelands of housing, all rather poor examples of concepts abstracted from the Ville Radieuse, provided clues as to how to approach redevelopment of the area. From this viewpoint it appeared obvious that some attempt should be made to make the many housing projects appear as if they were designed to co-exist with each other and with the context. This was accomplished by either "springing loose" the projects into zones of predominate void and defining these zones with hard edges, or by "wrapping up" the projects in order to give them back a context. The areas of great activity, where important new spaces were created, adjusted themselves to the existing context via multi-functioning buildings. The complex of buildings on the major east-west axis of 125th Street adheres on one side to the blocks opposite and on the other side reacts almost violently to various pressures on its "garden" facade which front an immense plaza.

These schemes have assumed a level of abstraction which permits the idealization of buildings either as particular urban symbols or as building programs. There is, therefore, a reliance on certain modern architecture parti-types. Although in many instances at the Urban Design Studio at Cornell buildings have been given functions roughly relating to their form type, it should be emphasized that the primary intention has been to create a formal "shorthand" which explains site pressures to an imaginary project architect. Thus, when presented with a design problem against which to measure the pre-deformed shapes given as the urban design exercise, the individual architect is in possession of an input which shows him how to start making decisions. The process can function only if the designer is willing to recognize the ultimate flexibility of any program and its ability to imply any number of partis. The process is also aided by the designer's knowledge of parti-types for traditional building programs.

1   This approach to urban design is the result of collaboration of graduate students at Cornell University under the guidance of Colin Rowe, between 1963 and the present. Professor Rowe is responsible for many of the points made in this paper. The term "Contextualism" was first used by Stuart Cohen and Steven Hurtt in an unpublished masters thesis entitled "Le Corbusier: The Architecture of City Planning."
2   The assumption of the Modern Movement was that existing Western forms had to be completely replaced. Van Doesburg's *Europe is Lost* and Le Corbusier's *There Can be No New Architecture Without New City Planning* are but two examples among many.
3   See Robert A.M. Stern, *New Directions in American Architecture* (New York: George Braziller, 1969).
4   This approaches the theories of Julien Guadet. See Colin Rowe, "Review of Talbot Hamlin's Forms and Functions of 20th-Century Architecture," *Art Bulletin* (May 1953). Also see Reyner Banham, *Theory and Design in the First Machine Age* (1959).

5   See Christian Norberg-Schulz, "Meaning in Architecture," in Charles Jencks and George Baird, eds., *Meaning in Architecture* (New York: George Braziller, 1969).

6   Luigi Moretti, "Form as Structure," *AA Journal Arena* (1967).

7   Alberti discusses the siting of temples separated from their surroundings, as does Palladio.

8   Sitte has shown how, in the nineteenth century, of 225 churches in Rome, only 6 were free-standing. Camillo Sitte, *City Planning According to Artistic Principles*, Collins, trans. (New York: Random House, 1965), 26.

9   Robert Venturi, *Complexity and Contradiction in Architecture* (New York: Museum of Modern Art), 22.

10 Literal urban collage is probably a semantic impossibility, except in an instance like the placing of a Claes Oldenburg lipstick in an urban landscape. For my purposes here, collage is taken to mean the placement of formally disparate elements in a given context.

11 Wayne Copper, *The Figure-Grounds* (Ithaca: Cornell University Press, 1967).

12 Venturi, *Complexity and Contradiction*, op. cit., 38.

13 See Cohen and Hurtt, "Le Corbusier," op. cit., 22.

14 Buffalo Waterfront Project: Colin Rowe, Werner Seligmann, Jerry Alan Wells, critics; Richard Baiter, Richard H. Cardwell, David W. K. Chan, Wayne Copper, Harris N. Forusz, Alfred H. Koetter, Maketo Miki, Elpidio F. Olimpio, Franz G. Ozwald, student collaborators.

15 *The New City: Architecture and Urban Renewal* (New York: Museum of Modern Art, 1967).

INTRODUCTION

A Significance for A&P Parking Lots or
Learning from Las Vegas
Robert Venturi and Denise Scott Brown

In this essay, incorporated into the book *Learning from Las
Vegas* (written with Steven Izenour, 1972), Robert Venturi
and Denise Scott Brown argue that architects should simply
"enhance" what exists in the environment, instead of assuming (in elitist, modernist fashion) that everything there is bad.
As an extension of the provocative critique of *Complexity
and Contradiction in Architecture* to the urban realm, the
article proposes a "revolutionary" approach for architects.
The authors expect that this more modest and tolerant
approach will be difficult for high-brow architects trained to
embrace Daniel Burnham's dictum: "Make no small plans."

In arguing for inclusion of the commercial highway
"strip" as valid American urbanism, the architects assert
that the Las Vegas strip is analogous to the Roman piazza. This analogy is intentionally inflammatory since the
piazza is a cherished paradigm of enclosed urban
space, and Venturi and Scott Brown admit that the image
of the strip is open and chaotic. Similarly provocative is
their comparison of the ubiquitous A&P grocery store parking lot to the formal landscape architecture of Versailles.
The authors describe the parking lot as part of the "current
phase in the evolution of vast space," thereby reducing
sophisticated French gardens to residual open space.

Humor aside, the outrageousness of these analogies
and statements, which appear not to recognize qualitative
differences, is part of their rhetorical strategy to force a
reconsideration of aspects of the architectural discipline
they deem to be marginalized or underrated. While they
appear to use logical argument brilliantly, their conclusions cast doubt on the process: the results caricature
logic and legitimate discourse, and leave responsible
architects wondering how to use their "contribution."

It is troubling but revealing of their intentions that
Venturi and Scott Brown issue a disclaimer about the content of their polemic: "Las Vegas is analyzed here only as
a phenomenon of architectural communication; its values
are not questioned." The medium of communication interests them (more than the implications of the message) as
part of the larger postmodern issue of meaning. Thus, the
semiotic role of advertising signs in the landscape receives
attention and is aggrandized to *become* the architecture.
(See semiotics, ch. 2) They claim that "If you take the signs
away there is no place," challenging phenomenologists'

earnest insistence on *place-making* as the architect's contribution to dwelling. (See Norberg-Schulz, ch. 9; Gregotti, ch. 7; Frampton, ch. 11) Thus for Venturi, Scott Brown and Associates, buildings and their spatial qualities are inconsequential, except insofar as they provide a wall that can be used as a billboard. This idea develops into their preference for the "decorated shed" (a dumb box with applied symbolism), over the "duck," (an expressionist, functionalist form), proclaimed in another collaborative article a few months later. The iconographic power of this opposition and its succinct terms have made it one of the memorable, if controversial, images of recent theory.

The VSBA office investigated the communicative possibilities of the wall surface in some of their architectural projects, including the infamous "billding board" Football Hall of Fame. As is often the case with projects that operate at the limits of the discipline, these remain unbuilt. But this does not diminish their impact as ironic provocations.

Emphasizing that their essay is only "a study on method," the authors disseminated their analysis technique in a design studio at Yale, taught with Izenour in 1968. In their avoidance of a critical position, the authors can be seen as apologists for the proliferation of the strip in America. This depressing, unecological condition of sprawl gained legitimacy through the indulgent, even approving, attitude expressed by these influential theorists and educators. Understandably, VSBA has been criticized for the opinions represented in their essay and book. James Howard Kunstler's *Geography of Nowhere* (1993) takes an angry look at the ubiquity of the strip phenomenon and its sociocultural impact on American towns from the perspective of a journalist and citizen. Other architects have vehemently opposed VSBA's theoretical direction as cynical and condescending, including Demetri Porphyrios and Kenneth Frampton. Objections like the following permeate Frampton's writings on the postmodern period:

The rhetoric [of *Learning from Las Vegas*]...is ideology in its purest form....Venturi and Scott Brown [ambivalently] exploit this ideology as a way of bringing us to condone the ruthless kitsch of Las Vegas.[1]

Frampton's published debate with Venturi and Scott Brown is legendary. On the other hand, one might detect sympathy toward their position in Dutch architect Rem Koolhaas, who makes a similar plea for appreciation of "edge cities" in this chapter.

1   Kenneth Frampton, *Modern Architecture: A Critical History* (New York: Thames and Hudson, 1985), 291.

ROBERT VENTURI AND DENISE SCOTT BROWN

A SIGNIFICANCE FOR A&P PARKING LOTS OR LEARNING FROM LAS VEGAS

Substance for a writer consists not merely of those realities he thinks he discovers;
it consists even more of those realities which have been made available to him by the literature and idioms of his own day and by the images that still have vitality in the
literature of the past.
Stylistically, a writer can express his feeling about this substance either by imitation, if
it sits well with him, or by parody, if it doesn't.
Richard Poirier[1]

Learning from the existing landscape is a way of being revolutionary for an architect. Not
the obvious way, which is to tear down Paris and begin again, as Le Corbusier suggested
in the 1920s, but another way which is more tolerant: that is to question how we look
at things.

The Commercial Strip, the Las Vegas Strip in particular—it is the example par
excellence—challenges the architect to take a positive, non-chip-on-the-shoulder view.
Architects are out of the habit of looking nonjudgmentally at the environment because
orthodox Modern architecture is progressive, if not revolutionary, utopian and puristic;
it is dissatisfied with *existing* conditions. Modern architecture has been anything but
permissive: architects have preferred to change the existing environment rather than
enhance what is there.

But to gain insight from the commonplace is nothing new: fine art often follows
folk art. Romantic architects of the eighteenth century discovered an existing and
conventional rustic architecture. Early Modern architects appropriated an existing and

From *Architectural Forum* 128, no. 2 (March 1968): 36–43, 91. Reprinted in *Lotus International* 5
(1968): 70–91. Courtesy of the authors and the publisher.

conventional industrial vocabulary without much adaptation. Le Corbusier loved grain elevators and steam ships; the Bauhaus looked like a factory; Mies refined the details of American steel factories for concrete buildings. Modern architects work through analogy, symbol, and image—although they have gone to lengths to disclaim almost all determinants of their forms except structural necessity and the program—and they derive insights, analogies, and stimulation from unexpected images. There is a perversity in the learning process: we look backward at history and tradition to go forward; we can also look downward to go upward.

Architects who can accept the lessons of primitive vernacular architecture, so easy to take in an exhibit like "Architecture Without Architects," and of industrial, vernacular architecture, so easy to adapt to an electronic and space vernacular as elaborate neo-Brutalist or neo-Constructivist megastructures, do not easily acknowledge the validity of the commercial vernacular. Creating the new for the artist may mean choosing the old or the existing. Pop artists have relearned this. Our acknowledging existing, commercial architecture at the scale of the highway is within this tradition.

Modern architecture has not so much excluded the commercial vernacular as it has tried to take it over by inventing and enforcing a vernacular of its own, improved and universal. It has rejected the combination of fine art and crude art. The Italian landscape has always harmonized the vulgar and the Vitruvian: the *contorni* around the *duomo*, the *pottere's* laundry across the *padrone's portone*, Supercortemaggiore against the Romanesque apse. Naked children have never played in *our* fountains and I. M. Pei will never be happy on Route 66.

ARCHITECTURE AS SPACE

Architects have been bewitched by a single element of the Italian landscape: the piazza. Its traditional, pedestrian-scaled, and intricately enclosed space is easier to take than the spatial sprawl of Route 66 and Los Angeles. Architects have been brought up on Space, and enclosed space is the easiest to handle. During the last forty years, theorists of Modern architecture ([Frank Lloyd] Wright and Le Corbusier sometimes excepted) have focused on space as the essential ingredient which separates architecture from painting, sculpture, and literature. Their definitions glory in the uniqueness of the medium, and although sculpture and painting may sometimes be allowed spatial characteristics, sculptural or pictorial architecture is unacceptable. That is because space is sacred.

Purist architecture was partly a reaction against nineteenth-century eclecticism. Gothic churches, Renaissance banks, and Jacobean manors were frankly picturesque. The mixing of styles meant the mixing of media. Dressed in historical styles, buildings evoked explicit associations and Romantic allusions to the past to convey literary, ecclesiastical, national, or programmatic symbolism. Definitions of architecture as space and form at the service of program and structure were not enough. The overlapping of disciplines may have diluted the architecture, but it enriched the meaning.

Modern architects abandoned a tradition of iconology in which painting, sculpture, and graphics were combined with architecture. The delicate hieroglyphics on a bold pylon, the archetypal inscriptions on a Roman architrave, the mosaic processions in Sant' Apollinare, the ubiquitous tatoos over a Giotto chapel, the enshrined hierarchies around a Gothic portal, even the illusionistic frescoes in a Venetian villa all contain messages beyond their ornamental contribution to architectural space. The integration of the arts in Modern architecture has always been called a good thing. But one didn't paint *on* Mies. Painted panels were floated independently of the structure by means of shadow joints; sculpture was in or near but seldom on the building. Objects of art were used to reinforce architectural space at the expense of their own content. The Kolbe in the Barcelona Pavilion was a foil to the directed spaces: the message was mainly architectural. The diminutive signs in most modern buildings contained only the most necessary messages, like "Ladies," minor accents begrudgingly applied.

ARCHITECTURE AS SYMBOL

Critics and historians who documented the "decline of popular symbols" in art, supported orthodox Modern architects who shunned symbolism of form as an expression or reinforcement of content: meaning was to be communicated through the inherent, physiognomic characteristics of form. The creation of architectural form was to be a logical process, free from images of past experience, determined solely by program and structure, with an occasional assist, as Alan Colquhoun has suggested,[2] from intuition.

But some recent critics have questioned the possible level of content to be derived from abstract forms. And others have demonstrated that the functionalists despite their protestations, derived a formal vocabulary of their own, mainly from current art movements and the industrial vernacular; latter-day followers like the Archigram group have turned, while similarly protesting, to Pop Art and the space industry. Indeed, not only are we

> not free from the forms of the past, and from the availability of these forms as typological models, but...if we assume we are free, we have lost control over a very active sector of our imagination, and of our power to communicate with others.[3]

However, most critics have slighted a continuing iconology in popular commercial art: the persuasive heraldry which pervades our environment from the advertising pages of the *New Yorker* to the super-billboards of Houston. And their theory of the "debasement" of symbolic architecture in nineteenth-century eclecticism has blinded them to the value of the representational architecture along highways. Those who acknowledge this roadside eclecticism denigrate it because it flaunts the cliché of a decade ago as well as the style of a century ago. But why not? Time travels fast today.

The Miami-Beach Modern motel on a bleak stretch of highway in southern Delaware reminds the jaded driver of the welcome luxury of a tropical resort, persuading him, perhaps, to forgo the gracious plantation across the Virginia border called Motel Monticello. The real hotel in Miami alludes to the international stylishness of a Brazilian resort, which, in turn, derives from the International Style of middle Corbu. This evolution from the high source through the middle source to the low source took only thirty years. Today, the middle source, the neo-Eclectic architecture of the 1940s and 1950s is less interesting than its commercial adaptations. Roadside copies of Ed Stone are more interesting than the real Ed Stone.

The sign for the Motel Monticello, a silhouette of an enormous Chippendale highboy, is visible on the highway before the motel itself. This architecture of styles and signs is antispatial; it is an architecture of communication over space; communication dominates space as an element in the architecture and in the landscape. But it is for a new scale of landscape. The philosophical associations of the old eclecticism evoked subtle and complex meanings to be savored in the docile spaces of a traditional landscape. The commercial persuasion of roadside eclecticism provokes bold impact in the vast and complex setting of a new landscape of big spaces, high speeds, and complex programs. Styles and signs make connections among many elements, far apart and seen fast. The message is basely commercial, the context is basically new.

A driver thirty years ago could maintain a sense of orientation in space. At the simple crossroad a little sign with an arrow confirmed what he already knew. He knew where he was. Today the crossroad is a cloverleaf. To turn left he must turn right, a contradiction poignantly evoked in the print by Allan D'Arcangelo. But the driver has no time to ponder paradoxical subtleties within a dangerous, sinuous maze. He relies on signs to guide him—enormous signs in vast spaces at high speeds.

The dominance of signs over space at a pedestrian scale occurs in big airports. Circulation in a big railroad station required little more than a simple axial system from taxi to train, by ticket window, stores, waiting room, and platform, virtually without signs. Architects object to signs in buildings: "if the plan is clear you can see where to go." But complex programs and settings require complex combinations of media beyond the purer architectural triad of structure, form, and light at the service of space. They suggest an architecture of bold communication rather than one of subtle expression.

THE ARCHITECTURE OF PERSUASION

The cloverleaf and airport communicate with moving crowds in cars or on foot, for efficiency and safety. But words and symbols may be used in space for commercial persuasion. The Middle Eastern bazaar contains no signs, the strip is virtually all signs. In the bazaar, communication works through proximity. Along its narrow aisles buyers feel and smell the merchandise, and explicit oral persuasion is applied by the merchant. In the narrow streets of the medieval town, although signs occur, persuasion is mainly through the sight and smell of the real cakes through the doors and windows of the bakery. On Main Street, shop-window displays for pedestrians along the sidewalks, and exterior signs, perpendicular to the street for motorists, dominate the scene almost equally.

On the commercial strip the supermarket windows contain no merchandise. There may be signs announcing the day's bargains, but they are to be read by the pedestrians approaching from the parking lot. The building itself is set back from the highway and half hidden, as is most of the urban environment, by parked cars. The vast parking lot is in front, not at the rear, since it is a symbol as well as a convenience. The building is low because air conditioning demands low spaces, and merchandising techniques discourage second floors; its architecture is neutral because it can hardly be seen from the road. Both merchandise and architecture are disconnected from the road. The big sign leaps to connect the driver to the store, and down the road the cake mixes and detergents are advertised by their national manufacturers on enormous billboards inflected toward the highway. The graphic sign in space has become the architecture of this landscape. Inside, the A&P has reverted to the bazaar except that graphic packaging has replaced the oral persuasion of the merchant. At another scale, the shopping center off the highway returns in its pedestrian mall to the medieval street.

HISTORICAL TRADITION AND THE A&P

The A&P parking lot is a current phase in the evolution of vast space since Versailles. The space which divides high-speed highway and low, sparse buildings produces no enclosure and little direction. To move through a piazza is to move between high enclosing forms. To move through this landscape is to move over vast expansive texture: the megatexture of the commercial landscape. The parking lot is the parterre of the asphalt landscape. The patterns of parking lines give direction much as the paving patterns, curbs, borders, and *tapis verts* give direction in Versailles; grids of lamp posts substitute for obelisks and rows of urns and statues, as points of identity and continuity in the vast space. But it is the highway signs through their sculptural forms or pictorial silhouettes, their particular positions in space, their inflected shapes, and their graphic meanings which identify and unify the megatexture. They make verbal and symbolic connections through space, communicating a complexity of meanings through hundreds of associations in few seconds from far away. Symbol dominates space. Architecture is not enough. Because the spatial relationships are made by symbols more than by forms, architecture in this landscape becomes symbol in space rather than form in space. Architecture defines very little: the big sign and the little building is the rule of Route 66.

The sign is more important than the architecture. This is reflected in the proprietor's budget: the sign at the front is a vulgar extravaganza, the building at the back, a modest necessity. The architecture is what's cheap. Sometimes the building *is* the sign: the restaurant in the shape of a hamburger is sculptural symbol and architectural shelter. Contradiction between outside and inside was common in architecture before the Modern Movement, particularly in urban and monumental architecture. Baroque domes were symbols as well as spatial constructions, and they were bigger in scale and higher outside than inside in order to dominate their urban setting and communicate their symbolic message. The false fronts of western stores did the same thing. They were bigger and taller than the interiors they fronted to communicate the store's importance and to enhance the quality and unity of the street. But false fronts are of the order and scale of Main Street. From the desert town on the highway in the West of today we can learn new and vivid lessons about an impure architecture of communication. The little low buildings, grey brown like the desert, separate and recede from the street which is now the highway, their false fronts disengaged and turned perpendicular to the highway as big high signs. If you take the signs away there is no place. The desert town is intensified communication along the highway.

Las Vegas is the apotheosis of the desert town. Visiting Las Vegas in the mid-1960s was like visiting Rome in the late 1940s. For young Americans in the 1940s, familiar only with the auto-scaled, gridiron city, and the antiurban theories of the previous architectural generation, the traditional urban spaces, the pedestrian scale, and the mixtures yet continuities of styles of the Italian piazzas were a significant revelation. They rediscovered the piazza. Two decades later architects are perhaps ready for similar lessons about large open space, big scale, and high speed. Las Vegas is to the Strip what Rome is to the Piazza.

There are other parallels between Rome and Las Vegas: their expansive settings in the Campagna and in the Mojave Desert, for instance, which tend to focus and clarify their images. Each city vividly superimposes elements of a supranational scale on the

View of the Las Vegas Strip, c.1968. Photograph by Denise Scott Brown.

local fabric: churches in the religious capital, casinos and their signs in the entertainment capital. These cause violent juxtapositions of use and scale in both cities. Rome's churches, off streets and piazzas, are open to the public; the pilgrim, religious or architectural, can walk from church to church. The gambler or architect in Las Vegas can similarly take in a variety of casinos along the Strip. The casinos and lobbies of Las Vegas which are ornamental and monumental and open to the promenading public are, a few old banks and railroad stations excepted, unique in American cities. Nolli's map of the mid-eighteenth century, reveals the sensitive and complex connections between public and private space in Rome. Private building is shown in gray hatching which is carved into by the public spaces, exterior *and* interior. These spaces, open or roofed, are shown in minute detail through darker poché. Interiors of churches read like piazzas and courtyards of palaces, yet a variety of qualities and scales is articulated. Such a map for Las Vegas would reveal and clarify the public and the private at another scale, although the iconology of the signs in space would require other graphic methods.

A conventional map of Las Vegas reveals two scales of movement within the gridiron plan: that of Main Street and that of the Strip. The main street of Las Vegas is Fremont Street, and the earlier of two concentrations of casinos is located along three or four blocks of this street. The casinos here are bazaar-like in the immediacy of their clicking and tinkling gambling machines to the sidewalk. The Fremont Street casinos and hotels focus on the railroad depot at the head of the street; here the railroad and main street scales of movement connect. The bus depot is now the busier entrance to town, but the axial focus on the rail depot from Fremont Street is visual, and possibly symbolic. This contrasts with the Strip, where a second and later development of casinos extends southward to the airport, the jet-scale entrance to town.

One's first introduction to Las Vegas architecture is a replica of Eero Saarinen's TWA Terminal, which is the local airport building. Beyond this piece of architectural image, impressions are scaled to the car rented at the airport. Here is the unraveling of the famous Strip itself, which, as Route 91, connects the airport with the downtown.

SYSTEM AND ORDER ON THE STRIP

The image of the commercial strip is chaos. The order in this landscape is not obvious. The continuous highway itself and its systems for turning are absolutely consistent. The median strip accommodates the U-turns necessary to a vehicular promenade for casino-crawlers, as well as left turns onto the local street pattern which the Strip intersects. The curbing allows frequent right turns for casinos and other commercial enterprises and eases the difficult transitions from highway to parking. The street lights function super-fluously along many parts of the Strip which are incidentally but abundantly lit by signs; but their consistency of form and position and their arching shapes begin to identify by day a continuous space of the highway, and the constant rhythm contrasts effectively with the uneven rhythms of the signs behind.

This counterpoint reinforces the contrast between two types of order on the Strip: the obvious visual order of street elements and the difficult visual order of buildings and signs. The zone *of* the highway is a shared order. The zone *off* the highway is an individual order. The elements of the highway are civic. The buildings and signs are private. In combination they embrace continuity *and* discontinuity, going *and* stopping, clarity *and* ambiguity, cooperation *and* competition, the community *and* rugged individualism. The system of the highway gives order to the sensitive functions of exit and entrance, as well as to the image of the Strip as a sequential whole. It also generates places for individual enterprises to grow, and controls the general direction of that growth. It allows variety and change along its sides, and accommodates the contrapuntal, competitive order of the individual enterprises.

There is an order along the sides of the highway. Varieties of activities are juxtaposed on the Strip: service stations, minor motels, and multimillion dollar casinos. Marriage chapels ("credit cards accepted") converted from bungalows with added neon-lined steeples are apt to appear anywhere toward the downtown end. Immediate proximity of related uses, as on Main Street where you walk from one store to another, is not required along the Strip since interaction is by car and highway. You *drive* from one casino to another even when they are adjacent because of the distance between them, and an intervening service station is not disagreeable.

THE ARCHITECTURE OF THE STRIP

A typical casino complex contains a building which is near enough to the highway to be seen from the road across the parked cars, yet far enough back to accommodate driveways, turnarounds, and parking. The parking in front is a token: it reassures the customer but does not obscure the building. It is prestige parking: the customer pays. The bulk of the parking, along the sides of the complex, allows direct access to the hotel, yet stays visible from the highway. Parking is never at the back. The scales of movement and space of the highway determine distances between buildings: they must be far apart to be comprehended at high speeds. Front footage on the Strip has not yet reached the value it once had on main street and parking is still an appropriate filler. Big space between buildings is characteristic of the Strip. It is significant that Fremont Street is more photogenic than the Strip. A single post card can carry a view of the Golden Horseshoe, the Mint Hotel, the Golden Nugget, and the Lucky Casino. A shot of the Strip is less spectacular; its enormous spaces must be seen as moving sequences.

The side elevation of the complex is important because it is seen by approaching traffic from a greater distance and for a longer time than the facade. The rhythmic gables on the long, low, English medieval style, half-timbered motel sides of the Aladdin Casino read emphatically across the parking space and through the signs and the giant statue of the neighboring Texaco station, and contrast with the modern Near-Eastern flavor of the casino front. Casino fronts on the Strip often inflect in shape and ornament toward the right, to welcome right-lane traffic. Modern styles use a porte-cochère which is diagonal in plan. Brazilianoid International styles use free forms. Service stations, motels, and other simpler types of buildings conform in general to this system of inflection toward the highway through the position and form of their elements. Regardless of the front, the back of the building is styleless because the whole is turned toward the front and no one sees the back.

Beyond the town, the only transition between the Strip and the Mojave Desert is a zone of rusting beer cans. Within the town the transition is as ruthlessly sudden. Casinos whose fronts relate so sensitively to the highway, turn their ill-kept backsides toward the local environment, exposing the residual forms and spaces of mechanical equipment and service areas.

Signs inflect toward the highway even more than buildings. The big sign—independent of the building and more or less sculptural or pictorial—inflects by its position, perpendicular to and at the edge of the highway, by its scale and sometimes by its shape. The sign of the Aladdin Casino seems to bow toward the highway through the inflection in its shape. It also is three dimensional and parts of it revolve. The sign at the Dunes is more chaste: it is only two-dimensional and its back echoes its front, but it is an erection twenty-two stories high which pulsates at night. The sign for the Mint Casino on Route 91 at Fremont Street inflects towards the Casino several blocks away. Signs in Las Vegas use mixed media—then words, pictures, and sculpture—to persuade and inform. The same sign works as polychrome sculpture in the sun and as black silhouette against the sun; at night it is a source of light. It revolves by day and moves by the play of light at night. It contains scales for close up and for distance. Las Vegas has the longest sign in the world, the Thunderbird, and the highest, the Dunes. Some signs are hardly distinguishable at a distance from the occasional highrise hotels along the Strip. The sign of the Pioneer Club on Fremont Street talks. Its cowboy, sixty feet high, says "Howdy Pardner" every thirty seconds. The big sign at the Aladdin has spawned a little sign with similar proportions to mark the entrance to the parking. "But such signs!" says Tom Wolfe. They soar in shapes before which the existing vocabulary of art history is helpless. I can only attempt to supply names—Boomerang Modern, Palette Curvilinear, Flash Gordon Ming-Alert Spiral, McDonald's Hamburger Parabola, Mint Casino Elliptical, Miami Beach Kidney.[4]

Buildings are also signs. At night on Fremont Street whole buildings are illuminated, but not through reflection from spotlights; they are made into sources of light by closely-spaced neon tubes.

LAS VEGAS STYLES

The Las Vegas casino is a combination form. The complex program of Caesar's Palace—it is the newest—includes gambling, dining, and banqueting rooms, night clubs and auditoria, stores, and a complete hotel. It is also a combination of styles. The front colonnade is San Pietro Bernini in plan, but Yamasaki in vocabulary and scale; the blue and gold mosaic work is Early Christian, tomb of Galla Placidia. (Naturally the Baroque symmetry of its prototype precludes an inflection toward the right in this facade.) Beyond and above is a slab in Gio Ponti, Pirelli-Baroque, and beyond that, in turn, a lowrise in neo-Classical Motel Moderne. Each of these styles is integrated by a ubiquity of Ed Stone screens. The landscaping is also eclectic. Within the Piazza San Pietro is the token parking lot. Among the parked cars rise five fountains rather than the two of Carlo Maderno. Villa d'Este cypresses further punctuate the parking environment. Gian da Bologna's Rape of the Sabine Women, and various statues of Venus and David, with slight anatomical exaggerations, grace the area around the porte-cochère. Almost bisecting a Venus is an Avis: a sign identifying No. 2's office on the premises.

The agglomeration of Caesar's Palace and of the Strip as a whole approach the spirit if not the style of the late Roman Forum with its eclectic accumulations. But the sign of Caesar's Palace with its Classical, plastic columns is more Etruscan in feeling than Roman. Although not so high as the Dunes sign next door or the Shell sign on the other side, its base is enriched by Roman Centurians, lacquered like Oldenburg hamburgers, who peer over the acres of cars and across their desert empire to the mountains beyond. Their statuesque escorts, carrying trays of fruit, suggest the festivities within, and are a background for the family snapshots of Middle Westerners. A massive Miesian light-box announces square, expensive entertainers like Jack Benny in 1930s-style marquis lettering appropriate for Benny, if not for the Roman architrave it almost ornaments. The light-box is not in the architrave; it is located off-center on the columns in order to inflect toward the highway.

THE INTERIOR OASIS

If the back of the casino is different from the front for the sake of visual impact in the autoscape, the inside contrasts with the outside for other reasons. The interior sequence from the front door back, progresses from gambling areas to dining, entertainment, and shopping areas to hotel. Those who park at the side and enter there can interrupt the sequence, but the circulation of the whole focuses on the gambling rooms. In a Las Vegas Hotel the registration desk is invariably behind you when you enter the lobby; before you are the gambling tables and machines. The lobby is the gambling room.

The interior space and the patio, in their exaggerated separation from the environment, have the quality of an oasis.

LAS VEGAS LIGHTING

The gambling room is always very dark; the patio, always very bright. But both are enclosed: the former has no windows, the latter is open only to the sky. The combination of darkness and enclosure of the gambling room and its subspaces makes for privacy, protection, concentration, and control. The intricate maze under the low ceiling never connects with outside light or outside space. This disorients the occupant in space and time. He loses track of where he is and when it is. Time is limitless because the light of noon and midnight are exactly the same. Space is limitless because the artificial light obscures rather than defines its boundaries. Light is not used to define space. Walls and ceilings do not serve as reflective surfaces for light, but are made absorbent and dark. Space is enclosed but limitless because its edges are dark. Light sources, chandeliers, and the glowing, juke-box-like gambling machines themselves, are independent of walls and ceilings. The lighting is antiarchitectural. Illuminated baldachini, more than in all Rome, hover over tables in the limitless shadowy restaurant at the Sahara Hotel.

The artificially lit, air conditioned interiors complement the glare and heat of the agoraphobic auto-scaled desert. But the interior of the motel patio behind the casino is literally the oasis in a hostile environment. Whether Organic Modern or neo-Classical Baroque, it contains the fundamental elements of the classic oasis: courts, water, greenery, intimate scale, and enclosed space. Here they are a swimming pool, palms, grass, and other horticultural importations set in a paved court surrounded by hotel suites balconied or terraced on the court side for privacy. What gives poignancy to the beach umbrellas and chaises lounges is the vivid, recent memory of the hostile cars poised in the asphalt desert beyond. The pedestrian oasis in the Las Vegas desert is the princely enclosure of the Alhambra, and it is the apotheosis of all the motel courts with swimming pools more symbolic than useful, the plain, low restaurants with exotic interiors, and the shopping malls of the American strip.

THE BIG, LOW SPACE

The casino in Las Vegas is big, low space. It is the archetype for all public interior spaces whose heights are diminished for reasons of budget and air conditioning. (The low, one-way mirrored ceilings also permit outside observation of the gambling rooms.) In the past, volume was governed by structural spans: height was relatively easy to achieve. For us, span is easy to achieve, and volume is governed by mechanical and economic limitations on height. But railroad stations, restaurants, and shopping arcades only ten feet high reflect as well a changing attitude to monumentality in our environment. In the past, big spans with their concomitant heights were an ingredient of architectural monumentality. But our monuments are not the occasional tour de force of an Astrodome, a Lincoln Center, or a subsidized airport. These merely prove that big, high spaces do not automatically make architectural monumentality. We have replaced the monumental space of Pennsylvania Station by a subway aboveground, and that of Grand Central Terminal remains mainly through its magnificent conversion to an advertising vehicle. Thus, we rarely achieve architectural monumentality when we try; our money and skill do not go into the traditional monumentality which expressed cohesion of the community through big scale, united, symbolic, architectural elements. Perhaps we should admit that our cathedrals are the chapels without the nave; that apart from theaters and ball parks the occasional communal space which is big is a space for crowds of anonymous individuals without explicit connection with each other. The big, low mazes of the dark restaurant with alcoves combine being together and yet separate as does the Las Vegas casino. The lighting in the casino achieves a new monumentality for the low space. The controlled sources of artificial and colored light within the dark enclosures, by obscuring its physical limits, expand and unify the space. You are no longer in the bounded piazza but in the twinkling lights of the city at night.

INCLUSION AND THE DIFFICULT ORDER

Henri Bergson called disorder all order we cannot see. The emerging order of the Strip is a complex order. It is not the easy, rigid order of the Urban Renewal project or the fashionable megastructure—the medieval hilltown with technological trappings. It is, on the contrary, a manifestation of an opposite direction in architectural theory: Broadacre City—a travesty of Broadacre City perhaps, but a kind of vindication of Frank Lloyd Wright's predictions for commercial strip within the urban sprawl is, of course, Broadacre City with a difference. Broadacre City's easy, motival order identified and unified its vast spaces and separate buildings at the scale of the omnipotent automobile. Each building, without doubt, was to be designed by the Master or by his Taliesin Fellowship, with no room for honky-tonk improvisations. An easy control would be exercised over similar elements within the universal, Usonian vocabulary to the exclusion, certainly, of commercial vulgarities. But the order of the Strip *includes*: it includes at all levels, from the mixture of seemingly incongruous advertising media plus a system of neo-Organic or neo-Wrightian restaurant motifs in Walnut Formica. It is not an order dominated by the expert and made easy for the eye. The moving eye in the moving body must work to pick out and interpret a variety of changing, juxtaposed orders, like the shifting configurations of a Victor Vasarely painting. It is the unity which "maintains, but only just maintains, a control over the clashing elements which compose it. Chaos is very near; its nearness, but its avoidance, gives...force."[5]

Las Vegas is analyzed here only as a phenomenon of architectural communication; its values are not questioned. Commercial advertising, gambling interests, and competitive instincts are another matter. The analysis of a drive-in church in this context would match that of a drive-in restaurant because this is a study of method not content. There is no reason, however, why the methods of commercial persuasion and the skyline of signs should not serve the purpose of civic and cultural enhancement. But this is not entirely up to the architect.

ART AND THE OLD CLICHÉ

Pop Art has shown the value of the old cliché used in a new context to achieve new meaning: to make the common uncommon. Richard Poirier has referred to the "de-creative impulse" in literature:

Eliot and Joyce display an extraordinary vulnerability...to the idioms, rhythms, artifacts associated with certain urban environments or situations. The multitudinous styles of *Ulysses* are so dominated by them that there are only intermittent sounds of Joyce in the novel and no extended passage certifiably is his as distinguished from a mimicked style.[6]

Eliot himself speaks of Joyce's doing the best he can "with the material at hand."[7] A fitting requiem for the irrelevant works of Art which are today's descendants of a once meaningful Modern architecture are Eliot's lines in *East Coker*:

> "That was a way of putting it—
> not very satisfactory:
> A periphrastic study in a worn-
> out poetical fashion,
> Leaving one still with the
> intolerable wrestle
> With words and meanings.
> The poetry does not matter."[8]

1   Richard Poirier, "T. S. Eliot and the Literature of Waste," *The New Republic* (20 May 1967): 21.
2   Alan Colquhoun, "Typology and Design Method," *Arena, Architectural Association Journal* (June 1967).
3   Ibid.: 14.
4   Tom Wolfe, *The Kandy-Kolored Tangerine Flake Streamline Baby* (New York: Farrar, Straus and Giroux, 1965), 8.
5   August Heckscher, *The Public Happiness* (New York: Atheneum Publishers, 1962).
6   Poirier, "T. S. Eliot and the Literature of Waste," op. cit.: 20.
7   Ibid.: 21.
8   T. S. Eliot, *Four Quartets* (New York: Harcourt, Brace and Co., 1943), 13.

INTRODUCTION

Postscript: Introduction for New Research
"The Contemporary City"
Rem Koolhaas

Rem Koolhaas's 1978 book *Delirious New York: A Retroactive Manifesto for Manhattan* (reissued 1994), presents a surreal postmodern architect's view of New York. Written while the Dutch architect was a fellow at the Institute for Architecture and Urban Studies, the text's cultish popularity is emblematic of renewed interest in the city. The book had lapsed from print, prompting the Japanese journal *Architecture and Urbanism* to excerpt it and include this retrospective reflection by its author.

Like many Europeans, Koolhaas is fascinated by New York's mythic power. While not a typical American city, it nonetheless epitomizes and exaggerates aspects of American character. He finds in Manhattan's "Culture of Congestion" a model for understanding the development of modern architecture. It is more difficult, however, to delineate the contemporary "urban" condition of sprawl, which appears to be a global phenomenon. His recent research, intended for publication as "The Contemporary City," notes fragmentation, a shift of emphasis from center to the periphery, and "spontaneous processes at work" in what have been termed "edge cities": Atlanta, Singapore, and the new towns around Paris. Resistant to classification or rules, these postindustrial landscapes, according to Koolhaas, contain an "unrecognized beauty" worthy of further contemplation. He claims these ubiquitous conditions have been ignored. A similar motivation prompted Robert Venturi, Denise Scott Brown, and Steven Izenour (VSBA) to write about the American strip in *Learning from Las Vegas* over twenty years ago. Koolhaas and VSBA share a contagious enthusiasm and wit in their theoretical work.

Koolhaas consciously situates his research in opposition to the various postmodern urban proposals of Colin Rowe (collage city), Aldo Rossi (the analogical city), and Leon Krier (the reconstruction of the European city), which focus to different degrees on the premodern European city as paradigm. Koolhaas is interested in continuing the modern project with revisions, instead of abandoning it. His formal vocabulary derives from Russian Constructivism and the Modern Movement, but without the agenda of social reform that characterized both. His firm, the Office for Metropolitan Architecture, actively engages urban design issues in projects for the new city center for Lille, France and built work such as the Nexus Housing in Fukuoka, Japan. Supported by this experience, his next treatise is likely to be an influential commentary on the postindustrial condition.

REM KOOLHAAS
POSTSCRIPT: INTRODUCTION FOR NEW RESEARCH "THE CONTEMPORARY CITY"

Delirious New York was a search in the influence of the metropolitan masses and culture on architecture and urbanism. It was directed towards the connection between new programmes—as an expression of new social demands and new forms. The research proved the existence in Manhattan of a reservoir of popular enthusiasm for "the new age," upon this a number of architects reacted with virtuosity.

The—never expressed—conclusion of the book is, that between the two World Wars architecture did undergo a definitive change. The cultural significance of traditional forms had lost unmistakably its univocability. Today there is no equivalent of that New York architecture, that—starting from mutations and rapid changes—influenced contemporary developments.

The *Contemporary City* is a research into the emerging forms of architecture in the city of today, and wants to search in the consequences and possibilities of actual mutations. This will not be directed to the "official debate," but to documentation and interpretation of a number of apparently spontaneous and independent processes, at work in cities as different as Paris, Atlanta, or Tokyo.

These processes all seem to lead to an unavoidable fragmentation of the existing city, a displacement of the centre of gravity of urban dynamics from the city centre to the urban periphery and a remarkable ingenuity in avoiding urbanistic rules.

After a period of almost exclusive interest in the historical city—and in relation to this: "housing"—a number of architects direct themselves to new territories.

Many of these projects are located in a modern "contemporary" environment, abandoned industrial sites, the periphery of the city or farther away in "new towns" or open landscapes. Programmatically existing subjects are treated in a new way, parks, company

From *Architecture and Urbanism* no. 217 (October 1988): 152. Courtesy of the author and publisher.

headquarters,...and clients change their demands. Possibilities that are still unclear, but that contain the beginning of new forms in architecture and urbanism, without post-modern nostalgia or modern tabula rasa. The common characteristic is an absence of preconceived theories, an eager liberation of a number of self-inflicted dogmas and a new sensibility for the qualities of the surrounding environment.

The Contemporary City will be a retro-active manifesto for the yet to be recognized beauty of the late twentieth-century urban landscape.

INTRODUCTION

Toward the Contemporary City
Rem Koolhaas

This polemic, published in an issue of *Design Book Review* devoted to postmodern urbanism, develops Rem Koolhaas's "paramodern alternative" as outlined in the previous essay. A significant part of his critique is the idea that while "purity" (for example, the closure or definition of the autonomous object) may have been desirable in modern buildings, it caused disorienting problems at the urban scale. Modern architecture in the form of urban renewal had devastated historic city centers. Vast, undifferentiated "open space," intended to suggest freedom, replaced the traditional, symbolic, public realm. The automobile changed the pace of experience of the city and ripped its pedestrian-scaled density apart with expressways.

Colin Rowe suggests that urban problems result from modernism's inversion of an important hierarchical relationship: the simple house versus the complex city. Along the same lines, Koolhaas notes that Modern Movement architects like Le Corbusier neglected complexity in their urban schemes. The reduction of complexity, combined with the modern schemes' partial realization, leads Koolhaas to claim that the modern city has yet to be realized. (This parallels Peter Eisenman's claim in chapter four that modernism in architecture has yet to be realized.) Thus, Koolhaas insists on withholding judgement on modern urbanism's potential. His proposed "contemporary" urbanism will be neither "contextual-traditional" nor "urban renewal-modern."

Like Robert Venturi, Denise Scott Brown, and Steven Izenour, Koolhaas accepts the given conditions of the "edge city" and metropolitan sprawl as characteristic of a significant portion of the territory in which architects work. But his strategy of amelioration is different from their proposal in *Learning from Las Vegas*: Koolhaas seeks to intensify and clarify the existing "neomodern" condition, primarily through the provision of open space ("urban voids"), which would contrast with more dense development.

Furthermore, the essay criticizes the naiveté of "utopian" approaches (such as the large-scale reconstruction of the traditional city proposed by Leon Krier) for not recognizing the determinants of what actually gets built. Koolhaas's global architectural practice offers him the chance to test his strategies by building in varied contexts. Whether his "paramodern" proposals can improve upon the ad hoc postindustrial landscape remains to be seen.

REM KOOLHAAS
TOWARD THE CONTEMPORARY CITY

For me, the key moments of modernist composition come from Mies, certainly over Le Corbusier, and from [Ivan Ilyich] Leonidov, much before [Walter] Gropius. I could continue to make a list, but I doubt this would seem very original. Every time I flip through this series of modernist images, however, what strikes me is the extraordinary incongruity between the perfection and instant completeness in their architectural plans (take for instance Mies's Barcelona Pavilion or [Giuseppe] Terragni's Danteum) and the inflexible, nearly infantile, simplicity of their urban projects, imagined as if the complexity of daily life could be accommodated right away through the freedom offered by the free plan, or as if all the experience of fragmentation and what this meant to perspective could occur without disturbing the territory of the city. This is quite clear even in Otto Wagner's deceptive plans for the extension of Vienna. Thus, for me, the most visionary architect, the one who best understood the ineluctable disorder in which we live, remains Frank Lloyd Wright and his Broadacre City.

In the last ten years, the projects I have been working on have been situated in a territory that can no longer be called suburbia but must be referred to as the borders or limits of the periphery. It is here on the edge of the periphery that we should observe how things take shape. The contemporary city, the one composed of these peripheries, ought to yield a sort of manifesto, a premature homage to a form of modernity, which when compared to cities of the past might seem devoid of qualities, but in which we will one day recognize as many gains as losses. Leave Paris and Amsterdam—go look at Atlanta, quickly and without preconceptions: that's all I can say.

From *Design Book Review* no. 17 (Winter 1989): 15–16. First published in *L'Architecture d'Aujourd'hui* (April 1989). Courtesy of the author and publisher.

Excepting certain airports and a few patches of urban peripheries, the image of the modern city—at least as it was projected—has nowhere been realized. The city that we have to make do with today is more or less made of fragments of modernity—as if abstract formal or stylistic characteristics sometimes survived in their pure state, while the urban program didn't come off. But I wouldn't cry over this failure: the resulting strata of neo-modern, which literally negates the traditional city as much as it negates the original project of modernity, offers new themes to work with. In them one can confront the buildings of this period and the different types of space—something that was impermissible in the pure doctrine of modernism. One can also learn from them to play with a substrata, mixing the built with the ideal project. This is a situation comparable to one for which the nineteenth century was much criticized, when in Milan, Paris, or Naples the strategy of remodeling without destroying the preexisting city was applied.

In the last fifteen years there has been an immense production of images for pieces of cities, which dense or not, have a power of attraction that cannot be denied. The problem is that they have been conceived in a sort of unconscious utopia, as if the powers that be, the decision mechanisms, and the means that are really available might be enchanted by the beauty or interest they portray. As if reality were going to latch onto these schemes and come to see how important it was to build them, which as far as I know is still not happening. Rather than count on this sort of fascination, or bet on the absolute authority of architecture, I think you have to ask yourself which way the forces that contribute to defining space are heading. Are they urban-oriented or the opposite? Do they ask for order or disorder? Do they play on the continuous or the discontinuous? Whatever the answer may be, there's a movement there and dynamics that you have to get to know, because they are the matter of the project.

Take for instance the IBA (Internationale Bauausstellung) in Berlin. In 1977, before the final programming of the exhibit, Oswald Ungers and I were the lone dissenting voices from [Leon] Krier, [Aldo] Rossi, [Josef Paul] Kleihues, and the others, who had already decided to make Berlin a test-case city for the reconstruction of the European city. Ungers and I pleaded for a quite different route, one that put history first: the city was destroyed, torn apart, punctured, and *this* was its memory. Second was the economy: West Berlin was stagnating, losing population ever since the construction of the wall despite thousands of institutional and fiscal incentives, and thus one could not see how a sufficient turnaround would suddenly occur to economically justify a project of general reurbanization. These were strong enough reasons to suggest that the IBA should not have taken place. Instead one had the chance in Berlin to enhance reality, to adapt to what already existed. Above all, Berlin provided the occasion to make of the city a sort of territorial archipelago—a system of architectural islands surrounded by forests and lakes in which the infrastructures could play without causing damage. It could have been realised in an almost picturesque mode (like [Gustav] Peichl's stations) with a free periphery from which one slides into great vegetal interstices. In the long run, the historical accidents (Berlin destroyed by the war, and redestroyed by the 1950s) could have offered a metaphoric role very much the opposite of the one chosen by IBA.

Remembering the projects of Mies, of [Bruno] Taut, the twin towers of Leonidov, and the like, one must also remember that these projects were first great distributors of space, more spatial definers than mere objects. I admit that there was a utopia in this vision that was just as strong, and perhaps in symmetry to the current desire to densify, construct, and give at all costs an architectural dimension. Nowadays every empty space is prey to the frenzy to fill, to stop up. But in my opinion there are two reasons that make urban voids at least one of the principal lines of combat, if not the only line, for people interested in the city. The first is quite simple: it is now easier to control empty space than to play on full volumes and agglomerate shapes that, though no one can rightly say why, have become uncontrollable. The second is something I've noticed: emptiness, landscape, space—if you want to use them as a lever, if you want to include them in a scheme—can serve as a battlefield and can draw quite general support from everyone. This is no longer the case for an architectural work, which today is always suspect and inspires prior distrust.

One of the current projects of OMA is the reurbanization of Bijlmermeer, the largest of the modernist *grands ensembles* constructed in Holland in the 1960s—it's something like Le Corbusier without talent, but conceived according to impeccable doctrine. It is an immense territory—just one of its twelve sections equals the area of the historic center of Amsterdam. Today on this immense surface where twelve capital cities might have been built, nothing is happening. The apartments are empty, people live there only in hopes of moving somewhere else, and there were serious discussions to demolish the whole project. But when looking closer, it seemed to us that these negative elements were beyond removal. It turned out that a lot of people—singles, couples, divorcees, those dedicated to the arts, and all of them necessarily motorized—were quite attached to Bijlmermeer and preferred to stay there. They enjoyed the light and space, and the indissociable feeling of freedom and abandonment. Thus it wasn't the spaces and buildings that were insufferable but rather the system of aberrant streets and garage connections that radically cut off people from their dwellings. For twenty years neither public nor private initiative has proposed anything to improve this forgotten territory. Our decision was not to alter the housing units but rather to try to give a force or intensity to the open spaces, superimposing on the original project (a giant beehive structure filled with trees) a design where the highways, the parking garages, the schools, and the stadiums would be articulated on islands of greenery and relate to a central armature of new services, including laboratories, research centers, and movie studios. This would constitute an indispensable investment if one wants to start national campaign to deal with what at the moment is a huge blight in the middle of Holland.

If my interest in the banal architecture of the 1950s and 1960s, the derivatives Ernesto Rogers and Richard Neutra, seems a somewhat boring source, I can only answer that to die of boredom is not so bad. There were much worse architects than Neutra. But let's face it, I like that kind of architecture, and quite often it has been magnificently built. It has also at times reached a carefreeness and a freedom that interests me—not that I'm the only one to take an interest in it. But the question at stake is what Bruno Vayssière and Patrice Noviant have defined as "statistic architecture": power architecture whose power is easy, that has moved without transition from the isolated experience to the series, from the series to repetition, and so on until you get sick of it. I'm trying to live with but also to detach myself from it. And since nostalgia disturbs me, I'm trying more and more not to be modern, but to be contemporary.

INTRODUCTION

Beyond Delirious
Rem Koolhaas

This recent article of Rem Koolhaas's is an excerpt from a lecture (University of Toronto School of Architecture, November 1993) in which the architect discussed his recent large-scale projects for the city, and the urban strategies devised by his firm. For a competition for the Parisian suburb of Melun-Sénart, the architect comes upon "a new conception of the city, a city no longer defined by its built space but by its absence or empty spaces." The metaphor of an "archipelago" of green spaces, places reserved from development, recurs in these essays. This idea signals his concern about unmitigated expansion into the landscape. For example, in the urban design project for Lille, the architect advocates resistance to sprawl through very high density building. Furthermore, he designed this project without the limitation of specific function, in order to maintain flexibility. (William McDonough also promotes planning for flexibility to allow reuse of buildings, which is more ecological than new construction; see ch. 8.) Flexibility underlies the modernist "open plan" (with connotations of honesty and freedom) and characterizes of investigations of shelter by Buckminster Fuller and others in the 1960s. Koolhaas's earlier projects combined functions not usually found in a single program; the results of this "cross-programming" were often surreal. (See Tschumi, ch. 3)

Now directing an immense urban development initiative, Koolhaas reflects with modesty on his "generation of May 1968," the student radicals. He expresses surprise at being entrusted with such authority. Will the Lille project actually advance beyond the modernist model of the "tower in the park," or will it simply exceed it in scale?

REM KOOLHAAS
BEYOND DELIRIOUS

I want to talk about a number of urban projects and to hint at certain problems in the contemporary urban condition which our work tries to address.

We all know the image of [Giovanni Battista] Piranesi's reconstruction of the Roman forum and we are all aware that it represents a very intense form of the city. We recognize a number of major geometrical forms associated with the major public elements, and between these we recognize smaller debris, programmatic plankton in which presumably the less formal activities of the city are accommodated. This mixture of formal and informal elements and the mixture of order and disorder which this single image represents are the essential conditions of the city.

We also know this second kind of city, and although it happens to be a part of the belt of new cities around Paris, it could as well be a part of Toronto or Tokyo or South Korea or Singapore. What is ironic is that latent underneath this model of the city you still see the major geometrical figures, the attempt at a degree of coherence, strangely Piranesian forms and organization, but without any evidence of the urban condition that Piranesi suggested or imagined. There is evidence of the debris filling the fault lines between the major figures. Where the first image inspires a certain amount of enthusiasm, we all feel degrees of disappointment if not revulsion for the second kind of city (even though it is now the dominant form and even though it is important that we declare it "city" because otherwise we are part of a culture and civilization which is simply unable to make the city.) The works I am showing have to be read against this background.

From *Canadian Architect* no. 39 (January 1994): 28–30. Courtesy of the author and publisher. This essay was presented as a lecture in November 1993 at the University of Toronto School of Architecture.

I also want to talk about my generation, as a kind of caricature of the generation of May 1968 which shouldn't be taken too seriously but shouldn't be ignored. Our generation has had two reactions to this contemporary urban condition. One basically ignored it, or to give a more positive interpretation, courageously resisted it, as Leon Krier's big theoretical reconstruction of Washington. There is a rediscovery of the city, a new loyalty to the idea of the city and our generation has been very important in claiming the city as a very essential territory of activity. But what is paradoxical in this reclamation is that it seems as if we have completely lost the power and ability to operate on and with the city.

The other part of my generation has taken the exact opposite track. For example, take Coop Himmelblau's project for a new town just outside Paris called Melun-Sénart. Where Leon Krier and his half of the generation are rebuilding the city, Coop Himmelblau and the other half is abandoning any claims that the city can be rebuilt, throwing up their arms about our ability to even reconstruct any recognizable form of the city. Out of this debate, they make spectacle—a rhetorical play where instead of a series of formal axes there is just composition, inspired on the unconscious and an essentially chaotic aesthetic.

What is painful in this having on the one hand a kind of delusion of power cut off from operational effectiveness, and on the other hand an abandonment of any claims to operational effectiveness, is that a completely devastated territory is left, which, in retrospect, our generation rediscovered but with which it was unable to find a significant relationship. And that is of course a pretty tragic condition.

Our office also participated in the competition for Melun Sénart and wrestled with the same condition, the same hopelessness of the contemporary form of the city. Paris is now encircled by a ring of new towns. Melun-Sénart is the last part of the ring, and when we started we found an incredibly beautiful French landscape. Essentially we were confronted with an innocent scene where we as architects had to imagine a new city. We felt like criminals because with the present powerlessness to imagine, build and construct a new city, and knowing the hopelessness of creating a new city with the present substance and conditions, it felt almost repulsive to have to imagine a new town on this canvas.

Using this moment of revulsion, we started to ask ourselves whether there was a new technique, a way of working with this weakness or incompetence, a potential to reverse the situation, whereby we could no longer claim that we could build a city, but could find other elements with which we could nevertheless create a new form of urban condition. We were not so much thinking about what we could build as analyzing the situation to determine where we would under no circumstances build.

To enjoy the forests, we decided not to build on the edges to the north and south. Between them was a superb zone of landscape with a number of smaller forests that French kings had used to chase deers from one forest to another and then shoot them in between, so we decided not to build there. Also, we decided not to build near the highway. We acquired by this systematic series of eliminations a kind of Chinese figure where we would make a statement about certainty—we are not going to be building here and we are not interested in building here. As we controlled this system of void spaces or landscape spaces, we systematically and enthusiastically abandoned any claim of control over the residual lands and thought that they would probably turn into what the French call "merde." The more sublime quality of the green spaces, in contrast, might give us a new conception of the city, a city no longer defined by its built space but by it absences or empty spaces.

We were quite pleased with this project, done in 1989, in that we were imagining a way of turning incompetence into the beginning of a new relationship with the city where this weakness could be incorporated and become part of an engine of recuperation.

Another recent investigation is the idea that in certain conditions, buildings of incredible density might be important instruments to contradict or resist the expansion of every city.

We have been experimenting with types of buildings which are frankly inspired by the Forbidden City in Hong Kong, which was destroyed last year. It was an incredible block—it was only approximately 180 by 120 metres but almost solid building, with minute air shafts separating buildings, sometimes not even air shafts. The total surface of the buildings was something like 300,000 square metres, and in this illegal development there was no programmatic stability. Any program here would, over time, undergo a series of perpetual modifications, so it could start as a house, then become a brothel, then a factory, then a heroin plant, then become a hospital. The liberating formula of such a clump of a building could be that we would no longer have to be very intense about making buildings for specific programs.

If we consider these clumps of buildings mainly as permanent accommodation for provisional activities, there is a whole zone of potential relaxation for the architectural profession. We no longer have to look for the rigid coincidence between form and program, and we can simply plan new masses which will be able to absorb whatever our culture generates.

So here, around an intersection outside Antwerp, a massive cluster of buildings which is specifically designed to keep the area around it free. The area is maybe a million and a half square metres, which we calculated would then liberate two square kilometres.

Next year the tunnel between England and the Continent opens. The French imagine that the combined effort of the tunnel and the TGV high speed rail will be drastic. The train from Lille to Paris used to take two hours thirty minutes. It's now fifty minutes. Disneyland is forty-five minutes. Lille to London was thirteen hours; it will be reduced to one hour and ten minutes. It will be forty minutes to Brussels, under two hours to Germany. These facts completely redesign or reinvent this area of Europe, for instance to the point that the English will buy houses here because it will be faster to go from Lille to the centre of London than from its own periphery. If you imagine not distance as a crucial given but time it takes to get somewhere then there is an irregular figure which represents the entire territory that is now less than one hour and thirty minutes from Lille. If you add up all the people in this territory, it turns out to be 60 million people. So the TGV and the tunnel could fabricate a virtual metropolis spread in an irregular manner, of which Lille, now a fairly depressing unimportant city, becomes, somehow by accident, completely artificially, the headquarters. And, equally accidentally, we became the planners of this whole operation in 1989.

We were selected and then surrounded by a table of experts looking with incredible expectation at us. Giving us a blank sheet of paper, they asked us, can you please resolve this conflict between the TGV tunnel and highway, because this is the Gordian knot of our project. That was a very important moment for me in terms of my position as a member of this May '68 generation, because I realized that I was simply not prepared for this kind of question. In my subconscious, as an architect, I never anticipated that a position as important as this one would be entrusted to a member of my generation. Somehow, I thought that highways were designed by uncles, by people with more robust nervous systems than myself, and by more plodding horses, and I felt in comparison like a race horse and therefore free of this kind of demand. That was an important moment in realizing how our generation had conceptually cut itself off from an operational world. Because I thought that the French were simply megalomaniacs and this whole project would probably never happen, and because I was surrounded by this rope of expectant experts, I decided to bluff and said, we know exactly how to resolve this problem: where the two lane TGV railway widens to six, we will run the highway parallel to the station. We will also run it underground, and in between, we will create the largest parking lot in the history of Christendom—8,000 places, and in this way, an unbelievable metropolitan concentrate of infrastructure. We used this underground literally as the basis for our project. The advantage of having this whole thing hidden underground was that it would co-exist with the scale of Europe and would not necessarily be too oppressive for the existing city.

The project in the first phase was supposed to contain a previously unimaginable 1.5 million square metres, so we had to prove to Europe that the towers could be nice, you didn't have to be afraid of towers. We also decided that the triangular area between the old station and the new station which we first imagined as a kind of plaza, could be interpreted as a plane, and that we could tilt the plane in. As tilted, part of it could become a building, toward the city, but another part, on a shear line with the tunnel, could be pushed down so that we could liberate the flank of the tunnel, creating a window so that the arrival of the TGV train (and therefore the reason for its drastic transformation) could be revealed and made part of the urban understanding.

We proposed, in terms of pure symbolism, to put a number of towers on the station itself, integrated with the station. The French in their Cartesian manner calculated that it would be eight percent more expensive to build them as bridges over the station, but that was a justified investment in symbolism. What we could symbolize was that it was not important that the presence of these towers was in Lille (actually their being in Lille is almost a coincidence or arbitrary condition), but that the really important and defining aspect of this address is its simultaneous distance of sixty minutes to both London and Paris. It's not where this building is, but the places with which it is connected that define its importance.

We were not the architects of the entire scheme. We proposed in the first instance a series of very sober and neutral envelopes for the towers, saying that the different architects could then liberate individual buildings from this envelope. We remained in a strange mixture of power and powerlessness, the *architecte en chef*, which meant that we would negotiate with the other architects without ever really imposing anything. We had a very strange relationship with all these buildings in the sense that we established the entire section and all the relationships, but we were not the architects.

There was one interesting moment when I asked the director, a brilliant developer with whom we worked closely, why he never said no in the beginning when we came with all our insane proposals—putting the towers over the station, the sinking of the highway. He said his strategy to succeed into the twenty-first century was to create within a limited territory what he called a *dynamique d'enfer*—a dynamic from hell, which is so relentlessly complex that all the partners are involved in it like prisoners chained to each other so that nobody would be able to escape. Unwittingly but enthusiastically we had worked on developing a *dynamique d'enfer* so that is now one of the items on our palette.

This first part of the project, which stared its initial planning in 1989, will be finished next year and the whole thing is now one of the largest building sites in Europe. What was exciting here was that we introduced buildings on a scale that Europe had almost never seen, therefore we could experiment with completely new typologies. More and more our major interest is not to make architecture but to manipulate the urban planes to create maximum programmatic effect.

7. THE SCHOOL OF VENICE

INTRODUCTION

Territory and Architecture
Vittorio Gregotti

Vittorio Gregotti is an architect and theorist who serves as editor in chief of the Italian journals *Casabella* and *Rassegna*. Through these activities, he has been responsible for introducing and framing many of the themes that have been important to the Italian critique of the Modern Movement and beyond. Gregotti, Aldo Rossi, and Manfredo Tafuri, all represented in this chapter, are associated with the "School of Venice," officially the Architectural Institute of the University of Venice, or IAUV. The Institute's members include neorationalists and neo-Marxists, who have in common a concern for "the fundamentally social role of architecture" and intend their work as a critique of modernism and modernization.[1]

Gregotti's editorials from the 1980s, such as "The Necessity of Theory" and "The Exercise of Detailing," (ch. 12) along with his untranslated 1966 book, *Il territorio dell'architettura*, are characteristic expressions of the neorationalist movement. Known collectively as *La Tendenza*, the Italian neorationalists attempt to "restate theoretical foundations of architectural design" and develop a logical design method.[2] Kenneth Frampton often cites Gregotti's book as one of the fundamental texts of the postmodern movement in architecture. This essay, reprinted from the British journal *Architectural Design*, brings to an English-speaking audience a few of the significant ideas from his book, along with a brief description of his award-winning 1974 design for the University of Calabria campus.

As the title suggests, Gregotti adds two important ideas (*place* and *genius loci*) to the neo-rationalist agenda of the city and form-making typologies. (ch. 5) His theory of *place* and *genius loci* derives from Heideggerian phenomenology. (ch. 9, 10) Following philosopher Martin Heidegger, the author asserts an origin for architecture in placing the first stone on the ground to recognize a *place*. This is consistent with Gregotti's general definition of the architect's task: to create "an architecture of context" by revealing nature through modification, measurement, and utilization of the landscape.

Gregotti's emphasis on *measure* is similar to Heidegger, who says, "The taking of measure is what is poetic in dwelling."[3] Formal interventions reveal the poetic truth of the site ("the essence of the environmental context"), which is necessitated by the fact that landscape and nature are broadly seen as "the sum total of all things" geographical and historical. Examples of this modification include ordering nature geometrically, idealizing it, and invoking it as a mirror of truth.[4] Gregotti's site strategy is suggestive of the "constructed site," or what might be seen as a tectonic approach to making a landscape.[5] This is consistent with his approach to building; in the design project shown, it is evident that Gregotti, like Rossi, is interested in morphology.

While his writings reference phenomenologists Heidegger and Edmund Husserl, they also cite Claude Lévi-Strauss. Gregotti's position is not simple; one detects the influence of structural linguistics in his emphasis on the constitution of architecture by the measurement of intervals, rather than by isolated objects. (ch. 2) In a definition of space that parallels semiologist Ferdinand de Saussure's discussion of language, Gregotti says, "space is composed of differences, discontinuities considered as value and as experience." In sum, Gregotti's theory is synthetic. He recognizes the whole web of relations in which one makes an architectural intervention.

1   Alan Colquhoun, "Postmodernism and Structuralism: A Retrospective Glance," in *Modernity and the Classical Tradition: Architectural Essays 1980–1987* (Cambridge: MIT Press, 1989), 251.
2   Ignasi de Solà-Morales Rubió, "Neo-Rationalism and Figuration," *Architectural Design* 54, no. 5–6 (1984): 15–20.
3   Martin Heidegger, "...Poetically Man Dwells...," in *Poetry, Language, Thought*, Albert Hofstadter, trans. (New York: Harper and Row, 1971), 221.
4   Vittorio Gregotti, "Architecture, Environment, Nature," in Joan Ockman, ed., *Architecture Culture* (New York: Rizzoli, 1993), 400.
5   Carol Burns, "On Site," in Andrea Kahn, ed., *Drawing Building Text* (New York: Princeton Architectural Press, 1991), 146–167.

VITTORIO GREGOTTI

TERRITORY AND ARCHITECTURE

While presenting my project for the University of Calabria, I thought again of some of the theoretical reflections I had made in *The Territory of Architecture* ten years earlier, in 1966, for they seemed relevant to many aspects of the overall layout of the Calabria project.

The theory of the materials of architecture and the pre-eminence of the figure as their organisational structure was central to *The Territory of Architecture*, but it did not resolve the specific organisational problems at Calabria. It concerned itself primarily with questions of theory and history, whether as hypotheses of the organisation of personal and group memory, or as a specific history of the discipline—the vacillations of its margins and the shifts in its centre of interests, its territory, and its privileged relations with other disciplines. However, the physical spirit of history is the built environment which surrounds us, the manner of its transformation into visible things, its gathering of depths and meanings which differ not only because of what the environment appears to be, but also because of what it *is* structurally. The environment is composed of the traces of its own history. If geography is therefore the way in which the signs of history solidify and are superimposed in a form, the architectural project has the task of drawing attention to the essence of the environmental context through the transformation of form.

From 1963–64 onwards I began to put these problems at the centre of my reflections on architecture: my first opportunity to experiment with their consequences in planning was at the XIIIth Triennale in Milan in 1964. Since then, I have always tried to keep the relationship between my theory and my work open, if not consistent. I have attempted, for instance, to understand what one could conclude from reflecting on the area of landscape and nature as the sum total of all things and of their past configurations. Nature, in this sense, is not seen as an indifferent, inscrutable force or a divine cycle of creation,

From *Architectural Design Profile* 59, no. 5–6 (1985): 28–34. Courtesy of the author and publisher.

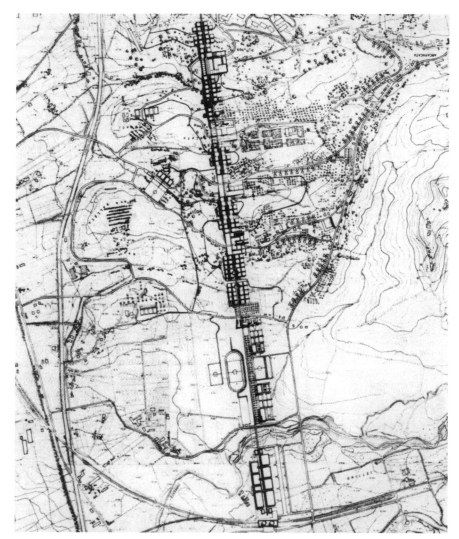

Vittorio Gregotti, site plan of the project for the University of Calabria.

but rather as a collection of material things whose reasons and relations architecture has the task of revealing. We must therefore modify, redouble, measure, situate, and utilise the landscape in order to know and meet the environment as a geographical totality of concrete things which are inseparable from their historical organisation.

This can only be done if we abandon the sociological or ecological or administrative notion of the environment as an imprisoned element and think of it instead as material for architecture. It should be made clear that this idea of the environment is not a system in which architecture is dissolved, but is on the contrary a load-bearing material for the architectural project, enabling new planning principles and methods to accommodate the spirit of the specific terrain.

The spirit behind these new methods is *modification*. Modification reveals an awareness of being part of a pre-existing whole, of changing one part of a system to transform the whole. Through its etymological root, *modus*, modification is linked to the concept of measure and the geometrical world of regulated things. It is modification which transforms *place* into *architecture* and establishes the original symbolic act of making contact with the earth, with the physical environment, with the idea of nature as a totality. Such a concept of the project sees architecture as a system of relations and distances, as the measurement of intervals rather than as isolated objects. Thus the specificity of the solution is closely related to differences in situation, context, or environment. We do not, therefore, conceive of space as a uniform and infinite extension where no place is privileged: space is not of identical value in all directions, but rather is composed of differences, discontinuities considered as value and as experience. The organisation of space, therefore, starts from the idea of *place*: the project transforms *place* into *settlement*.

The origin of architecture does not lie in the hut, the cave or in the mythical "Adam's house in paradise." Before a support was transformed into a column, a roof into a pediment, and stone heaped upon stone, man put stone on the ground in order to recognise place in the midst of the unknown universe and thereby measure and modify it. Like every aspect of measuring, this required a radical simplicity. From this point of view, there are essentially two ways to place oneself in relation to the context. The instruments of the first way are mimetic imitation, organic assimilation, and visible complexity. The second way uses measurement: distance, definition, rotation within complexity.

In the first case the problem is mirroring reality, in the second it is establishing the double. The latter mode is based on restless division: putting up a wall, building an enclosure, defining regions, producing a densely articulated interior which will correspond to the fragmentation and differences of behaviour. A simple exterior will thus appear as a measure of the larger environment's complexity. For this reason a material is not actually a thing of nature: it is more earthly and more abstract, alluding to the form of the place, to things as they are combined, but also to what is beneath, to the stable geological support, to a nature which is historically transformed, to a nature which is the product of thought, and which as a result of being frequented or settled has become a shared memory.

The project, then, must be established upon the regulating tradition of style and métier. But what gives architectural truth and concreteness to this tradition is its meeting with the site, for only by perceiving the site as a specific environment can those exceptions which generate architecture emerge.

My current work explores the implications of developing an architecture of context. This has led me to confront the problem of implementing large-scale works and to examine which principles and methods would stand up to the realities of production. I have been especially concerned with work environments in industry and universities, and was involved with the important competition for the University of Calabria. The project's main proposal was to base the design of the new university on a principle of settlement. This principle is evinced by an irregular alignment and by the connection between it and the sinuous terrain of the countryside. It functions as a way of gauging the landscape and regulating and characterising a large-scale design. Alignment and discontinuity are, moreover, ancient and characteristic methods of regulating settlements in Calabria.

The project also attempts to bring about an interaction between morphological and functional systems. The first system consists of a linear succession of university departments running across the hill system to the plain of the River Crati. The blocks housing the departmental activities accommodate the varying levels of the land and are laid out on a square plan on the axis of a bridge. The second system considers the morphology of the hills, the succession of their slopes and peaks (which carry the local road system), and their relationship to the fabric of the low-tiered houses along the northern slope intended as university residences. Since the southern slopes are cultivated with olive trees, an alternating succession of residential units and natural spaces results. The university services, which are open towards the exterior, are situated at the junctures between the bridge system and the hilltop roads.

The 7m-wide upper lane of the bridge caters for public transport and goods traffic; the lower lane is for pedestrians and internal student traffic. Between the two lanes, the various installations run along a conduit with a triangular section. The tall blocks of the university departments are linked to the bridge by a narrow body of services placed perpendicular or parallel to the bridge depending on the type of cube.

The whole layout of the university is regulated by a grid of 25.20 x 25.20m extended over two modules to the two sides of the axis, forming a settlement strip 110m wide. The tall blocks vary between two and five storeys to maintain a constant height of 232.40m above sea-level and project onto the line of transverse section of the valley below. They are enclosed by load-bearing reinforced concrete walls measuring 21.60 x 25.20m at distances of 3.60m on centre. The horizontal structures are supported by metal beams with a span of 19.60m for internal linkage. These control the positioning of the structures of the floors, spaces between floors, and intermediate floors. In the second type, the internal structures are also reinforced concrete, and pillars divide the interior into two different articulated spaces: on the one hand, small spaces for studies and offices; on the other, large collective spaces for laboratories, lecture halls, libraries, etc.

The natural lighting for the interiors is obtained through large openings in the perimeter wall and the transparent, partially sun-screened roofing. This strategically regulates the view of the natural landscape and external architecture.

The outer modules of the grid are occupied by the extension of the tall blocks on the ground floor to form a support base and house the more cumbersome technical equipment. The 250-seat lecture halls are suspended between the volumes of two lateral blocks in order to leave the continuity of the slope unbroken and form a passageway below the tiered arches. The blocks which house the various departments and a whole range of teaching and research activities form the basic element in the grouping and set up a morphological referent for the university's future growth and change of layout. The final phase of the project, providing accommodation for 12,000 students, suggested the doubling of the departmental spaces. In this projection, a rapid link-up service would replace the bridge and would continue both to the new station with parking facilities at the mouth of the Paola tunnel and to additional parking at the Cozenza tunnel. The level part of the northern area would house the buildings and supply areas of the main regional sports centre and the laboratories of the national research centre.

At this stage in its development, the university organism would be making full use of two access systems deriving from the settlement system: the two ends of alignment would be linked by a fast, efficient urban transport system while the hill roads would continue to function as they had in the first phase. The squares would be the meeting point of the two systems.

The plan for the University of Calabria was the result of a competition won in 1974 by a group consisting of E. Battisti, V. Gregotti, H. Matsui, P. Nicolin, F. Purini, C. Rusconi Clerici. Urban Planning was by Laris.
Collaborators on the project:
P. Cerri, V. Gregotti, H. Matsui (Gregotti Associati); G. Grandori, G. Ballio, A. Castiglioni, G. Colombo (Structural Engineers); Tenke VRC (Engineers).

INTRODUCTION

An Analogical Architecture
Aldo Rossi

A leader in the Italian neorationalist movement *La Tendenza*, Aldo Rossi earned international acclaim for *The Architecture of the City*, published in Italian in 1966 and translated to English and published by Oppositions Books (the Institute for Architecture and Urban Studies) in 1982. This central postmodern text is supported by the body of influential architectural work, both drawn and built, that Rossi has produced since the 1960s. The embodiment of his theoretical ideas in design work explains the impact of Rossi's architecture.

His involvement at the Architectural Institute of the University of Venice (IAUV or "School of Venice"), began with research in 1963–65 and resumed with teaching in 1975. In the interim, he taught for five years at the Milan Polytechnic, had four solo exhibitions, and edited a number of publications. This article and the companion piece that follows, "Thoughts about My Recent Work," appeared in *Architecture and Urbanism* as part of a special feature.[1]

"An Analogical Architecture" is an explication of Rossi's design method, which relies on the "logical-formal operation" of analogy as defined by psychoanalyst Carl Jung:

> "logical" thought is what is expressed in words directed to the outside world in the form of discourse. "Analogical" thought is sensed yet unreal, imagined yet silent; it is not a discourse but rather a meditation on themes of the past, an interior monologue.

Rossi uses analogical in the sense of retrieving the "archaic, unexpressed, and practically inexpressible" thought in memory. Kenneth Frampton's discussion of "analogical form" as part of his program of Critical Regionalism (ch. 11) may derive from Rossi, in its recall of primitive building forms and their associations.

Analogy explains Rossi's recourse to types, and to "certain forms of the utmost clarity [which] awaken a kind of collective memory."[2] Alan Colquhoun observes that Vittorio Gregotti and Rossi use type in different ways:

> Remaining open to contingency, Gregotti seems to display the "type" in the process of being eroded or transformed; Rossi displays it at such a level of generality that, no longer vulnerable to technological or social interference, it stands frozen in a surreal timelessness.[3]

The neorationalists were introduced to typology in the early 1960s through Giulio Carlo Argan's published research on Quatremère de Quincy, the nineteenth-century theorist whose distinction between ideal type (*type*) and physical model (*modèle*) they have adopted. (ch. 5)

Rossi is a self-proclaimed rationalist, but his work is nonetheless poetic because of the super-imposition of something surreal (or "abnormal" in Colquhoun's words) on a geometric order. (His exquisite collages are vivid postmodern interpretations, even appropriations, of the work of surrealist painter Giorgio Di Chirico.) Rossi's buildings are "abnormal" in terms of their typological signification of function; for example, his Gallaratese housing and Modena cemetery designs use uncannily similar forms for radically different programs.

Asserting that relationships or context determine meaning, Rossi says that fixed objects (forms) can be subject to changing meaning. Elemental architectural forms can thus be reused for different purposes, as in the above example. This parallels structuralist ideas of the role of fixed elements (received structures) in language. (ch. 2) To confirm this connection, Rossi cites structuralist Claude Lévi-Strauss in *The Architecture of the City*. In this book, Rossi points to the presence of morphological types with flexibility of function in the urban context. Semiotician Umberto Eco's "Function and Sign: Semiotics of Architecture" challenges Rossi's notion that a building's function can change without loss of meaning. Because for

Eco, function is the primary meaning denoted by architecture. Eco's theory of architectural meaning does allow, however, for the secondary (symbolic, aesthetic, etc.) functions connoted by architecture to change with the passage of time.

Rossi's interventions in the traditional city aim to shock by making their differences clear, rather than attempting to blend in. (Solà-Morales Rubió discusses this strategy of "contrast" in chapter four.) Rossi reasserts the significance of context indirectly, quoting Walter Benjamin; the Frankfurt School theorist says, "I am unquestionably deformed by relationships with everything that surrounds me." This citation suggests a link between the IAUV and the Frankfurt School, a link made more explicit in the historical work of Manfredo Tafuri and Francesco Dal Co.

1   The Japanese magazine, then five years old, had already asserted itself as an important critical and theoretical venue.
2   Alan Colquhoun, "Rational Architecture," *Architectural Design* 45, no. 6 (1975): 368.
3   Ibid.: 366.

ALDO ROSSI

AN ANALOGICAL ARCHITECTURE

Although in my architecture things are seen in a fixed way, I realize that in recent projects certain characteristics, memories, and above all associations have proliferated or become clearer, often yielding unforeseen results.

Each of these designs has been due increasingly to that concept of the "analogical city" about which I wrote sometime ago; meanwhile that concept has developed in the spirit of analogy.

Writing on that subject, I stated that it was mainly a matter of a logical-formal operation that could be translated as a design method.

In order to illustrate this concept, I cited the example of the view of Venice by Canaletto in the Parma Museum, in which Palladio's project for the Rialto Bridge, the Basilica, and the Palazzo Chiericati arranged and depicted as if the painter had reproduced an actual townscape. The three monuments, of which one is only a project, constitute an analogue of the real Venice composed of definite elements related to both the history of architecture and that of the city itself. The geographical transposition of the two existing monuments[†] to the site of the intended bridge forms a city recognizably constructed as a locus of purely architectonic values.

This concept of the analogical city has been further elaborated in the spirit of analogy toward the conception of an analogical architecture.

In the correspondence between [Sigmund] Freud and [Carl] Jung, the latter defines the concept of analogy in the following way:

From *Architecture and Urbanism* 56 (May 1976): 74–76. Translated by David Stewart. Courtesy of the author and publisher.

I have explained that "logical" thought is what is expressed in words directed to the outside world in the form of discourse. "Analogical" thought is sensed yet unreal, imagined yet silent; it is not a discourse but rather a meditation on themes of the past, an interior monologue. Logical thought is "thinking in words." Analogical thought is archaic, unexpressed, and practically inexpressible in words.

I believe I have found in this definition a different sense of history conceived of not simply as fact, but rather as a series of things, of affective objects to be used by the memory or in a design.

Thus, I believe I have also discovered the fascination of the picture by Canaletto in which the various works of architecture by Palladio and their removal in space constitute an analogical representation that could not have been expressed in words.

Today I see my architecture within the context and limits of a wide range of associations, correspondences, and analogies. Whether in the purism of my first works or the present investigation of more complex resonances, I have always regarded the object, the product, the project as being endowed with its own individuality that is related to the theme of human and material evolution. In reality research into architectural problems signifies little more to me than research of a more general nature, whether it be personal or collective, applied to a specific field.

My associates and I are striving to create new interests and alternatives.

The quotation from Walter Benjamin: "I am unquestionably deformed by relationships with everything that surrounds me," might be said to contain the thought underlying this essay. It also accompanies my architecture today.

There is a continuity in this, even though in the most recent projects general and personal tensions emerge with greater clarity, and in various drawings the uneasiness of different parts and elements can be felt to have superimposed itself on the geometrical order of the composition.

The deformation of the relationships between those elements surrounding, as it were, the main theme, draws me toward an increasing rarefaction of parts in favor of more complex compositional methods. This deformation affects the materials themselves and destroys their static image, stressing instead their elementality and superimposed quality. The question of things themselves, whether as compositions or components—drawings, buildings, models, or descriptions—appears to me increasingly more suggestive and convincing. But this is not to be interpreted in the sense of "*vers une architecture*" nor as a new architecture. I am referring rather to familiar objects, whose form and position are already fixed, but whose meanings may be changed. Barns, stables, sheds, workshops, etc. Archetypal objects whose common emotional appeal reveals timeless concerns.

Such objects are situated between inventory and memory. Regarding the question of memory, architecture is also transformed into autobiographical experience; places and things change with the superimposition of new meanings. Rationalism seems almost reduced to an objective logic, the operation of a reductive process which in time produces characteristic features.

In that respect I consider one of the studies realized in the course of the work on the Modena Cemetery competition as especially important. In redrawing this design and in the very process of rendering the various elements and applying the colors to parts that required emphasis, the drawing itself acquired a complete autonomy vis-à-vis the original design, so much so that the original conception might be said to be only an analogue of the finished project. It suggested a new idea based on the labyrinth and the contradictory notion of the distance traveled. In formal terms this composition is like the game of "royal goose."[††] In fact, I believe this resemblance explains its fascination and the reason why we produced several variations of the same form. Afterwards, it occurred to me that the "death" square is particularly noticeable as if it contained some profound automatic mechanism quite apart from the painted space itself.

No work, other than by its own technical means, can entirely resolve or liberate the motives that inspired it; for this reason, a more or less conscious repetition is produced in the work of anyone who labors continuously as an artist. In the best of cases, this can lead to a process of perfection but it can also produce total silence. That is the repetition of objects themselves.

In my design for the residential block in the Gallaratese district of Milan there is an analogical relationship with certain engineering works that mix freely with both the corridor typology and a related feeling I have always experienced in the architecture of the traditional Milanese tenements, where the corridor signifies a life-style bathed in everyday occurrences, domestic intimacy, and varied personal relationships. However, another aspect of this design was made clear to me by Fabio Reinhart driving through the San Bernardino Pass, as we often did, in order to reach Zurich from the Ticino Valley; Reinhart *noticed* the repetitive element in the system of open-sided tunnels, and therefore the inherent pattern. I understood on another occasion how I must have been conscious of that particular structure—and not only of the forms— of the gallery, or covered passage, without necessarily intending to express it in a work of architecture.

In like fashion I could put together an album relating to my designs and consisting only of things already seen in other places: galleries, silos, old houses, factories, farmhouses in the Lombard countryside or near Berlin, and many more—something between memory and an inventory.

I do not believe that these designs are leading away from the rationalist position that I have always upheld; perhaps it is only that I see certain problems in a more comprehensive way now.

In any case I am increasingly convinced of what I wrote several years ago in the "Introduction to Boullée": that in order to study the irrational it is necessary somehow to take up a rational position as observer.

Otherwise, observation—and eventually participation—give way to disorder.

The slogan of my entry in the competition for the Trieste Regional Office was taken from the title of a collection of poems by Umberto Saba; *Trieste e una Donna* (Trieste and a Woman). By this reference to one of the greatest modern European poets I attempted to suggest both the autobiographical quality of Saba's poetry and my own childhood associations of Trieste and Venice, as well as the singular character of the city that brings together Italian, Slav, and Austrian traditions.

My two years in Zurich had a great influence upon this project in terms of precise architectonic images: the idea of a great glazed cupola (*Lichthof*) such as the one at Zurich University by [Kolo] Moser or that of the *Kunsthaus*. I have combined the concept of a public building with this idea of a large, centrally illuminated space; the public building, like the Roman bath or gymnasium, is represented by a central space; here, in fact, three large central spaces related to one another, above which are the corridors of the upper storeys that lead to the offices.

The large spaces can either be divided or used as a single area for general assemblies; they are indoor plazas. Each is lit through large panes of glass recalling those I referred to in Zurich.

An important feature is the raised stone platform. This actually exists and represents the foundations of the old Austrian railway depots. It has been modified only by the openings through which one is able to enter a series of spaces occupying the lower level of the building.

I retained this basement level as a good way of expressing the physical continuity between old and new: by the texture of the stone; its color; and the perspective of the street running along the sea.

This project is closely related to that for the students' hostel made at about the same time, which represents a link between the design for Casa Bay, of which I shall speak more at length, and the Gallaratese block.

From Gallaratese it borrows the typology of rectilinear volumes with outside corridors, containing the students' living quarters, while with Casa Bay it shares the relationship with a sharply sloping site. The blocks of students' rooms are enclosed within an open framework of steel galleries linked at various points, and the whole building may be seen as an elevated construction anchored to the ground. The factory-like blocks are joined to a social services building (dining room, bar, reading and study rooms, etc.) standing on the level ground at the head of the site and connected with the residential wings by a T-shaped bridge.

The social services building is also developed on a centralized plan, the focus of which is a large open space with various rooms arranged above; the central room functions as the dining and assembly hall. It, too, is lit from above like the Regional Office Building. This steeply pitched roof of glass points toward the foot of the hill and, as can be seen from the drawings, is the focal point of the entire complex.

The use of light materials and, in particular, the contrast between steel and glass—combined in a way that emphasizes their technological or engineering qualities—and other materials suggestive of masonry (stone, plaster, and reinforced concrete) is expressed with clarity, and the design is restated by means of its specific relation with nature. The preference for light materials and open structural work corresponds to the space over the slope, like a bridge in other words, while the heavy part reposes directly on solid ground.

In a way this sort of contrast was already introduced in the design for a pedestrian bridge at the XIIIth Triennale (1963), in which the metal bridge enclosed in transparent steel netting contrasted with the static mass of the piers echoing the arcade behind. This same netting reappears in the housing at Gallaratese. The project for a bridge at Bellinzona in Switzerland followed a similar development; this was part of the overall scheme for the restoration of the castle, carried out by Reichlin and Reinhart, and the bridge was intended to connect the upper part of the fortifications with the part situated near the river passing over the via Sempione.

In that design the two concrete supports, that would probably have been varnished, were supposed to resemble the gray stone of the castle walls and the bridge was once more covered in metallic netting.

By means of such examples, I hope to be able to illustrate the problem of new building in historic town centers and the relationship between old and new architecture in general. I believe that this relation, or bond as it can be understood in the broader sense, is most satisfactorily expressed through the careful use of contrasting materials and forms, and not through adaptation or imitation.

But the same principles serve as an introduction to the contrasting relationship with nature pursued in the house at Borgo Ticino (Casa Bay).

I have a special fondness for this design because it seems to express a fortunate condition. Perhaps it is the fact of living suspended in mid-air among the trees of the forest, or the similarity to those riverbank constructions, including even fishermen's shacks, which for functional reasons but also owing to the basic repetition of their form remind us of prehistoric lake dwellings.

The typological image of the building is of elements growing along the slope but forming an independent horizontal line above it, the relationship to the earth being shown only by the varying height of the supports.

The architectural elements are like bridges suspended in space. The suspension or aerial construction allows the house an existence within the forest at its most secret and unattainable point amongst the branches of the trees.

The windows in each room open at the same level as the branches themselves, and viewed from certain parts of the house (the entry, the hall, and the bedrooms) the relation between earth, sky, and trees is unique.

The positioning of the building in the natural environment operates in this unusual fashion not because the building imitates or mimics nature but rather by the fact of being superimposed, almost as an addition to nature itself (trees, earth, sky, meadow).

†   [Actually situated in Vicenza.—Trans.]
††   [The playing board consists of sixty-three divisions painted in a spiral, each ninth space depicting a goose.—Trans.]

INTRODUCTION

Thoughts About My Recent Work
Aldo Rossi

Aldo Rossi discusses some of his projects in this companion piece to the preceding essay, "An Analogical Architecture." Both appeared in the Japanese magazine *Architecture and Urbanism* as part of a special feature on Rossi's work. Architect, educator, and theorist, Rossi also worked as an editor beginning in 1955, while still a student, at *Casabella Continuità*.

In the mid 1960s, Rossi translated, edited, and introduced Étienne-Louis Boullée's *Architecture: Essai sur l'art* for an Italian audience. His personal connection with the architecture of the Enlightenment is evident in his pursuit of the timeless, rational, and universal in design. The neorationalism of Rossi and the *Tendenza* group seeks to establish a continuity with the history of Italian architecture through an emphasis on the essence of architecture, or the internal aspects of the discipline.[1] The notion of a self-referential, autonomous architectural discipline is fundamental to understanding this movement, which recognizes the limitations of architecture's ability to promote social change. It is nonetheless considered possible for architecture to comment on or critique modern architecture. The Modern Movement's doctrine of functionalism, which considered form to be *determined* by function, is thus targeted by neorationalism.

The neorationalist return to typology is part of a larger postmodern critique emphasizing a continuous history (symbolized by the existence of *a priori* types) in lieu of modernist historicism. (ch. 4, 5) For Rossi, type is also a rejection of modern eclecticism and individual expressionism. Furthermore, type is not bound to function, as much as it is associated with an inventory of ideal forms with meanings resonant in "the collective memory." Rossi's recognition of the social significance of architecture takes the place of more overt connections to the political realm. The essay makes a plea for the significance of the general (societal) over the personal:

I consider that the assumptions contained in a building—technological, architectural, and typological—can offer a solution capable of generalization. In comparison, the repetition of characteristic personal architectural features has no special validity and correspondingly little interest.

Has Rossi managed to avoid the assertion of personality or style, which seems to be his stated intention for architecture? Does his use of simple forms constitute what Roland Barthes might call "degree zero" architecture?[2]

1   Rossi was responsible for organizing the XV Milan Triennale in 1973, entitled "Architettura Razionale," in which the work of the neorationalists was profiled.
2   Roland Barthes, *Writing Degree Zero* (New York: Hill and Wang, 1968).

ALDO ROSSI
THOUGHTS ABOUT MY RECENT WORK

These projects were designed between 1969 and 1973; until now, only some of them have been built and none is well known, even in Italy, except the housing at Gallaratese and the project for the city hall competition at Muggiò.

I think there is little more to be said here about the building at Gallaratese: it has been reproduced in reviews all over the world, with positive or negative comments, even copied or imitated, so that the image it has acquired is almost independent from the physical reality of the project as it was built. However, I believe that what I wrote about the design in 1970, when it was published in *Lotus* 7 is still true. I insisted then on a typology of linear galleries in contrast with the enclosed courtyard spaces used in the San Rocco scheme. Nevertheless, I must admit that the autonomy of the image and the reactions it has evoked has enriched the design even in my own eyes. Unfortunately, the photos published here show the building still not lived in and scarcely even finished. Only very recently, walking in front of it, I saw the first open windows, some laundry hung out over the balustrades to dry...those first shy hints of the life it will take on when fully inhabited. I am convinced that the spaces intended for daily use—the front portico, the open corridors meant to function as streets, the perches—will cast into relief, as it were, the dense flow of everyday life, emphasizing the deep popular roots of this kind of residential architecture. For this "big house" might be set alongside the Naviglio in Milan or any other canal in Lombardy.

Quite different to that tenement typology with its open corridors are the one-family houses at Broni with their paired entrances. With balconies, small gardens, and a characteristic curved roof, these houses are conceived as a single terrace in the main street

From *Architecture and Urbanism* 65 (May 1976): 83. Translated by David Stewart. Courtesy of the author and publisher.

of a new municipal housing scheme. The area has, in fact, been planned around this large central street which connects the new development with the old village center. Here the one-family house typology enabled me to create a long, low building overlooked by the hill and the vineyard behind. The semi-circular roofs interrupted by the sections of white wall that separate each pair of dwellings lead the eye across the Po River to the countryside in the direction of Pavia.

I also enlarged and restored an old school building at Broni. The building, which only became a school at the end of the last century, possesses an attractive Umbertine† façade, but the hall, the main stairway, and courtyard have been completely rebuilt. This work, despite its small scale, is particularly important because of the meaning my work assumes through direct confrontation with the old building. Most of all I tried, from the very first, to stress the contrast between two separate bodies, one taking form inside the other. By retaining the small courtyard, I was able to emphasize its vertical elements expressed in the portico on the ground floor and covered gallery above; these elements form a partial screen through which the yellow of the Umbertine courtyard façade is visible. Thus, both internal and external surfaces are revealed without being entirely separated. In the hall I tried to make the best use of the available space by lighting the central stairs from the courtyard; as a result, light is diffused and penetrates the entire hall. The outer wall of this staircase also provides the backdrop for the small court, emphasized by the large central window and triangular fountain.

The life of the edifice has already fused the two bodies, the old and new, into a single—yet, slightly ambiguous—whole. It now seems as if my intervention might have been a suggestion for viewing the entire building in a new way. The same method can serve as an approach to the conservation of ancient buildings and the renovation of historical town centers. In such cases, each new addition, however independent in its conception, exists physically within a pre-determined context. Not only is this context different in formal terms but also it has its own dimension in time, which must be taken into account whenever the context is to be modified. To proceed by any other method in a work of "restoration" can only signify destruction with all the sadness that destruction brings. The recent tendency toward environmental improvements, preservation, maintaining old façades—a sort of false embalming process—leads to the eventual decomposition of both architecture and townscape. Finally, I think that the importance of the school project at Broni—as I was saying at the beginning—lies precisely in the kind of associations that developed in the course of the work itself and, therefore, in the extension of the theme in new and unforeseen directions.

In the Fagnano Olona school a series of elements, which in the other projects had been divided, reunited, and approached in linear terms by means of a street, a bridge, a wall...were organized around a central court. The resulting enclosed square became the basic form of the building. This square is composed of two levels connected by a wide flight of steps with the gymnasium above. As in the central section of the project for the Modena Cemetery a skeletal image emerges from the plan. I cannot make out how much this design will be apparent to a person inside the school itself but certainly all the main elements, including the conical chimney, can be seen from the enclosure at the center. I have always imagined this central space a red color: it can be lined with either brick tiles or porphyry. Moreover, the walls of the courtyard will have the same large cross-mullioned windows that characterize the external façade.

There is certainly a marked connection between this project and that for the Muggiò city hall competition; in a sense the Fagnano project reorders the central space of the Muggiò building. This competition offered an occasion to combine different historical elements: the palatial blocks in the town center, a neoclassical villa standing to one side, and the park behind. It may be that the attempt to put them all together in a single project has brought into play a new sense of topography stressed by the diagonal arms of the city hall at the center.

Finally, any statement of the relationship between new buildings and the pre-existing configuration of the town and its architecture is more than a mere correlation between different qualities and quantities. (The attempt to discover that relationship in external facts stems from a mechanical point of view.) Any such statement to be capable of affording a solution to more general problems, must be generated from within the project according to the limits of the theme developed. This is a task for the architect as well as the critic; in the projects shown here it has been the main consideration and fundamental objective, even though each project in its final form may have been influenced by other factors of a personal nature.

This point is important for the purposes of the present discussion and essential for the development of an eventual teaching approach. Therefore, as I was saying about Gallaratese at the beginning, I consider that the assumptions contained in a building—technological, architectural, and typological—can offer a solution capable of generalization. In comparison, the repetition of characteristic personal architectural features has no special validity and correspondingly little interest. Such values are mainly of concern to the historian. Nevertheless, it is difficult for the architect to determine *a priori* whether any given formal relationship offers a chance for further creative development or whether a repeated feature may acquire unforeseen significance.

†   [Umbertino refers to the architectural style—corresponding to Victorian or Meiji—
practiced during the late nineteenth century in Italy during the reign of Umberto I of Savoy.
—Trans.]

INTRODUCTION Problems in the Form of a Conclusion
Manfredo Tafuri

This essay was published as the final chapter of
Manfredo Tafuri's book, *Architecture and Utopia:
Design and Capitalist Development* (originally
published as *Progetto e Utopia*. Bari: Guiseppe
Laterza and Figli, 1973), in which he situates the
crisis of modern architecture in the failure of its
ideology. Tafuri was a neo-Marxist theorist and
member of the "School of Venice." He was educated at the architecture school in Rome, where
he was greatly influenced by Giulio Carlo Argan.
(ch. 5) In 1968, the year of the student revolutions in Europe, Tafuri founded the Institute of
Architectural History within the Architectural
Institute of the University of Venice (IAUV); he
directed the history department until his death in
1994. A contribution to the critique of the
Modern Movement, *Architecture and Utopia* looks
rather pessimistically at the possible roles for
architecture and the theorist.

Fundamental to Tafuri's view of the history of
architecture is a Marxist suspicion of ideologies
(systems of legitimizing and naturalizing beliefs),
which mask the operation of capitalism. Tafuri
attributes the crisis that architecture experienced
in the late 1960s to the ineffectiveness of the
modernist ideology in coping with economic
realities. Like Diana Agrest (ch. 2, 13), Tafuri
defines his task as follows:

> ideological criticism is to do away with
> impotent and ineffectual myths, which so
> often serve as illusions that permit the survival
> of anachronistic "hopes in design."

Having undertaken a coherent Marxist
"demystification of reality," Tafuri finds that
modern architecture attempted to solve problems
beyond the scope of the discipline. This idea is
common to numerous postmodern views, especially with regard to architecture's elaborate program
for the large-scale improvement of society. Diane
Ghirardo has pointed out that the failure of modernism's overly ambitious agenda is used by some
postmodernists to justify a retreat from social

engagement to formalism. (ch. 8) Tafuri would thus seem to be advocating a narrow definition of architectural problems. To this extent, his theory directly opposes Robert Venturi in *Complexity and Contradiction*, who maintains that modern architecture achieved a (boring) purity of expression by excluding many legitimate architectural problems from its purview. (ch. 1)

Tafuri's extreme skepticism about the possibility of a critical ("class") architecture, or even of an *image* for a "class architecture," prevents him from prescribing a specific methodology for architectural activity. Many architects and theorists included in this anthology would find it very difficult to work within the restricted definition of architecture which Tafuri implies. For example, the interdisciplinarity and intertextuality of Bernard Tschumi's work (ch. 3, 13), and Philip Bess's effort to revive ethical positions (ch. 8) would fall outside Tafuri's scope. And yet, Tafuri would not accept descriptive criticism as adequate. Aldo Rossi's image "L'architecture assassinée" accompanies the text, which suggests that Rossi thinks Tafuri's disciplinary limits will be the death of architecture rather than its solution. In his essay "Architecture and the Critique of Ideology," Frederic Jameson responds to Tafuri's pessimism with the idea of "enclave theory," a localized resistance to capitalist optimization.[1]

Tafuri and his colleagues at the IAUV, including collaborator Francesco Dal Co, have been influenced by Walter Benjamin and other Frankfurt School members, and have disseminated the latters' ideas to the architectural community.

1   Frederic Jameson, "Architecture and the Critique of Ideology," in Joan Ockman, ed., *Architecture Criticism Ideology* (Princeton: Princeton Architectural Press, 1985), 51–87.

MANFREDO TAFURI

PROBLEMS IN THE FORM OF A CONCLUSION

It is certainly not easy, however, to integrate the aforementioned useful criticism with a type of designing that deliberately flees confrontation with the most pressing problems of the present situation.

Undeniably, we are here faced with various concomitant phenomena. On the one hand, building production taken as an element of comprehensive planning continues to reduce the usefulness of architectural ideology. On the other hand, economic and social contradictions, which explode in an always more accelerated way within urban agglomerations, seem to halt capitalist reorganization. Faced with the rationalization of the urban order, present-day political-economic forces demonstrate that they are not interested in finding the ways and means to carry out the tasks indicated by the architectural ideologies of the Modern Movement.

In other words, the ineffectiveness of ideology is clear. Urban approximations and the ideologies of the plan appear as old idols, to be sold off to collectors of antique relics.

Faced with the phenomenon of capital's direct management of land, the "radical" opposition (including portions of the working class) has avoided a confrontation with the highest levels attained by capitalist development. It has instead inherited the ideologies which capital used in the first phases of its development, but has since rejected. In this way it mistakes secondary contradictions for primary and fundamental ones.

The difficulty of the struggle for urban legislation, for the reorganization of building activity, and for urban renewal, has created the illusion that the fight for planning could in itself constitute an objective of the class struggle.

From *Architecture and Utopia: Design and Capitalist Development*, Barbara Luigia La Penta, trans. (Cambridge: MIT Press, 1980), 170–182. Courtesy of the publisher.

Aldo Rossi, "L'architecture assassinée," hand-painted etching, 1975. M. Tafuri, Rome.

And the problem is not even that of opposing bad plans with good ones. If, however, this were done with the cunning of the lamb, so to speak, it could lead to an understanding of the factors conditioning the structures of the plan that in each case correspond with the contingent objectives of the working class. This means that giving up the dream of a "new world" arising from the realization of the principle of Reason become the Plan involves no "renunciation." The recognition of the uselessness of outworn instruments is only a first necessary step, bearing in mind the ever-present risk of intellectuals taking up missions and ideologies disposed of by capital in the course of their rationalization.[1]

It is clear, however, that any struggle whatsoever on the part of the working class over the urban and regional structure must today reckon with programs of great complexity. This is true even when that complexity is due to the contradictions within the economic cycle as a whole, as in the case of the processes presently apparent in the area of building activity. Beyond the criticism of ideology there exists the "partisan" analysis of such a reality, in which it is always necessary to recognize the hidden tendencies, the real objectives of contradictory strategies, and the interests connecting apparently independent economic areas. It seems to me that, for an architectural culture that would accept such a terrain of operations, there exists a task yet to be initiated. This task lies in putting the working class, as organized in its parties and unions, face to face with the highest levels achieved by the dynamics of capitalist development, and relating particular moments to general designs.

But to do that it is necessary to recognize, even in the area of planning techniques, the new phenomena and new participant forces.

I have mentioned earlier the crisis, in the disciplines related to programming, of what we might define as the ideology of *equilibrium*. It is, on the one hand, the history of the Soviet five-year plans and, on the other, the teachings of post-Keynesian economic theories which sanction this crisis.[2] Even equilibrium is seen to be an unfeasible idol when applied to the dynamics of a given region. Indeed the present efforts to make equilibriums work, to connect crisis and development, technological revolution, and radical changes of the organic composition of capital, are simply impossible. To aim at the pacific equilibration of the city and its territory is not an alternative solution, but merely an anachronism.

The analytic models and the prognostications of the localization of productive centers prepared from the thirties up to today, by [Paul Oskar] Kristeller, [August] Lösch, [Jan] Tinbergen, [Dieter] Bos, etc., should be judged, not so much for their specific insufficiencies or with ideological criteria, but rather for the economic hypothesis they presuppose. Significant indeed is the ever-growing interest in [Evgenii Alekseevich] Preobrazensky, a Soviet theorist of the Twenties. Increasingly clear is the role Preobrazensky played as forerunner of a theory of the plan based explicitly on dynamic development, on organized disequilibrium, on interventions that presuppose a continual revolution of mass production.[3]

It should be observed, however, that programming in individual areas—also for the closed circle that is formed between the technique of intervention and its particular ends—has for the most part up to today operated on the basis of eminently static models, following a strategy based on the elimination of disequilibriums. The change from the use of static models to the creation of dynamic models seems to be the task posed today by the necessity of capitalist development to update its programming techniques.

Instead of simply reflecting a "moment" of development, the plan now takes on the form of a new political institution.[4]

It is in this way that interdisciplinary exchange pure and simple—a failure even at the practical level—is to be radically surpassed.

Horst Rittel has clearly demonstrated the implications of the insertion of "decision theory" into self-programming cybernetic systems. (And it is logical to take for granted that such a level of rationalization still in large part represents a utopian model.) Rittel has written:

> Systems of values can no longer be considered established for long periods. What can be wanted depends on what can be made possible, and what must be made possible depends on what is wanted. Ends and functions of utility are not independent measures. They have a relationship of implication in the decisional ambit. Representations of value are controllable within broad limits. Faced with the uncertainty of future alternative developments, it is absurd to wish to construct rigid decisional models that furnish strategies over long periods.[5]

Decision theory must assure the flexibility of the "systems that make decisions." It is clear that the problem is here no longer purely that of the criteria of value. The question to which an advanced level of programming must respond is, "What systems of values are generally coherent and guarantee the possibility of adaptation and therefore of survival?"[6]

For Rittel it is thus the very structure of the plan that generates its systems of evaluation. All opposition between plan and "value" falls away, precisely as recognized in Max Bense's lucid theorizing.[7]

The consequences of such phenomena, here barely touched upon, for the structure of planning and for the organization of designing, constitute a still completely open problem. It is, however, a problem which must be faced today and in regard to which didactic experimentation must take a position.

Viewed in this light, what remains of the role played historically by architecture? Up to what point does architecture's immersion in these processes render it a pure economic factor? And to what extent are decisions taken in its own specific sphere reflected in larger systems? The present-day situation in architecture makes it difficult to find coherent answers to these questions.

The fact is that, for architects, the discovery of their decline as active ideologists, the awareness of the enormous technological possibilities available for rationalizing cities and territories, coupled with the daily spectacle of their waste, and the fact that specific design methods become outdated even before it is possible to verify their underlying hypotheses in reality, all create an atmosphere of anxiety. And ominously present on the horizon is the worst of the evils: the decline of the architect's "professional" status and his introduction into programs where the ideological role of architecture is minimal.

This new professional situation is already a reality in countries of advanced capitalism. The fact that it is feared by architects and warded off with the most neurotic formal and ideological contortions is only an indication of the political backwardness of this group of intellectuals.

Architects, after having ideologically anticipated the iron-clad law of the plan, are now incapable of understanding historically the road travelled; and thus they rebel at the extreme consequences of the processes they helped set in motion. What is worse, they attempt pathetic "ethical" relaunchings of modern architecture, assigning to it political tasks adapted solely to temporarily placating preoccupations as abstract as they are unjustifiable.

Instead, there is a truth that must be recognized. That is that the entire cycle of modern architecture and of the new systems of visual communication came into being; developed, and entered into crisis as an enormous attempt—the last to be made by the great bourgeois artistic culture—to resolve, on the always more outdated level of ideology, the imbalances, contradictions, and retardations characteristic of the capitalist reorganization of the world market and productive development.

Order and disorder, understood in this way, no longer oppose each other. Seen in the light of their real historical significance there is no contradiction between Constructivism and the "art of protest"; between the rationalization of building production and the subjectivism of abstract expressionism or the irony of pop art; between capitalist plan and urban chaos; between the ideology of planning and the "poetry of the object."

By this standard, the fate of capitalist society is not at all extraneous to architectural design. The ideology of design is just as essential to the integration of modern capitalism in all the structures and suprastructures of human existence, as is the illusion of being able to oppose that design with instruments of a different type of designing, or of a radical "antidesign."

It is even possible that there exist many specific tasks for architecture. What is of greater interest to us here is to inquire how it is possible that up to now Marxist-inspired culture has, with a care and insistence that it could better employ elsewhere, guiltily denied or covered up a simple truth. This truth is, that just as there cannot exist a class political economy, but only a class criticism of political economy, so too there cannot be founded a class aesthetic, art, or architecture, but only a class criticism of the aesthetic, of art, of architecture, of the city itself.

A coherent Marxist criticism of the ideology of architecture and urbanism could not but demystify the contingent and historical realities, devoid of objectivity and universality, that are hidden behind the unifying terms of art, architecture, and city. It would likewise recognize the new levels attained by capitalist development, with which recognitions the class movements should be confronted.

First among the intellectual illusions to be done away with is that which, by means of the image alone, tries to anticipate the conditions of an architecture "for a liberated society." Who proposes such a slogan avoids asking himself if, its obvious utopianism aside, this objective is pursuable without a revolution of architectural language, method, and structure which goes far beyond simple subjective will or the simple updating of a syntax.

Modern architecture has marked out its own fate by making itself, within an autonomous political strategy, the bearer of ideals of rationalization by which the working class is affected only in the second instance. The historical inevitability of this phenomenon can be recognized. But having been so, it is no longer possible to hide the ultimate reality which renders uselessly painful the choices of architects desperately attached to disciplinary ideologies.

"Uselessly painful" because it is useless to struggle for escape when completely enclosed and confined without an exit. Indeed, the crisis of modern architecture is not the result of "tiredness" or "dissipation." It is rather a crisis of the ideological function of architecture. The "fall" of modern art is the final testimony of bourgeois ambiguity, torn between "positive" objectives and the pitiless self-exploration of its own objective commercialization. No "salvation" is any longer to be found within it: neither wandering restlessly in labyrinths of images so multivalent they end in muteness, nor enclosed in the stubborn silence of geometry content with its own perfection.

For this reason it is useless to propose purely architectural alternatives. The search for an alternative within the structures that condition the very character of architectural design is indeed an obvious contradiction of terms.

Reflection on architecture, inasmuch as it is a criticism of the concrete "realized" ideology of architecture itself, cannot but go beyond this and arrive at a specifically political dimension.

Only at this point—that is after having done away with any disciplinary ideology—is it permissible to take up the subject of the new roles of the technician, of the organizer of building activity, and of the planner, within the compass of the new forms of capitalist development. And thus also to consider the possible tangencies or inevitable contradictions between such a type of technical-intellectual work and the material conditions of the class struggle.

The systematic criticism of the ideologies accompanying the history of capitalist development is therefore but one chapter of such political action. Today, indeed, the principal task of ideological criticism is to do away with impotent and ineffectual myths, which so often serve as illusions that permit the survival of anachronistic "hopes in design."

1   In a seminal essay Mario Tronti has written: "We have before us no longer the great abstract syntheses of bourgeois thought, but the cult of the most vulgar empiricism as the practices of capital; no longer the logical system of knowledge, the scientific principles, but a mass without order of historical facts, disconnected experiences, great deeds that no one ever conceived. Science and ideology are again mixed and contradict one another; not, however, in a systematization of ideas for eternity, but in the daily events of the class struggle....All the functional apparatus of bourgeois ideology has been consigned by capital into the hands of the officially recognized working class movement. Capital no longer manages its own ideology; it has it managed by the working class movement....This is why we say that today the criticism of ideology is a task that concerns the working class point of view and that only in a second instance regards capital" (M. Tronti, "Marx, forza lavoro, classe operaia," in *Operai e capitale* [Turin: Einaudi, 1966], 171ff.)

2   In regard to the economic history of the USSR in the initial phase of the first five-year plan, see *Contropiano* no. 1 (1971), dedicated entirely to the problems of industrialization in the Soviet Union; in particular, M. Cacciari, "Le teorie dello sviluppo," 3ff, and F. Dal Co, "Sviluppo e localizzazione industriale," 81ff.

3   See M. Cacciari, "Le teorie dello sviluppo," op. cit. A systematic study of the theories of Preobrazensky is presently being prepared by M. Cacciari and C. Motta.

4   The appeal recently made by Pasquale Saraceno, to go beyond what he calls programs of objectives to programmed action of a general type, falls within that conception of the plan which does away with the schematizations and compartmented theories of planning elaborated between 1950 and 1960. Saraceno writes: "If programming is of a general

character it has in substance the goal—completely different [in respect to the vast projects that cover various given sectors of public action]—of composing into a system all the actions undertaken in the public sphere. Programming thus becomes a procedure providing a means of comparing the costs of all the various proposed governmental undertakings, as well as of comparing the total of such costs to the total foreseeable resources. The adoption of a similar procedure would make it more appropriate to speak of a programmed society than of a programmed economy" (P. Saraceno, *La programmazione negli anni '70* [Milan: Etas Kompass, 1970], 28). It should be noted that Saraceno's "general program" does not at all constitute a binding plan: its only official duty is to make known from time to time probably at intervals not longer than one year—the state of the system." (p. 32) Significant is the request for new institutions capable of realizing the coordination. The positive evaluation of the method followed in the formulation of *Progetto 80* (a report on the economic and urban situation in Italy, and on the possibilities of development by 1980, prepared by a team of economists and town planners in 1968–1969 for the Ministry of Development) confirms the line of thinking adopted. Saraceno asks: "What, in fact, is *Progetto 80*? It is a systematic review of the national problems that at *this* moment are judged of greatest importance, as well as of the new institutions which could better than those existing set in motion the means to a solution of these problems. If our public spheres were already ordered in a *system* in the sense defined above, the authors of that document would have produced what has been termed a *"program-verification."* (p. 52) Despite the fact that even Saraceno's technical prospectives are not without a utopian residue—see his plea for "an ordinance by virtue of which the social forces might morally [sic] adhere to the process of utilization of resources required for the solution of the problems" (p. 26)—his criticism of the five-year plan of 1966–1970 adheres to an institutional transformation of the control of development, correctly singled out in the note by Sandro Mattiuzzi and Stefania Potenza, "Programmazione e piani territoriali: l'esempio del Mezzogiorno," *Contropiano* no. 3 (1969): 685–717. That Saraceno's opinions are part of a vast current restructuring of the practice and theory of programming is proven by the whole series of voices raised in favor of the *plan* as a "continually and completely exercised policy." See G. Ruffolo, "Progetto 80 scelte, impegni, strumenti," *Mondo economico* no. 1 (1969).

5   H. Rittel, *Überlegungen zur wissenschaftlichen und politischen Bedeutung der Entscheidungstheorien*, report of the Studiengruppe für Systemforschung, Heidelberg, 29ff, now available in the volume edited by H. Krauch, W. Kunz, and H. Rittel, Forschungsplannung (Munich: Oldenbourg Verlag, 1966), 110- 129.

6   Ibid.

7   Pasqualotto has written "The various steps followed by Bense in his analysis represent the necessary premise and the very basis of his general conclusions, and at the same time demonstrate the absolute inadequacy of the policy proposed by Benjamin to the reality of technological integration. The chain of processes which constitute the radical formalization of the elements and structures, of the value and judgments that belong to the area of aesthetics and that of ethics, has proved to be completely functional in revealing the technical intentionality (*technische Bewusstsein*) which represents its foundation. In turn, that technical intentionality presents itself as the determining factor in the construction of a "new subjectivity," which works for the final goal of a "new synthesis": the thread of technical intentionality which weaves its way through the technological civilization ends in *integration*. But the realization of this integration evidently does not depend solely on the organic character of an ideology of technology but, rather, in large part on the elaboration of a policy of technology." (G. Pasqualotto, *Avanguardia e tecnologia*, 234–235.)

8. POLITICAL AND ETHICAL AGENDAS

Communitarianism and Emotivism: Two Rival
Views of Ethics and Architecture
Philip Bess

The postmodern period is characterized by a
renewed interest in ethical issues in architecture.
The five essays in this chapter span almost twenty
years of theory and represent diverse emphases,
but they share a common ethical stance. The first
piece, by architect Philip Bess, a former contributing editor of *Inland Architect*, adds to the critique
of modern urbanism.

Philip Bess's philosophical position follows
Aristotle in insisting on moral virtue as the necessary condition for community and for the fulfillment of the individual's potential. He contrasts
these ideas with "Nietzschean individualism,"
seen as the root of all evil in modern society. Of
particular interest to him as a practicing architect
and critic is the notion that buildings and cities
embody an ethic, whether communitarian or individualist. Today, manifestations of individualism in
the built world of city and suburb are rampant.
Regulated by proscriptive measures like zoning
and building codes designed to prevent harm to
the public, there is a startling absence of positive
values or virtues asserted. The community of individualists requires the restraint of rules, whereas
the Aristotelian scenario depends on the virtue of
community members in pursuit of their agreed-
upon ends. Bess advocates not only reviving this
latter idea of civic life, but also representing it in
the manner of the traditional city, which symbolized legitimate authority and civic virtue. (Here,
the influence of his education at the University of
Virginia, is evident.) Bess points out that the hierarchy and clarity of relations found in the traditional city between backdrop buildings, figural
public space, monuments, and institutions is lacking in the alienating contemporary city.

Contemporary architectural theory does not
help, Bess maintains. In fact, he claims it is guilty
of a pluralist retreat from judgement and therefore
from accountability, and it denies the possibility of
authority. In place of objective standards that can
be applied, recent theory offers only individual
taste, or "emotivism." Much of Bess's argument

taste, or "emotivism." Much of Bess's argument makes sense and parallels the neotraditional proposals of James Howard Kunstler (*The Geography of Nowhere*) and the Congress for the New Urbanism. However, one might question Bess's neotraditional stylistic prescription and more generally, the solution's viability. Bess himself asks, is architecture that expresses civic virtue necessarily capable of inspiring virtuous behavior? He seems to fear that a cause-and-effect relationship does not exist between providing certain urban forms and inspiring certain behavior. Further, is it realistic to expect that society will take the ethical turn toward the communitarian values Bess promotes? To reverse the increasing tendency towards individualism would certainly require a fundamental shift in values.

PHILIP BESS

COMMUNITARIANISM AND EMOTIVISM
TWO RIVAL VIEWS OF ETHICS AND ARCHITECTURE

Nietzsche's moral philosophy is matched specifically against Aristotle's by virtue of the historical role which each plays. For...it was because a moral tradition of which Aristotle's thought was the intellectual core was repudiated during the transitions of the fifteenth to seventeenth centuries that the Enlightenment project of discovering new rational secular foundations for morality had to be undertaken. And it was because that [Enlightenment] project failed, because...[it] could not be sustained in the face of rational criticism that Nietzsche and...[his] successors were able to mount their apparently successful critique of all previous morality. Hence the defensibility of the Nietzschean position turns *in the end* on the answer to the question: was it right in the first place to reject Aristotle? For if Aristotle's position in ethics and politics—or something very like it—could be sustained, the whole Nietzschean enterprise would be pointless....It is an understatement to call this a large and complex question.

Alasdair MacIntyre, *After Virtue*

"Ethics is money. Morals is sex." Thus did a Chicago lawyer once instruct novelist and Nobel laureate Saul Bellow in the wisdom of the world. These characterizations aptly summarize what is generally meant when we read in the papers that someone has been accused of ethical improprieties or arrested on a morals charge. They also correspond specifically to those items typically the concern of various professional codes of ethics, including the AIA's.

Bellow's lawyer acquaintance apparently felt no need to add that, beyond this very restricted sense of professional ethics, neither ethics nor morality have anything to do with architecture and urban design. And, had he made such an assertion, he surely would

From *Inland Architect* 5/6 (May/June 1993): 74–83. Courtesy of the author and publisher.

have been expressing a widely held opinion. Nevertheless, among design professionals and educators, there seems to be a fair amount of interest in the subject of ethics and architecture, and opinion on the matter is not at all settled.

On the one hand, schools of architecture at universities such as Virginia, Miami (Florida), Notre Dame, and Maryland enthusiastically promote a more or less strictly defined traditional architecture and/or urbanism as emblematic of and conducive to a species of morality known as civic virtue. On the other hand, at universities like Columbia, Princeton, and Ohio State, and at the Cranbrook Educational Community, a distinctly nontraditional architecture intentionally *dis*sociated from conventional notions of morality is promoted, although it is not always clear whether what is desired is a reassociation of architecture and urbanism with a new and improved morality, or their complete dissociation from morality altogether.

Local scholars and architects from the University of Illinois at Chicago (UIC) have recently weighed in with their own not entirely concordant opinions. Within the past year, in the pages of this magazine, Stanley Tigerman has blasted the new Chicago Public Library and cried out for a reconception of architecture as "a moral undertaking based on the problems of the day," unsullied by nostalgia and traditional forms "falsely reenlivened through picturesqueness debilitated by longing." Similarly, UIC's Roberta Feldman and Martin Jaffe, sounding a similar theme, have solemnly accused neo-traditionalist architects and town planners of a trivial aestheticism that diverts attention from the reclamation of our cities and from the social and ecological costs of suburban sprawl. Historian Robert Bruegmann, on the other hand, sounds a populist note, and tweaks moralizing critics of strip malls and regional shopping centers. He suggests that such critics, of whatever ideological bent, are antidemocratic snobs who should wise up and accept the plain truth that most Americans simply love their cars, their malls, and their suburbs. Bruegmann echoes the increasingly heard assertion that all types of retail centers now constitute the premiere public and/or civic spaces of contemporary society.

Yet another take on ethics and architecture comes from critic James Krohe, Jr., in the August 14, 1992, edition of the Chicago *Reader*. Krohe finds it a particular fault (and implicit moral failing) that UIC's architecture program allegedly fails to give adequate attention in its curriculum to the various practical concerns of building users, concerns traditionally subsumed under the Vitruvian heading of *commoditas*. In many cities across the country, a revival of advocacy architecture, focusing upon environmental issues and the pressing concerns of less affluent clients, is evident in the activities of organizations, such as Architects, Designers, and Planners for Social Responsibility (ADPSR) and the Mad Housers. The former promotes socially responsible design and the latter engages in localized guerrilla construction projects that result in portable individual shelters for the homeless.

Considering all of the above, perhaps the best that one can say about ethics and architecture is that interest exists, but there is neither clarity nor consensus on the subject, either within or beyond the practices of architecture and urban design or moral philosophy. Nevertheless, in the absence of consensus, one can still hope for greater clarification of intellectual differences, even perhaps for a more expansive understanding of ethics and morality (if not architecture) than that exhibited by Bellow's lawyer acquaintance. It is toward these latter more modest ends that I have invoked the names Aristotle and Nietzsche.

ARISTOTLE AND NIETZSCHE

Historically, when architects and urban designers have looked to Classical antiquity for intellectual support (as opposed to aesthetic inspiration), they have more often turned to Plato than to Aristotle. This is not surprising. Plato is more fun to read, and has interesting notions about ideal forms that readily lend themselves to the formalist and utopian inclinations of architects and urban designers. Platonism as a philosophy, however, has some internal difficulties accounting for both the material world and the phenomenon of change. For considering things like the design and construction of real architecture and real cities—practices that involve material artifacts, develop over time, and exhibit continuity and discontinuity—Aristotle's general interest in and emphasis upon material objects, and upon types rather than ideal forms, seems insufficiently appreciated by architects and architectural theorists.

Even less appreciated by theorists, however, is Aristotle's emphasis upon the necessity and centrality of various moral and intellectual virtues to the achievement of human well-being, their relationship to the life of the city, and their possible formal implications. Several years ago, philosopher Russell Hittenger commented that since the 1981 publication of Alasdair MacIntyre's *After Virtue* "it has become professionally respectable to take Aristotle seriously." For this, every traditionalist or neotraditionalist architect and urban designer is in MacIntyre's debt.

MacIntyre contends that Aristotle and the nineteenth-century German philosopher Friedrich Nietzsche provide the core concepts for two different and incommensurate understandings of the moral life that are in cultural competition at the dawn of the twenty-first century. Nietzsche's is now regnant, and Aristotle's is currently subject to reconsideration; both are critical of Kantian/Enlightenment moral rationalism and agree that it has failed. I would like to suggest that this competition in the realm of moral philosophy has (perhaps not surprisingly) a nearly exact parallel in the theory and practice of contemporary architecture and urban design; it sheds light on the not always obvious but nevertheless genuine and intrinsic relationship between architecture and ethics.

Buildings and cities both possess and represent a certain *ethos*, or character; in so doing, they embody (if often only implicitly) a certain ethic. In an early 1988 essay marking the (1987) centenary of the birth of Le Corbusier, *New Republic* architecture critic Herbert Muschamp noted (correctly, in my view) the historic affinities of the universalizing rationalism of Modernist architecture with the universalizing rationalism of Enlightenment moral and political philosophy. In like manner, I would suggest, on the one hand, that the spatial and formal hierarchies of traditional architecture and urbanism are physical manifestations of a communitarian culture and social ethic most accurately described and intelligently promoted by the Aristotelian intellectual tradition. On the other hand, the relative absence of spatial and formal hierarchies in contemporary architecture and urban and suburban design embodies an individualist/emotivist ethic best articulated by Nietzsche and his intellectual heirs.

ARISTOTELIAN COMMUNITARIANISM

A fundamental contention of the Aristotelian/communitarian viewpoint is that individual human well-being is impossible apart from the duties and privileges attendant to a variety of specific human practices, relationships, and roles. It is only in such roles and within such relationships that, over the course of a lifetime, individuals will discover (or fail to discover) the meaning of, and achieve (or fail to achieve), their well-being. Such relationships—families, churches, and schools; sailboat crews, dance companies, football teams, chess clubs, choirs, the starship Enterprise—are communities insofar as their individual members seek a common end or *telos* and will vary in size depending upon the specific goods and ends for which the communities exist.

For Aristotle himself, the foremost community was the city, which he understood as a community of communities, the chief end of which is the best life possible for its citizens. Even though some of the functions of the Greek *polis* can and have been allocated to other institutions in historical developments since Aristotle (for example, a degree of moral authority and autonomy to religious institutions or military defense to the nation-state), this understanding of the character and role of the city remains at the core of the Aristotelian intellectual tradition.

In that tradition, reason is the distinctively human faculty by which individuals are able to participate in the life of their several communities. The moral life is understood less in terms of being obedient to *rules* (there is almost no mention of rules in either Aristotle's *Ethics* or *Politics*) than in terms of developing various character habits of excellence; or *virtues*, by means of which one is able to pursue and achieve the goods and ends specific to any particular community. Education and success in virtually every type of human practice—success being the achievement of the particular goods unique and internal to the practice itself, to the best of one's natural abilities—require the virtues of courage, justice, and honesty, whether the practice be medicine, golf, architecture, flying, physics, or shoemaking. But in addition to these virtues, specific practices also require other specific virtues. The making and sustaining of families, for example, require the virtues of charity, patience, and steadfastness. And the making and sustaining of cities require of citizens (rulers and ruled) the virtues of temperance, friendship, magnanimity, and prudence: virtues that are specifically civic and which simultaneously support and restrain the individual pursuit of lesser goods in other practices.[1] This also implies a certain hierarchy of practices and virtues with respect to achieving the common good of the city.

In all communities, large and small, authority, while carrying connotations of power, is essentially a synonym for trustworthiness. The legitimacy of authority (or lack thereof) is a function of the ability *and* the trustworthiness of leaders seeking to achieve and advance the ends held in common by them and by those over whom they exercise leadership.

From this brief outline of the Aristotelian understanding of the relationship between virtues, practices, and the city, we may now begin to understand how and why traditional architecture and urban design are precisely the *formal expression* of this communitarian ethos. For the buildings that in traditional cities shelter the familial and economic activities—houses and housing, retail and office spaces—are typically backdrops to figural public spaces and to the buildings sheltering those governmental, religious, and educational institutions that promote and sustain the moral virtues and intellectual practices that simultaneously support and constrain the pursuit of private interest. And it is because the goods promoted by such institutions are goods *common* to denizens of the city, and necessary for the achievement of its common goals, that such institutions have been rightly regarded as *civic*. It is, therefore, neither a surprise nor an accident to find these institutions prominently sited and architecturally monumentalized in traditional cities and towns. Not merely symbolizing power, architecture in the traditional city aspired to symbolize legitimate authority in general, and specific (institutionally promoted) virtues in particular.

NIETZSCHEAN INDIVIDUALISM

In recent years, the banner of the Nietzschean/individualist view has been paraded most conspicuously by thinkers such as Michel Foucault, Jacques Derrida, Gilles Deleuze, Stanley Fish, and Richard Rorty, and in architecture by those such as Peter Eisenman and Bernard Tschumi. The Nietzschean/individualist view vigorously challenges Aristotelian assumptions about human well-being, the city, the nature of the moral life, the role of reason, and the characterization of authority. Individual well-being, rather than something achieved in the context of communal life, is realized by the self's increasing emancipation and inner detachment from various communal roles and commitments. The city is essentially an economic enterprise, affording individuals the material goods and the anonymity necessary for the pursuit of their own individual projects. The moral life is understood primarily in terms of rules: to be followed when convenient, invoked when necessary to protect oneself, and disregarded when they conflict with the pursuit of one's own particular projects.

Persons insufficiently detached from common morality so conceived (which Nietzsche sneeringly dismissed as slave morality) do so out of weakness, in fear and resentment of those superior individuals who make their own rules. Reason, in this view, is the ancient cultural mask that disguises (especially from its wearers) that primary instinct that Nietzsche called the will-to-power. For Nietzsche, power is the irreducible category in understanding human social relations, and the notion of legitimate authority is, therefore, inherently suspect. Where the Aristotelian might challenge authority in order to determine whether it is truly trustworthy, the Nietzschean cultivates "the art of mis-trust" from a conviction that *no* authority is trustworthy—that all authority conceals arbitrary power.[2]

I have suggested that much of contemporary social life, some of it quite conspicuously, can be understood as expressions of a Nietzschean point of view. This is not to imply, however, that most Moderns are self-conscious Nietzscheans or have even heard of Nietzsche. Many who would be sympathetic to some of the features I have characterized as Nietzschean would, nevertheless, recoil from the Nietzschean implication that mutual nonmanipulative social relations (friendship or love, for example) are impossible. So, today, although not that many people are Nietzscheans, Nietzschean categories seem to aptly encompass and explain much of contemporary social thought and behavior. But it is precisely to the extent that most people continue to believe in the possibility of mutual nonmanipulative social relations that, according to the Nietzscheans, they remain blind to their true motives.

I have characterized this point of view as individualist, but the term emotivist is equally descriptive. Emotivism reigns in many areas of contemporary life—from law and politics to literary criticism and religion—but especially in the areas of moral discourse and of art. For, where we find ourselves today is in a social setting in which specific disagreements about ethics and aesthetics—the good and the beautiful—are incapable of rational resolution. Hence, since modern societies lack a general agreement about such issues, opinion about them is increasingly and necessarily left to individual taste—to how individuals *feel* about such matters rather than what they *think* about them. This is not to say that individuals are unable to offer *reasons* for their opinions. It is rather to observe that an emotivist society is one in which there is no consensus about either a common good or the nature of reason itself. Consequently, disagreements (about, say, abortion, gun control, historic preservation, or whether urban buildings should be deferentially contextual or aggressively assertive) inevitably come down to the contestants *feeling strongly* about the matters in question but unable to reach rational consensus.

Just as the formal ordering of the traditional city can be seen as the physical expression of a moral sensibility focused primarily upon virtues and shared ends, the formal ordering of the modern city and suburb (at least in America) can be understood as the physical expression of an individualist/emotivist moral sensibility focused upon power and rules. No longer expressing a widely shared conception of a good and beautiful city (one built by small communities of craftsmen directed less by statute than by custom and habit), the developing formal condition of contemporary cities and suburbs is an individualist phenomenon governed by zoning ordinances and building codes intended as prophylactic measures employed (not always success-fully) to prevent individuals and corporations from infecting the city and landscape with rude and dangerous buildings.

ETHICS AND ARCHITECTURE

Commentary upon American inclinations toward individualism goes back at least as far as Alexis de Tocqueville in the 1830s. Individualist tendencies have been evident in American suburban development since the nineteenth century and are especially clear today in the post-World War II automobile suburb of functionally zoned and isolated office buildings, shopping centers, and single-family housing developments. But, even cities, no longer regarded by most Americans as desirable places to live, have increasingly come to be built by (and, perhaps more significantly, *for*) persons whose concerns are clearly more private than communal. Increasingly, cities are seen and valued almost exclusively as commercial and/or entertainment zones. The most prominent urban architecture today is built by developers, and architecture itself has come to be seen, and prized most highly by its owners, as a sales and marketing tool. In an individualist social order, it is perhaps plausible to praise contemporary retail centers—urban and suburban—as communal or civic spaces, insofar as they are places where large numbers of people gather. But this obscures an essential difference between contemporary and traditional architecture and urbanism. Only in an individualist social order can a hot-house architecture designed to shelter and promote the relentless stoking of consumer passions be counted as some sort of civic achievement.

As in contemporary architectural practice, individualist and emotivist themes increasingly dominate architectural theory. Some manifestations are more obvious than others. The heroic, rule-breaking, convention-defying architect as an ideal personality type is now so much a staple of architectural education and popular journalism as to have become a convention, albeit largely fictional. But, in addition to this perhaps too familiar motif, topics of postmodernist architectural discourse—pluralism, uncertainty, the post-Cartesian flight from the human subject, the problematic nature of personal identity, the retreat from accountability, and the denial of legitimate authority—are overtly and consistently emotivist. Architecture critic Jeffrey Kipnis has remarked that the cultural significance of Peter Eisenman's work is that it is increasingly: "directed toward...design which no longer seeks to embody any specific meaning, architectural or nonarchitectural, but rather to create a formal and material environment capable of engendering many meanings." In a similar vein, Chicago architect Joseph Valerio, writing about the new Chicago Public Library—an historicist building whose formal characteristics are far removed from Eisenman's Deconstructivist buildings—suggests that the work

> is purposely ambiguous because ambiguity is, after all, a symbol of modern times....
> [T]he library is successful as a mechanism for tapping people's emotions. This emotional
> connection signals a more modern way of understanding a building....Emotions may be
> the only way to understand buildings in modern times.

Interestingly, both Kipnis ("It is both possible and desirable to work in such a way as to respect undecidability") and Valerio ("Ambiguity should be both a condition and an objective") seem decidedly and unambiguously eager to justify an emotivist architecture as being somehow appropriate to an emotivist society. The possibility that such a society might *not* be most conducive to individual well-being appears scarcely to have occurred to them. Besides, why should I or anyone else be interested in an emotivist architecture? Because they wish it to be so?

It is just such emotivist formal and theoretical developments that have given rise to the neotraditionalist movement in architecture and urban design. Neotraditionalism in its origins undoubtedly was (and remains) the expression of an aesthetic preference for traditional architecture and urbanism over Modern architecture and suburbia. But, some neotraditionalists have come to see that traditional architecture and urbanism expresses and embodies a different, specifically communal, way of life—one not necessarily dismissive of modern amenities, but a way of life in their view clearly preferable to the individualism embodied in contemporary architecture, cities, and suburbs. From this recognition has come the argument for neotraditional architecture and urbanism that its advocates repeat with increasing frequency: that neotraditionalism is meritorious not only for its practical and aesthetic virtues but also because it promotes and expresses civic virtue.

I am sympathetic to neotraditionalists and the intuition that informs their civic virtue claims; but, the latter argument has clear problems that, if not addressed, severely impair the credibility of the movement it is intended to support. One such problem is that the meaning and content of civic virtue as propounded by most neotraditionalists is notoriously vague. Another is that while it may be true that traditional architecture and urbanism *express* (and even reinforce) communal ways of life, it is quite another to say that they *cause* them. Yet another is an intellectual objection: In an admittedly emotivist social context, and in the absence of a compelling nonemotivist social theory, neotraditionalism seems to be an individualist preference for which no more rational argument can be made than that its proponents happen to like it. And, finally, if this is true, there is the further objection—implicitly a communitarian objection, though it is occasionally made by individualists, sometimes without irony—that since neotradition-alist buildings and planning projects are likely to be developer-sponsored, and marketed to those individuals with similar irrational aesthetic preferences who are able to pay for them, neotraditionalism seems less likely to promote new social forms of communal life than to create traditional physical forms for contemporary individualist life. In short, neotraditionalists, if they wish to persuade intelligent people with an argument that is in part moral, need a better argument: in my view, an Aristotelian argument—one for which I can here provide no more than the barest outline.[3]

The Aristotelian intellectual tradition recommends itself for reasons both method-ological and substantive. Aristotelian methodology is inductive: Both rational and highly empirical, it begins with everyday experience and draws conclusions that are provisional, subject to change as more information becomes available. Considering the information we do have, however, I would suggest that the substance of a neotraditionalist commu-nitarian argument focus upon the following: 1) the formal and intellectual implications that follow from a careful consideration of the nature of various human practices; 2) the character virtues required for individuals to realize the goods internal to such practices; 3) the city as a collection of practices conducive to the best life for human beings; and 4) architecture as a symbol of legitimate authority in the city. The product of these deliberations would be a provisional, but substantive, communitarian theory of archi-tecture as a "civic art," set in opposition to individualist theories of architecture as an "autonomous art."[4]

The opposing arguments occur at two different levels. At one level is an argument about whether the specific goods internal to architecture include the traditional Vitruvian categories of durability, convenience, and beauty, or whether the former two categories are the exclusive concern of building, and the latter (most often expressed as a concern for form rather than beauty) the exclusive and more rarified domain of architecture. Communitarians and individualists will agree that formal concerns at the scale of indi-vidual buildings are absolutely essential to the definition of architecture. What is worth noting here is that traditionalist/communitarian architects tend to hold these three goods together in their definition of architecture. Conversely, Modernist/Rationalist and post-modernist/individualist architects have been more willing to fragment these categories, emphasizing (as have structural expressionists, user-needs advocates, and various types of formalists) one or two of the three goods to the diminishment of the others.

The second and more pertinent argument is whether individual buildings are to be designed with a concern for and deference to the larger formal order of the city, and whether this concern is *itself* another architecture's internal goods. For if it is, it necessarily implies communal constraints upon the autonomy of architects to pursue their formal concerns. Or, to put it another way, the formal concerns highly specific to the architectural community will themselves be informed by other concerns specific to a larger community of which the architect is (perhaps) a member. If, however, such concern and deference to the city are *not* one of architecture's internal goods, then the physical form of the city will exhibit not communal concerns but, rather, the particular formal concerns of individual architects and the economic and status concerns of their patrons—as, increasingly, it does today. It is, therefore, whether architecture is or is not necessarily conceived with reference to some larger urban formal order that determines whether it is to be understood as civic or autonomous. In today's world, one cannot promote a theory of architecture without simultaneously promoting a theory (at least implicit) of the city.

What is, or should be, the neotraditionalist architect's theory of and objective for the city? It is a common criticism that neotraditionalist architecture and urbanism is little more than nostalgia and that it seeks traditional communitarian forms for postmodernity's nonexistent communities. But, it is simply untrue that there are no communities today, though such as do exist tend to be small and voluntary. What *is* true is that the postmodern suburbanized world has dramatically accelerated the divorce of community from place. It seems to me, therefore, a legitimate objective of neotraditionalism to reconcile and/or remarry these two ideas.

Neotraditionalists seek, or should seek, to help create new neighborhoods and towns that encourage a participatory common life that is, for the most part, freely chosen. Here, individual lives of learning, piety, filial affection and obligation, respect for others, the pursuit of excellence, and the competitive creation of wealth can be pursued largely in practices sustained by families, the workplace, religious institutions, schools, libraries, and other political and voluntary associations; these pursuits can take place in a beautiful, multicentered, pedestrian-scaled physical environment of background buildings, monumental buildings, and public spaces conducive to the common good, in which automobiles are conveniences rather than necessities. In this scenario, neotraditionalist town plans would be meritorious in part for their aesthetic and sound environmental attributes. More valuable would be their ability to strengthen the communal practices and institutions that currently exist, but in a weakened and fragmented state, in contemporary cities and suburbs.

There is, of course, a danger in this scenario, which others have pointed out and that I alluded to earlier. Many such communities may already be terminally infected with individualism; developer-sponsored neighborhoods and new towns are, therefore, likely to create class-specific communities in which the primary communal end is the maximization of real estate values; and such developments will, therefore, constitute the refinement and extension of, rather than a partial antidote to, the individualist cultural tendencies of which American suburban life has long been an expression.

Committed neotraditionalists might try even more vigorously to identify and seek work not from *developers*, but from *founders*: leaders of intentional communities in which the primary criteria for membership are factors other than class. Many such communities might, perhaps likely will, be marginal to contemporary life, insofar as they consciously opt out of the individualist ethos. What are some examples of such communities, in which there might be unexplored affinities between the community's purposes and traditional architecture and urban form? These might include religious communities; academic communities; the military; communities organized around the creation and distribution of specific goods and services; and, perhaps, medical, health care, and hospice communities.

We know, however, that many such communities ostensibly committed to such ends are currently troubled to the point of dysfunction—and that what troubles them, in part, stems from individual members caring too much about securing for themselves wealth, status, comfort, or fame and too little about achieving the specific internal goods for which particular communities exist. Thus is it the case that too often the purpose of government is to maintain the power of the governors, of medicine, the perquisites of doctors, and of architecture, the aggrandizement of architects.

Such deficiencies are unavoidably about character, which is to say that they are unavoidably about ethics; but, they are ills about which individualist theorists can say nothing and for which they can offer no remedy without violating the logic of their own intellectual premises. Indeed by, individualist premises, they cannot be regarded as ills. Individualists, therefore, have no standing to complain about declining standards of excellence in these or other kinds of human practices. As C.S. Lewis noted long ago, one cannot mock honor and then be surprised to find oneself in the midst of traitors; nor castrate, and expect the geldings to be fruitful.

For communitarians, the only cure for such maladies is a greater appreciation of and attendance to the various moral virtues central to success in various human practices. These include the artistic practices of architecture and urban design, as well as the political practice of sustaining and advancing the goods of city life. How and in what way these three practices and their virtues are related, and the formal implications and consequences of such relations, are the perennial subject matter of ethics and architecture.

1   Note that virtue is a secondary concept. For example, it is not true that a virtuous person is always cooperative, gentle, and self-effacing. Neither is it true that he or she is always competitive and aggressive. Rather, any specific virtue requires for its understanding and application some prior social context in terms of which it is to be explained and valued. The notion of a virtue only makes sense in a teleological framework, as a habit the exercise of which is conducive to the achievement of some purpose or end pursued (almost always) in the company of others. The ends pursued may require cooperation, competitiveness, or both.

2   It is important to understand the implications of this. If there are no social relations in which power may be willingly conferred upon individuals authorized to exercise it—and held accountable for exercising it—in the pursuit of *common ends*, nor any social circumstances in which reason may be conceived as a persuasive faculty employable for the pursuit and attainment of common rather than merely private ends, then there are no mutual, nonmanipulative social relationships. That is to say that in the Nietzschean view, other persons cannot *logically* be regarded as ends in themselves but only as means to be used toward the fulfillment of one's own ends. Thus conceived, various social relations are *necessarily* only so many exercises in the engineering of consent. This does not mean that Nietzscheans are necessarily incapable of, say, friendship or love; it only means that their theory is incapable of explaining their behavior.

3   To imply, as I am, that such an argument—or any argument—might be rationally compelling is to necessarily imply that there are means of escape from emotivist social order. But, it is precisely this claim that Nietzsche and his intellectual heirs would deny. In just this sense then, the claims of Nietzscheans and the claims of Aristotelians are *incommensurate*; disputes between them cannot be resolved rationally by an appeal to their own major premises. It may, however, be possible to make a rational judgement of the me its of incommensurable theories by an evaluation of their *internal* logic—that is, by examining whether such theories are consistent with their own premises. The power of the Nietzschean critique of contemporary life derives from the fact that much of it rings true. But, it seems only one of its several inherent dilemmas that it denies validity to the concept

of truth, and, therefore, has no internally consistent way to press its claims. For an Aristotelian critique to triumph rationally over Nietzsche, it must address and explain in a more convincing and internally consistent way the very conditions that the Nietzschean critique purports to describe. This is the splendidly bodacious task that MacIntyre has described and undertaken, first in *After Virtue* (1981) and subsequently in his Gifford Lectures of 1988, later published as *Three Rival Versions of Moral Enquiry*; it entails returning the Aristotelian moral tradition's emphasis upon character virtues to the center of contemporary moral discourse and public debate.

4   To suggest that communitarian architects will not conceive of architecture as an "autonomous art" is not to deny to architecture a degree of autonomy. Architecture is a kind of practice, and to acknowledge it as such is precisely to acknowledge that it possesses a certain independence and its practitioners a certain expertise. Like most practices, architecture has a history, standards of excellence and authority, and specific internal goods as its desired end (even though such goods have themselves evolved over time in the course of being pursued). We can reasonably expect architecture to be to a certain degree self-referential. Indeed, it is when architects fail to refer and attend to architecture's internal standards of excellence, when in the studio and the academy trustworthy authority is replaced by authoritarianism, and when architecture's unique and particular internal goods become obscured, that we can recognize and measure its decline as a practice. At issue here is whether a concern for a building's proper place in an urban hierarchy not necessarily of the individual architect's (or the client's) own making is a good internal to architecture, comparable to other internal architectural goods, such as durability and beauty. To answer this in the affirmative is to argue for architecture as a "civic art."

INTRODUCTION   The Architecture of Deceit
                     Diane Ghirardo

In this essay, educator and theorist Diane
Ghirardo raises a question that seemed to have
been sidelined in the economic downturn of the
1970s and in the rush to build in the prosperous
1980s: is architecture an art or a service? The
development of Ghirardo's critique of various
strains of postmodern architecture makes clear
that she feels it must be a service profession,
engaged in the socio-political realm. Services are
to be rendered accompanied by a critical attitude
about architecture's role in society. She asks why
architecture doesn't confront real issues in the discipline and in the world, why architecture tries to
remain "pure," and what is being concealed in
this pursuit. In neglecting to respond to or even
acknowledge "the relationship between political
intentions, social realities, and building," architects avoid responsibility for issues like racism,
white flight, and the exploitative manipulation of
land development to benefit a power elite. The
net result of what Ghirardo sees as an abdication
of responsibility is the narrowing of the sphere of
architecture to superficial fashion. (She alludes to
"larger questions about our current cultural situation" without explanation.)

    Architects are not alone in their fetishistic
involvement with formal concerns: critics and historians promote and reward architects for formalist finesse. The critical establishment also defuses
architecture's potential for subversion and amelioration by presenting it as consumer commodity in
the latest style.

    Ghirardo recognizes that architectural pro-
duction is economically dependent on capital
and thus tends to be conservative. Her comparison of American architects' retreat into fantasy
during the recession in the 1970s with the post-
World War I situation in Europe, however, is
questionable. The housing crisis after the destructive war precipitated a European building boom,
necessitating the involvement of architects in
designing large master plans. Thus, the schemes
of Walter Gropius and Bruno Taut were not only
altruistic utopian visions, but also more or less

pragmatic professional responses to a specific crisis. In addition to the fact that American modern architecture has rarely associated itself with the social agenda of its European counterpart,[1] there was no comparable crisis here: large-scale building was neither required nor affordable in the 1970s.

The essay does not offer a prescription for ethical behavior, and leaves open for further investigation the following intriguing questions. Can one build while critical of the power structures that support building activity? Is there a way to work from within the system to initiate change, for example, by persuasion? This is, in fact, the route chosen by architect William McDonough, (this chapter) who takes his environmental agenda directly to the source of the pollution problem: industry. Through collaboration and persuasion, he institutes change in industrial and architectural practice.

---

1   Colin Rowe, introduction to *Five Architects: Eisenman, Graves, Gwathmey, Hejduk, Meier* (New York: Wittenborn, 1972).

DIANE GHIRARDO

THE ARCHITECTURE OF DECEIT

The town itself is peculiarly built, so that someone can live in it for years and travel into it and out of it daily without ever coming into contact with a working-class quarter or even with workers—so long, that is to say, as one confines himself to his business affairs or to strolling about for pleasure. This comes about mainly in the circumstances that through an unconscious, tacit agreement as much as through conscious, explicit inten- tion the working-class districts are most sharply separated from the parts of the city reserved for the middle class....Manchester's monied aristocracy can now travel from their houses to their places of business in the center of the town by the shortest routes, which run right through all the working-class districts, without even noticing how close they are to the most squalid misery which lies immediately about them on both sides of the road. This is because the main streets which run from the Exchange in all directions out of the city are occupied almost uninterruptedly on both sides by shops, which are kept by members of the middle and lower-middle classes. In their own interests these shop-keepers should keep up their shops in an outward appearance of cleanliness and respectability; and in fact they do so....Those shops which are situated in the commer- cial quarter or in the vicinity of the middle-class residential districts are more elegant than those which serve to cover up the worker's grimy cottages. Nevertheless, even these latter adequately serve the purpose of hiding from the eyes of wealthy gentlemen and ladies with strong stomachs and weak nerves the misery and squalor that form the com- pleting counterpart, the indivisible complement, of their riches and luxury. I know per- fectly well that this deceitful manner of building is more or less common to all big cities....I have never elsewhere seen a concealment of such fine sensibility of every thing that might offend the eyes and nerves of the middle classes. And yet it is precisely Manchester that has been built less according to a plan and less within the limitations of official regulations—and indeed more through accident—than any other town.[1]

From *Perspecta: The Yale Architectural Journal* 21 (1984): 110–115. Courtesy of the author and publisher.

In *The Condition of the Working Class in England in 1844*, Friedrich Engels exposed the effects of capitalism on the laboring classes. In his analysis of Manchester he also offered one of the first sustained critiques of the built environment. Engels discerned a relationship among political intentions, social realities, and building. Although he was not the last to perceive nature of this relationship, his approach to building has had little influence on the architecture, construction, and real estate industries in the twentieth century.

Both as a profession and as an academic discipline, architecture prefers not to be directly associated with the construction and real estate industries. All three deal with building and enjoy an enormously beneficial symbiotic relationship, and all three share an atrophied social conscience. Architecture offers itself as different from the other two by virtue of being an "art" rather than a trade or a business and to this end contemporary practice—through highly refined mechanisms of dissimulation—conspires to preserve that precarious pretense.

ARCHITECTURE AS ART

William Curtis articulates a particularly cogent version of what amounts to a traditional art-historical position in his *Modern Architecture Since 1900*. Curtis insists on "a certain focused interest on questions of form and meaning." He selects what he believes to be the masterpieces of modern architecture—"I make no apologies for concentrating on buildings of high visual and intellectual quality"—and sets out to write—"a balanced, readable, overall view of modern architecture from its beginnings until the recent past." To Curtis, balance implies exorcising political, social, and ideological considerations of the sort that he finds in the versions of history offered by Kenneth Frampton or Manfredo Tafuri and Francesco Dal Co, who "emphasized ideology at the expense of other matters."[2]

This critical position—which is by far the dominant one in America—at most admits only passing reference to any larger cultural, political, and social considerations. Instead it involves extended visual analysis, concentrating primarily on a few "important" buildings—the Robie House, the Villa Savoye, the Kimball Art Museum. Such singular masterpieces transcend not only political, social, and ideological contingencies, but their own time as well. In Curtis's words, "To slot them into the Modern Movement is to miss much of their value."[3] Set like jewels into the diadem of architecture, they become aesthetic objects par excellence and above reproach.

However appealing it may seem, a critical position predicated on formal qualities remains problematical. The standards of judgement are reduced to categories—"formal resolution," "integration," and "authenticity"—concepts which are more opaque than most critics will concede. Except on the most general level, none of these categories denote an objectively verifiable criterion, despite an unspoken assumption to that effect. Even if, in the best of both cases, there is a general agreement to canonize a few works, considerable disagreement usually attends the decision about the particular works to be so embalmed. Indeed, the criteria for selecting one work over another are often arbitrary precisely because judgement based on formal analyses boil down to nothing more than matters of taste. One critic may find a certain degree of mathematical complexity necessary to make a building great; another may focus on the effects of massing techniques; and yet a third may demand an elegant series of references to or comments on the past.

Though there is no denying the interest or significance of any of these aspects, it remains clear that assessing them depends as much upon personal taste as do preferences for a particular style.[4]

Edoardo Persico remarked on this situation nearly half a century ago, when he surveyed the bitter factional rivalries in Fascist Italy between classicizing traditionalists and Modern Movement rationalists. Persico concluded that, although they appeared to reflect dramatically different positions, the polemics in fact masked an underlying consensus. Since all sides took their cues from Fascism, the stylistic debates that flourished in the architectural press concerned matters of taste rather than substance.[5] It was no more than a preference for white walls and ribbon windows competing with a predilection for traditional columns and arches. Persico's critique addressed an unspoken corollary—that both factions fell over themselves to give architectural expression to the ideals of Italian Fascism: to provide luxury apartments for the bourgeoisie, or to design urban settlements that permitted close surveillance of the lowest classes.

Lobotomized history surfaces in contemporary criticism in a variety of guises. Curtis, for example, faults the "whites" (formalists) and the "greys" (informalists) of the 1970s for having nothing to say about the current state of American society; and he does this in a 400-page text devoted to formalist analysis.[6] Other historians laboriously criticize the naive and utopian visions of early European modernists who associated their architecture with radical opposition to existing political and social systems; at the same time they lament the fate of the Modern Movement under the totalitarian pressures of Stalinist Russia and Nazi Germany.

To be sure, the high aspirations of the European early modernists were often unrealistic, as were their exaggerated claims for the role of the architect in shaping the new societies they envisioned. Further, many critics have correctly diagnosed an authoritarian strain in the social programs of Le Corbusier and others. Yet the extraordinary power of Le Corbusier's architecture—sprang in part from their passionate searches for an architecture that would confront contemporary social realities.

ARCHITECTURE AS FASHION

A telling contrast can be drawn between the responses of contemporary architects to the economic decline of the 1970s and the attitude adopted by the radical architects who confronted the economically uncertain aftermath of the First World War. In the immediate postwar period architects turned to dreaming up new worlds to replace the old one; Bruno Taut and Walter Gropius come to mind as architects who attempted to reformulate architecture's role in society, and they are only two of a large and distinguished group active in Weimar Germany.

Conversely, when building opportunities dwindled in the United States in the 1970s, architects turned to drawings—not even designs of a different and better world, but instead a set of increasingly abstract, pretty (and marketable) renderings of their own or of antique works and recycled postclassical picturesque sites. Like much building of the decades just preceding, these aesthetic indulgences simply masquerade as architecture. They reveal architects in full retreat from any involvement with the actual world of buildings.

ARCHITECTURE AS FEELING

Another approach attempts to evade the trap of taste and fashion by explicitly setting itself apart from the current postmodernist discourse. Christopher Alexander, an ardent advocate of this view, maintains that "the core of architecture depends on feeling." Alexander talks about the "primitive feeling" evoked by a steeply pitched roof; he believes that the pitched roof may be the "most natural and simple" thing to build, and he contrasts it with the arid forms of contemporary architecture, which are prized precisely because they lack feeling. The task of the architect, Alexander argues, is to produce a harmonious work that feels "absolutely comfortable—physically, emotionally, practically," and indeed, "architects are entrusted with the creation of that harmony in the world."[7]

Like the formalists, this group arrogates to itself the power to decide what you and I will find "authentic," "integrated," "natural," and "comfortable." Underlying this archaeology of primitive forms is a desperate search, shared with the formalists, for a universal architecture and a universal standard of value; there is a concomitant aggressive hostility toward critical positions that engage in dialogue with the unresolved, uncomfortable, politically explosive, and unharmonious.

The contemporary discourse on architecture thus fashions the discipline's own neutron bomb, which promises to leave nothing but the vacant buildings intact—an empty bric-a-brac landscape in both style and substance, a literally empty reminiscence of a bygone culture.

THE CRITIC'S COMPLICITY

The responsibility for having cultivated this hardy bloom belongs at least as much to critics and historians as it does to architects. Because they assign priority to the unique formal features of individual monuments, historians and critics diminish interest in anything else. Criticism today borrows the already inadequate tools of art history as traditionally practiced, substitutes description for analysis, and turns architecture into a harmless but ultimately meaningless and consumable artifact. As society's arbiters of taste, critics also help to distribute society's rewards—prestige and money—to those architects who are willing to produce fresh new fashions destined for elite consumption.

The architectural profession seems deeply divided between those who conceive it as an art and those who perceive it as a service. Few would argue that either of these components can safely be jettisoned, but exactly what their proper relationship ought to be is not clear—nor is it likely to become so. Moreover, anything beyond purely formal concerns in the work of architecture is seen as sullying architecture's purity and rendering it no more than a billboard for political beliefs or the tool of class conflict and competing ideologies.[8] While banal or badly built work presents less of a problem ([Albert] Speer's Berlin, for example), a widely acclaimed, complex, and interesting work such as Giuseppe Terragni's Casa del Fascio in Como is deeply troubling, for its explicit and undeniably political matrix cannot successfully be evaded.

Sometimes architecture *is* an explicit political billboard; at other times it sets itself in opposition to dominant class interests; and still elsewhere it constitutes an unconscious—but no less real—expression of political and social realities and aspirations. Certainly aesthetic and formal considerations come into play in any understanding of a building; but the inescapable truth is that these categories are culturally conditioned, often arbitrary, and only two among a number of components that determine the value of architecture.

ARCHITECTURE AND EVASIVE MANEUVERABILITY

What accounts for the architectural community's pervasive refusal to confront real issues in the realm of architecture and the world that circumscribes it? When so much energy is devoted to maintaining architecture's privilege and its purity, one has to wonder what is being concealed.

Academic politics are so bitter because the stakes are so small; in a case where stakes are immeasurably larger—as in the politics of a building—the apparent strategy is to place something innocuous at center stage in order to divert attention from more important concerns. Formal elements—style, harmony of parts, call them what you will—are sufficiently trivial to be awarded top billing in architectural discourse. It is also far easier and far more tidy to persevere in formalist critiques, thereby avoiding the risk of antagonizing moneyed interest. In turn, architects choose the safer course by designing buildings that evade issues of substance.

The position that only formal elements matter in architecture bespeaks a monumental refusal to confront serious problems; it avoids a critique of the existing power structure, of the ways power is used, and of the identity of those whose interests power serves. To do otherwise might entail opening a Pandora's box of far more complicated issues: racism and white flight, exploitation and the manipulation of land values, prices, resources, building permits, zoning, and taxes on behalf of a small power elite—as well as larger questions about our current cultural situation. At the same time, to suggest that the world contains an ineluctable harmony which an architect need only discover in the realm of forms and feelings is dangerously naive.[9] An architecture predicated solely upon such principles finds its objective correlative in a Walt Disney movie: soothing in the promise of happy endings, simplified with clear-cut villains and heroes, and seductive in the presentation of a world that in so many ways simply does not correspond to the one in which we live.

In none of its manifestations does the profession dare question the politics of building: who builds what, where, for whom, and at what price. Although arguably one of the most important issues for all architects to consider—and for the discipline to emphasize—it is addressed by few. Certainly as professionals, architects do little to gain a voice in these important decisions—they do not, for example, organize political action committees; by default they are left with the trivial issues of fashion and taste. The anemic architecture that issues from this acquiescence overwhelms our cities. Nowhere is this more grotesquely apparent than in the tenements of the South Bronx in New York. Officials chose to deal with socially troubled, abandoned, and physically scarred public housing projects by spending thousands of dollars to replace broken and boarded up windows with decorative panels depicting houseplants and window shades, thereby avoiding a serious confrontation with the community's problems. Public officials in effect aped the activities of prominent architects who currently undertake the same kind of window dressing in their own work.

Only when architects, critics, and historians accept the responsibility for building— in all of its ramifications—will we approach an architecture of substance.

1   Friedrich Engels, *The Condition of the Working Class in England in 1844* (Stuttgart: 1992; reprint, Moscow: 1973), 84–86.

2   William J.R. Curtis, *Modern Architecture Since 1900* (New Jersey: 1982), 6–11, 389–392.

3   Ibid., 388.

4   Postmodernists defend the use of formal elements from ancient or Renaissance classicism, for example, with the argument that meaning inheres only in historical forms—that is, pr modern forms. With this claim they impale themselves on the horns of a dilemma since it leads them to incorporate historical forms into their works in such a way as to drain the forms of their highly precise historical associations. (In the designs of Michael Graves, for example, the keystone is hollowed out to become a window or raised high to become a scupper.) However contradictory the two positions, postmodernists do indeed want it both ways, and the point remains that they stand on the shifting grounds of arbitrary fashion.

5   Eduardo Persico "Punto e da capo per l'architettura," *Domus* VII (1934).

6   Curtis, *Modern Architecture*, op. cit., 355.

7   Christopher Alexander in debate with Peter Eisenman in *HGSD News* (March/April 1983): 12–17. Alexander, Sara Ishikawa, and Murray Silverstein, *A Pattern Language: Towns, Building, Construction* (New York: 1977); Alexander, *The Timeless Way of Building* (New York: 1979).

8   If we look at the recent Diana Agrest and Mario Gandelsonas building in Buenos Aires, for example, we recognize the references to historical forms that avoid banal imitation, and we can appreciate it as a highly intelligent, accomplished structure, with a high degree of sensitivity to the site, to the urban context, to contemporary building practice, and specifically, to building traditions in Buenos Aires. But what if we ask for whom it was built or inquire into its urban context in the political turbulence of Buenos Aires? Altogether too many critics and architects today would dismiss this line of questioning as irrelevant.

9   Louis Sullivan, "The Young Man in Architecture," address to the Architecture League of Chicago (June 1900); *Kindergarten Chats and Other Writings* (New York: 1947), 223.

The Ethical Function of Architecture
Karsten Harries

Like Philip Bess and William McDonough, Karsten Harries, a philosopher at Yale University, blames modern architecture for the degradation of contemporary life. Also like Bess, he is concerned in his writings on architecture about the loss of *place* and community. He takes a phenomenological position, arguing that the "objectivity" characteristic of modernity has contributed two unfortunate ideas: first, that the physical environment is material for humans to manipulate indiscriminately, and second, that architecture is part of a technological culture that demands (Corbusian) "machines for living," instead of (Heideggerian) "dwellings."

Harries argues that modern science has led to the transformation of man from embodied self to pure thinking subject. Objectivity has also led to a loss of hierarchical space, and to "displacement," which produces freedom, but also homelessness and disorientation. Electronic media (television, radio) have rendered proximity, intimacy, and place meaningless. Anthony Vidler's "spatial uncanny" addresses similar issues from a radically different perspective. (ch. 14)

Harries follows Martin Heidegger's phenomenological notion that the human *ethos*, or moral purpose, is to *dwell*. This is close to impossible, he argues, under contemporary conditions of "the terror of [endless, homogenized, modern] space" which renders life insignificant. In this contribution to the postmodern critique, he notes that modern architecture has neither reconciled technology with aesthetic considerations, nor successfully established a formalist position of autonomy. The purpose of his essay is to reintroduce the idea that architecture's ethical function is to articulate and establish the ethos, to permit humankind to dwell. Harries argues for involving the body and human scale in architecture, for "heterogeneity and boundaries," and for distinctiveness of place. Architecture is to express the "character" of place, neighborhood, and region, and to establish "unity." Provocative and brief, Harries's proposal prompts the following concerns: Is his a nostalgic

position that dictates or depends on a style?
Is unity possible or desirable, or repressive?
Will there be any "need" or desire to experience
these distinctive places, should they be built,
considering the overwhelming hegemony of the
electronic paradigm that gives one the ability to
be, virtually, everywhere at once? Questions of
place are also discussed by Kenneth Frampton,
Christian Norberg-Schulz, and Vittorio Gregotti in
chapters seven, nine, and eleven; Peter Eisenman
touches upon the impact of electronic communication on architecture in chapter thirteen.

KARSTEN HARRIES

THE ETHICAL FUNCTION OF
ARCHITECTURE

It has been stated over and over again. Through the discovery yesterday of the railway,
the motor car and the aeroplane, the physical influence of each man, formerly restricted
to a few miles, now extends to hundreds of leagues or more. Better still: thanks to the
prodigious biological event represented by the discovery of electro-magnetic waves, each
individual finds himself henceforth (actively and passively) simultaneously present, over
land and sea, in every corner of the earth.
Teilhard de Chardin, *The Phenomenon of Man*

Man has always tried to overcome distance, to bring things closer, to grasp them, and to
make them his own. But only modern man has carried this effort so far that with some
justice he can liken himself to God, to whom all things are equally close. The full consequences of this attack on distance are still uncertain: while it promises man almost
divine power, it also threatens him with a never before known homelessness. There are
indeed those who expect a new intimacy from the revolution of transportation and communication: man will feel at home on the earth and with others as he never could before.
But Marshall McLuhan's metaphor of the "global village" is misleading. Consider, for
example, today's "mobile homes" and the often pathetically ineffective attempts to transform them into houses. Or television: there is indeed a sense in which it negates distance:
the faraway and the nearby are equally brought into our living room, but only as pictures
from which the observer is excluded. The attack on distance and distancing devices has
to turn against intimacy, for intimacy requires distance; eliminate one and you eliminate
the other. Instead of genuine proximity we are offered increasingly only its perverted

From *Journal of Architectural Education* 29, no. 1 (September 1975): 14–15. Courtesy of the author
and publisher.

analogue: the equidistance and thus the homogeneity and indifference of place. When all places count the same we cannot place ourselves and become displaced persons. The ease with which we relocate ourselves and replace our buildings is witness to this displacement.

It would be a mistake to see in this displacement only the result of technological progress. This progress realizes a displacement which is implicit in the commitment to the objectivity on which science and technology rest. First of all man finds himself caught up in the world; the nature of his engagement establishes proximity and distance. But as soon as he begins to reflect on what happens to be his point of view and how it structures and limits what he sees, he has taken a first step towards objectivity which must transform his sense of space. Already in the fifteenth century Cusanus asks whether, when we take the earth to be the center of the cosmos, we are not deceived by perspectival appearance; what we take to be central and fixed depends on where we happen to be. With this reflection the closed world of the Middle Ages which allowed man to dwell near the center has been shattered. Objectivity demands homogeneity of place. Both have their foundation in a self-displacement which transforms man from an embodied self into a pure thinking subject.

The reward of this displacement is a new freedom, its price a new homelessness. The pure subject cannot locate itself. Depending on his specialty a scientist may be as much at home in New Guinea as he is in Connecticut. But "home" is not the right word. The equidistance of place implies that there is no particular place which can be called "home." Infinitely mobile, the pure subject can acquire roots only by incarnating itself. To reason such incarnation and the limits it establishes will always seem arbitrary. Why should I be bound by the accident of location? The attack on distance is born of the resentment expressed by this question. If the destruction of boundaries is welcomed by freedom, it also renders man's place arbitrary. [Blaise] Pascal, [Arthur] Schopenhauer, [Friedrich] Nietzsche, [Ivan] Turgenev, and [Rainer Maria] Rilke give voice to the dread of post-Copernican man lost in the silence of infinite space.

Eliade speaks of the terror of history; equally well we can speak of the terror of space, for like the homogeneity of endless time that of endless space renders life contingent and insignificant. We demand heterogeneity and boundaries, periods and regions, sacred events and central places which can gather a manifold into a meaningful whole. Time and space must be shaped in such a way that man is assigned a dwelling place, an *ethos*. Pure reflection is unable to discover or establish such a place for reflective man is as such displaced. The effort to place man has to address itself to the entire person, especially to the body. Consider the way in which a Greek temple or a medieval cathedral gathers the surrounding landscape into a region which lets men dwell together on the earth instead of leaving them to drift across it as strangers. From the very beginning architecture has had an *ethical function*, helping to articulate and even to establish man's *ethos* — our use of the word "edify" still hints at the relationship between building and ethics. The architecture of the baroque was perhaps the last to preserve this ethical function; the past two centuries have lost sight of it. Only recently has the seriousness of this loss been recognized by historians of architecture like [Hans] Sedlmayr and philosophers like [Martin] Heidegger.

Like language, architecture is on one hand a product of human activity while on the other it helps to create the environment which gives shape to man's activities. To build is to help decide how man is to dwell on the earth or indeed whether he is to dwell on it at all, rather than drift aimlessly across it. And yet, since the Enlightenment we have found it difficult to take seriously the ethical function of architecture. This difficulty is a consequence of the emphasis which has been placed on reason and objectivity. Is it not objective reasoning rather than architecture which should assign man his place? And is it not from reason that the architect must receive his tasks? As reason triumphs in science and technology, art withdraws from the totality of life and asserts its own autonomy as art for art's sake or becomes mere entertainment and decoration. Of all the arts architecture alone is unable to participate in this withdrawal. The world forces it into its service. Caught between engineering and art, modern architecture has been unable to achieve a convincing and lasting reconciliation of pragmatic-technological and aesthetic considerations. Indeed there can be no such reconciliation as long as art insists on its own autonomy and the essential connection between displacement and technological thinking is not recognized.

[Christian] Norberg-Schulz has suggested that the confused state of architecture today "necessarily implies that the training of architects is unsatisfactory. The schools have shown themselves incapable of bringing forth architects able to solve the actual tasks." (*Intentions in Architecture*) Unfortunately the problem is much more basic. The chaotic state of our architectural environment which yet goes along with a high degree of interchangeability and uniformity is part of our technological culture, which insists not so much on dwellings as on machines for working and living. Are the tasks posed by this culture "the actual tasks?" To decide what is involved in building one has to understand first what it is to dwell. But there is no genuine dwelling without both intimacy and distance. We have to discover the importance of neighborhoods and regions and of an architecture which will articulate their character and establish their unity. The attempt to impose on nature the order of a disembodied reason has to lead to an inhuman architecture. The spherical house projected by [Claude-Nicolas] Ledoux offers an early and frightening example. Only the measure provided by the human body lets us feel at home on the earth; only when we cease to consider the physical environment as material to be manipulated and controlled, but open ourselves to the natural language of place and time will we receive hints which may lead to a re-establishment of the lost ethos, of environments which will make a genuine dwelling possible. But no one is better equipped than the architect to contribute to such a re-establishment, even if the condition of our culture leaves little room for optimism.

INTRODUCTION

Design, Ecology, Ethics, and the Making of Things
William McDonough

In this polemic (originally presented in 1993 as a sermon at the Cathedral of St. John the Divine, New York City), architect William McDonough offers new ethical standards for the profession of architecture. Based on respect for human life, the natural world, and its complex processes, his agenda is another critique of modern architecture and the conditions of modernity. His research has revealed that the entire system of contemporary building construction is toxic. Given this knowledge, he finds it unethical for architects to continue practicing business as usual. Taking this message to the public, he is emerging as the major contemporary spokesman for a "sustainable" approach to design.

McDonough's ecological point of view requires that society resist the short-sighted thinking of some capitalists and elected officials to consider the long-term environmental implications of its actions. The ethical implications include acknowledging the rights of other species and of future generations in a "Declaration of Interdependence." While these issues have been raised in many fields since the first Earth Day in 1970, the author claims that architects have a special role to play, using "design as the first signal of human intention." It is now clear that nature is not immutable. The new role for architects is one of leadership in developing new definitions and measures of prosperity, productivity, and quality of life (in terms other than accumulation of material goods). In brief, his proposed criteria for evaluating a design solution, material, or product are: is it safe and just, and does it operate from current solar income?

McDonough advocates dwelling in a Heideggerian sense, when he says that we must "come to peace with our place in the natural world." (ch. 9) This also means dealing equitably (not imperialistically) with our immediate neighbors and with Third World countries. McDonough holds industry globally accountable for pollution, resulting in "freedom from remote tyranny." His firm has successfully worked with industry to redesign products and processes to make them nontoxic, while saving money for the manufacturer. This economic incentive offers the best hope of voluntary compliance in a market economy.

As laudable as these objectives are, one wonders whether their implementation can be achieved without the coercive power of a strong centralized government. Can we change the "individualist" values which lead us to assume the right to maximize profits from the use of private property, to societal values which recognize the common good? This last question overlaps with the issue of "civic virtue," as discussed by Philip Bess in this chapter.

WILLIAM McDONOUGH

DESIGN, ECOLOGY, ETHICS, AND THE MAKING OF THINGS

The following "sermon" was delivered by Dean McDonough in the Cathedral of St. John the Divine at the celebration of that institution's 100th anniversary. The speech was adapted to written form by Mr. McDonough and his friend and collaborator, Paul Hawken.

It is humbling to be an architect in a cathedral because it is a magnificent representation of humankind's highest aspirations. Its dimension is illustrated by the small Christ figure in the western rose window, which is, in fact, human scale. A cathedral is a representation of both our longings and intentions. This morning, here at this important crossing in this great building, I am going to speak about the concept of design itself as the first signal of human intention and will focus on ecology, ethics, and the making of things. I would like to reconsider both our design and our intentions.

When Vincent Scully gave a eulogy for the great architect Louis Kahn, he described a day when both were crossing Red Square, whereupon Scully excitedly turned to Kahn and said, "Isn't it wonderful the way the domes of St. Basil's Cathedral reach up into the sky?" Kahn looked up and down thoughtfully for a moment and said, "Isn't it beautiful the way they come down to the ground?"

If we understand that design leads to the manifestation of human intention, and if what we make with our hands is to be sacred and honor the earth that gives us life, then the things we make must not only rise from the ground but return to it, soil to soil, water to water, so everything that is received from the earth can be freely given back without causing harm to any living system. This is ecology. This is good design. It is of this we must now speak.

If we use the study of architecture to inform this discourse, and we go back in history, we will see that architects are always working with two elements, mass and

From *Colonnade* 10, no. 3 (Fall 1994): 9–14. Courtesy of the author and publisher.

membrane. We have the walls of Jericho, mass, and we have tents, membranes. Ancient peoples practiced the art and wisdom of building with mass, such as an adobe-walled hut, to anticipate the scope and direction of sunshine. They knew how thick a wall needed to be to transfer the heat of the day into the winter night, and how thick it had to be to transfer the coolness into the interior in the summer. They worked well with what we call "capacity" in the walls in terms of storage and thermal lags. They worked with resistance, straw, in the roof to protect from heat loss in the winter and to shield the heat gain in summer from the high sun. These were very sensible buildings within the climate in which they are located.

With respect to membrane, we only have to look at the Bedouin tent to find a design that accomplishes five things at once. In the desert, temperatures often exceed 120 degrees. There is no shade, no air movement. The black Bedouin tent, when pitched, creates a deep shade that brings one's sensible temperature down to 95 degrees. The tent has a very coarse weave, which creates a beautifully illuminated interior, having a million light fixtures. Because of the coarse weave and the black surface, the air inside rises and is drawn through the membrane. So now you have a breeze coming in from outside, and that drops the sensible temperature even lower, down to 90 degrees. You may wonder what happens when it rains, with those holes in the tent. The fibers swell up and the tent gets tight as a drum when wet. And of course, you can roll it up and take it with you. The modern tent pales by comparison to this astonishingly elegant construct.

Throughout history, you find constant experimentation between mass and membrane. This cathedral is a Gothic experiment integrating great light into massive membrane. The challenge has always been, on a certain level, how to combine light with mass and air. This experiment displayed itself powerfully in modern architecture, which arrived with the advent of inexpensive glass. It was unfortunate that at the same time the large sheet of glass showed up, the era of cheap energy was ushered in, too. And because of that, architects no longer rely upon the sun for heat or illumination. I have spoken to thousands of architects, and when I ask the question, "How many of you know how to find true South?" I rarely get a raised hand.

Our culture has adopted a design stratagem that essentially says that if brute force or massive amounts of energy don't work, you're not using enough of it. We made glass buildings that are more about buildings than they are about people. We've used the glass ironically. The hope that glass would connect us to the outdoors was completely stultified by making the buildings sealed. We have created stress in people because we are meant to be connected with the outdoors, but instead we are trapped. Indoor air quality issues are now becoming very serious. People are sensing how horrifying it can be to be trapped indoors, especially with the thousands upon thousands of chemicals that are being used to make things today.

Le Corbusier said in the early part of this century that a house is a machine for living in. He glorified the steamship, the airplane, the grain elevator. Think about it: a house is a machine for living in. An office is a machine for working in. A cathedral is a machine for praying in. This has become a terrifying prospect, because what has happened is that designers are now designing for the machine and not for people. People talk about solar heating a building, even about solar heating a cathedral. But it isn't the cathedral that is asking to be heated, it is the people. To solar-heat a cathedral, one should heat people's feet, not the air 120 feet above them. We need to listen to biologist John Todd's idea that we need to work with living machines, not machines for living in. The focus should be on people's needs, and we need clean water, safe materials, and durability. And we need to work from current solar income.

There are certain fundamental laws that are inherent to the natural world that we can use as models and mentors for human designs. Ecology comes from the Greek roots Oikos and Logos, "household" and "logical discourse." Thus, it is appropriate, if not imperative, for architects to discourse about the logic of our earth household. To do so, we must first look at our planet and the very processes by which it manifests life, because therein lie the logical principles with which we must work. And we must also consider economy in the true sense of the word. Using the Greek words Oikos and Nomos, we speak of natural law and how we measure and manage the relationships within this household, working with the principles our discourse has revealed to us.

And how do we measure our work under those laws? Does it make sense to measure it by the paper currency that you have in your wallet? Does it make sense to measure it by a grand summation called GNP? For if we do, we find that the foundering and rupture of the Exxon Valdez tanker was a prosperous event because so much money was spent in Prince William Sound during the clean-up. What then are we really measuring? If we have not put natural resources on the asset side of the ledger, then where are they? Does a forest really become more valuable when it is cut down? Do we really prosper when wild salmon are completely removed from a river?

There are three defining characteristics that we can learn from natural design. The first characteristic is that everything we have to work with is already here—the stones, the clay, the wood, the water, the air. All materials given to us by nature are constantly returned to the earth without even the concept of waste as we understand it. Everything is cycled constantly with all waste equaling food for other living systems.

The second characteristic is that the one thing allowing nature to continually cycle itself through life is energy, and this energy comes from outside the system in the form of perpetual solar income. Not only does nature operate on "current income," it does not mine or extract energy from the past, it does not use its capital reserves, and it does not borrow from the future. It is an extraordinarily complex and efficient system for creating and cycling nutrients, so economical that modern methods of manufacturing pale in comparison to the elegance of natural systems of production.

Finally, the characteristic that sustains this complex and efficient system of metabolism and creation is biodiversity. What prevents living systems from running down and veering into chaos is a miraculously intricate and symbiotic relationship between millions of organisms, no two of which are alike.

As a designer of buildings, things, and systems, I ask myself how to apply these three characteristics of living systems to my work. How do I employ the concept of waste equals food, of current solar income, of protecting biodiversity in design? Before I can even apply these principles, though, we must understand the role of the designer in human affairs.

In thinking about this, I reflect upon a commentary of [Ralph Waldo] Emerson's. In the 1830's, when his wife died, he went to Europe on a sailboat and returned in a steamship. He remarked on the return voyage that he missed the "Aeolian connection."

If we abstract this, he went over on a solar-powered recyclable vehicle operated by craftspersons, working in the open air, practicing ancient arts. He returned in a steel rust bucket, spilling oil on the water and smoke into the sky, operated by people in a black dungeon shoveling coal into the mouth of a boiler. Both ships are objects of design. Both are manifestations of our human intention.

Peter Senge, a professor at M.I.T.'s Sloan School of Management, works with a program called the Learning Laboratory where he studies and discusses how organizations learn. Within that he has a leadership laboratory, and one of the first questions he asks CEOs of companies that attend is, "Who is the leader on a ship crossing the ocean?" He gets obvious answers, such as the captain, the navigator, or the helmsman. But the answer is none of the above. The leader is the designer of the ship because operations on a ship are a consequence of design, which is the result of human intention. Today, we are still designing steamships, machines powered by fossil fuels that have deleterious effects. We need a new design.

I grew up in the Far East, and when I came to this country, I was taken aback when I realized that we were not people with lives in America, but consumers with lifestyles. I wanted to ask someone: when did America stop having people with lives? On television, we are referred to as consumers, not people. But we are people, with lives, and we must make and design things for people. And if I am a consumer, what can I consume? Shoe polish, food, juice, some toothpaste. But actually, very little that is sold to me can actually be consumed. Sooner or later, almost all of it has to be thrown away. I cannot consume a television set. Or a VCR. Or a car. If I presented you with a television set and covered it up and said, "I have this amazing item. What it will do as a service will astonish you. But before I tell you what it does, let me tell you what it is made of and you can tell me if you want it in your house. It contains 4,060 chemicals, many of which are toxic, two hundred of which off-gas into the room when it is turned on. It also contains 18 grams of toxic methyl mercury, has an explosive glass tube, and I urge you to put it at eye-level with your children and encourage them to play with it." Would you want this in your home?

Michael Braungart, an ecological chemist from Hamburg, Germany, has pointed out that we should remove the word "waste" from our vocabulary and start using the word "product" instead, because if waste is going to equal food, it must also be a product. Braungart suggests we think about three distinct product types:

> First, there are consumables, and actually we should be producing more of them. These are products that when eaten, used, or thrown away, literally turn back into dirt, and therefore are food for other living organisms. Consumables should not be placed in landfills, but put on the ground so that they restore the life, health, and fertility of the soil. This means that shampoos should be in bottles made of beets that are biodegradable in your compost pile. It means carpets that break down into CO_2 and water. It means furniture made of lignin, potato peels, and technical enzymes that looks just like your manufactured furniture of today except it can be safely returned to the earth. It means that all "consumable" goods should be capable of returning to the soil from whence they came.

Second are products of service, also known as durables, such as cars and television sets. They are called products of service because what we want as customers is the service the product provides—food, entertainment, or transportation. To eliminate the concept of waste, products of service would not be sold, but licensed to the end-user. Customers may use them as long as they wish, even sell the license to someone else, but when the end-user is finished with, say, a television, it goes back to Sony, Zenith, or Philips. It is "food" for their system, but not for natural systems. Right now, you can go down the street, dump a TV into the garbage can, and walk away. In the process, we deposit persistent toxins throughout the planet. Why do we give people that responsibility and stress? Products of service must continue beyond their initial product life, be owned by their manufacturers, and be designed for disassembly, re-manufacture, and continuous re-use.

The third type of product is called "unmarketables." The question is, why would anyone produce a product that no one would buy? Welcome to the world of nuclear waste, dioxins, and chromium-tanned leather. We are essentially making products or subcomponents of products that no one should buy, or, in many cases, do not realize they are buying. These products must not only cease to be sold, but those already sold should be stored in warehouses when they are finished until we can figure out a safe and non-toxic way to dispose of them.

I will describe a few projects and how these issues are implicit in design directions. I remember when we were hired to design the office for an environmental group. The director said at the end of contract negotiations, "By the way, if anybody in our office gets sick from indoor air quality, we're going to sue you." After wondering if we should even take the job, we decided to go ahead, that it was our job to find the materials that wouldn't make people sick when placed inside a building. And what we found is that those materials weren't there. We had to work with manufacturers to find out what was in their products, and we discovered that the entire system of building construction is essentially toxic. We are still working on the materials side.

For a New York men's clothing store, we arranged for the planting of 1,000 oak trees to replace the two English oaks used to panel the store. We were inspired by a famous story told by Gregory Bateson about New College in Oxford, England. It went something like this. They had a main hall built in the early 1600s with beams forty feet long and two feet thick. A committee was formed to try to find replacement trees because the beams were suffering from dry rot. If you keep in mind that a veneer from an English oak can be worth seven dollars a square foot, the total replacement costs for the oaks were prohibitively expensive. And they didn't have straight forty foot English oaks from mature forests with which to replace the beams. A young faculty member joined the committee and said, "Why don't we ask the College Forester if some of the lands that had been given to Oxford might have enough trees to call upon?" And when they brought in the forester he said, "We've been wondering when you would ask this question. When the present building was constructed 350 years ago, the architects specified that a grove of trees be planted and maintained to replace the beams in the ceiling when they would suffer from dry rot." Bateson's remark was, "That's the way to run a culture." Our question and hope is, "Did they replant them?"

For Warsaw, Poland, we responded to a design competition for a high-rise building. When the client chose our design as the winner after seeing the model, we said, "We're not finished yet. We have to tell you all about the building. The base is made from concrete and includes tiny bits of rubble from World War II. It looks like limestone, but the rubble's there for visceral reasons." And he said, "I understand, a phoenix rising. " And we said the skin is recycled aluminum, and he said, "That's O.K., that's fine." And we said, "The floor heights are thirteen feet clear so that we can convert the building into housing in the future, when its utility as an office building is no longer. In this way, the building is given a chance to have a long, useful life. "And he said, "That's O.K." And we told him that we would have opening windows and that no one would be further than twenty-five feet from a window, and he said that was O.K., too. And finally, we said, "By the way, you have to plant ten square miles of forest to offset the building's effect on climate change." We had calculated the energy costs to build the structure, and the energy cost to run and maintain it, and it worked out that 6,400 acres of new forest would be needed to offset the effects on climate change from the energy requirements. And he said he would get back to us. He called back two days later and said, "You still win. I checked out what it would cost to plant ten square miles of trees in Poland and it turns out it's equivalent to a small part of the advertising budget."

The architects representing a major retail chain called us a year ago and said, "Will you help us build a store in Lawrence, Kansas?" I said that I didn't know if we could work with them. I explained my thoughts on consumers with lifestyles, and we needed to be in the position to discuss their stores' impact on small towns. Click. Three days later we were called back and were told, "We have a question for you that is coming from the top. Are you willing to discuss the fact that people with lives have the right to buy the finest-quality products, even under your own terms, at the lowest possible price?" We said, "Yes." "Then we can talk about the impact on small towns."

We worked with them on the store in Kansas. We converted the building from steel construction, which uses 300,000 BTUs per square foot, to wood construction, which uses 40,000 BTUs, thereby saving thousands of gallons of oil just in the fabrication of the building. We used only wood that came from resources that were protecting biodiversity. In our research we found that the forests of James Madison and Zachary Taylor in Virginia had been put into sustainable forestry and the wood for the beams came from their and other forests managed this way. We also arranged for no CFC's to be used in the store's construction and systems, and initiated significant research and a major new industry in daylighting. We have yet to fulfill our concerns about the bigger questions of products, their distribution, and the chain's impact on small towns, with the exception that this store is designed to be converted into housing when its utility as a retail outlet has expired.

For the City of Frankfurt, we are designing a day-care center that can be operated by the children. It contains a greenhouse roof that has multiple functions: it illuminates, heats both air and water, cools, ventilates, and shelters from the rain, just like a Bedouin tent. One problem we were having during the design process was the engineers wanted to completely automate the building, like a machine. The engineers asked, "What happens if the children forget to close the shades and they get too hot?" We told them the children would open a window. "What if they don't open a window?" the engineers wanted to know. And we told them that in that case, the children would probably close the shade. And then they wanted to know what would happen if the children didn't close the shade. And finally we told them the children would open windows and close shades when they were hot because children are not dead but alive. Recognizing the importance for children to look at the day in the morning and see what the sun is going to do that day and interact with it, we enlisted the help of teachers of Frankfurt to get this one across because the teachers had told us the most important thing was to find something for the children to do. Now the children have ten minutes of activity in the morning and ten minutes of activity when they leave the building, opening and closing the system, and both the children and teachers love the idea. Because of the solar hot-water collectors, we asked that a public laundry be added to the program so that parents could wash clothes while awaiting their children in school. Because of advances in glazing, we are able to create a day-care center that requires no fossil fuels for operating the heating or cooling. Fifty years from now, when fossil fuels will be scarce, there will be hot water for the community, a social center, and the building will have paid back the energy "borrowed" for its construction.

As we become aware of the ethical implications of design, not only with respect to buildings, but in every aspect of human endeavor, they reflect changes in the historical concept of who or what has rights. When you study the history of rights, you begin with the Magna Carta, which was about the rights of white, English, noble males. With the Declaration of Independence, rights were expanded to all landowning white males. Nearly a century later, we moved to the emancipation of slaves, and during the beginnings of this century, to suffrage, giving the right to women to vote. Then the pace picks up with the Civil Rights Act in 1964, and then in 1973, the Endangered Species Act. For the first time, the right of other species and organisms to exist was recognized. We have essentially "declared" that Homo Sapiens are part of the web of life. Thus, if Thomas Jefferson were with us today, he would be calling for a Declaration of Interdependence which recognizes that our ability to pursue wealth, health, and happiness is dependent on other forms of life, that the rights of one species are linked to the rights of others and none should suffer remote tyranny.

This Declaration of Interdependence comes hard on the heels of realizing that the world has become vastly complex, both in its workings and in our ability to perceive and comprehend those complexities. In this complicated world, prior modes of domination have essentially lost their ability to maintain control. The sovereign, whether in the form of a king or nation, no longer seems to reign. Nations have lost control of money to global, computerized trading systems. The sovereign is also losing the ability to deceive and manipulate, as in the case of Chernobyl. While the erstwhile Soviet Republic told the world that Chernobyl was nothing to be concerned about, satellites with ten-meter resolution showed the world that it was something to worry about. And what we saw at the Earth Summit was that the sovereign has lost the ability to lead even on the most elementary level. When Maurice Strong, the chair of the United Nations Conference on the Environment and Development, was asked how many leaders were at the Earth Summit, he said there were over 100 heads of state. Unfortunately, we didn't have any leaders.

When Emerson came back from Europe, he wrote essays for Harvard on Nature. He was trying to understand that if human beings make things and human beings are natural, then are all the things human beings make natural? He determined that Nature was all those things which were immutable. The oceans, the mountains, the sky. Well, we now know that they are mutable. We were operating as if Nature is the Great Mother who never has any problems, is always there for her children, and requires no love in return. When you think about Genesis and the concept of dominion over natural things, we realize that even if we want to get into a discussion of stewardship versus dominion, in the end, the question is, if you have dominion, and perhaps we do have dominion, isn't it implicit that we have stewardship too, because how can you have dominion over something you've killed?

We must face the fact that what we are seeing across the world today is war, a war against life itself. Our present systems of design have created a world that grows far beyond the capacity of the environment to sustain life into the future. The industrial idiom of design, failing to honor the principles of nature, can only violate them, producing waste and harm, regardless of purported intention. If we destroy more forests, burn more garbage, drift-net more fish, burn more coal, bleach more paper, destroy more topsoil, poison more insects, build over more habitats, dam more rivers, produce more toxic and radioactive waste, we are creating a vast industrial machine, not for living in, but for dying in. It is a war, to be sure, a war that only a few more generations can surely survive.

When I was in Jordan, I worked for King Hussein on the master plan for the Jordan Valley. I was walking through a village that had been flattened by tanks and I saw a child's skeleton squashed into the adobe block and was horrified. My Arab host turned to me and said, "Don't you know what war is?" And I said, "I guess I don't." And he said, "War is when they kill your children." So I believe we're at war. But we must stop. To do this, we have to stop designing everyday things for killing, and we have to stop designing killing machines.

We have to recognize that every event and manifestation of nature is "design," that to live within the laws of nature means to express our human intention as an interdependent species, aware and grateful that we are at the mercy of sacred forces larger than ourselves, and that we obey these laws in order to honor the sacred in each other and in all things. We must come to peace with and accept our place in the natural world.

INTRODUCTION

The Hannover Principles
William McDonough Architects

The Hannover Principles represent an attempt by William McDonough Architects to establish some broad ethical guidelines for sustainable design. The firm was commissioned by the city of Hannover, Germany to develop standards for the millennial World's Fair with the theme "Humanity, Nature, and Technology." The Principles were first announced at the Earth Summit in Rio de Janeiro, Brazil in June 1992.

The principles are not a prescription for designers, but also ideals to pursue in the complex process of working in today's environment. They succinctly summarize the recommendations that derive from the ethical position stated in "Design, Ecology, Ethics, and the Making of Things." The guidelines begin by stating the significance of nature as the primary support to human life, while acknowledging its susceptibility to degradation by our activities. The concept of responsibility for the consequences of design is then expanded to include protecting natural systems, human settlements, and future generations. Reuse, reassembly, and recycling will help attain the goal of eliminating waste with regard to manufactured products. For example, in a plan endorsed by McDonough's firm, Herman Miller now accepts returns of its furniture for recycling of parts and materials into new pieces.

Perhaps most difficult for architects, engineers, and planners to accept, given the constantly shifting and growing knowledge base, is the idea that design and technology cannot solve all the problems they create. McDonough and company urge accepting the limitations of human ingenuity, instead of maintaining a positivist view of the role of science. Solutions to environmental problems will be found once humankind ceases its attempt to dominate nature and, instead, views it as a model. Architects must step forward to lead interdisciplinary teams in this newly reoriented problem-solving.

WILLIAM McDONOUGH
THE HANNOVER PRINCIPLES

1. Insist on rights of humanity and nature to co-exist in a healthy, supportive, diverse, and sustainable condition.

2. Recognize interdependence. The elements of human design interact with and depend upon the natural world, with broad and diverse implications at every scale. Expand design considerations to recognizing even distant effects.

3. Respect relationships between spirit and matter. Consider all aspects of human settlement including community, dwelling, industry, and trade in terms of existing and evolving connections between spiritual and material consciousness.

4. Accept responsibility for the consequences of design decisions upon human well-being, the viability of natural systems, and their right to co-exist.

5. Create safe objects of long-term value. Do not burden future generations with requirements for maintenance or vigilant administration of potential danger due to the careless creation of products, processes, or standards.

6. Eliminate the concept of waste. Evaluate and optimize the full life-cycle of products and processes, to approach the state of natural systems, in which there is no waste.

7. Rely on natural energy flows. Human designs should, like the living world, derive their creative forces from perpetual solar income. Incorporate this energy efficiently and safely for responsible use.

8. Understand the limitations of design. No human creation lasts forever and design does not solve all problems. Those who create and plan should practice humility in the face of nature. Treat nature as a model and mentor; not an inconvenience to be evaded or controlled.

From *The Hannover Principles: Design for Sustainability* (New York: William McDonough Architects, 1992), 5. Courtesy of the author.

9. Seek constant improvement by the sharing of knowledge. Encourage direct and open communication between colleagues, patrons, manufacturers, and users to link long term sustainable considerations with ethical responsibility, and re-establish the integral relationship between natural processes and human activity.

The Hannover Principles should be seen as a living document committed to the transformation and growth in the understanding of our interdependence with nature, so that they may adapt as our knowledge of the world evolves.

9. PHENOMENOLOGY
OF MEANING AND PLACE

INTRODUCTION

The Phenomenon of Place
Christian Norberg-Schulz

Christian Norberg-Schulz, a Norwegian architectural theorist, is closely associated with the espousal of a phenomenology of architecture. From his early writings in the 1960s to the more recent *Architecture: Meaning and Place* (1988), he develops a textual and pictorial interpretation of the ideas of Martin Heidegger (1889–1976), based primarily on Heidegger's essay "Building Dwelling Thinking." *Intentions in Architecture* (1963) uses linguistics, perceptual (Gestalt) psychology, and phenomenology to construct a comprehensive theory of architecture. It appeared just before Robert Venturi's *Complexity and Contradiction in Architecture*, another important postmodern text. An increasingly clear interest in phenomenology is evident in Norberg-Schulz's later books.

Initially defined by Edmund Husserl (1859–1938) as a systematic investigation of consciousness and its objects,[1] Norberg-Schulz refers to phenomenology as a "method" that urges a " 'return to things,' as opposed to abstractions and mental constructions." At the time this essay was published, few efforts had been made to study the environment phenomenologically. He identifies phenomenology's potential in architecture as the ability to make the environment meaningful through the creation of specific places. He reintroduces the ancient Roman idea of the *genius loci*, the spirit of a particular place, (creating a link to the sacred), which provides an "other" or opposite that humanity must confront in order to dwell. He interprets dwelling as being at peace in a protected place. Thus, enclosure, the act of marking or differentiating a *place* within *space* becomes the archetypal act of building and the true origin of architecture. Norberg-Schulz emphasizes the importance of basic architectural elements like wall, floor, or ceiling, experienced as horizon, boundary, and frame for nature. Architecture clarifies the location of human existence, which as Heidegger describes it, is between the sky and the earth, in front of the divinities. Phenomenologists such as

Vittorio Gregotti also argue the need for the site to intensify, condense, and make precise the structure of nature and man's understanding of it. (ch. 7) The celebration of the particular qualities of place is also fundamental to Kenneth Frampton's Critical Regionalism. (ch. 11)

In addition to a focus on site, phenomenology engages tectonics because, as Norberg-Schulz says, "the detail explains the environment and makes its character manifest." (ch. 10–12) Because of its embrace of site and tectonics, phenomenology has proven an extremely influential school of thought for contemporary designers such as Tadao Ando, Steven Holl, Clark and Menefee, and Peter Waldman. It has led to a renewed interest in the sensuous qualities of materials, light, and color, and in the symbolic, tactile significance of the joint. These aspects contribute to the poetic quality that Heidegger says is essential to dwelling.

Norberg-Schulz is led by his admiration for Robert Venturi into misreading him as a phenomenologist because of the latter's interest in "the wall between the inside and the outside." Certainly there is little doubt after *Learning from Las Vegas* that Venturi and his collaborators are more interested in surface ("decorated shed") than in spatial concerns like bounded places.

1   Anthony Flew, *A Dictionary of Philosophy*, rev. 2d ed. (New York: St. Martin's Press, 1984), 157.

CHRISTIAN NORBERG-SCHULZ
THE PHENOMENON OF PLACE

Our everyday life-world consists of concrete "phenomena." It consists of people, of animals, of flowers, trees and forests, of stone, earth, wood and water, of towns, streets and houses, doors, windows, and furniture. And it consists of sun, moon, and stars, of drifting clouds, of night and day and changing seasons. But it also comprises more intangible phenomena such as feelings. This is what is "given," this is the "content" of our existence. Thus Rilke says: "Are we perhaps *here* to say: house, bridge, fountain, gate, jug, fruit tree, window,—at best: Pillar, tower."[1] Everything else, such as atoms and molecules, numbers, and all kinds of "data," are abstractions or tools which are constructed to serve other purposes than those of everyday life. Today it is common to mistake the tools for reality.

The concrete things which constitute our given world are interrelated in complex and perhaps contradictory ways. Some of the phenomena may for instance comprise others. The forest consists of trees, and the town is made up of houses. "Landscape" is such a comprehensive phenomenon. In general we may say that some phenomena form an "environment" to others. A concrete term for environment is *place*. It is common usage to say that acts and occurrences *take place*. In fact it is meaningless to imagine any happening without reference to a locality. Place is evidently an integral part of existence. What, then, do we mean with the word "place?" Obviously we mean something more than abstract location. We mean a totality made up of concrete things having material substance, shape, texture, and colour. Together these things determine an "environmental character," which is the essence of place. In general a place is given as such a character or "atmosphere." A place is therefore a qualitative, "total" phenomenon, which we cannot reduce to any of its properties, such as spatial relationships, without losing its concrete nature out of sight.

From *Architectural Association Quarterly* 8, no. 4 (1976): 3–10. Courtesy of the author and publisher.

Everyday experience moreover tells us that different actions need different environments to take place in a satisfactory way. As a consequence, towns and houses consist of a multitude of particular places. This fact is of course taken into consideration by current theory of planning and architecture, but so far the problem has been treated in a too abstract way. "Taking place" is usually understood in a quantitative, "functional" sense, with implications such as spatial distribution and dimensioning. But are not "functions" inter-human and similar everywhere? Evidently not. "Similar" functions, even the most basic ones such as sleeping and eating, take place in very different ways, and demand places with different properties, in accordance with different cultural traditions and different environmental conditions. The functional approach therefore left out the place as a concrete "here" having its particular identity.

Being qualitative totalities of a complex nature, places cannot be described by means of analytic, "scientific" concepts. As a matter of principle science "abstracts" from the given to arrive at neutral, "objective" knowledge. What is lost, however, is the everyday life-world, which ought to be the real concern of man in general and planners and architects in particular.[2] Fortunately a way out of the impasse exists, that is, the method known as *phenomenology*. Phenomenology was conceived as a "return to things," as opposed to abstractions and mental constructions. So far phenomenologists have been mainly concerned with ontology, psychology, ethics, and to some extent aesthetics, and have given relatively little attention to the phenomenology of the daily environment. A few pioneer works however exist but they hardly contain any direct reference to architecture.[3] A phenomenology of architecture is therefore urgently needed.

Some of the philosophers who have approached the problem of our life world, have used language and literature as sources of "information." Poetry in fact is able to concretize those totalities which elude science, and may therefore suggest how we might proceed to obtain the needed understanding. One of the poems used by [Martin] Heidegger to explain the nature of language, is the splendid "A Winter Evening" by Georg Trakl.[4] The words of Trakl also serve our purpose very well, as they make present a total life-situation where the aspect of place is strongly felt:

A Winter Evening
Window with falling snow is arrayed,
long tolls the vesper bell,
The house is provided well,
The table is for many laid.
Wandering ones, more than a few,
Come to the door on darksome courses,
Golden blooms the tree of graces
Drawing up the earth's cool dew.
Wanderer quietly steps within;
Pain has turned the threshold to stone.
There lie, in limpid brightness shown,
Upon the table bread and wine.[5]

We shall not repeat Heidegger's profound analysis of the poem, but rather point out a few properties which illuminate our problem. In general, Trakl uses *concrete* images which we all know from our everyday world. He talks about "snow," "window," "house," "table," "door," "tree," "threshold," "bread and wine," "darkness," and "light," and he characterizes man as a "wanderer." These images, however, also imply more general structures. First of all the poem distinguishes between an *outside* and an *inside*. The *outside* is presented in the first two lines of the first stanza, and comprises *natural* as well as *man-made* elements. Natural place is present in the falling snow which implies winter, and by the evening. The very title of the poem "places" everything in this natural context. A winter evening, however, is something more than a point in the calendar. As a concrete presence, it is experienced as a set of particular qualities, or in general as a *Stimmung* or "character," which forms a background to acts and occurrences. In the poem this character is given by the snow falling on the window, cold, soft and soundless, hiding the contours of those objects which are still recognized in the approaching darkness. The word "falling" moreover creates a sense of *space*, or rather: an implied presence of earth and sky. With a minimum of words, Trakl thus brings a total natural environment to life. But the outside also has man-made properties. This is indicated by the vesper bell, which is heard everywhere, and makes the "private" inside become part of a comprehensive, "public" totality. The vesper bell, however, is something more than a practical man-made artifact. It is a symbol, which reminds us of the common values which are at the basis of that totality. In Heidegger's words: "the tolling of the evening bell brings men, as mortals, before the divine."[6]

The *inside* is presented in the next two verses. It is described as a house, which offers man shelter and security by being enclosed and "well provided." It has, however, a window, an opening which makes us experience the inside as a complement to the outside. As a final focus within the house we find the table, which "is for many laid." At the table men come together, it is the *centre* which more than anything else constitutes the inside. The character of the inside is hardly told, but anyhow present. It is luminous and warm, in contrast to the cold darkness outside, and its silence is pregnant with potential sound. In general the inside is a comprehensible world of *things*, where the life of "many" may take place.

In the next two stanzas the perspective is deepened. Here the *meaning* of places and things comes forth, and man is presented as a wanderer on "darksome courses." Rather than being placed safely within the house he has created for himself, he comes from the outside, from the "path of life," which also represents man's attempt at "orienting" himself in the given unknown environment. But nature also has another side: it offers the grace of growth and blossom. In the image of the "golden" tree, earth and sky are unified and become a *world*. Through man's labour this world is brought inside as bread and wine, whereby the inside is "illuminated," that is, becomes meaningful. Without the "sacred" fruits of sky and earth, the inside would remain "empty." The house and the table receive and gather, and bring the world "close." *To dwell in a house therefore means to inhabit the world.* But this dwelling is not easy; it has to be reached on dark paths, and a threshold separates the outside from the inside. Representing the "rift" between "otherness" and manifest meaning, it embodies suffering and is "turned to stone." In the threshold, thus, the *problem* of dwelling comes to the fore.[7]

Trakl's poem illuminates some essential phenomena of our life-world, and in particular the basic properties of place. First of all it tells us that every situation is local as well as general. The winter evening described is obviously a local, nordic phenomenon, but the implied notions of outside and inside are general, as are the meanings connected with this distinction. The poem hence concretizes basic properties of existence. "Concretize" here means to make the general "visible" as a concrete, local situation. In doing this the poem moves in the opposite direction of scientific thought. Whereas science departs from the "given," poetry brings us back to the concrete things, uncovering the meanings inherent in the life-world.[8]

Furthermore Trakl's poem distinguishes between natural and man-made elements, whereby it suggests a point of departure for an "environmental phenomenology." Natural elements are evidently the primary components of the given, and places are in fact usually defined in geographical terms. We must repeat however, that "place" means something more than location. Various attempts at a description of natural places are offered by current literature on "landscape," but again we find that the usual approach is too abstract, being based on "functional" or perhaps "visual" considerations.[9] Again we must turn to philosophy for help. As a first, fundamental distinction Heidegger introduces the concepts of "earth" and "sky," and says: "Earth is the serving bearer, blossoming and fruiting, spreading out in rock and water, rising up into plant and animal..." "The sky is the vaulting path of the sun, the course of the changing moon, the glitter of the stars, the year's seasons, the light and dusk of day, the gloom and glow of night, the clemency and inclemency of the weather, the drifting clouds and blue depth of the ether..."[10] Like many fundamental insights, the distinction between earth and sky might seem trivial. Its importance however comes out when we add Heidegger's definition of "dwelling:" "the way in which you are and I am, the way in which we humans are on the earth, is dwelling..." But "on the earth" already means "under the sky."[11] He also calls what is *between* earth and sky *the world*, and says that "the world is the house where the mortals dwell."[12] In other words, when man is capable of dwelling the world becomes an "inside."

In general, nature forms an extended comprehensive totality, a "place," which according to local circumstances has a particular identity. This identity, or "spirit," may be described by means of the kind of concrete, "qualitative" terms Heidegger uses to characterize earth and sky, and has to take this fundamental distinction as its point of departure. In this way we might arrive at an existentially relevant understanding of *landscape*, which ought to be preserved as the main designation of natural places. Within the landscape, however, there are subordinate places, as well as natural "things" such as Trakl's "tree." In these things the meaning of the natural environment is "condensed."

The man-made parts of the environment are first of all "settlements" of different scale, from houses and farms to villages and towns, and secondly "paths" which connect these settlements, as well as various elements which transform nature into a "cultural landscape." If the settlements are organically related to their environment, it implies that they serve as *foci* where the environmental character is condensed and "explained." Thus Heidegger says: "the single houses, the villages, the towns are works of building which within and around themselves gather the multifarious in-between. The buildings bring the earth as the inhabited landscape close to man, and at the same time place the closeness of neighbourly dwelling under the expanse of the sky."[13] The basic property of man-made places is therefore concentration and enclosure. They are "insides" in a full sense, which means that they "gather" what is known. To fulfill this function they have openings which relate to the outside. (Only an *inside* can in fact have openings.) Buildings are furthermore related to their environment by resting on the ground and rising towards the sky. Finally the man-made environments comprise artifacts or "things," which may serve as internal foci, and emphasize the gathering function of the settlement. In Heidegger's words: "the thing things world," where "thinging" is used in the original sense of "gathering," and further: "Only what conjoins itself out of world becomes a thing."[14]

Our introductory remarks give several indications about the *structure* of places. Some of these have already been worked out by phenomenologist philosophers, and offer a good point of departure for a more complete phenomenology. A first step is taken with the distinction of natural and man-made phenomena. A second step is represented by the categories of earth-sky (horizontal-vertical) and outside-inside. These categories have spatial implications, and "space" is hence re-introduced, not primarily as a mathematical concept, but as an existential dimension.[15] A final and particularly important step is taken with the concept of "character." Character is determined by *how* things are, and gives our investigation a basis in the concrete phenomena of our everyday life-world. Only in this way we may fully grasp the *genius loci*; the "spirit of place" which the ancients recognized as that "opposite" man has to come to terms with, to be able to dwell.[16] The concept of *genius loci* denotes the essence of place.

THE STRUCTURE OF PLACE

Our preliminary discussion of the phenomena of place led to the conclusion that the structure of place ought to be described in terms of "landscape" and "settlement," and analyzed by means of the categories "space" and "character." Whereas "space" denotes the three-dimensional organization of the elements which make up a place, "character" denotes the general "atmosphere" which is the most comprehensive property of any place. Instead of making a distinction between space and character, it is of course possible to employ one comprehensive concept, such as "lived space."[17] For our purpose, however, it is practical to distinguish between space and character. Similar spatial organizations may possess very different characters according to the concrete treatment of the space-defining elements (the *boundary*). The history of basic spatial forms have been given ever new characterizing interpretations.[18] On the other hand it has to be pointed out that the spatial organization puts certain limits to characterization, and that the two concepts are interdependent.

"Space" is certainly no new term in architectural theory. But space can mean many things. In current literature we may distinguish between two uses: space as three-dimensional geometry, and space as perceptual field.[19] None of these however are satisfactory, being abstractions from the intuitive three-dimensional totality of everyday experience, which we may call "concrete space." Concrete human actions in fact do not take place in an homogeneous isotropic space, but in a space distinguished by qualitative differences, such as "up" and "down." In architectural theory several attempts have been made to define space in concrete, qualitative terms. [Sigfried] Giedion, thus uses the distinction between "outside" and "inside" as the basis for a grand view of architectural history.[20]

Kevin Lynch penetrates deeper into the structure of concrete space, introducing the concepts of "node" ("landmark"), "path," "edge," and "district," to denote those elements which form the basis for man's orientation in space.[21] Paolo Portoghesi finally defines space as a "system of places," implying that the concept of space has its roots in concrete situations, although spaces may be *described* by means of mathematics.[22] The latter view corresponds to Heidegger's statement that "spaces receive their being from locations and not from 'space.'"[23] The outside-inside relation which is a primary aspect of concrete space, implies that spaces possess a varying degree of *extension* and *enclosure* Whereas landscapes are distinguished by a varied, but basically continuous extension, settlements are enclosed entities. Settlement and landscape therefore have a *figure-ground* relationship. In general, any enclosure becomes manifest as a "figure" in relation to the extended ground of the landscape. A settlement loses its identity if this relationship is corrupted, just as much as the landscape loses its identity as comprehensive extension. In a wider context any enclosure becomes a *centre*, which may function as a "focus" for its surroundings. From the centre space extends with a varying degree of continuity (rhythm) in different directions. Evidently the main directions are horizontal and vertical, that is, the directions of earth and sky. *Centralization, direction*, and *rhythm* are therefore other important properties of concrete space. Finally it has to be mentioned that natural elements (such as hills) and settlements may be clustered or grouped with a varying degree of *proximity*.

All the spatial properties mentioned are of a "topological" kind, and correspond to the well-known "principles of organization" of Gestalt theory. The primary existential importance of these principles is confirmed by the researches of Piaget on the child's conception of space.[24] Geometrical modes of organization only develop later in life to serve particular purposes, and may in general be understood as a more "precise" definition of the basic topological structures. The topological enclosure thus becomes a circle, the "free" curve a straight line, and the cluster a grid. In architecture geometry is used to make a general comprehensive system manifest, such as an inferred "cosmic order."

Any enclosure is defined by a boundary: Heidegger says: "A boundary is not that at which something stops but, as the Greeks recognized, the boundary is that, from which something begins its presencing."[25] The boundaries of a built space are known as *floor, wall*, and *ceiling*. The boundaries of a landscape are structurally similar, and consist of ground, horizon, and sky. This simple structural similarity is of basic importance for the relationship between natural and man-made places. The enclosing properties of a boundary are determined by its *openings*, as was poetically intuited by Trakl when using the images of window, door, and threshold. In general the boundary, and in particular the wall, makes the spatial structure visible as continuous and/or discontinuous extension, direction and rhythm.

"Character" is at the same time a more general and a more concrete concept than "space." On the one hand it denotes a general comprehensive atmosphere, and on the other the concrete form and substance of space-defining elements. Any real *presence* is intimately linked with a character.[26] A phenomenology of character has to comprise a survey of manifest characters as well as an investigation of their concrete determinants. We have pointed out that different actions demand places with a different character. A dwelling has to be "protective," an office "practical," a ball-room "festive," and a church "solemn." When we visit a foreign city, we are usually struck by its particular character, which becomes an important part of the experience. Landscapes also possess character, some of which is of a particular "natural" kind. Thus we talk about "barren" and "fertile," "smiling" and "threatening" landscapes. In general we have to emphasize that *all places have character*, and that character is the basic mode in which the world is "given." To some extent the character of a place is a function of time; it changes with the seasons, the course of the day, and the weather, factors which above all determine different conditions of *light*.

The character is determined by the material and formal constitution of the place. We must therefore ask: *how* is the ground on which we walk, *how* is the sky above our heads, or in general: *how* are the boundaries which define the place. How a boundary is depends upon its formal articulation, which is again related to the way it is "built." Looking at a building from this point of view, we have to consider how it rests on the ground and how it rises towards the sky. Particular attention has to be given to its lateral boundaries, or walls, which also contribute decisively to determine the character of the *urban* environment. We are indebted to Robert Venturi for having recognized this fact, after it had been considered for many years "immoral" to talk about "facades."[27] Usually the character of a "family" of buildings which constitute a place, is "condensed" in characteristic *motifs*, such as particular types of windows, doors, and roofs. Such motifs may become "conventional elements," which serve to transpose a character from one place to another. In the boundary, thus, character and space come together, and we may agree with Venturi when he defines architecture as "the wall between the inside and the outside."[28]

Except for the intuitions of Venturi, the problem of character has hardly been considered in current architectural theory. As a result, theory has to a high extent lost contact with the concrete life-world. This is particularly the case with technology, which is today considered a mere means to satisfy practical demand. Character however, depends upon *how things are made*, and is therefore determined by the technical realization ("building"). Heidegger points out that the Greek word *techne* meant a creative "re-vealing" (*Entbergen*) of truth, and belonged to *poiesis*, that is, "making."[29] A phenomenology of place therefore has to comprise the basic modes of construction and their relationship to formal articulation. Only in this way architectural theory gets a truly concrete basis.

The structure of place becomes manifest as environmental totalities which comprise the aspects of character and space. Such places are known as "countries," "regions," "landscapes," "settlements," and "buildings." Here we return to the concrete "things" of our everyday life-world, which was our point of departure, and remember Rilke's words: "Are we perhaps *here* to say..." When places are classified we should therefore use terms such as "island," "promontory," "bay," "forest," "grove," or "square," "street," "courtyard," and "floor," "wall," "roof," "ceiling," "window," and "door."

Places are hence designated by *nouns*. This implies they are considered real "things that exist," which is original meaning of the word "substantive." Space, instead, as a system of relations, is denoted by *prepositions*. In our daily life we hardly talk about "space," but about things that are "over" or "under," "before," or "behind" each other, or we use prepositions such as "at," "in," "within," "on," "upon," "to," "from," "along," "next." All these prepositions denote topological relations of the kind mentioned before. Character, finally, is denoted by *adjectives*, as was indicated above. A character is a complex totality, and a single adjective evidently cannot cover more than one aspect of this totality. Often, however, character is so distinct that one word seems sufficient to grasp its essence. We see, thus, that the very structure of everyday language confirms our analysis of place.

Countries, regions, landscapes, settlements, buildings (and their sub-places) form a series with a gradually diminishing scale. The steps in this series may be called "environmental levels."[30] At the "top" of the series we find the more comprehensive natural places which "contain" the man-made places on the "lower" levels. The latter have the "gathering" and "focussing" function mentioned above. In other words, man "receives" the environment and makes it focus in buildings and things. The things thereby "explain" the environment and make its character manifest. Thereby the things themselves become meaningful. That is the basic function of *detail* in our surroundings.[31] This does not imply, however, that the different levels must have the same structure. Architectural history in fact shows that this is rarely the case. Vernacular settlements usually have a topological organization, although the single houses may be strictly geometrical. In larger cities we often find topologically organized neighbourhoods within a general geometrical structure, etc. We shall return to the particular problems of structural correspondence later, but have to say some words about the main "step" in the scale of environmental levels: the relation between natural and man-made places.

Man-made places are related to nature in three basic ways. Firstly, man wants to make the natural structure more precise. That is, he wants to *visualize* his "understanding" of nature, "expressing" the existential foothold he has gained. To achieve this, he *builds* what he has seen. Where nature suggests a delimited space he builds an enclosure; where nature appears "centralized," he erects a *Mal*;[32] where nature indicates a direction, he makes a path. Secondly, man has to *symbolize* his understanding of nature (including himself). Symbolization implies that an experienced meaning is "translated" into another medium. A natural character is for instance translated into a building whose properties somehow make the character manifest.[33] The purpose of symbolization is to free the meaning from the immediate situation, whereby it becomes a "cultural object," which may form part of a more complex situation, or be moved to another place. Finally, man needs to *gather* the experienced meanings to create for himself an *imago mundi* or *microcosmos* which concretizes his world. Gathering evidently depends on symbolization, and implies a transposition of meanings to one place, which thereby becomes an existential "centre."

Visualization, symbolization and gathering are aspects of the general processes of settling; and dwelling, in the existential sense of the word, depends on these functions. Heidegger illustrates the problem by means of the *bridge*, a "building" which visualizes, symbolizes, and gathers, and makes the environment a unified whole. Thus he says:

> The bridge swings over the stream with ease and power. It does not just connect banks that are already there, the banks emerge as banks only as the bridge crosses the stream. The bridge designedly causes them to lie across from each other. One side is set off against the other by the bridge. Nor do the banks stretch along the stream as indifferent border strips of the dry land. With the banks, the bridge brings to the stream the one and the other expanse of the landscape lying behind them. It brings stream and bank and land into each other's neighbourhood. The bridge gathers the earth as landscape around the stream.[34]

Heidegger also describes *what* the bridge gathers and thereby uncovers its value as a symbol. We cannot here enter into these details, but want to emphasize that the landscape as such gets its value *through* the bridge. Before, the meaning of the landscape was "hidden," and the building of the bridge brings it out into the open.

"The bridge gathers Being into a certain 'location' that we may call a 'place.' This 'place,' however, did not exist as an entity before the bridge (although there were always many 'sites' along the river-bank where it could arise), but comes-to-presence with and as the bridge."[35] The existential purpose of building (architecture) is therefore to make a site become a place, that is, to uncover the meanings potentially present in the given environment.

The structure of a place is not a fixed, eternal state. As a rule places change, sometimes rapidly. This does not mean, however, that the *genius loci* necessarily changes or gets lost. Later we shall show that *taking place* presupposes that the places conserve their identity during a certain stretch of time. *Stabilitas loci* is a necessary condition for human life. How then is this stability compatible with the dynamics of change? First of all we may point out that any place ought to have the "capacity" of receiving *different* "contents," naturally within certain limits.[36] A place which is only fitted for one particular purpose would soon become useless. Secondly it is evident that a place may be "interpreted" in different ways. To protect and conserve the genius loci in fact means to concretize its essence in ever new historical contexts. We might also say that the history of a place ought to be its "self-realization." What was there as possibilities at the outset, is uncovered through human action, illuminated and "kept" in works of architecture which are simultaneously "old and new."[37] A place therefore comprises properties having a varying degree of invariance.

In general we may conclude that *place* is the point of departure as well as the goal of our structural investigation; at the outset place is presented as a given, spontaneously experienced totality, at the end it appears as a structured world, illuminated by the analysis of the aspects of space and character.

THE SPIRIT OF PLACE

Genius loci is a Roman concept. According to ancient Roman belief every "independent" being has its *genius*, its guardian spirit. This spirit gives life to people and places, accompanies them from birth to death, and determines their character or essence. Even the gods had their *genius*, a fact which illustrates the fundamental nature of the concept.[38] The *genius* thus denotes what a thing is, or what it "wants to be," to use a word of Louis Kahn. It is not necessary in our context to go into the history of the concept of *genius* and its relationship to the *daimon* of the Greeks. It suffices to point out that ancient man experienced his environment as consisting of definite characters. In particular he recognized that it is of great existential importance to come to terms with the *genius* of the locality where his life takes place. In the past survival depended on a "good" relationship to the place in a physical as well as a psychic sense. In ancient Egypt, for instance, the country was not only cultivated in accordance with the Nile floods, but the very structure of the landscape served as a model for the lay-out of the "public" buildings which should give a man a sense of security by symbolizing an eternal environmental order.[39]

During the course of history the *genius loci* has remained a living reality, although it may not have been expressively named as such. Artists and writers have found inspiration in local character and have "explained" the phenomena of everyday life as well as art, referring to landscapes and urban milieu. Thus Goethe says: "It is evident, that the eye is educated by the things it sees from childhood on, and therefore Venetian painters must see everything clearer and with more joy than other people."[40] Still in 1960 Lawrence Durrell wrote: "As you get to know Europe slowly tasting the wines, cheeses and characters of the different countries you begin to realize that the important determinant of any culture is after all—the spirit of place."[41] Modern tourism proves that the experience of different places is a major human interest, although also this value today tends to get lost. In fact modern man for a long time believed that science and technology had freed him from a direct dependence on places.[42] This belief has proved an illusion; pollution and environmental chaos have suddenly appeared as a frightening *nemesis*, and as a result the problem of place has regained its true importance.

We have used the word "dwelling" to denote the total man-place relationship. To understand more fully what this word implies, it is useful to return to the distinction between "space" and "character." When man dwells, he is simultaneously located in space and exposed to a certain environmental character. The two psychological functions involved, may be called "orientation" and "identification."[43] To gain an existential foothold man has to be able to *orientate* himself; he has to know where he is. But he also has to *identify* himself with the environment, that is, he has to know *how* he is in a certain place.

The problem of orientation has been given a considerable attention in recent theoretical literature on planning and architecture. Again we may refer to the work of Kevin Lynch, whose concepts of "node," "path," and "district" denote the basic spatial structures which are the object of man's orientation. The perceived interrelationship of these elements constitute an "environmental image," and Lynch asserts: "A good environmental image gives its possessor an important sense of emotional security."[44] Accordingly all cultures have developed "systems of orientation," that is, spatial structures which facilitate the development of a good environmental image. "The world may be organized around a set of focal points, or be broken into named regions, or be linked by remembered routes."[45] Often these systems of orientation are based on or derived from a given natural structure. Where the system is weak, the image-making becomes difficult, and man feels "lost." "The terror of being lost comes from the necessity that a mobile organism be oriented in its surroundings."[46] To be lost is evidently the opposite of the feeling of security which distinguishes dwelling. The environmental quality which protects man against getting lost, Lynch calls "imageability," which means "that shape, colour, or arrangement which facilitates the making of vividly-identified, powerfully-structured, highly useful mental images of the environment."[47] Here Lynch implies that the elements which constitute the spatial structure are concrete "things" with "character" and "meaning." He limits himself, however, to discuss the spatial function of these elements, and thus leaves us with a fragmentary understanding of dwelling.

Nevertheless, the work of Lynch constitutes an essential contribution to the theory of place. Its importance also consists in the fact that his empirical studies of concrete urban structure confirm the general "principles of organization" defined by Gestalt psychology and by the researches into child psychology of [Jean] Piaget.[48]

Without reducing the importance of orientation, we have to stress that dwelling above all presupposes *identification* with the environment. Although orientation and identification are aspects of one total relationship, they have a certain independence within the totality. It is evidently possible to orientate oneself well without true identification; one gets along without feeling "at home." And it is possible to feel at home without being well acquainted with the spatial structure of the place, that is, the place is only experienced as a gratifying general character. True belonging however presupposes that both psychological functions are fully developed. In primitive societies we find that even the smallest environmental details are known and meaningful, and that they make up complex spatial structures.[49] In modern society, however, attention has almost exclusively been concentrated on the "practical" function of orientation, whereas identification has been left to chance. As a result true dwelling, in a psychological sense, has been substituted by alienation. It is therefore urgently needed to arrive at a fuller understanding of the concepts of "identification" and "character."

In our context "identification" means to become "friends" with a particular environment. Nordic man has to be friends with fog, ice, and cold winds; he has to enjoy the creaking sound of snow under the feet when he walks around, he has to experience the poetical value of being immersed in fog, as Hermann Hesse did when he wrote the lines: "strange to walk in fog! Lonely is every bush and stone, no tree sees the other, everything is alone..."[50] The Arab, instead, has to be a friend of the infinitely extended, sandy desert, and the burning sun. This does not mean that his settlements should not protect him against the natural "forces"; a desert settlement in fact primarily aims at the exclusion of sand and sun. But it implies that the environment is experienced as *meaningful.* [Otto Friedrich] Bollnow says appropriately: "Fede Stimmung ist Übereinstimmung," that is, every character consists in a correspondence between outer and inner world, and between body and psyche.[51] For modern urban man the friendship with a natural environment is reduced to fragmentary relations. Instead he has to identify with man-made things, such as streets and houses. The German-born American architect Gerhard Kallmann once told a story which illustrates what this means. Visiting at the end of the Second World War his native Berlin after many years of absence, he wanted to see the house where he had grown up. As must be expected in Berlin, the house had disappeared, and Mr. Kallmann felt somewhat lost. Then he suddenly recognized the typical pavement of the sidewalk: the floor on which he had played as a child! And he experienced a strong feeling of having returned home.

The story teaches us that the objects of identification are concrete environmental properties and that man's relationship to these is usually developed during childhood. The child grows up in green, brown, or white spaces; it walks or plays on sand, earth, stone, or moss, under a cloudy or serene sky; it grasps and lifts hard and soft things; it hears noises, such as the sound of the wind moving the leaves of a particular kind of tree; and it experiences heat and cold. Thus the child gets acquainted with the environment, and develops perceptual *schemata* which determine all future experiences.[52] The schemata comprise universal structures which are inter-human, as well as locally-determined and culturally-conditioned structures. Evidently every human being has to possess schemata of orientation as well as identification.

The *identity* of a person is defined in terms of the schemata developed, because they determine the "world" which is accessible. This fact is confirmed by common linguistic usage. When a person wants to tell who he is, it is in fact usual to say: "I am a New Yorker," or "I am a Roman." This means something much more concrete than to say: "I am an architect," or perhaps: "I am an optimist." We understand that human identity is to a high extent a function of places and things. Thus Heidegger says: "Wir sind die Be-Dingten."[53] It is therefore not only important that our environment has a spatial structure which facilitates orientation, but that it consists of concrete objects of identification. *Human identity presupposes the identity of place.*

Identification and orientation are primary aspects of man's being-in-the-world. Whereas identification is the basis for man's sense of *belonging*, orientation is the function which enables him to be that *homo viator* which is part of his nature. It is characteristic for modern man that for a long time he gave the role as a wanderer pride of place. He wanted to be "free" and conquer the world. Today we start to realize that true freedom presupposes belonging, and that "dwelling" means belonging to a concrete place.

The word to "dwell" has several connotations which confirm and illuminate our thesis. Firstly it ought to be mentioned that "dwell" is derived from the Old Norse *dvelja*, which meant to linger or remain. Analogously, Heidegger related the German "wohnen" to "bleiben" and "sich aufhalten."[54] Furthermore he points out that the Gothic *wunian* meant to "be at peace," "to remain in peace." The German word for "peace," *Friede*, means to be free, that is, protected from harm and danger. This protection is achieved by means of an *Umfriedung* or enclosure. *Friede* is also related to *zufrieden* (content), *Freund* (friend), and the Gothic *frijōn* (love). Heidegger uses these linguistic relationships to show that *dwelling means to be at peace in a protected place*. We should also mention that the German word for dwelling *Wohnung*, derives from *das Gewohnte*, which means what is known or habitual. "Habit" and "habitat" show an analogous relationship. In other words, man knows what has become accessible to him through dwelling. We here return to the *Übereinstimmung* or correspondence between man and his environment, and arrive at the very root of the problem of "gathering." To gather means that the everyday life-world has become "gewohnt" or "habitual." But gathering is a concrete phenomenon, and thus leads us to the final connotation of "dwelling." Again it is Heidegger who has uncovered a fundamental relationship. Thus he points out that the Old English and High German word for "building," *buan*, meant to dwell, and that it is intimately related to the verb *to be*. "What then does *ich bin* mean? The old word *bauen*, to which the *bin* belongs, answers: *ich bin, du bist*, mean: I dwell, you dwell. The way in which you are and I am, the manner in which we humans *are* on earth, is *buan*, dwelling."[55] We may conclude that dwelling means to gather the world as a concrete building or "thing," and that the archetypal act of building is the *Umfriedung* or enclosure. Trakl's poetic intuition of the inside-outside relationship thus gets its confirmation, and we understand that our concept of *concretization* denotes the essence of dwelling.[56]

Man dwells when he is able to concretize the world in buildings and things. As we have mentioned above, "concretization" is the function of the work of art, as opposed to the "abstraction" of science.[57] Works of art concretize what remains "between" the pure objects of science. Our everyday life-world *consists of* such "intermediary" objects, and we understand that the fundamental function of art is to gather the contradictions and complexities of the life-world. Being an *imago mundi,* the work of art helps man to dwell. [Friedrich] Hölderlin was right when he said:

> *Full of merit, yet poetically, man*
> *Dwells on this earth.*

This means: man's merits do not count much if he is unable to dwell *poetically,* that is, to dwell in the true sense of the word. Thus Heidegger says: "Poetry does not fly above and surmount the earth in order to escape it and hover over it. Poetry is what first brings man onto the earth, making him belong to it, and thus brings him into dwelling."[58] Only poetry in all its forms (also as the "art of living") makes human existence meaningful, and *meaning* is the fundamental human need.

Architecture belongs to poetry, and its purpose is to help man to dwell. But architecture is a difficult art. To make practical towns and buildings is not enough. Architecture comes into being when a "total environment is made visible," to quote the definition of Suzanne Langer.[59] In general, this means to concretize the *genius loci.* We have seen that this is done by means of buildings which gather the properties of the place and bring them close to man. The basic act of architecture is therefore to understand the "vocation" of the place. In this way we protect the earth and become ourselves part of a comprehensive totality. What is here advocated is not some kind of "environmental determinism." We only recognize the fact that man is an integral part of the environment, and that it can only lead to human alienation and environmental disruption if he forgets that. To belong to a place means to have an existential foothold, in a concrete everyday sense. When God said to Adam: "You shall be a fugitive and a wanderer on the Earth"[60] he put man in front of his most basic problem: to cross the threshold and regain the lost place.

1   R. M. Rilke, *The Duino Elegies,* IX Elegy, (New York: 1972).
2   The concept "everyday life-world" was introduced by Husserl in *The Crisis of European Sciences and Transcendental Phenomenology* (1936).
3   Martin Heidegger, "Bauen Wohnen Denken"; Bollnow, "Mensch und Raum"; Merleau-Ponty, "Phenomenology of Perception"; Bachelard, "Poetics of Space"; also L. Kruse, *Räumliche Umwelt* (Berlin: 1974).
4   Heidegger, "Language," in Albert Hofstadter, ed., *Poetry, Language, Thought* (New York: 1971).
5   Ein Winterabend
        Wenn der Schnee ans Fenster fällt,
        Lang die Abendglocke läutet,
        Vielen ist der Tisch bereitet
        Und das Haus ist wohlbestellt.
        Mancher auf der Wanderschaft
        Kommt ans Tor auf dunklen Pfaden.
        Golden blüht der Baum der Gnaden
        Aus der Erde kühlem Saft.
        Wanderer tritt still herein;
        Schmerz versteinerte die Schwelle.
        Da erglänzt in reiner Helle
        Auf dem Tische Brot und Wein.

6   Heidegger, *Poetry*, op. cit., 199.
7   Ibid., 204.
8   Christian Norberg-Schulz, "symbolization," in *Intentions in Architecture* (Oslo and London: 1963).
9   See for instance J. Appleton, *The Experience of Landscape* (London: 1975).
10 Heidegger, *Poetry*, op. cit., 149.
11 Ibid., 147, 149.
12 Heidegger, *Hebel der Hausfreund* (Pfullingen: 1957), 13.
13 Ibid., 13.
14 Heidegger, *Poetry*, op. cit., 181–182.
15 Norberg-Schulz, *Existence, Space and Architecture* (London and New York: 1971), where the concept "existential space" is used.
16 Heidegger points out the relationship between the words *gegen* (against, opposite) and *Gegend* (environment, locality).
17 This has been done by some writers such as K. Graf von Dürckheim, E. Straus, and O.F. Bollnow.
18 We may compare with Alberti's distinction between "beauty" and "ornament."
19 Norberg-Schulz, *Existence*, op. cit., 12ff.
20 S. Giedion, *The Eternal Present: The Beginnings of Architecture* (London: 1964).
21 K. Lynch, *The Image of the City* (Cambridge: 1960).
22 P. Portoghesi, *Le inibizioni dell'architettura moderna* (Bari: 1975), 88ff.
23 Heidegger, *Poetry*, op. cit., 154.
24 Norberg-Schulz, *Existence*, op. cit., 18.
25 Heidegger, *Poetry*, op. cit., 154. "Presence is the old word for being."
26 O.F. Bollnow, *Das Wesen der Stimmungen* (Franfurt am Mein: 1956).
27 Robert Venturi, *Complexity and Contradiction in Architecture* (New York: 1967), 88.
28 Ibid., 89.
29 Heidegger "Die Frage nach der Technik," in *Vorträge und Aufsätze Pfullingen* (1954), 12.
30 Norberg-Schulz, *Existence*, op. cit., 27.
31 Ibid., 32.
32 D. Frey, *Grundlegung zu einer vergleichenden Kunstwissenschaft* (Vienna and Innsbruck: 1949).
33 Norberg-Schulz, *Intentions*, op. cit.
34 Heidegger, *Poetry*, op. cit., 152.
35 W. J. Richardson, *Heidegger, Through Phenomenology to Thought* (The Hague: 1974), 585.
36 For the concept of "capacity" see Norberg-Schulz, *Intentions*, op. cit.
37 Venturi, *Complexity and Contradiction*, op. cit.
38 Paulys, *Realencyclopedie der Klassischen Altertumwissenschaft* VII, I, col. 1155ff.
39 Norberg-Schulz, *Meaning in Western Architecture* (London and New York: 1975), 10ff.
40 Goethe, *Italienische Reise* 8 (October 1786).
41 L. Durrell, *Spirit of Place* (London: 1969), 156.
42 See M.M. Webber, *Explorations into Urban Structure* (Philadelphia: 1963), who talks about "non-place urban realm."
43 Norberg-Schulz, *Intentions*, op. cit., where the concepts "cognitive orientation" and "cathectic orientation" are used.
44 Lynch, *The Image of the City*, op. cit., 4.
45 Ibid., 7.
46 Ibid., 125.
47 Ibid., 9.
48 For a detailed discussion, see Norberg-Schulz, *Existence*, op. cit.
49 A. Rapoport, "Australian Aborigines and the Definition of Place," in P. Oliver, ed., *Shelter, Sign and Symbol* (London: 1975).
50 Seltsam, *im Nebel zu wandern! Einsam ist jeder Busch und Stein, kein Baum sieht den anderen, jeder ist allein.*
51 Bollnow, *Stimmungen*, op. cit., 39.

52   Norberg-Schulz, *Intentions*, op. cit., 41ff.
53   Heidegger, *Poetry*, op. cit., 181. "We are the be-thinged," the conditioned ones.
54   Heidegger, "Building Dwelling Thinking," in *Poetry*, op. cit., 146ff.
55   Ibid., 147.
56   Norberg-Schulz, *Intentions*, op. cit., 61ff, 68.
57   Ibid., 168ff.
58   Heidegger, *Poetry*, op. cit., 218.
59   S. Langer, *Feeling and Form* (New York: 1953).
60   *Genesis*, chapter 4, verse 12.

Heidegger's Thinking on Architecture
Christian Norberg-Schulz

This lucid explication of "Heidegger's Thinking on
Architecture" closely analyzes several of the philosopher's writings linguistically, following Martin
Heidegger's own interest in the etymology of words in
current usage. Broadly speaking, it develops Christian
Norberg-Schulz's critique of modern architecture,
which, he claims, has created a crisis of meaning by
creating a diagrammatic, functionalist environment that
does not allow for *dwelling*. Pointing to "a moment of
confusion and crisis," Norberg-Schulz acknowledges
that the problem of meaning in architecture has been
approached by others, some using semiology (studying
architecture as a system of conventional *signs*), a
method he finds inadequate to explain architecture.
His alternative is to understand architecture through a
reading of Heideggerian phenomenology.

The purpose of architecture, he states, is to provide an "existential foothold," one which provides "orientation" in space and "identification" with the specific
character of a place. The opposite of alienation, the
concept of an "existential foothold" suggests that the
environment is experienced as meaningful. (Very different approaches to the problem of alienation are taken
by Peter Eisenman and Anthony Vidler in their essays
on the grotesque and the uncanny in chapter 14.) He
demonstrates an understanding of the significance of
difference in the production of meaning: "a boundary
may also be understood as a threshold, i.e., as an
embodiment of a difference." In "The Phenomenon of
Place," Norberg-Schulz cites the influence of Kevin
Lynch's *Image of the City* (1960), in which he
describes the elements that make the city "legible."
Lynch's elements—node, landmark, path, edge, district—are thus orienting features of the city, functioning
like Norberg-Schulz's *place*.

For Norberg-Schulz, architecture makes the world
visible and spatial, gathering its presence in a *thing*.
In other words, the work of architecture presents, or
"brings something into presence"; it is not representational. Phenomenological positions are taken by writers
in this and the following three chapters, including
Kenneth Frampton, Juhani Pallasmaa, Tadao Ando,
Raimund Abraham, Vittorio Gregotti, and Marco
Frascari. In addition, Karsten Harries speaks as a
phenomenologist on ethical issues in chapter eight.

CHRISTIAN NORBERG-SCHULZ
HEIDEGGER'S THINKING ON ARCHITECTURE

Heidegger did not leave us any text on architecture, yet it plays an important role in his philosophy. His concept of being-in-the-world implies a man-made environment, and when discussing the problem of "dwelling poetically," he explicitly refers to the art of building. An exposition of [Martin] Heidegger's thinking on architecture therefore ought to be a part of our interpretation of his philosophy. Such an exposition may also contribute to a better understanding of the complex environmental problems of our time.

In his essay "The Origin of the Work of Art," a major example is taken from architecture, which we shall use as our point of departure:

> A building, a Greek temple, portrays nothing. It simply stands there in the middle of the rock-cleft valley. The building encloses the figure of the god, and in this conceal-ment lets it stand out into the holy precinct through the open portico. By means of the temple, the god is present in the temple. This presence of the god is in itself the exten-sion and delimitation of the precinct as a holy precinct. The temple and its precinct, however, do not fade away into the indefinite. It is the templework that first fits togeth-er and at the same time gathers around itself the unity of those paths and relations in which birth and death, disaster and blessing, victory and disgrace, endurance and decline acquire the shape of destiny for human being. The all-governing expanse of this open relational context is the world of this historical people. Only from and in this expanse does the nation first return to itself for the fulfillment of its vocation.
> Standing there, the building rests on the rocky ground. This resting of the work draws up out of the rock the mystery of that rock's clumsy yet spontaneous support. Standing there, the building holds its ground against the storm raging above it and so first makes

From *Perspecta: The Yale Architectural Journal* 20 (1983): 61–68. Courtesy of the publisher.

the storm itself manifest in its violence. The luster and gleam of the stone, though itself apparently glowing only by the grace of the sun, yet first brings to light the light of the day, the breadth of the sky, the darkness of the night. The temple's firm towering makes visible the invisible space of air. The steadfastness of the work contrasts with the surge of the surf, and its own repose brings out the raging of the sea. Tree and grass, eagle and bull, snake and cricket first enter into their distinctive shapes and thus come to appear as what they are. The Greeks called this emerging and rising in itself and in all things *phusis*. It clears and illuminates, also, that on which and in which man bases his dwelling. We call this ground the *earth*. What this word says is not to be associated with the idea of a mass or matter deposited somewhere, or with the merely astronomical idea of a planet. Earth is that whence the arising brings back and shelters everything that arises without violation. In the things that arise, earth is present as the sheltering agent. The temple-work, standing there, opens up a world and at the same time sets this world back again on earth, which itself only thus emerges as native ground. But men and animals, plants and things, are never present and familiar as unchangeable objects, only to represent incidentally also a fitting environment for the temple, which one fine day is added to what is already there. We shall get closer to what *is*, rather, if we think of all this in reverse order, assuming of course that we have, to begin with, an eye for how differently everything then faces us. Mere reversing, done for its own sake, reveals nothing. The temple, in its standing there, first gives to things their look and to men their out-look on themselves.[1]

What does this passage tell us? First of all we have to consider the context in which the quotation is used. When Heidegger mentions the temple, he does so to illuminate the nature of the work of art. Deliberately he chooses to describe a work "that cannot be ranked as representational." That is, the work of art does not represent; rather it presents; it brings something into presence. Heidegger defines this something as "truth."[2] The example moreover shows that a building according to Heidegger is, or may be, a work of art. As a work of art the building "preserves truth." *What* is thus preserved, and *how* is it done? The quotation indicates answers to both questions, but we shall also have to refer to other writings of Heidegger's to arrive at the needed understanding.

The *what* in our question comprises three components. First, the temple makes the god present. Second, it fits together what shapes the destiny of human being. Finally, the temple makes all the things of the earth visible: the rock, the sea, the air, the plants, the animals, and even the light of the day and the darkness of the night. In general, the temple "opens up a world and at the same time sets this world back again on earth." In doing this, it sets truth into work.

To understand what all this means, we may look at the second question, the *how*. Four times Heidegger repeats that the temple does what it does by "standing there." Both words are important. The temple does not stand anywhere, it stands *there*, "in the middle of the rock-cleft valley." The words rock-cleft valley are certainly not introduced as an ornament. Rather they indicate that temples are built in particular, prominent places. By means of the building the place gets extension and delimitation, whereby a holy precinct for the god is formed. In other words, the given place possesses a hidden meaning which is revealed by the temple. How the building makes the destiny of the people present, is not explicit, but it is implied that this is done simultaneously with the housing of the god, that is: the fate of the people is also intimately related to the place. The visualization of the earth, finally, is taken care of by the temple's standing. Thus it *rests* on the ground, and *towers* into the air. In doing this, it gives to things their look. Heidegger also emphasizes that the temple is not added to what is already there, but that the building first makes the things emerge as what they are.

Heidegger's interpretation of architecture as a "setting-into-work of truth" is new, and may even seem bewildering. Today we are used to thinking of art in terms of expression and representation, and consider man or society its origin. Heidegger, however, emphasizes that "it is not the 'N.N. fecit' that is to be made known. Rather, the simple 'factum est' is to be held forth into the Open by the work."[3] This factum is revealed when a world is opened up to give things their look. *World* and *thing* are hence interdependent concepts, which we have to consider to arrive at a better understanding of Heidegger's theory. In "The Origin of the Work of Art" Heidegger does not offer any true explanation and he even remarks that "here, the nature of world can only be indicated." In *Being and Time*, however, he defines world ontically as the totality of things, and ontologically as the Being of these things. In particular, the word means the *wherein* a human being is living.[4] In his later writings he offers an interpretation of this wherein as a fourfold of earth, sky, mortals, and divinities. Again we may feel bewilderment, being used to thinking of world in terms of physical, social, or cultural structures. Evidently Heidegger wants to remind us of the fact that our everyday life-world really consists of concrete *things*, rather than the abstractions of science. Thus he says:

Earth is the building bearer, nourishing with its fruits, tending water and rock, plant and animal.

The sky is the sun's path, the course of the moon, the glitter of the stars, the year's seasons, the light and dusk of day, the gloom and glow of night, the clemency and inclemency of the weather, the drifting clouds and blue depth of the ether.

The divinities are the beckoning messengers of the godhead. Out of the hidden sway of the divinities the god emerges as what he is, which removes him from any comparison with beings that are present. The mortals are human beings. They are called mortals because they can die. To die means to be capable of death as death.[5]

Each of the four is what it is because it mirrors the others. They all belong together in a "mirror-play" which constitutes the world.[6] The mirror-play may be understood as an open "between," wherein things appear as what they are. In his essay on Johan Peter Hebel, Heidegger in fact talks about man's stay "between earth and sky, between birth and death, between joy and pain, between work and word," and calls this "multifarious between" the *world*.[7] We see, thus, that Heidegger's world is a concrete totality, as was already suggested by the references made in the discussion of the Greek temple. Rather than being conceived as a distant world of ideas, it is given here and now.

As the totality of things, the world is however not a mere collection of objects. When Heidegger understands the thing as a manifestation of the fourfold he revives the original meaning of *thing* as a coming together or "gathering."[8] Thus he says: "Things visit mortals with a world."[9] Heidegger also offers examples to illustrate the nature of the thing. A jug is a thing, as is a bridge, and they gather the fourfold each in their own way. Both examples are relevant in our context. The jug, thus, forms part of that equipment which constitutes man's proximal environment, whereas the bridge is a building which discloses more comprehensive properties of the surroundings. Thus Heidegger says:

> The bridge *gathers* the earth as landscape around the stream....It does not just connect banks that are already there. The banks emerge as banks only as the bridge crosses the stream.[10]

The bridge thus makes a *place* come into presence, at the same time as its elements emerge as what they are. The words "earth" and "landscape" are not used here as mere topographical concepts, but to denote *things* that are disclosed through the gathering of the bridge. Human life takes place on earth, and the bridge makes this fact manifest. What Heidegger wants to reveal in his examples, is the *thingness* of the things, that is, the world they gather. In *Being and Time* the technique used was called "phenomenology."[11] Later, however, he introduced the term *Andenken* to indicate that kind of genuine thought which is needed to disclose a thing as a gathering. In this kind of thought *language* comes to play a primary role as a source of understanding.

When Heidegger wrote "The Origin of the Work of Art" he had not yet arrived at the concept of the fourfold, but in the description of the Greek temple all the elements are there: the god, the human beings, the earth, and, implicitly, the sky. As a thing, the temple relates to all of them, and makes them appear as what they are, at the same time as they are united into a "simple onefold." The temple is manmade, and is deliberately created to reveal a world. Natural things, however, also gather the fourfold, and ask for an interpretation which discloses their thingness. This disclosure happens in poetry, and in general in language which "itself is poetry in the essential sense."[12] Language, by naming beings for the first time, first brings beings to word and to appearance.[13]

The last quotation shows that in order to grasp Heidegger's theory of art we also have to consider his notion of language. Just as he does not understand art as representation, he cannot accept the interpretation of language as a means of communication, based on habit and convention. When things are named for the first time, they are recognized as what they are. Before they were just transient phenomena, but the names *keep* them, and a world is opened up. Language is therefore the original art, and discloses "that into which human being as historical is already cast. This is the earth and, for an historical people it's earth, the self-closing ground on which it rests together with everything that already is, though still hidden from itself. It is, however, its world, which prevails in virtue of the relation of human being to the unconcealedness of Being."[14]

The quotation is important because it tells us that the earth and the world of an historical people are what they are because they are related to the earth and the world in general. Language keeps *the* world but is used to say *a* world. Heidegger accordingly defines language as the "House of Being." Man *dwells* in language, that is: when he listens to and responds to language the world which he is, is opened up, and an authentic existence becomes possible. Heidegger calls this to "dwell poetically."[15] Thus he says:

But where do we humans get our information about the nature of dwelling and poetry? ....[We receive] it from the telling of language. Of course, only when and only as long as [we respect] language's own nature.[16]

Language's own nature is poetical, and when we use language poetically the house of being is opened.

Poetry speaks in images, Heidegger says, and "the nature of the image is to let something be seen. By contrast, copies and imitations are mere variations on the genuine image...which lets the invisible be seen..."[17] What this means is beautifully shown by Heidegger in his analysis of [Georg] Trakl's poem "A Winter Evening."[18] What, then, is the origin of poetical images? Heidegger answers explicitly: "Memory is the source of poetry."[19] The German word for memory, *Gedächtnis*, means "what has been thought." Here we must, however, understand "thought" in the sense of *Andenken*, that is, as the disclosure of "thingness" or the Being of beings." Heidegger points out that the Greeks already understood the relation between memory and poetry. To them the goddess Mnemosyne, memory, was the mother of the Muses, with Zeus as the father. Zeus needed memory to bring forth art: Mnemosyne herself was the daughter of the earth and the sky, which implies that the memories which give rise to art are our understanding of the relationship between earth and sky. Neither earth alone nor sky alone produces a work of art. Being a goddess Mnemosyne is also simultaneously human and divine, and her daughters are hence understood as the children of a complete world: earth, sky, humans, and divinities. The poetic image is therefore truly integral, and radically different from the analytic categories of logic and science. "Only image formed keeps the vision," Heidegger says and he adds: Yet image formed rests in the poem."[20] In other words, memory is kept in language.

What a poem and a work of art have in common is the quality of image. A work is in addition a thing, whereas a thing proper does not possess the quality of image. As a gathering it mirrors the fourfold in its way, but its thingness is hidden and has to be disclosed by a work.[21] In "The Origin of the Work of Art" Heidegger shows how [Vincent] van Gogh's painting of a pair of peasant shoes reveals the thingness of the shoes. By themselves, the shoes are mute, but the work of art speaks for them. Van Gogh's painting may be called a representational image, but we have to emphasize that its quality as a work of art does not reside in its being a representation. Other works of art, in particular works of architecture, do not portray anything, and are hence to be understood as non-representational images. What is a non-representational image? To answer this question we first have to say a few more words about man-made things as such.

Although poetry is the original art it does not exhaust the disclosure of truth. In poetic language truth is brought "to word." But it also has to be "set-into-work." Human life takes place between earth and sky in a concrete sense and the things which constitute the place have to be disclosed in their immediate presence. It is this kind of disclosure which is accomplished by the Greek temple. Thus Heidegger says that a man dwells "between work and word." The word opens up the world, the work gives the world presence. In the work the world is set back on earth, that is, it becomes part of the immediate here and now, whereby the latter is disclosed in its being. Heidegger in fact emphasizes that "Staying with things is the only way in which the fourfold stay within the fourfold is accomplished at any time..."[22] When man stays with things in a fourfold way, he "saves the earth, receives the sky, awaits the divinities, and initiates the mortals."[23] Therefore "mortals nurse and nurture things that grow and specially construct things that do not grow."[24] Buildings are such constructed things, which gather a world and allow for dwelling. In the Hebel essay Heidegger says:

> The buildings bring the earth as the inhabited landscape close to man and at the same time place the nearness of neighbourly dwelling under the expanse of the sky.[25]

This statement offers a clue to the problem of architectural gathering. What is gathered, Heidegger says, is the "inhabited landscape." An inhabited landscape obviously is a *known* landscape, that is, something that is *gewohnt*. This landscape is brought close to us by the buildings,[26] or in other words, the landscape is revealed as what it is in truth.

What, however, is a landscape? A landscape is a space where human life takes place. It is therefore not a mathematical, isomorphic space, but a "lived space" between earth and sky. In *Being and Time* Heidegger points out that "what is within-the-world is also within space,"[27] and explains the concrete nature of this space referring to *above* as what is on the ceiling and *below* as what is on the floor. He also mentions sunrise, midday, sunset, and midnight, which he relates to the regions of life and death.[28] Already in his early *magnum opus*, the notion of the fourfold was implicit. In general he points out that spatiality (*Räumlichkeit*) is a property of being-in-the-world. The discussion of the Greek temple indicates the nature of spatiality. Thus the building defines a precinct or a space in the narrower sense of the word, at the same time as it discloses the nature of this space by standing there. In his essay "Building Dwelling Thinking" Heidegger makes this more precise, saying that buildings are *locations* and that "the location *admits* the fourfold and *installs* the fourfold."[29] Admittance (*Einräumen*) and installment (*Einrichten*) are the two aspects of spatiality as location. The location makes room for the fourfold and simultaneously discloses the fourfold as a built thing. Space is therefore not given a priori, but is provided for by locations. "Building never shapes pure 'space' as a single entity...(but) because it produces things as locations, building is closer to the nature of space and to the origin of the nature of 'space' than any geometry and mathematics."[30] A location or "lived space" is generally called a *place*, and architecture may be defined as the *making of places*.

In a late essay "Art and Space," Heidegger in more detail discusses the twofold nature of spatiality.[31] First he points out that the German word *Raum*, (space) originates from *räumen*, that is, the "freeing of places for human dwelling." "The place opens a domain, in gathering things which here belong together."[32] "We must learn to understand that the things themselves are the places and that they do not simply belong to the place."[33] Second, the places are embodied by means of sculptural forms. These embodiments are the characters which constitute the place.[34] Sculptural embodiment is therefore the "incarnation of the truth of Being in a work which founds its place."[35] Heidegger's statements here may be related to his description of the temple as a body which stands, rests, and towers. The thingness of a building is hence determined by its being between earth and sky as a sculptural form. In general this lines up with Heidegger's saying that the building sets the world back on earth. Setting back on earth means embodiment, or in other words, that the fourfold is brought into a thing through the act of building, in the sense of *poiesis*. The earth thus *keeps* the world that is opened up.

The simultaneous opening and keeping may be understood as a conflict which Heidegger calls the "rift" (*Riss*). "The conflict, however, is not a rift as a mere cleft is ripped open; rather, it is the intimacy with which opponents belong together." "The rift does not let the opponents break apart; it brings the opposition of measure and boundary into their common outline."[36] The world, thus, offers a measure to things, whereas the earth as embodiment provides a boundary. If we refer this to our context, we may say that a place is determined (*be-dingt*) by its boundary. Architecture occurs in the boundary as an embodiment of world. Thus Heidegger says: "A boundary is not that at which something stops but, as the Greeks recognized, the boundary is that from which something begins its presencing."[37] A boundary may also be understood as a threshold, that is, as an embodiment of a *difference*. In his analysis of Trakl's "A Winter Evening," Heidegger shows how the threshold carries the unity and difference of world and thing (earth).[38] In a building the threshold separates and simultaneously unites an outside and an inside, that is, what is alien and what is habitual. It is a gathering middle where an outlook on the world is opened up and set back on earth.

Boundary and threshold are constituent elements of place. They form part of a figure which discloses the spatiality in question. In German its nature is beautifully shown by language itself, as the word *Riss* means rift as well as plan. The rift is fixed in place by a *Grund-riss* as well as an *Auf-riss*, that is, by a plan and an elevation, whereby the twofold nature of spatiality again becomes apparent. Together, plan and elevation make up a figure or *Gestalt*. "Gestalt is the structure in whose shape the rift composes and submits itself."[39] The word Gestalt evidently could be replaced by "image," whereby we gain an important clue to the understanding of the architectural image. As the image comprises an elevation, it is a thing rather than a mere geometrical diagram. "Standing there" as elevation, the architectural image sets the rift "back into the heavy weight of stone, the dumb hardness of wood, the dark glow of colours."[40]

Here Heidegger's thinking on the art of building stops. In a certain sense it stops outside architecture itself, as it does not treat the problems of the architectural Gestalt as such. And in fact Heidegger starts his essay "Building Dwelling Thinking," saying: "This thinking on building does not presume to discover architectural ideas, let alone give rules for building."[41] The statement clearly shows that for Heidegger the arts have their particular professional problems, which he, as a philosopher, did not feel qualified to discuss. His aim was not to offer any explanation, but to help man get back to authentic dwelling. All the same, he certainly laid a foundation for the field, and demonstrated that his *Andenken* may bring us far "on the way to architecture."[42] To sum up, we may repeat the main points of Heidegger's thinking on architecture. The general point of departure is the thought that the world only emerges as what it is, when it is "said" or "set into work." The discussion of the Greek temple illustrates this idea, stating that the work "opens up a world" and "first gives to things their look." Already in *Being and Time*, Heidegger emphasized that "discourse is existentially equiprimordial with state-of-mind and understanding."[43] In other words, it is impossible to consider the world separately from language, which is understood as the *House of Being*. Language names things which "visit man with a world," and man's access to the world is through listening and responding to language. Thus Heidegger quotes [Friedrich] Hölderlin's dictum: *Wat bleibt aber, stiften die Dichter*, what remains, the *factum est*, is founded by the poets.

To give the world immediate presence, however, man also has to set truth into work. The primary purpose of architecture is hence to make a world visible. It does this as a thing, and the world it brings into presence consists in what it gathers. Evidently a work of architecture does not make a total world visible, but only certain of its aspects. These aspects are comprised in the concept of spatiality. Heidegger explicitly distinguishes spatiality from space in a mathematical sense. Spatiality is a concrete term denominating a domain (*Gegend*) of things which constitute an inhabited landscape.[44] The Greek example in fact starts with the image of a rock-cleft valley and later refers to several concrete elements of earth and sky. But it also suggests that landscape cannot be isolated from human life and from what is divine. The inhabited landscape therefore is a manifestation of the fourfold, and comes into presence through the buildings which bring it close to man. We could also say that inhabited landscape denominates the spatiality of the fourfold. This spatiality becomes manifest as a particular *between* of earth and sky, that is, as a *place*.[45]

When we say that life takes place, we imply that man's being-in-the-world mirrors the between of earth and sky. Man *is* in this between, standing, resting, and acting. The natural and man-made things which constitute the boundaries of the between, also stand, rest, and tower, to recall the terms used in Heidegger's description of the Greek temple. Thus they embody characters which mirror man's state-of-mind (*Befindlichkeit*), at the same time as they delimit a precinct which admits man's actions. A work of architecture therefore discloses the spatiality of the fourfold through its standing there. Standing there, it admits life to happen in a concrete place of rocks and plants, water and air, light and darkness, animals and men.[46] Standing there, however, implies that what is standing must be understood as a materialized image. It is the "luster and gleam of the stone which brings to light the light of the day, the breadth of the sky, the darkness of the night." A work of architecture is therefore not an abstract organization of space. It is an embodied Gestalt, where the *Grundriss* mirrors the admittance and the *Aufriss* the mode of standing.[47] Thus it brings the inhabited landscape close to man, and lets him dwell poetically, which is the ultimate aim of architecture.

We have already pointed out that Heidegger does not offer any further explanation of the architectural Gestalt or image. The discussion of the Greek temple, however, suggests its nature. The words "extension," "delimitation," "standing," "resting," and "towering," refer to modes of being-in-the-world in terms of spatiality. Although the possibilities are infinite, the modes always appear as variations on archetypes. We all know some of these, as column, gable, arch, dome, or tower. The very fact that language names these things, proves their importance as types of images which visualize the basic structure of spatiality.[48] But here we go beyond the limits of the present essay, and enter the field of architectural theory proper.

Heidegger's thinking on architecture is of great immediate interest. At a moment of confusion and crisis, it may help us to arrive at an authentic understanding of our field. Between the two wars, architectural practice was founded on the concept of "functionalism," which got its classical definition in the slogan "Form follows function."[49] The architectural solution should, thus, be derived directly from the patterns of practical use.

During the last decades it has become increasingly clear that this pragmatic approach leads to a schematic and characterless environment, with insufficient possibilities for human dwelling. The problem of *meaning* in architecture has therefore come to the fore.[50] So far, it has mostly been approached in semiological terms, whereby architecture is understood as a system of conventional signs.[51] Considering architectural forms as representations of something else, semiological analysis has, however, proved incapable of explaining works of architecture as such. Here Heidegger comes to our rescue. His thinking on architecture as a visualization of truth restores its artistic dimension and hence its human significance.[52] By means of the concepts of world, thing, and work, he leads us out of the impasse of scientific abstraction, and back to what is concrete, that is, to the *things themselves.*

This does not mean, however, that the problems are solved. Today we are only at a beginning. This is apparent in architectural practice, where functionalism is being abandoned while a new architecture of images is emerging.[53] Heidegger's thinking may help us to understand what this implies, and his *Andenken* is certainly the method we need to gain a fuller understanding of the things themselves. In his essay "Building Dwelling Thinking," Heidegger in fact concludes that "thinking itself belongs to dwelling in the same sense as building....Building and thinking are, each in its own way, inescapable for dwelling."[54] In other words, we have to give thought to the thingness of things in order to arrive at a total vision of our world. Through such a poetical *Andenken* we take "the measure for architecture, the structure of dwelling."[55]

1   Martin Heidegger, *Poetry, Language, Thought,* Hofstadter, ed. (New York: Harper & Row, 1971), 41ff.
2   Ibid., 36.
3   Ibid., 65.
4   Martin Heidegger, *Being and Time* (New York: Harper, 1962), 93.
5   Heidegger, *Poetry,* op. cit., 178.
6   Ibid., 179.
7   Martin Heidegger, *Hebel der Hausfreund* (Pfullingen: G. Neske, 1957), 13.
8   Heidegger, *Poetry,* op. cit., 174.
9   Ibid., 200.
10 Ibid., 152.
11 Heidegger, *Being and Time,* op. cit., 58ff.
12 Heidegger, *Poetry,* op. cit., 74.
13 Ibid., 73.
14 Ibid., 75.
15 We may in this context be reminded of Rilke's IX Elegy: Are we perhaps *here* to say: house, bridge, fountain, gate, jug, fruit tree, window—at best: column, tower..."
16 Heidegger, *Poetry,* op. cit., 215.
17 Ibid., 226.
18 Ibid., 194ff.
19 Martin Heidegger, *Vorträge und Aufsätze* II (Pfullingen: G. Neske, 1954), 11.
20 Heidegger, *Poetry,* op. cit., 7.
21 We may again recall Rilke's IX Elegy: "And these things, that live only in passing...look to us, the most fugitive, for rescue."
22 Heidegger, *Poetry,* op. cit., 151.
23 Ibid., 150.

24 Ibid., 151.

25 Heidegger, *Hebel der Hausfreund,* op. cit., 13.

26 In *Hebel der Hausfreund,* Heidegger explicitly considers villages and cities "buildings" in this context.

27 Heidegger, *Being and Time,* op. cit., 135.

28 Ibid., 137.

29 Heidegger, *Poetry,* op. cit., 158.

30 Ibid., 158.

31 Martin Heidegger, *Die Kunst und der Raum* (St. Gallen: 1969).

32 Ibid., 10.

33 Ibid., 11.

34 Ibid., 12.

35 Ibid., 13.

36 Heidegger, *Poetry,* op. cit., 63.

37 Ibid., 154.

38 Ibid., 202.

39 Ibid., 64.

40 Ibid., 63.

41 Ibid., 145.

42 It is interesting to notice that Heidegger's basic ideas on world, thing, spatiality and building were implicit already in *Being and Time* (1927). "The Origin of the Work of Art" (1935) does not represent a new departure, but rather brings us a step further on the way. The later essays on "The Thing" (1950) and "Building Dwelling Thinking" (1951) as well as the late text on "Art and Space" (1969), clarify and organize the thoughts contained in "The Origin of the Work of Art." In our opinion, therefore, Heidegger's thinking shows great consistency and may certainly be understood as a "way," a metaphor he himself liked to use.

43 Heidegger, *Being and Time,* op. cit., 203.

44 Heidegger's term *Gegund* (in *Gelassenheit* [Pfullingen: 1959], 38ff) may be translated with "domain" or "region."

45 On several occasions Heidegger uses the German word *Ort,* for instance in "Art and Space" where we read: "Der Ort öffnet jeweils eine Gegend, indem er die Dinge auf das Zusammengehören in ihr versammelt." This sentence presents Heidegger's thinking on architecture in a nutshell!

46 This is also how the world is described in *Genesis* I.

47 It is therefore something more than a matter of convenience when architects present their projects by means of plans and elevations.

48 We may infer that a theory and history of archetypes is urgently needed.

49 Louis Sullivan, who coined the phrase, hardly intended it in a radical functionalist sense.

50 See C. Jencks and G. Baird, eds., *Meaning in Architecture* (London: Design Yearbook Limited, 1969).

51 See G. Broadbent, R. Bunt, and C. Jencks, eds., *Signs, Symbols and Architecture* (Chichester: Wiley, 1980).

52 This was also accomplished by Louis Kahn, whose conception of architecture comes surprisingly close to Heidegger's thinking. See C. Norberg-Schulz, "Kahn, Heidegger and the Language of Architecture," *Oppositions* 18 (New York: 1979).

53 See C. Norberg-Schulz, "Chicago: vision and image," in *New Chicago Architecture* (Chicago: Rizzoli, 1981).

54 Heidegger, *Poetry,* op. cit., 150.

55 Ibid., 227.

INTRODUCTION

On Reading Heidegger
Kenneth Frampton

This essay (which precedes the others in this chapter) only touches peripherally on Martin Heidegger, but offers the phenomenological idea of *place* as a solution to the many urban and environmental problems that theorist and educator Kenneth Frampton observes. The operations of capitalism, emphasizing short term planning, have produced a "motopic" suburban sprawl of maximum profit and maximum consumption of land and energy. Architects seem unable, at present, to create places, and planners rush to rationalize the commercial strip. The lack of differentiation in the built world leads Frampton to the realization "that should we stop, there are few places which any of us might significantly choose to be." This statement brings to mind Italo Calvino's *Invisible Cities*, in which one is not sure if one has arrived or left the surreal, "continuous city" of Penthesilea.[1]

Within the discipline, Frampton notices four contemporary conditions that diminish the potential contribution of architecture to dwelling. First is the failure to distinguish between architecture and building, and an assumption that all work is architecture. (This assumption contrasts with Adolf Loos's restriction of architecture to just the monument and the tomb, and with Hannes Meyer's idea that everything is building.) Second is the passive acceptance of industrialized construction, in lieu of demanding craftsmanship. Third is the pursuit of an autonomous practice, which is counter to "place-making," and to "being in the world." Fourth, and equally significant, is the loss of rapport with nature, evident in the efficient, relentless, technological destruction of resources, which diminishes the possibility of a fulfilling life. Frampton sees all of these conditions as having ethical implications. (ch. 8)

The primary aspect of his proposal is a renewed attention to the spatial quality of containment by which architecture demarcates a *place*. In addition to its quality of enclosure or boundedness, place as envisioned by Heidegger and Aristotle has an important symbolic and political role representing the structure of social relations, or the *res publica*. Next he calls for "an environmental dialectic of production," a sort of cost-benefit analysis considering qualitative as well as quantitative aspects. (This attempt at different, nonmonetary means of valuation is currently receiving much attention in the field of environmental ethics.) Frampton develops his response to these concerns in his theory of Critical Regionalism, (1983, ch. 11) hints of which are found in this article. Persisting as important themes in his work are the necessity of tempering the products of industrialization with a craft sensibility; the resistance to "optimization," "the tyranny of technique," and kitsch; and the search for meaning and cultural association with place.

1   Italo Calvino, *Invisible Cities*, William Weaver, trans. (New York: Harcourt Brace Jovanovich, Inc., 1972).

KENNETH FRAMPTON
ON READING HEIDEGGER

> The nature of building is letting dwell. Building accomplishes its nature in the raising
> of locations by the joining of their spaces. Only if we are capable of dwelling, only then
> can we build.
> Martin Heidegger, "Building Dwelling Thinking"

It becomes increasingly clear, as the utopian hallucinations of the Enlightenment fade, that we have long been in the habit of using too many synonyms; not only in our everyday speech but also in our more specialized languages. We still fail, for example, to make any satisfactory distinction between architecture and building, despite the fact that we are, at the same time, inconscionably aware that such a distinction should be made. We know, for instance, that Mies van der Rohe was at pains throughout his life to recognize this distinction and that in his own work he asserted the mediatory realm of *Baukunst* (the "art of building"), a Teutonic term for which there is no satisfactory English equivalent. All of this would be mere etymological speculation were we not constantly being reminded of the issue by those cultural and operational discrepancies that invariably arise between the generation of built form and its reception by society. This *lapsus* is sufficient to suggest that these every-day disjunctions must have at least some of their origins in our persistent failure to make such a distinction in building practice. There, in the physical realm of the built world, we seem to be presented with dramatic proof of the paradoxical Heideggerian thesis that language, far from being the servant of man, is all too often his master. We would, for instance, invariably prefer to posit the ideal of architecture—the monument in every circumstance be it public or private, the major opus—for situations that simply demand "building" and we are commonly led to realize the irreducibility of this fact, fatally after the event.

From *Oppositions* 4 (October 1974): unpaginated. Courtesy of the author and publisher.

As with that which we would fain idealize in the projection, so with that which we would rationalize after the misconception and here we find that the ironic mystifications of Candide have much in common with the deception of our own more recent ideologies. Surely this was never more evident than in, say, Daniel Bell's presumptuous announcement of the end of ideology or in Melvin Webber's ingenious celebration of the "non-place urban realm"; that apotheosis of late liberal capitalism posited, not to say "deposited," as the existing paradise of Los Angeles. In this last context, we are supposed (according to the received program of the idealogues) not only to recognize but further even to welcome with enthusiasm the utopian advent of this "community without propinquity," to quote yet another appealing phrase of more than a decade ago.

The intervening lapse of time has done little to neutralize such rationalizations. The actual phrases may have passed from our lips but the mental sets largely remain and it is these that unavoidably condition us as we go about our work. Should we choose, through some inner inadequacy or protracted sense of responsibility, to eschew autonomous art or the liberating promise of the poetic intellect, then all too often, we will find ourselves conflating in the name of populism the objects of elitist culture with elaborate rationalizations of the environments as found. In such a vein, we will seek to sublimate the frustrations of utopia with the sadness of suburbia or with the enervations of the strip; and while we will self-consciously appeal, by way of justification, to an illusory vernacular, the true nature of our Western predicament will continue to escape us. Between the Charybdis of elitism and the Scylla of populism, the full dimension of our historical dilemma will remain hidden.

Nowhere are the turns of this labyrinth more evident, as Heidegger tries to make clear, than in our language, than in our persistent use of, say the Latin term "space" or "*spatium*" instead of "place" or the Germanic word "*Raum*"—the latter carrying with it, as it does, the explicit connotations of a clearing in which to be, a place in which to come into being. We have only to compare the respective *Oxford English Dictionary* definitions to appreciate the abstract connotations of "space" as opposed to the socially experienced nature of "place"; to confront construction *in extensio* with the act of significant containment.

This, again, would be empty speculation could we not point directly to our present all but total incapacity to create places; an incapacity that is as prevalent in our architectural schools and in the monuments of the elite, as it is in "motopia" at large. Place now appears as inimical to our received mental set, not only as architects but also as a society. In our ubiquitous "non-place" we congratulate ourselves regularly on our pathological capacity for abstraction; on our commitment to the norms of statistical coordination; on our bondage to the transactional processes of objectification that will admit to neither the luxury nor the necessity of place. We exonerate the strip, ever fearful to admit that we might have eliminated, once and for all, the possibility of ever being anywhere. We vaunt our much prized mobility, our "rush city," to coin [Richard] Neutra's innocent phrase, our consumption of frenetic traction, only to realize that should we stop, there are few places within which any of us might significantly choose to be. Blithely, we exchange our already tenuous hold on the public sphere for the electronic distraction of the private future. Despite this, outside the "mass" engineered somnambulism of the television, we still indulge in the proliferation of roadside kitsch—in the fabricated mirage of "somewhere" made out of billboard facades and token theatrical paraphernalia the fantasmagoria of an escape clause from the landscape of alienation. In all this, the degeneration of the language speaks for itself. Terms such as "defoliation" and "pedestrianization" enter everyday speech as categories drawn from the same processes of technological rationalization. With "newspeak" overtones, they testify to a fundamental break in our rapport with nature (including our own), they speak of a laying waste that can only find its ultimate end in ourselves.

Against this, it would seem that the apparent universal triumph of the "non-place urban realm" may only be modified through a profound consciousness of history and through a rigorous socio-political analysis of the present, seen as a continuing fulfillment of the past. We have no choice but to reformulate the dialectical constituents of the world, to determine more consciously the necessary links obtaining between *place* and *production*, between the "what" and the "how." This reciprocation of ends and means binds us to an historical reality wherein the *tabula rasa* fantasies of the Enlightenment lose a good deal of their authority. With the manifest exhaustion of non-renewable resources the technotopic myth of unlimited progress becomes somewhat discredited and, at this juncture, the *production of place* returns us by way of economic limit not to architecture but to *Baukunst* and to that which Aldo Van Eyck has already called the "timelessness of man."

Accepting the limits of our historical circumstance and the perennial conflict of ends with means and of freedom with necessity, that which remains critical is the process by which decisive priorities are established; for in the last analysis, as Jürgen Habermas and Giancarlo de Carlo have reminded us, design goals, as the motives of our instrumentality, may only be legitimized through the activation of the public sphere—a political realm that, in its turn, is reciprocally dependent on the representational and physical embodiment of the collective. Place, at this juncture, irrespective of its scale, takes on its archetypal aspect, its ancient attribute which is as much political as it is ontological. Its sole legitimacy stems, as it must, from the social constituency it accommodates and represents.

The minimum physical pre-condition for place is the conscious placement of an object in nature, even if that artifice be nothing more than an object in the landscape or the rearrangement of nature herself. At the same time, the mere existence of an object in and of itself guarantees nothing. The cyclical processes of modern production and consumption seem to be more than adequately matched for the exhaustion of every resource and for the laying waste to all production irrespective of the rate at which it is generated. To rationalize this so-called optimization in the name of human adaptability and progress is to ideologize the self alienation of man. One has to recognize the dialectical opposition of place and production and not confuse the one with the other, that is, ends with means. For where *place* is essentially qualitative and in and of itself concrete and static, *production* tends to stress quantity and to be in and of itself dynamic and abstract.

Place, as an Aristotelian phenomenon, arises at a symbolic level with the conscious signification of social meaning and at a concrete level with the establishment of an articulate realm on which man or men may come into being. The receptivity and sensitive resonance of a place—to wit its sensate validity *qua* place—depends first on its stability in the everyday sense and second, on the appropriateness and richness of the socio-cultural experiences it offers.

Production, on the other hand, clearly has its own laws, which are tied into a reality that none of us can escape. But the margin of choice that always remains, demands to be fully exploited, less we arrive by default at the government of nobody, at that so-called utilitarian tyranny of technique. Since the "what" is fatally tied to the "how," everything resides in how and to what end we choose to modify the relevant optimal sub-categories of production, not only those of the built form itself, but also those structurally productive forces that implacably shape the built environment as elements in the general economy of our relations to nature.

A state of affairs, in which on the threshold of famine large amounts of prime agricultural land are continually lost to urbanization and mining without the exercise of adequate restraint, can hardly be regarded as economic in any fundamental sense, just as the proliferation of suburban sprawl can have little significance beyond stimulating land speculation and maximizing the amortization of investment in certain lines of consumer production. Certainly the creation of place, in both an ontological and political sense, is generally ill-served by our persistent policies of laissez-faire dispersal, and what is true for the essence of the *res publica* applies with equal force to the "catchment" limits of public transportation. All discourse on the built environment that does not make at least a reference to these kinds of basic contradictions, between the so-called short and long term interests in the society, tends towards a mystification of the historical circumstances in which we work.

At the more specific level of built form, production considered solely as an economy of method has the unfortunate tendency of inhibiting rather than facilitating the creation of receptive places. A case in point is the universal tendency towards stereo-metric high-rise flat slab construction where economy in erection is granted absolute priority over any other morphological consideration. By a similar token, the industrialization or rationalization of building, as the unavoidable consequence of the inviability of high craft production in a mass society, should not be regarded as beneficial in itself, particularly where such methods lead, through an abstract optimization, to a manifest impoverishment of the environment. And here, in this hypothetical confrontation between the *macro-scaled environmental desirability* of urban containment and *micro-scaled environmental undesirability* of high-rise construction, we have perhaps a convenient if highly schematic example of what one might regard as *an environmental dialectic of production*, that is, a state of affairs wherein the quantitative and qualitative gains at one level should be evaluated against the quantitative and qualitative losses at another.

The necessary relations obtaining between *place, production, and nature* implacably suggest the biological concept of the "homeostatic plateau," wherein the energy feedback loops of an organic metabolism serve to sustain the steady state of its overall system— the "zero-growth" feedback syndrome in nature. Comparable structural models in the field of the built environment have long since been posited at varying levels of detail from N.A. Maliutin's linear agro-industrial city to Ralph Knowles's metabolic profiling of the built environment, as though it were a climatic and topographic extension of the landscape itself. The rooted ecological nature of such otherwise abstract models finds its reflection in the direct recycling of body-waste for the purpose of horticultural production, or in the conservation of the overall energy required for the tasks of heating and cooling. It should come as no surprise that up to now, despite the current fad for solar energy studies, short-term interests have effectively inhibited anything but the most limited application of such models and one may take it as a reflection of these interests that architectural schools have largely ceased to concern themselves with such matters.

This aloof critique of current design praxis and its pedagogical substance brings us to the question once again of the full nature of the art of building. The present tendency to polarize the quintessence of built form as though it were of necessity one single thing appears to my mind to be nothing other than an ideological refusal to confront historical reality. The building task intrinsically resists such polarization. It remains fatally situated at that phenomenological interface between the infrastructural and superstructural realms of human production. There it ministers to the self-realization of man in nature and mediates as an essential catalyst between the three states of his existence: first, his status as an organism of primal need; second, his status as a sensate, hedonistic being; and finally, his status as a cognitive, self-affirmative consciousness. Autonomous artistic production certainly has its many provinces but the task of *place creation*, in its broadest sense, is not necessarily one of them. The compensatory drive of autonomous art tends to remove it from the concrete realization of man in the world and to the extent that architecture seeks to preempt all culture it consciously divorces itself from both building and the realm of historical reality. This much Adolf Loos has already intimated by 1910, when he wrote with characteristic but understandable overstatement: "Only a very small part of architecture belongs to art: the tomb and the monument."

The Geometry of Feeling: A Look at the
Phenomenology of Architecture
Juhani Pallasmaa

Like Christian Norberg-Schulz, Finnish architect
and theorist Juhani Pallasmaa is concerned with
architecture's loss of communicative power. This
essay, published in Finnish and Danish architectural journals with English translations, establishes a
phenomenological position. Meaning in architecture, Pallasmaa asserts, depends on its ability to
symbolize human existence or presence, and as
modern architects appear to have overlooked, on
the spatial experience of the work. Forms themselves are meaningless, but can transmit meaning
via images enriched by association. Science and
reason, he maintains, have contributed limiting
mindsets like analysis, elementarism, and reductionism, with unfortunate consequences for architecture. By contrast, the experience of architecture
is synthetic, operating at many levels simultaneously: mental/physical, cultural/biological, col-
lective/individual, etc. Based on readings of
Edmund Husserl, Martin Heidegger, and Gaston
Bachelard, Pallasmaa formulates a theoretical
position about experience's reliance on memory,
imagination, and the unconscious.
In "The Phenomenon of Place," Norberg-
Schulz asserts that "to dwell in a house is to
inhabit the world." This idea of the house as a
condensation of broader, worldly experience is
echoed in the significance Pallasmaa gives to the
dwelling place:

> A house in fact is a metaphysical instrument,
> a mythical tool with which we try to intro-
> duce a reflection of eternity into our momen-
> tary existence.

The author purports that the richest interpretations come from the simplest archetypal forms:
column, gable, arch, dome, tower. Concerns that
this indicates a nostalgic, stylistic agenda (postmodern historicism) are contradicted by
Pallasmaa's own sensuous, abstract "architecture
of silence" and his criticism of postmodern collage as superficial formalism.

JUHANI PALLASMAA
THE GEOMETRY OF FEELING
A LOOK AT THE PHENOMENOLOGY OF ARCHITECTURE

Why do so very few modern buildings appeal to our feelings, when almost any anonymous house in an old town or the most unpretentious farm outbuilding gives us a sense of familiarity and pleasure? Why is it that the stone foundations we discover in an overgrown meadow, a broken-down barn or an abandoned boathouse can arouse our imagination, while our own houses seem to stifle and smother our daydreams? The buildings of our own time may arouse our curiosity with their daring or inventiveness, but they hardly give us any sense of the meaning of our world or our own existence.

Efforts are today being made to revitalize the debilitating language of architecture both through a richer idiom and by reviving historical themes, but despite their effusive diversity, avant-garde works are just as bereft of meaning as the coldly technical approach to building that they are rebelling against.

The impoverishment of the inner meaning of architecture has also been pondered in numerous writings on architectural theory recently. Some writers think our architecture is too poor in terms of form, others that its form is too abstract or intellectual. From the viewpoint of cultural philosophy our entire hedonistic materialism seems to be losing the mental dimension that might in general be worthy of perpetuation in stone.

ARCHITECTURE AS PLAY WITH FORM
In turning into a specialist profession, architecture has gradually detached itself from its intentional background, becoming a discipline which is more and more fully determined by its own rules and value systems. Architecture has come to be a field of technology which still ventures to believe itself a form of free artistic expression.

From *Skala: Nordic Journal of Architecture and Art* 4 (June 1986): 22–25. Courtesy of the author and publisher.

But additional proof can be offered of how architecture has detached itself from its proper background and purpose. I would like here to consider one viewpoint, the relationship between architectural form and how architecture is experienced. I am basing myself on the argument that planning has become so intensively a kind of game with form, that the reality of how a building is experienced has been overlooked. We make the mistake of thinking of and assessing a building as a formal composition, no longer understanding that it is a symbol or experiencing the other reality that lies behind the symbol.

It is time that we considered whether forms or geometry in general can give rise to architectural feeling. Are forms the real basic elements of architecture at all? Are even such elements of building such as walls, windows or doors the real units of architectural effect?

THE ILLUSION OF ELEMENTARISM

The advance of modern science has been dominated by the principle of elementarism and reductionism. Every phenomenon considered is divided into its basic elements and relations and is viewed as the sum of these elements.

The elementarist view has also been dominant in the theory, teaching, and practice of art and architecture. These have at the same time been reduced solely to arts of the visual sense. On the basis of the ideology taught by the Bauhaus school, architecture is taught and analysed as a play with form combining various visual elements of form and space. This is thought to acquire a character which stimulates our visual senses from the dynamics of visual perception as studied by perceptual psychology. A building is considered to be a concrete composition built up out of a selection of given basic elements but no longer in touch with the reality of experience outside itself, not to mention striving consciously to depict and articulate the sphere of our consciousness.

But is not an artistic work actually the opposite of the whole elementarist idea? Surely the meanings of an artistic work are born out of the whole, from a vision that integrates the parts, and are in no way the sum of the elements.

Analysis of the formal structure of an architectural work does not necessarily reveal the artistic quality of the building or how it makes its effect.

THE ARCHITECTURE OF IMAGERY

The artistic dimension of a work of art does not lie in the actual physical thing; it exists only in the consciousness of the person experiencing it. Thus analysis of a work of art is at its most genuine introspection by the consciousness subjected to it. Its meaning lies not in its forms, but in the images transmitted by the forms and the emotional force that they carry. Form only affects our feelings through what it represents.

Thus as long as teaching and criticism do not strive to clarify the consciously grasped dimensions of architecture they will hardly have anything to do with the artistic essence of architecture. The efforts being made today to restore the richness of architectural idiom through diversity of form are based on lack of understanding of the essence of art. The richness of a work of art lies in the vitality of the images it arouses, and—paradoxically—the images open to most interpretations are aroused by the simplest, most archetypal forms. Post-Modernism's return to ancient themes lacks emotive power because these collages of architectural motifs are no longer linked with phenomenologically authentic feelings true to architecture.

Ezra Pound said that music degenerates if it moves too far away from dance, and poetry shrivels if it becomes too remote from music and song. In the same way, architecture has its own origins, and if it moves too far away from them it loses its effectiveness. The renewal of an art means rediscovering its deepest essence.

The language of art is the language of symbols that can be identified with our existence. If it lacks contact with the sensory memories that live in our subconscious and link our various senses, art could not but be reduced to mere meaningless ornamentation. The experience of art is an interaction between our embodied memories and our world. In one sense all art originates from our body, as the perceptive art essayist Adrian Stokes has pointed out.

It is also vital if we are to experience architectural meaning and sense that the effect of the building should find a counterpart in the world of the viewer's experience.

THE EIDOS OF ARCHITECTURE

As architects we do not primarily design buildings as physical objects, but the images and feelings of the people who live in them. Thus the effect of architecture stems from more or less common images and basic feelings connected with building.

It is basic feelings like these that phenomenology analyses, and it has become a more common method of examining architecture, too, in the last few years. A philosophical approach attached most closely to the names of Edmund Husserl and Martin Heidegger, it is introspective in nature, in contrast to the desire for objectivity of the positivist standpoint. Phenomenology strives to depict phenomena appealing directly to the consciousness as such without any theories and categories taken from the natural sciences or psychology. Phenomenology thus means examining a phenomenon of the consciousness in its own dimension of consciousness. That, using Husserl's concept, means "pure looking at" the phenomenon, or "viewing its essence." Phenomenology is a purely theoretical approach to research in the original sense of the Greek word *theoria*, which means precisely "a looking at."

The phenomenology of architecture is thus "looking at" architecture from within the consciousness experiencing it, through architectural feeling in contrast to analysis of the physical proportions and properties of the building or a stylistic frame of reference. The phenomenology of architecture seeks the inner language of building.

There is on the whole great suspicion of an introspective approach to art because it is thought to lack objectivity. But people do not seem to demand the same kind of objectivity from the artist's creative work. A work of art is a reality only when it is experienced, and experiencing a work of art means recreating its dimension of feeling.

One of the most important "raw materials" of phenomenological analysis of architecture is early childhood memory. We are used to thinking of childhood memories as products of the naive consciousness and imprecise memory capacity of the child, something with great appeal but of as little real value as our dreams. But both of these preconceived ideas are wrong. Surely the fact that certain early memories retain their personal identifiability and emotional force throughout our lives provides convincing proof of the importance and authenticity of these experiences, just as our dreams and daydreams reveal the most real and spontaneous contents of our minds.

ARCHITECTURE WITHOUT ARCHITECTS

Fruitful material for a phenomenological analysis of architectural experience is also offered by the ways in which architecture is presented and depicted in other branches of the arts. In poetry, images connected with buildings are common, and are the actual material of Gaston Bachelard's work "La Poétique de l'Espace." Bachelard has also written a phenomenological work on the poetics of daydreams ("La Poétique de la Rêverie"), which has many points of contact with the art of building in spite of its nonarchitectural subject. In novel writing, film, photography, and painting the secret language by which landscape, buildings, and objects influence people also often plays a crucial role. There are examples in the classics of Russian literature, the films of [Alfred] Hitchcock and [Andre] Tarkovski, Walker Evans's photographs, or the architecture shown in paintings, from medieval miniatures to Edward Hopper's landscapes of metaphysical loneliness and Balthus's rooms full of erotic anxiety. A writer, film director, or painter has to give the human event he is presenting a setting, a place, and thus in fact to perform a job of architectural design without a client, structural calculations, or a building permit. The presentation of architecture in other arts is the "pure looking" of a child's way of experiencing things, for the rules of architectural discipline do not regulate the experience or the way it is presented.

THE ARCHITECTURE OF MEMORY

The inner architecture of the mind emerging out of feelings and memory images is built on different principles from the architecture developed out of professional approaches. I personally, for instance, cannot bring to mind from my own childhood a single window or door as such but I can sit down at the windows of my many memories and look out at a garden that has long disappeared or a clearing now filled with trees. I can also step through the innumerable doors of my memory and recognise the dark warmth and special smell of the rooms that are there on the other side.

THE PRIMARY FEELINGS OF ARCHITECTURE

I have said that architecture cannot be a mere play with form. This view does not spring from the self-evident fact that architecture is tied to its practical purpose and many other external conditions. But if a building does not fulfill the basic conditions formulated for it phenomenologically as a symbol of human existence it is unable to influence the emotional feelings linked in our souls with the images a building creates. Architectural effect is based on a number of what we could call primary feelings. These feelings form the genuine "basic vocabulary" of architecture and it is by working through them that a work becomes architecture and not, for instance, a large-scale sculpture or scenography.

Architecture is a direct expression of existence, of human presence in the world. It is a direct expression in the sense that it is largely based on a language of the body of which neither the creator of the work nor the person experiencing it is aware.

The following types of experience could well be among the primary feelings produced by architecture:

—the house as a sign of culture in the landscape, the house as a projection of man and a point of reference in the landscape;

—approaching the building, recognising a human habitation or a given institution in the form of a house;

—entrance into the building's sphere of influence, stepping into its territory, being near the building;

—having a roof over your head, being sheltered and shaded;

—stepping into the house, entering through the door, crossing the boundary between exterior and interior;

—coming home or stepping inside the house for a specific purpose, expectation and fulfillment, sense of strangeness and familiarity;

— being in the room, a sense of security, a sense of togetherness or isolation;

—being in the sphere of influence of the foci that bring the building together, such as the table, bed, or fireplace;

—encountering the light or darkness that dominates the space, the space of light;

—looking out of the window, the link with the landscape.

I should think that experiencing loneliness is one of the basic feelings given by architecture, just like the experiences of silence and light often found in [Louis] Kahn's texts. A strong architectural experience always produces a sense of loneliness and silence irrespective of the actual number of people there or the noise. Experiencing art is a private dialogue between the work and the person experiencing it which excludes all other interaction.

The natural landscape can never express solitude in the same way as a building. Nature does not need man to explain itself, but a building represents its builder and proclaims his absence. The harrowing feeling of being left alone achieved by the metaphysical painters is based precisely on signs of man which are a reminder of the viewer's solitude.

The most comprehensive and perhaps most important architectural experience is the sense of being in a unique place. Part of this intense experience of place is always an impression of something sacred: this place is for higher beings. A house may seem built for a practical purpose, but in fact it is a metaphysical instrument, a mythical tool with which we try to introduce a reflection of eternity into our momentary existence.

Architecture exists in another reality from our everyday life and pursuits. The emotional force of ruins, of an abandoned house or rejected objects stems from the fact that they make us imagine and share the fate of their owners. They seduce our imagination to wander away from the world of everyday realities. The quality of architecture does not lie in the sense of reality that it expresses, but quite reverse, in its capacity for awakening our imagination.

Architecture is always inhabited by spirits. People known to us may well live in the building, but they are only understudy actors in a waking dream. In reality architecture is always the home of spirits, the dwelling place of metaphysical beings.

The defenders of the humanization of architecture today are completely mistaken when they claim that buildings should be designed for the needs of real people. I would like them to name a single great building in the history of architecture that was not built for the idealized man. The primary condition for the production of good architecture is the creation of an ideal client for the commission at hand.

MULTISENSORY EXPERIENCE

An impressive architectural experience sensitizes our whole physical and mental receptivity. It is difficult to grasp the structure of feeling because of its vastness and diversity. In experience we find a combination of the biological and the culturally derived, the collective and the individual, the conscious and the unconscious, the analytical and the emotional, the mental and the physical.

The symbols and associations in the language of art can be interpreted in many ways and make our consciousness shift from one possible interpretation to another. Adrian Stokes refers, for instance, to the close connection between experience of marble and low relief, and water fantasies.

Then how about the sound space created by drops of water falling occasionally in a dark, damp vault, the urban space created by the sound of church bells, the sense of distance that we feel when the sound of a night train pierces our dreams, or the smell space of a bakery or sweet shop? Why do abandoned, unheated houses have the same smell of death everywhere? Is it because the smell we sense is in fact one created through our eyes?

THE BEGINNING

I talked once with a church official about church design. He stressed the importance of knowing about the liturgy, iconography, and other internal rulings of the church. He seemed upset when I said that only a heathen can design a really expressive church. In my view the symbol of faith can only be turned into stone by someone who is being newly introduced to the dimensions of faith. A person for whom the design of a church is merely the organization of given forms can produce only empty sentimentality.

10. ARCHITECTURE, NATURE, AND THE CONSTRUCTED SITE

INTRODUCTION

Toward New Horizons in Architecture
Tadao Ando

This polemic, the title of which pays homage to Le Corbusier's famous manifesto, comments succinctly on the failings of both modern and postmodern architecture. Furthermore, the title's reference to the horizon indicates the need for a broad perspective. The word "horizon" is not casually chosen; it can be read as a signal of the importance of phenomenology and site in Tadao Ando's design process and theory. As we enter the last decade of the millennium, Ando suggests that what is needed is a "development through and beyond modernism," which can be accomplished only through "critical action." Some aspects of the critique are the deliberate distancing of his design work from function ("my spaces are not always given clear functional articulation"[1]), the quietude derived from simplicity of form, and the introduction of nature. The confrontation with nature and the concrete actuality of materials are intended to provoke reflection.

Ando recognizes that architecture produces a new landscape and thus has a responsibility to draw out the particular characteristics of a given place. He has said, "The purpose of architecture is basically the construction of place."[2] Through this reading of the interaction of landscape and building, Ando finds a vital tension that allows for spiritual awakening, similar perhaps to Martin Heidegger's conception of dwelling. While Ando's vocabulary draws upon phenomenological notions, he does not often refer specifically to this philosophical tradition.[3] One can surmise that he is familiar with Christian Norberg-Schulz's and Kenneth Frampton's writings on Heidegger and architecture, and perhaps with Vittorio Gregotti's. (ch. 9, 7) His intense involvement with site is similar to Gregotti's and Raimund Abraham's.

Despite apparent similarities with these theorists, Ando points out a significant distinction between Eastern and Western attitudes to nature: Japanese culture emphasizes a spiritual *threshold* between the building and nature, as opposed to a physical *boundary* in Western culture.

In aspiring to "a level of the abstract and universal" while recognizing the distinctive character of regional culture, the self-taught Ando has been cited as an exemplar of Frampton's Critical Regionalism. (ch. 11)

The internationally respected architect's work is tectonically lucid and resolved. While it often appears that concrete is his sole material, Ando would point to the use of light and wind as other physical elements of his constructions. Like his buildings, his theoretical writings attain a poetic level.

1   Kenneth Frampton, ed., *Tadao Ando: Buildings Projects Writings* (New York: Rizzoli, 1984), 134.
2   Ibid., 133.
3   Ibid., 134. In another essay, he cites Gaston Bachelard.

TADAO ANDO
TOWARD NEW HORIZONS IN ARCHITECTURE

Architectural thought is supported by abstract logic. By abstract I mean to signify a meditative exploration that arrives at a crystallization of the complexity and richness of the world, rather than a reduction of its reality through diminishing its concreteness. Were not the best aspects of modernism produced by such architectural thinking?

Postmodernism emerged in the recent past to denounce the poverty of modernism at a time when that movement was deteriorating, becoming conventionalized, and had abandoned its self-ordained role as a revitalizing cultural force. Modernist architecture had become mechanical, and postmodernist styles endeavored to recover the formal richness that modernism appeared to have discarded. This endeavor undeniably was a step in the right direction—utilizing history, taste, and ornament—and restored to architecture a certain concreteness. Yet this movement, too, has quickly become mired in hackneyed expression, producing a flood of formalistic play that is only confusing rather than inspiring.

The most promising path open to contemporary architecture is that of a development through and beyond modernism. This means replacing the mechanical, lethargic, and mediocre methods to which modernism has succumbed with the kind of abstract, meditative vitality that marked its beginnings, and creating something thought-provoking that will carry our age forward into the twenty-first century. The creation of an architecture able to breathe new vigor into the human spirit should clear a road through the present architectural impasse.

From *Tadao Ando* (New York: Museum of Modern Art, 1991), 75–76. Courtesy of the author and publisher.

TRANSPARENT LOGIC

Architectural creation is founded in critical action. It is never simply a method of problem-solving whereby given conditions are reduced to technical issues. Architectural creation involves contemplating the origins and essence of a project's functional requirements and the subsequent determination of its essential issues. Only in this way can the architect manifest in the architecture the character of its origins.

In envisioning the Chikatsu-Asuka Historical Museum, Osaka, on a site central to early Japanese history, I came to realize the vital importance of establishing an architecture that didn't mar the grandeur of the existing landscape. Therefore, I focussed on architecture's power to introduce a new landscape, and sought to create a museum that would embrace the entire landscape within the scope of its exhibitions.

In contemporary society, architecture is determined by economic factors and for the most part ruled by standardization and mediocrity. The serious designer must question even the given requirements, and devote deep thought to what is truly being sought. This kind of inquiry will reveal the special character latent in a commission and cast sharp light on the vital role of an intrinsic logic, which can bring the architecture to realization. When logic pervades the design process the result is clarity of structure, or spatial order—apparent not only to perception but also to reason. A transparent logic that permeates the whole transcends surface beauty, or mere geometry, with its intrinsic importance.

ABSTRACTION

The real world is complex and contradictory. At the core of architectural creation is the transformation of the concreteness of the real through transparent logic into spatial order. This is not an eliminative abstraction but, rather, an attempt at the organization of the real around an intrinsic viewpoint to give it order through abstract power. The starting point of an architectural problem—whether place, nature, lifestyle, or history—is expressed within this development into the abstract. Only an effort of this nature will produce a rich and variable architecture.

In designing a residence—a vessel for human dwelling—I pursue precisely that vital union of abstract geometrical form and daily human activity.

In the Row House (Azuma Residence), Suniyoshi, I took one of three wood row houses and reconstructed it as a concrete enclosure, attempting to generate a microcosm within it. The house is divided into three sections, the middle section being a courtyard open to the sky. This courtyard is an exterior that fills the interior, and its spatial movement is reversed and discontinuous. A simple geometric form, the concrete box is static; yet as nature participates within it, and as it is activated by human life, its abstract existence achieves vibrancy in its meeting with concreteness. In this house my chief concern was the degree of austerity of geometric form that could be fused with human life. This concern predominates in my Koshino House, Kidosaki House, in other residential works, and in other types of buildings as well. Geometric abstraction collides with human concreteness, and then the apparent contradiction dissolves around their incongruity. The architecture created at that moment is filled with a space that provokes and inspires.

Tadao Ando, Children's Museum, Himeji, Hyogo, 1987–89. Exterior view. Photo: Mitsuo Matsuoka.

NATURE

I seek to instill the presence of nature within an architecture austerely constructed by means of transparent logic. The elements of nature—water, wind, light, and sky—bring architecture derived from ideological thought down to the ground level of reality and awaken man-made life within it.

The Japanese tradition embraces a different sensibility about nature than that found in the West. Human life is not intended to oppose nature and endeavor to control it, but rather to draw nature into an intimate association in order to find union with it. One can go so far as to say that, in Japan, all forms of spiritual exercise are traditionally carried out within the context of the human interrelationship with nature.

This kind of sensibility has formed a culture that de-emphasizes the physical boundary between residence and surrounding nature and establishes instead a spiritual threshold. While screening man's dwelling from nature, it attempts to draw nature inside. There is no clear demarcation between outside and inside, but rather their mutual permeation. Today, unfortunately, nature has lost much of its former abundance, just as we have enfeebled our ability to perceive nature. Contemporary architecture, thus, has a role to play in providing people with architectural places that make them feel the presence of nature. When it does this, architecture transforms nature through abstraction, changing its meaning. When water, wind, light, rain, and other elements of nature are abstracted within architecture, the architecture becomes a place where people and nature confront each other under a sustained sense of tension. I believe it is this feeling of tension that will awaken the spiritual sensibilities latent in contemporary humanity.

At the Children's Museum, Hyogo, I have arranged each of the architectural elements to allow congenial meetings with water, forest, and sky under ideal conditions. When the presence of architecture transforms a place with a new intensity, the discovery of a new relationship with nature is possible.

PLACE

The presence of architecture—regardless of its self-contained character—inevitably creates a new landscape. This implies the necessity of discovering the architecture which the site itself is seeking.

The Time's Building, situated on the Takase River in Kyoto, originated out of the involvement with the delicate current of the nearby river. The building's plaza where one can dip a hand in the water, the bridge-like attitude of its deck above the current, the horizontal plan of approach from along the river rather than from a road—these elements serve to derive the utmost life from the character of the building's unique setting. The Rokko Housing project was born from attention to an equally singular site, in this case one pitched on a maximum sixty-degree slope. Underlying its design was the idea of sinking the building in along the slope, governing its projection above the ground in order to merge it into the surrounding cover of dense forest. This affords each dwelling unit an optimal view of the ocean from a terrace provided by its neighbor's roof. Each of my projects, whether the Children's Museum, Hyogo, the Forest of Tombs Museum, Kumamoto, the Raika Headquarters Building, or Festival, Okinawa, results from an endeavor to create a landscape by bringing the character of place fully into play.

I compose the architecture by seeking an essential logic inherent in the place. The architectural pursuit implies a responsibility to find and draw out a site's formal characteristics, along with its cultural traditions, climate, and natural environmental features, the city structure that forms its backdrop, and the living patterns and age-old customs that people will carry into the future. Without sentimentality, I aspire to transform place through architecture to the level of the abstract and universal. Only in this way can architecture repudiate the realm of industrial technology to become "grand art" in its truest sense.

INTRODUCTION

Negation and Reconciliation
Raimund Abraham

The two authors in this chapter are among others (such as Vittorio Gregotti and William McDonough, ch. 7, 8) concerned with architecture's relationship with nature. It is interesting to contrast Raimund Abraham's phenomenological point of view with that of Tadao Ando; both develop a design process based on an appreciation of modern architecture.

The site has great significance for both Abraham and Ando, but their approaches are opposed. While Ando seeks to draw nature into a union or association with mankind through a carefully structured confrontation, Abraham speaks of conquest and negation of the site and its topography. Abraham clearly operates from a Western, anthropocentric frame of mind, one which does not question the rights of the human species to manipulate the environment at large. Abraham bases his position on Martin Heidegger's discussion of the site's ability to "gather in and preserve [or install]" the fourfold of man, divinities, sky, and earth. But the architect's aggressive "intervention and collision" seems to oppose the Heideggerian notion of *sparing* (freeing something to become its essence). Christian Norberg-Schulz and others have interpreted sparing as a call for cultivating and nurturing the earth. Abraham admits that the design process, in his case, is secondary and can only attempt to "reconcile the consequences" of his destructive first act.

Other aspects of Abraham's search for meaning in architecture are more compelling. Rejecting "formal speculation" as an origin, he chooses instead to investigate "the primal architectural event": interaction with site. This is an origin beyond history, aesthetics, and style; it engages metaphysical issues. Like Juhani Pallasmaa (ch. 9), Abraham finds richness in architecture, which by juxtaposing the ideal and the material, commemorates both the absence and presence of man, and the eternal and the temporal. His pencil-rendered projects hauntingly illustrate the power of associations evoked by both grotesque excavations into the earth and bounded spatial precincts. The body inhabits and informs these spaces and the architect's representations.

RAIMUND ABRAHAM
NEGATION AND RECONCILIATION

The sensuous and the spiritual which struggle as opposites in the common understanding are revealed as reconciled in the truth expressed by art.
G. W. F. Hegel, *On the Arts*

A place in which everything comes together, is concentrated, the site gathers unto itself, supremely and radically. Its gathering power, gathers in and preserves all it had gathered, not like an encapsulating shell but rather by penetrating with its light all it had gathered, and only thus releasing it into its own nature.
Martin Heidegger, "On the Way to Language"

If we conceive of time as a process of transformation through continuous negation, then the basis of time is self-criticism and its products are ceaseless division and separation. The form in which time manifests itself is the repeated interpretation of an eternal truth or an archetype.

The modern age began as criticism of all mythologies, and therefore modern architecture is the first in history to predicate itself not only on the criticism of cultural antecedents but also on the criticism of art *per se*. Modern architecture provided neither a new treatise nor a new style. Instead, it brought about a radical break in the continuity of history. This radical form of critique indicated the possibility of an irreversible termination of style:

From *Perspecta: The Yale Architectural Journal* no. 19 (1982): 5–6. Courtesy of the author and the publisher.

Everything varies both with time and by place, and we can not fix anywhere upon an invariant quality such as the idea of style supposes, even when we separate things by their setting. But when duration and setting are retained in view, we have shifting relations, passing moments, and changing places in historic life. Any imaginary dimensions or continuities like style fade from view as we look for them. Style is like a rainbow. We can see it only briefly while we pause between the sun and the rain, and it vanishes when we go to the place where we thought we saw it.

George Kubler, *The Shape of Time*

The termination of style becomes synonymous with the repudiation of formal speculation as a possible generating force for a new beginning in architecture.

If anything, my own work owes its origin to the principle of intervention and decomposition as the quintessence of the primal architectural event, a principle which is totally antithetical to any form of aesthetic or historical manipulation. *Ort* ("site") originally meant, in the German language, the pointed end of a lance and suggests a gathering together.

It is the conquest of the site, the transformation of its topographical nature, that manifests the ontological roots of architecture. The process of design is only a secondary and subsequent act, whose purpose is to reconcile and harmonize the consequences of the initial intervention, collision, and negation.

I see the process of architectural creation as one that oscillates between negation and reconciliation: it is a continuous confrontation between ideal and matter, idea and image, intellectual and physiological, technological and spiritual. More specifically, architectural space can only be defined as the collision of geometric and physiological space or of ideal and matter, and while the ideal represents the notion of infinity or the eternal, matter can be regarded as the symbolic representation of the body—its presence and its absence. While man's conceptual powers aspire to the infinite, his body is essentially fragile, temporal, a corpus which will be laid waste, like material itself, by the unremitting and critical action of time.

Every civilization is a metaphor of time, a version of change. The preeminence of the now could, perhaps, reconcile us with the reality that the religion of progress, with the same zeal as the old religions, tried to conceal or disguise: that of death.

Octavio Paz, "The New Analogy"

Architecture has always been and will always be a monument to the eternal, commemorating both the absence and presence of man. If there remains any hope for the reengendering of the iconic in the modern world, then this will only derive from a reinterpretation of the archetypal existence of man: that is to say, new icons cannot possibly be established on the basis of signs and objects drawn or transposed from lost historical epochs. New icons in architecture will either come from the recognition of our intrinsic ontological limits or they will not arise at all.

11. CRITICAL REGIONALISM
LOCAL CULTURE VS. UNIVERSAL CIVILIZATION

INTRODUCTION

Prospects for a Critical Regionalism
Kenneth Frampton

This essay appeared in *Perspecta: The Yale Architectural Journal* in 1983, expanding a theme in Kenneth Frampton's theoretical agenda indicated in "The Isms of Contemporary Architecture."[1]

Since its publication, "Critical Regionalism" has proven immensely influential on practitioners. The term, borrowed from theorists Alexander Tzonis and Liane Lefaivre (this chapter) indicates in part the approach he advocates. Frampton synthesizes aspects of the Frankfurt School's "Critical Theory" as well as a phenomenological interest in the specificity of place. Phenomenological, political, and cultural issues concerning boundaries also surface as important.

Consistent with Frampton's writings here and elsewhere is a Marxist concern about the manipulation of the consumer ("admass seduction") and the problem of architecture conceived and perceived as fashion ("individualist forms of narcissism") or scenography. This commodification of shelter negates local identity and expression. His critique offers an alternative, authentic architecture, based on two essential aspects of architecture: an understanding of place, and tectonics. He aims to re-ground architecture without prescribing a singular strategy. Thus, an exemplary work of architecture "evokes the oneiric essence of the site, together with the inescapable materiality of building."

Ideas about "building the site," credited to Vittorio Gregotti (ch. 7) and evident in the work of Louis Kahn and Alvar Aalto, are central to Critical Regionalism. The engagement with and accentuation of topography, (the *constructed* site model), stands in sharp contrast to the International Style ideal of a flat, *cleared* site. Raimund Abraham, Tadao Ando, (both, ch. 10) and Mario Botta all demonstrate the former, postmodern landscape strategy.

Equally significant are the use of local materials and craftsmanship, and responsiveness to light and climate. These points promote architecture that is spatial and experiential, rather than image-oriented. Later articulations of Critical Regionalism emphasize climatic issues more forcefully and stress that architecture based in regional building customs is more ecologically sound, as well as aesthetically differentiated. For example, Frampton reacts against the ubiquitous use of air conditioning, which has made it possible to export a universal architecture around the world.

In general, Critical Regionalism proposes *resistance* to the homogenization of the built environment that results from the modernization of product manufacturing and construction techniques. Frampton is not, however, urging the embrace of vernacular stylistic elements, nor is he opposed to modern architecture. He aims to establish:

> an alternative theoretical position with which to continue the critical practice of architecture ...able to build on the liberative and poetic legacy of the pre-war Modern Movement.[2]

He seeks an architecture with the "capacity to condense the artistic potential of the region while reinterpreting cultural influences coming from the outside." The critique of universal modernization he proposes should well up from local "enclaves" or pockets of resistance. Architecture can support this expression of political identity through clarification of place.

The version of Frampton's theory published in *Perspecta* cites more architects and works, and focuses more on the city and on democracy than later articles on the same subject. Another distinguishing aspect of his piece is the examination of "analogical forms," an idea which may have come from Aldo Rossi. (ch. 7) Additionally, in this version, Paul Ricoeur's distinction between *culture* (a local, particular phenomenon) and a dominant universal *civilization* is framed as an opposition between nature and technology. Critical Regionalism seeks an architectural synthesis of the two.

1   Kenneth Frampton, "The Isms of Contemporary Architecture," in *Modern Architecture and the Critical Present, Architectural Design Profile* (1982), 61–82
2   "Place-form and Cultural Identity," in John Thackara, ed., *Design After Modernism: Beyond the Object* (New York: Thames and Hudson, 1988).

KENNETH FRAMPTON

PROSPECTS FOR A CRITICAL REGIONALISM

The phenomenon of universalization, while being an advancement of mankind, at the same time constitutes a sort of subtle destruction, not only of traditional cultures, which might not be an irreparable wrong, but also of what I shall call for the time being the creative nucleus of great civilizations and great cultures, that nucleus on the basis of which we interpret life, what I shall call in advance the ethical and mythical nucleus of mankind. The conflict springs up from there. We have the feeling that this single world civilization at the same time exerts a sort of attrition or wearing away at the expense of the cultural resources which have made the great civilizations of the past. This threat is expressed, among other disturbing effects, by the spreading before our eyes of a mediocre civilization which is the absurd counterpart of what I was just calling elementary culture. Everywhere throughout the world, one finds the same bad movie, the same slot machines, the same plastic or aluminum atrocities, the same twisting of language by propaganda, etc. It seems as if mankind, by approaching *en masse* a basic consumer culture, were also stopped en masse at a subcultural level. Thus we come to the crucial problem confronting nations just rising from underdevelopment. In order to get on to the road toward modernization, is it necessary to jettison the old cultural past which has been the *raison d'être* of a nation?...Whence the paradox: on the one hand, it has to root itself in the soil of its past, forge a national spirit, and unfurl this spiritual and cultural revindication before the colonialist's personality. But in order to take part in modern civilization, it is necessary at the same time to take part in scientific, technical, and political rationality, something which very often requires the pure and simple abandon of a whole cultural past. It is a fact: every culture cannot sustain and absorb the shock

From *Perspecta: The Yale Architectural Journal* 20 (1983): 147–162. Courtesy of the author and publisher.

of modern civilization. There is the paradox: how to become modern and to return to sources; how to revive an old, dormant civilization and take part in universal civilization....

No one can say what will become of our civilization when it has really met different civilizations by means other than the shock of conquest and domination. But we have to admit that this encounter has not yet taken place at the level of an authentic dialogue. That is why we are in a kind of lull or interregnum in which we can no longer practice the dogmatism of a single truth and in which we are not yet capable of conquering the skepticism into which we have stepped. We are in a tunnel, at the twilight of dogmatism and the dawn of real dialogues.[1]

The term critical regionalism is not intended to denote the vernacular, as this was once spontaneously produced by the combined interaction of climate, culture, myth, and craft, but rather to identify those recent regional "schools" whose aim has been to represent and serve, in a critical sense, the limited constituencies in which they are grounded. Such a regionalism depends, by definition, on a connection between the political consciousness of a society and the profession. Among the pre conditions for the emergence of critical regional expression is not only sufficient prosperity but also a strong desire for realising an identity. One of the mainsprings of regionalist culture is an anti-centrist sentiment—an aspiration for some kind of cultural, economic, and political independence.

The philosopher Paul Ricoeur has advanced the thesis that a hybrid "world culture" will only come into being through a cross-fertilization between rooted *culture* on the one hand and universal *civilization* on the other. This paradoxical proposition, that regional culture must also be a form of world culture, is predicated on the notion that development *in se* will, of necessity, transform the basis of rooted culture. In his essay "Universal Civilization and National Cultures" of *1961*, Ricoeur implied that everything will depend in the last analysis on the capacity of regional culture to recreate a rooted tradition while appropriating foreign influences at the level of both culture and civilization. Such a process of cross-fertilization and reinterpretation is impure by definition. This much is at once evident, say, in the work of the Portugese architect Alvaro Siza y Viera. In Siza's architecture [Alvar] Aalto's collage approach to building form finds itself mediated by normative typologies drawn from the work of the Italian Neo-rationalists.

It is necessary to distinguish at the outset between critical regionalism and the simplistic evocation of a sentimental or ironic vernacular. I am referring, of course, to that nostalgia for the vernacular which is currently being conceived as an overdue return to the ethos of a popular culture; for unless such a distinction is made one will end by confusing the resistant capacity of Regionalism with the demagogic tendencies of Populism. In contradistinction to Regionalism, the primary goal of Populism is to function as a *communicative or instrumental sign.*[2] Such a sign seeks to evoke not a critical perception of reality, but rather the sublimation of a desire for direct experience through the provision of information. Its tactical aim is to attain, as economically as possible, a preconceived level of gratification in behavioristic terms. In this regard, the strong affinities of Populism for the rhetorical techniques and imagery of advertising is hardly accidental.

On the other hand, Critical Regionalism is a dialectical expression. It self-consciously seeks to deconstruct universal modernism in terms of values and images which are locally cultivated, while at the same time adulterating these autochthonous elements with paradigms drawn from alien sources. After the disjunctive cultural approach practised by Adolf Loos, Critical Regionalism recognizes that no living tradition remains available to modern man other than the subtle procedures of synthetic contradiction. Any attempt to circumvent the dialectics of this creative process through the eclectic procedures of historicism can only result in consumerist iconography masquerading as culture.

It is my contention that Critical Regionalism continues to flourish sporadically within the cultural fissures that articulate in unexpected ways the continents of Europe and America. These borderline manifestations may be characterized, after Abraham Moles, as the "interstices of freedom."[3] Their existence is proof that the model of the hegemonic center surrounded by dependent satellites is an inadequate and demagogic description of our cultural potential.

Exemplary of an explicitly anti-centrist regionalism was the Catalonian nationalist revival which first emerged with the foundation of the Group R in the early Fifties. This group, led by J. M. Sostres and Oriol Bohigas, found itself caught from the beginning in a complex cultural situation. On the one hand, it was obliged to revive the Rationalist, anti-Fascist values and procedures of GATEPAC (the pre-war Spanish wing of CIAM); on the other, it remained aware of the political responsibility to evoke a realistic regionalism; a regionalism which would be accessible to the general populace. This double-headed program was first publicly announced by Bohigas in his essay, "Possibilities for a Barcelona Architecture,"[4] published in 1951. The various impulses that went to make up the heterogeneous form of Catalonian Regionalism exemplify, in retrospect, the essentially hybrid nature of an authentic modern culture. First, there was the Catalonian brick tradition which evidently dates back to the heroic period of the *Modernismo*; then there was the influence of Neoplasticism, an impulse which was directly inspired by Bruno Zevi's *La poetica della architettura neoplastica* of 1953 and, finally, there was the *revisionist* style of Italian Neo-Realism—as exemplified above all in the work of Ignazio Gardella.[5]

The career of the Barcelona architect J. A. Coderch has been typically Regionalist inasmuch as it has oscillated, until recent date, between a mediterraneanized, modern brick vernacular—Venetian in evocation—apparent, say, in his eight-storey brick apartment block built in Barcelona in the Paseo Nacional in 1952–54 (a mass articulated by full-height shutters and overhanging cornices), and the avant-gardist, Neoplastic composition of his Casa Catasús completed at Sitges in 1957. The work of Martorell, Bohigas and Mackay has tended to oscillate between comparable poles; between, on the one hand, an assumed brick vernacular close to the work of Coderch and Gardella[6] and, on the other, their Neo-Brutalist public manner; this last being best exemplified in the technical rationalism of their Thau School built in the suburbs of Barcelona in 1975.

The recent deliquescence of Catalonian Regionalism finds its most extreme manifestation in the work of Ricardo Bofill and the Taller de Arquitectura. For where the early work of Bofill (for example, the Calle Nicaragua apartments of 1964) displayed evident affinity for the re-interpreted brick vernacular of Coderch, the Taller was to adopt a more exaggerated rhetoric in the Seventies. With their Xanadu complex built in Calpe (1967), they entered into a flamboyant romanticism. This castellated syntax reached its apotheosis in their heroic, but ostentatious, tile-faced Walden 7 complex at Saint-Just Desvern (1975). With its twelve-storey voids, underlit living rooms, miniscule balconies, and its now disintegrating tile cladding, Walden 7 denotes that delicate boundary where an initially sound impulse degenerates into an ineffective Populism—a Populism whose ultimate aim is not to provide a liveable and significant environment but rather to achieve a highly photogenic form of scenography. In the last analysis, despite its passing homage to Gaudí, Walden 7 is devoted to a form of *admass* seduction. It is architecture of narcissism *par excellence*, for the formal rhetoric addresses itself mainly to high fashion, and to the marketing of Bofill's flamboyant personality. The Mediterranean hedonistic utopia to which it pretends collapses on closer inspection, above all at the level of the roofscape where a potentially sensuous environment has not been borne out by the reality of its occupation.

Nothing could be further from Bofill's intentions than the architecture of the Portugese master Alvaro Siza y Viera, whose career, beginning with his swimming pool at Quinta de Conceicad, completed in 1965, has been anything but photogenic. This much can be discerned not only from the fragmentary evasive nature of the published images but also from a text written in 1979.

> Most of my works were never published, some of the things I did were only carried out in part, others were profoundly changed or destroyed. That's only to be expected. An architectonic proposition whose aim is to go deep...a proposition that intends to be more than a passive materialisation, refuses to reduce that same reality, analysing each of its aspects, one by one; that proposition can't find support in a fixed image, can't follow a linear evolution....Each design must catch, with the utmost rigour, a precise moment of the flittering image, in all its shades, and the better you can recognize that flittering quality of reality, the clearer your design will be....That may be the reason why only marginal works (a quiet dwelling, a holiday house miles away) have been kept as they were originally designed. But something remains. Pieces are kept here and there, inside ourselves, perhaps fathered by someone, leaving marks on space and people, melting into a process of total transformation.6

It could be argued that this hypersensitivity toward the fluid and yet specific nature of reality renders Siza's work more layered and rooted than the eclectic tendencies of the Barcelona School for, by taking Aalto as his point of departure, he seems to have been able to ground his building in the configuration of a given topography and in the fine-grained specificity of the local context. To this end his pieces are tight responses to the urban fabric and marinescape of the Porto region. Other important factors are his extraordinary sensitivity towards local materials, craft work, and, above all, to the subtleties of local light—his sense for a particular kind of filtration and penetration. Like Aalto's Jyväskylä University (1957), or his Säynätsalo City Hall (1949), all of Siza's buildings are delicately layered and inlaid into their sites. His approach is patently tactile and materialist, rather than visual and graphic, from his Bircs House built at Povoa do Varzim in 1976 to his Bouca Resident's Association Housing of 1977. Even his small bank buildings, of which the best is probably the Pinto branch bank built at Oliveira de Azemeis in 1974, are topographically conceived and structured.

The theoretical work of the New York-based Austrian architect Raimund Abraham may also be seen as having latent regionalist connotations inasmuch as this architect has always stressed place creation and the topographic aspects of the built environment. The House with Three Walls (1972) and the House with Flower Walls (1973) are typical onto-logical works of the early Seventies, wherein the project evokes the oneiric essence of the site, together with the inescapable materiality of building. This feeling for the tectonic nature of built form and for its capacity to transform the surface of the earth has been carried over into Abraham's recent designs made for International Bauausstellung [the IBA] in Berlin, above all his recent projects for South Friedrichstadt, designed in 1981.

An equally tactile but more specifically regionalist approach is obtained in the case of the veteran Mexican architect Luis Barragán, whose finest houses (many of which have been erected in the suburb of Pedregal) are nothing if not topographic. As much a land-scape designer as an architect, Barragán has always sought a sensual and earthbound architecture; an architecture compounded out of enclosures, stelae, fountains, water courses, color saturation; an architecture laid into volcanic rock and lush vegetation; an architecture that refers only indirectly to the Mexican colonial *estancia*. Of Barragán's feeling for mythic and rooted beginnings it is sufficient to cite his memories of the apoc-ryphal *pueblo* of his youth:

> My earliest childhood memories are related to a ranch my family owned near the village of Mazamitla. It was a *pueblo* with hills, formed by houses with tile roofs and immense eaves to shield passersby from the heavy rains which fall in that area. Even the earth's color was interesting because it was red earth. In this village, the water distribution sys-tem consisted of great gutted logs, in the form of troughs, which ran on a support struc-ture of tree forks, five meters high, above the roofs. This aqueduct crossed over the town, reaching the patios, where there were great stone fountains to receive the water. The patios housed with stables, with cows and chickens, all together. Outside, in the street, there were iron rings to tie the horses. The channeled logs, covered with moss, dripped water all over town, of course. It gave this village the ambience of a fairy tale.
> No, there are no photographs. I have only its memory.[7]

This remembrance has surely been filtered through Barragán's life-long involvement with Islamic architecture. Similar feelings and concerns are evident in his opposition to the invasion of privacy in the modern world and in his criticism of the subtle erosion of nature which has accompanied postwar civilization

> Everyday life is becoming much too public. Radio, T.V., telephone all invade privacy. Gardens should therefore be enclosed, not open to public gaze....Architects, are forget-ting the need of human beings for half-light, the sort of light that imposes a tranquility, in their living rooms as well as in their bedrooms. About half the glass that is used in so many buildings—homes as well as offices—would have to be removed in order to obtain the quality of light that enables one to live and work in a more concentrated manner ....Before the machine age, even in the middle of cities, Nature was everybody's trusted companion....Nowadays, the situation is reversed. Man does not meet with Nature, even when he leaves the city to commune with her. Enclosed in his shiny automobile, his

spirit stamped with the mark of the world whence the automobile emerged, he is, within Nature, a foreign body. A billboard is sufficient to stifle the voice of Nature. Nature becomes a scrap of Nature and man a scrap of man.[8]

By the time of his first house and studio built in Tacubaya, Mexico D.F. in 1947, Barragán had already made a subtle move away from the universal syntax of the so-called International Style. And yet his work has always remained committed to that abstract form which has so characterized the art of our era. Barragán's penchant for large, almost inscrutable abstract planes set in the landscape is perhaps at its most intense in his garden for Las Arboledas of 1961 and his freeway monument, Satellite City Towers, designed with Mathias Goertiz in 1967.

Regionalism has, of course, manifested itself in other parts of the Americas; in Brazil in the 1940s, in the early work of Oscar Niemeyer and Alfonso Reidy; in Argentina in the work of Amancio Williams—above all in Williams's bridge house in Mar del Plata of 1945 and more recently perhaps in Clorindo Testa's Bank of London and South America, built in Buenos Aires in 1959; in Venezuela, in the Ciudad Universitaria built to the designs of Carlos Raoul Villanueva between 1945 and 1960; in the West Coast of the United States, first in Los Angeles in the late 1920s in the work of [Richard] Neutra, [Rudolph] Schindler, [Ken] Weber, and [Irving] Gill, and then in the so-called Bay Area and Southern California schools founded by William Wurster and Hamilton Harwell Harris respectively. No-one has perhaps expressed the idea of a Critical Regionalism more discretely than Harwell Harris in his address, "Regionalism and Nationalism," which he gave to the North West Regional Council of the AIA, in Eugene, Oregon in 1954:

Opposed to the Regionalism of Restriction is another type of regionalism; the Regionalism of Liberation. This is the manifestation of a region that is *especially in tune with the emerging thought of the time.* We call such a manifestation "regional" *only because it has not yet emerged elsewhere.* It is the genius of this region to be more than ordinarily aware and more than ordinarily free. Its virtue is that its manifestation has *significance for the world outside itself.* To express this regionalism architecturally it is necessary that there be building,—preferably a lot of building—at one time. Only so can the expression be sufficiently general, sufficiently varied, sufficiently forceful to capture people's imaginations and provide a friendly climate long enough for a new school of design to develop.

San Francisco was made for Maybeck. Pasadena was made for Greene and Greene. Neither could have accomplished what he did in any other place or time. Each used the materials of the place; but it is not the materials that distinguish the work....

A region may develop ideas. A region may accept ideas. Imaginations and intelligence are necessary for both. In California in the late Twenties and Thirties modern European ideas met a still developing regionalism. In New England, on the other hand, European Modernism met a rigid and restrictive regionalism that at first resisted and then surrendered. New England accepted European Modernism whole because its own regionalism had been reduced to a collection of restrictions.[9]

Despite an apparent freedom of expression, such a level of liberative regionalism is difficult to sustain in North America today. Within the current proliferation of highly individualistic forms of narcissism—a body of work which is ultimately cynical, patronising and self-indulgent rather than rooted—only two firms today display any consistent sensitivity towards the evolution of a regional culture which is both specific and critical.

The first example would be the simple, site-responsive houses designed by Andrew Batey and Mark Mack for the Napa Valley area in California; the second would be the work of the architect Harry Wolf, whose work, which has so far been largely restricted to North Carolina, is designed out of Charlotte. Wolf's sensitivity to the specificity of place has perhaps been most intensely demonstrated in his recent competition entry for the Fort Lauderdale Riverfront Plaza. The description of this work at once displays both a feeling for the specificity of the place and a self-conscious reflection on the locus of Fort Lauderdale in history:

> The worship of the sun and the measurement of time from its light reach back to the earliest recorded history of man. It is interesting to note in the case of Fort Lauderdale that if one were to follow a twenty-six degree latitudinal line around the globe, one would find Fort Lauderdale in the company of Ancient Thebes—the throne of the Egyptian sun god, Ra. Further to the East, one would find Jaipur, India, where heretofore, the largest equinoctal sundial in the world was built 110 years prior to the founding of Fort Lauderdale.
>
> Mindful of these magnificent historical precedents, we sought a symbol that would speak of the past, present and future of Fort Lauderdale....To capture the sun in symbol a great sundial is incised on the Plaza site and the gnomon of the sundial bisects the site on its north-south axis. The gnomon of the double blade rises from the south at twenty-six degrees five minutes parallel to Fort Lauderdale's latitude....
>
> Each of (the) significant dates in Fort Lauderdale's history is recorded in the great blade of the sundial. With careful calculation the sun angles are perfectly aligned with penetrations through the two blades to cast brilliant circles of light, landing on the otherwise shadowy side of the sundial. These shafts of light illuminate an appropriate historical marker serving as annual historical reminders.
>
> Etched into the eastern side of the plaza, an enlarged map of the City shows the New River as it meets the harbor. The eastern edge of the building is eroded in the shape of the river and introduces light into the offices beneath the Plaza along its path.
>
> The River continues until it meets the semicircle of the water court where the river path creates a wall of water even with the level of the Plaza, providing a sixteen-foot cascade into the pool below. The map follows the river upstream until it reaches the gnomon where, at map scale, the juncture of the blade and the river coincide exactly with the site on which the blade stands.[10]

In Europe the work of the Italian architect Gino Valle may also be classified as critical and regionalist inasmuch as his entire career has been centered around the city of Udine, in Italy. From here Valle was to make one of the earliest post-war reinterpretations of the Italian Lombardy vernacular in the Casa Quaglia built at Sutrio in 1956. Throughout the Fifties, Valle dedicated himself to the evolution of an industrial format for the Lombardy region. This development reached its zenith in his Zanussi Rex factory built at Pordenone in 1961. Aside from this, he was to extend his capacity for a more richly-textured and inflected regional expression in his thermal baths, built at Arta in 1964 and in his project for the Udine Civic Theatre submitted one year before. Regionalism, as we have seen, is often not so much a collective effort as it is the output of a talented individual working with commitment towards some sort of rooted expression.

Apart from the Western United States, Regionalism first became manifest in the post-war world in the vestigial city-states of the European continent. A number of regional architects seem to have had their origins in this middle ground in the first decade after the war. Among those of the pre-war generation who have somehow remained committed to this regional inflection one may count such architects as Ernst Gisel in Zurich, Jørn Utzon in Copenhagen, Vittorio Gregotti in Milan, Gino Valle in Udine, Peter Celsing in Stockholm, Mathias Ungers in Cologne, Sverre Fehn in Oslo, Aris Konstantinides in Athens, Ludwig Leo in Berlin, and the late Carlo Scarpa in Venice. Louis Kahn may also be considered to be a regionally-oriented architect inasmuch as he was to remain committed to Philadelphia, both as myth and reality, throughout his life. It is symptomatic of his concern for preserving the urban qualities of downtown Philadelphia that he should show the central city area as a citadel; as a sector walled in like Carcassonne by an autoroute instead of a bastion and studded on its perimeter with cylindrical parking silos instead of castellated towers.

Switzerland, with its intricate linguistic and cultural boundaries and its tradition of cosmopolitanism, has always displayed strong regionalistic tendencies; ones which have often assumed a critical nature. The subtle cantonal combination of admission and exclusion has always favored the cultivation of extremely dense forms of expression in quite limited areas, and yet, while the cantonal system serves to sustain local culture, the Helvetic Federation facilitates the penetration and assimilation of foreign ideas. Dolf Schnebli's Corbusian, vaulted villa at Campione d'Italia on the Italo-Swiss frontier (1960) may be seen as initiating the resistance of Swiss regional culture to the rule of international Miesianism. This resistance found its echo almost immediately in other parts of Switzerland, in Aurelio Galfetti's equally Corbusian Rotalini House, in Bellinzona, and in the Atelier 5 version of the Corbusian *béton brut* manner, as this appeared in private houses at Motier and Flamatt and in Siedlung Halen, built outside Bern in 1960. Today's Ticinese Regionalism has its ultimate origins not only in this pioneering work of Schnebli, Galfetti and Atelier 5, but also in the Neo-Wrightian work of Tita Carloni.

The strength of provincial culture surely resides in its capacity to condense the artistic potential of the region while reinterpreting cultural influences coming from the outside. The work of Mario Botta is typical in this respect, with its concentration on issues which relate directly to a specific place and with its adaptation of various Rationalist methods drawn from the outside. Apprenticed to Carloni and later educated under Carlo Scarpa in Venice, Botta was fortunate enough to work, however briefly, for both Kahn and Le Corbusier during the short time that they each projected monuments for that city. Evidently influenced by these men, Botta has since appropriated the methodology of the Italian Neo-Rationalists as his own, while simultaneously retaining, through his apprenticeship with Scarpa, an uncanny capacity for the craft enrichment of both form and space. Perhaps the most striking example of this last occurs in his application of *intonocare lucido* (polished plaster) to the fireplace surrounds of a converted farmhouse that was built to his designs at Ligrignano in 1979.

Two other primary traits in Botta's work may be seen as testifying to his Regionalism; on the one hand, his constant preoccupation with what he terms *building the site*, and, on the other, his deep conviction that the loss of the historical city can only now be compensated for on a fragmentary basis. His largest work to date, namely his school at Morbio Inferiore, asserts itself as a micro-urban realm; as a cultural compensation for the evident loss of urbanity in Chiasso, the nearest large city. Primary references to the culture of the Ticino landscape are also sometimes evoked by Botta at a typical level. An example of this would be the house at Riva San Vitale, which refers obliquely to the traditional country summer house or *rocoli* which was once endemic to the region.

Aside from this specific reference, Botta's houses often appear as markers in the landscape, either as points or as boundaries. The house in Ligornetto, for example, establishes the frontier where the village ends and the agrarian system begins. The visual acoustics of its plan stem from the gun-sight aperture of the house which turns away from the fields and towards the village. Botta's houses are invariably treated in this way, as bunkerbelvederes, where the fenestration opens towards selected views in the landscape, thereby screening out, with stoic pathos, the rapacious suburban development that has taken place in the Ticino region over the past twenty years. Finally, his houses are never layered into the contours of a given site, but rather "build the site"[11] by declaring themselves as primary forms, set against the topography and the sky. Their surprising capacity to harmonize with the still partially agricultural nature of the region stems directly from their *analogical form* and finish; that is to say, from the fair-faced, concrete block of their structure and from the silo or barn-like shell forms in which they are housed, these last alluding to the traditional agricultural structures from which the form derives.

Despite this demonstration of a convincing, modern, domestic sensibility, the most critical aspect of Botta's achievement does not reside in his houses, but rather in his public projects; in particular in the two large-scale proposals which he designed in collaborative with Luigi Snozzi. Both of these are "viaduct" buildings and as such are certainly influenced to some degree by Kahn's Venice Congress Hall project of 1968 and by [Aldo] Rossi's first sketches for Gallaratese of 1970. The first of these projects, their Centro Direzionale di Perugia of 1971, is projected as a "city within a city" and the wider implications of this design clearly stem from its potential applicability to many Megalopolitan situations throughout the world. Had it been realized, this regional center, built as an arcaded galleria, would have been capable of signaling its presence to the urban region without compromising the historic city or fusing with the chaos of the surrounding suburban development. A comparable clarity and appropriateness was obtained in their Zurich Station proposal of 1978. The advantages of the urban strategy adopted in this instance are so remarkable as to merit brief enumeration. This multileveled bridge structure would have not only provided four separate concourse levels to accommodate shops, offices, restaurants, etc., but would have also constituted a new head building at the end of the covered platforms. At the same time it would have emphasized an indistinct urban boundary without compromising the historic profile of the existing terminus.

In the case of the Ticino, one can lay claim to the actual presence of a Regionalist School in the sense that, after the late 1950s, this area produced a body of remarkable buildings, many of which were collectively achieved. This much is clear, not only from the diversity of Botta's own collaborators but also from associations which took place without his participation. Once again credit is due to the older generation such as Galfetti, Carloni, and Schnebli, who frequently collaborated with younger architects. There is no room here to list all the architects involved, but some idea of the scope of this endeavor may be obtained from the fact that the Ticinese "school" comprised well over twenty architects who were variously to build some forty buildings of note between 1960 and 1975.

It is hardly surprising that Tadao Ando, who is one of the most regionally conscious architects in Japan should be based in Osaka rather than Tokyo and that his theoretical writings should formulate more clearly than any other architect of his generation a set of precepts which come close to the idea of Critical Regionalism. This is most evident in the tension that he perceives as obtaining between the process of universal modernization and the idiosyncrasy of rooted culture. Thus we find him writing in an essay entitled, "From Self Enclosed Modern Architecture toward Universality,"

> Born and bred in Japan, I do my architectural work here. And I suppose it would be possible to say that the method I have selected is to apply the vocabulary and techniques developed by an open, universalist Modernism in an enclosed realm of individual lifestyles and regional differentiation. But it seems difficult to me to attempt to express the sensibilities, customs, aesthetic awareness, distinctive culture, and social traditions of a given race by means of an open, internationalist vocabulary of Modernism....[12]

As Ando's argument unfolds we realize that for him an *Enclosed Modern Architecture* has two meanings. On the one hand he means quite literally the creation of enclaves or, to be specific, court-houses by virtue of which man is able to recover and sustain some vestige of that time honoured triad,—*man, nature, culture*—against the obliterating onslaught of Megalopolitan development. Thus Ando writes:

> After World War II, when Japan launched on a course of rapid economic growth, the people's value criteria changed. The old fundamentally feudal family system collapsed. Such social alterations as concentration of information and places of work in cities led to overpopulation of agricultural and fishing villages and towns (as was probably true in other parts of the world as well); overly dense urban and suburban populations made it impossible to preserve a feature that was formerly most characteristic of Japanese residential architecture; intimate connection with nature and openness to the natural world. What I refer to as an Enclosed Modern Architecture is a restoration of the Unity between house and nature that Japanese houses have lost in the process of modernization.[13]

In his small courtyard block houses, often set within dense urban fabric, Ando employs concrete in such a way as to stress the taut homogeneity of its surface rather than its weight, since for him it "is the most suitable material for realizing surfaces created by rays of sunlight...(where)...walls become abstract, are negated, and approach the ultimate limit of space. Their actuality is lost, and only the space they enclose gives a sense of really existing."[14]

While the cardinal importance of light is present in theoretical writings of Louis Kahn and Le Corbusier, Ando sees the paradox of spatial limpidity emerging out of light as being peculiarly pertinent to the Japanese character and with this he makes explicit the second and broader meaning which he attributes to the concept of a self-enclosed modernity. He writes:

> Spaces of this kind are overlooked in utilitarian affairs of everyday living and rarely make themselves known. Still they are capable of stimulating recollection of their own inner-most forms and stimulating new discoveries. This is the aim of what I call closed mod-ern architecture. Architecture of this kind is likely to alter with the region in which it sends out roots and to grow in various distinctive individual ways, still, though closed, I feel convinced that as a methodology it is open in the direction of universality.[15]

What Ando has in mind is the development of a trans-optical architecture where the richness of the work lies beyond the initial perception of its geometric order. The tac-tile value of the tectonic components are crucial to this changing spatial revelation, for as he was to write of his Koshino Residence in 1981:

> Light changes expressions with time. I believe that the architectural materials do not end with wood and concrete that have tangible forms but go beyond to include light and wind which appeal to our senses....Detail exists as the most important element in expressing identity....Thus to me, the detail is an element which achieves the physical com-position of architecture, but at the same time, it is a generator of an image of architecture.[16]

That this opposition between universal civilization and autochthonous culture can have strong political connotations has been remarked on by Alex Tzonis in his article on the work of the Greek architects Dimitris and Susana Antonakakis, entitled, "The Grid and Pathway," in which he demonstrates the ambiguous role played by the universality of the *Schinkelschuler* in the founding of the Greek state. Thus we find Tzonis writing:

> In Greece, historicist regionalism in its neo-classical version had already met with oppo-sition before the arrival of the Welfare State and of modern architecture. It is due to a very peculiar crisis which explodes around the end of the nineteenth century. Historicist regionalism here had grown not only out of a war of liberation; it had emerged out of interests to develop an urban elite set apart from the peasant world and its rural "back-wardness" and to create a dominance of town over country: hence the special appeal of historicist regionalism, based on the book rather than experience, with its monumen-tality recalling another distant and forlorn elite. Historical regionalism had united peo-ple but it had also divided them.[17]

While the various reactions which followed the nineteenth-century triumph of the Greek Nationalist, Neo-classical style varied from vernacular historicism in the Twenties to a more thorough-going modernist approach which, immediately before and after the Second World War, first proclaimed modernity as an ideal and then directly attempted to participate in the modernization of Greek society.

As Tzonis points out, Critical Regionalism only began in Greece with the Thirties projects of Dimitri Pikionis and Aris Konstantinidis, above all in the latter's Eleusis house of 1938 and his garden exhibition built in Kifissia in 1940. It then manifested itself with great force in the pedestrian zone that Dimitri Pikionis designed for the Philopappus Hill, in 1957, on a site immediately adjacent to the Acropolis in Athens. In this work, as Tzonis points out:

> Pikionis proceeds to make a work of architecture free from technological exhibitionism and compositional conceit (so typical of the mainstream of architecture of the 1950s) a stark naked object almost dematerialized, an ordering of "places made for the occasion," unfolding around the hill for solitary contemplation, for intimate discussion, for a small gathering, for a vast assembly.
>
> To weave this extraordinary braid of niches and passages and situations, Pikionis identifies appropriate components from the lived-in spaces of folk architecture, but in this project the link with the regional is not made out of tender emotion. In a completely different attitude, these envelopes of concrete events are studied with a cold empirical method, as if documented by an archaeologist. Neither is their selection and their positioning carried out to stir easy superficial emotion. They are platforms to be used in an everyday sense but to supply that which, in the context of contemporary architecture, everyday life does not. The investigation of the local is the condition for reaching the concrete and the real, and for rehumanizing architecture.[18]

Unlike Pikionis, Konstantinidis, as his career unfolded, moved closer to the rationality of the universal grid and it is this affinity that now leads Tzonis to regard the work of Antonakakis as lying somewhere between the autochthonous pathway of Pikionis and universal grid of Konstantinidis. Are we justified in seeing this dualism as yet a further manifestation of the interaction between culture and civilization, and if so, what are the general consequences? Tzonis writes of Antonakakis's work and of critical regionalism in general that: "...(it) is a bridge over which any humanistic architecture of the future must pass, even if the path may lead to a completely different direction."[19]

Perhaps the one work of Antonakakis which expresses this conjunction of grid and the pathway more succinctly than any other is the Benakis Street apartment building completed to their designs in Athens in 1975; a building wherein a concept of labyrinthine path-movement, drawn from the islands of Hydra, is woven into the structural fabric of a rationalist grid—the ABA concrete frame which sustains the form of the building.

If any central principle of critical regionalism can be isolated, then it is surely a commitment to *place* rather than *space*, or, in Heideggerian terminology, to the nearness of *raum*, rather than the distance of *spatium*. This stress on place may also be construed as affording the political *space of public appearance* as formulated by Hannah Arendt. Such a conjunction between the *cultural* and the *political* is difficult to achieve in late capitalist society. Among the occasions in the last decade on which it has appeared on more general terms, recognition should be given to the development of Bologna in the Seventies. In this instance, an appraisal was made of the fundamental morphology and typology of the city fabric, and *socialist* legislation was introduced to maintain this fabric in both *old* and *new* development. The conditions under which such a plan is feasible must of necessity be restricted to those surviving traditional cities which have remained subject to responsible forms of political control. Where these *cultural* and *political* conditions are absent, the formulation of a creative cultural strategy becomes more difficult. The universal Megalopolis is patently antipathetic to a dense differentiation of culture. It intends, in fact, the reduction of the environment to nothing but commodity. As an abacus of development, it consists of little more than a hallucinatory landscape in which nature fuses into instrument and vice versa. Critical Regionalism would seem to offer the sole possibility of resisting the rapacity of this tendency. Its salient cultural precept is "place" creation; the general model to be employed in all future development is the *enclave* that is to say, the bounded fragment against which the ceaseless inundation of a place-less, alienating consumerism will find itself momentarily checked.

1   Paul Ricoeur, "Universalization and National Cultures," in *History and Truth* (Evanston, IL: Northwestern University Press, 1961), 276–283.

2   Jan Mukarovsky, *Structure, Sign and Function* (New Haven: Yale University Press, 1970), 228. Perhaps I am overstating the case. However, Mukarovsky writes: "The artistic sign, unlike the communicative sign, is not serving, that is, not an instrument."

3   Abraham Moles, "The Three Cities," in Anthony Hill, ed., *Directions in Art, Theory and Aesthetics* (London: Faber and Faber Limited, 1968), 191.

4   Oriel Bohigas, "Posibilidades de una arquitectura Barcelona," in *Destino* (Barcelona: 1951). See also Oriel Bohigas, "Disenar para un publico o contra un publico," in Seix Barral, *Contra una arquitectura adjetivida* (Barcelona: 1969).

5   See Ignazio Gardella's Casa Borsalino Apartments built in Alexandria in 1951.

6   Alvaro Siza, "To Catch a Precise Moment of Flittering Images in All its Shades," *Architecture and Urbanism* no. 123 (December 1980): 9.

7   Emilio Ambasz, *The Architecture of Luis Barragán* (New York: Museum of Modern Art, 1976), 9.

8   C. Banford-Smith, *Builders in the Sun: Five Mexican Architects* (New York: Architectural Book Publishing Co., 1967), 74.

9   Harwell H. Harris, "Regionalism and Nationalism," *Student Publication of the School of Design, North Carolina State of the University of North Carolina at Raleigh* vol. 14, no. 5.

10   Description submitted by Harry Wolf Associates on September 3, 1982 for the Fort Lauderdale Riverfront Plaza Competition.

11   Vittorio Gregotti, *L'Architettura come territoria.* Botta took his notion of building the site from the thesis that Gregotti advanced in this book.

12   Tadao Ando, "From Self-Enclosed Modern Architecture Toward Universality," *The Japan Architect* no. 301 (May 1982): 8–12.

13   Ibid.

14   Ibid.

15   Ibid.

16   Ibid.

17   Alexander Tzonis and Liane Lefaivre, "The Grid and the Pathway: An Introduction to the Work of Dimitris and Susana Antonakakis, with Prolegomena to a History of the Culture of Modern Greek Architecture," *Architecture in Greece* no. 15 (1981): 164–178.

18   Ibid.

19   Ibid.

INTRODUCTION

Why Critical Regionalism Today?
Alexander Tzonis and Liane Lefaivre

The inventors of the term "Critical Regionalism," architect Alexander Tzonis and historian Liane Lefaivre here offer a history of regionalism in the twentieth century and a defense of its continued viability as a critical paradigm. Fending off accusations that regionalist architecture leads to chauvinistic nationalism and kitsch, they describe a strategy of self-examination in the tradition of the "Critiques" of philosopher Immanuel Kant and the Frankfurt School. Critical, in this specialized usage, means to challenge both the world as it exists and underlying world views. In architecture, Tzonis and Lefaivre say this is accomplished when a building is "self-reflective, self-referential, when it contains, in addition to explicit statements, implicit metastatements."

Their idea of region is not static or closed. Furthermore, their Critical Regionalism is differentiated from past regionalist episodes, except with regard to a common concern for place and use of regional design elements to confront a universalizing architecture. The modernist technique of defamiliarization is used to represent regional elements in an unfamiliar light. The use of this poetic device forces a dialogue between building and viewer. Tzonis and Lefaivre assert that all architects have the skills for defamiliarization ("identifying, decomposing, recomposing elements"), and that regionalism does not limit architects to working in their own regions.

Tzonis and Lefaivre acknowledge a debt for their idea of regionalism to Lewis Mumford, the architectural and urban historian. In Mumford's writing of the 1940s, he was similarly concerned about the domination of technology and the limitations of the International Style. Regionalism is seen by all three writers as a secondary thread of modernism. "Why Critical Regionalism Today?" is historical, as opposed to the more polemical tone and intent of Kenneth Frampton's essay. Tzonis and Lefaivre do not propose a nostalgic recapitulation of local traditions, nor do they completely reject these traditions. A critical reevaluation of local culture, employing modernist strategies, elevates their proposed regionalism above the parochial. Finally, Critical Regionalism's acknowledgement of local environments has particular relevance as the world faces a growing ecological crisis.

ALEXANDER TZONIS AND LIANE LEFAIVRE
WHY CRITICAL REGIONALISM TODAY?

In the last ten years, since the term was introduced,[1] critical regionalism has emerged as one of the alternatives to a clearly aging modernism and to postmodernism's younger but prematurely ailing sibling, deconstruction.

Yet for many people, even for those who believe that postmodernism is eclipsing and that deconstruction is no substitute for it, the meaning and appropriateness of regionalism is questionable. How can one be regionalist in a world that is increasingly becoming one global economically and technologically interdependent whole, where universal mobility is taking architects and users of architecture across borders and through continents at an unprecedented speed? More pointedly, how can one be regionalist today when regions in the cultural, political, social sense, based on the idea of ethnic identity, are disintegrating before our eyes? And anyway, how can one be critical and regionalist at the same time? It sounds like a contradiction in terms.

Indeed no building today is capable of arousing feelings like the ones the Cathedral of Strasbourg did in the heart of the first *Romantic Regionalist*, the young Goethe in 1772, that sense of individual and local architectural values symbolizing an aspiration for emancipation against universal alien design canons, a sense of belonging to a single racial community. No building can talk to the viewer directly and immediately "without the aid of a translator" as it did to him, and make the viewer rush to embrace it as Goethe wanted to embrace the Cathedral of Strasbourg.[2] Nor can contemporary buildings possess as buildings and for John Ruskin, a mid-nineteenth century Romantic Regionalist, that strong quality of "sympathy," "affinity," "memory," and "familiarity" a "deep sense of voicefulness" that convincingly speaks of past as if it were one with the present, telling us "all we need to know of national feeling or achievement." Even less can a building still

From *Architecture and Urbanism* no. 236 (May 1990): 22–33. Courtesy of the authors and publisher.

evoke that same sense of revolt and righteousness? To look again to the topography of the region as a source of inspiration as [Eugène Emmanuel] Viollet-le-Duc did when he took the Mont-Blanc as an archetypal image, a paradigmatic building on which to base his design for his one single building "La Vedette"[3] can only be an exercise in anachronism today. Even less can one go back to cultivating the *genius loci* in the manner of the early eighteenth-century *Picturesque Regionalists*,[4] those "brave Britons" who in the words of Alexander Pope used local elements as a means of manifesting their desire for emancipation from "despised" "foreign laws" and the "formal mockery" of the absolutist classical order.

Surely [Marcel] Proust, whose very different ideas about the mechanisms of familiarization and memory evolved out of an early apprenticeship to Ruskin[5] is right. *Swann's Way* (1913), the first volume of *À la recherche du temps perdu*, finishes with the hero reflecting sadly on the houses and avenues of Combray and of the Paris of his youth that are now "all fugitive," mere memories, irretrievable things of the past. "The reality I have known no longer exists," he sighs. This is the sigh of a culturally, politically, ethnically, sexually ambivalent "Cosmopolitan" intellectual, but it is also the sign of a civilization that has lost identifiable regions, collective social structures, and the collective representations that went with them, a syndrome of the magic realization that community and place cannot be recaptured.

Given this loss of region, how is it possible for regionalist architecture to be anything more than, at best, a sentimental cosy indulgence in nostalgia for a bygone era, having nothing to do with Proust's art and everything to do with what we have called Proust's syndrome, citing highly typified regional fragments and gluing them together in a fake, a pastiche, kitsch, good only for commercial facilities, restaurants, hotels, and other emporia; or, at worst, a form of atavism, a setting for a xenophobic, neo-tribal racist hallucination. How is it possible for such a regionalist architecture, whether libertarian or totalitarian, commercial or propagandistic, in its *"as-if" overfamiliarity* to be anything but a kind of architectural pornography?

We would like to argue that one contemporary trend of Regionalist architecture— Critical Regionalism—is a more original movement which has come about as a response to new problems posed by contemporary global development of which it is strongly critical, and that the poetics of this new movement are to a great extent different from if not antithetical to other architectural regionalist techniques of the past. In fact the beginning of this new kind of regionalism has coincided with the realization of the obsolescence of traditional perceptions of regions as static closed entities corresponding to similarly invariant, insular groups and the outworn character of traditional regionalist architectural modes of expression. These realizations have mounted as universal culture, economy, and technology have expanded, and as regions have melted and fused into capitals, capitals into metropolises, metropolises into Patrick Geddes's "conurbations"[6] and Jean Gottmann's "megalopolises,"[7] and these in turn into Melvin Webber's ultimate postindustrial "world-realms."[8]

This new trend of regionalism is not only a defense against the obsolescence of the region itself but also a reaction to a perverse mutation of Romantic Regionalism, the commercial as well as the totalitarian *Heimatsarchitektur* regionalism we referred to above which spread during the decade before the Second World War. From the outset, it is clear that this new regionalism shares with the entire tradition of regionalism since its earliest inception—Romantic Regionalism and Picturesque Regionalism—a commitment to "placeness" and a use of regional design elements as a means of confronting a universalist order of architecture that is seen as dominating or oppressive. But it also contains a new idea, one which is essential to critical regionalism that of "place" whose definition goes beyond ethnicity, not to say against the grain of nationalist insularity. Much of this discussion is to be found first in the writings of Lewis Mumford.

In his *South in Architecture*,[9] he evokes the architecture of [Henry Hobson] Richardson as an example of regionalism in architecture. The work is not without an element of dramatizing simplicity in its account of certain complex historical phenomena. But its importance lies in Mumford's interpretation of Richardson's architecture, largely unknown at that time, as regionalist. Mumford praises his buildings for the critical confrontation and alternative they offer to the "despotic" Beaux-Arts architecture that Mumford links en masse to the imperial "exploitation and colonialization and conquest of Asia, Africa, and the Americas" as well as to what had been during Richardson's time, the East Coast banking establishment which in its architectural expression had "placed a premium upon the facade." Mumford hails Richardson for his refusal "to place the premium upon the facade" and for carrying out through regionalism the "social task of architecture."

In addition, Mumford opposes Richardson's regionalism to the totalitarian type of regionalism that is being propounded in Nazi Germany at the time. He shows that an architecture can provide an identity and express the specifics of a program without the "deification of Heimatsarchitektur," the "cult of the relics of another imperial age," and on a neo-tribal creation of a "deep unbridgeable gulf between the peoples of the earth." Mumford puts forth a concept of regionalism that upholds, on the contrary, the idea of a common humanity, explicitly free of racial or tribal or ethnic dimensions. Last but not least Mumford uses the example of Richardson to juxtapose regionalism polemically to another kind of "despotism," that of the "mechanical order" and of the absurdities of a mindless use of technology.

After the war Mumford does not return to the attack on Heimat. His regionalist position focuses on the developing post-war International Style which he feels has deviated from the original objectives of the Modern Movement in architecture and succumbed to the very forces it was created to reform. He reacts to an architecture of false modernity that emulates modernity through the rote repetition of surface effects where once more "the premium is placed upon the facade." Thus the International Style replaces Beaux-Arts as the target of Mumford's criticism. In 1947, in his famous column "Skyline" of *The New Yorker*,[10] the tone is provocative and polemical, almost pugnacious. Referring to Henry-Russell Hitchcock's turn to "personalism" and Sigfried Gideon's new enthusiasm for "the monumental and the symbolic," he complains that modern architecture is being subverted from within by critics who had been so closely identified with the Modern Movement's preoccupations with objectivity and plain reality. As a critical confrontation to what he sees as a debased post-war "modernism," he proposes the so-called Bay Region Style of California of William Wurster and his associates calling it a "native and humane form of modernism" which a "product of the meeting of Oriental and Occidental traditions" is "far more truly a universal style than the international style of the 1930s," because it permits *regional* adaptations."

The article creates an enormous stir which leads to an open debate at the Museum of Modern Art on the evening of February 11, 1948. The title "What is happening to Modern Architecture?" reflects the concerns of the organizers.[11] The speakers include some of the main figures of post war modernism: Alfred Barr Jr., the director of the museum, Henry-Russell Hitchcock, Philip Johnson, Walter Gropius, Marcel Breuer, Serge Chermayeff, George Nelson among others, and Mumford himself.

Most of the participants completely miss Mumford's redefinition of regionalism. In spite of Mumford's insistence that "it is a sample of internationalism, not a sample of localism and limited effort,"[12] Alfred Barr refers to it dismissively as the *Neue Gemutlichkeit*, the International Cottage Style; as for Gropius, he reads into it "a chauvinistic sentimental national prejudice." The one exception is Hitchcock. He is sensitive to the real critical impact of the notion. "Criticism—for it is criticism—that is implicit" in Mumford's article is, according to Hitchcock, "a criticism of the International Style conceived in the limited sense..." But then he comments "that this criticism and the steps that have been taken are to be subsumed in a more general problem" which in his familiar formalist way identifies as "the problem of expression in architecture."[13]

Mumford's ideas are read, praised, and dutifully ignored. Or they are subverted, as in the case of the "regionalist" epidermic concrete lace screened facades of such new projects, at that time widely published, as Edward Durrell Stone's Pakistan Institute of Science and Technology, Walter Gropius's University of Bagdad and Yamasaki's entry for the United States Embassy in London. While these efforts to restore the "imperial facade" are being deployed, technocracy, bureaucracy, and real estate get their equally imperial way, with as sole result widespread anomie and atopy.

It is in Europe that the new approach to regionalism is used as a critical confrontation of the state of architecture after the Second World War, although the word "regionalism" is rarely used. It emerges a few years after Mumford's polemic at the MoMA. In at least one sense the Europeans develop the Mumford thesis further, the "architecturalness" with which they carry out their analysis and their capability to implement these ideas in concrete projects of often considerable scale.

In an article entitled "Regionalism and Modern Architecture"[14] the young James Stirling juxtaposes regionalism to what he calls "the so-called International Style combined with a strong dose of monumental eclectic neo-historicism" that was dominant and promoted the "new traditionalism" taking into account the local technological and economic realities. Furthermore, Stirling designs projects for his Village Project (1955) and for his Preston Infill Housing (1957–59), which in their respective incorporation of regional and working class neighbourhood elements, make a strong implicit critique of the post-war New Monumentality.[15]

A number of other interesting regionalist projects are designed across the same lines in England by the "new empiricists" whose regionalist outlook is influenced by Scandinavian architecture or by [Alvar] Aalto. The issue of regionalism is also discussed by Team X as a critique of New Monumentality and finds its way into several of their projects, especially in the early work of Candilis, Josic and Woods in North Africa. Also critical of the neo-formalist and technocratic architecture of the International style of the 1950s are many Italians practitioners and theoreticians, the architects of INA-Casa. Giancarlo de Carlo especially in his shops and apartment buildings in Matera, and last but not least Ernesto Rogers, both as editorialist at *Casabella* and as designer of the Torre Velasca (1958) in Milan.

The Torre Velasca is widely covered by the press internationally and its regionalist expression as a critique of International Style was acknowledged. Gerhard Kallman writes one of the most trenchant reviews in *Architectural Forum* in February 1958. He sees it as "a valiant essay in the neglected art of fitting modern architecture into a historic continuity of building" while avoiding "folkloristic revivalism" and "sentimental eclecticism." Rogers himself in his own article for *Casabella* on "Our Responsibility toward Tradition" (August 1954) attacks the dogmatism of those modernists who "fail to realize that the modern style contrasts with the old precisely because it laid the ground for a dynamic approach to the problems" as well as of "neo-arcadian populism," which was "anachronistic if not hypocritical or downright demagogic lying."

Kenzo Tange's work in the second part of the 1950s, particularly his Kagawa Prefectural Office of 1956, the project with which Japan definitely enters the international architectural forum, significantly contributes to the specific post-war development of regionalism and to the search to redefine modern architecture in an exchange which took place in 1959 when the building was presented at the Otterlo meeting of CIAM. In response to Ernesto Rogers's enthusiastic praise of the building's regionalism as "a very good example of what we have to do," Tange's response is guarded. "I cannot accept the concept of total regionalism," he asserts, adding that "tradition can be developed through challenging its own shortcomings," implying the same for regionalism.

This last statement of Tange's encapsulates the antinomy in the thinking, partly an attachment, partly a rejection of regional elements, typical of the current practice of what we have called Critical Regionalism. This antinomy is the second essential element that goes into the definition of Critical regionalism. "Critical" here does not connote a "confrontational" attitude only. After all, as we have seen, Mumford's post war regionalism was confrontational with respect to the facadist, anomic, atopic modernism, and the attitude of romantic nineteenth-century regionalists was in open rebellion against the "imperialist" spread of the classical canon. But this does not necessarily make them critical in the more specialized sense we now apply, that is as a regionalism that is self-examining, self-questioning, self-evaluating, that not only is confrontational with regard to the world but to itself.

The idea of "critical" in this second sense, originates in the serene essays of [Immanuel] Kant[16] and is developed in the agitated writings of the Frankfurt School.[17] Critical works challenge not only the established actual world as confrontational works do, but the very legitimacy of the possible world views which interpret it in the mind. One might say, borrowing [Jürgen] Habermas's expression, that they "dissolve the objective illusion" in architecture. This occurs when a building is self-reflective, self-referential, when it contains, in addition to explicit statements, implicit *metastatements* that make the beholder aware of the artificiality of her or his way of looking at the world.

An essential characteristic of critical regionalist buildings is that they are critical in two senses then. In addition to providing contrasting images to the anomic, atopic, misanthropic ways of a large number of current mainstream projects constructed world wide, they raise questions in the mind of the viewer about the legitimacy of the very regionalist tradition to which they belong.

The poetics of critical regionalism carry out its self-reflective function through the method of defamiliarization. "Defamiliarization" is a concept coined by the Russian literary theoretician Victor Shklovsky.[18] It was initially applied to literature, but it can be also applied to architecture as we have demonstrated in our studies on classical architecture.[19] But as it relates to regionalism, defamiliarization is instrumental only in its current critical phase.

Romantic regionalism, despite its confrontational stance, employed *familiarization*. It selected regional elements linked in memory with forlorn eras and inserted them into new buildings, constructing scenographic settings for arousing affinity and "sympathy" in the viewer, forming familiarized scenes which, although contrasting, mostly emotionally, with the actual despotic architecture, rendered consciousness insensible. The mawkish, gushing, sentimental regionalism with its overfamiliarizing, immediate easy, titillating "as if" narcissistic *Heimat* settings, has had an even more narcotic—if not hallucinatory—effect on consciousness.

Critical regionalism for its part reacts—more polemically than the period of the 1950s we referred to before—to this explosion of counterfeit regionalist settings which are even more widespread in its commercial version today than its totalitarian one in the 1930s. It selects these regional elements for their potential to act as support, physical or conceptual, of human contact and community, what we may call "place-defining" elements, and incorporates them "strangely" rather than "familiarly." In other words it makes them appear distant, hard to grasp, difficult, even disturbing. It frames as if it were the sense of place in a strange sense of displacement. It disrupts the sentimental "embrace" between buildings and their consumers, "de-automatizing" perception and thus "pricking the conscious," to use another of Shklovsky's expressions. Hence, through appropriately chosen poetic devices of defamiliarization critical regionalism makes the building appear to enter into an imagined dialogue with the viewer. It sets up a process of hard cognitive negotiation in place of the fantasized surrender that follows from familiarization and the seduction that follows from overfamiliarization. It leads the viewer to a *metacognitive* state, a democracy of experience as Jerome Bruner might have called it, it conjures up a "forum of possible worlds."[20]

Current critical regionalism, emerging with Mumford's censoring of the fake modernism of the International Style, in contrast to previous phases of regionalism, does not support the emancipation of a regional group nor does it set up one group against another. It tries to forge the identity of a "global group" in opposition to "them," "them" being the alien occupation army of technocracy and bureaucracy imposing the illegitimate rule of anomie and atopy. Furthermore, critical regionalism not only alerts us through the poetics of its forms to the loss of place and community but also to our "reflective" incapability to become aware of this loss while it was occurring. Its relation to a global practice of architecture is also special. The operations of identifying, decomposing, recomposing regional elements in a "defamiliarizing" way is part of the universal set of skills of architects. They can be carried out by any knowledgeable, responsible, competent architect committed to the understanding of local constraints not only by "local" ones. Critical regionalism does not imply professional parochialism.

In this brief sketch of the poetics of critical regionalism, we have not tried to identify any general criteria of style. We have not provided answers to the pragmatic questions such as "are wooden houses less atopic than concrete ones?" or "are concrete cafeterias more anomic than brick ones?" We have not made check lists of physical design criteria of how to be a critical regionalist. And for a good reason. The poetics of critical regionalism does not include a set of design rules of partitioning, motifs and *genera* as does the definition of classicism, the picturesque or de Stijl. Rather, as with Neue Sachlichkeit architecture, it draws its forms from the context. In other words its general poetics become specific drawing from the regional, circumscribed constraints which have produced places and collective representations in given bound areas. To cite just one example, in the case of Spanish critical regionalism these design elements include the prismatic purity and vivid color of jointless brick facades, the inner courts of apartment houses called *corrala*, the *manzana* patios, the *miradores*. These are regional elements which are historically linked with the formation of concrete urban *genius loci* which are selected, defamiliarized, and recomposed in new projects.[21]

There is also another mode in the critical regionalist poetics, found more often in the United States, through which regional characteristics—natural rather than cultural— enter into design. This is the case of optimally composing buildings as shelters, respecting regional environmental constraints, and accepting regional resources. This is the reverse of the anomy and atopy resulting when nature is violated through brute force to control environmental conditions—not force as such, but as a cause of the *hubris* of mind spent on nothing, a hubris present even when there is money and machinery to spend, combined with the hubris of the mean view of the world which the project in its "gluttony" implies. In other words, placeness and the containment of anomie and atopy are supported by the implicit messages of a well tempered, "economical," "ecological" design.

One cannot say on the other hand by looking at a building, as one can do for classical temples for instance, this is a well-formed critical regionalist building. As Kenneth Frampton, the critic whose writings have helped raise and spread the issue of critical regionalism more than any other today, has made the point very clearly:

> The fundamental strategy of Critical Regionalism is to mediate the impact of universal civilization with elements derived indirectly from the peculiarities of a particular place. It is clear from the above that Critical Regionalism depends upon maintaining a high level of critical self-consciousness. It may find its governing inspiration in such things as the range and quality of the local light, or in a tectonic derived from a peculiar structural mode, or in the topography of a given site.[22]

Neither have we tried to argue that critical regionalism should be seen as contradictory to trends towards higher technology and a more global economy and culture. It merely opposes their undesirable contingent byproducts borne of private interests and public mindlessness.

It seems that after two highly creative but also frustrating decades, during which architecture has oscillated between dreaming socially engaged visions completely outside the conceptual and practical framework of architecture and actualizing socially vacuous exercises within the autonomous formal framework of architecture, we are coming closer to a more balanced outlook, closer to reality. One of the issues which identify this new outlook is the problem of the architecture of place, the articulation of a critical statement in terms of shape and space about community in a world of global mobility and integration. Critical regionalism appears as a movement seriously engaged in this problem. This gives us enough ground to claim that it has emerged as one of the most exciting approaches in architecture today.

1   See A. Tzonis, L. Lefaivre "The grid and the pathway," *Architecture in Greece* no. 5 (1981); A. Tzonis, L. Lefaivre, and A. Alofsin, "Die Frage des Regionalismus"; N. Andritzky, I. Burckhardt, and O. Hoffman, (hrsg.) *Für eine andere Architektur* (Frankfurt: Fischer, 1981).

2   See W. Goethe's *Von deutscher Baukunst*, N. Pevsner, trans., in *Architectural Review* XCVIII, 155ff. In the text Goethe argues, erroneously, that the Gothic was German. In fact the Gothic was French. It is generally accepted that the first Gothic building was the abbey church of St. Denis in the Île de France, supervised by the abbot Suger for his patrons, the Capetian dynasty. For a general background on the subject of the role of Goethe in the Gothic revival in Germany see W.D. Robson-Scott, *The Literary Background of the Gothic Revival in Germany* (Oxford: Oxford University Press, 1965).

3   This point has been made by Jacques Gubler in his penetrating study "Viollet-le-Duc et l'Architecture Rurale," in the exhibition catalogue *Viollet-le-Duc, Continuité de la Mort à Lausanne*, Exposition au Musée de l'Ancien Évêche (Lausanne: 1979).

4   For an outline of the biography of regionalism starting from its earliest, "emblematic" phase in the early renaissance and continuing through to the Picturesque Regionalism of the eighteenth century and the Romantic Regionalism of the nineteenth century, see our "El Regionalismo critico y la arquitectura espanola actual," in *A & V* 3 (Madrid: 1985): 4–19.

5   Proust translated Ruskin's *Bible of Amiens* into French, and the overt and implicit references to Ruskin in *À la recherche du temps perdu* constitute an important pattern in the fabric of the novel. For an indication of the extent of Ruskin's influence on Proust, see the excellent Marcel Proust, *On Reading Ruskin* (New Haven: Yale University Press, 1987), edited and translated by J. Autret, W. Burford, and P. Wolfe, and introduced by R. Macksey.

6   Patrick Geddes, *Cities in Evolution* (London: 1915).

7   Jean Gottmann, *Megalopolis* (Cambridge: MIT Press, 1961).

8   Melvin Webber, "The Urban Place and the Nonplace Urban Realm," in M. Webber et al., eds., *Explorations into Urban Structure* (Philadelphia: University of Pennsylvania Press, 1964), 79–137. For a contemporary extensive critique of the Webber thesis see S. Chermayeff and A. Tzonis, *Advanced Studies in Urban Environments* (New Haven: Yale University Press, 1967).

9   L. Mumford, *The South in Architecture* (New York: Harcourt, Brace & Co. 1941).

10   L. Mumford, "Skyline," *The New Yorker* (11 October 1947).

11   *The Museum of Modern Art Bulletin* vol. XV, no. 3 (Spring 1948): 35ff.

12   Ibid.: 18.

13   Ibid.: 9.

14   See *Architect's Year Book* no. 8 (1957).

15   New Monumentality is an expression coined by Giedion to the monumental architecture of the 1950s.

16   I. Kant, *The Critique of Pure Reason* (1791).

17   For a synoptic coverage of the development of the idea of a critical theory, see Raymond Geuss, *The Idea of a Critical Theory. Habermas and the Frankfurt School* (Cambridge: Cambridge University Press, 1981).

18   Shklovsky was a member of the "Russian Formalists," the avant-garde group of literary theoreticians active around the time of the Russian revolution. See Shklovsky's "Art as technique," in L.T. Lemon and M. Reis, eds., *Russian Formalist Critique* (Lincoln: University of Nebraska Press, 1965).

19 A. Tzonis and L. Lefaivre, *Classical Architecture: The Poetics of Order* (Cambridge: MIT Press, 1986). See in particular the last chapter, "Critical Classicism: the tragic function."

20 Jerome Bruner, *Actual Minds, Possible Worlds* (Cambridge: Harvard University Press, 1986).

21 See our "El Regionalismo Critico y la Arquitectura espanola actual," in *A & V* no. 3, op. cit.

22 In "Towards a Critical Regionalism: Six Points for an Architecture of Resistance," in H. Foster, ed., *The Anti-Aesthetic, Essays on Postmodern Culture* (Port Townsend: Bay Press, 1983), 21.

12. TECTONIC EXPRESSION

INTRODUCTION

The Exercise of Detailing
Vittorio Gregotti

In the postmodern critique, an interest in tectonics is common to divergent theoretical and stylistic components. Demetri Porphyrios, for example, presents an argument for tectonics, (ch. 1) promising:

> to construct slowly an ontology of building...
> a tectonic discourse which, while addressing
> the pragmatics of shelter, could at the same
> time represent its very tectonics as myth.

He specifically advocates classical architecture's mimetic transformation and mythification of vernacular building.[1]

One finds a similar interest in *making* in very different postmodern work—such as that of Tadao Ando (ch. 10) and Juhani Pallasmaa (ch. 9), Morphosis and Frank Israel, Stephen Holl and Mario Botta. The current significance of making is based on the idea that amplification of construction can be a source of meaning. It reflects a phenomenological interest in the "thingness" of architecture, and its ability to *gather*. (ch. 9) For these architects, tectonics and the significant detail register a criticism of both formulaic corporate modernism and superficial postmodern historicism. Construction as a process of "becoming" sometimes develops as a material narrative, for example, in the partially clad roof of Faye Jones's Pinecote Pavilion. The revealing of structure, associated with authenticity in some modern and postmodern architecture, coincides with Martin Heidegger's *unconcealing* as the poetic act.

For Vittorio Gregotti, architecture (as distinguished from building) resides in the details, and he laments that contemporary architects seem to have forgotten this point. Detailing demonstrates the attributes of materials through application of the laws of construction; it renders design decisions articulate. The detail also raises the issue of hierarchy, in suggesting a relationship between part and whole.

Since the time of the skilled details of modernists Carlo Scarpa and Franco Albini, there has been a loss of the capacity to signify structural changes in architecture through the detail. In place of the detail, Gregotti finds historicist stylistic quotation and accessible populist imagery, underscoring "the crisis of architectural language." Gregotti cites classicism to establish that details can provide the meaningful ornament wrongly sought now in pastiche. While Porphyrios advocates and pursues an authentic classical revival for this reason, Gregotti's design work is neorationalist, building on the modern and classical traditions. (ch. 7)

The author says the self-reflexive nature of the discipline requires that detailing be resituated as an essential architectural problem. This essay, the following by Marco Frascari, and Kenneth Frampton's "Prospects for a Critical Regionalism," all published between 1983 and 1984, both reflected and stimulated the tectonic "return to things." The tectonic expression of architecture is capable of enhancing the sensual and intellectual experience of building

1   Demetri Porphyrios, "Classicism is not a Style," *Architectural Design. Classicism is not a Style* 5–6 (1982): 56.

VITTORIO GREGOTTI
THE EXERCISE OF DETAILING

Detailing is, surely, one of the more revealing components of changing architectural language. We have often stated our opinion on how this language has, in recent years, lost its capacity to signify structural changes in the architectural field. Its manifest redundance and its obsession with the new and the different, has nullified any meaningful differences. Nevertheless, things that get made are given a form, which automatically has a capacity to communicate through language.

For this reason it is important to examine its constitution which, to take August Perret's famous saying "Il n'y a pas de détail dans la construction," detail is certainly not just a matter of detail. Obviously detailing does not necessarily depend on an overall guiding concept; even if it has inherent relations with such a concept, it is not simply a declination of general decisions; but gives them form, rendering them recognizable and articulated in their various parts.

In the Fifties and Sixties the detail had some great and very diverse protagonists in Italy such as Franco Albini, Carlo Scarpa, and Mario Ridolfi, in which the analysis and displays of material, provided by the laws of construction and formation of the architectural object, constituted its principal support. One can easily see how the eloquent detail of that period has been followed by one of reduced expressive content, one could say the return of the architectural detail to guiding concept.

It was not a case of its elimination but a different approach to the hierarchy of the detail to the whole, which was occasionally a great deal more sophisticated and complex. The connection between the floors, the relation of the materials and the differences in the use, both practical and symbolic, thus became more explicit and for the first time expressive. This has taken on a double meaning. On the one hand, a negation of the

From *Casabella* no. 492 (June 1983): 11. Courtesy of the author and publisher.

value of construction as a subject of importance regarding architectural expression, resulting in a gradual increase in the abstraction of detailing, and the progressive lack of interest in the handling of materials according to a model of modernity, going back to the architecture of the end of the nineteenth century and that of the Enlightenment. On the other hand, there has been discussion, not so much of the detail's possible eloquence as its different expressive value and technical composition, in relation to a crisis of architectural language as an objectual language, towards the revaluation of the notion of relation and modification, of physical and historical place and context of specificity and difference. In both cases the resulting eloquent aphasia, though with very different meanings, has been hastily taken over by a reawakening of interest in decoration, or the ornate (according to [Ernesto N.] Rogers's distinction between these two terms) in the peculiar acceptance of stylistic quotation, often as a breaking of the constitutional methodological rules of contemporary architecture.

There have been hurried reconciliations with tradition and history, false cures derived from communication processes, searching for a consent at the lowest level of mass culture, as well as, and worse for architecture, the loss of practice, tradition, and knowledge. There was the illusion that quotation is a sufficient substitute for the detail as a system of articulation in architectural language, and that an overall "grand conception" can dominate and automatically permeate every aspect of the project and its realization, but the very abstention of the detail, thus polemically underlining the lack of influence of building techniques as an expressive component. Often the outcome of this idea in built terms is an unpleasant sense of an enlarged model, a lack of articulation of the parts at different scales: walls that seem to be made of cut out cardboard, unfinished windows and openings; in sum, a general relaxing of tension from the drawing to the building. It is false to think that culture of industry or building (by now distant cultures from design) could solve the problem of detailing; this might be convenient or economic to the architect, but lead to unprecedented downfall of architecture. There is no wonder that in classical architecture, on the contrary, the "general, the proportioned, and the measured project" (i.e. the outline sketch project, the project to scale and the model, according to [Antonio Averlino] Filarete) were coupled with very few indications of detail: both construction detail and decorative detail were expressions of a cultural heritage common to design and building in a unity of intent unknown today.

With regard to this point, we know that the dissociation between decoration and detail was practiced for many centuries, sometimes with great success. This was in the past the acting out of a continuing dialogue about classical rules on "ornament in architecture," whose object lay in their comprehension and re-articulation. But according to theories held by someone, the notion of ornament was, for example with [Leon Battista] Alberti, much closer in meaning to expressive form than that of the ornate, and the memory of the original links between ornament and construction was always there to testify to the integrity of architecture. Even the marvellous medieval use of classical fragments, as exemplary architectural details, was the testimony of the perfection of that integrity. Both technology and culture of design (in the production sense from industry's point of view) have "improperly" flooded the architectural field. This is due to the weakness of our discipline and its inability to reintegrate the sum of those techniques, which certainly form an indestructible base of today's building process, and therefore of the exercise in detailing, to architectural horizons.

INTRODUCTION

The Tell-the-Tale Detail
Marco Frascari

Architect Marco Frascari, like Vittorio Gregotti, locates the source of architectural meaning in construction, in particular in the "formal and actual joints" between materials or spaces. In this influential essay, Frascari privileges the joint—the original detail—as the generator of construction, and therefore of meaning. The tectonic detail is thus the site of innovation and invention. Frascari defines architecture as the result of the design of details and their resolution and substitution.

While functioning pragmatically, the "fertile" detail can also be seen as an aesthetic expression of structure and use. Frascari's semiological reading suggests that the detail is the minimum unit of signification within the architectural production of meaning. As in Gregotti's "The Exercise of Detailing," (this chapter) Carlo Scarpa's work is chosen as exemplary because "each detail tells us the story of its making, of its placing, of its dimensioning." The idea of narrative permeates the article, for instance, in the intriguing idea that joints are pretexts for generating new texts. This is possible, Frascari claims, because the detail or joint can impose its order on the whole. Thus, located within tectonics is an endless set of architectural ideas.

The "techne of logos," which can be understood as the production of discourse, is the aspect Frascari calls *construing*. Like Martin Heidegger, Frascari is interested in the etymological connections between words, in this case between *constructing* (building) and *construing* (giving order and intelligibility to the world, i.e., constructing meaning).

In Heidegger's discussion, building (*bauen*) is linked to constructing, dwelling, and cultivating, with connotations of edifying. Furthermore, Heidegger asserts that dwelling is the purpose of life and depends on building. The linguistic connection to phenomenology lends credibility to Frascari's link between constructing (details and meaning) and construing meaning. A slight digression into perceptual psychology nonetheless makes a contribution to his argument, in positing the detail as the perceptual structure for apprehending architecture as meaningful. In its emphasis on returning architecture to its origin in tectonics, seen as generative of meaning, Frascari's essay touches on several important postmodern themes.

MARCO FRASCARI

THE TELL-THE-TALE DETAIL

The architectural community has traditionally ascribed the maxim "God lies in the detail" to Mies van der Rohe.[1] The German version of the adage, *Der liebe Gott steckt in Detail,* perhaps the original source of Mies's maxim, was used by Aby Warburg to indicate the foundation of the iconographical method for researching in art history. The French version has been attributed to Gustave Flaubert, and in this case the maxim indicates a manner of literary production.[2] The common denominator in these different forms and uses indicates that the detail expresses the process of signification; that is, the attaching of meanings to man-produced objects. The details are then the *locii* where knowledge is of an order in which the mind finds its own working, that is, *logos*.[3]

The aim of this paper is to indicate the role of details as generators, a role traditionally ascribed to the plan, and to show that technology, with its double-faced presence as "*techné of logos*" and "*logos of techné*"[4] is the basis for the understanding of the role of details. That is to say the "construction" and the "construing" of architecture are both in the detail. Elusive in a traditional dimensional definition, the architectural detail can be defined as the union of construction, the result of the *logos of techné*, with construing, the result of the *techné of logos*.

Details are much more than subordinate elements; they can be regarded as the minimal units of signification in the architectural production of meanings. These units have been singled out in spatial cells or in elements of composition, in modules or in measures, in the alternating of void and solid, or in the relationship between inside and outside.[5] The suggestion that the detail is the minimal unit of production is more fruitful because of the double-faced role of technology, which unifies the tangible and the intangible of architecture. As Jean Labatut, a French Beaux-Arts-trained Princeton professor

From *VIA 7: The Building of Architecture* (1984): 23–37. Courtesy of the author and publisher.

of architecture notes: "Whatever the air spaces, areas and dimensions involved, it is the precise study and good execution of details which confirm architectural greatness. 'The detail tells the tale.'"[6]

In the details are the possibilities of innovation and invention, and it is through these that architects can give harmony to the most uncommon and difficult or disorderly environment generated by a culture.[7] The notion that architecture is a result of the resolution, substitution, and design of details has always been a latent concept in architects' minds. That is to say, there is truth in the classical commonplace of architectural criticism: "That might have been great architecture if only somebody had worked out the details...." Careful detailing is the most important means for avoiding building failure, on both dimensions of the architectural profession—the ethical and the aesthetic. The art of detailing is really the joining of materials, elements, components, and building parts in a functional and aesthetic manner. The complexity of this art of joining is such that a detail performing satisfactorily in one building may fail in another for very subtle reasons.[8]

The discussion of the role of detail in the architectural process of signification will be developed in two parts. These inquiries analyze the understanding of the role of the detail within two different but interlocking realms, the theoretical and the empirical.

The first part is a search for an understanding of the concept of details in different levels of architectural production. The result of this inquiry is the conceptual identification of the detail with the making of the joint and the recognition that details themselves can impose order on the whole through their own order. Consequently, the understanding and execution of details constitute the basic process by which the architectural practice and theories should be developed.

The second part is an analysis of the architecture of Carlo Scarpa (1906–1979), a Veneto architect. In Scarpa's architecture, as Louis Kahn pointed out, "detail is the adoration of nature." The architectural production of this architect, in which the adoration of the making of joints is almost obsessive, allows an empirical interpretation of the role of detail in the process of signification, seen within culturally definable modes of construction and construing. In Scarpa's works the relationships between the whole and the parts and the relationships between craftsmanship and draftsmanship allow a direct substantiating *in corpore vili* of the identity of the processes of perception and production, that is, the union of the construction with the construing in the making and use of details.

Dictionaries define "detail" as a small part in relation to a larger whole. In architecture this definition is contradictory, if not meaningless. A column is a detail as well as it is a larger whole, and a whole classical round temple is sometimes a detail, when it is a lantern on the top of a dome. In architectural literature, columns and capitals are classified as details, but so are *piani nobili*, porches, and pergolas. The problem of scale and dimension in those classifications and the relationship between aediculas and edifices makes the dictionary definition useless in architecture. However, it is possible to observe that any architectural element defined as detail is always a joint. Details can be "material joints," as in the case of a capital, which is the connection between a column shaft and an architrave, or they can be "formal joints," as in the case of a porch, which is the connection between an interior and an exterior space. Details are then a direct result of the multifold reality of functions in architecture. They are the mediate or immediate expressions of the structure and the use of buildings.[9]

The etymological origin of the word "detail" does not help at all in understanding the architectural use of the term.[10] In architectural literature the term appeared in the French theoretical works of the eighteenth century and from France spread all over Europe. This spread was caused by the coupling of the term with the concept of "style" and by the active influence of French literary criticism and theory on the French neo-classical architects. In 1670 Despreaux Nicolas Boileau, in the first part of his *L'Art Poétique*, warning against the use of superfluous details in poems, set an analogy between an overdetailed palace and an overdetailed poem.[11] By the eighteenth century this analogy was commonplace and, ascribing it to Montesquieu, Giovanni Battista Piranesi attacked it as trivial in his defense of his architectural theory of overdetailed buildings.[12]

The French theoreticians of the *architecture parlante* were the ones who formally consolidated the role of detail in architectural production. In the analogy of the "speaking architecture," the architectural details are seen as words composing a sentence. And, as the selection of words and style gives character to the sentence, in a similar way the selection of details and style gives character to a building. This powerful role of the detail as generator of the character of a building was also pointed out by John Soane in one of his lectures on architecture: "Too much attention can not be given to produce a distinct Character in every building, not only in great features, but in minor detail likewise; even a moulding, however diminutive, contributes to increase or lessen the Character of the assemblage of which it forms a part."[13]

In the Beaux-Arts tradition the understanding of the role of detail as a generator of the character of buildings determined a very peculiar graphic means for the study of it, the *analytique*. In this graphic representation of a designed or surveyed building the details play the predominant role. They are composed in different scales in the attempt to single out the dialogue among the parts in the making of the text of the building. Sometimes the building as a whole is present in the drawing, and generally it is represented on a minuscule scale, and so it seems a detail among details. The origin of the *analytique* and its role in the construing of architecture can be traced back to the technique of graphic representation and composition developed by Piranesi in his etchings surveying the *Magnificenza* of Roman architecture. These are a graphic interpretation, with a stronger Vichian bias, of Carlo Lodoli's understanding of the built environment as a sum of inadequate details to be substituted with more appropriate ones.[14] Another form of the *analytique*, illustrating the architecture of Italy, can be found on the back of Italian lire notes today.

It is important to notice that the *analytique* as graphic analysis of details had its development in a period in which architects did not have to prepare working drawings showing the construction of the details. The drawings carried few if any details and dimensions. The designer could be almost entirely dependent on his craftsmen. Builders had no need for drawings to show details whose execution was a matter of common knowledge. Construction of details was parceled out among the various tradesmen, who supplied the necessary knowledge for making them. The same craftsmen who furnished the information for the [Denis] Diderot and [Jean le Rond] D'Alambert *Encyclopédie* were able to construct the drawing with the exact eye of the artist, and the *analytique* was simply the source for the understanding of the ordering role of a single detail in the overall composition.[15]

The production of details, as it was established before the development of the industrial society and motivated by different cultural needs, began to become problematic in a predominantly economically motivated society. No longer considered as long-lasting cultural and social repositories, buildings came to be viewed as economic investments with an intentionally planned short existence. Two polar reactions had developed from the change that occurred in the scope of edifices. One of the reactions was that the various building trades no longer inferred the construction of the detail from design drawings The details were studied and resolved on the drawing boards. Draftsmanship was substituted for workmanship, and the development of "real details" was replaced by "virtual" procedures. From this point of view the detail was no longer part of the building. The detail was no longer seen as a joint; instead, it was seen as a production drawing. In an *American Glossary of Building* the term "detail" is defined as "the delineation to full size or a large scale of any portion of an architectural design."[16] A French glossary was even more precise in this understanding of detail: "Detail: Specification or description of the work to be performed in the execution of a building."[17] In this interpretation "details" are verbal and graphic means for controlling the work of variable crews of vocationless workers who are unprepared for their own jobs and possibly even financially dishonest.

The second reaction to the change that occurred in the role of detail is the one that can be exemplified by the architecture produced by the Arts and Crafts Movement. The detail, in this movement, was seen as the means for the redemption of workers. The skill and knowledge of the making of details were given back to the workers. Workmanship was seen as the sole parameter for the details, which in themselves were seen as refinement of building tradition. The knowledge of details and of the related skills was the necessary means for the architect to practice his profession, since it was his task to select the appropriate workers for the appropriate details.

This duality in the physical production of detail is also found in the mental production. Using a conceptual analogy, it is possible to define architecture as a system in which there is a "total architecture," the plot, and a detailed architecture, the tale. The detailed architecture is based on "the constant process of drawing extrasystematic elements into the realm of the system and of expelling systematic elements into the area of not system....The stone that the builders of a formed and stabilized system reject for being, from their point of view, superfluous and unnecessary, turns out to be the cornerstone of subsequent system."[18] From this point of view architecture becomes the art of appropriate selection of details in the devising of the tale. A plot with the appropriate details becomes a fully developed and successful "tale."

Architecture as art of the appropriate is the theme of Leon Battista Alberti's architectural theory. Alberti sees architecture as the art of the selection of appropriate details whose result is beauty, which is a meaningful goal. He defines beauty as "the 'concinnity' of all the details in the unity to which they belong"; in other words, beauty is the skillful joining of parts by a normative by which nothing can be added, subtracted, or altered for the worse. Generally this principle has been interpreted as stating that a building should be a complete and finished whole, a total architecture. Alberti, however, does not apply this concept to the actual edifice, but, rather, to the mental one.[19] The joint, that is, the detail, is the place of the meeting of the mental construing and of the actual construction. A perfect instance of this union of mental function and physical representation is in the façade of Palazzo Rucellai, designed by Alberti in Florence. Although the façade is incomplete and its incompleteness is clearly shown, the detailed architecture is complete, and nothing can be added or subtracted for the worse. The grooves of the joints of the stone slabs composing the thick veneer of the Florentine *schiacciato* (representing the post and beam structure of the three superimposed classical Orders, related with arched windows and infilling walls) are the solution of the mathematical problem set by the relationships existing among the parts of the façade. In many cases the joints are not real ones, and the shapes of the stones are not as regular as they appear; fake grooves were carved in the stone to make the detailed architecture complete and to offer at the same time its own proof.

Alberti's search for "Beauty" is the setting of a precise relationship between the detail and the attached meaning. Beauty is the result of the process of signification, and *concinnity* is the process for achieving it. Concinnity is the correspondence of three basic requirements: 1) Number, 2) Finishing, 3) Collocation.[20]

Number is a system of calculation. "The technique of calculation is part of the technique of house building."[21] Numbers in this way are tools for giving meaning. In architecture there are elements, and, in order to build, it is necessary to draw numerical correlation among them. In a triforium, three arches are correlated to four columns to make a serliana. The proof is in the details, and it is expressed in terms of mouldings, capitals, bases, and keystone. "Numerology," then, is for Alberti a technique for the selection of figures, thereby signalling that the details are related to memorable shapes such as the human body or cosmological figures.[22]

Finishing is a mathematical procedure for the definition of the dimensions of the directions in which the space of architectural objects is articulated. The edges of the tri-dimensional bodies of architecture are defined by a system of proportions. Proportion or "analogy" is the use of relations in a measurement.[23] An analogical system is a set of norms for the creation and combination of details. A basic measure, or module, is the norm from which all the lengths, widths, and heights are derived, and any single detail is measured after it. Then all the parts of the building will stand to each other in a direct and intelligible relationship. This relationship stands even when its form does not yet have a verbalized expression.

Collocation is the composing by place, that is, the functional placement of the details. The function in this case not only is limited to the practical and structural dimensions but it embodies, as well, historical and aesthetic dimensions.[24] The placing of details, then, is deeply related to the other two requirements: numbers and analogies. The detail in this manner is not defined by scale, but, rather, the scale is the tool for controlling it.

The geometrical and mathematical construction of the architectural detail is in no sense a technical question. The matter should be regarded as falling within the philosophical problem of the foundation of architecture or geometry, and ultimately within the theories of perception.

The processes of designing, ordering materials, and building a house are techniques in the same way geometry is a technique by which the designer, the builder, and the user of a house transform the appropriate sign with a view to predicting the occurrence of certain events. This technique (geometry) provides us with a structure for describing the built world, a conceptual framework into which the designer, the builder, and the user can fit their empirical experience. Geometry shows how to derive a shape from another shape by transformation.

In this guise geometry does not state facts, but gives us the forms in which to state facts. It provides us with a linguistic or conceptual structure for the construction and the construing of a building. The geometrical structures embodied in the architectural details do not state facts but rather provide a structure for stating facts within a "scale." They give us a way of making comparisons that meaningfully relate visually perceived architectural details. The notion of the individually perceived details can be illustrated with the phenomenon of "indirect vision" as explained by Hermann von Helmholtz:

> The eye represents an optical instrument of a very large field of vision, but only a small very narrowly confined part of that field of vision produces clear images. The whole field corresponds to a drawing in which the most important part of the whole is carefully rendered but the surrounding is merely sketched, and sketched the more roughly the further it is removed from the main object. Thanks to the mobility of the eye, however, it is possible to examine carefully every point of the visual field in succession.[25]

Helmholtz's research on visual perception persuaded him that sensory stimuli only supply signs of the presence of architecture, but do not give us an adequate understanding of it. Such signs, that is, the details, acquire a meaning by virtue of which they become a vehicle of knowledge through a long process of association and comparison and through a set of geometric relationships.[26]

The geometrical relationships embodied in the details in a built environment as well as in a natural environment set the understanding of the large field of vision. The geometrical relationship or proposition at the base of the compound pier of the High Gothic architecture expresses in itself every feature of the imposed superstructure. Such relationships are the results of the transformation in stone of the second requirement of Scholastic writing, of an "arrangement according to a system of homologous parts and parts of parts."[27] The details in this way, while forming an indivisible whole, are individually perceived and understood.

The problem of perception of details within the sphere of architectural appropriation is stated by Walter Benjamin:

> Buildings are appropriated in a twofold manner: by use and by perception or rather by touch and sight....Tactile appropriation is accomplished not so much by attention as by habit. As regards architecture, habit determines to a large extent even optical reception.[28]

This is an empirical theory that regards all perception of space as depending upon conventions and takes not only qualities, but even details as nothing more than signs, the meanings of which are learned only by experience. These conventions are the basis for architecture understood as existence, form, and location of external objects. These Helmholtz calls perceptions.[29] Perceptions are the ideas or signs of objects resulting from an interpretation of sensations that is carried out by processes of unconscious geometrical inference. The placing of details has a key role in these processes of inference. The visual sensations guided by the tactile sensations are the generator of the geometrical propositions. In architecture, feeling a handrail, walking up steps or between walls, turning a corner, and noting the sitting of a beam in a wall, are coordinated elements of visual and tactile sensations. The location of those details gives birth to the conventions that tie a meaning to a perception. The conception of the architectural space achieved in this way is the result of the association of the visual images of details, gained through the phenomenon of indirect vision, with the geometrical proposition embodied in forms, dimensions, and location, developed by touching and by walking through buildings.

The art of detail is in its most sophisticated and learned form in the work of Carlo Scarpa. An analysis of the concept of detail in Scarpa's architecture can best be begun with the words of Louis Kahn:

> In the work of Carlo Scarpa
> Beauty
> the first sense
> Art
> the first word
> then wonder
> then the inner realization of Form
> the sense of wholeness of inseparable elements.
> Design consults Nature
> to give presence to the elements.
> A work of art makes manifest
> the wholeness of Form of the
> symphony of the selected shapes
> of the elements. In the elements
> the joint inspires ornament, its
> celebration.
> The detail is the adoration of Nature.[30]

The "adoration of the joint," in Scarpa's architecture, is a perfect realization of Alberti's concinnity. Each detail tells us the story of its making, of its placing, and of its dimensioning. The selection of the appropriate details is the result of singling out its functional roles. The details of Scarpa's architecture solve not only practical functions, but also historical, social, and individual functions.[31]

Scarpa's architecture can be generically classified as the merging of the principles of the organic architecture as expressed by Frank Lloyd Wright with a learned distilling of Veneto craftsmanship with a blend modern and ancient technologies. However, the definition is inadequate; whereas Scarpa's understanding of Wright's architecture was passive, based on an appreciation of photographs and drawings, his understanding of Veneto craftsmanship was active, based on his daily working and dealing with the stonecutters, masons, carpenters, glassmakers, and smiths of Venice. The result is a modern architecture that is more than rational structures and functional spaces. The teaching of functionalism is present in Scarpa's work, but the functionality is mediated by the search for representation and expression through the making. Scarpa's architecture stands against the bare structure of logic; it stands for the union of *res* and *verba*, that is, for the union of representation and function. This concept rules Scarpa's architecture from structure to expression. In his architectural objects the *techné of the logos*, the construing, becomes the manner of production of signs that are the details. The *logos of the techné*, the constructing, which results from the expression of Veneto craftsmanship, becomes the dialectical counterpart in the generation of the details as signs. Scarpa's buildings show indeed a constant search set between the actual form (the built one), and the virtual form (the perceived one). The constant manipulation of the discrepancies between virtual and actual forms is the method used for achieving expression. "In architecture," Scarpa once said, "there is no such thing as a good idea. There is only expression."[32]

The analysis of Scarpa's detail can be satisfactorily managed visually only by a continuous comparison between drawings and built objects, on the one hand, and the historical, practical, and formal reference that generated any single detail, on the other. It is also necessary to see Scarpa's details from two different sides. On one side, his detailing is the result of interfacing of design and craftsmanship on the site and of the constant "sensorial verification" of details during the assembly of the building. Scarpa made a practice of visiting the building site during the night for verification with a flashlight, thereby controlling the execution and the expression of the details. In the normal daylight it would indeed be impossible to focus on details in such a selective manner. It is also a procedure by which the phenomenon of the indirect vision becomes an element in the process of decision in the design. The flashlight is a tool by which is achieved an analog of both the process of vision and the eye's movement in its perception field (with only one spot in focus and the eye darting around). Another Veneto architect, Piranesi, used the same technique in visiting the sites of the buildings he was going to survey and represent in his etchings of the *Antichita Romane*. To single out the "expression of the fragments," that is, the details, he used the light of a candle.[33]

On the other side, Scarpa's details are the result of an intellectual game performed on the "working drawings" that are the result of the interfacing of design and draftsmanship. That game is the matching of the construction of a representation with a construction of an edifice. The relationship between architectural drawings and buildings is generally thought of as a Cartesian representation based on visual matching of lines. However, Scarpa's drawings show the real nature of architectural drawings, that is, the fact that they are representations that are the results of constructions. They are a construing of perceptual judgments interfaced with the real process of physical construction of an architectural object. The lines, the marks on the paper, are a transformation from one system of representation to another. They are a transformation of appropriate signs with a view to the predicting of certain architectural events, that is, on the one hand the phenomena of construction and the transformation by the builders, and on the other hand, the phenomena of construing and the transformation by the possible users. Consequently, on the same drawing there are present several layers of thought.

A design is developed by the same technique in which the drawing is made. The continuous inference process on which the design process is based is transformed in a sequence of marks on paper that are an analog for the processes of construction and construing. The piece of drawing paper selected for supporting the slow process of the construction of a design presents concurrently vertical and horizontal sections, as well as elevations of the designed piece. These drawings are surrounded by unframed vignettes that analyze tri-dimensionally any joint of the object, as in a prediction of the role of each detail in generating the whole text and in the perception of them in the "indirect vision." Scarpa's drawings do not define future architectural pieces as a simple sum of lines, surfaces, and volumes. Rather they present the process of transformation of the details from one system of representation to another, from drawing to building.

In Scarpa's drawings it is also possible to have the "proof" of the system of appropriation that rules the perception of architecture. These representations of three-dimensional structures on a two-dimensional surface result from the interaction existing between visual and tactile perceptions. The central part of the drawings generally presents graphic constructions that might be labeled a technical drawing. But they are not what are traditionally identified as plans, sections, and elevations. Scarpa's drawings are not merely devices of Cartesian descriptive geometry; rather, they are descriptions of the future perception in relationship to the making of the architectural object. The visual components of perception are analyzed for a detail and not for the whole, whereas the tactile perceptions are verified for the whole. These drawings present components that are not visible but that are the result and the projection of construction and construing, Alberti's mental edifice. They are the result of the memory effects of the organs of touch and sight in the making and using of architecture. These drawings are never fully rendered. Only fragments and parts of them are. This practice shows by analogy that, while it is whole, Scarpa's architecture cannot be characterized as complete. An architectural whole is seen as a phenomenon composed by details unified by a "device," a structuring principle. This principle, in Scarpa's architecture, is the order generated by the use and the understanding of classical architectural ideas such as façade design.[34]

Scarpa is a *Magister Ludi,* and his buildings are texts wherein the details are the minimal unit of signification. The joints between different materials and shapes and spaces are pretexts for generating texts. The interfacing of commentaries with preceding texts in the architecture of Scarpa is always a problem of joints, and in the joint he achieves the change of conventions. That possibility is a consequence of the fact that many of his architectural texts are learned commentary to preceding texts and in many cases, as in a medieval *scholium,* the commentary in its interfacing with the original text is generating a new text. In the design of the addition to Gipsoteca Canoviana in Possagno, Scarpa was able to change the convention that asks for the background walls of a collection of gypsum casts to be tinted. Scarpa's solution was to put the white casts against a white background wall that was washed with light, without directly lighting the casts. The problem and the solution are in the use of light. Scarpa solves it in a detail in the joint of three walls in a corner made of glass. In a lecture given at the University of Venice (1976) he described the architectural making of this corner. The achievement of the effect of light occurs by a formal manipulation. The solution of the formal cause solves the final cause. He described it as "clipping off the blue of the sky," a formal cause, but the result was the lighting of the wall, the final cause. His own words are the best description of the making of an architectural detail:

I love a lot of...natural light: I wanted to clip off the blue of the sky. Then what I wanted was an upper glass recess....The glass corner becomes a blue block pushed up and inside [the building], the light illuminates all the four walls. My bias for formal solutions made me prefer an absolute transparency. Consequently I did not want the corner of glass to tie in a frame. It had been a *tour de force* because it was not possible to obtain this idea of pure transparency. When I overlap the glasses I see the corner anyway especially if the glass is thick. One may as well put in the frame. Then, besides this, if it is a clear day one may see the reflection. Look, when I saw the reflection I hated myself. I did not think of it. These are mistakes which one makes in thinking, acting, and making, and therefore [it] is necessary to have a double mind, a triple mind, the mind like that of a robber, a man who speculates, who would like to rob a bank, and it is necessary to have that which I call wit, an attentive tension toward understanding all that is happening.[35]

The development of architecture in the works designed by Scarpa proceeds by steps and stages. These are in the details. Each detail represents an interim result that cannot be considered a final result. Scarpa would invent details the precise architectural functions of which would become clear only after they had been used in several different designs. The range of those architectural functions goes from the immediate to the mediate understanding of the meaning of the detail. This creative use of details in design is fully in accordance with [Ludwig] Wittgenstein's understanding of a creative use of language. The "exact" meaning, that is, the function of words, would only become known by a later use. A function of detail in a design becomes clear by re-presentation, that is, by re-use. The detail often appears incomplete and vague in its structuring principle. But, unifying in itself function and representation, the re-use of a detail becomes a creative catalyst. It becomes a fertile detail. The re-use of details is analogous to Richard Wagner's re-use of *leitmotifs*.[36] The *leitmotifs* are structural devices used by Wagner to assemble and reconstruct the architecture of opera from within and are the smallest units of signification in the musical text. Scarpa's details are structural devices used to assemble architectural text from within.

A case of *fertile* details in Scarpa's architecture is the use of the "ziggurat" motif. The architectural function of these fertile details emerge in the Brion Cemetery at S. Vito d'Altivole and in the façade and the interiors of the Banca Popolare di Verona. In the Cemetery, the ziggurat is executed in cast concrete, and it is a celebration of the possibility of casting as generator of mouldings. In the bank, especially in the façade, the ziggurat detail is a *prima donna* in Rosso Verona, the brocade-like local red marble in which it is executed.

Scarpa's first use of this detail was a cosmetic treatment of a temporary façade executed by piling up concrete blocks in front of the Italian Pavilion at the 1962 Biennale in Venice. But as Heraclitus has pointed out, the primary root of "cosmesis" is "cosmos." This same cosmetic detail becomes the principle of order in Scarpa's Museum of Castelvecchio in Verona. The ziggurat motif becomes the solution for terminating the layers of the wall of the façade to show the virtual joint between the original walls and the Romantic replica of the façade wall constructed by Antonio Avena in 1924. In the Museum of Castelvecchio, the medieval equestrian statue of Cangrande and

Carlo Scarpa, Museo di Castelvecchio, Verona. Joint, with Cangrande statue.

the structure which supports it are set in a spatial location that allows a view from the balcony, the bridge, and the court below. This location allows one to view the statue from close-up as well as from below, as it was seen in its original location on Cangrande shrine. This joint originates the full text of the spatial organization of the Castelvecchio Museum. It thus becomes the cause for the formal solution of the museum and the text in the context.

An early design of the platform holding the statue of Cangrande shows it as the pre-text for a celebration of the virtual joint determined by its collocation. This drawing shows the idea of the ziggurat as a generator of the wall. The layers of the wall become independent units and each one of them is expressed in a vertical ziggurat. The space opened up by the cutting of the façade wall helps the whole composition of the new arrangement of the museum devised by Scarpa. The space, a virtual joint, is then the key articulation in the museum's path, but at the same time becomes a "negative joint" in the articulation of the masses of Castelvecchio. The open space, instead of separating, helps connect the left and the right masses of the castle. These are situated on the sides of the tower which articulates the joint between the bridge on the river Adige and the castle. The selection of the ziggurat as the ending of the wall mediates the transition between inside and outside of the articulation. It exposes the materials of this complex architec-tural hinge composed of vertical planes defined by their framing relationship with the statue of Cangrande, the visual pin of the hinge. The ziggurat detail is also used in many other parts of the museum. In a study plan of the entry, this fertile detail is used in solv-ing the joining of the stones used for the floor as well as in solving the deep reveal of the windows in the thick medieval wall.

The ziggurat detail is also used extensively in the Brion Cemetery. The material, cast in place concrete, gives new meaning to the detail. The interaction between form and material moves the fertile detail from the realm of a production *sub specie utilitatis* to a production of *sub specie aeternitatis*. It is construed as a "ruin" loaded with memories before time. It becomes a perfect detail for the architecture of a cemetery, a place of memories. In this use the ziggurat finds its proof of being a fertile detail. A detail proves its fertility when it moves out of a private architectural language and becomes available through a collective production. A famous case of this is the Serliana Window that after being used by Palladio became a standard detail known as the Palladian Window. The Scarpian Ziggurat has indeed been used by many architects in their designs, but now is used in collective architecture. It has become a standard detail of Veneto cemetery archi-tecture. The neoclassical temple *in antis* which has been the type for many family chapels has been modified by a new model reference. The detailing of the Tuscan or Doric Orders has been replaced by a new detailing, a concrete cast-in-place Scarpian Ziggurat, a New Order.

To conclude this discussion on the role of detail as a minimal unit in the process of signification (that is, the manipulation of meaning), it is useful to restate that archi-tecture is an art as well as a profession. This is because of the understanding generated by the detail as joint. Architecture is an art because it is interested not only in the origi-nal need of shelter but also in putting together spaces and materials in a meaningful manner. This occurs through formal and actual joints. The joint, that is the fertile detail, is the place where both the construction and the construing of architecture take place.

(Furthermore, it is useful to complete our understanding of this essential role of the joint as the place of the process of signification to recall that the meaning of the original Indo-European root of the word *art* is "joint.") As Kahn has said,

> The joint is the beginning of ornament
> And that must be distinguished from
> decoration which is simply applied.
> Ornament is the adoration of the joint.[37]

1   Philip Johnson. "Architectural Details," *Architectural Record* (1964): 137–147.
2   W.S. Heckscher, "Petites Perceptions," *Journal of Medieval and Renaissance Studies* 4 (1974): 101ff. The idea of the process of signification in the details can be traced through Leibniz to Ramon Lull.
3   In jotting down those data concerning the adage, I had a *lapsus calami*, and instead of spelling God with one *o*, I spelled it with two os. Later on the same page of my notebook I scribbled down a note taken from a passage from Vitruvius's treatise on architecture, *De Architettura*, S. Ferri, ed. and comm. (Rome: 1960), 10. A few days later, while reviewing those notes, I was amazed by the presence of the quasi-Platonic transcription of a quasi-Aristotelian maxim—i.e., "Good lies in the detail"—next to a note stating that Callimacus, the mythical designer of the Corinthian capital, whose name in Greek means "He who fights strongly for beauty," had been nicknamed *Katatexitechnos* by the Athenians. By this long and complicated alias the Athenians recognized Callimacus's work as the result of an activity that proceeded with rational method toward a specific productive aim and is a knowing in the doing. *Techné* is reflection in action embodied in the details (M. Isardi Parente, *Techné* [Florence: 1966]). This curious misspelling accident and association of words brought me to consider the role of *techné* in the production of architecture and in the process of architectural signification.
4   In the architectural detail, the practical norms (technology) and the aesthetic norms (semiotics) come together in a dialectical relationship. The detail is the unit of architectural production. See for the origin of this theory in the eighteenth century: Marco Frascari, "*Sortes Architectii* in the Eighteenth-Century Veneto," Ph.D. diss., University of Pennsylvania, 1981.
5   For a survey and a discussion of the different elements and theories developed in architectural semiotics see: Martin Krampen, *Meaning in the Urban Environment* (London: 1979), 6–91.
6   J. Labatut, "An Approach to Architectural Composition," *Modulus* 9 (1964): 55–63.
7   See for a different approach, but reaching the same conclusion: Roger Scruton, *Aesthetics of Architecture* (Princeton: 1979), 77ff.
8   A case is the collapse of the Marciana Library in Venice. In his first Venetian building J. Sansovino, indeed a skillful "proto," used Roman detailing (*maniera Romana*), which indeed did not work in Venice. See T. Temanza, *Vite dei piu celebri architetti e scultori Veneziani* (Venice: 1778).
9   Functions in architecture depend on both the building itself and on who uses it or organizes its use. Custom and repeated usages are the base of functions. Architecture not only performs but also signifies its functions and can be organized in four functional horizons: the practical, the historical, the social, and the individual. For a discussion of the four functional horizons and a typology of functions see J. Mukarovsky, "The Place of the Aesthetic Function Among the Other Functions in Architecture" in *Structure, Sign and Function* (New Haven: 1978), 240–243.

10   The French commercial origin of the word, which differentiates between the selling of slices of pizzas and the sale of whole ones, besides clarifying that details are parts, does not help in the understanding of the detail as joint and its nonsubordinate relationship with wholes. A better and meaningful term is the Italian, *particolari architettonici*, which is also connected with the literary theories of the eighteenth century, for instance, Antonio Conti's idea on *particolareggiamento*.

11   Despreaux Nicolas Boileau, *L'Art Poétique* I (1670; repr. Paris, 1966), 158.

12   G. B. Piranesi. "Parere," (1765) in J. Wilton-Ely, ed., *The Polemical Works* (Farnborough: 1972).

13   J. Soane, *Lectures on Architecture* (London: 1929), 177.

14   For a discussion of the origin of the *analytique* in Lodoli's garden at S. Francesco della Vigna see Frascari, "*Sortes Architectii*," op. cit.

15   For this role of the *analytique* and the process of detailing see the discussion of Antonio Conti's theory of *particolareggiamento* in Frascari, "*Sortes Architectii*," op. cit., 141–150.

16   G.O. Garney, *The American Glossary of Architectural Terms* (Chicago: 1887).

17   D. Ramée, *Dictionnaire général des termes d'architecture* (Paris: 1868).

18   J. Lotman, "The Dynamic Model of a Semiotic System," *Semiotica* 21, no. 3/4 (1977): 194.

19   Leon Battista Alberti, *De Re Aedificatoria* (Bologna: 1782). The principle of the *nihil addi* is presented in the first book, but it is theoretically developed in the sixth and seventh books. For this new interpretation of the concept see the discussion of the role of "decoration: in the small temples: *'eti pare che, & vi si possa, & vi si debbu aggiunere.'*"

20   This tripartite discussion of beauty is developed by Alberti in his seventh book (IX, 5), 229–230.

21   Ludwig Wittgenstein, *Remarks on the Foundation of Mathematics* (A, II, 14, j; cf. II, 47 and V, 46) (Oxford: 1956).

22   On the use of the human body as basic design reference and generator of measures see Marco Frascari, "The Search for Measure in Architecture," to be published in *Res*.

23   For the concept of analogy in architecture see Vitruvius (Ferri, ed.), 50ff.

24   Mukarovsky, "The Place of the Aesthetic Function," op. cit., 240–243.

25   H. Von Helmholtz, *Über Geometrie* (Darmstadt: 1968), 218.

26   R. Torretti, *Philosophy of Geometry* (Dordrecht: 1978), 162–171.

27   Erwin Panofsky, *Gothic and Scholasticism* (New York: 1946).

28   Walter Benjamin, *Illuminations* (New York: 1968), 242.

29   Torretti, *Philosophy of Geometry*, op. cit., 168.

30   Accademia Olimpica, *Carlo Scarpa* (Vicenza: 1974), 1.

31   Mukarovsky, "The Place of the Aesthetic Function," op. cit., 240–243.

32   Carlo Scarpa, "Frammenti, 1926–78," *Rassegna* 7 (1981): 82.

33   H. Focillon, *Piranesi* (Bologna: 1962), 166.

34   Scarpa, "Frammenti," op. cit.: 83–84.

35   Ibid.: 83–84.

36   For a discussion of the use of "fertile details" see the analysis of the "fertile motif" in Anton Ehrenzweig, *The Hidden Order of Art* (London: 1962).

37   Louis Kahn, *Light is the Theme* (Fort Worth: 1975), 43.

BIBLIOGRAPHY

Accademia Olimpica. *Carlo Scarpa*. Vicenza: 1974.
Alberti, Leon Battista. *De Re Aedificatoria*. 1485; repr. Milan: 1966.
Benjamin, Walter. *Illuminations*. New York: 1968.
Blomfield, Reginald. *The Mistress Art*. London: 1908.
Boileau, Despreaux Nicolas. *Art poétique* I. 1670; repr. Paris: 1966.
Brusatin, Manlio. "Carlo Scarpa," *Controspazio* 3/4 (1972): 2–85.
"Details," *Construction Details* (January 1914): 1.
Ehrenzweig, Anton. *The Hidden Order of Art*. London: 1962.

Focillon, H. *Piranesi*. Bologna: 1967.

Frascari, Marco. "*Sortes Architectii* in the Eighteenth-Century Veneto." Ph.D. diss., University of Pennsylvania, 1981.

———. "The True and the Appearance; The Italian Facadism and Carlo Scarpa," *Daedalus* 6 (December 1982): 37–46.

Garvey, C.O. *The American Glossary of Architectural Terms*. Chicago: 1887.

Helmholtz, H. Von. *Über Geometrie*. Darmstadt: 1968.

Heckscher, W. "Petites Perceptions," *Journal of Medieval and Renaissance Studies* 4 (1974): 100–142.

Johnson, Philip. "Architectural Details," *Architectural Record* (April 1964): 137–147.

Kahn, Louis. *Light is the Theme*. Fort Worth: 1975.

Krampen, M. *Meaning in the Urban Environment*. London: 1979.

Labatut, Jean. "An Approach to Architectural Composition," *Modulus* 9 (1964): 55–63.

Lotman, J. M. "The Dynamic Model of a Semiotic System," *Semiotica* 21, no. 3/4 (1977): 193–210.

Mukarovsky, Jan. *Structure, Sign and Function*. New Haven: 1978.

Panofsky, Erwin. *Gothic and Scholasticism*. New York: 1946.

Parente, M. Isardi. *Techné*. Florence: 1966.

Piranesi, G. B. *Polemical Works*. J. Wilton-Ely, ed. Farnborough: 1972.

Ramée, Daniel. *Dictionnaire général des termes d'architecture*. Paris: 1868.

Scarpa, Carlo. "Frammenti. 1926–78," *Rassegna* 7 (1981).

Scruton, R. *Aesthetics of Architecture*. Princeton: 1979.

Serlio, S. *Trattato di architettura*. 1619.

Soane, J. *Lectures on Architecture*. London: 1929.

Torretti, R. *Philosophy of Geometry from Riesmann to Poincaré*. London: 1978.

Van Pelt, J. V. "Architectural Detail," *Pencil Point* (May 1921, June 1921).

Vitruvius. *De Architettura*, 7 vols. S. Ferri, ed. and comm. Rome: 1960.

Wittgenstein, Ludwig. *Remarks on the Foundation of Mathematics*. Oxford: 1956.

INTRODUCTION

Rappel à l'ordre, the Case for the Tectonic
Kenneth Frampton

In this "call to order," Kenneth Frampton maintains that building is first an act of construction, a tectonic and not a scenographic activity. Building is ontological, a presence or a "thing," as opposed to a sign. This approach can be put in the context of other attempts to define the "essence" of architecture, for example as function, or as type. For Frampton, the essence is the poetic manifestation of structure implied in the Greek (and Heideggerian) *poesis*: an act of making and revealing that is the tectonic. In this polemical essay, he identifies "the structural unit as the irreducible essence of architectural form." It thus deserves more attention than spatial invention and the pursuit of novelty.

A poetics of construction, Frampton says, offers the possibility of resisting the *commodification* of shelter, and the prevalent postmodern "decorated shed" approach to architectural design promulgated by Robert Venturi, Denise Scott Brown, et al. Tectonics is a potent antidote because it is astylistic, internal to the discipline (i.e., autonomous) and mythical.

Consistent with Martin Heidegger's recognition of the placement of humankind on the earth and under the sky, Frampton proposes that architects need to consider the ontological consequences of building with heavy mass walls or with light frames. The two systems represent cosmological opposites, with connotations of earth versus sky, and solidity versus dematerialization. To reinforce the value of such distinctions, he also asserts the importance of Gottfried Semper's alternative myth of origin, described in *The Four Elements of Architecture* (1852). Semper counters the typological basis of Marc-Antoine Laugier's classically-derived "Primitive Hut" with his four tectonically-based elements, all deduced from a vernacular Caribbean hut: earthwork (mound), hearth, (framework and) roof, and enclosing membrane. In lieu of a frame construction in a single material, Semper offers a grounded, heavy foundation condition, with a light frame and infill above, and the requisite connections between the two. Frampton links Heidegger's phenomenology to Semper's materially-specific origin of architecture to argue for tectonics as expressive of its own making and of its relationship to the earth and sky.

Semper emphasizes the textile origins of tectonics and suggests that the knot was the first joint. For Frampton, the joint is "the nexus around which the building comes into being and is articulated as a presence." It can have ideological and referential roles, in that cultural differences emerge in the articulated transitions and joints making up a tectonic syntax. Vittorio Gregotti and Marco Frascari also posit a symbolic role for the detail in this chapter.

The joint is essential, not gratuitous, and it thus avoids the possibility of conspicuous consumption that plagues contemporary architecture and reduces it to fashion. Tectonics plays a part in the argument Frampton constructs in the earlier essays on Critical Regionalism. (ch. 11) While he now seems to have distanced himself from Critical Regionalism, tectonics continues as an important path of resistance to the homogenization of the built environment. Frampton's 1995 book, *Studies in Tectonic Culture*, presents an expanded discussion of this essential part of architecture.

KENNETH FRAMPTON

RAPPEL À L'ORDRE, THE CASE FOR THE TECTONIC

I have elected to address the issue of tectonic form for a number of reasons, not least of which is the current tendency to reduce architecture to scenography. This reaction arises in response to the universal triumph of Robert Venturi's decorated shed; that all too prevalent syndrome in which shelter is packaged like a giant commodity. Among the advantages of the scenographic approach is the fact that the results are eminently amortisable with all the consequences that this entails for the future of the environment. We have in mind, of course, not the pleasing decay of nineteenth-century Romanticism but the total destitution of commodity culture. Along with this sobering prospect goes the general dissolution of stable references in the late-modern world; the fact that the precepts governing almost every discourse, save for the seemingly autonomous realm of techno-science, have now become extremely tenuous. Much of this was already foreseen half a century ago by Hans Sedlmayr, when he wrote, in 1941:

> The shift of man's spiritual centre of gravity towards the inorganic, his feeling of his way into the inorganic world may indeed legitimately be called a cosmic disturbance in the microcosm of man, who now begins to show a one-sided development of his faculties. At the other extreme there is a disturbance of macrocosmic relationships, a result of the especial favour and protection which the organic now enjoys—almost always at the expense, not to say ruin, of the inorganic. The raping and destruction of the earth, the nourisher of man, is an obvious example and one which in its turn reflects the distortion of the human microcosm for the spiritual.[1]

Against this prospect of cultural degeneration, we may turn to certain rearguard positions, in order to recover a basis from which to resist. Today we find ourselves in a

From *Architectural Design* 60, no. 3–4 (1990): 19–25. Courtesy of the author and publisher.

similar position to that of the critic Clement Greenberg who, in his 1965 essay "Modernist Painting," attempted to reformulate a ground for painting in the following terms:

> Having been denied by the Enlightenment of all tasks they could take seriously, they (the arts) looked as though they were going to be assimilated to entertainment pure and simple, and entertainment itself looked as though it were going to be assimilated, like religion, to therapy. The arts could save themselves from this levelling down only by demonstrating that the kind of experience they provided was valuable in its own right, and not to be obtained from any other kind of activity.[2]

If one poses the question as to what might be a comparable ground for architecture, then one must turn to a similar material base, namely that architecture must of necessity be embodied in structural and constructional form. My present stress on the latter rather than the prerequisite of spatial enclosure stems from an attempt to evaluate twentieth-century architecture in terms of continuity and inflection rather than in terms of originality as an end in itself.

In his 1980 essay, "Avant Garde and Continuity," the Italian architect Giorgio Grassi had the following comment to make about the impact of avant-gardist art on architecture:

> ...as far as the vanguards of the Modern Movement are concerned, they invariably follow in the wake of the figurative arts...Cubism, Suprematism, Neoplasticism, etc. are all forms of investigation born and developed in the realm of the figurative arts, and only as a second thought carried over into architecture as well. It is actually pathetic to see the architects of that "heroic" period and the best among them, trying with difficulty to accommodate themselves to these "isms"; experimenting in a perplexed manner because of their fascination with the new doctrines, measuring them, only later to realise their ineffectuality...[3]

While it is disconcerting to have to recognise that there may well be a fundamental break between the figurative origins of abstract art and the constructional basis of tectonic form, it is, at the same time, liberating to the extent that it affords a point from which to challenge spatial invention as an end in itself: a pressure to which modern architecture has been unduly subject. Rather than join in a recapitulation of avant-gardist tropes or enter into historicist pastiche or into the superfluous proliferation of sculptural gestures all of which have an arbitrary dimension to the degree that they are based in neither structure nor in construction, we may return instead to the structural unit as the irreducible essence of architectural form.

Needless to say, we are not alluding here to mechanical revelation of construction but rather to a potentially poetic manifestation of structure in the original Greek sense of *poesis* as an act of making and revealing. While I am well aware of the conservative connotations that may be ascribed to Grassi's polemic, his critical perceptions none the less cause us to question the very idea of the new, in a moment that oscillates between the cultivation of a resistant culture and a descent into value-free aestheticism. Perhaps the most balanced assessment of Grassi has been made by the Catalan critic, Ignasi de Solà-Morales Rubió, when he wrote:

> Architecture is posited as a craft, that is to say, as the practical application of established knowledge through rules of the different levels of intervention. Thus, no notion of architecture as problem-solving, as innovation, or as invention *ex novo*, is present in Grassi's thinking, since he is interested in showing the permanent, the evident, and the given character of knowledge in the making of architecture.
>
> ...The work of Grassi is born of a reflection upon the essential resources of discipline, and it focuses upon specific media which determine not only aesthetic choices but also the ethical content of its cultural contribution. Through these channels of ethical and political will, the concern of the Enlightenment...becomes enriched in its most critical tone. It is not solely the superiority of reason and the analysis of form which are indicated, but rather, the critical role (in the Kantian sense of the term) that is, the judgement of values, the very lack of which is felt in society today...
>
> In the sense that his architecture is a meta-language, a reflection on the contradictions of its own practice, his work acquires the appeal of something that is both frustrating and noble...[4]

The dictionary definition of the term "tectonic" to mean "pertaining to building or construction in general; constructional, constructive used especially in reference to architecture and the kindred arts," is a little reductive to the extent that we intend not only the structural component *in se* but also the formal amplification of its presence in relation to the assembly of which it is a part. From its conscious emergence in the middle of the nineteenth century with the writings of Karl Bötticher and Gottfried Semper the term not only indicates a structural and material probity but also a poetics of construction, as this may be practiced in architecture and the related arts.

The beginnings of the Modern, dating back at least two centuries, and the much more recent advent of the Post-Modern are inextricably bound up with the ambiguities introduced into Western architecture by the primacy given to the scenographic in the evolution of the bourgeois world. However, building remains essentially *tectonic* rather than scenographic in character and it may be argued that it is an act of construction first, rather than a discourse predicated on the surface, volume and plan, to cite the "Three Reminders to Architects," of Le Corbusier. Thus one may assert that building is *ontological* rather than *representational* in character and that built form is a presence rather than something standing for an absence. In Martin Heidegger's terminology we may think of it as a "thing" rather than a "sign."

I have chosen to engage this theme because I believe it is necessary for architects to re-position themselves given that the predominant tendency today is to reduce all architectural expression to the status of commodity culture. In as much as such resistance has little chance of being widely accepted, a "rearguard" posture would seem to be an appropriate stance to adopt rather than the dubious assumption that it is possible to continue with the perpetuation of avant gardism. Despite its concern for structure, an emphasis on tectonic form does not necessarily favor either Constructivism or Deconstructivism. In this sense it is astylistic. Moreover it does not seek its legitimacy in science, literature or art.

Greek in origin, the term *tectonic* derives from the term *tekton*, signifying carpenter or builder. This in turn stems from the Sanskrit *taksan*, referring to the craft of carpentry and to the use of the ax. Remnants of a similar term can also be found in Vedic, where it again refers to carpentry. In Greek it appears in Homer, where it again alludes to carpentry and to the art of construction in general. The poetic connotation of the term first appears in Sappho where the *tekton*, the carpenter, assumes the role of the poet. This meaning undergoes further evolution as the term passes from being something specific and physical, such as carpentry, to the more generic notion of construction and later to becoming an aspect of poetry. In Aristophanes we even find the idea that it is associated with machination and the creation of false things. This etymological evolution would suggest a gradual passage from the ontological to the representational. Finally, the Latin term *architectus* derives from the Greek *archi* (a person of authority) and *tekton* (a craftsman or builder).

The earliest appearance of the term "tectonic" in English dates from 1656 where it appears in a glossary meaning "belonging to building" and this is almost a century after the first English use of the term *architect* in 1563. In 1850 the German oriental scholar K. O. Muller was to define the term rather rudely as "A series of arts which form and perfect vessels, implements, dwellings and places of assembly." The term is first elaborated in a modern sense with Karl Bötticher's *The Tectonic of the Hellenes* of 1843–52 and with Gottfried Semper's essay *The Four Elements of Architecture* of the same year. It is further developed in Semper's unfinished study, *Style in the Technical and Tectonic Arts or Practical Aesthetic*, published between 1863 and 1868.

The term "tectonic" cannot be divorced from the technological, and it is this that gives a certain ambivalence to the term. In this regard it is possible to identify three distinct conditions: 1) the *technological object* that arises directly out of meeting an instrumental need, 2) the *scenographic object* that may be used equally to allude to an absent or hidden element, and 3), the *tectonic object* that appears in two modes. We may refer to these modes as the ontological and representational *tectonic*. The first involves a constructional element, that is shaped so as to emphasise its static role and cultural status. This is the tectonic as it appears in Bötticher's interpretation of the Doric column. The second mode involves the representation of a constructional element which is present, but hidden. These two modes can be seen as paralleling the distinction that Semper made between the *structural-technical* and the *structural-symbolic*.

Aside from these distinctions, Semper was to divide built form into two separate material procedures: into the *tectonics* of the frame in which members of varying lengths are conjoined to encompass a spatial field and the *stereotomics* of compressive mass that, while it may embody space, is constructed through the piling up of identical units: the term *stereotomics* deriving from the Greek term for solid, *stereotos* and cutting, *-tomia*. In the first case, the most common material throughout history has been *wood* or its textual equivalents such as bamboo, wattle, and basket-work. In the second case, one of the most common materials has been brick, or the compressive equivalent of brick such as rock, stone or rammed earth and later, reinforced concrete. There have been significant exceptions to this division, particularly where, in the interest of permanence, stone has been cut, dressed, and erected in such a way as to assume the form and function of a frame. While these facts are so familiar as to hardly need repetition, we tend to be unaware of the ontological consequences of these differences: that is to say, of the way in which framework tends towards the aerial and the dematerialisation of mass, whereas the mass form is telluric, embedding itself ever deeper into the earth. The one tends towards light and the other towards dark. These gravitational opposites, the immateriality of the frame and the materiality of the mass, may be said to symbolise the two cosmological opposites to which they aspire: the sky and the earth. Despite our highly secularised technoscientific age, these polarities still largely constitute the experiential limits of our lives. It is arguable that the practice of architecture is impoverished to the extent that we fail to recognise these transcultural values and the way in which they are intrinsically latent in all structural form. Indeed, these forms may serve to remind us, after Heidegger, that inanimate objects may also evoke "being," and that through this analogy to our own corpus, the body of a building may be perceived as though it were literally a physique. This brings us back to Semper's privileging of the joint as the primordial tectonic element as the fundamental nexus around which building comes into being, that is to say, comes to be articulated as a presence in itself.

Semper's emphasis on the joint implies that fundamental syntactical transition may be expressed as one passes from the *sterotomic* base to the tectonic frame, and that such transitions constitute the very essence of architecture. They are the dominant constituents whereby one culture of building differentiates itself from the next.

There is a spiritual value residing in the particularities of a given joint, in the "thingness" of the constructed object, so much so that the generic joint becomes a point of ontological condensation rather than a mere connection. We need only to think of the work of Carlo Scarpa to touch on a contemporary manifestation of this attribute.

The first volume of the fourth edition of Karl Bötticher's *Tektonik der Hellenen* appeared in 1843, two years after [Karl Friedrich] Schinkel's death in 1841. This publication was followed by three subsequent volumes which appeared at intervals over the next decade, the last appearing in 1852, the year of Semper's *Four Elements of Architecture*. Bötticher elaborated the concept of the tectonic in a number of significant ways. At one level he envisaged a conceptual juncture, which came into being through the appropriate interlocking of constructional elements. Simultaneously articulated and integrated, these conjunctions were seen as constituting the body-form, the *Körperbilden* of the building that not only guaranteed the material finish, but also enabled this function to be recognised, as a symbolic form. At another level, Bötticher distinguished between the *Kernform* or nucleus and the *Kunstform* or decorative cladding, the latter having the purpose of representing and symbolising the institutional status of the work. According to Bötticher, this shell or revetment had to be capable of revealing the inner essence of the tectonic nucleus. At the same time Bötticher insisted that one must always try to distinguish between the indispensable structural form and its enrichment, irrespective of whether the latter is merely the shaping of the technical elements as in the case of the Doric column or the cladding of its basic form with revetment. Semper will later adapt this notion of *Kunstform* to the idea of *Bekleidung*, that is to say, to the concept of literally "dressing" the fabric of a structure.

Bötticher was greatly influenced by the philosopher Josef von Schelling's view that architecture transcends the mere pragmatism of building by virtue of assuming symbolic significance. For Schelling and Bötticher alike, the inorganic had no symbolic meaning, and hence structural form could only acquire symbolic value by virtue of its capacity to engender analogies between tectonic and organic form. However, any kind of direct imitation of natural form was to be avoided since both men held the view that architecture was an imitative art only in so far as it imitated itself. This view tends to corroborate Grassi's contention that architecture has always been distanced from the figurative arts, even if its form can be seen as paralleling nature. In this capacity architecture simultaneously serves both as a metaphor of, and as a foil to, the naturally organic. In tracing this thought retrospectively, one may cite Semper's "Theory of Formal Beauty" of 1856, in which he no longer grouped architecture with painting and sculpture as a plastic art, but with dance and music as a cosmic art, as an ontological world-making art rather than as representational form. Semper regarded such arts as paramount not only because they were symbolic but also because they embodied man's underlying erotic-ludic urge to strike a beat, to string a necklace, to weave a pattern, and thus to decorate according to a rhythmic law.

Semper's *Four Elements of Architecture* of 1852 brings the discussion full circle in as much as Semper added a specific anthropological dimension to the idea of tectonic form. Semper's theoretical schema constitutes a fundamental break with the four-hundred year-old humanist formula of *utilitas, firmitas, venustas*, that first served as the intentional triad of Roman architecture and then as the underpinning of post-Vitruvian architectural theory. Semper's radical reformulation stemmed from his seeing a model of a Caribbean hut in the Great Exhibition of 1851. The empirical reality of this simple shelter caused Semper to reject Laugier's primitive hut, adduced in 1753 as the primordial form of shelter with which to substantiate the pedimented paradigm of Neoclassical architecture. Semper's Four Elements countermanded this hypothetical assumption and asserted instead an anthropological construct comprising 1) a hearth, 2) an earthwork, 3) a framework and a roof, and 4) an enclosing membrane.

While Semper's elemental model repudiated Neoclassical authority it none the less gave primacy to the frame over the loadbearing mass. At the same time, Semper's four part thesis recognised the primary importance of the earthwork, that is to say, of a telluric mass that serves in one way or another to anchor the frame or the wall, or Mauer, into the site.

This marking, shaping, and preparing of ground by means of an earthwork had a number of theoretical ramifications. On the one hand, it isolated the enclosing membrane as a differentiating act, so that the *textural* could be literally identified with the proto-linguistic nature of textile production that Semper regarded as the basis of all civilisation. On the other hand, as Rosemary Bletter has pointed out, by stressing the earthwork as the fundamental basic form, Semper gave symbolic import to a nonspatial element, namely, the hearth that was invariably an inseparable part of the earthwork. The term "breaking ground" and the metaphorical use of the word "foundation" are both obviously related to the primacy of the earthwork and the hearth.

In more ways than one Semper grounded his theory of architecture in a phenomenal element having strong social and spiritual connotations. For Semper the hearth's origin was linked to that of the altar, and as such it was the spiritual nexus of architectural form. The hearth bears within itself connotations in this regard. It derives from the Latin verb *aedisficare*, which in its turn is the origin of the English word *edifice*, meaning literally "to make a hearth." The latent institutional connotations of both hearth and edifice are further suggested by the verb *to edify*, which means to educate, strengthen, and instruct.

Influenced by linguistic and anthropological insights of his age, Semper was concerned with the etymology of building. Thus he distinguished the massivity of a fortified stone wall as indicated by the term *Mauer* from the light frame and infill, wattle, and daub say, of mediaeval domestic building, for which the term *Wand* is used. This fundamental distinction has been nowhere more graphically expressed than in Karl Gruber's reconstruction of a mediaeval German town. Both *Mauer* and *Wand* reduce to the word "wall" in English, but the latter in German is related to the word for dress, *Gewand*, and to the term *Winden*, which means to embroider. In accordance with the primacy that he gave to textiles, Semper maintained that the earliest basic structural artifact was the knot which predominates in nomadic building form, especially in the Bedouin tent and its textile interior. We may note here in passing Pierre Bourdieu's analysis of the Bedouin house wherein the loom is identified as the female place of honour and the sun of the interior.[5] As is well known, there are etymological connotations residing here of which Semper was fully aware, above all, the connection between *knot* and *joint*, the former being in German *die Knoten* and the latter *die Naht*. In modern German both words are related to *die Verbindung* which may be literally translated as "the binding." All this evidence tends to support Semper's contention that the ultimate constituent of the art of building is the joint.

The primacy that Semper accorded to the knot seems to be supported by Gunther Nitschke's research into Japanese binding and unbinding rituals as set forth in his seminal essay, "*Shi-Me*" of 1979. In Shinto culture these proto-tectonic binding rituals constitute agrarian renewal rites. They point at once to that close association between building, dwelling, cultivating, and being, remarked on by Martin Heidegger in his essay "Building Dwelling Thinking" of 1954.

Semper's distinction between tectonic and stereotomic returns us to theoretical arguments recently advanced by the Italian architect Vittorio Gregotti, who proposes that the marking of ground, rather than the primitive hut, is the primordial tectonic act. In his 1983 address to the New York Architectural League, Gregotti stated:

> ...The worst enemy of modern architecture is the idea of space considered solely in terms of its economic and technical exigencies indifferent to the idea of the site.
>
> The built environment that surrounds us is, we believe, the physical representation of its history, and the way in which it has accumulated different levels of meaning to form the specific quality of the site, not just for what it appears to be, in perceptual terms, but for what it is in structural terms.
>
> Geography is the description of how the signs of history have become forms, therefore the architectural project is charged with the task of revealing the essence of the geo-environmental context through the transformation of form. The environment is therefore not a system in which to dissolve architecture. On the contrary, it is the most important material from which to develop the project.
>
> Indeed, through the concept of the site and the principle of settlement, the environment becomes the essence of architectural production. From this vantage point, new principles

and methods can be seen for design. Principles and methods that give precedence to the siting in a specific area. This is an act of knowledge of the context *that comes out of architectural modification* [KF italics]. The origin of architecture is not the primitive hut, the cave or the mythical "Adam's House in Paradise." Before transforming a support into a column, roof into a tympanum, before placing stone on stone, man placed a stone on the ground to recognise a site in the midst of an unknown universe, in order to take account of it and modify it. As with every act of assessment, this one required radical moves and apparent simplicity. From this point of view, there are only two important attitudes to the context. The tools of the first are mimesis, organic imitation, and the display of complexity. The tools of the second are the assessment of physical relations, formal definition, and the interiorisation of complexity.[6]

With the tectonic in mind it is possible to posit a revised account of the history of modern architecture, for when the entire trajectory is reinterpreted through the lens of *techne* certain patterns emerge and others recede. Seen in this light a tectonic impulse may be traced across the century uniting diverse works irrespective of their different origins. In this process well-known affinities are further reinforced, while others recede and hitherto unremarked connections emerge asserting the importance of criteria that lie beyond superficial stylistic differences. Thus for all their stylistic idiosyncrasies a very similar level of tectonic articulation patently links Hendrik Petrus Berlage's Stock Exchange of 1895 to Frank Lloyd Wright's Larkin Building of 1904 and Herman Hertzberger's Central Beheer office complex of 1974. In each instance there is a similar concatenation of span and support that amounts to a tectonic syntax in which gravitational force passes from purlin to truss, to pad stone, to corbel, to arch, to pier, and to abutment. The technical transfer of this load passes through a series of appropriately articulated transitions and joints. In each of these works the constructional articulation engenders the spatial subdivision and vice versa and this same principle may be found in other works of this century possessing quite different stylistic aspirations. Thus we find a comparable concern for the revealed joint in the architecture of both August Perret and Louis Kahn. In each instance the joint guarantees the probity and presence of the overall form while alluding to distinct different ideological and referential antecedents. Thus where Perret looks back to the structurally rationalised classicism of the Graeco-Gothic ideal, dating back in France to the beginning of the eighteenth century, Kahn evokes a "timeless archaism," at once technologically advanced but spiritually antique.

The case can be made that the prime inspiration behind all this work stemmed as much from Eugène Viollet-le-Duc as from Semper, although clearly Wright's conception of built form as a petrified fabric writ large, most evident in his textile block houses of the 1920s derives directly from the cultural priority that Semper gave to textile production and to the knot as the primordial tectonic unit. It is arguable that Kahn was as much influenced by Wright as by the Franco-American Beaux-Arts line, stemming from Viollet-le-Duc and the École des Beaux Arts. This particular genealogy enables us to recognise the links tying Kahn's Richards' Laboratories of 1959 back to Wright's Larkin Building. In each instance there is a similar "tartan," textile-like preoccupation with dividing the enclosed volume and its various appointments into *servant* and *served* spaces. In addition to this there is a very similar concern for the *expressive rendering of mechanical services* as though they were of the same hierarchic importance as the structural frame. Thus the monumental brick ventilation shafts of the Richards' Laboratories are anticipated, as it were, in the hollow, ducted, brick bastions that establish the four-square monumental corners of the Larkin Building. However dematerialised there is a comparable discrimination between servant and served spaces in Norman Foster's Sainsbury Centre of 1978 combined with similar penchant for the expressive potential of mechanical services. And here again we encounter further proof that the *tectonic* in the twentieth century cannot concern itself only with structural form.

Wright's highly tectonic approach and the influence of this on the later phases of the modern movement have been underestimated, for Wright is surely the primary influence behind such diverse European figures as Carlo Scarpa, Franco Albini, Leonardo Ricci, Gino Valle, and Umberto Riva, to cite only the Italian Wrightian line. A similar Wrightian connection runs through Scandinavia and Spain, serving to connect such diverse figures as Jørn Utzon, Xavier Saenz de Oiza, and most recently Rafael Moneo, who as it happens was a pupil of both.

Something has to be said of the crucial role played by the joint in the work of Scarpa and to note the syntactically tectonic nature of his architecture. This dimension has been brilliantly characterised by Marco Frascari in his essay on the mutual reciprocity of "constructing" and "construing":

> Technology is a strange word. It has always been difficult to define its semantic realm. The changes in meaning, at different times and in different places of the word "technology" into its original components of techne and logos, it is possible to set up a mirror-like relationship between the *techne of logos* and the *logos of techne*. At the time of the Enlightenment the rhetorical *techne of logos* was replaced by the scientific *logos of techne*. However, in Scarpa's architecture this replacement did not take place. Technology is present with both the forms in a chiastic quality. Translating this chiastic presence into a language proper to architecture is like saying that there is no construction without a construing, and no construing without a construction.[7]

Elsewhere Frascari writes of the irreducible importance of the joint not only for the work of Scarpa but for all tectonic endeavours. Thus we read in a further essay entitled "The Tell-the-Tale Detail":

> Architecture is an art because it is interested not only in the original need for shelter but also in putting together, spaces and materials, in a meaningful manner. This occurs through formal and actual joints. The joint, that is the fertile detail, is the place where both the construction and the construing of architecture takes place. Furthermore, it is useful to complete our understanding of this essential role of the joint as the place of the process of signification to recall that the meaning of the original Indo-European root of the word *art* is joint...[8]

If the work of Scarpa assumes paramount importance for stress on the joint, the seminal value of Utzon's contribution to the evolution of modern tectonic form resides in his reinterpretation of Semper's Four Elements. This is particularly evident in all his "pagoda/podium" pieces that invariably break down into the earthwork and the surrogate hearth embodied in the podium and into the roof and the textile-like infill to be found in the form of the "pagoda," irrespective of whether this crowning roof element comprises a shell vault or a folded slab (cf the Sydney Opera House of 1973 and the Bagsvaerd Church of 1977). It says something for Moneo's apprenticeship under Utzon that a similar articulation of earthwork and roof is evident in his Roman archaeological museum completed in Merida, Spain in 1986.

As we have already indicated, the tectonic lies suspended between a series of opposites, above all between the *ontological* and the *representational*. However, other dialogical conditions are involved in the articulation of tectonic form, particularly the contrast between the culture of the heavy-*stereotomics*, and the culture of the light-*tectonics*. The first implies load-bearing masonry and tends towards the earth and opacity. The second implies the dematerialised A-frame and tends towards the sky and translucence. At one end of this scale we have Semper's earthwork reduced in primordial times, as Gregotti reminds us, to the marking of ground. At the other end we have the ethereal, dematerialised aspirations of Joseph Paxton's Crystal Palace, that which Le Corbusier once described as the victory of light over gravity. Since few works are absolutely the one thing or the other, it can be claimed that the poetics of construction arise, in part, out of the inflection and positionings of the tectonic object. Thus the earthwork extends itself upwards to become an arch or a vault or alternatively withdraws first to become the cross wall support for a simple light-weight span and then to become a podium, elevated from the earth, on which an entire framework takes its anchorage. Other contrasts serve to articulate this dialogical movement further such as *smooth* versus *rough* at the level of material (cf Adrian Stokes) or *dark* versus *light* at the level of illumination.

Finally, something has to be said about the signification of the "break" or the "dis-joint" as opposed to the signification of the joint. I am alluding to that point at which things break against each other rather than connect: that significant fulcrum at which one system, surface or material abruptly ends to give way to another. Meaning may be thus encoded through the interplay between "joint" and "break" and in this regard rupture may have just as much meaning as connection. Such considerations sensitise architecture to the semantic risks that attend all forms of articulation, ranging from the over-articulation of joints to the under-articulation of form.

POSTSCRIPTUM: TECTONIC FORM AND CRITICAL CULTURE

As Sigfried Giedion was to remark in the introduction to his two-volume study, *The Eternal Present* (1962), among the deeper impulses of modern culture in the first half of this century was a "transavantgardist" desire to return to the timelessness of a prehistoric past; to recover in a literal sense some dimension of an eternal present, lying outside the nightmare of history and beyond the processal compulsions of instrumental progress. This drive insinuates itself again today as a potential ground from which to resist the commodification of culture. Within architecture the tectonic suggests itself as a mythical category with which to acquire entry to an anti-processal world wherein the "presencing" of things will once again facilitate the appearance and experience of men. Beyond the aporias of history and progress and outside the reactionary closures of Historicism and the Neo-Avant-Garde, lies the potential for a *marginal* counter-history.

This is the primaeval history of the logos to which Vico addressed himself in his *Nuova Scienza* in an attempt to adduce the poetic logic of the institution. It is a mark of the radical nature of Vico's thought that he insisted that knowledge is not just the province of objective fact but also a consequence of the subjective "collective" elaboration of archetypal myth, that is to say an assembly of those existential symbolic truths residing in the human experience. The critical myth of the tectonic joint points to just this timeless, time-bound moment, excised from the continuity of time.

1   Hans Sedlmayr, *Art in Crisis: The Lost Centre* (New York and London: Hollis and Carter Spottiswoode, Ballantyne & Co., Ltd., 1957), 164.
2   Clement Greenberg, "Modernist Painting," (1965) in Gregory Battcock, ed., *The New Art* (New York: Dalton Paperback, 1966), 101–102.
3   Giorgio Grassi, "Avant-Garde and Continuity," *Oppositions* 21 (Summer 1980): 26–27.
4   Ignasi de Solà-Morales Rubió, "Critical Discipline," *Oppositions* 23 (Winter 1981): 148–150.
5   Vittorio Gregotti, "Lecture at the New York Architectural League," *Section A* vol. 1, no. 1 (Montreal: February/March 1983).
6   Marco Frascari, "Technometry and the work of Carlo Scarpa and Mario Ridolf," *Proceedings of the ACSA National Conference on Technodoom* (Washington: 1987).
7   Marco Frascari, "The Tell-the-Tale Detail," *VIA* 7.
8   See Joseph Mali, "Mythology and Counter-History: The New Critical Art of Vico and Joyce."

13. FEMINISM, GENDER, AND THE PROBLEM OF THE BODY

INTRODUCTION

The Pleasure of Architecture
Bernard Tschumi

Bernard Tschumi's concern with the "exclusion of the body and its experience from all discourse on the logic of form" was encountered in "Architecture and Limits III." This earlier essay takes a more extreme stance in calling attention to the sensual aspects of space through sexual analogy. Like Roland Barthes's *Le Plaisir du Texte*, to which the title refers, the author feels a need to embrace the Dionysian along with the Apollonian. This call for the inclusion of the irrational is dramatically and graphically stated by illustrations from Tschumi's "Advertisements for Architecture" posters.

Equally provocative is his assertion that architecture's necessity is its uselessness. This challenge to the significance of function constitutes a transgression of the rules of architecture, for instance, the aspect of accommodation as laid down in the Vitruvian triad. Transgression, limits, and excess are themes to which Tschumi often returns, in this case for their links with forbidden sexual pleasure.

The equivalent of pleasure in the triad (delight), he finds best represented in the garden. His claim that the garden anticipates the city sheds light on his design for Parc de la Villette, with its grid of points and networks of paths. He discusses the seductive appeal of the mask, in terms reminiscent of Michel Foucault; he describes the revelation of the layered "systems of knowledge" that lie behind the mask. Coinciding with the excavation of these systems are constantly shifting levels of meaning.

While writing this article, Tschumi was involved in performance art activities with London collaborator Roselee Goldberg. His ongoing critique of the architectural program, and emphasis on the *event*, orchestrated by architectural space, was served by this work. At the same time, theater (Fluxus) and dance companies (Merce Cunningham) were staging performances in untraditional arenas such as city squares, to investigate the impact of different spaces on performance. Tschumi's works must be seen in light of surrealist and dadaist actions, especially because of his regular habit of juxtaposition.[1] Throughout, the language of this polemic is that of the classical avant-garde, including the conclusion that architecture can only save itself through negation of the conservative expectations of society. Radical uselessness, Tschumi claims, offers the best hope of critique.

1   Bernard Tschumi "Architecture and Its Double," *Architectural Design* 48, no. 2–3 (1978): 111–116.

BERNARD TSCHUMI
THE PLEASURE OF ARCHITECTURE

INTRODUCTION TO THE FRAGMENTS

Functionalist dogmas and the puritan attitudes of the Modern Movement have often come under attack. Yet the ancient idea of pleasure still seems sacrilegious to modern architectural theory. For many generations any architect who aimed for or attempted to experience pleasure in architecture was considered decadent. Politically, the socially conscious have been suspicious of the slightest trace of hedonism in architectural endeavours and have rejected it as a reactionary concern. And in the same way, architectural conservatives have relegated to the Left everything remotely intellectual or political, including the discourse of pleasure. On both sides, the idea that architecture can possibly exist without either moral or functional justification, or even responsibility, has been considered distasteful.

Similar oppositions are reflected throughout the recent history of architecture. The avant-garde has endlessly debated oppositions that are mostly complementary: order and disorder, structure and chaos, ornament and purity, rationality and sensuality. And these simple dialectics have pervaded architectural theory to such an extent that architectural criticism reflected similar attitudes: the Purists' ordering of form versus Art Nouveau's organic sensuousness; [Peter] Behrens's ethic of form versus [Josef Maria] Olbrich's impulse to the formless.

Often these oppositions have been loaded with moral overtones. Adolf Loos's attack on the criminality of ornament masked his fear of chaos and sensual disorder. And de Stijl's insistence on elementary form was not only a return to some anachronistic purity but also a deliberate regression to a secure order.

So strong were these moral overtones that they even survived Dada's destructive attitudes and the Surrealists' abandonment to the unconscious. [Tristan] Tzara's ironical

From *Architectural Design* 47, no. 3 (1977): 214–218. Courtesy of the author and publisher.

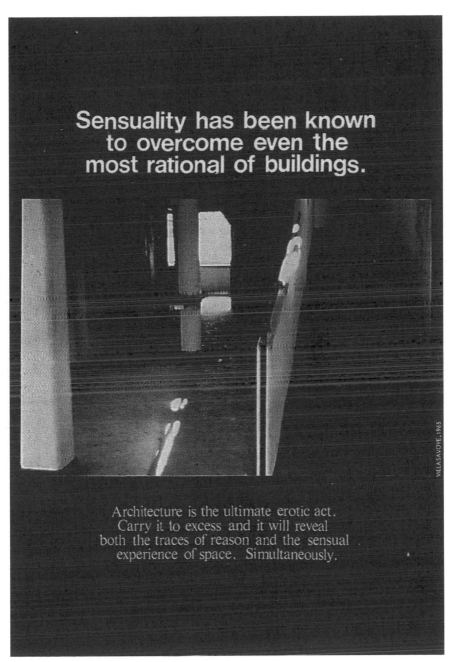

Bernard Tschumi, "Advertisements for Architecture," 1975.

contempt for order found few equivalents among architects too busy replacing the Système des Beaux-Arts by the Modern Movement's own set of rules. In 1920—despite the contradictory presences of Tzara, [Hans] Richter, Ball, [Marcel] Duchamp, and [André] Breton—Le Corbusier and his contemporaries chose the quiet and acceptable route of Purism. Even in the early 1970s, the work of the architectural school circles, with their various brands of irony or self-indulgence, ran counter to the moral reminiscences of 1968 radicalism, although both shared a dislike for established values.

Beyond such opposites lie the mythical shadows of Apollo's ethical and spiritual mindscapes versus Dionysus's erotic and sensual impulses. Architectural definitions, in their surgical precision, reinforce and amplify the impossible alternatives: on the one hand, architecture as a thing of the mind, a dematerialised or conceptual discipline with its typological and morphological variations, and on the other, architecture as an empirical event that concentrates on the senses, on the experience of space.

In the following paragraphs, I will attempt to show that today the pleasure of architecture may lie both inside *and* outside such oppositions—both in the dialectic *and* in the disintegration of the dialectic. However, the paradoxical nature of this theme is incompatible with the accepted and rational logic of classical arguments; as Roland Barthes puts it in *The Pleasure of the Text*: "pleasure does not readily surrender to analysis," hence there will be no theses, antitheses, and syntheses here. The text instead is composed of fragments that only loosely relate to one another. These fragments— *geometry, mask, bondage, excess, eroticism*—are all to be considered not only within the reality of ideas but also in the reality of the reader's spatial experience: a silent reality that cannot be put on paper.

FRAGMENT 1: A DOUBLE PLEASURE (REMINDER)

The pleasure of space. This cannot be put into words, it is unspoken. Approximately: it is a form of experience—the "presence of absence"; exhilarating differences between the plane and the cavern, between the street and your living room; symmetries and dissymmetries emphasizing the spatial properties of my body: right and left, up and down. Taken to its extreme, the pleasure of space leans toward the poetics of the unconscious, to the edge of madness.

The pleasure of geometry and, by extension, the pleasure of order—that is, the pleasure of concepts. Typical statements on architecture often read like the one in the first edition of the *Encyclopedia Britannica* of 1773: "architecture, being governed by proportion, requires to be guided by rule and compass." That is, architecture is a "thing of the mind," a geometrical rather than a pictorial or experiential art, so the problem of architecture becomes a problem of ordinance—Doric or Corinthian order, axes or hierarchies, grids or regulating lines, types or models, walls or slabs, and, of course, the grammar and syntax of the architecture's sign become pretexts for sophisticated and pleasurable manipulation. Taken to its extreme, such manipulation leans toward a poetic of frozen signs, detached from reality, into a subtle and frozen pleasure of the mind.

Neither the pleasure of space nor the pleasure of geometry is (on its own) the pleasure of architecture.

FRAGMENT 2: GARDENS OF PLEASURE

In his *Observations sur l'Architecture*, published in The Hague in 1765, Abbé Laugier suggested a dramatic deconstruction of architecture and its conventions. He wrote:

> Whoever knows how to design a park well will have no difficulty in tracing the plan for the building of a city according to its given area and situation. There must be regularity and fantasy, relationships and oppositions, and casual, unexpected elements that vary the scene; great order in the details, confusion, uproar, and tumult in the whole.

Laugier's celebrated comments, together with the dreams of Capability Brown, William Kent, [Jean-Jacques] Lequeu, or [Giovanni Battista] Piranesi, were not merely a reaction to the Baroque period that preceded them. Rather, the deconstruction of architecture that they suggested was an early venture into the realm of pleasure, against the architectural order of time.

Take Stowe, for example. William Kent's park displays a subtle dialectic between organised landscape and architectural elements: the Egyptian Pyramid, the Italian Belvedere, the Saxon Temple. But these "ruins" are to be read less as elements of a picturesque composition than as the dismantled elements of order. Yet, despite the apparent chaos, order is still present as a necessary counterpart to the sensuality of the winding streams. Without the signs of order, Kent's park would lose all reminders of "reason." Conversely, without the traces of sensuality—trees, hedges, valleys—only symbols would remain, in a silent and frozen fashion.

Gardens have had a strange fate. Their history has almost always anticipated the history of cities. The orchard grid of man's earliest agricultural achievements preceded the layout of the first military cities. The perspectives and diagonals of the Renaissance garden were applied to the squares and colonnades of Renaissance cities. Similarly, the romantic, picturesque parks of English empiricism pre-empted the crescents and arcades of the rich urban design tradition of nineteenth-century English cities.

Built exclusively for delight, gardens are like the earliest experiments in that part of architecture that is so difficult to express with words or drawings: pleasure and eroticism. Whether romantic or classical, gardens merge the sensual pleasure of space with the pleasure of reason, in a most *useless* manner.

FRAGMENT 3: PLEASURE AND NECESSITY

"Uselessness" is associated only reluctantly with architectural matters. Even at a time when pleasure found some theoretical backing ("delight" as well as "commodity" and "firmness"), utility always provided a practical justification. One example among many is Quatremère de Quincy's introduction to the entry on architecture in the *Encyclopédie méthodique* published in Paris in 1778. There you will read a definition of architecture that contends that

> amongst all the arts, those children of *pleasure and necessity*, with which man has formed a partnership in order to help him bear the pains of life and transmit his memory to future generations, it can certainly not be denied that architecture holds a most outstanding place. Considering it only from the point of view of *utility*, architecture

surpasses all the arts. It provides for the salubrity of cities, guards the health of men, protects their property, and works only for the safety, repose, and good order of civil life.

If de Quincy's statement was consistent with the architectural ideology of his time, then two hundred years later, the social necessity of architecture has been reduced to dreams and nostalgic utopias. The "salubrity of cities" is now determined more by logic of land economics, while the "good order of civil life" is more often than not the order of corporate markets.

As a result, most architectural endeavors seem caught in a hopeless dilemma. If, on one hand, architects recognize the ideological and financial dependency of their work, they implicitly accept the constraints of society. If, on the other hand, they sanctuarize themselves, their architecture is accused of elitism.

Of course, architecture will save its peculiar nature, but only wherever it questions itself, wherever it denies or disrupts the form that a conservative society expects of it. For if architecture is useless, and radically so, this very uselessness will mean strength in any society where profit is prevalent. Once again, if there has lately been some reason to doubt the necessity of architecture, then the necessity of architecture may well be its non-necessity.

Rather than an obscure "artistic supplement" or a cultural justification for financial manipulation, architecture recalls the "fireworks" example. Fireworks produce a pleasure that cannot be sold or bought, that cannot be integrated in any production cycle. Such totally gratuitous consumption of architecture is ironically *political* in that it disturbs established structures. It is also pleasurable.

FRAGMENT 4: METAPHOR OF ORDER—BONDAGE

Unlike the necessity of mere building, the non-necessity of architecture is undissociable from architectural histories, theories, and other precedents. These bonds enhance pleasure. The most excessive passion is always methodical. In such moments of intense desire, organization invades pleasure to such an extent that it is not always possible to distinguish the organizing constraints from the erotic matter. For example, the Marquis de Sade's heroes enjoyed confining their victims in the strictest convents before mistreating them according to rules carefully laid down in a precise and obsessive logic.

Similarly, the game of architecture is an intricate play with rules that one may accept or reject. Indifferently called Système des Beaux-Arts or Modern Movement precepts, this pervasive network of binding laws entangles architectural design. These rules, like so many knots that cannot be untied, are generally a paralyzing constraint. When manipulated, however, they have the erotic significance of bondage. To differentiate between rules or ropes is irrelevant here. What matters is that there is no simple bondage technique: the more numerous and sophisticated the restraints, the greater the pleasure.

FRAGMENT 5: RATIONALITY

In *Architecture and Utopia*, the historian Manfredo Tafuri recalls how the rational excesses of Piranesi's prisons took Laugier's theoretical proposals of "order and tumult" to the extreme. The classical vocabulary of architecture is Piranesi's self-chosen form of bondage. Treating classical elements as fragmented and decaying symbols, Piranesi's architecture battled against itself, in that the obsessive rationality of building types was "sadistically" carried to the extremes of irrationality.

FRAGMENT 6: EROTICISM

We have seen that the ambiguous pleasure of rationality and irrational dissolution recalled erotic concerns. A word of warning may be necessary at this stage. Eroticism is used here as a theoretical concept, having little in common with fetishistic formalism and other sexual analogies prompted by the sight of erect skyscrapers or curvaceous doorways. Rather, eroticism is a subtle matter. It does not mean simply the pleasure of the senses, nor should it be confused with sensuality. Sensuality is as different from eroticism as a simple spatial perception is different from architecture. *Eroticism is not the excess of pleasure, but the pleasure of excess.* This popular definition should make my point clear. Just as contentment of the senses does not constitute eroticism, so the sensual experience of space does not make architecture. On the contrary, "the pleasure of excess" requires consciousness as well as voluptuousness. The pleasure of architecture simultaneously contains (and dissolves) both mental constructs and sensuality. Neither space nor concepts alone are erotic, but the junction between the two is.

The ultimate pleasure of architecture is that impossible moment when an architectural act, brought to excess, reveals both the traces of reason and the immediate experience of space.

FRAGMENT 7: METAPHOR OF SEDUCTION—THE MASK

There is rarely pleasure without seduction, or seduction without illusion. Consider: sometimes you wish to seduce, so you act in the most appropriate way in order to reach your ends. You wear a disguise. Conversely, you may wish to change roles and *be* seduced: you consent to someone else's disguise, you accept his or her assumed personality, for it gives you pleasure, even if you know that it dissimulates "something else."

Architecture is no different. It constantly plays the seducer. Its disguises are numerous: facades, arcades, squares, even architectural concepts become the artifacts of seduction. Like masks, they place a veil between what is assumed to be reality and its participants (you or I). So sometimes you desperately wish to read the reality behind the architectural mask. Soon, however, you realise that no single understanding is possible. Once you uncover that which lies behind the mask, it is only to discover another mask. The literal aspect of the disguise (the facade, the street) indicates other systems of knowledge, other ways to read the city: formal masks hide socioeconomic ones, while literal masks hide metaphorical ones. Each system of knowledge obscures another. Masks hide other masks, and each successive level of meaning confirms the impossibility of grasping reality.

Consciously aimed at seduction, masks are of course a category of reason. Yet they possess a double role: they simultaneously veil and unveil, simulate and dissimulate. Behind all masks lie dark and unconscious streams that cannot be dissociated from the pleasure of architecture. The mask may exalt appearances. Yet by its very presence, it says that, in the background, there is something else.

FRAGMENT 8: EXCESS

If the mask belongs to the universe of pleasure, pleasure itself is no simple masquerade. The danger of confusing the mask with the face is real enough never to grant refuge to parodies and nostalgia. The need for order is no justification for imitating past orders. Architecture is interesting only when it masters the art of disturbing illusions, creating breaking points that can start and stop at any time.

Certainly, the pleasure of architecture is granted when architecture fulfills one's spatial expectations as well as embodies architectural ideas, concepts, or archetypes, with intelligence, invention, sophistication, irony. Yet there is also a special pleasure that results from conflicts: when the sensual pleasure of space conflicts with the pleasure of order.

The recent widespread fascination with the history and theory of architecture does not necessarily mean a return to blind obedience to past dogma. On the contrary, I would suggest that the ultimate pleasure of architecture lies in the most forbidden parts of the architectural act; where limits are perverted and prohibitions are *transgressed*. The starting point of architecture is distortion—the dislocation of the universe that surrounds the architect. Yet such a nihilistic stance is only apparently so: we are not dealing with destruction here, but with excess, differences, and left-overs. *Exceeding* functionalist dogmas, semiotic systems, historical precedents, or formalized products of past social or economic constraints is not necessarily a matter of subversion but a matter of preserving the erotic capacity of architecture by disrupting the form that most conservative societies expect of it.

FRAGMENT 9: ARCHITECTURE OF PLEASURE

The architecture of pleasure lies where concept and experience of space abruptly coincide, where architectural fragments collide and merge in delight, where the culture of architecture is endlessly deconstructed and rules are transgressed. No metaphorical paradise here, but discomfort and the unbalancing of expectations. Such architecture questions academic (and popular) assumptions, disturbs acquired tastes and fond architectural memories. Typologies, morphologies, spatial compressions, logical constructions—all dissolve. Such architecture is perverse because its real significance lies outside utility or purpose and ultimately is not even necessarily aimed at giving pleasure.

The architecture of pleasure depends on a particular feat, which is to keep architecture obsessed with itself in such an ambiguous fashion that it never surrenders to good conscience or parody, to debility or delirious neurosis.

FRAGMENT 10: ADVERTISEMENTS FOR ARCHITECTURE

There is no way to perform architecture in a book. Words and drawings can only produce paper space and not the experience of real space. By definition, paper space is imaginary: it is an image. Yet for those who do not build (whether for circumstantial or ideological reasons—it does not matter), it seems perfectly normal to be satisfied with the representation of those aspects of architecture that belong to mental constructs—to imagination. Such representations inevitably separate the sensual experience of a real space from the appreciation of rational concepts. Among other things, architecture is a function of both. And if either of these two criteria is removed, architecture loses something. It nevertheless seems strange that architects always have to castrate their architecture whenever they do not deal with real spaces. So the question remains: why should the paper space of a book or magazine replace an architectural space?

The answer does not lie in the inevitability of media or in the way architecture is disseminated. Rather it may lie in the very nature of architecture. Let's take an example. There are certain things that cannot be reached frontally. These things require analogies, metaphors, or round-about routes in order to be grasped. For instance, it is through *language* that psychoanalysis uncovers the unconscious. Like a mask, language hints at something else behind itself. It may try to hide it, but it also implies it at the same time.

Architecture resembles a masked figure. It cannot easily be unveiled. It is always hiding: behind drawings, behind words, behind precepts, behind habits, behind technical constraints. Yet it is the very difficulty of uncovering architecture that makes it intensely desirable. This unveiling is part of the pleasure of architecture.

In a similar way, reality hides behind its advertising. The usual function of advertisements reproduced again and again, as opposed to the single architectural piece—is to trigger desire for something beyond the page itself. When removed from their customary endorsement of commodity values, advertisements are the ultimate magazine form, even if somehow ironically. And, as there are advertisements for architectural products, why not for the production (and the reproduction) of *architecture?*

FRAGMENT 11: DESIRE/FRAGMENTS

There are numerous ways to equate architecture with language. Yet such equations often amount to a *reduction* and an *exclusion*. A reduction, insofar as these equations usually become distorted as soon as architecture tries to produce meaning (which meaning? whose meaning?), and thus end up reducing language to its mere combinatory logic. An exclusion, insofar as these equations generally omit some of the important findings made in Vienna at the beginning of the century, when language was first seen as a condition of the unconscious. Here, dreams were analysed as language as well as through language; language was called "the mainstreet of the unconscious." Generally speaking, it appeared as a series of fragments (the Freudian notion of fragments does not presuppose the breaking of an image, or of a totality, but the dialectical multiplicity of a process). So, too, architecture when equated with language can only be read as a series of *fragments* which make up an architectural reality.

Fragments of architecture (bits of walls, of rooms, of streets, of ideas) are all one actually sees. These fragments are like beginnings without ends. There is always a split between fragments that are real and fragments that are virtual, between memory and fantasy. These splits have no existence other than being the passage from one fragment to another. They are relays rather than signs. They are traces. They are in-between.

It is not the clash between these contradictory fragments that counts, but the movement between them. And this invisible movement is neither a part of language nor of structure (language or structure are words specific to a mode of reading architecture which does not fully apply in the context of pleasure); it is nothing but a constant and mobile relationship inside language itself.

How such fragments are organized matters little: volume, height, surface, degree of enclosure, or whatever. These fragments are like sentences between quotation marks. Yet they are not quotations. They simply melt into the work. (We are here at the opposite of the collage technique.) They may be excerpts from different discourses, but this only demonstrates that an architectural project is precisely where differences find an overall expression.

An old film of the 1950s had a name for this movement between fragments. It was called desire. Yes, *A Streetcar Named Desire* perfectly simulated the movement toward something constantly missing, toward absence. Each setting, each fragment, was aimed at seduction, but always dissolved at the moment it was approached. And then each time it would be substituted by another fragment. Desire was never seen. Yet it remained constant. The same goes for architecture.

In other words, architecture is not of interest because of its fragments and what they represent or do not represent. Nor does it consist in *exteriorizing*, through whatever forms, the unconscious desires of society or its architects. Nor is it a mere representation of those desires through some fantastic architectural image. Rather it can only act as a recipient in which your desires, my desires, can be reflected. Thus a piece of architecture is not architectural because it seduces, or because it fulfills some utilitarian function, but because it sets in motion the operations of seduction and the unconscious.

A word of warning. Architecture may very well activate such motions, but it is not a dream (a stage where society's or the individual's unconscious desires can be fulfilled). It cannot satisfy your wildest fantasies, but it may exceed the limits set by them.

For a detailed discussion of some of these fragments, please see:
Fragments 1 and 3: "Questions of Space," in *Studio International* (September/October 1975).
Fragment 2: "The Garden of Don Juan," *L'Architecture d'Aujourd'hui* (October/November 1976).
Fragments 6 and 8: "Architecture and Transgression," *Oppositions* 7 (February 1977).

INTRODUCTION

Architecture from Without: Body, Logic, and Sex
Diana I. Agrest

Feminist readings of architecture raise political concerns,
framed by critical paradigms including post-structuralism,
psychoanalysis, and Marxism. Following Freudian and
Derridean analysis, architectural theorist and educator
Diana Agrest believes the "system" of architecture is
defined both by what it includes and what it excludes, or
represses. Her analysis in "Architecture from Without:
Body, Logic, and Sex" finds the body of woman repressed
by the Western architectural tradition and its anthropomorphism. When she asks the question, "Which body is projected as the model for architectural imagery?" she finds
the male body, promoted by images from Renaissance
theory, from which measurements like the foot and cubit
are derived. Vitruvius and Alberti have, she claims:

> elaborated a system for the transformation [of the
> male body] into a *system* of architectural syntactic
> rules, elements, and meanings.

The system has both surreptitiously appropriated the
female body as the locus of reproduction and creativity
and marginalized it as a model for the production of
architectural imagery. The repression is accomplished symbolically: the creator-persona of the male architect appro-
priates the female role of mother of the building. Similarly,
the navel as the center of the body (within the square within the circle) "becomes a metonymic object or a *shifter* in
relation to gender."

The goal of Agrest's critique is the recuperation of the
female body in architecture. As a female architect, she has
experienced the exclusion of the "system." She suggests in
the introduction to her collection of theory essays that an
outside position may be an advantage, given her goal:

> It is from without architecture that one can take a
> true critical distance. Outside means from the city,
> from other fields, from other cultural and representa-
> tional systems. [1]

In synthesizing the influences of Sigmund Freud and
Julia Kristeva, Roland Barthes and Jacques Derrida, Agrest
constructs a potent interdisciplinary critical position.

---

1   Diana I. Agrest, *Architecture from Without: Theoretical Framings
     for a Critical Practice* (Cambridge: MIT Press, 1993).

DIANA I. AGREST
ARCHITECTURE FROM WITHOUT
BODY, LOGIC, AND SEX

Somewhere every culture has an imaginary zone for what it excludes and it is that zone that we must try to remember today.[1]

For something to be excluded two parts are necessary: something inside, some defined entity, and something outside. In our world of architecture and architectural ideology there is such an inside, the body of texts and rules developed in the Renaissance that, as a reading of the classics, established the foundations for Western architecture, and which I call the "system of architecture." This inside has been transformed throughout history, sometimes more profoundly than at others; and even through the apparent breaks of the first decades of this century, it has remained at the very base of Western architectural thought.

Logocentrism and anthropomorphism, in particular male anthropomorphism, have underlain the system of architecture ever since Vitruvius, read and rewritten in the Renaissance and through the Modern Movement.[2] This system is defined not only by what it includes, but also by what it excludes, inclusion and exclusion being parts of the same construct. Yet that which is excluded, left out, is not really excluded but rather repressed; repression neither excludes nor repels an exterior force for it contains within itself an interior of representation, a space of repression.[3] The repressed, the interior representation in the system of architecture that determines an outside (of repression) is woman and woman's body. The ideological construct of the architectural system determined by an idealistic logic and a concomitant system of repressions becomes apparent in the role sex plays within it. The logic in the system of architecture represses sex in two different ways: sex is understood in positive and negative terms, and woman assigned the

From *Assemblage* 7 (1988): 29–41. Courtesy of the author and publisher.

negative term (phallocentrism); and sex is neutralized or erased through the medium of the artist, who, sexless, engenders by himself and gives birth to a work, the product of creation.

Society establishes a certain kind of symbolic order where not everyone has an equal chance of fitting. Those who do not fit have to find their place between symbolic orders, in the interstices; they represent a certain symbolic instability. These are the people often called odd, abnormal, perverse or who have been labeled neurotics, ecstatics, outsiders, witches, or hysterics.[4] In strange ways, woman has been placed in this category when she has tried to establish her presence rather than limit herself to finding a way of "fitting" within the established symbolic order.

Woman has been allowed to surface from the space of her repression as a witch or as a hysteric and thus has been burned or locked up, ultimately representing the abnormal. Women who are the bearers of the greatest norm, that of reproduction, paradoxically embody also the anomaly.[5] It is through her body and through the symbolic order that woman has been repressed in architecture, and in dealing with body and architecture the obvious question, What body? is the key to the unveiling of many mysterious ideological fabrications. Asking what body is synonymous to asking which gender, for a genderless body is an impossible body.

In many of the important texts of the Renaissance, that is, the founding texts of Western architectural ideology, the body in architecture is not only an essential subject, but one, moreover, indissolubly linked to the question of gender and sex, a question that has generated the most extraordinary metaphors in the elaboration of an architectural ideology. The reading of these texts is a fundamental operation in the understanding of a complex ideological apparatus that has systematically excluded women through an elaborate mechanism of symbolic appropriation of the female body.

Two scenes will be presented here, two scenes of architecture: Scene I, The Book of the Renaissance, and Scene II, The Text of the City.

SCENE I: THE BOOK OF THE RENAISSANCE
THE SCENE OF THE REPRESSED: ARCHITECTURE FROM WITHIN

Architecture in the Renaissance establishes a system of rules that forms the basis of Western architecture. The texts of the Renaissance, which in turn draw upon the classic Vitruvian texts, develop a logocentric and anthropocentric discourse that establishes the male body at the center of the unconscious of architectural rules and configurations. The body is inscribed in the system of architecture as a male body replacing the female body. The Renaissance operations of the symbolization of the body are paradigmatic of the operations of the repression and exclusion of woman by means of the replacement of her body. Throughout the history of architecture, woman has been displaced/replaced not simply at a general social level, but, more specifically, at the level of the body's relation to architecture.

ARCHITECTURE AS A REPRESENTATION OF THE BODY

The texts of the Renaissance offer a certain clue to the mode in which man's appropriation of woman's place and body in architecture has occurred in a complex process of symbolization that works at the level of architectural ideology, therefore at an almost unconscious level. Several texts are exemplary of this procedure in various degrees, particularly [Leon Battista] Alberti's *De re aedificatoria,* [Antonio Averlino] Filarete's *Trattato d'architettura,* [Francesco] di Giorgio Martini's *Trattato di architettura civile e militare* and his *Trattati di architettura, ingegneria e arte militare.* And, of course, we cannot forget Vitruvius, whose *De architectura libri* decem is at the base of every Renaissance text.

In the several steps in the operation of symbolic transference from the body to architecture, the first is the relationship established between man and nature through the notions of natural harmony and perfection.[6] Man is presented as having the attribute of perfect natural proportions. Thus the analogical relationship between architecture and the human body appears to ensure that the natural laws of beauty and nature are transferred into architecture. The body thus becomes a mediator, a form of "shifter."[7]

It is in Vitruvius that we first encounter the significant notions that will later be variously reelaborated. His text clearly posits the issue of the human body as a model for architecture, particularly in his chapter "On Symmetry in Temples and the Human Body," where he relates symmetry to proportion:

> The design of a temple depends on symmetry, the principles of which must be carefully observed by the architect. They are due to proportion, in Greek *avanoyia.* Proportion is a correspondence among measures of the members of an entire work, and of the whole to a certain part selected as standard. From this result the principles of symmetry. Without symmetry and proportion there can be no principles in the design of any temple; that is, if there is no precise relation between its members, as in the case of those of a well-shaped man. Further, it was from the members of the body that they derived the fundamental ideas of the measures which are obviously necessary in all works, such as the finger, palm, foot, and cubit.[8]

The relationship between architecture and the human body becomes particularly important at the moment in which the issue of the center—a preoccupation that filters throughout the history of art and architecture in its many symbolic roles—acquires a very specific meaning.

> Then again, in the human body the central point is naturally the navel. For if a man be placed flat on his back, with his hands and feet extended, and a pair of compasses centered at his navel, the fingers and toes of his two hands and feet will touch the circumference of a circle described therefrom. And just as the human body yields a circular outline, so too a square figure maybe found from it. For if we measure the distance from the soles of the feet to the top of the head, and then apply that measure to the outstretched arms, the breadth will be found to be the same as the height, as in the case of plane surfaces which are perfectly square.[9]

The center is represented by the navel, which becomes a metonymic object or a "shifter" in relation to gender. It is a true shifter in that it transforms the body into geometry, nature into architecture, the "I" of the subject into the "I" of the discourse. The relationship between these two "I's" is what allows the constant shifting of genders.[10]

This type of formal relationship between the body of man and architecture, developed by Vitruvius, will be everpresent in the Renaissance texts.

An analogical relationship between the body (of man) and architecture can also be found in Alberti's *De re aedificatoria*:

> The whole Force of the invention and all our skill and Knowledge in the Art of Building, it is required in the Compartition: Because the distinct Parts of the entire Building, and, to use such a Word, the Entireness of each of those parts and the Union and Agreement of all the lines and Angles in the Work, duly ordered for Convenience, Pleasure, and Beauty are disposed and measured out by the Compartition alone: For if a City, according to the Opinion of Philosophers, be no more than a great House and, on the other hand, a House be a little City; why may it not be said that the Members of that House are so many little Houses...and as the Members of the Body are correspondent to each other, so it is fit that one part should answer to another in a Building; whence we say, that great Edifices require great Members.[11]

Alberti is never as direct in his analogies as Vitruvius or as other architects of the Renaissance. His text offers a far more elaborate system of metaphorical transformation by which he develops specific notions that allow for the development of an abstract system in a discourse that incorporates the "laws of nature."

> If what we have here laid down appears to be true, we may conclude Beauty to be such a Consent and Agreement of the Parts of the Whole in which it is found, as to Number, Finishing, and Collocation, as Congruity, that is to say, the principal law of Nature, requires. This is what Architecture chiefly aims at, and by this she obtains her Beauty, Dignity, and Value. The Ancients knowing from the Nature of Things, that the Matter was in fact as I have stated it, and being convinced, that if they neglected this main Point they should never produce any Thing great or commendable, did in their Works propose to themselves chiefly the Imitation of Nature, as the greatest Artist of all Manner of Composition;...
>
> Reflecting therefore upon the Practice of Nature as well with Relation to an entire Body, as to its several Parts, they found from the very first Principles of Things, that Bodies were not always composed of equal parts of Members; whence it happens, that of the Bodies produced by Nature, some are smaller, some are larger, and some middling.[12]

The process of symbolization takes place by relating the body as a system of proportion to other systems of proportion. The body, transformed into an abstract system of formalization, is thus incorporated into the architectural system as form, through the orders, the hierarchies, and the general system of formal organization that allows for this anthropocentric discourse to function at the level of the unconscious.

TRANSSEXUAL OPERATIONS IN ARCHITECTURE

Vitruvius and Alberti point the way to the incorporation of the body as an analogue, model, or referent, elaborating a system for its transformation into a system of architectural syntactic rules, elements, and meanings. Filarete and di Giorgio Martini, further, eliminate the original ambiguity of the gender of the body in question by making explicit that the human figure is synonymous with the male figure. A different ambiguity will appear instead, the ambiguity of gender or sex itself. In a rather complex set of metaphorical operations throughout these texts, the gender of the body and its sexual functions are exchanged in a move of cultural transsexuality whereby man's everpresent procreative fantasy is enacted.

Filarete starts by making sure we understand that when he refers to the "human" figure or body, he means the male figure:

> As I have said, the building is constructed as a simile for the human figure. You see that I have shown you by means of a simile that a building is derived from man, that is, from his form, members, and measure.
>
> Now as I have told you above, I will show you how the building is given form and substance by analogy with the members and form of man. You know that all buildings need members and passages, that is, entrances and exits. They should all be formed and arranged according to their origins. The exterior and interior appearance of the building is arranged effectively in such a way that the members and passages are suitably located, just as the exterior and interior parts and members are correct for the body of man.[13]

Here the conditions are present for the development of a double analogy and for possible exchanges and combinations in the body considered as interior and/or exterior. In the most common and apparent analogical relationship between the body of man and architecture we are faced with the exterior. In bringing about the interior, another set of metaphors will be possible, particularly those that allow for the permutation of gender. In order to elaborate on the question of the interior of man, Filarete does not stop at the formal analogy; his symbolic operations lead him to develop his most extraordinary metaphor, that of the building as living man:

> [When they are] measured, partitioned, and placed as best you can, think about my statements and understand them clearly. I will [then] show you [that] the building is truly a living man. You will see it must eat in order to live, exactly as it is with man. It sickens or dies or sometimes is cured of its sickness by a good doctor. In the first book you have seen, as I have demonstrated to you, the origins of the building and its origins in my opinion, how it is proportioned to the human body of man, how it needs to be nourished and governed and through lack it sickens and dies like man.[14]

In this manner he slowly and steadily builds up a symbolic argument that unfolds from the building created as a formal analogue of the male body, from which even the orders are derived, to the building as a living body. If the building is a living man the next necessary step in the argument is its birth and its conception. It is at this critical point that another body will be incorporated: that of the architect himself.

> You perhaps could say, you have told me that the building is similar to man. Therefore, if this is so it needs to be conceived and then born. As [it is] with man himself, so [it is]

with the Building. First it is conceived, using a simile such as you can understand, and then it is born. The mother delivers her child at the term of nine months or sometimes seven; by care and in good order she makes him grow.[15]

If the building is a living man, someone must give birth to it—and here the architect appears in the role of the mother. The figure of the architect becomes feminized in the act of procreation:

The building is conceived in this manner. Since no one can conceive himself without a woman, by another simile, the building cannot be conceived by one man alone. *As it cannot be done without woman, so he who wishes to build needs an architect.* He conceives it with him and then the architect carries it. When the architect has given birth *he becomes the mother* of the building. Before the *architect gives birth*, he should dream about his conception, think about it, and turn it over in his mind in many ways for seven to nine months, just as a woman carries her child in her body for seven to nine months. He should also make various drawings of this conception that he has made with the patron, according to his own desires. As the woman can do nothing without the man, so the architect is the mother to carry this conception. When he has pondered and considered and thought [about it] in many ways, he ought to choose (according to his own desires), what seems most suitable and most beautiful to him according to the terms of the patron. When this birth is accomplished, that is, when he has made, in wood, a small relief design of its final form, measured and proportioned to the finished building, then he shows it to the father.[16]

Filarete takes this transsexual operation to its extreme by transforming the architect into a woman—or better, mother. He proceeds to state that just like a mother, the architect must also be a nurse, and "with love and diligence" he will help the building grow to its completion:

As I have compared the architect to the mother, he also needs to be nurse. He is both mother and nurse. As the mother is full of love for her son, so he will rear it with love and diligence, cause it to grow, and bring it to completion if it is possible, if it is not, he will leave it ordered.[17]

Filarete pushes his argument all the way to cover the various aspects involved in the building:

A good mother loves her son and with the aid of the father strives to make him good and beautiful, and with a good master to make him valient and praiseworthy. So the good architect should strive to make his buildings good and beautiful.[18]

First woman is excluded (repressed) by making architecture an image of man as an analogue to man's body and, as we have seen, to the point of turning it into a living organism. Then, in an extraordinary operation that I call here architectural transsexuality, for which her repression is essential, woman is replaced—her place usurped by man, who, as the architect, possesses the female attributes necessary for conception and reproduction.

Filarete's texts are greatly complemented by those of Francesco di Giorgio Martini. In his *Trattato di architettura civile e militare* and *Trattati di architettura, ingegneria e arte militare*, di Giorgio uses similar analogies between the human body and architecture, but in his case the analogy is proposed at the scale of the city.

> One should shape the city, fortress, and castle in the form of a human body, that the head with the attached members have a proportioned correspondence and that the head be the rocca, the arms its recessed walls that, circling around, link the rest of the whole body, the vast city.
>
> And thus it should be considered that just as the body has all its members and parts in perfect measurements and proportions, in the composition of temples, cities, rocche, and castles the same principles should be observed.[19]

Di Giorgio further develops this argument so that the ideology can be better translated into specific formal systems:

> Cities have the reasons, measurements, and form of the human body. I am going to describe precisely their perimeters and partitions. First the human body stretched on the ground should be considered. Placing a string at the navel, the other end will create a circular form. This design will be squared and angles placed in similar fashion...
>
> Thus it should be considered just as the body has all the parts and members in perfect measurement and circumference, the center in the cities and other buildings should be observed....The palms and the feet would constitute other temples and squares. And as the eyes, ears, nose, and mouth, the veins, intestines, and other internal parts and members that are organized inside and outside the body according to its needs, in the same way this should be observed in cities, as we shall show in some focus.[20]

The reading and reuse of Vitruvius takes on a new dimension in di Giorgio, for it is not only part of an analogical discourse between the body (male) and the city, it is at the same time central in a representational discourse where the roles and places of male and female body in relation to architecture are swiftly exchanged. It is in shifting from the external appearance to the internal functions and order of the body that we will be faced once more with a transsexual operation.

> And so as it has been said that all the internal parts [of the human body] are organized and divided for its government and subsistence, in the same way that inside and outside parts of the body are necessary, it is that each member of the city should be distributed to serve its subsistence, harmony, and government...
>
> I therefore say that first of all the main square [piazza] should be placed in the middle and the center of that city or as close as possible, just as the navel is to man's body; convenience should go second to this. The reason for this similitude could be the following; just as it is through his navel that human nature gets nutrition and perfection in its beginnings, in the same way by this common place the other particular places are served.[21]

But this can only be an analogy after some operations of substitution are performed: The umbilical cord is the tie to the mother, the woman. Di Giorgio says "like the navel is to a man's body," yet the relationship of the man's body to the umbilical cord is one of dependence. He does not provide nourishment; rather, he is nourished by the mother at the beginning of life. Thus for this analogy to work for the city, the female body should be taken as the symbolic reference; instead, it is replaced by the male body and man's navel is transformed into the city's "womb." In the production of this architectural analogy man's body is functionally transformed, feminized.

Although di Giorgio never mentions the sexual organs, they have an analogical presence in some of his designs for cities, where the male sexual organ occupies the place previously analogically assigned to the various parts of the body. That which has been taken must be negated; it is the denial that goes with repression.

I propose three instances in this play of substitutions:

First, the male body is projected, represented, and inscribed in the design of buildings and cities and in the texts that establish their ideology. The female body is suppressed or excluded. Second, the architect himself is presented as a woman in relation to the reproductive creative functions, operating as a "literal" sexual replacement. And third, the male body becomes the female body in its functions of giving nourishment, that is, life, to the city; man's navel becomes woman's womb.

It is remarkable that the replacement of the female body by the male body always occurs in relation to the maternal function: reproduction. It has been said that we live in a civilization in which the consecrated—religious or secular—representation of femininity is subsumed by the maternal.[22] In this perspective, the whole operation appears to be a veiled representation of the myth of Mary.

In Filarete, the architect, a man, gives birth like a woman. In di Giorgio, the center of the city, based on the configuration of man's body, gives subsistence, like a woman's body, through the umbilical cord from the womb to the rest of the city. In one case men's fantasies of conception and reproduction are placed in the figure of the architect, in the other they are set in the principles organizing the formal configuration of the city. Woman is thus suppressed, repressed, and replaced.

Suppressed, in the analogical relation between body and architecture. It is man's body that is, according to the classic texts, the natural and perfectly proportioned body from which architectural principles and measurements derive.

Repressed, in the model of the city. Woman's unique quality, that of motherhood, is projected onto the male body. Thus woman is not only suppressed, but indeed her whole sexual body is repressed.

Replaced, by the figure of the architect. The male, through a transsexual operation, has usurped the female's reproductive qualities, in the desire to fulfill the myth of creation.

Motherhood more than womanhood has been appropriated, but motherhood has always been confused with womanhood as one and the same: the representation of femininity is subsumed by the maternal.

In the art of the Renaissance, Mary, Queen of the Heavens and Mother of the Church, was an everpresent figure. It is in this ideological context, that of Christianism, that the treatises of Alberti, di Giorgio Martini, and Filarete were developed. (Fantasies of male conception can also be found in the texts of other men, including Saint Augustine.)[23]

The power of this ideology was evidenced in the mode of representing religion and its concomitant myths. A most powerful one was that of the Virgin Mary. The nature of the mother/son relationship between Mary and Christ and the belief in the immaculate conception leads toward the possibility of pregnancy without sex: woman, rather than being penetrated by a male, conceives with a non-person, the spirit. This conception without sex (sin) is the negation of sex as an essential part in the reproductive process, and ultimately, in the birth of Christ.

This religious ideology was all-encompassing. In a move of perfect ideological representation in a particular subregion of ideology, that of architecture, the architect, by usurping the female body, can give birth to buildings or cities, and just like Mary, he can conceive without sex, through spirit alone. Man is thus placed at the center of creation.

The architectural treatises mentioned here develop a system of rules elaborating an ideology that allows for the transformation in philosophy, Christianity, and the power structure of the Church to filter through the subregion of architecture.[24]

Woman (mother/Mary) was necessary as an imposing image within the system; woman outside that system, if not suppressed, had to be burned. On the one hand, Mary; on the other, heretics and witches, those who pointed out the system of repressions and the possibility of a certain demystification. Men's mechanism of the assumption of the maternal role, through Christianity, may also be a mechanism of masculine sublimation.[25]

SCENE II: THE TEXT OF THE CITY
THE RETURN OF THE REPRESSED: ARCHITECTURE FROM WITHOUT

The system of architecture from within is characterized by an idealistic logic that can assume neither contradiction nor negation and, therefore, is based upon the suppression of either one of two opposite terms. This is best represented by the consistent repression and exclusion of woman. Woman does not fit the symbolic order. She is offside, in the cracks of symbolic systems, an outsider.

It is in that outside that we stand. It is from that outside that we can project better than anyone the critical look. Woman can place herself from without the system of architecture by accepting heterogeneity and by including positively the negated, woman herself. In the ideological realm of architecture this implies the negation of the "system of architecture" through a critical work and the inclusion of the denied, the excluded, the hidden, the repressed.

This discourse from without incorporates heterogeneous matter, includes negation, and is psychoanalytical and historical. Woman, representing both the heterogeneity of matter through her body[26] and the historical negation of her gender, is in the perfect position to develop such a discourse. Woman, a discourse of heterogeneity, "represents the negative in the homogeneity of the community."[27]

To take a place from without the system is not simply to include what has been negated, or excluded, or to surface the repressed: a more complex process occurs. The classic architectural project of the city (as a body) is a reflection in the mirror of a totally formed, closed, and unitary system. We are dealing now instead with a representation of a fragmented body.[28] The architect cannot recognize himself or his system of rules in the mirror of the city as did di Giorgio or Filarete. The body as a metaphor of the fragmented architectural body, which cannot be recomposed within the system of architectural rules, will be that referential outside.

It is the explosion, the fragmented unconscious, where the "architectural body" does not reflect the body of the subject, as it did in the Renaissance, but instead reflects the perception of the fragmented body as the built text, a set of fragments of languages and texts, the city. The body cannot be reconstructed, the subject architect/man does not recognize itself in architecture as an entity in front of the mirror. The system has been broken; architecture cannot be recognized again as a whole.

We will take that built social unconscious of architecture, the city, a text, for it is not the result of the creation of a subject, product of a logocentric, anthropomorphic system. There is no subject. Here are only fragments of texts and languages to be read, and in this reading they traverse the subject, in the position of reader-writer.

THE STREET: STREETWALKERS
The city presents itself as a fragmentary text escaping the order of things and of language, a text to be "exploded," taken in pieces, in fragments, to be further decomposed in so many possible texts, open in a metonymy of desire.

To design is not to reclose but to affect the openings and be affected by them to play an intersection between the two subjects, that of the reader and that of the writer, by an operation of shifting through the "I." The subject gets caught in the text and becomes part of the text.

This subject, woman, writes as she reads, where the repression has failed, where the system is fragmented, and where she does not want to be reconstructed by finding in it the reflection of an enclosed, homogeneous, unitary system. She reads there and activates the absence of the repression/replacement of her body.

The street is the scene of her writing, with her body following the role that she is given in the evaluation of her body as merchandise. The street is the scene of architectural writing. The private realm is the scene of the institution, where woman and her body have an assigned place: the house.

WIFE IN THE KITCHEN. WHORE IN THE STREET.
Rather than worshiping the monuments, we take the streets, we "play house," taking a critical view of the family as a hierarchical system and of the rules of architecture that go with it.

The city is the social scene where woman can publicly express her struggle. She was/is not accepted in the institutions of power; she is dispossessed (of her body) and is with the dispossessed. The public place is a no-man's-land ready to be appropriated. The scene of the city, of the street, of the public place is that of the dispossessed; there she is "at home."

(A place outside the accepted institutions is taken and assumed through various texts and readings of an open and heterogeneous quality.)

READING FROM WITHOUT
I think of this project. I have a vision, a realist image of unreal events. It flows without knowing like a mystic pad; the city like an unconscious of architecture unveils itself,

three modes of time in three analogues of experience: permanence, succession, simultaneity.

A register of urban inscriptions, these three together—now I am reading, now I am writing—the boundaries are not clear. I can read the words, the unsaid, the hidden, there where no man wants to read, where there are no monuments to speak of an established and unitary system of architecture.

Like an optical illusion the grid becomes an object, then the fabric, then the object again. The apparent contradiction and undialectical opposition between object and fabric at the base of this process develops a text from the inclusions and juxtaposition of these opposite terms.

All of a sudden an erasure, the erasure necessary to remark, reinstate the obvious not seen, the *tabula rasa* that could become fabric, the object that would rather be a public place.

The *refoules* (repressed) of architecture, the public, the negation all become the material of my fictional configuration. The (project) marks I make are organized through a contradiction—a negation through an affirmation. Negate the city to affirm the city. It is the affirmation of the erasure of the city in order to reinstate its trace. The critical reading is taken from the subject: I am spoken through the city and the city is read through me.

This text originated in the fall of 1971 as a proposal for an article to be entitled "Architecture from Without: Matter, Logic, and Sex." Although my interest in the material was very strong at that time, I did not have the opportunity to develop it until 1986–87. The original abstract was only four pages long, but it contained all the elements necessary to develop this article. During the process of development, I realized that the second part, "Architecture from Without," could not be expanded in the same manner as the first part, "Architecture from Within." For the latter section posits a premise for and an approach to critical work. I believe that this critical approach to architecture is present in my work produced throughout these years in practice, theory, criticism, and teaching. I want to thank Amy Miller and David Smiley and especially Judy O'Buck Gordon for her initial incentive and persistent interest in this essay.

1   Catherine Clément, "La Coupable," in *La Jeune née union* (Paris: Union Générale d'Editions, 1975).
2   Even Le Corbusier's Modulor is entirely based on a male body.
3   Jacques Derrida, "Freud et la scène de l'écriture," in *L'Écriture et la différence* (Paris: Éditions de Seuil, 1967); English ed., "Freud and the Scene of Writing," in *Writing and Difference*, Alan Bass, trans. (Chicago: University of Chicago Press, 1978).
4   See Clément, "La Coupable," op. cit.
5   Ibid.
6   Françoise Choay, "La Ville et le domaine bati comme corps," *Nouvelle revue de psychanalyse* 9 (1974).
7   For this notion, see Diana Agrest, "Design Versus Non-Design," *Oppositions* 6 (1976).
8   Marcus Vitruvius Pollio, *De architectura libri decem*; English ed., *The Ten Books of Architecture*, Morris Hicky Morgan, trans. (New York: Dover Publications, 1960).
9   Ibid.
10   Roman Jakobson, "Shifters, Verbal Categories and the Russian Verb," paper delivered at Harvard University, 1957.

11   Leon Battista Alberti, *De re aedificatoria* (1485); *Architecture of Leon Battista Alberti in Ten Books*, facsimile reprint from the Giacomo Leoni translation of 1726, with a reprint of the "Life" from the 1739 edition, Joseph Rykwert and Alex Tiranti, eds. (London: 1955).

12   "You have seen briefly the measures, understood their names and sources, their qualities and forms. I told you they were called by their Greek names, Doric, Ionic, and Corinthian. The Doric I told you is one of the major quality; the Corinthian is in the middle, the Ionic is the smallest for the reasons alleged by the architect Vitruvius in his book [where] he shows how they were in the times of the emperor Octavian. In these modes the Doric, Ionic, and Corinthian corresponded in measure to the form or, better, to the quality of the form to which they are proportioned. As the building is derived from man, his measures, qualities, form, and proportions, so the column also derives from man: The polished columns, according to Vitruvius, were derived from the nude man and fluted from that well-dressed young woman, as we have said. Both are derived from the form of man. Since this is so, they take their qualities, form and measure from man. The qualities, or better Ionic, Doric, and Corinthian, are three, that is large, medium, and small forms. They should be formed, proportioned, and measured according to their quality. Since man is the measure of all, the column should be measured and proportioned to his form" (Alberti, *De re aedificatoria,* op. cit.).

13   Antonio Averlino Filarete, *Trattato d'architettura* (1461 63); *Treatise on Architecture,* translated, with an introduction and notes, by John R. Spencer, 2 vols. (New Haven: Yale University Press, 1965).

14   Ibid.

15   Ibid.

16   Ibid. Agrest's emphasis.

17   Ibid.

18   Ibid.

19   Francesco di Giorgio Martini, *Trattati di architettura, ingegneria e arte militare* (1470–92); Italian ed., edited by Corrado Maltese and transcribed by Livia Maltese Degrassi, 2 vols. (Milan: Edizioni Il polifilo, 1967). Translations here are my own.

20   Ibid.

21   Ibid.

22   Julia Kristeva, "Stabat Mater," in *Histoires d'amour* (Paris: Éditions Denoël, 1983); English ed., *Tales of Love*, Leon S. Roudiez, trans. (New York: Columbia University Press, 1987).

23   Ibid.

24   This question of the relationship between humanism, Christianism, and the Church is an entire subject on its own and should be treated at length outside the context of this article.

25   Kristeva, "Stabat Mater," op. cit.

26   Julia Kristeva, "Matière, sens, dialectique," *Tel Quel* 44 (1971).

27   Ibid.

28   Jacques Lacan, "Le Stade du miroir comme formateur de la fonction du Je," in *Écrits* I (Paris: Éditions du Seuil, 1966); English trans., "The Mirror Stage as Formative of the Function of the I," in *Écrits: A Selection* (New York: Norton, 1977).

INTRODUCTION   Visions' Unfolding: Architecture in the Age of
                 Electronic Media
                 Peter Eisenman

In this essay from the Italian magazine *Domus*,
Peter Eisenman argues that a major paradigm
shift has taken place in the second half of the
twentieth century that has not been acknowledged by architecture. The shift from mechanical
to electronic media (for example, from camera to
facsimile machines) has been ignored, he contends, because architecture depends upon statics
and mechanical construction. The electronic paradigm has implications for architecture's role in the
visual representation of society's values, especially
with regard to ideas of reality, the original, and
their perception.

Eisenman challenges the body's projection
through our primary interpretive faculty, vision.
Speaking from a poststructuralist position, he
says, "the seeing human subject—monocular and
anthropocentric—remains the primary discursive
term of architecture." His analysis indicates that
rationalizing vision has determined architectural
drawing, especially perspective, and that these
drawing conventions limit our ideas of form and
space. Sounding a familiar theme, (ch. 4) he suggests that architecture will never move beyond the
Renaissance world view unless it challenges representation fundamentally, as was accomplished
in Cubist painting and in some sculpture from the
1960s. One type of challenge is to invert the
classical aesthetic categories of the beautiful and
the grotesque, as outlined in "En Terror Firma."
(ch. 14) Diana Agrest's critique in this chapter
also urges a challenge to Renaissance representation, in particular its *anthropomorphic* aspects. In
her case, the critique is motivated by concern
about the suppression of the female body in
architectural imagery.

Eisenman thus seeks a new kind of non-projective drawing and a new relationship between
subject and object that could confront the "ocular
centrist" and anthropocentric bias of the Western
culture. He says that architecture must problematize vision in order to critique the current dominant condition and come to a new understanding

of "folded" space. The latter concept is borrowed from Gilles Deleuze, a contemporary French film and cultural critic. Folded space is to be an alternative to normative, gridded, Cartesian space. In place of the traditional projection of vision into space, Eisenman offers "inscribe[ing] space in such a way as to endow it with the possibility of looking back at the subject."

PETER EISENMAN

VISIONS' UNFOLDING
ARCHITECTURE IN THE AGE OF ELECTRONIC MEDIA

During the fifty years since the Second World War, a paradigm shift has taken place that should have profoundly affected architecture: this was the shift from the mechanical paradigm to the electronic one. This change can be simply understood by comparing the impact of the role of the human subject on such primary modes of reproduction as the photograph and the fax; the photograph within the mechanical paradigm, the fax within the electronic one.

In photographic reproduction the subject still maintains a controlled interaction with the object. A photograph can be developed with more or less contrast, texture, or clarity. The photograph can be said to remain in the control of human vision. The human subject thus retains its function as interpreter, as discursive function. With the fax, the subject is no longer called upon to interpret, for reproduction takes place without any control or adjustment. The fax also challenges the concept of originality. While in a photograph the original reproduction still retains a privileged value, in facsimile transmission the original remains intact but with no differentiating value since it is no longer sent. The mutual devaluation of both original and copy is not the only transformation affected by the electronic paradigm. The entire nature of what we have come to know as the reality of our world has been called into question by the invasion of media into everyday life. For reality always demanded that our vision be interpretive.

How have these developments affected architecture? Since architecture has traditionally housed value as well as fact, one would imagine that architecture would have been greatly transformed. But this is not the case, for architecture seems little changed at all. This in itself ought to warrant investigation, since architecture has traditionally been a bastion of what is considered to be the real. Metaphors such as house and home: bricks

From *Domus* no. 734 (January 1992): 20–24. Courtesy of the author and publisher.

and mortar; foundations and shelter, attest to architecture's role in defining what we consider to be real. Clearly, a change in the everyday concepts of reality should have had some affect on architecture. It did not because the mechanical paradigm was the *sine qua non* of architecture; architecture was the visible manifestation of the overcoming of natural forces such as gravity and weather by mechanical means. Architecture not only overcame gravity, it was also the monument to that overcoming; it interpreted the value society placed on its vision.

The electronic paradigm directs a powerful challenge to architecture because it defines reality in terms of media and simulation, it values appearance over existence, what can be seen over what is. Not the seen as we formerly knew it, but rather a seeing that can no longer interpret. Media introduce fundamental ambiguities into how and what we see. Architecture has resisted this question because, since the importation and absorption of perspective by architectural space in the fifteenth century, architecture has been dominated by the mechanics of vision. Thus architecture assumes sight to be pre-eminent and also in some way natural to its own processes, not a thing to be questioned. It is precisely this traditional concept of sight that the electronic paradigm questions.

Sight is traditionally understood in terms of vision. When I use the term *vision* I mean that particular characteristic of sight which attaches seeing to thinking, the eye to the mind. In architecture, vision refers to a particular category of perception linked to monocular perspectival vision. The monocular vision of the subject in architecture allows for all projections of space to be resolved on a single planimetric surface. It is therefore not surprising that perspective, with its ability to define and reproduce the perception of depth on a two-dimensional surface, should find architecture a waiting and wanting vehicle. Nor is it surprising that architecture soon began to conform itself to this monocular, rationalizing vision—in its own body. Whatever the style, space was constituted as an understandable construct, organized around spatial elements such as axes, places, symmetries, etc. Perspective is even more virulent in architecture than in painting because of the imperious demands of the eye *and* the body to orient itself in architectural space through processes of rational perspectival ordering. It was thus not without cause that [Filippo] Brunelleschi's invention of *one-point* perspective should correspond to a time when there was a paradigm shift from the theological and theocentric to the anthropomorphic and anthropocentric views of the world. Perspective became the vehicle by which anthropocentric vision crystallized itself in the architecture that followed this shift.

Brunelleschi's projection system, however, was deeper in its effect than all subsequent stylistic change because it confirmed vision as the dominant discourse in architecture from the sixteenth century to the present. Thus, despite repeated changes in style from the Renaissance through Post Modernism and despite many attempts to the contrary, the seeing human subject—monocular and anthropocentric—remains the primary discursive term of architecture.

The tradition of planimetric projection in architecture persisted unchallenged because it allowed the projection and hence, the understanding of a three-dimensional space in two dimensions. In other disciplines—perhaps since [Gottfried Wilhelm] Leibniz and certainly since [Jean-Paul] Sartre—there has been a consistent attempt to demonstrate the problematic qualities inherent in vision, but in architecture the sight/mind construct has persisted as the dominant discourse.

In an essay entitled "Scopic Regimes of Modernity," Martin Jay notes that. "...Baroque visual experience has a strongly tactile or haptic quality, which prevents it from turning into the absolute ocular centrism of its Cartesian perspectivalist rival." Norman Bryson in his article, "The Gaze in the Expanded Field" introduces the idea of the gaze (le regard) as the looking back of the other. He discusses the gaze in terms of Sartre's intruder in *Being and Nothingness* or in terms of [Jacques] Lacan's concept of a darkness that cuts across the space of sight. Lacan also introduces the idea of a space looking back which he likens to a disturbance of the visual field of reason.

From time to time architecture has attempted to overcome its rationalizing vision. If one takes for example the church of San Vitale in Ravenna one can explain the solitary column almost blocking the entry or the incomplete groin vaulting as an attempt to signal change from a Pagan to a Christian architecture. [Giovanni Battista] Piranesi creates similar effects with his architectural projections. Piranesi diffracted the monocular subject by creating perspectival visions with multiple vanishing points so that there was no way of correlating what was seen into a unified whole. Equally, Cubism attempted to deflect the relationship between a monocular subject and the object. The subject could no longer put the painting into some meaningful structure through the use of perspective. Cubism used a non-monocular perspectival condition: it flattened objects to the edges, it upturned objects, it undermined the stability of the picture plane. Architecture attempted similar dislocations through Constructivism and its own, albeit normalizing, version of Cubism—the International Style. But this work only *looked* cubistic and modern, the subject remained rooted in a profound anthropocentric stability, comfortably, upright, and in place on a flat, tabular ground. There was no shift in the relationship between the subject and the object. While the object looked different it failed to displace the viewing subject. Though the buildings were sometimes conceptualized, by axonometric or isometric projection rather than by perspective, no consistent deflection of the subject was carried out. Yet modernist sculpture did in many cases effectuate such a displacement of the subject. These dislocations were fundamental to minimalism: the early work of Robert Morris, Michael Heizer, and Robert Smithson. This historical project, however, was never taken up in architecture. The question now begs to be asked: Why did architecture resist developments that were taking place in other disciplines? And further, why has the issue of vision never been properly problematized in architecture?

It might be said that architecture never adequately thought the problem of vision because it remained within the concept of the subject and the four walls. Architecture, unlike any other discipline, concretized vision. The hierarchy inherent in all architectural space begins as a structure for the mind's eye. It is perhaps the idea of interiority as a hierarchy between inside and outside that causes architecture to conceptualize itself ever more comfortably and conservatively in vision. The interiority of architecture more than any other discourse defined a hierarchy of vision articulated by inside and outside. The fact that one is actually both inside and outside at architecture, unlike painting or music, required vision to conceptualize itself in this way. As long as architecture refuses to take up the problem of vision, it will remain within a Renaissance or Classical view of its discourse. Now what would it mean for architecture to take up the problem of vision? Vision can be defined as essentially a way of organizing space and elements in space. It is a way of looking *at*, and defines a relationship between a subject and an object.

Traditional architecture is structured so that any position occupied by a subject provides the means for understanding that position in relation to a particular spatial typology, such as a rotunda, a transept crossing, an axis, an entry. Any number of these typological conditions deploy architecture as a screen for looking-at.

The idea of a "looking-back" begins to displace the anthropocentric subject. Looking back does not require the object to become a subject, that is to anthropomorphosize the object. Looking back concerns the possibility of detaching the subject from the rationalization of space. In other words to allow the subject to have a vision of space that no longer can be put together in the normalizing, classicizing or traditional construct of vision; an other space, where in fact the space "looks back" at the subject. A possible first step in conceptualizing this "other space," would be to detach what one sees from what one knows—the eye from the mind. A second step would be to inscribe space in such a way as to endow it with the possibility of looking back at the subject. All architecture can be said to be already inscribed. Windows, doors, beams, and columns are a kind of inscription. These make architecture known, they reinforce vision. Since no space is uninscribed, we do not see a window without relating it to an idea of window, this kind of inscription seems not only natural but also necessary to architecture. In order to have a looking back, it is necessary to rethink the idea of inscription. In the Baroque and Rococo such an inscription was in the plaster decoration that began to obscure the traditional form of functional inscription. This kind of "decorative" inscription was thought too excessive when undefined by function. Architecture tends to resist this form of excess in a way which is unique to the other arts, precisely because of the power and pervasive nature of functional inscription. The anomalous column at San Vitale inscribes space in a way that was at the time foreign to the eye. This is also true of the columns in the staircase at the Wexner Center. However most of such inscriptions are the result of design intention, the will of an authorial subjective expression which then only reconstitutes vision as before. To dislocate vision might require an inscription which is the result of an outside text which is neither overly determined by design expression or function. But how could such an inscription of an outside text translate into space?

Suppose for a moment that architecture could be conceptualized as a Moebius strip, with an unbroken continuity between interior and exterior. What would this mean for vision? Gilles Deleuze has proposed just such a possible continuity with his idea of the fold. For Deleuze, folded space articulates a new relationship between vertical and horizontal, figure and ground, inside and out—all structures articulated by traditional vision. Unlike the space of classical vision, the idea of folded space denies framing in favor of a temporal modulation. The fold no longer privileges planimetric projection; instead there is a variable curvature. Deleuze's idea of folding is more radical than origami, because it contains no narrative, linear sequence; rather, in terms of traditional vision, it contains a quality of the unseen. Folding changes the traditional space of vision. That is, it can be considered to be *effective*; it functions, it shelters, it is meaningful, it frames, it is aesthetic. Folding also constitutes a move from *effective* to *affective* space. Folding is not another subject expressionism, a promiscuity, but rather unfolds in space alongside of its functioning and its meaning in space—it has what might be called an excessive condition or *affect*. Folding is a type of *affective* space which concerns those aspects that are not associated with the *effective*, that are more than reason, meaning and function.

In order to change the relationship of perspectival projection to three-dimensional space it is necessary to change the relationship between project drawing and real space. This would mean that one would no longer be able to draw with any level of meaningfulness the space that is being projected. For example, when it is no longer possible to draw a line that stands for some scale relationship to another line in space, it has nothing to do with reason, of the connection of the mind to the eye. The deflection from that line in space means that there no longer exists a one-to-one scale correspondence.

My folded projects are a primitive beginning. In them the subject understands that he or she can no longer conceptualize experience in space in the same way that he or she did in the gridded space. They attempt to provide this dislocation of the subject from effective space; an idea of presentness. Once the environment becomes affective, inscribed with another logic or an ur-logic, one which is no longer translatable into the vision of the mind, then reason becomes detached from vision. While we can still understand space in terms of its function, structure and aesthetic—we are still within the "four walls"—somehow reason becomes detached from the affective condition of the environment itself. This begins to produce an environment that "looks back"—that is, the environment seems to have an order that we can perceive even though it does not seem to mean anything. It does not seek to be understood in the traditional way of architecture yet it possesses some sense of "aura," an ur-logic which is the sense of something outside of our vision. Yet one that is not another subjective expression. Folding is only one of perhaps many strategies for dislocating vision—dislocating the hierarchy of interior and exterior that preempts vision.

The Alteka Tower project begins simultaneously with an "el" shape drawn in both plan and section. Here, a change in the relationship of perspectival projection to three-dimensional space changes the relationship between project drawing and real space.

In this sense, these drawings would have little relationship to the space that is being projected. For example, it is no longer possible to draw a line that stands for some scale relationship to another line in the space of the project, thus the drawn lines no longer have anything to do with reason, the connection of the mind to the eye. The drawn lines are folded with some ur-logic according to sections of a fold in René Thom's catastrophe theory. These folded plans and sections in turn create an object, which is cut into from the ground floor to the top. When the environment is inscribed or folded in such a way the individual no longer remains the discursive function; the individual is no longer required to understand or interpret space. Questions such as what the space means are no longer relevant. It is not just that the environment is detached from vision, but that it also presents its own vision, a vision that looks back at the individual. The inscription is no longer concerned with aesthetics or with meaning but with some other order. It is only necessary to perceive the fact that this other order exists; this perception alone dislocates the knowing subject.

The fold presents the possibility of an alternative to the gridded space of the Cartesian order. The fold produces a dislocation of the dialectical distinction between figure and ground; in the process it animates what Gilles Deleuze calls a smooth space. Smooth space presents the possibility of overcoming or exceeding the grid. The grid remains in place and the four walls will always exist but they are in fact overtaken by the folding of space. Here there is no longer one planimetric view which is then extruded to provide a sectional space. Instead it is no longer possible to relate a vision of space in a two-dimensional drawing to the three-dimensional reality of a folded space. Drawing no longer has any scale value relationship to the three-dimensional environment. This dislocation of the two-dimensional drawing from the three-dimensional reality also begins to dislocate vision, inscribed by this ur-logic. There are no longer grid datum planes for the upright individual.

Alteka is not merely a surface architecture or a surface folding. Rather, the folds create an affective space, a dimension in the space that dislocates the discursive function of the human subject and thus vision, and at the same moment, creates a condition of time, of an event in which there is the possibility of the environment looking back at the subject, the possibility of the *gaze*.

The *gaze* according to Maurice Blanchot is that possibility of seeing which remains covered up by vision. The gaze opens the possibility of seeing what Blanchot calls the light lying within darkness. It is not the light of the dialectic of light/dark, but it is the light of an otherness, which lies hidden within presence. It is the capacity to see this otherness which is repressed by vision. The looking back, the gaze, exposes architecture to another light, one which could not have been seen before.

Architecture will continue to stand up, to deal with gravity, to have "four walls." But these four walls no longer need to be expressive of the mechanical paradigm. Rather they could deal with the possibility of these other discourses, the other affective senses of sound, touch, and of that light lying within the darkness.

14. CONTEMPORARY DEFINITIONS OF THE SUBLIME

INTRODUCTION

En Terror Firma: In Trails of Grotextes
Peter Eisenman

In the essay "En Terror Firma," published in the inaugural volume of the *Pratt Journal of Architecture*, architect Peter Eisenman develops some of the themes he has been working with in theoretical writings since the late 1970s. His broad interest in understanding the limits of the discipline of architecture emerge here in his consideration of architecture's relationship to nature and to beauty. Both are classical sources of meaning and embody societal ideals. It is Eisenman's stated purpose to challenge the premises that support nature as the "other," the opposite by which humans define themselves, and beauty, as the dominant aesthetic category.

Eisenman asserts that overcoming nature is no longer a pressing problem for architecture, although buildings must still physically do so. Technology has made nature a less urgent threat, leaving a new problem for the postindustrial era: overcoming knowledge. One instance of overcoming knowledge is displacing the architectural discourse, a theme running through Eisenman's later writings.

He suggests here that this displacement or deconstruction of the architectural discourse might be accomplished using the aesthetic category of the *grotesque*, considered a component of the sublime. Eisenman defines the architectural sublime as "airy qualities which resist physical occupation," while the grotesque deals with "real substance." The grotesque is characterized by the uncertain, the unspeakable, and the unphysical. He claims the grotesque will accomplish the desired displacement by challenging architecture's 500-year-long dependence on normative beauty.

Despite the advent of modernity, classical criteria for beauty (and classicism in general) have yet to be unseated. Eisenman critiques the traditional opposition between the qualities of the beautiful (the good, rational, and true) and of the terrifying sublime (the unnatural and unpresent). In lieu of this opposition, he proffers Immanuel Kant's model of *containing within*: thus, present within the beautiful is the grotesque, which encompasses "the idea of the ugly, the deformed, and the supposedly unnatural."

Eisenman is concerned that oppositional categories are inadequate to account for the complexity and irrationality of the occupation of space. (This echoes Bernard Tschumi's polemic in "The Pleasure of Architecture," ch. 13.) Furthermore, the grotesque challenges the consideration of architecture as *object*, a theme addressed in Eisenman's "The End of the Classical" by positing architecture as *text*. (ch. 4) Noting that the grotesque is a concept and not a design product or prescription, Eisenman hints at the difficulty of realizing this theoretical agenda. Similar difficulties would occur in the application of Anthony Vidler's ideas of the uncanny to design; both serve best as analytical tools.

PETER EISENMAN
EN TERROR FIRMA
IN TRAILS OF GROTEXTES

It is amazing how complete is the illusion that beauty is goodness.
Leo Tolstoy

Author's note: The following text is a series of notes which merely scratch the surface of a subject which will be taken up more fully in my forthcoming book *The Edge of Between.*

Recently a client said to me, "Peter, for the past five hundred years the discourse of science has been about man overcoming nature. Man overcomes nature through things which are rational, which are good, which are truthful, and ultimately these take on the characteristics of the natural itself, i.e. the beautiful. Obviously," he said to me, "it follows that architecture has been about this overcoming of the natural, because architecture symbolizes the structures, cosmological attitudes of the society: architecture mirrors what the society is about." Thus, though not explicitly, architecture has represented and symbolized this struggle of man to overcome nature. "Today," he said, "this is no longer the problem which science is addressing. This is no longer where the discourses on the forefront of thinking are." He said that the problem today for man is to overcome knowledge: "You see, computers have knowledge, robots have knowledge, the technological clones that we are developing have knowledge, but man has wisdom. The knowledge revolution, artificial intelligence, and the systems of knowledge have gotten out of hand, and have started to control man, rather than the reverse. Science today is trying to find a way to control knowledge, and the knowledge revolution." And my client then said to me, "Peter, you architects, for too long, have been solving a problem, representing and symbolizing a problem which is no longer where we are." He said,

From *Pratt Journal* 2 (1988): 111–121. Courtesy of the author and publisher.

"I want you to do a building which symbolizes man's capacity to overcome knowledge." I looked at him and thought, what is that? He said, "Do you know something, you are supposed to be an architect on the edge. Yet," he added, "there is nothing you could do toward this end that would upset me at all." He said, "I do not want you to merely illustrate the problem. I do not want you to decorate a facade with a computer chip, cut into the chip, and say, there—we have symbolized the overcoming of knowledge. No," he said, "I am not talking about that. I want something far more significant. I want something that challenges man's very occupation of space, not just the surface of that space." He said, "And I do not think that you can do it."

Now why is this? First of all, architects traditionally do not speculate on the here and now, on gravity, as scientists do. Architects have to deal with the real conditions of gravity, they have to build the here and now. They have to deal with physical presence. In fact, architects continually not only symbolize the overcoming of nature, they must overcome nature. It is not so simple for architecture merely to shift and say that overcoming nature is no longer the problem, because it obviously remains a problem.

However, it is possible to respond to my scientist client and at the same time still deal with the problems of presence and gravity. To do this the architectural discourse must be displaced. The issue is not merely as it was in the past, that architecture must withstand the forces of gravity, but the manner in which this overcoming is symbolized. In other words, it is not enough to suggest that building must be rational, truthful, beautiful, good, must in its mimesis of the natural suggest man's overcoming of the natural. Rather, as the architectural discourse changes its focus from nature to knowledge, a far more complex object emerges, which requires a more complex form of architectural reality. This is because knowledge (as opposed to nature) has no physical being. What is being represented in physical form when knowledge is being overcome? Nature, traditionally, was the liminal, the boundary definition; it mediated, in the anthropocentric world of the enlightenment, the lost certainty of God. The natural became a valued origin, both useful to explain the world metaphorically and as a process and an object to be emulated. Since architecture had set out to symbolize the overcoming of nature, it is more than reasonable to think that the overcoming of knowledge also could be symbolized. The uncertainty that is contained in something other than the liminal will certainly be part of the expression of man overcoming knowledge.

At the root of the present conceptual structure of architecture is the Vitruvian triad of commodity, firmness, and delight (use, structure, and beauty). The beautiful as a dialectical category has been understood as a singular and monovalent condition; it has been about goodness, about the natural, the rational, and the truthful. It is that to which architects are taught to aspire in their architecture. Thus they search for and manifest conditions of the beautiful as a form of delight in the Vitruvian sense. It was within such a desire that this form of the beautiful became as if natural for architecture over the past five hundred years. There were rules for the beautiful, for example, in classical ordination which, although modified through different periods of architecture, much as styles change in fashion, were never, even in Modern architecture, essentially displaced

In the eighteenth century, Immanuel Kant began to destabilize this singular concept of beauty. He suggested that there could be something else, another way to conceptualize beauty other than as goodness, other than as natural. He suggested that within the beautiful there was something else, which he called the sublime. When the sublime was articulated before Kant, it was in dialectical opposition to beauty. With Kant came the suggestion that the sublime was within the beautiful, and the beautiful within the sublime. This difference between opposition and being within is at the very heart of the argument to follow.

Now, interestingly, the sublime also has within it a condition which the conventionally beautiful represses. It is a condition of the uncertain, the unspeakable, the unnatural, the unpresent, the unphysical; taken together these constitute the condition which approaches the terrifying, a condition which lies within the sublime.

The terms of the grotesque are usually thought of as the negative of the sublime. However, this is not quite the case in architecture, where the sublime deals with qualities of the airy, qualities which resist physical occupation, the grotesque deals with real substance, with the manifestation of the uncertain in the physical. Since architecture is thought to deal with physical presence, then the grotesque in some sense is already present in architecture. And this condition of the grotesque was acceptable as long as it was as decoration; in the form of gargoyles and frescoes. This is because the grotesque introduces the idea of the ugly, the deformed, the supposedly unnatural as an always present in the beautiful. It is this condition of the always present or the already within, that the beautiful in architecture attempts to repress.

That the overcoming of nature, or the depiction of nature as other, preoccupied the Enlightenment and the technological and scientific revolutions, was obvious. In response, the grotesque as it was put forward in the Romantic movement in [William] Wordsworth, [John] Keats and [Percy Bysshe] Shelley, was concerned with rethinking this relationship between the self and nature. Therefore, today the "sublime" and the "grotesque" deal with this movement between self and the natural, and the representation of this unease in literature and painting. If the "naturalness" of nature is to be displaced in the uneasy movement between nature and self, then our ideas of the sublime and the grotesque must also be reconceptualized in terms of overcoming knowledge without losing the fear associated with the natural, and the fear of the uncertain, i.e. the fear of not overcoming nature, must be preserved in any displaced categories.

The fear or uncertainty is now doubly present; the previous uncertainty of the natural, as well as the uncertainty of something other than the liminal, that is the uncertainty of knowledge that is within knowledge. Since the conditions for the sublime and the grotesque evolved from the expression of man overcoming nature, other terms which contain this double uncertainty will have to be found; the form of expression for man overcoming knowledge becomes far more complex.

What does this mean for architecture? In order to achieve the necessary internal displacement, architecture would have to displace the former ways of conceptualizing itself. It would follow then that the notion of the house, or of any form of the occupation of space, requires a more complex form of the beautiful, one which contains the ugly, or a rationality that contains the irrational. This idea of containing within, necessitates a break from the tradition of an architecture of categories, of types which in their essence rely on the separation of things as opposites. There seem to be four aspects which begin to outline a condition of displacement. The following four aspects should be seen neither as comprehensive (there could be others) nor as a guarantee that their displacing capacities will produce a displaced architecture.

A major displacement concerns the role of the architect/designer and the design process. Something may be designed which can be called displacing, but it may be only an expressionism, a mannerist distortion of an essentially stable language. It may not displace the stable language, but on the contrary further stabilize its normative condition. This can be seen in many examples of current architectural fashion. There is a need for a process other than an intuition—"I like this," or "I like that." When the process is intuitive, it will already be known, and therefore complicit with the repressions inherent in architectural "knowledge." Intuitive design can never produce a state of uncertainty, only, at best, an illustration of uncertainty. While the concept of the grotesque or the uncanny can be conceptualized and imaged, it cannot be designed. Something designed is essentially non-textual, because design of necessity involves certainty; something always has to be made. To attempt to design between uncertainty or multivalency, produces only a superficial illustration of such a condition. If something can be designed it is no longer uncertain.

In the traditional idea of architectural design, form, function, structure, site, and meaning can all be said to be texts. But they are not textual. Texts are always thought to be primary or original sources. Textual or textuality is that aspect of text which is a condition of otherness or secondarity. An example of this condition of otherness in architecture is a trace. If architecture is primarily presence—materiality, bricks, and mortar—then otherness or secondarity would be trace, as the presence of absence. Trace can never be original, because trace always suggests the possibility of something *other* as original, as something *prior* to. In any text there are potential traces of otherness, aspects or structures which have been repressed by presence. As long as presence remains dominant i.e. singular, there can be no textuality. Therefore, by its very nature such a condition of trace requires at least *two* texts.

Thus the second aspect of this *other* architecture is something which might be called *twoness*. There are many different twonesses which exist in traditional architecture already: The twoness of form and function, and twoness of structure and ornament. But these are traditionally seen as hierarchical categories; one is always seen as dominant or original and the other as secondary (form follows function, ornament is added to structure). In the sense it is being used here, twoness suggests a condition where there is no dominance or originary value but rather a structure of equivalences, where there is uncertainty instead of hierarchy. When the one text is too dominant there is no displacement. When the other text becomes presence itself it obtrudes and loses its capacity for the uncertain. Equally the second text cannot obliterate the first text, but will be understood to be interior to it, thus as an already present "trace" usually suppressed by a single dominant reading. This second text thus will always be within the first text and thus between traditional presence and absence, between being and non-being.

Therefore, the third condition of this other architecture is *betweeness*, which suggests a condition of the object as a weak image. A strong image would give a primary dominant meaning to one or the other of the two texts. Not only must one or the other of the two texts not have a strong image; they will seem to be two weak images, which suggests a blurred third. In other words, the new condition of the object must be *between* in an imageable sense as well: It is something which is almost this, or almost that, but not quite either. The displacing experience is the uncertainty of a partial knowing.

Therefore, the object must have a blurring effect. It must look out of focus: almost seen, but not quite, seen. Again, this between is not a between dialectically, but a between *within*. The loss of the idea of architecture as a strong image undercuts the traditional categories of architecture associated with man overcoming nature; place, route, enclosure, presence, and the vertebrate, upright building—symbolic of overcoming gravity.

To deny traditional place or enclosure, suggests an other condition of this displaced architecture, that is interiority. Interiority has nothing to do with the inside or the inhabitable space of a building but rather of a condition of being within. However, as is the case with the grotesque, interiority deals with two factors; the unseen and the hollowed-out. Interiority also deals with the condition proposed by textuality that the symbolism or meaning of any sign refers, in such a displaced architecture, not outward but inward to an already present condition. Ultimately, each of these four conditions provoke an uncertainty in the object, by removing both the architect and the user from any necessary control of the object. The architect no longer is the hand and mind, the mythic originary figure in the design process. And the object no longer requires the experience of the user to be understood. No longer does the object need to look ugly or terrifying to provoke an uncertainty; it is now the distance between object and subject—the impossibility of possession which provokes this anxiety.

INTRODUCTION

Theorizing the Unhomely
Anthony Vidler

Anthony Vidler has been writing on the sublime for at least ten years, prompted perhaps by his study of the visionary architects Claude-Nicolas Ledoux and Étienne-Louis Boullée. In a series of lectures presented at the Institute for Architecture and Urban Studies in 1985, the architect and historian began to exhibit an interest in the sublime's dark side, the *uncanny*. This Freudian and aesthetic category foregrounds the body and the *subject* in relation to the experience of architecture and the city. In particular, the uncanny permits Vidler to look at the sources, meaning, and impact of fragmentation on the individual, an important aspect of both postmodern historicist and deconstructivist architecture. This essay from Columbia University's architecture school newsletter introduces many of the ideas that sustain his book, *The Architectural Uncanny* (1992).

The argument presented for the significance of the uncanny in architecture is a fascinating synthesis of several different points of view, or thought paradigms. In addition to the influence of phenomenology, (ch. 9) which he acknowledges, Vidler is affected by the psychoanalytic model. As described by Sigmund Freud in his 1919 essay, the uncanny is the rediscovery of something familiar that has been previously repressed: it is the uneasy recognition of the presence of an absence. The mix of the known and familiar with the strange surfaces in *unheimliche*, the German word for the uncanny, which literally translated means "unhomely." Thus, according to Vidler, architecture (especially residential) has the capacity to raise "unsettling problems of identity around the self, the other, the body and its absence." The uncanny provokes haunting sensations, the idea of the double, fear of dismemberment, and other terrors. Vidler notes that a common theme of the uncanny is the idea of the human body in fragments. This uncanny is the terrifying side of the sublime, with the fear being privation of the integrated body.

Another aspect of Vidler's position emerges with regard to his aesthetic agenda. He writes:

Consideration of the theory of the uncanny allows for a rewriting of traditional and modernist aesthetic theory as applied to categories such as imitation, repetition, the symbolic, and the sublime.

Because he sees the uncanny as emblematic of modern estrangement and alienation, Vidler claims that it is useful for analyzing and interpreting modernity. Estrangement offers a way to reexamine the exclusion of segments of the population on the basis of gender, race, etc. This notion suggests a poststructuralist orientation in Vidler's work.

Since the uncanny cannot be deliberately provoked or planned, this theory cannot be prescriptive. In that it cannot be instrumentalized in design, Vidler's uncanny is similar to Peter Eisenman's grotesque. Both are components of a postmodern redefinition of the classical aesthetic conception of the sublime, begun by poststructuralist theorists in other disciplines. (See Derrida, ch. 3) The contemporary sublime, also receiving attention in art since the 1980s, is the most significant aesthetic development on the horizon. Whether articulated as the psychoanalytic uncanny or the aesthetic grotesque (tied to ideas of beauty), the sublime in Jean-François Lyotard's words, is "the single artistic sensibility to characterize the Modern."[1]

1   Jean-François Lyotard, "The Sublime and the Avant-Garde," ArtForum 20, no. 8 (April 1982): 38.

ANTHONY VIDLER
THEORIZING THE UNHOMELY

Impelled by a need to confront the uncanny qualities of contemporary architecture, its fragmented new-Constructivist forms mimetic of dismembered bodies, its public representation buried in earthworks or lost in mirror reflection, its "seeing walls" reciprocating the passive gaze of domestic cyborgs, its spaces surveyed by moving eyes and simulating transparency, its historical monuments indistinguishable from glossy reproductions, I have been drawn to explore aspects of the spatial and architectural uncanny as articulated in literature, philosophy, psychology, and architecture from the beginning of the nineteenth century to the present. Taking as my starting point Sigmund Freud's 1919 essay "The Uncanny," I follow the double route indicated by Freud himself, returning to the sources of the notion in the theory and practice of Romanticism, then examining the different ways in which the concept has been operative in modern culture.

Architecture since the Romantic period has been intimately linked to the notion of the uncanny. On an obvious level, architecture has provided the site for endless explorations of haunting, doubling, dismembering, and other terrors in literature and art. It has opened its labyrinthine spaces to the relentless gaze of the modern detective deciphering the countless mysteries of urban life. It has engendered and mirrored atmospheres, moods, and metaphysical states as its stable forms have offered a more or less reassuring key to reality amid the flux of parapsychological manifestations.

As articulated theoretically by Freud and embedded in the literature of the uncanny from E.T.A. Hoffmann to the present, architecture reveals the deep structure of the uncanny in a more than analogical way, demonstrating a disquieting slippage between what seems *homely* and what is definitely *unhomely*. Rooted by etymology and usage in the peculiarly unstable environment of the domestic, the uncanny necessarily opens up

From *Newsline* 3 no. 3 (1990): 3. Courtesy of the author and publisher.

the unsettling problems of identity around the self, the other, the body, and its absence: thence its power to interpret the relations between the psyche and the dwelling, the body and the house, the individual and the metropolis. Linked by Freud to the death drive, to fear of castration, and to the impossible desire to return to the womb, the uncanny has been construed as a dominant constituent of modern estrangement and alienation, with a corresponding spatiality touching all aspects of urban life.

I do not intend an exhaustive historical or theoretical treatment of the subject; rather I have chosen themes provoked by a resurgent interest in the theory of the uncanny exhibited in literary criticism and, more recently, architectural theory. Beginning with an examination of the insistent recurrence of the uncanny in aesthetics and psychology from Friedrich Schelling to Freud, I explore the architectural uncanny as embedded in the myth of modern domesticity evinced in the writings of nineteenth- and twentieth-century authors including Freud's own favorite, E.T.A. Hoffmann. Selecting from the numerous "haunted houses" of the Romantic period, I then construct a phenomenology of the spatial uncanny, which I extend to the city as a locus of spatial fear through the reading of urban pathologists and sociologists from Legrand du Saule to Georg Simmel, Siegfried Kracauer, and Walter Benjamin. Agoraphobia and its complement, claustrophobia, are discussed in relation to the notion of metropolitan estrangement, while the question of the temporal uncanny is addressed through theories of memory and its opposite, amnesia, in the writings of Maurice Halbwachs, Eugène Minkowski, and Jean-Paul Sartre. An examination of the uncanny as a characteristic of bodily projection, of architectural embodiment, and of the expression of movement, corporeal fragmentation, reflection, and absorption in a world dedicated to simulacra, spectacle, and the suppression of phenomenological depth follows. Here the long tradition of anthropomorphic embodiment in classical architecture is revealed to be broken, with uncanny consequences for the present. The last chapter considers the recent theoretization of cybernetic culture and its relation to the notion of domesticity; the concept of the cyborg, a being that knows none of the nostalgia associated with birth but that presents all the spectral effects of the double, is offered as a characteristic manifestation of the uncanny that continues to haunt contemporary culture.

As a concept the uncanny has, not unnaturally, found its metaphorical home in architecture: first in the house—haunted or not—that pretends to afford the utmost security while opening itself to the secret intrusion of terror, and second in the metropolis, where what was once walled and intimate, the confirmation of community—one thinks of Jean-Jacques Rousseau's Geneva—has been rendered strange by the spatial incursions of modernity. In neither case, of course, is the "uncanny" a property of the space itself, nor can it be provoked by any particular spatial conformation; it is, in its aesthetic dimension, a representation of a mental state of projection that precisely elides the boundaries of the real and the unreal in order to provoke a disturbing ambiguity, a slippage between waking and dreaming.

In this sense, it is perhaps difficult to speak of an "architectural" uncanny as of a literary or psychological uncanny; certainly no single building, no special effect of design can be guaranteed to provoke an uncanny feeling. But in each moment of the history of the representation of the uncanny and at certain moments in its psychological analysis the buildings and spaces that have acted as sites of uncanny experiences have been invested with recognizable characteristics. These almost typical and eventually common-place qualities—the attributes of haunted houses in Gothic romances are the best known—while evidently not essentially uncanny in themselves, nevertheless have been seen as *emblematic* of the uncanny, as the cultural signs of estrangement for particular periods. An early stage of psychology even identified space as a *cause* of the fear or estrangement hitherto the privilege of fiction; for an early generation of sociologists, "spatial estrangement" was more than a figment of the imagination, representing pre-cisely that mingling of mental projection and spatial characteristics associated with the uncanny.

From this point of view the architectural uncanny invoked here is necessarily ambiguous, combining aspects of its fictional history, its psychological analysis, and its cultural manifestations. If actual buildings or spaces are interpreted through this lens, it is not because they themselves possess uncanny properties but rather because they act, historically or culturally, as representations of estrangement. If there is a single premise to be derived from the study of the uncanny in modern culture, it is that there is no such thing as an uncanny architecture but simply architecture that, from time to time and for different purposes, is invested with uncanny qualities.

The contemporary sense of the uncanny, as I will attempt to demonstrate, is not simply a survival of a Romantic commonplace or a feeling confined to the artistic genres of horror and ghost stories. Its theoretical exposition by Freud and later by Martin Heidegger places it among the categories that might be adduced to interpret modernity. In [*The Architectural Uncanny: Essays in the Modern Unhomely*] I explore those aspects of the uncanny's domain that touch on the spatial, the architectural, and the urban. As a frame of reference that confronts the desire for a home and the struggle for domestic security, with its apparent opposite—intellectual and actual homelessness—at the same time that it reveals the fundamental complicity between the two *das Unheimliche* captures the difficult conditions of the theoretical practice of architecture in modern times. As a concept that itself has recurred with differing effects in the last two centuries, it serves as an interpretative model that cuts through such historical periodizations as Romanticism, modernism, and post-modernism, providing a way of understanding an aspect of moder-nity that gives new meaning to the traditional Homeric notion of homesickness.

Consideration of the theory of the uncanny also allows for a re-writing of tradi-tional and modernist aesthetic theory as applied to categories such as imitation (the double), repetition, the symbolic, and the sublime. More radically, questions of gender and subject might be linked to the continuing discourse of estrangement and the Other in the social and political context of racial, ethnic, and minority exclusion. The resurgent problem of homelessness as the last traces of welfare capitalism are systematically demol-ished lends, finally, a special urgency to any reflection on the modern unhomely.

NOTES ON CONTRIBUTORS

RAIMUND ABRAHAM is Professor of Architecture at The Cooper Union, and principal of Atelier Raimund Abraham Architect in New York. He has written numerous articles on architecture and is author of *Elementare Architektur* (1963). His work has been exhibited throughout the United States and Europe, and has won awards internationally. Abraham has been the recipient of grants from the National Endowment for the Arts and the Graham Foundation. His current projects include the new Austrian Cultural Institute in New York.

DIANA AGREST is principal of Agrest and Gandelsonas Architects, New York, and Adjunct Professor of Architecture at Columbia University and The Cooper Union. From 1979 to 1984 she was Director of the Advanced Design Workshop in Architecture and Urban Form at the Institute for Architecture and Urban Studies. Her books include *Agrest and Gandelsonas: Works* (1994) and *Architecture from Without: Theoretical Framings for a Critical Practice* (1991). Agrest graduated from the University of Buenos Aires in Argentina, and did post-graduate work at the Centre de Recherche and at the École des Hautes Études en Sciences Sociales in Paris.

TADAO ANDO, Hon. FAIA, is founder and principal of Tadao Ando Architects & Associates in Osaka, Japan. His work has been the subject of exhibitions in Europe, Asia, and America, and of numerous monographs, including *Tadao Ando: Buildings, Projects, Writings* (1984) and *Tadao Ando: Details* (1991). A self-taught architect, he has been Visiting Professor of Architecture at Yale, Columbia, and Harvard. He is the recipient of the 1995 Pritzker Prize in Architecture, the Mainichi Art Prize for the Mt. Rokko Chapel, and the Japanese Cultural Design Prize for his Rokko Housing.

GIULO CARLO ARGAN (d.1992) was one of Italy's preeminent art historians, whose writings on the baroque and modern periods were published widely. From 1939 to

1955 Argan worked in the office of the Director General of Fine Arts in Rome, and from 1955 to 1979 he taught art history at the University of Rome. He is best known for his writings on Borromini and Gropius, and for *Storia dell'Arte* (1968–70). Argan received his Laureato in lettere from the University of Turin.

PHILIP BESS is a principal with Thursday Architects in Chicago. He has taught at the University of Illinois at Chicago, the University of Notre Dame, and the University of Michigan. He was a contributing editor to *Inland Architect*, and recently received a Graham Foundation grant. He earned a Masters in Architecture at the University of Virginia.

GEOFFREY BROADBENT has taught at Manchester, York, Sheffield, and Portsmouth Universities, and was Head of School at Portsmouth in 1967. He is the author of *Design in Architecture* (1973, 1988), and co-editor with Richard Bunt and Charles Jencks of *Signs, Symbols and Architecture* (1980). He is currently completing a book on composition in architecture. Broadbent received a B.A. in Architecture from Manchester University.

ALAN COLQUHOUN is Professor Emeritus of Architecture at Princeton University, where he began teaching as a visiting critic in 1966. Prior to that, he taught at the AA in London. Colquhoun has lectured and written extensively on architecture. He is author of *Essays in Architecture: Modern Architecture and Historical Change* (1981) and *Modernity and the Classical Tradition: Architectural Essays 1980–1987* (1989). He was educated at Edinburgh College of Art and at the Architectural Association in London.

JACQUES DERRIDA is Director of the École des Hautes Études en Sciences Sociales in Paris. From 1964 until this appointment in 1984, he was Professor of Philosophy at the École Normale Supérieure in Paris. Derrida has been Visiting Professor and lecturer at Cornell, Johns Hopkins and Yale Universities. Among his numerous books and essays are *Of Grammatology* (1976) and *Truth in Painting* (1987). Derrida attended the Université de Paris, Sorbonne, where he received his Doctorate en Philosophie and Doctorate d'État en Lettres.

PETER EISENMAN is principal of Eisenman Architects in New York, and is the Irwin S. Chanin Distinguished Professor of Architecture at The Cooper Union. He was the founder and Director of the Institute for Architecture and Urban Studies, and editor of *Oppositions* journal and Oppositions Books. He received his Masters of Architecture from Columbia University, and Masters of Arts and Ph.D. from the University of Cambridge. He is author of *Houses of Cards* (1987) and *Fin d'Ou T Hou S* (1985). In addition to a substantial body of theoretical projects, Eisenman's built works include the award-winning Wexner Center for the Visual Arts at Ohio State University and Koizumi Sangyo Corporation building in Tokyo.

KENNETH FRAMPTON is the Ware Professor of Architecture at Columbia University, where he has taught since 1972. From 1964 to 1972 he was a member of the faculty at Princeton University. He was also a Fellow at the Institute for Architecture and Urban Studies, and a founding editor of *Oppositions*. In addition to numerous articles, Frampton's books include *Modern Architecture: A Critical History* (1980) and *Modern*

Architecture 1851–1945 (1983). He has recently been working on a book on tectonics. The recipient of a Guggenheim Fellowship, the Topaz Award, and the AIA National Honors Award, Frampton was educated at the Architectural Association in London.

MARCO FRASCARI is Chair of the Ph.D. Program in Architecture and of the Design of the Environment Program at the University of Pennsylvania. He is the author of *Monsters in Architecture* (1991) and the forthcoming *Under the Sign of Wonder*. Frascari holds a Ph.D. in Architecture from the University of Pennsylvania. In addition, he received his Masters of Architecture and Masters of Science from the Istituto Universitario di Architettura di Venezia and the University of Cincinnati, respectively. He is a member of the Semiotic Society of America, and has written and lectured widely on the subject of semiotics.

MARIO GANDELSONAS is principal of Agrest and Gandelsonas Architects in New York and is Professor of Architecture at Princeton University. A Fellow at the Institute for Architecture and Urban Studies from 1971 to 1984, he was a founder and editor of *Oppositions* and served as Director of Educational Programs. Gandelsonas received his post-graduate education at the University of Buenos Aires School of Architecture and Urbanism, and at the Centre de Recherche d'Urbanisme in Paris. His recent work has focused on the analysis and planning of American cities, as represented in his book *The Urban Text* (1991).

DIANE GHIRARDO is Associate Professor of Architecture at the University of Southern California, where she has taught since 1984. She is Executive Editor of *Journal of Architectural Education* and past President of the Association of Collegiate Schools of Architecture. She has written and lectured widely on architecture; her books include *Out of Site: A Social Criticism of Architecture* (1991) and *Building New Communities: New Deal America and Fascist Italy* (1989). Ghirardo received her M.A. and Ph.D. from Stanford University, and is a Fellow of the American Academy in Rome.

MICHAEL GRAVES, FAIA, is the Schirmer Professor of Architecture at Princeton University, where he has taught since 1962. His built works include the Humana Corporate Headquarters, the Portland Municipal Building, and the San Juan Capistrano Library. Among other publications, his work appears in *Michael Graves: Buildings and Projects 1966–81* (1983) and *Five Architects* (1972). Graves studied architecture at the University of Cincinnati and at Harvard University, and is a Fellow of the American Academy in Rome.

VITTORIO GREGOTTI is Professor of Architecture at the Istituto Universitario di Architettura di Venezia, and principal of Gregotti Associati, with offices in Venice and Milan. As Editor-in-Chief of *Casabella*, he has written many significant theoretical editorials. He is the author of numerous books, including *Il territorio dell'architettura* (1966). Gregotti was Director of the Art and Architecture sections of the Venice Biennale from 1974 to 1976. He was educated at the Milan Polytechnic.

KARSTEN HARRIES is Professor of Philosophy at Yale University. He is past Chairman of the Philosophy Department at Yale (1973–78), and served as Acting Chair

(1987–88). He is on the editorial board of *The International Journal of Philosophical Studies* and has written widely on the subject of phenomenology in architecture. Harries received his B.A. and Ph.D. from Yale, and was the recipient of a Guggenheim Fellowship in 1971. His books include *The Meaning of Modern Art* (1968) and the forthcoming *The Ethical Function of Architecture*.

FRED KOETTER is Dean of the School of Architecture at Yale University and principal of Koetter, Kim and Associates in Boston. Prior to his appointment at Yale, Koetter was Professor of Architecture at Harvard University, and held teaching positions at Cornell University and the University of Kentucky. He is co-author of *Collage City* (1979) with Colin Rowe and has contributed numerous articles to architectural journals. Koetter received his Masters of Architecture from Cornell University.

REM KOOLHAAS is founder and principal of the Office for Metropolitan Architecture in Rotterdam. Currently Professor of Architecture at Harvard University, he was a Fellow at the Institute for Architecture and Urban Studies from 1975 to 1979, and has taught at Rice University, Cornell University, and the Architectural Association. He is author of *Delirious New York: A Retroactive Manifesto for Manhattan* (1974, 1994) and the forthcoming *OMA: S M L XL*. Koolhaas studied architecture at the Architectural Association. His built work includes the recently completed, award-winning Nexus Housing in Fukuoka, Japan.

LIANE LEFAIVRE is a writer who has published numerous books and articles on architecture. She is the co-author of *Classical Architecture: The Poetics of Order* (1986) with Alexander Tzonis, and is currently working on Leon Battista Alberti's *Hypnerotomachi Poliphili*. Lefaivre was educated at McGill University and at the Université de Strasbourg, where she earned degrees in psychology and comparative literature. In 1994, she and Alexander Tzonis were awarded an AIA Book Award for *Architecture in Europe Since 1968*.

WILLIAM McDONOUGH is Dean of the School of Architecture at the University of Virginia, and principal of William McDonough Architects, Charlottesville. He is a founding member of the AIA's Committee on the Environment and advises President Clinton's Council on Sustainable Development. McDonough received a Bachelor of Arts from Dartmouth College and a Master of Architecture from Yale University. He is currently working with the city of Chattanooga on "The Chattanooga Principles," a plan for environmentally sensitive development.

ROBERT MUGERAUER is Associate Professor of Architecture and Adjunct Professor of Geography and Philosophy at the University of Texas at Austin. He has written extensively on environmental perception and behavior, and on social and cultural factors in design. He is author of the forthcoming book *Environmental Interpretations: Tradition, Deconstruction, Hermeneutics*, and was a contributor to *Geography and Identity: Exploring and Living in the Geopolitics of Identity*, edited by Dennis Crow (1994). Mugerauer holds a Ph.D. in philosophy from the University of Texas at Austin.

CHRISTIAN NORBERG-SCHULZ was Professor of Architecture at the Oslo School of Architecture, where he began teaching in 1951. He is Co-Director of *Lotus*

International, and author of numerous books, including *Intentions in Architecture* (1963) and *Architecture: Meaning and Place* (1988). Norberg-Schulz received a Ph.D. from the Technical University of Trondheim, in Norway. He is currently working on two books, *The History of Modern Architecture in Norway* and *The Phenomenology of Modern Architecture*.

JUHANI PALLASMAA, Hon. FAIA, is Dean of the Faculty of Architecture at the Helsinki Institute of Technology and principal of his own firm in Helsinki. From 1978 to 1983 he was Director of the Museum of Finnish Architecture in Helsinki. He has taught at numerous universities, and was the Eero Saarinen Visiting Professor at Yale University in 1993. He is the co-editor of *Alvar Aalto: 1898–1976* (1978). Pallasmaa received his Masters of Science in Architecture from the Helsinki University of Technology in 1966.

DEMETRI PORPHYRIOS is principal of Porphyrios Associates in London. He has been the Thomas Jefferson Professor at the University of Virginia and the Davenport Professor at Yale University. His books include *Sources of Modern Eclecticism: Studies on Alvar Aalto* (1982) and *Classicism Is Not A Style* (1982). Porphyrios earned his Masters of Architecture, Masters of Arts, and a Ph.D. in the History and Theory of Architecture from Princeton University.

ALDO ROSSI (d.1997) Hon. FAIA, was principal of Studio di Architettura, Milan. He taught at the Istituto Universitario di Architettura di Venezia, and at Harvard, Rice, and Yale Universities. Rossi is past editor of *Casabella* and is author of *The Architecture of the City* (1966) and *A Scientific Autobiography* (1981). In 1990 Rossi won the Pritzker Prize for Architecture and in 1992, the Thomas Jefferson Medal in Architecture. He is known for his drawings and projects as well as his built work, which includes the award-winning Hotel Il Palazzo in Fukuoka, Japan. He was educated at the Milan Polytechnic.

COLIN ROWE is the Andrew Dickinson White Professor Emeritus at the Cornell University College of Architecture, Art, and Planning. Professor at Cornell since 1962, Rowe also taught at Harvard, Princeton, and Syracuse Universities, and at the University of Virginia. His writings include the introduction to *Five Architects* (1972), *The Mathematics of the Ideal Villa* (1976), and *Collage City* with Fred Koetter (1978). He is currently working on a collection of essays. Rowe holds Master of Architecture and Master of Art degrees from Cambridge University and the University of London, respectively.

THOMAS L. SCHUMACHER, R.A., is Professor of Architecture at the University of Maryland. Since 1972, he has taught at several schools, including Princeton University, the University of Michigan, and the University of Virginia. Prior to teaching, Schumacher was a research associate at the Institute for Architecture and Urban Studies. He is author of *The Danteum* (1985, 1993) and *Surface and Symbol: Giuseppe Terragni and the Architecture of Italian Rationalism* (1991). He earned a Masters of Architecture in Urban Design from Cornell University and is a Fellow of the American Academy in Rome.

DENISE SCOTT BROWN, RIBA, is principal of Venturi, Scott Brown and Associates in Philadelphia. She has taught and lectured at Harvard, Rice, and Yale Universities, and at the University of Pennsylvania. In 1991 she received a Distinguished Professor Award from the ASCA. Scott Brown has written extensively on architecture and urban planning and is the co-author of *Learning from Las Vegas* (1972, 1977) with Robert Venturi and Steven Izenour. She was educated at the Architectural Association in London and at the University of Pennsylvania, where she received her Masters in Architecture and City Planning.

IGNASI DE SOLÀ-MORALES RUBIÓ, Hon. FAIA, is principal of Ignasi de Solà-Morales Rubió Architect in Barcelona. He has taught and lectured throughout Europe, the United States, and South America. From 1980 to 1981, he was a faculty member at the Institute for Architecture and Urban Studies, and in 1993 was Visiting Professor of Architecture at Princeton University. He serves on the editorial board of *Lotus International* and has written numerous books. Solà-Morales Rubió holds degrees in Architecture and Philosophy, and a Ph.D. in Architecture from the Escuela Técnica Superior de Arquitectura in Barcelona.

ROBERT A.M. STERN, FAIA, is senior partner of Robert A.M. Stern Architects in New York and Professor of Architecture at the Graduate School of Architecture, Planning, and Preservation at Columbia University. Currently Director of the Historic Preservation Department, he is the former Director of Columbia's Temple Hoyne Buell Center for the Study of American Architecture. He is the author of *New Directions in American Architecture* (1969, 1977) and *Modern Classicism* (1988). Stern's work has been exhibited throughout the United States and is the subject of seven monographs. He received his Masters of Architecture from Yale University.

MANFREDO TAFURI (d.1994) was Director of the Institute of Architectural History at the Istituto Universitario di Architettura di Venezia from 1968 to 1994. He authored numerous books and essays on architecture and modern society, including *Theories and History of Architecture* (1968) and *Architecture and Utopia* (1973). From 1977 forward, Tafuri served on the Board of Directors of *Casabella* magazine. He was educated at the University of Rome, where he received his Masters of Architecture.

BERNARD TSCHUMI is Dean of the Columbia University Graduate School of Architecture, Planning, and Preservation and principal of Bernard Tschumi Architects in New York and Paris. He has been Visiting Professor at the Architectural Association, the Istituto Universitario di Architettura di Venezia, and at Princeton and Yale Universities. His books include *Manhattan Transcripts* (1981) and *Architecture and Disjunction* (1994). Tschumi graduated from the Federal Institute of Technology in Zurich. His projects include the ongoing Parc de la Villette in Paris.

ALEXANDER TZONIS is Professor of Architectural Theory and Chairman of the Department of History, Theory, Media, and Computers at the University of Technology at Delft, the Netherlands. From 1967 to 1982 he taught at the Harvard University Graduate School of Design. He is co-author of *Architecture in Europe Since 1968* (1993) with Liane Lefaivre, and the forthcoming *Architecture in North America* with

Lefaivre and Rosamund Diamond. Tzonis received his Masters of Architecture from Yale University.

ROBERT VENTURI, FAIA, Hon. FRIBA, is principal of Venturi, Scott Brown and Associates in Philadelphia. He has been Visiting Professor and Lecturer at Harvard and Rice Universities and at the University of Pennsylvania. In 1986–87, he was the Eero Saarinen Visiting Professor at Yale. Venturi is the author of *Complexity and Contradiction in Architecture* (1966) and co-author of *Learning from Las Vegas* (1972, 1977) with Denise Scott Brown and Steven Izenour. He received a Master of Fine Arts degree from Princeton University and is a Fellow at the American Academy in Rome.

ANTHONY VIDLER is Professor and Chair of the Department of Art History at the University of California at Los Angeles and Professor of Architecture at Princeton University. Since 1980, he has been Visiting Professor at the Architectural Association and at the Institute of Architectural History of the Istituto Universitario di Architettura di Venezia. From 1973 to 1993 Vidler taught and was Chair of the Ph.D. Program in Architecture at Princeton. Vidler has written and lectured extensively on architecture; his book *Claude Nicolas Ledoux: Architecture and Social Reform at the End of the Ancien Regime* (1990) won an AIA International Book Award in 1991. Vidler received a Diploma in Architecture from Cambridge University.

ILLUSTRATION SOURCES

COVER   Courtesy of Laurinda Spear and Bernardo Fort-Brescia of Arquitectonica; reprinted with permission of Timothy Hursley, the Arkansas Office.

p. 131   From *Five Architects: Eisenman, Graves, Gwathmey, Hejduk, Meier* (New York: Wittenborn, 1972). Courtesy of Peter Eisenman.

p. 269   From *Architectural Review* 158, no. 942 (August 1975). Reprinted with permission.

p. 275   From *Architectural Review* 158, no. 942 (August 1975). Reprinted with permission.

p. 276   From Francis D.K. Ching, *Architecture: Form, Space and Order* (New York: Van Nostrand Reinhold, 1979). Reprinted with permission.

p. 281   From *Architectural Review* 158, no. 942 (August 1975). Courtesy of Christopher Alexander.

p. 285   From Christoph Luitpold Frommel, *Der Römische Palastbau der Hochrenaissance* (Tübingen: Verlag Ernst Wasmuth GmbH & Co., 1973). Reprinted with permission.

p. 288   From *Architectural Review* 158, no. 942 (August 1975). Reprinted with permission.

p. 298   From *I Quattro libri dell'architettura* (Milan: Ulrico Hoepli, 1968).

p. 299   Theo van Doesburg, "Counter-Construction." Reprinted with permission of the Stedelijk Museum, Amsterdam.

p. 300 (top)   Reprinted with permission of Art Resources, Inc., New York.

p. 300 (bottom) Courtesy of the Fiske-Kimball Fine Arts Library, University of Virginia.

p. 304 (all)   From *Cornell Journal of Architecture* 2 (1983). Courtesy of Wayne Copper, "The Figure-Grounds."

p. 315   From *Architectural Forum* 128 no. 2 (March 1968). Courtesy of Denise Scott Brown.

p. 341   From *Architectural Design Profile* 59, no. 5–6 (1985). Reprinted with permission.

p. 363   From Manfredo Tafuri, *Architecture and Utopia: Design and Capitalist Development* (Cambridge: MIT Press, 1973, 1976). Reprinted with permission.

p. 460   From *MoMA Members Quarterly* (Fall 1991): 9–11. Also in *Tadao Ando* (New York: Museum of Modern Art, 1991). Reprinted with permission.

p. 510   From *VIA 7: The Building of Architecture* (1984). Reprinted with permission.

p. 533   From *Architectural Design* 47, no. 3 (1977). Courtesy of Bernard Tschumi.

BIBLIOGRAPHY

CULTURAL POSTMODERNISM

Adams, Hazard, and Leroy Searle, eds. *Critical Theory Since 1965*. Tallahassee: Florida State
   University Press, 1986.
Foster, Hal. "(Post) Modern Polemics," *Perspecta: The Yale Architecture Journal* 21 (1984). 144–153.
Habermas, Jürgen. "Modernity—An Incomplete Project," in Hal Foster, ed., *The Anti-Aesthetic:
   Essays on Postmodern Culture*. Port Townsend, WA: Bay Press, 1983.
Harrison, Charles, and Paul Wood, eds. *Art in Theory 1900–1990: An Anthology of Changing Ideas*.
   Oxford: Blackwell Publishers, 1992.
Huyssen, Andreas. "Mapping the Postmodern," *New German Critique* no. 33 (Fall 1984): 5–52.
Jameson, Frederic. "Postmodernism: or the Cultural Logic of Late Capitalism," *New Left Review*
   no. 146 (July/August 1984): 53–92.
Lyotard, Jean-François. "Defining the Postmodern," in Geoffrey Bennington...[et al.], *ICA
   Documents* 4: *Postmodernism*. London: Institute of Contemporary Arts, 1986.
——. *The Postmodern Condition: A Report on Knowledge*, Geoffrey Bennington and Brian
   Massumi, trans. Minneapolis: University of Minnesota Press, 1984.

1. POSTMODERNISM

Alexander, Christopher. *Notes on the Synthesis of Form*. Cambridge: Harvard University Press, 1964.
Colomina, Beatriz, ed. *Architectureproduction*. New York: Princeton Architectural Press, 1988.
Colquhoun, Alan. *Modernity and the Classical Tradition*. Cambridge: MIT Press, 1989.
Gandelsonas, Mario. "Neo-Functionalism," *Oppositions* 5 (Summer 1976): n. pp.
Horowitz, Jeffrey, and Michael L. Lauber. "Editorial," *Harvard Architecture Review, Beyond the
   Modern Movement* 1 (Spring 1980).
Jencks, Charles. *The Language of Postmodern Architecture*. London: Academy Editions, 1977.
——, and George Baird, eds. *Meaning in Architecture*. New York: Braziller, 1969.
Lillyman, William J., Marilyn Moriarty, and David J. Neuman, eds. *Critical Architecture and
   Contemporary Culture*. New York: Oxford University Press, 1994.
McLeod, Mary. "Architecture," in Stanley Trachtenberg, ed., *The Postmodern Moment:
   A Handbook of Contemporary Innovation in the Arts*. Westport, CT: Greenwood Press, 1985.
——. "Architecture and Politics in the Reagan Era: From Postmodernism to Deconstructivism,"
   Assemblage 8 (1989): 23–59.

Museum of Modern Art. *Five Architects: Eisenman, Graves, Gwathmey, Hejduk, Meier.* New York: Wittenborn, 1972.

Ockman, Joan. *Architecture Criticism Ideology.* Princeton: Princeton Architectural Press, 1985.

——, ed. *Architecture Culture 1943–1968: A Documentary Anthology.* New York: Rizzoli and The Trustees of Columbia University, 1993.

Stern, Robert A.M. "The Doubles of Post-Modern," *Harvard Architecture Review, Beyond the Modern Movement* 1 (Spring 1980).

2. SEMIOTICS AND STRUCTURALISM

Agrest, Diana. "Design versus Non-design," *Oppositions* 6 (Fall 1976): 45–68.

Barthes, Roland. "Semiology and Urbanism," in *Elements of Semiology,* Annette Lavers and Colin Smith, trans. New York: Hill and Wang, 1968.

——. "The Structuralist Activity," in Hazard Adams, ed., *Critical Theory Since Plato.* New York: Harcourt Brace Jovanovich, Inc., 1971.

Broadbent, Geoffrey, Richard Bunt, and Charles Jencks, eds. *Signs, Symbols and Architecture.* Chichester, UK: John Wiley & Sons Ltd., 1980.

Colquhoun, Alan. *Essays in Architectural Criticism: Modern Architecture and Historical Change.* Cambridge: Oppositions Books and MIT Press, 1981.

Eco, Umberto. "Function and Sign: Semiotics of Architecture," *VIA* 2: *Structures Implicit and Explicit* (1973): 130–153.

——. *A Theory of Semiotics.* Bloomington and London: Indiana University Press, 1976.

Foucault, Michel. "Of Other Spaces: Utopias and Heterotopias," in Joan Ockman, ed., *Architecture Culture 1943–1968: A Documentary Anthology.* New York: Rizzoli and The Trustees of Columbia University, 1993.

Gandelsonas, Mario. "On Reading Architecture," *Progressive Architecture* 53 (March 1972): 68–87.

——, and Diana Agrest. "Critical Remarks on Semiology and Architecture," *Semiotica* no. 6 (1973): 252–271.

——, and ——. "Letters." [Letters to the editor and responses from the authors with respect to their article "Semiotics and Architecture."] *Oppositions* 3 (May 1974): 110–119.

Guillerme, Jacques. "The Idea of Architectural Language," *Oppositions* 10 (Fall 1977): 21–26.

Hawkes, Terence. *Structuralism and Semiotics.* London: Methuen and Co., Ltd., 1977.

Jencks, Charles. "A Semantic Analysis of Stirling's Olivetti Centre Wing," *Architectural Association Quarterly* 6, no. 2 (1974): 13–15.

3. POSTSTRUCTURALISM AND DECONSTRUCTION

Barthes, Roland. "The Death of the Author," in *Image, Music, Text,* Stephen Heath, trans. New York: Hill and Wang, 1977.

Culler, Jonathan D. *On Deconstruction: Theory and Criticism After Structuralism.* Ithaca: Cornell University Press, 1982.

Derrida, Jacques. "Point de Folie—Maintenant l'Architecture," *Architectural Association Files* no. 12 (Summer 1986): 65–75.

Eagleton, Terry. *Literary Theory: An Introduction.* Minneapolis: University of Minnesota Press, 1983.

Eisenman, Peter. "The Futility of Objects: Decomposition and Differentiation," *Lotus* 42 (1984): 63–75.

——. "Post/El Cards: A Reply to Jacques Derrida," *Assemblage* 12 (August 1990): 14–17.

——, Rosalind E. Krauss, and Manfredo Tafuri. *Houses of Cards: Critical Essays.* New York: Oxford University Press, 1987.

Foucault, Michel. "What is an Author?" in Josüe V. Harari, ed., *Textual Strategies: Perspectives in Post-structuralist Criticism.* Ithaca: Cornell University Press, 1979.

Ghirardo, Diane. "Mind the Gap," *Architectural Review* 184, no. 1100 (October 1988): 4, 9.

Glusberg, Jorge, ed. *Deconstruction: A Student Guide.* London: Academy Editions, 1991.

Harari, Josüe V. *Textual Strategies: Perspectives in Post-structuralist Criticism.* Ithaca: Cornell University Press, 1979.

Johnson, Philip, and Mark Wigley. *Deconstructivist Architecture*. New York: Museum of Modern Art, 1988.

Martin, Louis. "Transpositions: On the Intellectual Origins of Tschumi's Architectural Theory," *Assemblage* 11 (1990): 23–36.

Nesbitt, Kate. "Construction/demolition, Object/process," in *Proceedings of the 1991 Association of Collegiate Schools of Architecture Southeast Regional Meeting*. Charlotte University of North Carolina, College of Architecture, 1992.

Pallasmaa, Juhani. "Contemporary Avant-Garde and the Wisdom of Architecture," *Skala* no. 28 (1993): 28–31.

Tschumi, Bernard. *Architecture and Disjunction*. Cambridge: MIT Press, 1994.

———. "Questions of Space," *Studio International* 190, no. 977 (September/October 1975): 136–142.

Vidler, Anthony. "After the End of the Line," *Arquitectura* 69, no. 270 (January/February 1988): 92–104.

———. "The Pleasure of the Architect," *Architecture and Urbanism* no. 216 (September 1988): 17–23.

Wigley, Mark. *The Architecture of Deconstruction: Derrida's Haunt*. Cambridge: MIT Press, 1993.

———. "The Translation of Architecture: The Product of Babel," *Architectural Design* 60, no. 9/10 (1990): 6–13.

4. HISTORICISM

Colquhoun, Alan. "Historicism and the Limits of Semiology," in *Essays in Architectural Criticism: Modern Architecture and Historical Change*. Cambridge: Oppositions Books and MIT Press, 1981.

Popper, Karl R. *The Poverty of Historicism*. Boston: Beacon Press, 1957.

Rowe, Colin. *The Mathematics of the Ideal Villa*. Cambridge: MIT Press, 1976.

Scully, Vincent J. *Modern Architecture; the Architecture of Democracy*. New York: Braziller, 1961.

Van Pelt, Robert Jan, and Carroll William Westfall. *Architectural Principles in the Age of Historicism*. New Haven: Yale University Press, 1991.

5. TYPOLOGY AND TRANSFORMATION

Bandini, Micha. "Typology as a Form of Convention," *Architectural Association Files* no. 6 (1984): 73–82.

Colquhoun, Alan. "Rationalism: A Philosophical Concept in Architecture," in *Modernity and the Classical Tradition*. Cambridge: MIT Press, 1989.

Moneo, Rafael. "On Typology," *Oppositions* 13 (Summer 1978): 22–45.

Rossi, Aldo. "The Urban Artifact as a Work of Art," and "Typological Questions," in *The Architecture of the City*, Diane Ghirardo and Joan Ockman, trans. Cambridge: MIT Press, 1982.

Vidler, Anthony. "The Idea of Type: The Transformation of the Academic Ideal, *1750–1830*," *Oppositions* 8 (Spring 1977): 95–115.

6. URBAN THEORY AFTER MODERNISM

Anyone Corporation. "Seaside and the Real World: A Debate on American Urbanism," *Architecture New York* no. 1 (July/August 1993).

Colquhoun, Alan. "Twentieth-Century Concepts of Urban Space," in *Modernity and the Classical Tradition*. Cambridge: MIT Press, 1989.

Dennis, Michael. *Court and Garden: From the French Hôtel to the City of Modern Architecture*. Cambridge: MIT Press, 1986.

Design Book Review. "Postmodern Urbanism," *Design Book Review* 17 (Winter 1989).

Frampton, Kenneth. "The City of Dialectic," *Architectural Design* 7/6 (October 1969): 541–546

Gandelsonas, Mario. *The Urban Text*. Chicago: Chicago Institute for Architecture and Urbanism, 1991; distributed by MIT Press.

Harvard Architecture Review. "Monumentality and the City," *Harvard Architecture Review, Monumentality and the City* 4 (Spring 1984).

Jacobs, Jane. *The Death and Life of Great American Cities.* New York: Random House, 1961.
Katz, Peter. *The New Urbanism.* New York: McGraw-Hill, Inc., 1994.
Koolhaas, Rem. *Delirious New York: A Retroactive Manifesto for Manhattan.* New York: Oxford
    University Press, 1978, The Monacelli Press, 1994.
———. "From 'Delirious New York,'" *Architecture and Urbanism* no. 217 (October 1988): 135–151.
Krier, Leon. "The Reconstruction of the City," in *Rational Architecture: The Reconstruction of the
    European City.* Brussels: Archives of Modern Architecture Editions, 1978.
———. "The Reconstruction of the European City: An Outline for a Charter," *Architectural
    Design* 54, no. 11–12 (1984): 16–21.
Kunstler, James Howard. *The Geography of Nowhere: The Rise and Decline of America's Man-Made
    Landscape.* New York: Simon and Schuster, 1993.
Lynch, Kevin. *Image of the City.* Cambridge: MIT Press, 1960.
Plattus, Alan J. "Emblems of the City: Civic Pageantry and the Rhetoric of Urbanism,"
    ArtForum 20, no. 1 (September 1981): 48–52.
Rossi, Aldo. *The Architecture of the City,* Diane Ghirardo and Joan Ockman, trans. Cambridge:
    MIT Press, 1982.
Rowe, Colin. "The Present Urban Predicament," *Cornell Journal of Architecture* 1 (Fall 1981): 17–33.
Scott Brown, Denise and Robert Venturi. "The Highway," *Modulus* 9 (1973): 6–15.
Venturi, Robert, Denise Scott Brown, and Steven Izenour. *Learning from Las Vegas.* Cambridge:
    MIT Press, 1972.

7. THE SCHOOL OF VENICE

Colquhoun, Alan. "Rational Architecture," *Architectural Design* 45, no. 6 (1975): 365–370.
Grassi, Giorgio. *Architecture, Dead Language.* New York: Electa/Rizzoli, 1988.
Solà-Morales Rubió, Ignasi de. "Neo-Rationalism and Figuration," *Architectural Design* 54,
    no. 5–6 (1984): 15–20.
Tafuri, Manfredo, and Francesco Dal Co. *Modern Architecture.* Robert Erich Wolf, trans.
    New York: Electa/Rizzoli, 1986.

8. POLITICAL AND ETHICAL AGENDAS

Beatley, Timothy. *Ethical Land Use: Principles of Policy and Planning.* Baltimore: John Hopkins
    University Press, 1994.
Ghirardo, Diane, ed. *Out of Site: A Social Criticism of Architecture.* Seattle: Bay Press, 1991.
McLeod, Mary. "Architecture or Revolution: Taylorism, Technology, and Social Change," *Art
    Journal* 43, no. 2 (Summer 1983): 132–147.
Pallasmaa, Juhani. "The Social Commission and the Autonomous Architect," *Harvard
    Architecture Review* 6 (1987): 115–121.
Westfall, Carroll William. "Architecture as Ethics," in Richard Economakis, ed., *Building
    Classical: A Vision of Europe and America.* London: Academy Editions, 1993.

9. PHENOMENOLOGY

Bachelard, Gaston. "The House. From Cellar to Garret. The Significance of the Hut," in
    The Poetics of Space, Maria Jolas, trans. Boston: Beacon Press, 1969.
Harries, Karsten. "Building and the Terror of Time," *Perspecta: The Yale Architecture Journal* 19
    (1982): 59–69.
———. "The Dream of the Complete Building," *Perspecta: The Yale Architecture Journal* 17 (1980):
    36–43.
Heidegger, Martin. "Building Dwelling Thinking" and "...Poetically Man Dwells...," in *Poetry,
    Language, Thought,* Albert Hofstadter, trans. New York: Harper & Row, 1971.
Merleau-Ponty, Maurice. *The Phenomenology of Perception,* Colin Smith, trans. New York:
    Humanities Press, 1962.
Norberg-Schulz, Christian. *Architecture: Meaning and Place.* New York: Rizzoli, 1988.
———. *The Concept of Dwelling: On the Way to Figurative Architecture.* New York: Rizzoli, 1985.

——. *Existence, Space and Architecture.* New York: Praeger, 1971.
——. *Genius Loci: Towards a Phenomenology of Architecture.* New York: Rizzoli, 1980.
——. *Intentions in Architecture.* Cambridge: MIT Press, 1965.
Vesely, Dalibor. "On the Relevance of Phenomenology," *Pratt Journal of Architecture* 2 (1988): 59–62.

10. ARCHITECTURE, NATURE, AND THE CONSTRUCTED SITE

Burns, Carol. "On Site: Architectural Preoccupations," in Andrea Kahn, ed.,
    Drawing/Building/Text: Essays in Architectural Theory. New York: Princeton Architectural
    Press, 1991.
Frampton, Kenneth, ed. *Tadao Ando: Buildings, Projects, Writings.* New York: Rizzoli, 1984.
Gregotti, Vittorio. "Excerpt from Territory and Architecture," in Joan Ockman, ed., *Architecture
    Culture 1943–1968: A Documentary Anthology.* New York: Rizzoli and The Trustees of
    Columbia University, 1993.
Meyer, Elizabeth K. "Landscape Architecture as Modern Other and Postmodern Ground," in
    Harriet Edquist and Vanessa Bird, eds., *The Culture of Landscape Architecture.* Melbourne,
    Australia: RMIT Press, 1994.
——. "The Public Park as Avant-Garde (Landscape) Architecture," *Landscape Journal* 10, no. 1
    (Spring 1991): 16–26.

11. CRITICAL REGIONALISM

Colquhoun, Alan. "Regionalism and Technology," in *Modernity and the Classical Tradition.*
    Cambridge: MIT Press, 1989.
Frampton, Kenneth. *Modern Architecture, a Critical History.* New York: Thames and Hudson, 1985.
——. "Place-form and Cultural Identity," in John Thackara, ed., *Design after Modernism:
    Beyond the Object.* New York: Thames and Hudson, 1988.
Schumacher, Thomas. "Regional Intentions and Contemporary Architecture: A Critique,"
    Center 3 (1987): 50–57.
Tzonis, Alexander, and Lefaivre, Liane. "The Grid and the Pathway: An Introduction to the
    Work of Dimitris and Susana Antonakakis," *Architecture in Greece* no. 15 (1981): 164–178.

12. TECTONIC EXPRESSION

Ando, Tadao. "Introduction," in Kenneth Frampton, ed., *Tadao Ando: Buildings, Projects,
    Writings.* New York: Rizzoli, 1984.
——. "The Wall as Territorial Delineation," in Kenneth Frampton, ed., *Tadao Ando: Buildings,
    Projects, Writings.* New York: Rizzoli, 1984.
Grassi, Giorgio. "On the Question of Decoration," *Architectural Design* 54, no. 5–6 (1984): 10–13,
    32–33.
Kahn, Louis. "An Architect Speaks his Mind," in Alessandra Latour, ed., *Louis I. Kahn Writings,
    Lectures, Interviews.* New York: Rizzoli, 1991.
Porphyrios, Demetri. "Building and Architecture," *Architectural Design* 54, no. 5–6 (1984): 6–9,
    30–31.
Rykwert, Joseph. "Ornament is No Crime," *Studio International* 190, no. 977 (October 1975): 91–97.

13. FEMINISM, GENDER, AND THE PROBLEM OF THE BODY

Agrest, Diana I. *Architecture from Without: Theoretical Framings for a Critical Practice.* Cambridge:
    MIT Press, 1993.
Bergren, Ann. "Architecture Gender Philosophy," in John Whiteman, Jeffrey Kipnis and Richard
    Burdett, eds., *Strategies in Architectural Thinking.* Cambridge: MIT Press, 1992.
Colomina, Beatriz. "The Split Wall: Domestic Voyeurism," in Beatriz Colomina, ed., *Sexuality
    and Space.* New York: Princeton Architectural Press, 1992.
MacAnulty, Robert. "Body Troubles," in John Whiteman, Jeffrey Kipnis and Richard Burdett,
    eds., *Strategies in Architectural Thinking.* Cambridge: MIT Press, 1992.
Torre, Susana. "Space as Matrix." *Heresies* 11, *Making Room: Women and Architecture* 3, no. 3
    (1981): 51–52.

Tschumi, Bernard. "Architecture and Transgression," *Oppositions* 7 (Winter 1976): 55–63.
——. "Violence of Architecture," *ArtForum* 20, no. 1 (September 1981): 44–47.
Weedon, Chris. *Feminist Practice and Poststructuralist Theory*. Oxford and New York: Blackwell Publishers, 1987.

14. CONTEMPORARY DEFINITIONS OF THE SUBLIME

Art and Design Profile. "The Contemporary Sublime: Sensibilities of Transcendence and Shock," *Art and Design Profile* 40, no. 1/2 (1995).
Lyotard, Jean-François. "Appendix," in *The Postmodern Condition: A Report on Knowledge*, Geoffrey Bennington and Brian Massumi, trans. Minneapolis: University of Minnesota Press, 1984.
——. *Lessons on the Analytic of the Sublime*, Elizabeth Rottenberg, trans. Stanford: Stanford University Press, 1994.
——. "Presenting the Unpresentable: The Sublime," *ArtForum* 20, no. 8 (April 1982): 36–43. Also published in *The Inhuman: Reflections on Time*. Oxford: Polity Press, 1991.
——. "The Sublime and the Avant-garde," ArtForum 22, no. 8 (April 1984): 64–69.
Nesbitt, Kate. "The Sublime and Modern Architecture: Unmasking (an Aesthetic of) Abstraction," *New Literary History* 26, no. 1 (Winter 1995): 95–110.
Vidler, Anthony. *The Architectural Uncanny*. Cambridge: MIT Press, 1992.
——. "The Architecture of Allusion: Notes on the Postmodern Sublime," *Art Criticism* 2, no. 1 (1985): 61–69.
——. "Notes on the Sublime," *Canon: The Princeton Journal* 3 (1988): 165–191.

INDEX

Pallasmaa, Juhani, 30, 462, 494
  "The Geometry of Feeling: A Look at the Phenomenology of Architecture," 447–453
Pane, Roberto, 134
parody, 93, 94, 96
Parthenon, 134
pastiche, 47–48
Paxton, Joseph
  Crystal Palace, 527
Paz, Octavio
  The New Analogy, 465
Pei, I. M., 135, 184, 193–194, 196
  Louvre project, 193–194
Peichl, Gustav, 329
perceptions, 505
Perez-Gomez, Alberto, 19, 30, 50, 64, 65
Perrault, Charles, 203
Perret, August, 496, 525
Persico, Edoardo, 388
Perspecta: The Yale Architectural Journal, 24, 25, 72, 248, 468, 469
Pevsner, Nikolaus, 125, 206
  Pioneers of Modern Design, 17
phallocentrism, 543
phenomenology, 28–30, 182, 308–309, 338–339, 392, 456, 462, 468, 494, 498, 517, 523, 572, 575
  "Phenomenology: Of Meaning and Place," 412–455
Piaget, Jean, 423
Picasso, Pablo, 286–287, 289
picturesque
  "Complexity versus Picturesqueness," 72, 74–76
Pierce, Charles Sanders, 33,122, 125–126, 135–136, 138
Pikionis, Dimitri, 481
  Philopappus Hall, 481
Piranesi, Giovanni Battista, 262, 332, 502, 507, 536–537, 558
  Antichita Romani, 507
  Carceri series, 19
place, 28, 29, 37, 40, 49–51, 55, 180, 309, 338, 342, 392, 395, 429, 433, 435–436, 440–441, 443–446, 452, 461, 468, 469, 481–482, 486, 480–491
Plater-Zyberk, Elizabeth, 58–59
  Seaside, Florida, 18, 58
Plato, 374
Platz, Gustav Adolf, 232
pleasure
  "The Pleasure of Architecture," 55, 64, 530–540
  see Vitruvian triad
pluralism, 16–17, 27, 200, 266–267

poetic, 86, 87, 222, 489
poiesis, 436, 516
politics, 59–65, 481–482
  "Political and Ethical Agendas," 370–411
Polshek, James, 104
Popper, Karl, 53, 267, 272–274, 279–280, 289–291
  Logic of Scientific Discovery, 280
  Notes on the Synthesis of Form, 280
  The Open Society, 44
  The Poverty of Historicism, 44, 280
  "Towards a Rational Theory of Tradition," 272
  "Utopia and Violence," 272
populism, 25, 52, 53, 57, 471, 473, 488
Porphyrios, Demetri, 46, 47–48, 79, 309, 494, 495
  "Classicism is Not a Style," 91
  "Relevance of Classical Architecture," 47, 91–96
Portoghesi, Paolo, 28, 419
  Postmodern: The Architecture of the Postindustrial Society, 28
positivism, 29, 31, 40, 42, 81, 83, 200, 204, 205, 214, 231
post-functionalism, 72, 102
  "Post-Functionalism," 78–83
postmodern classicism, 93, 94
postmodern deconstruction, 93, 94
postmodern high tech, 93–94
postmodern historicism, 24, 25–26, 31, 41–44, 47, 58, 85, 98, 122, 178, 200–201, 447, 494, 572
postmodernism, 16–17, 21, 72–109, 174, 179, 184–185, 189, 195–196, 200, 207, 208, 214, 240, 258, 308, 326, 338, 360, 370 379, 392, 449, 456, 458, 468, 494, 499, 520, 573
  historical description, 21–28
  major themes, 40–65
  theoretical paradigms, 28–40
poststructuralism, 19, 32, 34–36, 37, 39, 142–199, 541, 554, 573
potential ideal, 206
pragmatics, 129, 138
Pratt Journal of Architecture, 24, 48, 564
praxis, 446
precedent, 45, 57, 66, 72, 98, 103, 166, 181, 241, 246, 248, 257, 263, 476, 536, 538
Precis, 24
prescription, 17–19
presence, 28, 29, 30, 31, 33, 36, 46, 49, 50, 64, 88, 174, 176, 178, 179, 180, 181, 182, 185–196, 287, 289, 291, 416, 419, 422, 429, 431, 433, 434, 436, 447, 451, 460, 461, 462, 465, 508, 516, 517, 520, 522, 525, 526, 534, 537, 549, 561

Xenakis, Yannis 253

Yamasaki, Monoru, 22
     Pruitt-Igoe housing complex, St. Louis, 22
Yates, Francis
     Art of Memory, 217

zeitgeist, 41, 60, 200–201, 217, 218, 219, 220, 233
Zodiac, 245
zones, 51, 305–306